LEGAL OBLIGATIONS IN CONSTRUCTION

REVISED CONFERENCE PROCEEDINGS

Editors

John Uff
Nash Professor of Engineering Law
King's College London

Anthony Lavers
Professor of Law
Oxford Brookes University

Construction Law Press
London
1996

Construction Law Press ® is the imprint of the Centre of Construction Law and Management, King's College London.

Published in Great Britain by
Centre of Construction Law and Management
King's College London
The Old Watch House
Strand
London WC2R 2LS

020 7848 2685
020 7848 2638 (Fax)

First published 1992
Reprinted by Construction Law Press 1996 & 2007

ISBN 0-9514866-2-4

A copy of the CIP entry for this book is available from the British Library

Printed in Great Britain by CPI Antony Rowe

Preface

Over a period of almost exactly twenty years, "Building Contracts" and "Building and Civil Engineering Contracts" have not only become construction Law, but can also be said to have crossed over to the right side of the tracks. Not so long ago Construction Law was just a little unfashionable. It can now be mentioned in the same breath as commercial and chancery, has an outstanding body of case law in tort and contract, a growing number of Chairs, a substantial and expanding body of specialists in both branches of the English profession, and an international involvement which is extensive and progressive.

The Centre of Construction Law and Management is to be congratulated on the concept of persuading contributors from many disciplines to support the Annual conferences and then to publish their papers, thereby producing something far more useful and imaginative than a traditional "Casebook on the Law". Consider the List of contributors to the present volume: they include a former Lord Justice of Appeal, now President of the London Court of International Arbitration; a Judge who has been closely involved in introducing new technology to the judicial process describing current procedure in the court specialising in construction disputes; distinguished academics and authors, leading practitioners from both branches of the profession, and others giving the wider perspective of the United States, the European community and China.

This volume ranges widely, including as an addendum and noter-up to the preceding volume, the most recent developments in arbitration, with thoughts on the alternative resolution of disputes. Parts IV and V contain much useful and thought-provoking material on Comparative Law and EEC Law and practice. Part IV in particular makes stimulating reading and should interest many who are not construction law specialists.

Perhaps the bedrock of the volume is in Part I, II and III where the contributors enquire where we stand and where we are going now that the great flood tide of tort has receded. Those of us who were in practice from the mid-seventies onwards may be forgiven for thinking that we were participating in an astonishing evolution of common law which would ensure that almost any loss was matched by a corresponding duty in tort. We were wrong: contract must govern the majority of rights and remedies, often in very intricate contractual relationships. To what extent the Law Commission's deliberations on the rights and liabilities of third parties will enhance or stimulate development of this branch of the law remains to be seen, but Peter Barber's paper reminds us of the difficulties and uncertainties that can arise between a main contractor and subcontractors, nominated and domestic, skilled and unskilled, while Richard Winward asks whether the draftsmen really can supply the answers. One also asks whether, in practice, contracting parties would be prepared to be buried in a sea of complex (and expensive) drafting, but the thought remains that skimped contractual precautions can lead down the same primrose path as skimped soil surveys.

The general Introduction modestly describes this volume and its companions as "an available corpus of material of high academic quality for the use of students undertaking the King's College MSc in Construction Law and Arbitration" which at the same time can be made available to a wider audience. The value of the material is that it comes both from the coalface and the laboratory, and so far as the wider audience is concerned, provides what to the practising profession must be an invaluable back-up to the standard textbooks as a source of ideas and arguments while at the same time looking at particular issues with a breadth of vision that cannot be achieved in a standard work.

The Honourable Sir Patrick Garland
Queen's Bench Division
Royal Courts of Justice
July 1992

Contents

Part I - Contract

Part II - Tort

Section III - Remedies and Sanctions

General Introduction

This volume completes the set of three, representing the first four Annual Conferences and the first five years' development at the Centre of Construction Law and Management. The aim in publishing these proceedings has been to provide an available corpus of construction law materials of high academic quality, for the use of students undertaking the King's College MSc in Construction Law and Arbitration and at the same time to make the conference proceedings available to a wider audience.

This volume of proceedings contains the edited, revised and updated papers from the third and fourth annual conferences of the Centre of Construction Law and Management held in September 1990 and September 1992, which were generously sponsored and supported respectively by Linklaters & Paines, Solicitors, and by Lovell White Durrant, Solicitors. We take some satisfaction in the knowledge that our endeavours are in keeping with the views of commercial firms of such wide influence. It is not wholly by chance that it has been possible to amalgamate these two conferences. Both events covered a range of current topics which embrace the whole subject - Contract - Tort - Remedies and sanctions - European law and practice - Dispute resolution. In addition, we have been able to cover, albeit in an introductory way only, the potentially large subject of comparative construction law. With the impending open European market in 1993, it is particularly appropriate that this volume should contain papers which touch on a range of European legal systems as well as the law of the United States and the People's Republic of China.

These two conferences took place against a strong current of change. First, in the common law itself, the great cycle of development in the law of tort had just reached its (apparent) conclusion with the House of Lords' decisions in *D & F Estates* v. *Church Commissioners* and *Murphy* v. *Brentwood District Council*; and the subsequent revision of the papers prior to publication was able to take into account the decision of the court of Appeal in *St. Martin's Corporation* v. *Sir Robert McAlpine*. Such developments led Mr. Donald Keating QC in his Keynote Address to the third annual conference to observe:

"These conferences emphasise the outstanding importance of construction law in the body of English commercial and business law. Construction law either has already, or will in the futuɹ̯ become, the most important stimulus to the development of business law in its widest sense. It may replace the importance of shipping law as a prime generator of English law, a position which it held for the centuries when Britannia's rule was not limited to the last night of the Proms".

Secondly, and partly as a result of changes in the law of tort, there has been a new growth of interest in the law of contract, through the development of new devices such as the collateral warranty. Thirdly, publication of this volume will mark the twentieth anniversary of the passing of the European Communities Act 1972, by which the United Kingdom started its journey into Europe. Whatever reluctance there has been to accept the loss of sovereignty, it is clear that Europe now represents a major element of our legal system, and nowhere more than in the field of construction, which must look increasingly to the Community for its trade as well as its regulation.

The Editors wish to express their appreciation of the work of the sponsoring firms, of the Chairmen of the Conferences and of the Keynote speakers; and of the many contributors to these conferences whose work stands as its own tribute. We also express our thanks for the tireless organising skills of the Centre's Manager, Mrs. Pauline Gale, BA, and of her assistant Mrs. Helen Brownstone.

1 August 1992
JFU
AL

Centre of Construction Law and Management,
King's College London.

List of Contributors

Conference Chairmen: Adrian Montagu, Solicitor, Partner Linklaters & Paines.
HH Judge Peter Bowsher QC, Official Referee.
The Hon. Sir Philip Otton, Judge of the High Court of Justice.

Keynote Speakers: Donald Keating, QC, BA, FCIArb.
The Rt. Hon. Sir Michael Kerr, former Lord Justice of Appeal.

Contributors:

Leslie Ainsworth, BA, Partner, Lovell White Durrant, Solicitors.

John N. Barber, BA, MA, LLB, CEng, MICE, FCIArb., Research Fellow, Centre of Construction Law, King's College London.

Peter Barber, MA, BCL (Oxon), Solicitor with Freshfields, Solicitors.

Professor Hugh Beale, BA (Oxon), Barrister, Chairman of School of Law, University of Warwick.

Donald Bishop, CEng, MICE, ARICS, FCIOB, Emeritus Professor of Building, University of London.

Michael Bowsher, Barrister, Gleary Gottlieb Steen & Hamilton, Brussels.

HH Judge Peter Bowsher QC, Official Referee.

Phillip Capper, MA, BA, Partner, Masons, Solicitors Masons' Visiting Professor, Centre of Construction Law, King's College London.

John Cartwright, Tutor in law, Christ Church, Oxford.

Douglas Close, BA, BCL (Oxon).

Laurence W. Gormley, MA, MSc, LLD, Barrister, Professor, Department of European & Economic Law, Rijksuniversiteit Groningen.

George MacIlwaine, BSc, MA, C.Eng, MICE. Law Offices: Derek Elliott, Paris.

Nerys Jefford, MA (Oxon), LLM (Virginia), Barrister.

Elizabeth Jones, MA, LLB, ACIArb., Solicitor, Director, High-Point Schaer.

The Rt. Hon. Sir Michael Kerr, President of the London Court of International Arbitration.

Anthony Lavers, LLB, MPhil, PhD, Fishburn Boxer Reader in Law, Oxford Polytechnic.

Marshall F. Levine, LLB, Solicitor, Partner, Linklaters & Paines, Solicitors.

Charles B. Lewis, Juris Doctor (Univ. San Francisco) Head, Baker & McKenzie, Chicago, USA.

Mark McGaw, LLB, LLM (Cantab), Solicitor, Partner, Lovell White Durrant.

David R. Marks, LLB, LLM, Solicitor, McKennas, Brussels.

Arthur Marriot, Solicitor, FCIArb., Partner, Wilmer Cutler & Pickering.

John Powell, QC, MA, LLB (Cantab).

Christopher Thomas, QC, BA, Dip de Droit Comp.

John Turnbull, Solicitor, Partner, Linklaters & Paines, Solicitors.

John Uff, QC, PhD, FICE, FCIArb, Nash Professor of Engineering Law, Director, Centre of Construction Law & Management, KCL.

Ian N. Duncan Wallace, QC, Visiting Professor, Centre of Construction Law, King's College London.

Jeremy Winter, LLB, Solicitor, Partner Baker & McKenzie.

Richard Winward, LLB, Solicitor, Partner Winward Fearon & Co., Solicitors.

Table of Statutes

Table of Cases

Part I

Contract

Legal obligations in construction : 1
Privity of contract, formation
and third party rights

Hugh Beale

Synopsis

This paper sets out the general principles of the law of contract, particularly relating to formation and privity of contract and third party rights, as the background to the following papers in this section. The author rehearses the essential elements of a valid contract, being agreement, intention to create legal relations and consideration, noting that developments have occurred in each of these areas. The possibility of contractual liability being held to exist where it might not be anticipated on an orthodox analysis is discussed. Contract and tort are compared using the factual situation of *Donoghue* v. *Stevenson* for illustration, and the nature of contractual and tortious liabilities and their exclusion. The paper includes recoverability of loss and defences, including limitation, agency and acceptance of risk.

Introduction

Although we are accustomed to think of construction contracts as synonymous with the contract documents, it has to be remembered that the standard forms must always be read in the light of the general law of contract. Firstly, none of the forms gives a complete statement of the legal position of either party - for instance, often little is said about the obligations relating to the quality of the work and materials; so these are governed by terms implied into the contract by the Supply of Goods and Services Act 1982. Secondly, even where a point is dealt with by the standard form, the general law may provide additional or alternative remedies: for instance, if soil investigation reports fail to reveal the full extent of difficult strata on a site, there may be a remedy in misrepresentation as well as a claim under one of the contract clauses. Thirdly, many of the contract clauses can only be fully understood in the light of the general law: for example the provisions for objections to nominated suppliers are partly a response to the decision that the contractor is not responsible for defective materials supplied by a nominated supplier against whom the contractor had no right of objection,

3

at least if the supplier would only do business on limited liability terms.[1] Fourthly, the general law determines the scope of the contractual obligations: in particular, the question of who is entitled to enforce the contract and the effect of the contract on other forms of liability, especially liability in tort.

Common law and statute law

Although statute has had a considerable impact upon the law of contract and tort in recent years - for example, the Defective Premises Act 1972, the Unfair Contract Terms Act 1977 and the Consumer Protection Act 1987 - the foundations of the law are still decided cases. The basic principles of the common law in this area are still fundamentally the same, but there have been new developments and new applications. Meanwhile there has been great debate about the fundamental interrelationships of contract and tort, with the latest pronouncement of the House of Lords taking a very conservative approach.

Essential elements of contract

The essential elements of contractual liability are agreement, intention to create legal relations and consideration. It might be thought that any doubts about these would have been settled long ago, but in each area there have been interesting new developments.

Offer and acceptance

The basic rules here remain the same. Thus there will not be an offer if one party merely says that "it may be prepared to" contract.[2] Equally there must still be an exact fit between offer and acceptance, so that a "battle of the forms" will result in a series of counter-offers and, in the absence of one party signing a tear-off acceptance slip from the other party's form[3] there may be no contract until the goods are delivered or the services performed, when a contract will arise on the terms of the last form sent.[4] Problems still continue with unilateral contract offers. There can be no acceptance until the offeree starts performance, and though the courts have suggested that they

1 *Gloucestershire CC* v. *Richardson* [1969] 1 AC 480.
2 *Gibson* v. *Manchester City Council* [1979] 1 All ER 972.
3 As in *Butler Machine Tool Co Ltd* v. *Ex-Cell-O Corpn (England) Ltd* [1979] 1 All ER 965.
4 *Sauter Automation Ltd* v. *Goodman (Mechanical Services) Ltd* (1986) 34 BLR 81.

may imply a term to prevent the offeror revoking before the offeree has had a chance to complete the performance,[5] this will not be done if the court thinks the offeree was taking the risk.[6]

The vast majority of contracts are created deliberately, but the House of Lords has stressed that conduct may give rise to "unintended" contractual liability.

> "...if one party (O) so acts that his conduct, objectively considered, constitutes an offer, and the other party (A), believing that the conduct of O represents his actual intention, accepts O's offer, then a contract will come into existence, and on those facts it will make no difference if O did not in fact intend to make an offer, or if he misunderstood A's acceptance, so that O's state of mind is, in such circumstances, irrelevant.[7]"

Although it seems improbable that anyone would enter a construction contract unwittingly, the same may not be true of ancillary obligations. It is not clear, for instance, that Detel actually intended to give a contractual warranty when it stated to Shanklin Pier Co. that its paint would last for seven years; but when the Pier Co. relied on this in specifying Detel paint for repainting the pier and the paint turned out to be unsuitable, Detel were held liable in contract.[8]

Intention to create legal relations

The risk of incurring unintended contractual liability is reduced by the doctrine of intention to create legal relations. Although the courts have been prepared to find contractual liability where there has been a direct conversation between the parties before any contract has been made, and one party has clearly stated that it will do something, even if the occasion was fairly casual[9], they have not found contractual intention when a party has purchased goods from a retailer or wholesaler on the strength of a manufac-

---

5 See the judgment of Goff LJ in *Daulia* v. *Four Millbank Nominees Ltd* [1978] 2 All ER 557.
6 *Luxor (Eastbourne) Ltd* v. *Cooper* [1941] AC 108.
7 Robert Goff LJ in *The Leonidas D* [1985] 2 All ER 796, citing Lord Brightman in *The Hannah Blumenthal* [1983] 1 AC 854.
8 *Shanklin Pier* v. *Detel Products Ltd* [1951] 2 KB 854. Note that the painting contractor would not have been responsible as the paint was simply unfit for the particular purpose: see paper 2.
9 Eg *Evans & Son (Portsmouth) Ltd* v. *Andrea Merzario Ltd* [1976] 2 All ER 930 (undertaking to ship containers below decks given in course of "courtesy call").

turer's general publicity.[10] An assurance given to an employer by a nominated subcontractor during the course of a contract that its design for a television mast was safe was also said to be made without contractual intention.[11] In cases of doubt, the words used will be construed in the light of the circumstances of the case. Thus a notice in a shop that it is a shop's "policy" to give refunds on undamaged goods returned within 14 days might be contractual, whereas a statement in a "letter of comfort" that it was the defendant's "policy to ensure that the business of [a subsidiary] is at all times in a position to meet its liabilities to you" did not constitute a guarantee.[12]

Consideration

A promise will not be binding unless either it is made by deed[13] or it is supported by "consideration". The traditional requirements for consideration are that the promisor must receive a benefit, or the promisee incur a detriment, in exchange for the promise.[14] In practice the rules are changing. Firstly, where the promise relates to the granting of an interest in property, the courts are increasingly willing to enforce the promise not as a contract but via the doctrine of proprietary estoppel.[15] Secondly, in the area of contractual variations, which traditionally had to fulfil the same requirements as new contracts, the courts have effectively reached the position that a freely agreed variation will be binding without consideration. If one party promises not to enforce its contractual rights, the promise may be binding under the doctrine of promissory estoppel.[16] If one party promises to pay the other extra if the other will complete its original contractual obligation, it used to be thought that the promise would fail for want of consideration, but in *Williams* v. *Roffey Bros & Nicholls (Contractors) Ltd*[17] the Court of Appeal held that a practical benefit to the promisor - in that case, getting a subcontractor's work finished on time and thus avoiding liquidated damages on the head contract - was a sufficient benefit to constitute considera-

---

10 *Lexmead Ltd* v. *Lewis* [1982] AC 225, 262-263.

11 *IBA* v. *EMI Electronics Ltd and BICC Construction Ltd* (1980) 14 BLR 1.

12 *Kleinwort Benson Ltd* v. *Malaysian Mining Corpn Bhd* [1989] 1 All ER 785. Letters of intent are dealt with in paper 4.

13 Note that a seal is no longer required for a deed, but it must now be witnessed: Law of Property (Miscellaneous Provisions) Act 1989, s.1.

14 See eg *Dunlop Pneumatic Tyre Co Ltd* v. *Selfridge & Co Ltd* [1915] AC 847.

15 For a description see Treitel, *Law of Contract* (7th ed, 1987) pp.105-115.

16 *Central London Property Trust Ltd* v. *High Trees House Ltd* [1947] KB 130; *WJ Alan & Co Ltd* v. *El Nasr Import & Export Co* [1972] 2 QB 189. The promise will not be binding if it was the result of coercion by the party who stood to benefit from it: *D & C Builders Ltd* v. *Rees* [1966] 2 QB 617.

17 [1990] 1 All ER 512.

tion.[18] Whether this case heralds a fresh approach to completely new contracts also remains to be seen.

The courts have accepted that performance of an existing duty owed under contract to a third party can be good consideration for a promise.[19] As we shall see, this is of some importance when ancillary contracts are being made between various parties involved in a single project.

Finding contracts

In practice none of the three doctrines is a great barrier to the court finding contractual liability if it thinks this is appropriate. For instance the court can usually find consideration if it wants to do so. Thus there was no difficulty about consideration in the *Detel* case although it was the painting contractor rather than the plaintiffs who bought the paint from Detel. The indirect benefit to Detel of increased sales would be ample consideration.[20]

Contracts between parties not normally in contractual relationship

If it is desired deliberately to create contractual liability between two parties who are not obviously in an exchange relationship - eg. between a designer or contractor and the ultimate user of a building - there is no great difficulty in so doing, provided that the parties to be linked are identifiable at the time. A collateral agreement can be entered between them. Unless the language is vague, as in the letter of comfort case, the court will treat it as intended to create legal relations, and the doctrine of consideration is easily overcome by using a deed or by inserting nominal consideration. There is much greater difficulty if one of the parties cannot be identified at the time - eg a future purchaser or tenant - as it may be necessary for the present owner to enter the collateral warranty arrangement and then assign its rights. The problems will be explored in Mr. Cartwright's paper.

Contract and tort compared

It may be helpful to summarise some of the main differences between the two forms of liability in contract and tort. The way in which the two interrelate can be illustrated by taking the facts alleged in the famous tort

18 The CA limited this to the case where the promise to pay extra was voluntary, but if it was coerced it would be voidable anyway under the new doctrine of economic duress: see *The Atlantic Baron* [1979] QB 705.
19 *New Zealand Shipping Co Ltd* v. *Satterthwaite* [1975] AC 154.
20 Cf.*Carlill* v. *Carbolic Smoke Ball Co.* [1893] 1 QB 256.

case of *Donoghue* v. *Stevenson*.[21] The plaintiff and a friend entered Minchella's cafe in Paisley and the friend treated the plaintiff to a bottle of ginger beer, manufactured by Stevenson. The ginger beer was in a sealed glass bottle. Minchella poured out half of it, which the plaintiff drank. When she poured out the remainder, out came the decomposed remains of a snail. The plaintiff suffered illness as a result of drinking the ginger beer. Who had rights against whom? We will also explore some related questions which are of relevance to construction projects and which will form a useful background to the papers which follow.

The scope of contractual rights and duties

Underlying the essential requirements of agreement and consideration is a notion of private bargain. Only a party who is "privy" to the bargain may enforce it, even if the parties quite clearly intended a third party to benefit from the contract. Thus in *Beswick* v. *Beswick*[22] a nephew bought his uncle's coal business and promised to pay his uncle £6.10s a week for life and thereafter £5 per week to his widow, but after the uncle's death the nephew made only a couple of payments to his aunt. The House of Lords held that the doctrine of privity of contract prevented the widow from recovering the money in her own name. Equally in *Donoghue* v. *Stevenson* the plaintiff could not sue Minchella in contract because he had sold the ginger beer not to her but to her friend.

Agency

It is sometimes possible for the courts or contract drafter to avoid the privity doctrine by using agency. Thus if Donoghue's friend had merely ordered the ginger beer on her behalf, there would have been a contract between Donoghue and Minchella.[23] But this involves not only showing that the friend was acting on Donoghue's behalf but that Donoghue was providing consideration.[24] Thus it would have to be shown that she intended to pay for the drink herself.

Enforcement by promisee

Although the doctrine of privity of contract prevents the third party suing

21 [1932] AC 562.
22 [1968] AC 58.
23 *Lockett* v. *AM Charles Ltd* [1938] 4 All ER 170.
24 *Dunlop Pneumatic Tyre Co Ltd* v. *Selfridge & Co Ltd* [1915] AC 847.

the defaulting party for breach of contract, the other party to the contract may still sue. Thus in *Beswick* v. *Beswick* the uncle's personal representative was able to enforce the nephew's obligation by getting an order of specific performance against him, ordering him to pay his aunt - and as the aunt was the personal representative, justice was ultimately done. But this route will be of little help if the original promisee will not co-operate or no longer exists. Nor will it help when the plaintiff wants damages for a loss she has suffered, as in *Donoghue* v. *Stevenson*. The promisee can only recover for her own loss, and it was of course Donoghue not the friend who suffered the personal injury.[25] This point, that a party can only recover its own loss, is a fundamental one to remember when considering recovery against nominated subcontractors and in relation to assignment: these points will be taken up later.

Scope of duty in tort

Because she could not sue in contract, Donoghue brought an action in tort for negligence against the manufacturer, Stevenson; and it was that case that held that a manufacturer who is careless in the preparation of a product with the foreseeable result that a consumer of the product is injured is liable. The fact that the manufacturer might be liable in contract to someone else was immaterial. Subsequent interpretation of Lord Atkin's dicta in that case have established that, in cases involving physical injury or property damage, a person normally owes a duty to take reasonable care to avoid foreseeable harm to anyone who may be classified as a "neighbour": that is, anyone who may foreseeably be affected by his conduct. We shall see, however, that foreseeability of merely "economic loss", not consequent on physical injury or damage, is not sufficient to create liability in tort.

Nature of contractual rights and duties

The promises which form part of the contractual bargain must be strictly performed. In a contract for the sale of goods there is an implied term that the goods sold will be of merchantable quality[26] and liability is strict. Thus if Donoghue had been able to sue Minchella, the latter would have been liable even though he was not at fault in any way. There is also strict liability

---

25 See *Woodar Investment Development Ltd* v. *Wimpey Construction UK Ltd* [1980] 1 WLR 277, doubting dicta in *Jackson* v. *Horizon Holidays Ltd* [1975] 1 WLR 1468.
26 Sale of Goods Act 1979, s.14(2).

for the quality of materials supplied under a construction contract.[27] Contract liability is not always strict. Firstly, the contract itself may state that there is only to be liability if there has been a failure to use due skill and care. This is common in contracts with design professionals, though it leaves the professional responsible for seeing that reasonable care has been taken by any one to whom the work is delegated. Secondly the courts tend to hold that in contracts for professional services the professional's only implied obligation is to use reasonable care and skill to achieve the desired result, rather than a promise that the result will be achieved. Probably this is because the result is to some extent unpredictable.[28] A designer who agrees to provide a design meeting certain performance specifications has been held to be accepting strict responsibility for ensuring that the specifications are fulfilled;[29] but subsequent cases seem to treat this as exceptional.[30]

Nature of duties in tort

A person will not be liable in negligence unless he has failed to exercise the care that could reasonably be expected from someone in his position.[31] This applies both to actions and to advice. Where the action is done or the advice is given in pursuance of a contract, the terms of the contract may modify the general tortious duty of care as between the parties to the contract. Thus the property owner who has specifically contracted for a low cost, risky design cannot claim that the designer was negligent in not providing a risk-free design. But a third party who is injured as the result of the design failing will not be affected by the contract and can claim in negligence against the designer.[32] Liability under the Defective Premises Act 1972 and Consumer Protection Act 1987 is strict.[33]

Excluding liability

It is possible for the parties to limit or exclude their contractual liability, subject to the provisions of the Unfair Contract Terms Act 1977. This is not

27 See paper 2
28 Eg *Thake* v. *Maurice* [1986] QB 644.
29 *Greaves & Co (Contractors) Ltd* v. *Baynham, Meikle & Partners* [1975] 1 WLR 1095.
30 *Hawkins* v. *Chrysler (UK) Ltd and Burne Associates* (1986) 38 BLR 36.
31 The most frequently cited case is probably *Bolam* v. *Friern Hospital Management Committee* [1957] 1 WLR 582.
32 *Voli* v. *Inglewood Shire Council* (1963) 110 CLR 74.
33 Subject in the latter case to the "development risk defence": s.4(1)(e).

the place for a full review of the Act, but it will be remembered that:

(i) business liability for death or personal injury caused by negligence, including "contractual" negligence, cannot be excluded or restricted;[34]
(ii) business liability for other loss or damage so caused can be excluded or restricted but only if the clause is fair and reasonable;[35]
(iii) clauses in supply of goods contracts and contracts for work and materials excluding or restricting liability for quality, etc. of the goods will be void in consumer contracts and will be effective in other contracts only if fair and reasonable;[36]
(iv) exclusion or limitation clauses in other consumer contracts and in a party's "written standard terms of business" (still undefined) will have to be fair and reasonable in order to protect the business.[37]

The courts have shown themselves very ready to hold clauses unreasonable - for instance, if the party whose liability was limited in practice paid more than the clause allowed, or could insure more easily;[38] or if the other party did not have much chance to assess the risks and arrange insurance.[39] This may partly be due to the burden of proving reasonableness being on the proferens,[40] and to the reluctance of the courts to interfere with the decision at first instance.[41] However it suggests that the courts are still hostile to clauses even in business agreements unless the parties clearly went in "with their eyes open" and there are good reasons for the clause. It is perhaps worth noting that all the cases appear to involve standard form contracts, and all but one[42] have been of unilateral provenance.

Tortious liability may also be excluded by agreement with the defendant and sometimes by a notice to him but subject to the terms of the Act as set out above.

Nature of losses compensable in contract

The victim of a breach of contract may recover damages for any loss caused by the breach unless:

34 Section 2(1).
35 Section 2(2).
36 Sections 6 and 7.
37 Section 3.
38 *George Mitchell (Chesterhall) Ltd* v. *Finney Lock Seeds Ltd* [1983 1 All ER 108.
39 *Phillips Products Ltd* v. *Hyland* [1987] 2 All ER 620.
40 Section 11(5).
41 *Phillips Products* op.cit..
42 *Walker* v. *Boyle* [1982]1 WLR 495 (National Conditions of Sale).

(i) it could have been avoided by taking reasonable steps - the so called duty to mitigate;[43] or

(ii) the loss was not the natural and probable result of the type of breach which occurred and the party in breach was not warned at the time that the contract was made that such a loss might occur.[44]

The aim is to put the plaintiff, so far as money can do it, into the same position as if the contract had been performed.[45] No distinction is drawn between losses resulting from physical damage or injury and financial losses such as loss of value of the building or loss of profit. Thus on the facts of *Donoghue* v. *Stevenson* the friend could have recovered from Minchella the cost of a replacement bottle of ginger beer.

Nature of losses compensable in tort

There has been a great deal of difficulty over the kinds of loss which are compensable in the tort of negligence. Traditionally a distinction has been drawn between physical injury and property damage, on the one hand, and "economic loss" on the other. Financial losses directly consequent on physical injury - eg. loss of earnings and medical expenses - and on physical damage - eg. the cost of hiring a replacement car while the damaged one is repaired, or loss of rental value - have always been recoverable, but purely financial loss has not. Thus a factory which is unable to work because a contractor's negligence has deprived it of electric power without damaging the factory itself cannot recover loss of profit.[46] Economic loss is recoverable only in very limited (and ill-defined) circumstances. The current position seems to be that physical injury or property damage is recoverable on the foreseeability principle described earlier; but that economic loss is probably only recoverable if there is a "special relationship" between the parties.[47] Such a relationship, described as "equivalent to contract", will probably only exist if one party is relying on the other to give careful advice[48] or to carry out work skilfully[49] and the other knows this and accepts

---

43 See generally *British Westinghouse Electric and Manufacturing Co Ltd* v. *Underground Railways of London Ltd* [1912] AC 673.
44 *Hadley* v. *Baxendale* (1854) 9 Exch 341.
45 *Robinson* v. *Harman* (1848) 1 Exch 850, 855. Compensation is not given, however, for vexation or disappointment, unless the contract was one to provide enjoyment: *Jarvis* v. *Swan's Tours Ltd* [1973] 2 QB 233; *Bliss* v. *SETRHA* [1987] ICR 700.
46 *Spartan Steel & Alloys Ltd* v. *Martin & Co (Contractors) Ltd* [1973] QB 27.
47 Ibid.
48 *Hedley Byrne & Co Ltd* v. *Heller & Partners Ltd* [1964] AC 465.
49 *Junior Books Ltd* v. *Veitchi Co Ltd* [1983] 1 AC 520.

responsibility. The fact that economic loss is foreseeable if the advice is wrong or the work is not well done is not sufficient.

Carelessly constructed or designed items

In this context, physical damage to property does not include damage to a negligently built or designed item itself, but only damage to some other item of the plaintiff's property.[50] Thus if a defective appliance catches fire and your house is destroyed, you will have an action for loss of the house; but if the damage is simply that the appliance itself is destroyed, this is not normally compensable in tort. Equally the friend could not have sued Stevenson for the 6d she threw away on the defective ginger beer. There will only be liability in tort in such a case if the owner and the negligent manufacturer or builder were in a special relationship. Such a relationship has been held to exist between an employer and a nominated subcontractor,[51] but the scope of the decision is very much in doubt. Even then the plaintiff's rights are probably not fully equivalent to contract rights. Whereas in contract the damages should put the plaintiff into the same position as if the contract had been performed, so that it should recover the full cost of putting right the defects plus consequential loss, the measure in tort is to put it back to its earlier position. This may mean that if the cost of repair is now greater than the amount it originally paid for the work, the damages for the repair work may be limited to the latter figure.

Limitation in contract and tort

The limitation periods in contract and tort differ. In contract, time (6 years, or 12 years if the contract is by deed) runs from the date of breach. In tort, the broad position is that action must be commenced within six years or for latent damage within three years from the date by which the damage could reasonably have been discovered, with an overall longstop of 15 years from the date at which the negligent act occurred.

Privity and subcontractors

It may be helpful to explore the problems caused by the doctrine of privity when subcontractors are employed. Although a subcontractor's work is intended to be for the employer's benefit, the employer cannot sue a

50 *Murphy* v. *Brentwood DC* [1990] 2 All ER 908.
51 *Junior Books*, above.

subcontractor on either the main contract or the subcontract for defective work - nor can the subcontractor sue the employer for payments stated to be due to the subcontractor. Actions in tort are of course possible but, as we have seen, the employer's loss may not be compensable and the employer will have to prove negligence.

The chain of contracts

It is for this reason that liability "up and down the chain of contracts" is so vital. Unless the main contract forbids delegation, the contractor is entitled to employ subcontractors to carry out the work; but the contractor remains responsible for the work so that if it is done defectively the contractor will be liable. There are certain exceptions in the case of nominated subcontractors; for instance, the contractor may not be liable for the extra cost of completion caused by the subcontractor "dropping out". This can cause great difficulty of the type suggested earlier: if the contractor is not liable to the employer, the contractor's recovery against the subcontractor will be limited to its private loss, so that the employer's loss cannot be passed down the chain. These problems will be explored in detail in paper 2 below, but there are two general solutions to them. One is to make the contractor explicitly accept responsibility for these matters, as is done in the ICE conditions (5th ed). The other is for the employer to take a direct warranty from the subcontractor, for instance JCT80 NSC/2.

Protecting subcontractors from tortious liability

One party may be liable to another in both contract and tort - eg. if your private surgeon carelessly amputates the wrong leg you can sue the surgeon in either contract or tort. The parties sometimes wish to exclude or limit liability - the employer may prefer to bear some of the risks itself. Subject to the Unfair Contract Terms Act 1977,[52] contracting parties may agree that their liability in tort as well as in contract may be limited or excluded. Because of the doctrine of privity, a third party cannot usually be protected from liability in tort by a clause in a contract to which he is not privy.[53] Nor can he use a clause in a contract to which he is party as a defence against an

---

52 Especially s.2(1) (business liability for death or personal injury caused by negligence cannot be excluded or restricted); s.2(2) (business liability for other loss or damage may be restricted or excluded but only in so far as the term satisfies the requirement of reasonableness).

53 *Scruttons Ltd* v. *Midland Silicones Ltd* [1962] AC 446.

action for negligence by a plaintiff who is not privy to the contract.[54] The obverse of the doctrine that no one can enforce obligations under a contract to which he or she is not a party is that a contract cannot normally affect persons who are not party to it.

Agency as a way of limiting tortious liability

It may be desired to limit a subcontractor's liability in tort to the employer. For the reasons just explained, neither a clause in the main contract nor one in the subcontract may be effective to do this. A possible way out is for the main contractor to take an exclusion or limitation of liability clause on the subcontractor's behalf (ie as the subcontractor's agent). There will thus be a contract between employer and subcontractor, made through the agency of the main contractor, that the subcontractor's liability in tort will be limited according to the terms of the clause in consideration of the subcontractor doing the subcontract work.[55] This of course requires careful drafting in advance, and it is not a foolproof system of protecting the subcontractor. Firstly, the clause will not operate to protect the subcontractor from liability for any damage caused before the subcontract work has been started, since this is when the direct contract comes into existence.[56] Secondly and more seriously, the subcontractor must show that the main contractor was authorised to act on its behalf or that it has effectively ratified what has been done in its name. A principal can only ratify what the agent has done if at the time the agent acted it could have identified the principal for whom it was acting. Thus an "agency" clause in a Model A contract purporting to protect a nominated subcontractor failed to protect a subcontractor who was nominated only after the main contract had been signed.[57] Probably the only safe ways to protect subcontractors are for employers to contract directly with them or to set up a "circle of indemnities" under which the main contractor is obliged to indemnify the sub against any tortious liability to the employer and the employer agrees in turn to indemnify the main contractor.[58]

54 There are exceptions relating to the law of bailment: see most recently *Singer Co (UK) Ltd* v. *Tees & Hartlepool PA* [1988] 2 Lloyd's Rep 164.
55 *New Zealand Shipping Co Ltd* v. *Satterthwaite* [1975] AC 154.
56 *Raymond Burke Motors Ltd* v. *Mersey Docks & Harbour Board* [1986] 1 Lloyd's Rep 155.
57 *Southern Water Authority* v. *Carey* [1985] 2 All ER 1077.
58 See the judgment of Lord Reid in *Scruttons* and *Gore* v. *Van der Lann* [1967] 2 QB 31.

Acceptance of risk as a defence to liability in tort

There have for some time been suggestions that a defendant who is not a party to a contract may nonetheless be able to take advantage of clauses within it if the latter constitute an acceptance of the risk of damage by the party affected by the clause.[59] In *Norwich City Council* v. *Harvey*[60] The Court of Appeal seems to have come close to accepting this argument in holding that a subcontractor whose employee negligently set fire to the Employers' building was not liable because of cl.20C of the JCT 1963 conditions, which states that the Works shall be at the sole risk of the Employer as regards loss or damage by fire. This case is discussed in paper 2 below.

Conclusion

I have tried in this paper to suggest that, while contract is a flexible device, it is one which has to be used with care. This applies to questions of formation, to the contractual obligations and exclusions or restrictions of liability, and most of all to problems of privity. I believe that careful drafting can still deal with most of the difficulties encountered under construction contracts.

59 See *Wilson* v. *Darling Island Stevedoring Co* [1956] 1 Lloyd's Rep 346, 365.
60 [1989] 1 All ER 1180.

Liability for Default of 2
Sub-Contractors

Peter Barber

Synopsis

This paper reviews comprehensively the circumstances in which a main contractor may be liable (or not liable) to the Employer for default by a sub-contractor, either in contract or tort, and considers the possible defence of "no loss" under forms of management contract.

Introduction

The object of this paper is to examine the liability of a contractor who, having been charged with an obligation or duty, seeks by contract to obtain its performance by another, where that other fails to perform in some respect. The situation addressed here is where the original obligor retains its obligation or duty to the original obligee, notwithstanding that it imposes a new and independent obligation on a third party to perform some or all of the content of the original obligation or duty. This is to be distinguished at the outset from an outright assignment of the original obligation, which can only be effected by way of novation so as to substitute a new obligation owed directly by the third party to the original obligee. There, the question of the original obligor's liability for a failure by the new third party obligor will not arise, because as part of the novation the original obligor will normally have been released entirely from its obligation. Here, the original obligation is not substituted by a new and distinct obligation owed by someone else, but simply is performed wholly or in part by someone else, a sub-contractor, under a separate contract with the original obligor, the main contractor, to which the obligee is not privy.

The obligee may be the main contractor's employer, in which case liability, if any, will arise in contract; or it may be some third party with an interest in the contract project, in which case (in the absence of some direct contractual link) any liability of the main contractor will be owed in tort. The nature and extent of its liability for sub-contractors will vary considerably depending on how the cause of action on the original obligation arises.

Broadly speaking, where the obligation arises in tort, through a duty of care, the obligor can in most circumstances discharge its duty and thereby obtain relief from liability, by contracting another to perform it - subject, however, to certain exceptions. By contrast, where the obligation is created by contract, as a basic principle the obligor will not be able unilaterally to escape liability by sub-contracting some or all of the obligation - but, again, subject to (even more) exceptions. In each case it is the exceptions and the extent of limitation to the broad principles which give rise to interesting difficulties, and which are largely the subject of this paper.

Finally by way of introduction, one should note the relevance to this issue of the distinction between various types of sub-contractor, depending on the way in which they are appointed. That is to say, the nature and extent of a contractor's liability for its sub-contractors (whether in contract or in tort) may depend on whether they are "nominated" – designated by the employer or its professional consultants in accordance with the prescribed procedures under the contract for selecting sub-contractors for appointment by the main contractor; or "domestic" – selected entirely at the discretion of the main contractor and, so far as the employer is concerned, entirely within the household of the main contractor; or chosen through some intermediate procedure, in which the employer and/or its professional consultants take a greater or lesser role together with the main contractor (for example, "naming" of sub-contractors under the JCT's Intermediate Form of contract). The degree of involvement of the employer and its professional team in the selection of the sub-contractor can have a material effect on the nature of the main contractor's liability for that sub-contractor.

It is proposed in this paper to examine the position first in tort, then in contract, where there is more scope for difficulty owing to the possibility of self-created exceptions generated by the contract itself. Consideration will be given to exceptions created both through interpretation or implication of contract terms, and by express provisions. In the context of express contractual exceptions, the paper will conclude with a review of the House of Lords decision in "*The Padre Island*"[1] in the different but (it will be seen) analogous field of third party rights in marine insurance.

Tortious liability for Sub-Contractors – General Principle

As a general common law principle, a contractor under a duty of care (or certain other forms of private law tortious duties) to a third party can adequately discharge such a duty, and thus relieve itself from liability, by delegating it to a sub-contractor or independent contractor whom he has used reasonable care in selecting. Several cases have established this

---

1 *Firma C. Trade S.A.* v. *Newcastle Protection & Indemnity Assoc* [1991] A AC 1 A.L. (E).

proposition; perhaps one of the best known is *Haseldine* v. *C.A. Daw & Son Ltd.*[2] in which a main contractor was held not responsible for the negligent installation of a lift by independent contractors whom it had properly selected and could reasonably have expected competently to carry out their works. More recently, and emphatically, the principle was confirmed by the House of Lords in *D&F Estates Limited and Others* v. *Church Commissioners for England and Others*[3]. There, in considering the liability of the main contractors for the negligent workmanship of their sub-contracted plasterer, Lord Bridge said: "It is trite law that the employer of an independent contractor is, in general, not liable for the negligence or other torts committed by the contractor in the course of the execution of the work."

In this connection Lord Bridge referred to the recommendations of the Law Commission in paragraph 26 of its Report on "Civil Liability of Vendors and Lessors for Defective Premises"[4]. These recommendations included: "(a)that a builder of a dwelling... should be placed under a duty, similar to his common law obligations, to build properly and should not be able to contract out of this duty", and "(d)that those who (without being builders or otherwise concerned with work taken on for or in connection with the provision of the dwelling) arrange in the course of their business for the construction of dwellings for sale or letting to the public, should be placed under the same duty as builders towards persons who acquire interests in those dwellings...". Whilst considering that such conclusions as a matter of social policy might be "entirely admirable", Lord Bridge concluded that it was not open to the court to embody such a policy in the law without the assistance of the legislature, and that the Defective Premises Act of 1972 must be taken to have gone as far in that direction as the legislature had intended.

As also mentioned by Lord Bridge in *D & F Estates* there are, however, certain exceptions to the general rule that a contractor is not liable for the negligence of his carefully selected independent sub-contractors. Considered here are the principal such exceptions; whilst it is debatable (and has been suitably debated) whether they are in fact true "exceptions", they are on any reckoning circumstances which prevent the application of the general rule in a context where it might otherwise have been applicable.

Tortious liability for Sub-Contractors – Exceptions – Negligent Selection

The first of these "exceptions" follows from the way in which the rule was

---

2 [1941] KB 343
3 [1989] AC 177
4 Law Commission Report No.40 dated 15 December 1970

formulated in the first place, in referring to the careful or non-negligent, selection of independent contractors. It follows that if the independent contractor or sub-contractor to whom work is entrusted is not competently and carefully selected, then the original duty of care will not have been discharged; negligent selection of a sub-contractor can itself constitute a breach of a duty of care where one is held to have existed in the first place. Thus, in *Saper* v. *Hungate Builders Limited*,[5] a large builders' skip hired from and delivered by a plant hire company was inadequately lit by the contractors and their servant who had hired it, resulting in a car accident. The hire company were held to be as much under a duty to third parties to see that the skip was adequately lit, as the contractors who hired it; and the hire company were held not to have discharged their duty merely by having left it in the care and control of the contracting company and its servant – "They did nothing at all about lighting this obstruction; they simply left the skip there in the road with a man of whose capacity, experience and equipment they knew nothing, and to whom they never said a word about lighting."

Equally, failure to engage a sufficient quantity of labour will prevent a contractor from discharging its duty by entrusting work to an independent sub-contractor. For example, in *Pinn* v. *Rew*,[6] a drover engaged to drive cattle to a farm procured another man, who was intending to drive some bullocks in the same direction, to drive the cattle along with them. The drover was found liable for negligence when one of the cows, disturbed by a dog, tossed someone more than six feet in the air. Atkin J. upheld the County Court's finding that the defendant had been negligent in employing a single drover to drive the cattle when they clearly would have needed more supervision in order to keep them under control.

Tortious Liability for Sub-Contractors – Exceptions – Non-Delegable Duty

The second main exception to the general principle takes a number of different forms, all of which amount to a finding that the original duty is itself of such a particular nature as to be "non-delegable". There are a number of types of such duty and it is beyond the scope of this paper to attempt to analyse them in detail; in the main they amount to situations where the duty arises either through the inherently dangerous nature of operations being carried out, or from some kind of public law or statutory obligation. Operations in respect of which a duty arises may be inherently

5   [1972] RTR 3 80
6   [1916] 32 TLR 451

dangerous due to their situation – as for example, in the case of operations undertaken on (or in some circumstances near) the highway – or due to the nature of the substances or materials with which the operations are concerned. The public nature of a duty may arise from its being imposed by statute or from the general circumstances in which the duty arises.

In either case, the circumstances have to be such that the duty becomes "not merely a duty to take care but a duty to provide that care is taken" – *The Pass of Ballater*.[7] In that case a consulting engineer employed by a firm of ship repairers, when certifying that a vessel was gas free and fit for the use of naked light, omitted to mention a certain part of the ship which he had not properly inspected and which subsequently exploded when the ship repairers used an oxyacetylene burner in it. The duty to take care in circumstances involving the use of implements or substances dangerous in themselves, such as flame bearing instruments or explosives, was held to be a duty the burden of which could not be "thrown off". Similarly, in *Riverstone Meat Co. Pty. Limited* v. *Lancashire Shipping Co. Limited*,[8] the duty of ship owners to exercise "due diligence" to make a ship seaworthy was held not capable of delegation to an independent firm of ship repairers; it amounted to a duty to ensure that reasonable care was taken, rather than merely to take care.

The position regarding statutory duties depends on the construction of the statute in question; where a statutory duty is construed to be "absolute", it cannot be passed off onto independent contractors – *Smith* v. *Cammell Laird & Co Limited*.[9] The greater difficulty in this context has been to determine where and to what extent a statutory duty to ensure, for example, compliance with certain kinds of regulations, is enlarged to become a general private law duty, owed either to certain classes of people proximate to the authority concerned, or to the world at large. In *Murphy* v. *Brentwood District Council*,[10] the Court of Appeal had held that a local authority's duty to inspect and approve a property for compliance with building regulations could not be delegated to outside consultants: "The duty was imposed on the council, no matter from whom it sought or obtained expert advice" (Ralph Gibson LJ). The House of Lords[11], overruling *Anns* v. *Merton L.B.C.*[12], held there to be, after all, no private law duty on a local authority amounting to a duty owed to subsequent occupiers of the house to save them harmless from economic loss consequent on the discovery that the property does not

7 [1942] P 112
8 [1961] AC 807
9 [1940] AC 242
10 [1991] 1 WLR 414
11 [1991] 1 AC 398
12 [1978] AC 728

comply with building regulations. Consequently, the House of Lords found it unnecessary to decide whether a duty of that nature could be delegated to a subcontractor (Lords Keith and Oliver expressly and the other five Law Lords by implication).

However, in circumstances where a statutory obligation does still give rise to some private law duty of care, it is submitted that the position will still be the same as it was held to be by the Court of Appeal in *Murphy*; for example, where the duty consists in granting some form of approval then, although an authority may seek the advice of independent consultants in determining whether or not to grant the approval, the act of granting or withholding the approval is the act of the authority itself and cannot be delegated. In other words, even though the House of Lords in *Murphy* held that the particular private law duty contended for was not in fact owed, nevertheless duties of a similar nature to that contended for – whether based on statutory or "absolute" obligations or inherently dangerous circumstances – will still be subject to the principles enunciated by the Court of Appeal in *Murphy* as to the circumstances where duties cannot be delegated to sub-contractors.

Drawing the line in construing whether a duty does or does not fall into the non-delegable class may eventually prove difficult, as recognised in the *Riverstone Meat* case by Viscount Simonds[13]: "No one, I think, doubts that in some circumstances a defendant can escape liability for the negligence of an independent contractor; nor could he doubt that in other circumstances he cannot so escape ... I do not think it necessary to try and reconcile all the cases on this subject. It is surely sufficient to say that in the context of the Hague Rules it is patent that the obligation of the ship owner is in the latter category." It will not always be quite so "patent" into which category a duty or obligation falls, but it is at all events clear that the ordinary duty to exercise care and skill in building, or in advising in connection with the design or construction of a building, falls within the delegable category. Thus, in *D & F Estates*, Lord Bridge concluded that if the contractors in an ordinary building situation were to be held liable in tort for the negligent workmanship of their sub-contractors, it would have to be shown that in the circumstances "they had assumed a personal duty to all the world to ensure that [the building] should be free of dangerous effects". In fact, as concluded in *D & F Estates* and now emphasised in *Murphy*, the builder has no such general duty. In *D & F Estates*, Lord Bridge on this specific point expressly declined to follow the New Zealand Court of Appeal in *Mount Albert Borough Council* v. *Johnson*[14]. Their finding that the duty of a development company having homes built on development land for sale to the public was

13 [1961] AC 807, 845
14 [1979] 2 NZLR 234

"a duty to see that proper care and skill are exercised in the building of the houses" was rejected as a matter of social policy best left to the legislature rather than the judiciary to implement.

A final exception to the "non-delegable duty" principle: even if the duty is considered to be of such a nature as to be non-delegable, it will not be broken by mere "casual or collateral" negligence on the part of an employer's independent contractor or sub-contractor. Again, it is difficult to draw a precise line but it seems that negligence will be categorised as such if it arises outside the actual act which the independent contractor is employed to perform. In *Padbury* v. *Holliday and Greenwood Ltd.*[15], the employee of a sub-contractor fitting metal windows into a house placed a tool on the windowsill in such a position that it was knocked off by the window being blown shut by the wind. This was held (perhaps somewhat strangely) to be outside the scope of what the sub-contractors were employed to do and therefore outside the scope of the employer's otherwise non-delegable duty of ensuring that passers-by were not injured by the operation of the works in question.

Contractual Liability for Sub-Contractors – General Principle

In clear distinction to the position in tort, it is probably equally "trite law" that, although a contracting party can in many cases sub-contract performance to some other person, so as to bind the other contracting party provided the latter receives due performance, it will nevertheless remain liable for any breach that may happen; and the other contracting party will not be put to recovering from the sub-contractor for breach of contract. Whether or not a contractor is entitled to sub-contract the performance of any aspect of its work to someone else is another issue and beyond the scope of this paper to examine; but, whether or not so entitled, it will in the ordinary course remain fully responsible to its employer for any defective performance by its sub-contractor. Thus, for example, the repairer of a motor car will remain responsible to his customer for its proper repair even where a particular aspect of the repair such as the realigning of the brakes is sent, on the repairer's recommendation, to a specialist firm, and the customer agrees to this; the customer nevertheless relies on the repairer to procure the proper repair of the brakes and the repairer cannot not avoid that responsibility by using other specialists to perform, even with the customer's consent – *Stewart* v. *Reavell's Garage*[16].

That this principle is accepted for the most part as a "given", is reflected

15 [1912] 28 TLR 494
16 [1952] 2 QB 545

in those standard forms of main building contract which adopt the traditional system of building procurement on the basis of a lump sum for employer-designed works, or even a design and build system. For example, JCT 1980 Private With Quantities form clause 19.2 sets out the limitations on the Contractor's right to sub-contract and in clause 20.2 requires the Contractor to give an express indemnity to the Employer against liability for default of the Contractor's servants or agents. Adaptations of these forms sometimes add an express statement as to liability of the contractor for the performance of his sub-contractors but, in the absence of special circumstances such as those considered below, it is suggested that such statements do not add to the position as it would stand under the general law.

It is precisely the special circumstances and cases for exceptions to the general principle, which cause difficulty. In the case of liability in contract, as distinct from tort, in addition to the possibility of exceptions introduced by the general law, there is of course the possibility of exceptions introduced by the contract itself.

Contractual Liability for Sub-Contractors – Exceptions implied by law – reliance

The exceptions to the general principle consist mainly of situations where the person giving an order, or employer, has in some way not relied or has ceased to rely on the person accepting the order, the main contractor, in respect of some aspect of the work, and has instead relied on some other party, who may or may not have been a sub-contractor to the main contractor.

For example, in the context of an ordinary contract for work and materials a contractor will not be liable for defects in the materials if he has not himself been responsible for selecting them and if the owner has instead required him to use particular materials. In such circumstances, the contractor will not be taken to give a warranty that the materials supplied will be reasonably fit for their purpose (which would otherwise be the warranty implied in a contract for work and materials) but merely that the materials supplied have been obtained from the source stipulated. In *G H Myers & Co.* v. *Brent Cross Service Co.*[17], a car was repaired with connecting rods obtained by the repairers from the manufacturers of the car, and one of the rods later proved to be defective in a way which could have not been discoverable by the repairers with reasonable care or skill. It was not clear on the facts before the Court of Appeal whether the repairers had been instructed specifically to use new parts supplied by the manufacturer, or simply to effect the repairs

17 [1934] 1 KB 46

as best they might; the case was accordingly remitted to the County Court for determination of this. Du Parcq J said in the Court of Appeal: "A person contracting to do work and supply materials warrants that the materials which he uses will be of good quality and reasonably fit for the purpose for which he is using them, unless the circumstances of the contract are such as to exclude any such warranty". Such circumstances would cover a situation where the owner stipulates the course of parts for the repairs. This was followed by the House of Lords in *Young & Marten Ltd* v. *McManus Childs Ltd*[18], where a sub-contractor supplying and fixing roofing tiles was held to have given an implied warranty as to their quality notwithstanding the main contractor having specified the particular kind of tiles and their supplier.

In the context of construction work, the issue arises most prominently in the case of specialist design carried out by a nominated or other independently selected sub-contractor where, to the knowledge of all parties concerned, the employer is in fact relying on the sub-contractor for some element of specialist design rather than on the main contractor or upon his own architect or other consultants. In *University of Warwick* v. *Sir Robert McAlpine*[19] epoxy resin was injected to remedy problems found with white ceramic wall tile cladding; the resin itself caused further cracking of the cladding. The resin was recommended by the architects and supplied and injected by a sub-contractor selected by them; the main contractor was not involved in the decision to use it and expressed reservations as to its suitability. Garland J found that the employer had relied on the skill and judgement of the selected sub-contractor rather than that of the main contractor, and accordingly that no warranty of fitness of the resin could be implied into the main contract.

So far as the employer's architect is concerned, the position will usually be reasonably clear if he is appointed on conditions such as the RIBA form. In *Investors in Industry Limited* v. *South Bedfordshire DC*[20], Slade LJ held that the then current version of the RIBA conditions of engagement under consideration clearly contemplated that "where a particular part of the work involved in a building contract involves specialist knowledge or skill beyond that which an architect of ordinary competence may reasonably be expected to possess, the architect is at liberty to recommend to his client that a reputable independent consultant, who appears to have the relevant specialist knowledge or skill, shall be appointed by the client to perform this task. If following such a recommendation a consultant with these qualifications is appointed, the architect will normally carry no legal responsibility for the work to be done by the expert which is beyond the capability of an

18 [1969] 1 AC 454
19 (1988) 42 BLR 2
20 [1986] 1 All ER 787

architect of ordinary competence; in relation to the work allotted to the expert, the architect's legal responsibility will normally be confined to directing and coordinating the expert's work as a whole."

The position is likely to be the same whether the "expert" is directly appointed as a consultant to the client or is a sub-contractor or sub-consultant designated for employment by the main contractor. This is reflected in the current version of the RIBA conditions, of which condition 3.8 provides: "A specialist contractor, sub-contractor or supplier who is to be employed by the client to design any part of the works may be nominated by either the architect or the client, subject to acceptance by each party. The client will hold such contractor, sub-contractor or supplier, and not the architect, responsible for the competence, proper execution and perform-ance of the work thereby entrusted to that contractor, sub-contractor or supplier. The architect will have the authority to coordinate and integrate such work into the overall design." Needless to say, this condition or its equivalent is frequently the subject of amendment or substitution in negotiated architects' appointment agreements; but the general principle seems generally adhered to, that the architect's responsibility for design work carried out by sub-contractors or other consultants to the employer (in effect, anyone not actually appointed by the architect itself), is confined to coordinating and integrating their design work in that of the overall design of the project without responsibility for the efficacy of the specialist design itself.

The case of the main contractor who actually employs the specialist design sub-contractor is more difficult to evaluate. There are various possible permutations depending on the terms of both the main contract and the sub-contract, of which three may be mentioned here.

First, it seems established that where the main contract contains, however briefly or incidentally, an express imposition of a design responsibility on the main contractor, then the main contractor will still be liable in respect of specialist design performed by a sub-contractor in direct consultation with the employer and the employer's directly appointed consultants, even where there has been no practical involvement by the main contractor in the element of specialist design concerned and the employer cannot be said, as a matter of fact, to have "relied" exclusively or at all on the main contractor in respect of it. *IBA* v. *EMI and BICC*[21], concerned a contract between IBA and EMI for the supply and erection of a television mast, the design for which was required to be carried out by BICC as a subcontractor to EMI. EMI's quotation, and the basis on which the contract was placed with it, was "for the design, supply and delivery" of the mast, though the actual conditions of contract did not deal in detail or at all with the extent of any design responsibility of EMI. The Court of Appeal nevertheless held (and the House of Lords did not dissent from this, though eventually deciding the case on the grounds of negligence rather than contract) that EMI's obligation to the IBA included an absolute warranty of suitability of the mast based on the briefly expressed design obligation in the quotation, and notwithstanding that the actual design, as stipulated for by the IBA, was carried out by BICC. Roskill LJ rejected an argument that EMI had assumed no contractual obligations to the IBA in respect of the design of the mast, on the basis that this did not take account of the totality of the contract documents and ignored the express obligations assumed by EMI on acceptance of their tender by IBA, a tender which loaded 10% onto the sub-contract figure for the design, supply and delivery of the mast. Then, considering the nature of the main contractor's design obligation which had not been abrogated to the sub-contractor, he concluded, following *Young & Marten* v. *McManus Childs*, that there was no reason "for not importing an obligation as to reasonable fitness for the purpose into these contracts or for importing a different obligation in relation to design from the obligation which plainly exists in relation to materials".

The second situation to be considered in the context of an employer's reliance on a specialist sub-contractor for design, is that where, although specialist design is in fact carried out by a subcontractor, there is no express design obligation included in the main contract. This is of course the situation which arises more and more frequently in practice under the traditional employer-designed forms of contract, where the main contractor's obligation is confined to carrying out and completing the construction of the works supposedly to the employer's architect's design, but in fact a substantial amount of specialist design is performed by sub-contractors either nominated by the employer or its architect or other consultants, or somehow otherwise designated by those consultants. Frequent though such a situation is in practice, it does not appear yet to have been put to the test in the courts. The undetermined question is therefore whether in such circumstances an implied warranty regarding the element of specialist design is included in the main contract, by virtue of the main contractor's acceptance (even if such acceptance is imposed by the terms of the main contract) of the subcontractor, and by virtue of the inclusion, in the main contract scope of works, of sub-contract works which do include such design. Practitioners and commentators have expressed differing views on this, with Professor Duncan Wallace concluding that the question is to be regarded as still open[22], citing amongst others the Irish case of *Norta*

22 *Construction Contracts: Principles and Policies in Tort and Contract* (1986), p.327

Wallpapers Ltd v. *John Sisk Ltd*[23].

It is submitted, notwithstanding the *Norta Wallpapers* case, that the *IBA* case and cases referred to in it, and the subsequent case of *Viking Grain Storage Ltd.* v. *T.H. White Installations Limited*[24], do in fact point in the direction of such an implied term in the main contract, in order to complete the chain or "string" of liability from employer through to sub-contractor, even if they do not categorically dispose of the issue. Thus, in *Young & Marten*, Lord Upjohn said[25]: "The practical business effect and just solution to this type of breach of contract is that each vendor or contractor of labour and materials should warrant his supply of materials against patent and latent defects so that by the well-known chain of third party procedures the ultimate culprit, the manufacturer, may be made liable for his defective manufacture". Following and referring to this, in *IBA* v. *EMI* Roskill LJ said[26]: "It has been a striking feature of the development of this branch of the law in recent years that commercial contracts should be interpreted so that where there is a succession of contracts, as in the case of string contracts for the sale of goods on one of the London commodity markets, or as here, in the case of successive construction contracts, the ultimate liability if something goes wrong should rest where it properly belongs, and that the court should not be too astute to apply the rules of privity of contract or reliance on skill and judgement for the purposes of section 14(1) of the Sale of Goods Act 1893 or the equivalent obligation in relation to contracts for work and labour done and materials supplied so as to defeat obvious business intention by over-rigid adherence to strictly legal principle". In following *IBA* v. *EMI* in *Viking Grain Storage* v. *T.H. White*, Judge John Davies QC referred, again, to "the arguments against cutting the chain of responsibility in a case like this, with its tally of sub-contracts, which would be the consequence of not implying the terms sought".

The third situation, however, to consider in this context is where the chain of liability referred to is in fact broken, through inability of the main contractor to recover from its sub-contractor through the terms of the sub-contract in respect of the point of liability at issue. Again, this does not appear to have been tested in the courts, but, as pointed out by Professor Duncan Wallace[27], where there is an express design liability on the nominated sub-contractor through the terms of the sub-contract, any lack of actual reliance by the main contractor on the sub-contractor should not

---

23 (1980) 14 BLR 49
24 (1985) 33 BLR 103
25 at page 475
26 at page 52
27 op.cit. p. 327

operate so as to defeat that express term and prevent the benefit of it in turn passing up into the main contract, so as to complete the chain of liabilities.

Contractual Liability for Sub-Contractors – Exceptions created by the contract itself

Consideration of a contractor's liability for sub-contractors as a matter of contract rather than tort is subject to the extra dimension that exceptions to the general principle of liability can arise from an interpretation of, or be expressly created by, the terms of the contract itself. Some such exceptions can be implied as terms of the contract and some can arise from express terms. Some are difficult to classify either way, and so for the purposes of this discussion the distinction is drawn between, on the one hand, issues which arise as a result of a particular interpretation of the contract as well as from implied terms, and, on the other hand, express terms of the contract whose whole purpose in themselves is to create an exception to the general principle of liability for sub-contractors.

Contractual interpretations or implied terms relieving main contractor of liability

In the first place, it is clear that not every breach by a sub-contractor, even where it technically constitutes also a breach of contract by the main contractor, will necessarily bring upon the main contractor the consequences attributable to a breach of contract, if the contract on a proper reading provides only for certain specific consequences in relation to the sub-contractor's breach. In *John Jarvis Ltd.* v. *Rockdale Housing Association Ltd*[28], which was possibly the first case on the JCT 1980 standard form to reach the Court of Appeal, a nominated sub-contractor for piling work started late, failed to carry out the work properly and eventually withdrew from site leaving its work defective and unfinished. The contractor was given an instruction to postpone the works. After one month's postponement the contractor gave notice to terminate its employment under the contract relying on sub-clause 28.1.3.4 of the Conditions of Contract, which entitled such termination for suspension of a continuous period of one month by reason, *inter alia*, of "Architect's instructions issued under Clause 23.2 (the postponement instruction) unless caused by reason of some negligence or default of the Contractor." One of the issues in the case turned on whether "the Contractor" in that provision was to be interpreted as meaning only the main contractor or as including its sub-contractors. For the employer it was contended that "Contractor" in Sub-Clause 28.1.3.4 was to be interpreted as meaning in effect "the Contractor, his servants and agents and any sub-contractor and his servants and agents", and that since every breach by a sub-contractor necessarily put the contractor in breach of the main contract, the exception to 28.1.3.4 should be understood as if it read "unless caused by any breach by the Contractor of his obligations hereunder". For the contractor it was argued that "Contractor" covered only the directing mind or senior management of the company and did not include the contractor's servants or agents, or that at least it did not include the contractor's sub-contractors and their servants and agents; therefore, it was contended, either no "negligence or default" could be shown on the part of the contractor, or at least a breach by a sub-contractor did not necessarily constitute a breach by the contractor - until the contractor failed in its principal duty of handing over completed work complying with the requirements of the main contract, it could not be alleged to be in breach of the main contract, whether or not any nominated sub-contractor was in breach of its sub-contract.

Giving the judgment of the Court of Appeal and finding for the Contractor, Bingham LJ considered that the reference in the clause to "the Contractor" could not sensibly be taken as excluding the Contractor's servants and agents, but that the significant aspect of the clause was that it made no reference in express terms to breach of contract. "That is surprising if the existence of a breach of contract by the contractor is what determines his right or lack of right to rely on the sub-clause. In my view the language of the sub-clause is directed to a much more practical (and to men on the ground much more easily answered) question; whose fault is it that the architect's instruction to postpone the work was given?.... [The contractor] does not lose the right [to rely on the suspension of work as a ground for termination] because a nominated sub-contractor chosen by the employer has failed to perform his contract and so (on the assumption [made as a result of a concession by counsel]) put the contractor in breach of the main contract, despite the lack of any actual fault (as opposed to technical breach of contract) on the part of the contractor, his servants and agents."

"Negligence or default" are thus not necessarily to be construed as the same as "breach of contract"; and liability of a contractor for breach of contract by a sub-contractor, even if as a matter of fact it does technically constitute a breach of the main contract, will not necessarily imply liability of the main contractor for "negligence or default" of the sub-contractor. The editors of the Building Law Reports accordingly concluded, rightly, that this result would lead either to users amending the JCT 1980 Form by extending the Clause 28.1.3.4 reference to "the Contractor" so as expressly to include sub-contractors and suppliers of all descriptions and types, or to a further decrease in the use of the system of nomination. For this and many other reasons, it is the latter that seems to have occurred in practice.

It is also worth noting in passing that particular interpretations of terms which have the effect of relieving the main contractor of responsibility in some respect for its sub-contractors, or at least of putting the risk on the Employer for such matters, can even affect the nature of the sub-contractor's liability owed directly to the Employer in tort. In *Norwich City Council* v. *Harvey and Briggs Amasco*[29], Clause 20[C] of the JCT 1963 (July 1977 revision) Form was considered, which provided that as between employer and contractor the existing structures and works would be at the sole risk of the employer as regards loss or damage by, amongst other things, fire. This arose for consideration because in the course of felt roofing work being carried out by a sub-contractor, one of its employees set fire with a blow-torch both to the existing building and to the new extension works that were being constructed under the main contract. Garland J, after reviewing several different arguments as to the possible basis on which the sub-contractor could obtain the benefit of the contractor's relief provision constituted by Clause 20[C], eventually concluded that, simply as a matter of principle, the duty owed by the sub-contractors to the employer was in effect qualified by the relevant term of the employer's contract with the main contractor; the whole scheme of contract and sub-contract made it clear that the Employer was intended to bear the whole risk of damage by fire to existing structures, including fire caused by the negligence of the Contractor or sub-contractors.[30]

Interpretation of the terms of the contract or implication of new terms can, however, also work the other way; that is, it may be effective not only to relieve the main contractor of a liability for a sub-contractor which he would otherwise have had, but also so as to impose a particular obligation on the main contractor in respect of a sub-contractor, in an area in which he might otherwise have been excused of liability. Thus, even if a contractor were to be relieved in some measure of responsibility for specialist design carried out by a nominated sub-contractor, he could still be under a duty to warn the employer if and to the extent that any defective design by the nominated sub-contractor (or the architect) were to come to his attention. In *Victoria University of Manchester* v. *Hugh Wilson and Lewis Womersley (a firm) and others*[31], following his own judgement in *Equitable Debenture Assets*

---

29 (1988) 4 CLJ 217
30 This provision of the standard form has been subsequently modified, first in JCT 1980 and then in JCT Amendment 2 of 1986.
31 (1984) 1 CLJ 162

Corporation Ltd v. *William Moss Group Ltd and others*[32], Judge Newey QC, in an action involving claims for defects that had occurred in tiled cladding to buildings, specifically held that "a term was to be implied in each contract requiring the contractors to warn the architects as the [employer's] agents of defects in design, which they believe to exist. Belief that there were defects required more than mere doubt as to the correctness of the design, but less than actual knowledge of errors."

Contractual interpretations – repudiation by nominated sub-contractors

The prime example, however, of contractual interpretation creating an exception to the general principle of contractors' liability in contract for sub-contractors, is the series of decisions on the consequences of repudiation or failure to perform by a nominated sub-contractor. It is not proposed to examine these in detail here; they have been subject to a close analysis (and trenchant criticism) by Professor Duncan Wallace (*op.cit.*) and others. However it is worth noting them briefly as illustrative of the degree of confusion (even danger) that can result from creation of exceptions to the general principle by interpretation or implication.

In the first case of the series, *NW Metropolitan Regional Hospital Board* v. *T.A. Bickerton & Son Limited*[33] decided, broadly, that clause 27 of the JCT 1963 Form was to be interpreted as requiring a second nomination by the employer in the event of repudiation by a nominated sub-contractor; and that clause 3(5)(c) of that form was to be interpreted as stipulating that, in that event, the main contractor would be entitled to recover from the employer the second nominee's account for the work. Clause 27 provided that prime cost sums included in the contract bills in respect of persons to be nominated by the architect "shall be expended in favour of such persons as the architect... shall instruct", and clause 3(5)(c) provided that, in settling accounts, "the amounts paid or payable under the appropriate contracts by the contractor to nominated sub-contractors... shall be set against the relevant prime cost... and the balance... shall be added to or deducted from the contract sum." In considering the issue of construction, Lord Hodson noted the strong view against the interpretation contended for, in the then current 9th Edition of *Hudson*, expressed in these terms: "If no such term is implied, the contractor can recover as damages from the original sub-contractor the difference between the original and the later sub-contractor's price, whereas if such a term is to be implied the result must be that a nominated sub-contractor, provided he acts in good time, can repudiate his contract with impunity, since the main contractor will have suffered no damage as a result."

Lord Hodson nevertheless managed to find weightier considerations pointing in the opposite direction, in favour of the interpretation contended for by the contractor: "It is conceded by the employer that having nominated a sub-contractor to do prime cost work he cannot require the contractor to perform it. The repudiation by the sub-contractor makes no difference to that position. The employer must, it seems, if he wants the prime cost work done, either renominate or pay a reasonable sum to the persons called upon to do the work. There seems no way out of this impasse save by construing the relevant conditions as placing an obligation on the employer to renominate, in the event of the collapse of the first nomination, if he wants the work to be done."

The point made in *Hudson* quoted above can be seen as advance warning of the "no loss" difficulties which arise out of the express relieving provisions for main contractors, which are discussed later in this paper. However, so far as implied terms and interpretations of contract terms are concerned, the next issue to be resolved after *Bickerton* was the extent, if any, to which the main contractor's implied relief from a duty to renominate in the event of repudiation by a nominated sub-contractor, could be extended into a right to recover from the employer loss and damage suffered by the main contractor as a result of the delay and disruption caused by the nominated sub-contractor's repudiation. On this issue some limits were set in favour of the employer by the House of Lords' decision in *Percy Bilton Limited* v. *GLC*[34]. In that case, which in fact involved an employer's claim for liquidated damages rather than a contractor's claim for additional cost, Lord Fraser declined an invitation to build on dicta of Lord Reid in *Bickerton* to the effect that it would actually be a breach of contract by the employer "if his failure to nominate a sub-contractor impeded the contractor in the execution of his own work". Lord Fraser considered that if that were correct, "its effect would be to turn the employer's duty of nominating a sub-contractor, and if necessary a replacement, into a duty to ensure that the main contractor is not impeded by want of a nominated sub-contractor. That would be virtually a warranty that a nominated sub-contractor would carry on work continuously, or at least that he would be available to do so.... Such a warranty would... place an unreasonable burden on the employer, particularly as he has no direct contractual relationship with a nominated sub-contractor, and no control over him. When the nominated sub-contractor withdrew, the duty of the employer, acting through his architect was... limited to giving instructions for a nomination of a replacement within a reasonable time after receiving a specific application in writing from the main contractor". (It was then held that the employer had in fact in the circumstances failed to perform that duty).

However, at the end of his judgment in *Bilton* Lord Fraser expressed the opinion, in an *obiter dictum*, that the contractor "could have exercised its right of "reasonable objection" under clause 27(a) [of the JCT 1963 Form] to prevent the nomination of any new sub-contractor who did not offer to complete his part of the work within the overall completion period for the contract as a whole." This extension of the *Bickerton* principle was followed by the Court of Appeal in *Fairclough Building Limited* v. *Rhuddlan Borough Council[35]*. Fairclough also concerned the interpretation of clause 27 of the JCT 1963 Form; clause 27(a)(ii) provided that "the Architect... shall not nominate any person as a sub-contractor... who will not enter into a sub-contract which provides (*inter alia*); (ii)that the nominated sub-contractor shall observe, perform and comply with all the provisions of this Contract on the part of the Contractor to be observed, performed and complied with... so far as they relate and apply to the sub-contract works". Parker LJ, referring to the *Bilton* dictum, held that this entitled the contractor to object to a substitute nomination where the substitute's programme for completion of the sub-contract work extended beyond the original date for completion of the work under the main contract; and he declined to rewrite the contract to the extent of implying a term overcoming the difficulty of the extended sub-contract programme by admitting the possibility of an extension of time under the main contract to accommodate it. It was also held that, since it followed from the *Bickerton* reasoning that a main contractor was not himself entitled to carry out prime cost work nor the repair or removal of defective nominated sub-contract work, a substitute nomination was also invalid if it excluded the remedial work necessary in respect of the work done by the defaulting first nominee.

The cases above mentioned all concerned interpretation of aspects of the nomination provisions of the JCT 1963 Form, and produced a degree of stringent criticism of those provisions from the judiciary. The JCT 1980 Form in its original state omitted to address any of these points of criticism, as pointed out by Professor Duncan Wallace[36]. Amendments numbers 4 and 5 to JCT 1980 did eventually address some of the mechanical or procedural difficulties arising out of the previous omissions from the clauses and consequent need to interpret or import implied terms (and Amendment number 10 of 1991 has not made any significant changes on this aspect). Thus, clause 35.24.6.3 now expressly provides that, where (in effect) a first

35 (1985) 30 BLR 26
36 op.cit.

nominee has defaulted in the performance of its nominated sub-contract, and the various tortuous and complicated tripartite communication procedures have been gone through, then "the Architect shall make such further nomination of a Sub-Contractor in accordance with clause 35 as may be necessary to supply and fix the materials or goods or to execute the work and to make good or re-supply or re-execute as necessary any work executed by or any materials or goods supplied by the Nominated Sub-Contractor whose employment has been determined which were not in accordance with the relevant Sub-Contract". However the underlying "no loss" difficulty which results from the *Bickerton* interpretation has not been alleviated by the new JCT 1980 provisions but has rather been perpetuated, clause 35.24.9 providing expressly that "the amount properly payable to the Nominated Sub-Contractor under the Sub-Contract resulting from such further nomination under clause 35.24.6.3 shall be included in the amount stated as due in Interim Certificates and added to the Contract Sum."

This is still in marked contrast to the provisions of Form GC/Works/1 recently revised as Edition 3, which largely maintains the straightforward "pre-*Bickerton*" position, noted with approval by Professor Duncan Wallace, by reference to the previous edition of GC/Works/1. Clause 63(8) of the 3rd Edition now provides: "Subject to paragraph (9) if a nominated sub-contract is determined or assigned the Authority shall not be required to pay the Contractor any greater sums than would have been payable if determination or assignment had not occurred." Paragraph (9) provides for the Authority to bear the extra cost of completing the sub-contract work only where termination of the nominated sub-contract is due to the sub-contractor's insolvency.

There is perhaps little sign yet of the GC/Works/1 Form being used in private works contracts for the advantages it gives to employers; presumably this has been considered too unpalatable to the contracting industry. However, there does seem to have been a trend away from the use of the JCT nomination system and it may be speculated that this has been due as much to the *Bickerton* consequences perpetuated in that system, as to the exceedingly complicated procedures required to be followed when it is implemented (slightly alleviated by JCT Amendment number 10 of 1991).

Contractual liability for sub-contractors – Exception by express contract terms

Notwithstanding the difficulties encountered when attempting to interpret indirect terms or imply terms to deal with the contractor's position towards the employer in relation to default of sub-contractors, even more scope for problems lies in the use of express terms in the contract which, for a variety of reasons, are designed on their face to exclude or in some way to commute a main contractor's contractual liability for the performance of its sub-contractors. Such provisions have been seen most commonly in the past in relation to the position of, again, nominated sub-contractors. Thus, clause 35.21 of JCT 1980 expressly provides that the contractor is not to be responsible to the employer in respect of the nominated sub-contract works for anything to which the terms of the form of direct employer/nominated sub-contractor agreement relates, whether or not such an agreement has in fact been entered into. This covers the key areas of design, selection of materials and satisfaction of performance specification. Thus the employer's recourse in respect of problems in such areas will be against the nominated sub-contractor under the terms of such a direct agreement, or not at all.

Similarly, the old clause 27(e) of the JCT 1963 Form provided that, on final payment to a nominated sub-contractor, "save for latent defects the contractor shall be discharged from all liability for the work, materials or goods executed or supplied by such sub-contractor under the sub-contract." This was interpreted in *Victoria University of Manchester* v. *Wilson* as amounting to an exemption clause absolving the contractors from liability in respect of the sub-contractor's failures (though the contractors in that case were still held liable for failure to supervise the sub-contractor's work and therefore for having failed to detect such failures).

However, the best (or worst) example of the problems occasioned by the introduction of express clauses intended to create exceptions to the general principle of the contractor's liability for sub-contractors, is that of the "relief clauses" introduced into main contracts under systems of management contracting. In a paper written for the Society of Construction Law in 1988[37] the writer attempted to explore the anomalies that such clauses can create and to note the difficulties of the "no loss" and "different loss" logistical problems that can arise. In the remainder of this paper it is proposed to consider further the conceptual difficulties inherent in express contract provisions which seek to relieve a main, or management, contractor from liability for its sub-contractors (or trade contractors or works contractors) by means of a mechanism which seeks to restrict the main contractor's liability to the employer by reference to the extent of a sub-contractor's liability to the main contractor. In this context it will be relevant to consider the decision of the House of Lords in the combined case of *Firma C-Trade S.A.* v. *Newcastle Protection and Indemnity Association ("The Fanti")* and *Socony Mobil Oil Inc.* v. *West of England Ship Owners Mutual Insurance*

---

37 "Management Contracting – Low Risk for Contractor – Low Recovery by Employer"

Association (London) Ltd ("The Padre Island")[38], referred to below simply as *"The Padre Island"*. This was a case concerning marine insurance and the ability of third parties to recover from insurers, but the relationships involved between the various parties are an interesting parallel of those between employer, management contractor and sub-contractor in the context of a construction contract.

Express contract terms – conceptual problems

There seems to be a fundamental mechanical difficulty in a clause which seeks to express either:

(a) one person's contractual liability to another in terms of a third person's liability to the first, or

(b) one person's contractual remedy against another person in terms of that other's remedy against a third person.

This is because the exercise of determining liabilities and remedies involves questions of quantification of loss and damage which, by definition, are matters peculiar to the particular parties to a situation and the particular set of circumstances in which they are involved. This sort of determination may be distinguished from the exercise of establishing whether and to what extent a particular obligation or duty exists as between parties, since this is easier to express as an objective, abstract concept which may be considered to exist in a hypothetical fact situation without regard to the personal or financial circumstances of the parties involved.

Thus, if A's remedy against B (or B's liability to A) falls to be determined by reference to B's remedy against C (or C's liability to B), it follows that A's recovery from B will be limited or constrained by the practical, personal and financial circumstances obtaining as between B and C, which may be (though not necessarily) completely extraneous to the circumstances obtaining as between A and B. It is the same when the relationship between B and C is expressed as a "limitation" operating to govern the relationship between A and B; the circumstances of the two relationships may be entirely different yet, because of the limitation, the circumstances of the "limiting" relationship will prevail over those of the "limited" relationship.

Such is the case when an employer's rights against a main contractor are limited by reference to the main contractor's rights against its sub-contractors, as in forms of management contract (for example JCT 1987 Clause 3.21); or under collateral warranties, where the beneficiary's rights against the warrantor are limited by reference to the original employer's rights against the warrantor under the principal contract (particularly where this limitation is expressed in terms of the warrantor's "liability" to its original employer). By analogy, it is also the case with an insurance claim where the injured party's rights against the claimant's insurers, to the extent that he has any by virtue of the Third Party (Rights Against Insurers) Act 1930 ("the 1930 Act"), are limited by reference to the insured's own rights against its insurers, which was the situation considered in *The Padre Island*.

The Padre Island – the decision

The case concerned the effect of "pay to be paid" clauses contained in P&I club rules in the field of marine insurance, on the rights under the 1930 Act of cargo owners against two P&I clubs, where two of the clubs' respective members, against whom the cargo owners had claims covered by the members' insurance, had become insolvent. The rules of both clubs contained provisions to the effect that the club would only pay out on a claim by an insured member once the amount of the claim had been paid by the member to the injured third party. The two ship owner members having become insolvent prior to paying out such claims, the two cargo owner third parties sought to transfer their claims to the members' respective insurers.

The House of Lords held that the need for compliance with the pay when paid clauses in the rules could not be dispensed with, and the fact that neither of the members could now comply with the pay when paid clauses, because they were both insolvent, was not something that the injured third party cargo owners could do anything about. Under the 1930 Act, the third party cargo owners could acquire only whatever rights the insolvent members had had under the terms of their insurances; those rights, under the terms of the P&I clubs' rules, were contingent on the member having actually paid out the amount of the claim, which it had not done (and could not now do).

The Padre Island – effect of transfer of rights – "no loss"

The decision in *The Padre Island* is relevant in two ways to consideration of clauses seeking to exclude a main contractor's liability for the performance of sub-contractors. First, the decision places it beyond doubt that, if A's rights or remedies against B are expressed in terms of or are somehow dependent on B's rights or remedies against C, then A cannot acquire any greater rights against B than B has against C and cannot recover more than B can recover - even if A's actual losses, in respect of which it seeks to enforce its remedies against B, are considerably greater than B's rights against C admit.

Thus Lord Brandon, in considering the effect of the "pay to be paid" conditions upon the rights transferred under the 1930 Act on the members' insolvency, said: "Immediately before the members were ordered to be wound up they had only contingent rights against the clubs in respect of the liabilities to the third parties incurred by them. The rights were contingent in that it was a condition precedent to the members being indemnified by the clubs in respect to those liabilities that they should first have been discharged by the members themselves."

Lord Goff dealt with the issue at greater length and in doing so disposed of the argument that the "pay to be paid" condition had become somehow ineffective, because of impossibility of performance, once the insureds' rights under the policy and the claimants' rights against the insureds merged in the cargo-owning claimants by virtue of the transfer under the 1930 Act - which Lord Goff dubbed "the futility point": "The point is this. The member's right of indemnity in respect of any relevant claim or expense under the rules of either club is conditional upon his having first paid such claim or expense. The statutory transfer of that right of indemnity to a third party carries with it a transfer of the term that the member must first have paid such claim or expense. The third party cannot however pay himself; accordingly that term becomes, upon such transfer, of no effect, either (i) because it has become impossible of performance; or (ii) because it is futile to require a person to pay himself, and the law does not require the performance of the futile conditions; or (iii) because there is a merger of interests.... The point... is, to my mind, fundamentally flawed. I start from the position that what is transferred to and invested in the third party is the member's right against the club. That right is, at best, a contingent right to indemnity, the right being expressed to be conditional upon the member having in effect paid the relevant claim or expense. If that condition is not fulfilled, the member has no present right to be indemnified by the club. Here the relevant claim or expense was never paid, by the member or indeed by anybody else on his behalf. That condition not having been fulfilled, the member had no present right to indemnity, and the statutory transfer of his right to a third party cannot put the third party in any better position than the member. It is as simple as that. The fundamental flaw in the argument, as I see it, is that it assumes that the statutory transfer of the contingent right to the third party has the effect that the third party has then to pay himself.... What is transferred under the statute is the right. That right is expressed to be conditional upon the happening of a certain event; and the right as transferred remains so conditional.... There is no duty on the member to make prior payment; there is simply a contractual term that, if he does not do so, he has no right to be indemnified. The statutory transferee of the member's right is in no better position than the member; and so, if the condition is not fulfilled, he too has no right to be indemnified.... The argument of the cargo owners raises... a question not of futility but of impossibility. Furthermore I know of no general rule that the mere fact that a condition become impossible of performance renders the condition of no effect. Whether it does so or not must depend on the construction of the contract; and it may well be that, as here, the fact that it cannot be performed will simply mean that it is never fulfilled."

On the face of it the parallel is clear between the situation covered by *The Padre Island* and the situation arising under a management contract containing the usual "relief" provision for the management contractor. However it is necessary to examine it a little more closely to consider what exactly are the comparisons to be made. "A", the party who seeks to recover an original actual loss, is the third party cargo owner in the insurance case and the employer in the construction contract situation. "B", the intermediate party on whose rights A's rights depend, is the insured shipowner, the P&I club member, in the insurance case, and is the main contractor in the construction contract situation. "C", the party from whom it is ultimately sought to recover the loss, is the P&I club itself, the insurers, in the marine insurance situation, and the defaulting sub-contractor in the construction contract situation.

In the marine insurance example, the machinery which effects the transfer of rights of A against C via B, is the 1930 Act, which operates by creating rights in A against C which otherwise would not exist. The event here which removes B from the chain between A and C is its failure to satisfy the "pay to be paid" condition on which its rights, which become A's rights, are contingent, due to its insolvency - though that insolvency is itself the trigger for the transfer of its rights against C to A under the 1930 Act.

By contrast, in the management contract situation, the transfer of rights against C from B to A is effected by the particular clause in the contract, and this here operates not so as to create new rights but so as to limit rights which otherwise would exist, namely the employer's rights against the main contractor in respect of a breach of sub-contract by the sub-contractor. Here, the event which removes B, the main contractor, from the normal chain of recovery is its potential inability to recover anything from C, the sub-contractor, because it has suffered no loss to recover – the very limitation of liability (which is the obverse of the transfer of its rights to A) having arguably precluded it from asserting that it has suffered a recoverable loss.

So far as the management contract situation is concerned, therefore, the employer's position depends on whether the rights against the sub-contractor which he acquires from the management contractor are subject, in effect, to a similar "pay to be paid" condition which becomes incapable of fulfilment by virtue of the very instrument which transfers those rights to the employer. The management contractor's transferable rights, if any, in this situation, consist of a right to be indemnified by the sub-contractor against the management contractor's liability to the employer. Such an indemnity is expressed in various terms in different forms of sub-contract or works contract associated with a management contract, but it is usually fairly widely and generally drawn. The question therefore becomes whether a general indemnity of this nature is itself in effect subject to a "pay to be paid" condition implied by the general law.

The Padre Island – indemnities – treatment in equity

This introduces the second aspect in which the decision in *The Padre Island* is of assistance, namely in its close examination of the nature of rights under an indemnity. In particular, the argument and judgements in the case explore the ways in which equity may intervene to alleviate the difficulties arising from the purely logical attitude to indemnities taken by the common law, that a right to be indemnified can arise only once the event being indemnified against - usually the payment out of a sum of money - has actually occurred.

The argument was run on behalf of the cargo owners that, whilst at common law an indemnity did no more than protect the indemnified person against actual loss, equity would go further and in appropriate circumstances require the indemnifier either to pay the creditor direct or pay the indemnified person before he had paid the creditor. The point was eventually decided on the basis that, whatever relief against the strict common law rule might have been available in equity, it was clearly displaced by an express condition in the contract requiring prior payment as a condition of indemnification. It was therefore not material to the outcome of the decision to determine finally whether or not equity would in fact provide the relief contended for in the absence of such an express condition, but the remarks of the House of Lords on the issue are nonetheless interesting.

Lord Brandon expressed the issue as follows: "There is no doubt that before the passing of the Supreme Court of Judicature Acts 1873 and 1875, there was a difference between the remedies available to enforce an ordinary contract of indemnity (by which I mean a contract of indemnity not containing any express "pay to be paid" provision) at law on the one hand and in equity on the other. At law the party to be indemnified had to discharge the liability himself first and then sue the indemnifier for damages for breach of contract. In equity an ordinary contract of indemnity could be directed to be specifically performed by ordering that the indemnifier should pay the amount concerned directly to the third party to whom the liability was owed or in some cases to the party to be indemnified. *Johnston* v. *Salvage Association*[39], *per* Lindley L.J.; *British Union and National Insurance Co.* v. *Rowson*[40], per Pickford L.J. There is further no doubt that since the passing of the Supreme Court of Judicature Acts 1873 and 1875 the equitable remedy has prevailed over the remedy at law."

Lord Goff considered this aspect in the context of an argument that there was at common law a condition of prior payment implicit in a contract of indemnity, analogous to the express "pay to be paid" condition in the P&I Club's rules, but felt unable to accept this submission: "I accept that, at common law, a contract of indemnity gives rise to an action for unliquidated damages, arising from the failure of the indemnifier to prevent the indemnified person from suffering damage, for example, by having to pay a third party. I also accept that, at common law, the cause of action does not (unless the contract provides otherwise) arise until the indemnified person can show actual loss; see *Collinge* v. *Heywood*[41]. This is ...because a promise of indemnity is simply a promise to hold the indemnified person harmless against a specified loss or expense. On this basis, no debt can arise before the loss is suffered or the expense incurred; however, once the loss is suffered or the expense is incurred, the indemnifier is in breach of contract for having failed to hold the indemnified person harmless against the relevant loss or expense. There is no condition of prior payment; but the remedies available at law... were not efficacious to give full effect to the contract of indemnity. It is for this reason that equity felt that it could, and should, intervene. If there had been a clear implied condition of prior payment, operable in the relevant circumstances, equity would not have intervened to enforce the contract in a manner inconsistent with that term. Equity does not mend men's bargains; but it may grant specific performance of a contract, consistently with its terms, where the remedies at law are inadequate. This is what has happened in the case of contracts of indemnity. As a general rule, "Indemnity requires that the party to be indemnified shall never be called upon to pay" (see *In re Richardson*[42], *per* Buckley L.J.); and it is to give effect to that underlying purpose of the contract that equity intervenes, the common law remedies being incapable of achieving that result."Lord Jauncey considered and quoted from the same cases mentioned by Lords Brandon and Goff. He held that *"Collinge* v. *Heywood* was a procedural decision and it laid down no rule as to the common law rights of parties under a contract of indemnity", and noted Cozens-Hardy MR's view

39 [1887] 19 QBD 458, 460
40 [1916] 2 ch 476, 481
41 (1839) 9 Ad. & E. 633
42 [1911] 2KB 705, 716

from *In re Richardson*, as having restated "the view of the Court of Equity that it was not necessary for the person entitled to the indemnity to be ruined by having to pay the full amount in the first instance." He noted that "no other case [apart from *Collinge* v. *Heywood*] was cited to support the proposition that the common law would import a "pay to be paid" provision into all contracts of indemnity unless otherwise excluded", and therefore concluded that the P&I club rule in question did not "merely repeat what is already the position at common law but that they add a specific provision to what would otherwise be an ordinary contract of indemnity".

These observations of the House of Lords, though possibly strictly obiter, may be seen as giving considerable support in the face of the difficulties that could be encountered by employers - and management contractors - seeking to operate the relief/transfer of rights provisions of management contracts by seeking to enforce, for the employer's benefit, the rights of indemnity obtained by the management contractor from a sub-contractor. Equity, though it will be unable to supply the inevitable difference between the employer's and the management contractor's loss, may at least alleviate the problems of the "no loss" argument. There are, however, two areas of caution to be noted.

Equitable treatment of indemnities – reservations

First, equitable remedies will of course be granted only subject to the observance of equitable principles by those seeking them, and in any event will be available only at the discretion of the Court. An employer subject to the usual "relief" clause in a management contract is going to be in the position of attempting to enforce the subcontractor's indemnity given to the management contractor against the management contractor's liability to the employer, before the management contractor has actually sustained a loss against which to be indemnified, by actually paying out to the employer. The employer will therefore have to be confident that it has acted equitably in all the circumstances surrounding the claim situation and, more importantly, that its management contractor (on whose rights against the sub-contractor the employer's remedies will depend) has also so acted. At best, this must seem to subject the employer's remedies to a degree of uncertainty.

The second note of caution in welcoming the equitable remedies for indemnities discussed in *The Padre Island*, is that their Lordships do not appear to have had cited to them a number of cases, considerably more recent than the late 19th and early 20th century cases quoted in support of their propositions, which considered the equitable treatment of indemnities and which point in the opposite direction. These cases, which mostly concern the question when the cause of action on an indemnity arises for limitation

purposes, were considered in this writer's paper on Management Contracting previously referred to, and it is not proposed to repeat that analysis
here[43]. It will be sufficient here to quote at some length from the judgment
of Neill J in *Telfair Shipping Corp*; there, he also considered the Richardson
case quoted from in *The Padre Island*, but referred to, and drew the opposite
conclusion from, the third judgment in that case, that of Fletcher Moulton
LJ.

Having reviewed the cases on indemnities listed above, Neill J continued[44]:

> "From a consideration of these cases and other authorities to
> which my attention was directed, it seems to me that it is possible
> to identify at least three ways in which a person A who has
> become liable to B may be able to obtain redress from C.
>
> "The first way is by an action of damages for breach of contract
> (or warranty). In such a case A will be in a position to claim that
> the incurring of his liability to B flowed directly from an act of
> C which constituted a breach of a contract between A and C or
> of a warranty given by C to A. The damages will be assessed in
> accordance with Hadley v. Baxendale principles. The cause of
> action will date from the date of breach. The second way is by
> a claim on an express indemnity. In such a case the extent of the
> indemnity and the time at which the cause of action arises will
> depend on the construction of the contract. If the indemnity is an
> indemnity against liability..., the cause of action will come into
> existence when A incurs a liability to B. It may be that in certain
> circumstances a liability may be incurred for this purpose when
> the liability is still merely contingent... If, however, the indemnity
> is a general indemnity..., then time will not begin to run against
> A for the purpose of pursuing his indemnity against C until A's
> liability to B has been established and ascertained..."
>
> "The third way in which A may claim against C in respect of
> sums which he has had to pay to B is under an implied
> indemnity... Such an implied indemnity would prima facie be a
> general indemnity of the kind recognised by the common law.

43 *Biggin & Co Limited* v. *Permanite Limited* [1951] 1 KB 422; *County & District Properties Limited* v. *C. Jenner & Son Limited* [1976] 2 Lloyds Rep 728; *R&H Green & Silley Weir Limited* v. *British Railways Board* [1985] 1 All ER 237; *Gromal (UK) Limited* v. *W. T. Shipping Limited* [1984] CA Unrep. *Grand Bahama Petroleum Co Limited* v. *Manunited Companiera Naviera SA* [1985] Commercial Court Unrep. and *Telfair Shipping Corp* v. *Inersea Carriers* [1985] 1 All ER 243.
44 (1985) 1 All ER 243

The rules relating to what I have described as a general indemnity were explained by Fletcher Moulton LJ as follows in *Re Richardson*...:

"If, for instance, B was bound to pay a sum to A and C was bound to indemnify B... then B could not sue C unless he could aver payment to A. It was the same thing whether it was a case of suretyship, indemnity or contribution. In all cases before you could make a guarantor pay, you must prove that you had actually paid the money. No better example of this could be given than the case of *Collinge* v. *Heywood*... That was a contract to indemnify a Plaintiff against costs, and it was decided that the cause of action arose when he paid the costs, not when the costs were incurred or the attorney's bill was delivered to him... There the Court applied the well-known common law principle that before you can avail yourself of your right of indemnity you must show that you have paid the money... The rule in Chancery was somewhat different, and yet, to my mind, it emphasises the fundamental principle that you must have paid before you have a right to indemnity, because the remedy which equity gave was a declaration of a right. You could file a bill against the principal debtor to make him pay the debt so that you would not be called upon to pay it, and then you obtained a declaration that you were entitled to an indemnity. You could in certain cases have a fund set aside in order that you might be indemnified, to avoid the necessity of your having to pay and then to sue for the money you had paid, which perhaps would not repair your loss and credit even if it discharged the debt. But I do not think that equity ever compelled a surety to pay money to the person to whom he was surety before the latter had actually paid. He might be ordered to set a fund aside, but I do not think that he could be ordered to pay."

"It seems clear, however, that even in equity time does not begin to run for the purposes of any limitation period until the liability of the person to be indemnified has been ascertained."

Fletcher Moulton LJ thus seems to have taken a somewhat different view of equity's treatment of rights under a general indemnity, from that of Cozens-Hardy MR and Buckley LJ in *Re Richardson*, as cited in *The Padre Island*, and this was the view taken in the line of cases referred to, which do not appear to have been considered in *The Padre Island*. Again, therefore, there might be said to be at best some degree of uncertainty over the ability of an indemnified party to recover from the indemnifier before it has actually sustained the loss against which it claims to be indemnified. It is submitted that the employer's position under a management contract should accordingly still be viewed with some circumspection.

Express "no loss" clauses

Finally on this issue, there needs to be mentioned the device adopted by the JCT forms of nominated sub-contract and by the JCT 1987 form of Works Contract for use with a Management Contract, to attempt to overcome the "no loss" difficulties inherent in the relief provisions of the management contract or main contract in connection with a nominated sub-contract. These provide, broadly, an obligation on the sub-contractor or works contractor not to contend that the main or management contractor has suffered no loss merely by virtue of the provision which relieves the main or management contractor from liability to the employer unless and until it is recovered from the sub-contractor or works contractor. As noted in this writer's paper on Management Contracting previously referred to, it is felt that the efficacy of such a provision is, to put it at its highest, doubtful, since a contractor will still have to prove a recoverable loss even if the sub-contractor is somehow contractually debarred from disputing the loss once asserted.

Dr. John Parris, in *"Default by Sub-Contractors and Suppliers"*[45] makes the point more strongly: "The clause is likely to be greeted with hilarity, if not derision, by the Court. The idea that by a contractual term a defendant can be estopped from setting up a defence which is manifestly open to him, so that the Court thereby is induced to decide contrary to law, can in no way be supported. No defendant can by contract be pushed into a position where he says: 'I am precluded by my contract from saying that the law of England is what the law of England is.' There is a close analogy in those cases in which it has been held that the parties cannot by contract exclude the jurisdiction of the Court. Before a plaintiff can establish a right, he must prove to the satisfaction of the Court that he has a cause of action either under a contract or for breach of a contract, or that for a recognised tort he is entitled to damages. In the circumstances contemplated by this clause, the contractor cannot prove that he is entitled to any specific sum under his contract with the sub-contractor; nor that the sub-contractor was in breach of the contract; still less that he, the contractor, has suffered any loss whatsoever. He has not." (This comment was made concerning the provision on this issue that appears in the JCT intermediate sub-contract form NAM/SC). Again, therefore, there are grounds for, at least, caution as to the efficacy of the contractual mechanism provided to safeguard the employer's position, once the general principle of a contractor's liability for its sub-contractors is tampered with.

Conclusions

From the point of view of the potential obligee in relation to a construction project – the owner, employer, or purchaser etc. of a building – rights of recourse against main contractors can be fraught with difficulties. This will be the case either where those rights are framed in tort, because there is no other direct contractual link between obligor and obligee; or where, even though there is such a direct contractual link, the contract has built into it implied or – even more hazardous for the obligee – express exceptions or exclusions to the general principle of a main contractor's liability for its sub-contractors.

The solution from the obligee's point of view is simple – at least in theory, though by no means in practice. This has to be, to attempt to secure a direct contractual link, via a collateral agreement, with the sub-contractor who is responsible for any important aspect of design or construction of work in which the obligee has an interest. Hence the importance of an adequate employer/sub-contractor agreement in the case of works contractors under a management contract, or nominated sub-contractors under a main contract, and the importance that such agreements should cover not only design (as is the case with the standard forms of such agreement) but all aspects of the work. Hence also the proliferation (even before the House of Lords' decision in *Murphy* v. *Brentwood D.C.*) of requirements for collateral warranties by interested third parties who would otherwise have no contractual nexus at all with sub-contractors involved in significant aspects of projects.

3 Warranties and Duty of Care Documents: Problems of Enforcement

John Cartwright

Synopsis

The paper considers the enforceability of warranties/duty of care documents by assignees against the warrantor in three situations. First, the author considers the situation where the warrantee has let the building in question on a full repairing lease and in particular whether the warrantee could recover against a warrantor architect in respect of defects arising, for example, from negligent design. Secondly, the author discusses whether an assignee of the whole building for full value will receive the full benefit of the warranty given to the assignor. Thirdly, where the building is sold off in parts, the question arises as to whether the respective purchasers can receive the benefit of the warranty to the extent that it affects their parts of the building.

Introduction

Deeds of collateral warranty are already commonplace in the construction industry. They are used to give the benefit of contractual protection in respect of defects in the building, against those involved in the provision of a building, in favour of those who may suffer as a result of those defects, but who would not otherwise have the benefit of any direct contractual obligations. For example, an architect may be asked to execute a warranty in favour of a funding institution, the first purchaser of the freehold or the first tenants of a development.

Since the House of Lords has recently taken a restrictive approach to the liability of those involved in the provision of buildings in respect of defects in the buildings themselves,[1] purchasers and tenants are likely to be even

---

1 See *D & F Estates Ltd.* v. *Church Commissioners for England* [1989] A.C.177; *Murphy* v. *Brentwood District Council* [1990] 2 All E.R. 908; *Department of the Environment* v. *Thomas Bates and Son* [1990] 2 All E.R. 943. However, the potential liability of professionals in a development is wider: see the approval by Lord Keith in *Murphy* v. *Brentwood District Council* ([1990] 2 All E.R. 908 at p.919) of *Pirelli General Cable Works Ltd.* v. *Oscar Faber & Partners* [1983] 2 A.C. 1: "It would seem that in a case such as the *Pirelli General Cable Works* case, where the tortious liability arose out of

more keen to take direct contractual warranties. There are certain situations, however, where the enforceability of such warranties may be called into question. The purpose of this paper is to examine three such situations.

Consider the following facts. A is the architect of a new building. P1 is the first purchaser of the freehold. A executes a warranty in favour of P1.[2] If the design of the building is defective, because A has not exercised a sufficient degree of care in accordance with his warranty, P1 will have a direct action for breach of contract against A to recover his losses (typically, the cost of rectifying the defects, and such other losses as lost rental income during the remedial works).

However, by the time the defect is discovered, the following alternative situations may have occurred:

(a) P1 has let the whole building to T, on a full repairing lease. T has the obligation to rectify the defects under his lease; can P1 choose to recover the cost of the remedial works from A, or will A be able to avoid paying on the ground that P1 has an action against T?

(b) P1 has sold the whole building for its full value to P2, and has assigned to P2 the benefit of A's warranty. Can A avoid paying P2 under the assigned warranty on the ground that P1 has suffered no loss, and therefore P2 (standing in P1's shoes as assignee) also has no loss to claim?

(c) P1 has sold the freehold of the building in two separate parts, to P3 and P4. He has purported to assign the warranty to each insofar as it affects their respective parts of the building. Is this a valid assignment, and so can P3 or P4 sue A under the warranty?

Letting on a Full Repairing Lease

The situation here is that P1, who has the benefit of the contractual warranty against A, has retained his interest in the building, but has granted a lease to T, on terms which include a covenant by T to repair the premises.

a contractual relationship with professional people, the duty extended to take reasonable care not to cause economic loss to the client by the advice given. The plaintiffs built the chimney as they did in reliance on that advice. The case would accordingly fall within the principle of *Hedley Byrne & Co. Ltd.* v. *Heller & Partners Ltd.* [1964] A.C. 465. I regard *Junior Books Ltd.* v. *Veitchi Co.Ltd.* [1983] 1 A.C. 520 as being an application of that principle."

2   It is assumed that A executes a collateral warranty in favour of P1: i.e., that A and P1 are not already in any direct contractual relationship. There is no magic however in the warranty being collateral; the same issues would arise if P1 was the direct client of A. It is, however, in practice in the context of collateral warranties that the questions to be discussed in this paper have arisen.

The problem is that, when the defect is in due course discovered, and P1 sues A under the warranty, A will claim that P1 has no loss to remedy, since he has a right against T to have the building repaired; that the loss is therefore T's.

T's liability must cover the same ground as A's liability

The first point to notice is that the problem does not arise unless the liability of T covers the same ground as that of A In the light of *Post Office* v. *Aquarius Properties Ltd*,[3] T's covenant will have to be clear if it is to cover the remedying of inherent defects in the construction of the building, at least before the defects have caused some other damage. However, it will be assumed in this paper that T's covenant is sufficiently widely drawn.

Analogous Situations

There appears to be no direct authority on the question which we are considering. It is therefore necessary to look at certain other, analogous situations.

Tenant's covenant to yield up in repair

There is clear authority that, when a tenant breaches his covenant to yield up the demised premises in repair at the end of the lease, the landlord may recover damages to cover the cost of repairing the premises, even though it will not cost the landlord that sum, since he has obtained another tenant for the premises who has undertaken an obligation to repair.

In *Joyner* v. *Weeks*,[4] where a subsequent lease was entered into before the first lease ended (and therefore before the first tenant was in breach of his repairing covenant), Lord Esher M.R. said:[5]

> "The circumstances relied upon by the defendant [i.e., the fact of the covenant by the new tenant] did not affect the property as regards the relation between the lessor and the lessee in respect to it. They arose from a relation, the result of a contract between the plaintiff and a third person, to which the defendant was no party, and with which he had nothing to do. ... At the moment of

3 [1987] 1 All E.R. 1055: see particularly Slade L.J. at p.1066.
4 [1891] 2 Q.B. 31.
5 At p. 44.

the determination of the lease between the plaintiff and the defendant, the premises were out of repair. And, if we cannot look at the contract between the plaintiff and the third person, or anything that took place under it, there was nothing but the ordinary case of the breach of a covenant to leave the premises in repair. In my opinion the contract between the plaintiff and the third person cannot be taken into account; it is something to which the defendant is a stranger. So, also, anything that may happen between the plaintiff and the third person under that contract after the breach of covenant is equally matter with which the defendant has nothing to do, and which cannot be taken into account. These are matters which might or might not have happened, and, so far as the defendant is concerned, are mere accidents."

It should be noted that this goes even further than not requiring the landlord to sue the subsequent tenant to recoup his loss; it even requires the fact that the tenant has complied with his obligations under the subsequent lease to be disregarded.

A similar approach was also taken in *Haviland* v. *Long*,[6] where the landlord had again obtained, before the termination of the first lease, a covenant from a subsequent tenant to put the premises into repair, but had also agreed to pay to the second tenant any sum recovered by the landlord from the first tenant by way of dilapidations. Denning L.J. said,[7]

"The fact that the landlord has an undertaking from a new tenant to do the repairs does not go in diminution of damages. It is *res inter alios acta*."

The argument put by Somervell L.J. was more detailed. He took the view that:[8]

"The landlords, when they entered into the new lease, had certain rights against the tenants under the old lease, and these included the then contingent right of recovering damages from those tenants if they failed to put the premises into repair.... The new tenants would never have agreed to pay what was the economic rent for a repaired building and do the repairs unless they had been satisfied, quoad those repairs which were covered by the old

6 [1952] 2 Q.B. 80.
7 At p. 84.
8 At p. 83.

lease, that they would get, through the landlords, the sum, however it was quantified, which the old tenants were liable to pay as damages for the breach of their covenant."

This analysis is relevant to our case. T undertakes the repairing obligation in respect of the new building on the assumption that it is properly designed. T is not intending to be an insurer of the architect. Moreover, *Haviland* suggests that even if P1 undertook to pass on to T the fruits of any claim against A if T had incurred the expense of repairing the property, that undertaking would not diminish P1's loss which he could claim from A.

Repair of premises by a tenant following breach of covenant by the landlord

In both *Joyner* v. *Weeks* and *Haviland* v. *Long* the second lease was entered into before the tenant under the first lease was actually in breach of his covenant to repair. In *Naumann* v. *Ford*[9] the sequence of events was reversed. A landlord was in breach of his covenant under the lease by allowing his insurance of the demised premises to lapse. A fire occurred at the premises causing personal injury to the tenant and damage to the premises. After the fire, the tenant entered into an agreement with the insurance company whose policy had lapsed; the insurance company agreed to compensate the tenant for the cost of the fire damage, in consideration of the tenant taking proceedings against the landlord for breach of the covenant to insure. The tenant then carried out the necessary repairs to the premises. The landlord claimed that the fact that the repairs had now been effected pursuant to the arrangements between the tenant and the insurance company, subsequent to his breach of covenant, meant that the tenant was entitled only to nominal damages: that the tenant suffered no loss. Mr. Vivian Price QC[10] rejected this: the insurance company were "truly strangers" to the breach of covenant by the landlord.

> "[The tenant] was under no obligation to [the landlord] to repair the premises, but [the landlord] was under the obligation to [the tenant] to do so. The fact that [the tenant] made arrangements herself to have the premises repaired cannot, of itself, discharge [the landlord's] obligation and liability under the covenant.... In my judgment, the arrangements made between [the tenant] and

9 [1985] 2 E.G.L.R. 70.
10 Relying on *Haviland* v. *Long* [1952] 2 Q.B. 80; *British Westinghouse Electric and Manufacturing Co. Ltd.* v. *Underground Electric Railways Company of London Ltd.* [1912] A.C. 673 and passages from *McGregor on Damages* (14th ed.).

[the insurance company] for the repair of the premises are completely collateral and *res inter alios acta* to the obligation and liability of [the landlord] to [the tenant]."

Contracts for the sale of goods

There is authority that, where the seller supplies defective goods under a contract for the sale of goods, but the purchaser is able to resell the goods without loss under a sub-contract made before the breach of contract by the supplier, the purchaser can still recover damages for breach under the first contract. The sub-contract is disregarded: *Slater* v. *Hoyle & Smith* Ltd.[11] Scrutton L.J. said,[12]

> "it is *res inter alios acta*: "circumstances peculiar to the plaintiff," which cannot affect his claim one way or the other. If the buyer is lucky enough, for reasons with which the seller has nothing to do, to get his goods through on the sub-contract without a claim against him, this on principle cannot affect his claim against the seller any more than the fact that he had to pay very large damages on his sub-contract would affect his original seller."

Concurrent claims by a mortgagee against a valuer and the mortgagor; mitigation

In *London and South of England Building Society* v. *Stone*,[13] a valuer negligently failed to detect structural defects in a house; the building society, on the faith of his valuation, made a mortgage advance to their borrowers, who in the mortgage covenanted to repay the advance, to repair the property and to pay to the mortgagees the cost incurred by the mortgagees in repairing the property. The borrowers were financially stretched, and the mortgagees decided not to enforce their covenants in respect of the defects in the property. The valuer claimed that his liability in damages should be reduced to take account of the value to the mortgagees of being able to recover against the borrowers under their covenants. The

---

11 [1920] 2 K.B. 11.
12 At p. 23.
13 [1983] 1 W.L.R. 1242. See also the judgment of Sir Denys Buckley and a case-note by A.P.Lavers in (1983) *Construction Surveyor* Vol. 17 No. 50(17).

situation is clearly analogous to our case.[14]

The majority of the Court of Appeal held that the borrowers' covenants were not to be taken into account in calculating the damages payable by the valuer. O'Connor L.J. said,[15]

> "I can see no justification for the suggestion that the lenders were under any duty to the valuer to mitigate this loss by trying to extract money from the borrowers. Let me test the proposition in a simple way: assume that the borrower had agreed to contribute 5,000 towards these repairs, could the valuer have claimed credit for this or any part of this sum on the facts of this case? I am quite clear that he could not have done so."

Stephenson L.J. discussed the point at more length. His analysis appears to be that one must first decide whether the obligations of the borrowers are merely collateral to the valuer's liability, or can be taken into account. If they can be taken into account, the question is whether, on the facts, they should be taken into account, in that the mortgagee should have mitigated its loss by suing the borrowers. He said,[16]

> "the object of securing the loan by charging the property was to secure repayment of the sum lent with interest under the covenant to repay. The borrowers' obligation to repay was therefore not so collateral or remote as to be disregarded altogether in measuring the lenders' loss.... If, therefore, the borrowers had suddenly found themselves in sufficient funds to repay the lenders' advance, and had repaid it in full before the valuer's liability was established, I do not see how the lenders could have recovered more than nominal damages.... [I]f an advance secured by the borrower's reliance on a false valuation of a property becomes in fact an advance which needs no security, but is repaid without recourse to the property, then in my judgment the valuer may be fortunate enough to be able to rely on the borrower's

14 There are of course differences: the valuer's liability is for failing to take care in assessing the property as security for the loan, and not for producing a defective building; the basic measure of damages against the valuer is therefore the building society's loss in making an advance greater than they would have made had the true value been known. Also, the link between the borrowers' obligations and the valuer's negligence is close: both are designed to ensure the continuing worth of the property as security for the mortgagees.
15 At p. 1257.
16 At pp. 1261-1262.

repayment in diminution of the lender's loss and of the compensation he is legally liable to pay for it....

However, on the assumption that it would be permissible for the valuer to claim credit for any repayment of capital by the borrowers before action, can he also claim credit for what the borrowers have not repaid if the lender could have insisted on repayment in full or in part and could, if the borrowers refused, have sued them with a reasonable prospect of success? ... [T]he valuer is not merely asking the court to take account of what has actually been paid to the lenders; he is requiring the lenders to have taken action in claiming payment from the borrowers; and it is one thing for a wrongdoer to claim the benefit of a benefit obtained by the wronged party under a contract with another; it is quite another thing - and, in my judgment, a far stronger thing - to claim the valuation of the chance of such a benefit which the wronged party has deliberately chosen not to take."

Stephenson L.J. decided that there was no duty to mitigate on the facts, since the valuer had not proved that it was reasonable to require such action to be taken against the borrowers. He relied expressly on the propositions that

1) a plaintiff need not take the risk of starting an uncertain litigation against a third party: *Pilkington* v. *Wood*;[17]
2) a plaintiff need not take steps to recover compensation for his loss from parties who, in addition to the defendant, are liable to him: *The Liverpool (No. 2)*;[18]
3) a plaintiff need not act so as to injure innocent persons; and
4) a plaintiff need not prejudice its commercial reputation.

Applying the principles stated by Stephenson L.J. to our case, it might be said that there is no such close link between the obligations of A and T; as in the case of a tenant's covenant to yield up in repair, discussed above,[19] the arrangement with T is *res inter alios acta*. Even if that is not the case, provided that T has not in fact repaired the premises, P1 can still assert a loss enforceable against A, equal to the cost of repairs, provided that there is no duty to mitigate. On the facts of *London and South of England Building Society* v. *Stone*, the financial difficulties of the borrowers influenced the

17 [1953] Ch. 770.
18 [1963] P. 64.
19 Pp.3ff.

question of reasonableness in not enforcing their personal covenants. However, the other criteria mentioned by Stephenson L.J. could still apply to suggest that there is no duty to mitigate in our case.

Conclusion

All the above analogies suggest that P1 can still sue A for the full amount of the loss, provided, at least, that T has not already repaired the property in accordance with his covenant. *Joyner* v. *Weeks*, Haviland v. *Long*, *Naumann* v. *Ford* and the statement by O'Connor L.J. in *London and South of England Building Society* v. *Stone*, quoted above,[20] suggest that even if T has repaired, P1 may still recover substantial damages. The argument of Stephenson L.J. in *London and South of England Building Society* v. *Stone*, taking the point as one dealing with mitigation, tends however to the opposite view. These arguments hold, irrespective of whether the lease to T is entered into before or after A is in breach of warranty: contrast the sequence of events in *Joyner* v. *Weeks* with those in *Naumann* v. *Ford*, for example.

Sale of the building for value

Here, P1 has sold the whole building to P2, and has assigned to P2 the benefit of A's warranty of care in design. Not realising that the building is defective, P2 has paid to P1 the full market value of the building. Can P2 sue A for the loss he suffers by reason of the defects?

Are such warranties capable of assignment?

The first question to consider is whether such a warranty is on the facts capable of being assigned.[21] There is a general rule in the law of contract that a contract for services is incapable of assignment without the agreement of the other party, on account of its personal nature.[22] Might it be said that collateral warranties fall within this rule?

The first question must always be to look at the wording of the particular warranty, to see whether it makes provision in relation to assignment. If it indicates – expressly or impliedly – that the warranty may or may not be

20 P.8.
21 This question was raised in a letter by Elizabeth Jones of Messrs. Fox Williams in *Building*, 17 August 1990, p. 20.
22 Treitel, *The Law of Contract* (8th ed., 1991), pp. 597-8.

assigned, then the issue is resolved. For example, the model form of collateral warranty to be given to a company providing finance for a proposed development published by the British Property Federation provides:[23]

> "This Agreement may be assigned by the Company by way of absolute legal assignment to another company providing finance or re-finance in connection with the Development without the consent of the Client or the Firm being required and such assignment shall be effective upon written notice thereof being given to the Client and to the Firm. "

This expressly allows assignment by the financing company without having to ask for the consent of the consultant who gave the warranty or his employer. However, the permitted assignment is narrowly defined: there must be an absolute legal assignment with notice given to the consultant and the employer (an equitable assignment will not, it seems, suffice); and the assignment may only be to another company providing finance or re-finance. This may impliedly exclude assignments to persons who are not a "company" - such as a partnership or an unincorporated association; or where the assignee is not financing the Development.[24]

Once it is established that there is nothing in the wording of the warranty itself which provides (expressly or impliedly) for its assignment, the question to be addressed is whether of its nature it is a contract capable of assignment. The basic rule is that the benefit of a contract can be assigned without the consent of the other party only if "it can make no difference to the person on whom the obligation lies to which of two persons he is to discharge it."[25] So, for example, a painter cannot assign the benefit of a

---

23 Model Form CoWa/F 1990, clause 11 (italics added).SEE TEXT
24 See also, for example, the earlier form of warranty to be given to a funding institution, issued by the RIBA (1988, replaced by the 1990 British Property Federation model form), which provided that the warranty could be assigned only once, prior to practical completion, within three years of the giving of the warranty, subject to the express consent of the Consultant (not to be unreasonably withheld); and the draft form of collateral warranty to be given to tenants published by the RIBA (but never issued in final form, and since withdrawn), printed in Architects Liability, March 1989, which provided that the warranty was personal to the Tenant and could not be assigned. The new British Property Federation model form of collateral warranty for purchasers and tenants (CoWa/P & T 1992) allows an absolute legal assignment to a purchaser of the whole of the premises, but is so drafted as to invite the parties to place a limit on the number of assignments (or to exclude assignment altogether).
25 *Tolhurst* v. *The Associated Portland Cement Manufacturers* (1900) Ltd [1902] 2 K.B. 660 at p. 668 (Collins M.R.).

contract to paint a portrait: the person who has commissioned the painting must be allowed to decide who does the painting. And a contract of employment may not be assigned by the employer without the employee's consent.[26]

Whether the warranty can be assigned will therefore depend upon the nature of its terms. If A warrants to P1, on the completion of the building, simply that he exercised reasonable skill and care in the design, it is difficult to see why this should not be capable of assignment. It makes little difference to A whether it is P1 or P2 who can enforce the warranty.[27] If, however, the warranty, executed during the project, contains a right for P1 to take over the architect's appointment in the event of, for example, the developer's default, then it could well be argued that A should not be required to have another person – P2 – to whom he has not consented, taking over as his employer under his appointment.

The "no loss" argument[28]

In the example under consideration, A had already broken his warranty by the time it was assigned by P1 to P2, since he had already failed to take the warranted care in design. What P1 assigned to P2 was therefore an accrued right to sue for damages for breach of contract. There have been suggestions in the industry[29] that the assignment of the right of action might not yield full damages for P2 when he later sues to enforce it, and this argument might be at its strongest in a situation where P1 transfers the property for full value to P2 and *later* assigns the benefit of the warranty as a separate transaction: for then it would be arguable[30] that the warranty at

---

26 *Nokes* v. *Doncaster Amalgamated Collieries Ltd* [1940] A.C. 1014 at p. 1026; *Denham* v. *Midland Employers Mutual Assurance Ltd* [1955] 2 Q.B. 437 at p. 443.

27 As long, perhaps, as P2 can recover only that which P1 could have recovered had he not assigned the warranty: see the statement in n.50, below.

28 For a fuller, earlier account of the arguments on this issue, see the author's article, The Assignment of Collateral Warranties in (1990) 6 Const. L.J.14. Some of the points made in this section have been revised in the light of the decision of the Court of Appeal in *Linden Gardens Trust Ltd.* v. *Lenesta Sludge Disposals Ltd.* (consolidated with *St.Martin's Corporation Ltd.* v. *Sir Robert McAlpine & Sons Ltd.*, 13 February 1992; at the time of writing, reported only in (1992) CILL 731). It is understood that leave to appeal to the House of Lords was given.

29 For example, see a letter to *Building*, 20 April 1990 p.31.

30 A variation on such an argument was accepted by His Honour Judge Loyd QC in *Linden Gardens Trust Ltd.*v. *Lenesta Sludge Disposals Ltd.* (1990) 52 BLR 93 at p.106, although he failed to distinguish between the accrual of a right of action, and the incurring of expense to remedy the defect, before the assignment. Moreover, there is a dictum of His Honour Judge Newey QC in *Perry* v. *Tendring D.C.* [1985] 1 EGLR 260

the time of its assignment had no value to P1 – since by then he had already obtained the full value of the property independently of the warranty and so had no loss.

However, it now seems clear that this argument is incorrect. There are a number of approaches which can be taken: first, by looking at the statutory mechanism for assignment of choses in action, in section 136 of the Law of Property Act 1925, and then looking at case-law in support of the assignee's right of action for substantial damages. The most recent case in support is the Court of Appeal decision in *Linden Gardens Trust Ltd.* v. *Lenesta Sludge Disposals Ltd.*[31] However, it will still be worth looking at earlier cases which were relied upon by the Court of Appeal in coming to that decision.

The basic position in the case of an assignment of an accrued right of action is that the assignee steps into the shoes of the assignor – and so he can bring an action which the assignor could have brought, had he not assigned; the amount recoverable by the assignee in an action is the same that the assignor would have recovered, had he not made the assignment.

Section 136 Law of Property Act 1925

Section 136(1) of the Law of Property Act 1925, which deals with statutory assignments of debts and other legal choses in action,[32] uses language which appears to assume that the assignee's position is identical – both in terms of his rights and the remedies available to enforce the rights

at p.266 (italics added) - although that case concerned the assignment of a right to sue in the tort of negligence:

"when damage to a building occurs its owner acquires a cause of action immediately, even though he is not aware of it, and ... unless he assigns that right of action, when agreeing to convey or conveying the building to a successor ..., the successor has no right to sue.
I do not know how an assignment could be effected. For assignment under section 136 of the Law of Property Act 1925, notice to the "debtor" is required, but an assignor could not give notice to a tortfeasor if unaware of the existence of his cause of action ... I am also uncertain as to what damages the assignee could recover, since the assignor would not have expended money on the remedying of undiscovered defects and would presumably have obtained market price for his property."

This statement was, however, only obiter, and there is no detailed consideration of the problem in the judgment.

31 Consolidated with *St.Martin's Corporation Ltd.* v. *Sir Robert McAlpine & Sons Ltd.* see note 28 above.
32 Which will include the benefit of a contractual obligation, such as a collateral warranty.

– to that of the assignor:

> "Any absolute assignment by writing under the hand of the
> assignor (not purporting to be by way of charge only) of any debt
> or other legal thing in action, of which express notice in writing
> has been given to the debtor, trustee or other person from whom
> the assignor would have been entitled to claim such debt or thing
> in action, is effectual in law (subject to equities having priority
> over the right of the assignee) to pass and transfer from the date
> of such notice:
> (a) the legal right to such debt or thing in action;
> (b) all legal and other remedies for the same; and
> (c) the power to give a good discharge for the same without the
> concurrence of the assignor."

Moreover, consider the common situation of debt factoring, which
involves the assignment by a creditor to the factor of the benefit of a debt,
in return for (usually) a money payment discounted by reference to the
contingency of the debt's recovery by the factor: the fact that the assignor
has received value is irrelevant for the ability of the factor to sue for the
whole debt. What the factor recovers is the amount which the assignor could
have recovered immediately before he made the assignment, without any
reference to the price paid for the assignment.[33]

Case-law in support

There are three cases which should be considered in particular to support
the view that the assignee for value can recover in respect of the full (pre-
assignment) remedy. The first case, *Dawson* v. *Great Northern and City
Railway Company*,[34] was not concerned with assignment of the benefit of
a contract, but of the right to recover statutory compensation for compulsory
purchase of land. However, it contains a useful discussion of the nature of
assigned rights to sue.

In *Dawson*, the defendants had the right to purchase land compulsorily
- subject to paying compensation. They served a notice on Blake, the
freehold owner of land and buildings near the City Road, London, that they

---

33 Note also the case of a restrictive covenant given by an employee of a business on
   leaving his employment. The benefit of such a covenant, since it protects the goodwill
   of the business, may be assigned to a purchaser of the business, and (if so assigned) will
   be fully enforceable by him: *Jacoby* v. *Whitmore* (1883) 49 L.T. 335.
34 [1905] 1 K.B. 260.

intended to use the soil under his premises to build an underground railway. Blake later sold the freehold to Dawson, and assigned at the same time the benefit of the right to compensation. Dawson sought to enforce that right; she claimed damages in respect of "structural damage" to her other property and "damage to trade stock", to cover losses she incurred in her business as a draper on the premises. Had Blake not sold the land, he would have been able to recover damages from the defendants in respect of "structural damage"; but he was not carrying on a business which would have entitled him to recover damages in respect of trade stock. The Court of Appeal allowed Dawson, the assignee, to recover damages in respect of structural damage, but not in respect of damage to trade stock - that is, they allowed her to recover precisely the types of loss which Blake, the assignor, would have been able to recover. The fact that Blake (presumably[35]) received money for the sale to Dawson of the land and the assignment of the right to sue the defendants was not apparently considered of any relevance.

Passages in the judgment of the Court of Appeal show how the judges saw assignment as operating:[36]

> "Lord Lindley [in *Mercer* v. *Liverpool, St. Helen's and South Lancashire Railway Company*[37]]...says: "The broad principle appears to me to be that it is not competent for an owner of land who has received notice to treat to deal with any of his land either taken or injuriously affected by the company, so as to increase the burdens of the company as regards the compensation to be made in respect of such land or any of it." This principle, in our opinion, applies to the present case. The landowner, however, is only precluded from dealing with his property in such a way as to subject the company which has given the notice to a greater burden in respect of compensation for damage occasioned by their works. So long as he does not infringe this rule he may, as it seems to us, sell and convey his land to a purchaser; and the company cannot take advantage of such a conveyance to escape from any obligation on their part subsisting at the time of the conveyance in respect of the lands conveyed....
> [T]he intention of this deed[38] was to place the plaintiff precisely in the same position as regards the defendants with respect to the lands conveyed as was previously occupied by Blake, and in

---

35 The point was not discussed - but there is no evidence that the transaction was gratuitous (it is referred to in the report as a "sale").
36 [1905] 1 K.B. 260 at pp. 268-270.
37 [1904] A.C. 461 at p. 465.
38 That is, the deed which contained the assignment of the right to compensation.

particular to transfer to the plaintiff the compensation for structural damage to the conveyed property..."

The second case is *G.U.S. Property Management Ltd* v. *Littlewoods Mail Order Stores Ltd.*[39] Rest, a wholly owned subsidiary of Great Universal Stores Ltd., owned a building which had been damaged, allegedly by the fault of the defenders. In accordance with the G.U.S. group policy, it was decided to transfer all property into one particular wholly owned subsidiary, the pursuer. In 1975, Rest therefore transferred the building to the pursuer, at a price fixed for accounting purposes only. It was not a sale at arm's length for value. In 1976, Rest assigned the right of action against the defender to the pursuer. The question was whether the pursuer had any loss which it could claim against the defender. Lord Stewart[40] put the defender's argument as follows:

"Rest suffered no loss because that company disposed of the property at a book value which took no account of the damage done to the property. The pursuers acquired no title to sue merely because they became heritable proprietors of property previously damaged. As the purported assignation was about a year later than the disposition Rest had by that time nothing to assign and so the assignation was ineffective."

However, he refused to accept the argument; and although his decision was reversed by the First Division of the Court of Session, the House of Lords held that the pursuers, the assignees, did have the right to sue for substantial damages. Lord Keith said,[41]

"As was rightly said by the Lord President in giving the judgment of the Court,[42] the basic question at issue is whether in this action the pursuers are really seeking to pursue against the defenders a claim or claims which Rest itself could have pursued at the date of the assignation in favour of the pursuers. As he further rightly said, the only relevant loss which, by virtue of the assignation, the pursuers could claim title to recover is loss suffered by their cedent, Rest, for which Rest could at the date of the assignation have sought reparation....

39 [1982] S.C.(H.L.) 157. The author is grateful to Mr. J. H. Butler of Jaques & Lewis for drawing his attention to this case.
40 Hearing the case at first instance: [1982] S.C.(H.L.) 157 at p. 165.
41 At pp. 177-178.
42 I.e., the First Division.

Where specific property has been damaged by delict, it is a general rule that the owner of the property does not, by parting with it to another, lose his title and interest to pursue a claim for damages against the wrongdoer.... Where the property is disposed of in an arm's length transaction for the price which it is fairly worth in its damaged condition, the difference between that price and the price which it would have fetched in an undamaged condition is likely to be the best measure of the loss and damage suffered. But it may happen that the owner of the property disposes of it otherwise than by such a transaction. He may, for example, alienate it gratuitously.... It is absurd to suggest that in such circumstances the claim to damages would disappear, as the Lord Ordinary put it, into some legal black hole, so that the wrongdoer escaped scot-free....

In the present case I am of opinion that the price for which, in pursuance of Group policy, Rest conveyed the damaged building to the pursuers is entirely irrelevant for the purpose of measuring the loss suffered by Rest through the defenders' negligence, and is quite incapable of founding an argument that Rest suffered no loss at all. The figure of price was fixed, in an internal group transaction and for accounting purposes only, without any reference to the true value of the building. The transaction cannot in the circumstances lead properly to the inference that Rest suffered no loss through the defenders' negligence, but is for all practical purposes on the same footing as a gratuitous alienation, as regards its significance for the purpose of a claim to damages."

This case, like *Dawson*, suggests that the nature of the assignee's right is the same as that which the assignor had immediately before the assignment, and that the value received by the assignor is to be disregarded in assessing the damages recoverable by the assignee. However, it goes further than *Dawson*, in that it held that the assignment was valid even though it took place separately from - and later than - the transfer of the property. This view was applied by the Court of Appeal most recently in *Linden Gardens Trust Ltd.* v. *Lenesta Sludge Disposals Ltd.*[43]

In *Linden Gardens*, Stock Conversion were lessees of a building which was found to contain blue asbestos. They contracted with McLaughlin and Harvey plc for the removal of the asbestos, and these works were completed in March 1980. It was alleged that McLaughlin and Harvey plc were in breach of contract in failing to remove all the asbestos:[44] on this basis, Stock

Conversion would have an accrued right of action against McLaughlin and Harvey plc in 1980. In April 1985 and December 1986, Stock Conversion assigned to Linden Gardens Trust Ltd. the leases on separate parts of the building: by the end of 1986, therefore, Stock Conversion had divested itself of its legal estate in the building - and it was assumed in the action that Linden Gardens gave full value for the leases. However, it was not until 14 January 1987 that Stock Conversion purported to assign[45] to Linden Gardens their rights of action in respect of the defects.

However, although the rights of action against McLaughlin and Harvey plc were not assigned until after the property had been transferred, all three members of the Court of Appeal held that Linden Gardens, as assignee, had a good claim to damages for breach of contract: and it was made clear that this claim was the same as that which Stock Conversion would have been able to bring, had it not assigned the leases and the rights of action. Staughton L.J. said:[46]

> "Where the assignment is of a cause of action for damages, ... it is said that ... the assignee can recover no more as damages than the assignor could have recovered.
> That proposition seems to me well-founded. It stems from the principle already discussed, that the debtor is not to be put in any worse position by reason of the assignment. And it is established by *Dawson* v. *Great Northern & City Railway Co.*; see also *GUS Property Management Ltd.* v. *Littlewoods Mail Order Stores Ltd.* ... But in a case such as the present one must elucidate the proposition slightly: the assignee can recover no more damages than the assignor could have recovered if there had been no assignment, and if the building had not been transferred to the assignee ...
> Stock Conversion had an accrued cause of action against McLaughlin & Harvey by 25 March 1980, the date of practical completion of that company's works ... That claim was validly assigned to Linden Gardens Trust, who can recover in respect of

44 The action was on preliminary issues; many facts were therefore assumed, rather than proved. Another company, Ashwell Construction Company Ltd., was brought in in 1985 to remove the further asbestos which had been found: the action was also brought against Ashwell, because it was alleged that even after their remedial works, there was still asbestos present in the building.
45 A further issue which was raised in the action, and on which the Court of Appeal was divided, was the effect of a prohibition against "assignment of this Contract" contained in the contract by which McLaughlin and Harvey undertook the work. However, this issue is not material for our present argument.
46 Court of Appeal Transcript, pp.20-21; 39-40.

it.

In my opinion Stock Conversion acquired a right to substantial damages for those breaches of contract[47], and did not lose it when they disposed of the rest of their interest in the building for its sound market value, on 12 December 1986. After the assignment on 14 January 1987, Linden Gardens Trust as assignees became entitled to enforce Stock Conversion's claim."

Sir Michael Kerr took the same line:[48]

"It makes no difference that Stock Conversion had transferred the premises before assigning their rights under the contracts: see *G.U.S.*, where this was the position. Stock Conversion retained their rights against the defendants and could assign them later ...

The next point is then that an assignee can recover damages from the debtor to the same extent as his assignor could have done, but he cannot enforce any claims, let alone under new heads of damage, which would not have been available to his assignor. However, his right to damages, limited to that extent, is enforceable by him even though he is not accountable to his assignor. These principles are illustrated by *Dawson* v. *Great Northern & City Railway Co.* [1905] 1 K.B. 260 (C.A.) at pp.273, 274, and by *G.U.S.* v. *Littlewoods Mail Order Stores* (H.L.) [1982] S.L.T. 533."

Conclusion

The present position, on the authorities, is clearly in favour of the view that the assignee of an accrued[49] right to sue for breach of warranty can sue

---

47 At this point, Staughton L.J. is referring to claims both against McLaughlin and Harvey, dating from 1980, and against Ashwell Construction, who were alleged to have been in breach of contract for failing to execute adequate remedial works in 1985.

48 Quoted from the transcript of his judgment, at pp 5-6.

49 In the alternative situation, where the warranty has not yet been broken, it is the right to have the warrantor continue to perform his obligations under the warranty which will be transferred. This was the case in *St.Martin's Corporation Ltd.* v. *Sir Robert McAlpine & Sons Ltd.* (consolidated in the Court of Appeal with the action in Linden Gardens). A majority of the Court of Appeal held in that case that the assignment was not valid; and so there was no decision on the rights which the assignee of such a warranty would have, although Staughton L.J. (dissenting on the issue of the validity of the assignment) held that the assignee would have the right to sue for substantial damages (transcript, pp.41-42): "[the assignor] by the assignment transferred to [the

the warrantor for substantial damages - he is in the same position as his assignor would have been had he assigned neither the warranty nor the property to which it relates[50]. *G.U.S. Property Management Ltd.* v. *Littlewoods Mail Order Stores Ltd.* and the decision of the Court of Appeal in *Linden Gardens Trust Ltd.* v. *Lenesta Sludge Disposals Ltd.* go so far as to say that this is true even if the warranty is assigned later than the transfer of the property.[51]

Assignment of the warranty with separate parts of the building

The final situation to consider is where P1, the recipient of the warranty, sells the building in two separate parts, to P3 and P4 respectively. If a defect is subsequently found in the building, can either of the assignees enforce the warranty?

assignee] the contractual right to have the building property constructed. [The assignee] can sue for breach of that obligation and recover substantial damages - which they in fact incurred. The damages must be no more than [the assignor] would have suffered if there had been no assignment and no transfer of the property, since [the warrantor] must not be put in any worse position by reason of the assignment. That is established by *Dawson's* case." However, in *St.Martin's* the purported assignment was contemporaneous with the transfer of the property there was therefore no issue as to whether it matters if the property is transferred before the assignment of the warranty.

50 This does not necessarily mean that the assignee recovers exactly the same quantum of damages as his assignor would have recovered, in the event that he sues the architect for damages for breach of contract. The general rule is that the injured party can recover as damages for breach of contract the losses of a kind which the contract breaker ought reasonably to have contemplated (at the time that the contract was entered into) that the other party would suffer as a result of a breach: *Chitty on Contracts* (26th ed. 1989), Sections 794. *Dawson* v. *Great Northern and City Railway Company* [1905] 1 K.B. 260 at pp.268-269, and the Court of Appeal in *Linden Gardens Trust Ltd.* v. *Lenesta Sludge Disposals Ltd.* make clear that an assignment cannot increase the liability of the party in breach. However, it appears that this would be applied - as in *Dawson* itself - to mean that the assignee can recover the actual value of his own losses, provided that those losses can be characterised as being within categories which the architect ought reasonably to have had in contemplation at the time of the execution of the warranty.

51 Therefore apparently assuming that even though the assignor has received full value for the property, he still retains a right to sue for the loss. Given that there might still be room for argument on this point - particularly in the light of the appeal to the House of Lords pending in the *Linden Gardens* and *St. Martin's* cases, the prudent advice would be for an assignee of the property to take an assignment of the rights of action under the warranty as part of the same transaction: thus ensuring that there is no doubt that the price paid is consideration for the property plus the warranty (that is, the defective property plus the rights under the warranty to have the defects corrected).

What is to be "divided"?

The first point is to be clear what is being assigned. A collateral warranty executed by an architect will typically contain a number of different obligations. For example, there may be covenants:

(i) that the designer has exercised, and will continue to exercise, reasonable skill;
(ii) that it will not terminate its appointment without giving the covenantee notice and a chance to remedy any breach of contract by the designer's appointor;
(iii) that it grants to the covenantee a licence to use material which would be subject to copyright restrictions.

It is assumed that the question is not whether each of these obligations can be assigned separately (e.g. if P1 wishes to assign obligations (i), and (ii) to P2, and (iii) to P3) but whether the obligations can themselves be split. It would not generally make sense in this context to consider assigning obligations separately; what is required is to give the benefit of, for example, the designer's warranty of care to each owner of part, insofar as his part is affected by a breach of the warranty. The question therefore resolves itself into whether A's warranty of care, executed in favour of P1, can be assigned in part to each of P2 and P3, who together own the same estate as P1 owned at the time the warranty was given.

Legal and equitable assignments

There appears to be no authority directly in point. The courts have considered the assignment of parts of obligations, but only in the context of debts, and not the benefit of contractual obligations of the kind which we are considering. The cases relating to debts can, however, assist us. There are two methods of assignment: statutory assignment under section 136 of the Law of Property Act 1925, and assignment in equity. Section 136(1)[52] refers to

> "Any absolute assignment by writing under the hand of the assignor (not purporting to be by way of charge only) of any debt or other legal thing in action...."

Although the benefit of the warranty would be a "legal thing in action" for the purpose of the section, it has been decided that an assignment of part

52 See above.

of a debt cannot be an absolute assignment, and is therefore not within the section.[53] It is clear, then, that an assignment of part of a "legal thing in action" (if such a concept is possible) could not be within the section, either. It is, however, possible to assign part of a debt in equity.[54] One reason why the court will allow such an assignment, but not a statutory assignment, is the issue of joinder of parties. A statutory assignment, if it is operative, allows the assignee to sue the debtor without any reference to the assignor. He stands entirely in the same position as if he had been the original creditor, and the assignor drops out of the picture. Under an equitable assignment of part of the debt, however, the original creditor (and, presumably, any other present or previous assignee of any part of the original debt) must be a party to any action by the assignee. This enables the court to make a single judgment binding on all the parties concerned.[55]

Given this, it seems that a court might well be prepared to say that a warranty of the kind which we are discussing, which affects the whole of a building, can in equity be divided and assigned insofar as it affects each part, on a division of the building on sale.[56] This is also a sensible outcome. If the warranty has not, at the time of the assignment, been broken, P2 and P3, who presumably pay full value for their respective parts of the building, need the protection of the warranty when it is subsequently broken, and it is difficult to see why they should separately (given that they must both join in any action to enforce the warranty) be in a worse position than a single purchaser of the whole building. If the warranty has been broken by the time of the assignment, P1 will after the assignment have no loss to claim, if he has obtained the full value of a non-defective building, and P2 and P3 have (unknowingly) taken the assignment of an accrued right of action - i.e., a

---

53 *Re Steel Wing Company Ltd.* [1921] 1 Ch. 349 at p.354-355; *Forster* v. *Baker* [1910] 2 K.B. 636; *Williams* v. *Atlantic Assurance Co. Ltd.* [1933] 1 K.B. 81. Coleridge L.C.J. at first instance in *Brice* v. *Bannister* (1878) 3 Q.B.D. 569 at pp.574-5 had thought that there could be a statutory assignment of part of a debt, but this was doubted by Chitty L.J. in *Durham Bros.* v. *Robertson* [1898] 1 Q.B. 765 at p.774.

54 *Re Steel Wing Company Ltd.* [1921] 1 Ch. 349.

55 It was this consideration which led Chitty L.J. in *Durham Bros.* v. *Robertson* [1898] 1 Q.B. 765 at p. 774 to doubt whether a statutory assignment of part of a debt was possible: "If it be, it would seem to leave it in the power of the original creditor to split up the single legal cause of action for the debt into as many separate legal causes of action as he might think fit."

56 If one compares the position of restrictive covenants relating to land, similar provisions apply: a covenant could not at common law be split up and assigned in pieces; however equity will allow such an assignment if the land is divided: *Re Union of London and Smith's Bank Ltd.'s Conveyance* [1933] Ch. 611 at p. 630. Notice that if a warranty can be divided only by an equitable assignment, a warranty which is expressed to be capable of assignment only by a legal assignment - such as the British Property Federation collateral warranty for funding institutions, CoWa/F 1990 - cannot be so divided.

right to recover damages for breach of contract. Again, if a right to a debt can be severed in equity on assignment, it is difficult to see why the right to damages for breach of contract should not also be severable.[57]

There is, however, the overriding limitation that the assignments must not increase the overall burden of the covenantor, and hence the assignees, P2 and P3, can together recover only the damages[58] which the assignor, P1, could himself have recovered.[59] This emphasises again the need for a single determination binding all parties.

Conclusions

Where the warrantee lets the building to a tenant, he should still be able to sue the warrantor architect for defects arising from negligent design, notwithstanding the existence of covenants in a full repairing lease which afford the warrantee, as lessor, a right of action against the tenant to compel the repair of the property. It is suggested that even repair by the tenant might not deprive the warrantee of a right of action for substantial damages against the architect, although there are dicta to the contrary to set against the authority cited in support of that view.

Where there is an assignment of the whole interest of the warrantee, the architect might resist a claim against him by the assignee on the ground that the assignee could only claim to the same extent as the assignor - who would have suffered no loss. It is concluded that such warranties should be assignable, subject to any provision (express or implied) to the contrary and

57 Two objections might be that the right to damages is a right to an unliquidated sum, whereas a debt is ascertained; and that the form of assignment which we are considering involves a division by reference to the extent to which the warranty relates to each separate part of the building - a less precise formula than a division into, for example, particular fractions or "the first 1000 out of..." However, these need not be insuperable objections; there can, for example, be a valid equitable assignment of part of a debt which has not yet accrued and is therefore presently unascertainable (*Shepherd* v. *Commissioner of Taxation of the Commonwealth of Australia* (1965) 113 C.L.R. 385: assignment of 90% of royalties which would become due pursuant to an existing contractual right). And the difficulty relating to the division by reference to the separate parts of the building shows that there may be problems of drafting the assignments, but that ought not to be impossible. One further limitation is that the assignment of the right to sue must not be invalid on the grounds of maintenance or champerty; but, as long as the assignment is linked to the sale of the land affected by the breach of warranty, it should not be invalid: *Trendtex Trading Corporation* v. *Credit Suisse* [1982] A.C. 679.

58 Either the total quantum, or (more likely) the kind of loss, which A ought reasonably to have contemplated that P1 would have suffered: Chitty on Contracts (26th ed., 1989) section 1794; n.50 above.

59 *Dawson* v. *Great Northern and City Railway Company* [1905] 1 K.B. 260 at pp. 268-269.

provided that the provisions in the warranty are not of a personal nature; and that an assignee should be able to claim for substantial damages. The case-law is clearly against the "no loss" argument.

It does not seem possible to resolve the issue as to whether the assignee of a part, following division of the property, could take the benefit of a warranty. While no statutory legal assignment of part would be effective in permitting enforcement of the warranty, a warranty should and might be divisible and thus enforceable in equity.

Options, letters of intent and agreements to agree

4

Richard Winward

Synopsis

This paper discusses the difficulties involved in creating and attempting to enforce a variety of commercial arrangements which lie at the periphery of the law of contract as it presently stands.

Introduction

A contract is[1] "a promise or set of promises which the law will enforce". Unlike tort, where the standard of behaviour is imposed by the courts, in contract the relevant standards are a matter of private bargain. Provided that the subject matter of the bargain is not illegal or contrary to public policy, the courts adopt a negative role in contract and that role is to police a set of rules which determine whether or not an enforceable contract has come into existence. Subject to certain statutory exceptions, particularly in the consumer field, it is not the court's role to form views as to the fairness of the bargain and the court will not intervene to make a harsh but unambiguous contract more reasonable. For example in *Trollope and Colls Ltd* v. *North West Metropolitan Regional Hospital Board*[2] the contract provided for three phases of work, phase 1 to be completed by the 30th April 1969 and phase 3 to commence six months after the date of practical completion of phase 1 and to be completed on the 30th April 1972 i.e an overall construction period of 30 months for phase 3. The completion of phase 1 was delayed by a period of 59 weeks, 47 of which were not the fault of the contractor. Practical completion of phase 1 was not achieved until the 22nd June 1972 leaving a construction period of only 16 months, rather than 30 months for the completion of phase 3. The court took the view that the intention of the parties was perfectly clear from the wording of their contract and accordingly refused to relax the contractor's obligations by implication of a term that the time for completion of phase 3 should be extended by the same period as the extension of time granted in respect of phase 1.

Often construction contracts are complex documents comprising nu-

---

1 Pollock *Principles of Contract* (13th Edition)
2 [1973] 1 WLR 601, All E.R. 260

merous pages. It is important to bear in mind however that construction contracts are governed not by special rules but by the ordinary rules of formation. A basic understanding of those rules is a prerequisite to understanding the subject matter of this paper, namely options, letters of intent and agreements to agree. These matters are all facets of the formation of contract.

The essential requirements of a contract are as follows:
1. Two or more parties; and
2. An intention to create legal relations; and
3. An agreement; and
4. Consideration.

Options, letters of intent and agreements to agree require examination of the last two requirements, i.e. agreement and consideration.

Agreement

Agreement is evinced by offer and acceptance. An offer is a written or oral statement by a person of his willingness to enter into a contract upon terms which are certain or which are capable of being rendered certain. The offeror's intention to enter into a contract may be actual or apparent. An apparent intention is determined by an objective test that is to say that which a reasonable man would construe from a particular set of facts; it is not based upon the beliefs of the parties and indeed there may be an apparent intention to enter into a contract even though the parties themselves believed that they had not yet reached that stage. An offer must be accepted to form a contract. An acceptance is a written or verbal expression of assent to the terms of the offer. It must be unequivocal and unconditional. In *Peter Lind & Co Ltd* v. *Mersey Docks and Harbour Board*[3] the Harbour Board invited PL a building contractor to submit alternative tenders for the construction of a container freight terminal, one tender to be at a fixed price and the other at a price varying with the cost of labour and materials. The Harbour Board wrote to PL stating that they accepted "your tender". The court held that this letter was imprecise because it did not specify which tender was being accepted so that there was no concluded contract at that stage.

Consideration

Save for contracts made under seal i.e deeds, the courts will not enforce gratuitous promises. There must be valuable consideration. Valuable

3 [1972] 2 Lloyds L.R. 234

consideration is something of value in the eye of the law; *Roscorla* v. *Thomas*[4]. Clearly the payment of money or a promise to pay money is valuable consideration. However other acts even though insignificant may provide valuable consideration. For example a promise to give £50 "if you will come to my house" was held to be valuable consideration in *Gilbert* v. *Ruddeard*.[5] As a general rule a moral obligation does not provide valuable consideration for example a promise made "in consideration of natural love and affection"; *Bret* v. *J.S.*[6] It will be appreciated that valuable consideration is not value in the sense that the courts are concerned about the fairness or otherwise of the bargain between the parties; it is the distinction between gratuitous promises and non-gratuitous promises.[7]

Form of Contract

Construction contracts may be deeds or a simple contract. A simple contract may be a written contract or an oral contract, or partly in writing and partly oral. There are two essential differences between deeds and simple contracts. A deed is a specialty and does not require consideration. Further the limitation period [i.e the period after which claims for breach are no longer possible] is six years from the date on which the cause of action accrued in respect of a simple contract and twelve years from such date in respect of deeds: Section 5 of the Limitation Act 1980.

Much of the law relating to the execution of deeds was swept away on the 31st July 1990 by the Law of Property (Miscellaneous Provisions) Act 1989 and the Companies Act 1989. Section 1(3) of the Law of Property (Miscellaneous Provisions) Act provides that a deed must be signed by a person who is to be bound and the signature must be attested by a witness. Section 1(2)(a) of the Act provides that a document shall not be a deed unless it is made clear on its face that it is intended to be a deed by the person making it. If these provisions are not satisfied then the document will not take effect as a deed however may still take effect as a simple contract. The Companies Act 1989 has amended the rules for sealing of deeds by registered companies. Companies may still execute deeds by using their company seal, however Section 130 of the Companies Act [introducing a new Section 36A to the Companies Act 1985] provides that if a document is signed by a director and the secretary of the company or by two directors and the document is expressed (in what ever form of words) to be executed by the

4   [1842] 2 QB 851
5   (1608) 3 Dy. 276 b(n)
6   (1600) Cro.Eliz. 755
7   See also *Williams* v. *Roffey Bros.* [1991] 1 QB 1.

company it will have the same effect as if it had been executed under the common seal of the company i.e it is a deed. Further a document which makes it clear on its own wording that it is to be a deed will also take effect as a deed: for example a document described as "this deed" and signed by one director will operate as a deed.

It follows that extreme care must be taken when drafting documents to ensure that documents take effect as deeds and, as regards companies, that documents which are intended to be simple contracts do not take effect as deeds.

Options

As stated above agreement is established by the process of offer and acceptance. An offer can be withdrawn at any time prior to it being accepted. This rule applies even though the person who makes the offer, the promisor, states to the person whom the offer is made, the promisee, that the offer will be kept open for a particular period of time. In *Routledge* v. *Grant*[8] G offered to buy a house from R stating that R had six weeks in which to decide whether or not to sell. Before the end of the six week period G withdrew his offer and upon being sued by R the court held that the offer had been properly withdrawn before acceptance and therefore there was no binding contract. Again in *Offord* v. *Davies*[9] D made a written offer to O that, if O would discount bills for another Firm, then D would guarantee the payment of such bills to the extent of £600 during a period of twelve calendar months. Some bills were discounted by O and duly paid, but before the end of the twelve month period, D revoked their offer and notified O that they were no longer guarantee payment of the bills. O continued to discount bills some of which were not paid and then O sued D on their guarantee. The court held that D's revocation was a good defence. The guarantee was an offer, for a period of twelve months, of promises for acts (i.e the promise to guarantee payment of the bill in consideration of the act of discounting) and each discount turned the offer into a promise, pro tanto, but the entire offer could be revoked except as regards discounts made before the notice of revocation.

The common point in the *Routledge* and *Offord* cases was that a statement that an offer will be kept open for a particular period was held not to be legally binding. However such a statement will be binding if it forms part of a contract of option which is a contract having a separate legal existence to the main transaction. A contract of option is therefore a promise by the offeror, supported by consideration, usually the payment of money, whereby

8 (1828) 4 Bing 653
9 [1862] 12 CB.NS 748

the offeror binds himself to the offeree not to revoke his offer during a stated period. The question of whether or not consideration is necessary to make a contract of option legally binding has been the subject of much legal debate. Indeed in 1937 the Law Revision Committee in its Sixth Interim Report recommended that "an agreement to keep an offer open for a definite period of time or until the occurrence of some specified event should not be unenforceable by reason of the absence of consideration." Nevertheless the courts still require a contract of option to be supported by consideration. If however the promise to keep open an offer is made in a deed that is to say is a promise under seal, then consideration is not necessary: *Beesly* v. *Hallwood Estates Ltd*[10].

Option contracts are often used in the sale of development land, for example where the land has development potential but planning permission has not yet been obtained and the builder is prepared to purchase the land subject to planning consent. Also a developer may be trying to bring together various plots of land and does not wish to be bound in respect of any one plot until such time as he is certain that he can acquire all the plots. Until recently option contracts for the sale of land were governed by Section 40 of the Law of Property Act 1925 which required that such contracts should be in writing or evidenced in writing. Since September 1989 option contracts for the sale of land have been governed by Section 2 of the Law of Property (Miscellaneous Provisions) Act 1989. Section 2(1) of the Act provides that "a contract for the sale or other disposition of an interest in land can only be made in writing and only by incorporating all the terms which the parties have expressly agreed in one document or, where contracts are exchanged, in each." It is considered that an option contract falls within the words "other disposition of an interest in land" and accordingly the Act creates some pitfalls for current conveyancing practice. Traditionally option contracts have been granted by the seller signing a letter addressed to the purchaser and the purchaser exercising the option by sending a signed notice to the seller. It is suggested that such a letter or notice would not satisfy the requirements of the Act and would not be valid. Care must be taken therefore that both the grant of options by the seller and the exercise of an option by the purchaser should be contained in formal contracts signed by both parties.

An option for the purchase of land should be distinguished from a conditional contract for purchase or a right of pre-emption. A conditional contract binds the purchaser if the condition is satisfied. With an option contract the purchaser is not bound until he exercises the option which of course is a unilateral act on the part of the purchaser and therefore gives the purchaser greater flexibility. Whether a contract is a conditional contract or

10 [1961] Ch. 105

an option contract is a matter of substance and not simply a question of the title of the document. In *Re Longlands Farm, Long Common, Botley, Hants Alford* v. *Superior Developments Ltd*[11] the Plaintiff owned 57 acres of agricultural land. The Plaintiff and the Defendants, Superior Developments Ltd, signed a document which stated that the Defendants were "agreeable to the purchase" of the 57 acres for a price of £114,000 subject to the Defendants obtaining planning permission to their entire satisfaction for the development of the land and to questions of title being to their approval, the purchase to be completed within 8 weeks of those conditions being satisfied. The Plaintiff agreed and accepted those terms and he acknowledged receipt of £5 "In consideration to my holding the property for you." The court held that the document was not an option but was a conditional contract which would become absolute if the Defendants obtained planning permission to their satisfaction and approved the title.

A right of pre-emption is the giving of a right of first opportunity to buy certain land in the event that the purchaser decides to sell the land. Unlike an option contract, a right of pre-emption is merely a contractual right and not an interest in land. It follows that provided the requirements of registration have been satisfied (see paragraph 2.7 below) an option contract will take priority over a preemption right even though the former was dated later than the latter. In *Pritchard* v. *Briggs & Others*[12] L and his wife owned certain land on which there was an hotel, a house and garage premises. In 1945 they sold the hotel to R but retained the rest of the land ("the retained land"). The conveyance of the hotel to R contained a covenant giving a right of preemption to R and his successors by L and his wife, on behalf of themselves and their successors in title that so long as the survivor of them was alive and R was alive they would not sell the retained land without giving R or his successors in title the option of purchasing the retained land for £3,000 together with the fixtures and petrol pumps on the garage premises at valuation..On the 17th December 1944 the right of pre-emption was registered under the Land Charges Act 1925 as an estate contract. L and his wife retired to live in the house on the retained land. R subsequently sold the hotel and the benefit of the right of pre-emption to M who in turn in 1954 sold the hotel and the benefit of the right of pre-emption to the Defendant. In 1959 L and his wife granted the Plaintiff a lease of the garage premises for 5 years at a rent of £156 per annum. The lease contained a covenant by L and his wife, on behalf of themselves and their successors in title, that on the death of the survivor of them the Plaintiff was to have an option to purchase the whole of the retained land for £3,000 within 3 months of the

11 [1968] 3 All E.R. 552
12 [1980] Ch. 338; 1 AER 294

survivor's death. In February 1964 L and his wife granted the Plaintiff a further lease of the garage premises for a term of 21 years at an increased rental. This second lease also incorporated the option over the retained land granted by the previous lease. The option was registered as an estate contract on the 10th February 1964. In 1969 L's wife died and the legal and beneficial interest in the retained land became vested in L. In 1971 L became ill and was unable to manage his affairs and his nephew was appointed receiver of his estate under the Mental Health Act 1959. The nephew wished to realise L's only asset, the retained land, to provide for L. The nephew was aware both of the right of pre-emption under the 1944 conveyance and the Plaintiff's option under the lease. He negotiated a sale of the land to the party having the pre-emptive right. On the 15th January 1973 L died and on the 16th February the sale was completed by a conveyance dated that date. On the 12th March, within 3 months of L's death, the Plaintiff served notice on the executors purporting to exercise his option to purchase the retained land. The court held that on a true construction of the Plaintiff's option clause he had an unqualified right to call for the conveyance of the retained land if within 3 months of the death of the survivor of L and his wife he gave notice and paid £3,000. Further the right of pre-emption, unlike an option to purchase, did not create an interest in land because it did not give the grantee a present right, or even a contingent right, to call for the conveyance of the legal estate. It created a mere spes and could not become an interest in land until the condition on which it depended was satisfied (i.e by the grantor offering the land to the grantee) and the right was converted into an option. It followed that once the Plaintiff's option had been granted and registered it took priority over the right of pre-emption.

Both option contracts and rights of pre-emption are estate contracts which require to be registered under Section 10 of the Land Charges Act 1925. Failure to register invalidates the option or the pre-emptive right against a purchaser of the land. The date of registration also determines the order of priorities over competing options or competing pre-emption rights.

As a matter of practice options will invariably include a condition providing for the option to be exercised within a definite, usually limited, period. If the option is silent on this point or provides for a period greater than 21 years then the document may well contravene Section 9(2) of the Perpetuities and Accumulations Act 1964 which provides by Section 9(2) that options for the purchase of land for valuable consideration should be limited to a period of 21 years. It is important to note however that Section 3(3) of the Act provides a "wait and see" rule which will save the option if, as a matter of fact, it is exercised within the 21 years. Care must be taken when drafting options to incorporate all necessary conditions that will be relevant to the ultimate sale and also care needs to be taken on the part of the purchaser exercising the option to ensure that the precise requirements of the option are satisfied.

Letters of Intent

The process of offer and acceptance often involves protracted and complex negotiations. As stated in paragraph 1.6 above, in order to create a binding agreement there must be an unequivocal and unconditional acceptance of an offer. If a party to negotiations attempts to accept an offer but introduces new terms this is not an acceptance but a counter offer. It is not difficult therefore to imagine the situation where parties have made offers, counter-offers, counter counter offers etc each party trying to impose their own terms and conditions of trade or a standard form of contract which is more to their liking. It is this ebb and flow of commercial negotiations that sets the scene for considering the role of letters of intent.

As a general statement the purpose of a letter of intent is to express an intention to enter into a contract at a future date. Such letters are usually sent at a time when it is anticipated that the recipient will be incurring costs and overheads in respect of the project. It is important to bear in mind that the words "letter of intent" give rise to a term of convenience rather than a term having a substantive legal meaning for example "subject to contract" or "without prejudice". It is suggested that the legal effect of a letter of intent may fall into one or more of the following categories, namely:-

1.   The expression of an intention to enter into a contract at a future date which does not give rise to any legal obligation whether in contract or quasi ex contractu on a quantum meruit; or
2.   The expression of an intention to enter into a contract at a future date which does not give rise to any liability in contract but does not exclude or negative a right to recover on a quantum meruit; or
3.   The creation of a conditional or ancillary contractual obligation which may but not necessarily will be subsumed by a wider contractual obligation upon formal contracts being executed; or
4.   A legally binding executory contract in that the letter of intent is an offer capable of being accepted or the acceptance of an offer.

The essential test is one of substance not form. In *O.T.M. Limited* v. *Hydranautics*[13] H offered to sell OTM a device for tensioning chains on a monitoring buoy in the North Sea. The document of offer incorporated H's

---

13 [1981] 2 Lloyds L.R. 211

terms and conditions of sale. In response to the offer OTM telexed H stating "it is our intention to place an order for one chain tensioner... A purchase order will be prepared in the near future but you are directed to proceed with the tension and fabrication on the basis of this telex. The purchase order will be issued subject to our usual terms and conditions". The court held, inter alia, that OTM's telex was a letter of intent and did not constitute an acceptance of H's offer. In *British Steel Corporation* v. *Cleveland Bridge & Engineering Company*[14] Cleveland Bridge were sub-contractors for the fabrication of steelwork for the Sama Bank, Damman, Saudi Arabia. The design of the building was unusual, involving an exposed steel lattice-work frame to which were joined the main diagonal steel beams. The junction between the diagonal beams and the lattice-work was provided by 150 steel nodes. Cleveland Bridge entered into negotiations with British Steel for the casting and supply of the steel nodes. There were protracted discussions between Cleveland Bridge and British Steel as to the production of a specification for the steel nodes. Early on in these negotiations Cleveland Bridge had sent a letter to British Steel stating as follows:

> "We are pleased to advise you that it is the intention of Cleveland Bridge & Engineering Co Ltd to enter into a sub-contract with your Company for the supply and delivery of the steel castings which form the roof nodes on this project. The price will be as quoted in your telex dated the 9th February 1979... The form of sub-contract to be entered into will be our standard form of sub-contract for use in conjunction with the ICE General Conditions of Contract, copy of which is enclosed for your consideration... We request that you proceed immediately with the works pending the preparation and issuing to you of the official form of subcontract".

The court held that there was no contract between Cleveland Bridge and British Steel as the effect of the letter of intent was to ask British Steel to proceed immediately with the work pending the preparation and issuing of a form of sub-contract being a document which was plainly in a state of negotiation not least on the issues of price, delivery dates and applicable terms and conditions.

In contrast to OTM and British Steel the court found there was a binding contract in *Wilson Smithett & Cape (Sugar) Ltd* v. *Bangladesh Sugar & Food Industries Corporation*[15]. The Plaintiffs, who were sugar merchants,

14 [1981] 24 BLR 94
15 [1986] 1 Lloyds LR 375

responded by a tender to an invitation sent by the Defendants, a nationalised Bangladeshi corporation. The tender was for the sale of 10,000 tonnes of sugar cane. The Plaintiffs were the second lowest bidder. The Bangladeshi Government decided to import a further 10,000 tonnes and the Defendants were instructed to place an order with the second lowest tenderer i.e the Plaintiffs, if they were agreeable to matching the successful tenderer's bid. Negotiations were conducted between the Plaintiffs and Defendants and eventually the Plaintiffs sent to the Defendants a letter of offer which was to remain open until 2 pm local Dacca time on June 12th 1981. The same day the Defendants issued a letter of intent which stated:

> "We are pleased to issue this letter of intent to you for the supply of the following materials... All other terms and conditions as per your... offer dated June 12th 1981."

The Defendants decided not to proceed with their purchase and they contended that their letter of the 12th June was nothing more than an expression of a future intent to enter into a contract. The court rejected this submission and held that the letter although it used the phrase letter of intent was intended to have contractual significance and effect. The court held that there was a binding contract between the parties. Similarly in *Turriff Construction Ltd and Turriff Limited* v. *Regalia Knitting Mills Ltd*[16] the court held that a letter of intent had a contractual effect. In that case T were invited by R to submit a tender for the design and construction of a new factory for R at Corby, Northants. A tender was sent in December 1968 and after discussion it was finalised in May 1969. On the 2nd June 1969 a meeting took place at which R told T that they wanted them to carry out the project for them under one contract with a programme based on completion in 1972. In order to meet R requirements a considerable amount of work had to be undertaken by T and accordingly T requested "an early letter of intent... to cover Turriff Limited for the work they will now be undertaking." Because of outstanding detail it was not possible, at that time, to enter into a formal contract. On the 17th June 1969 R sent a letter to T stating:

> "As agreed at our meeting on the 2nd June 1969 it is the intention of Regalia to award a contract to Turriff to build a factory including production, stores, offices and canteen facilities to be built in four continuous phases.
> Phase I to be on a fixed price basis as agreed and phases II, III and IV to be calculated on the same basis as Phase I and completed

by 1972. The commencing date to be 1st August and the terms
of payment to be negotiated on a monthly form against bills of
quantities supplied by Regalia's surveyor.
All this to be subject to obtaining agreement on the land and
leases with the Corby Development Corporation, full building
and by-law consent, and the site investigation being undertaken
by Drilling and Prospecting International Limited.
The whole to be subject to agreement on an acceptable contract."

On the strength of that letter T undertook a considerable amount of work;
however the project was subsequently abandoned. On the issue of whether
or not a contract had come into existence between T and R entitling T to be
paid for the work they had undertaken, the court held that in June 1969 T had
made an offer which was an offer to carry out work with the urgency required
by R if R would assume liability for the work done thereafter and that this
offer was capable of being accepted by the receipt of the letter of intent.
Further that R's letter on the 17th June was a letter of intent and there was
nothing in it which negatived the apparent acceptance of T's offer and
accordingly an "ancillary" contract came into existence.

So far the cases have been considered from the point of view of the
contractor's entitlement to payment. It is important to note that even though
a letter of intent does not give rise to any contractual obligation a contractor
who carries out work at the request of a client during the course of
negotiations may still be entitled to recover costs, profit and overheads
expended on those works even if the negotiations do not ultimately lead to
a concluded contract. In the appropriate case a contractor will be entitled to
recover a reasonable sum on a quantum meruit which is an obligation arising
quasi ex contractu commonly referred to as "quasi contract". In the Turriff
case there was an unusual finding in so far as the Judge felt that the parties'
discussions had excluded the prospect of quasi contractual liability. It is
important to note that an entitlement to a quantum meruit arises not from the
actual intentions of the parties but as a matter of law. This was explained by
Greer L.J. in *Craven-Ellis* v. *Cannons Limited*[17] in the following words:

> "In my judgment the obligation to pay reasonable remuneration
> for the work done when there is no binding contract between the
> parties is imposed by a rule of law and not by inference of fact,
> arising from the acceptance of services or goods."

In *William Lacey (Hounslow) Limited* v. *Davis*[18] Barry J stated:

17 [1936] 2 KB 403
18 [1957] 1 WLR 932

"In these quasi contractual cases the court will look at the true facts and ascertain from them whether or not a promise to pay should be implied, irrespective of the actual views or intentions of the parties at the time when the work was done or the services rendered."

In *Lacey* one of the important findings was that the work carried out by the contractor fell outside the normal work which a builder performed gratuitously, for example the costs of preparing competitive tenders. Again in *British Steel* the court held that British Steel were entitled to recover a reasonable sum on a quasi contractual basis.

The *British Steel* case considered the effect of a letter of intent from a different stand point, namely, could it introduce performance obligations on the contractor for the benefit of the employer? That is to say was there some contractual halfway house between quantum meruit and contract whereby the letter of intent gave rise to what was described in the *British Steel* case as an "if" contract? In that case Goff J stated:

"As a matter of analysis the contract (if any) which may come into existence following a letter of intent may take one of two forms: either there may be an ordinary executory contract under which each party assumes reciprocal obligations to the other; or there may be what is sometimes called an "if" contract i.e a contract under which A requests B to carry out a certain performance and promises B that, if he does so, he will receive a certain performance in return, usually remuneration for his performance. The latter transaction is really no more than a standing order which, if acted upon before it lapses or is lawfully withdrawn, will result in a binding contract."

This is an interesting though somewhat difficult concept. On the facts of *British Steel* the Judge found that there was no contract and no "if" contract because the parties were still in a state of negotiation on essential terms such as price, delivery dates and applicable terms and conditions of sale.

Agreements to Agree

It is a principle of contract law that the courts will not enforce an agreement to agree. To give rise to a legally binding contractual obligation the process of offer and acceptance must, as a general rule, result in the parties agreeing on all the terms that are essential to their bargain; there must be a *"consensus ad idem"*. As a general rule the essential terms for a construction contract are parties, description of the works, price and period for construction. A failure to agree on price and period may not necessarily be fatal as the contract could be rescued by the courts construing an implied term to give the contract business efficacy. In any event terms as to reasonable price and reasonable period are now implied as a matter of statute by Sections 13 and 14 of the Supply of Goods and Services Act 1982.

The difficulties arise when the parties have clearly left an essential term to be settled by further agreement. The case of *May & Butcher* v. *The King*[19] was concerned with an agreement by MB to purchase from the Crown all its surplus tentage "at such prices as should be agreed upon between them as quantities of tentage become available for disposal and were offered for purchase". The House of Lords held that there was no concluded contract. Lord Buckmaster stated:

> "It has long been a well recognised principle of contract law that an agreement between two parties to enter into an agreement in which some critical part of the contract matter is left undetermined is no contract at all. It is of course perfectly possible for two people to contract that they will sign a document which contains all the relevant terms, but it is not open to them to agree that they will in the future agree upon a matter which is vital to the arrangement between them and has not yet been determined."

Viscount Dunedine added:

> "To be a good contract there must be a concluded bargain and a concluded contract is one which settles everything that is necessary to be settled and leaves nothing to be settled by agreement between the parties. Of course it may leave something which still has to be determined but then that determination must be a determination which does not depend upon the agreement between the parties... Therefore you may very well agree that a certain part of the contract of sale, such as price may be settled by someone else... as long as you have something certain it does not matter. For instance with regard to price it is a perfectly good contract to say that the price is to be settled by the buyer...".

There is an essential difference therefore between a contract which

19 [1929] reported [1934] 2 KB 17N

expressly leaves an essential term to be agreed and a contract which leaves that term to be determined by one of the parties or indeed is silent on that term. The first type of agreement is merely an agreement to agree and is unenforceable. The second type is an agreement subject to a determination and is enforceable. The third type is an agreement which may be rescued by an implied term.

The first type of agreement was considered in *Courtney & Fairbairn Limited* v. *Tolaini Bros (Hotels) Limited & Another*[20]. T wished to develop a site and discussed their plans with C who were building contractors. C were well placed to obtain finance for the development and it was proposed that C should introduce a third party to provide the finance and thereafter C would be employed to carry out the construction work. C subsequently wrote to T notifying T that they were able to introduce the third party financier and at the same time stressed that C's interest was as builders and enquired whether if their introduction led to an acceptable financial arrangement, T would instruct their quantity surveyor "to negotiate fair and reasonable sums" for the projects based on agreed estimates of net cost and overheads with a 5% profit margin. T wrote to C agreeing "to the terms specified". C introduced a financier and the necessary financial arrangements were agreed. Differences of opinion arose between C and T as to the price of the construction works and T engaged other contractors to do those works. The Court of Appeal held that since there had been no agreement upon such a fundamental matter as the price in a building contract, or the method by which it was to be calculated, there was no contract; there was merely a contract to negotiate.

In *Courtney* the emphasis was placed upon the words that T would instruct their quantity surveyor to negotiate fair and reasonable sums. If the letter had merely provided that T's quantity surveyor would determine those sums then it is suggested that the facts of Courtney would have fallen within the second type of agreement and would have given rise to an enforceable contract. This was the situation in *Sudbrook Trading Estate Limited* v. *Eggleton & Others*[21]. The facts of this case concerned four separate leases made in 1949, 1955, 1966 and 1968 whereby four adjacent industrial premises were demised for various terms of years all expiring on December 24th 1997. By clause 9 of the lease made in 1955 the lessees were granted an option, on giving to the lessors notice in writing of their desire "to purchase the reversion in fee simple in the premises hereby demised... at such price not being less than £2,000 as may be agreed upon by two valuers

20 [1975] 1 WLR 297; see also *Walford* v. *Miles* [1992] 1 All ER 453 (H.L.)
21 [1983] 1 AC 444

one to be nominated by the lessor and the other by the lessee and in defa of such agreement by an umpire appointed by the valuers." The other leases contained option clauses in identical terms save as to the minimum price. The lessees exercised their options to purchase the reversions but the lessors refused to appoint a valuer. On the issue of whether or not the options were valid the Judge at first instance considered that the options were both valid and had been properly exercised. On appeal to the Court of Appeal the court held that since the agreement was one where the parties had agreed the machinery for ascertaining the option price, the parties had come to an agreement to agree and therefore the options were unenforceable. The House of Lords, reversing the Court of Appeal, held that on its true construction the agreement was for sale at a fair and reasonable price by the application of objective standards and once the options had been exercised in accordance with the necessary pre-conditions, since the price was capable of being ascertained and was therefore certain, a complete contract for the sale and purchase of the freehold reversion was constituted; that as the price was to be ascertained by machinery which, on the true construction of the agreement was a subsidiary and non essential part of the contract, the court would, if the machinery broke down for any reason substitute its own machinery to ascertain a fair and reasonable price.

If the letter in *Courtney* had been silent on the matter of instructing a quantity surveyor then the third case may have applied and the agreement might have been rescued by an implied term that the price of the work was to be calculated by the addition of 5% to the fair and reasonable costs and overheads. In *Foley* v. *Classique Coaches Ltd*[22] the contract was rescued by the use of implied term. This case concerned an agreement by F to sell to C certain land which C intended to use for their business of motor coach operators. The sale was subject to a second agreement in which C agreed to purchase from F all the petrol required for the purpose of their business at "a price to be agreed by the parties in writing and from time to time". On the issue of whether or not that second agreement was binding the court held that a term must be implied in the agreement that the petrol supplied by F should be of a reasonable quantity and sold at a reasonable price and that if any dispute arose as to what was a reasonable price it was to be determined by an arbitration clause in the petrol agreement and accordingly the agreement was valid and binding. In *Hillas & Co* v. *Arcos Limited*[23] the agreement was rescued by custom and usage and from a previous course of dealings. H entered into an agreement with A for the sale to them in 1930

22 [1934] 2 KB 1
23 [1932] 147 L.T. 503

of a quantity of Russian softwood timber. The contract contained a clause giving H an option to purchase further timber in 1931 but the option gave no particulars as to the kind or size or quantity of the timber nor the manner of shipment. When H sought to exercise the option A argued that the clause was too indeterminate and uncertain to indicate an unequivocal intention to be bound and that it was merely an agreement to negotiate a future agreement. The court held that in the light of previous dealings there was sufficient intention to be bound: the terms left uncertain in the option could be ascertained by reference to those contained in the original contract and from the normal practice of the timber trade. Lord Wright stated:

> "Businessmen often record the most important agreements in crude and summary fashion; modes of expression sufficient and clear to them in the course of their business may appear to those unfamiliar with the business far from complete or precise. It is accordingly the duty of the court to construe such documents fairly and broadly without being too astute or subtle in finding defects...".

The above cases have been considering whether or not an enforceable agreement has come into existence. What is the position where an agreement to negotiate is one of the conditions of what is otherwise a binding contract? For example a condition in a construction contract that the contractor will enter into collateral warranties, in terms to be agreed, with third parties. Does a failure or refusal of a party to enter into negotiations give rise to a claim for damages for breach of contract? Certain statements made by Lord Wright in the *Hillas* case would appear to suggest a cause of action. Lord Wright stated:

> "...if however what is meant is that the parties agree to negotiate in the hope of effecting a valid contract, the position is different. There is then no bargain except to negotiate and negotiations may be fruitless and end without any contract ensuing; yet even then, in strict theory, there is a contract (if there is good consideration) to negotiate, though in the event of repudiation by one party the damages may be nominal..."

In *Mollozzi* v. *Carapelli*[24] there was a charter party for the shipment of maize and oats from the River Plate to Italy and the first port of discharge

---

to be mutually agreed between the parties. In the event the port was nominated unilaterally by the sellers. The Judge at first instance (who had not had the benefit of considering the Court of Appeal's decision in *Courtney* which rejected Lord Wright's statement in *Hillas* as being purely obiter) found that the term in the contract that the parties were to agree on the order as between the first and second ports of discharge meant or at any rate included an obligation that they must at least bona fide negotiate with a view to trying to reach agreement. The Judge also found that the sellers had committed a breach of contract in failing to go through the full process of consultation and negotiation in order to achieve agreement with the buyers and the buyers were at least entitled to nominal damages. The Court of Appeal reversed the Judge at first instance and held that there was no breach by the sellers of any obligation in respect of negotiations because there was no legally binding obligation to negotiate.

The scope of *Hillas* has been severely restricted by the recent decision of the House of Lords in *Walford* v. *Miles*[25]. In that case, an Agreement in two separate parts was considered: there was an Agreement between the owner of a factory and a prospective purchaser but the owner would not sell the factory to anyone else (called a "lock-out" Agreement) and there was an Agreement that the owner and the prospective purchaser should negotiate in good faith (called a "lock-in" Agreement). Both Agreements were held by the House of Lords to be unenforceable. In the case of the lock-out Agreement, it was simply because no time limit had been specified: interestingly the Court was unwilling to imply a term that the time allowed should be reasonable. The Court held that the lock-in Agreement was unenforceable in any event. Lord Ackner said:

> "... the concept of a duty to carry on negotiations in good faith is inherently repugnant to the adversarial position of the parties when involved in negotiations. Each party to the negotiations is entitled to pursue his (or her) own interest, so long as he avoids making misrepresentations. To advance that interest he must be entitled, if he thinks it appropriate, to threaten to withdraw from further negotiations, or to withdraw in fact in the hope that the opposing party may seek to re-open the negotiations by offering improved terms."

Lord Ackner specifically disapproved an American case (*Channel Homes Centers Division of Grace Retail Corp* v. *Grossman*[26]) which suggested that

25 [1992] 1 All ER 453
26 (1986) 795 F2D 291

an **Agreement** to negotiate could be regarded in the same light as an Agreement that a party would use its "best endeavours" to perform a particular task.

The Rosehaugh Stanhope decisions   5

Anthony Lavers

Synopsis

This paper reviews the decisions in *Rosehaugh Stanhope* v. *Redpath Dorman Long* and *Beaufort House* v. *Zimmcor* and considers the findings of the Court of Appeal on the provisions of the trade contracts used in a construction management system and on set-off. Specifically, the entitlement of an employer to obtain summary judgment on the basis of the construction manager's assessment of loss suffered due to a trade contractor's delay is considered in the light of wording in construction management contracts used particularly in the latter part of the 1980's. The perception that these decisions may affect the continued viability of construction management contracting or even construction contracts more widely, is addressed. It is argued that it is uncertain as to whether the Court of Appeal's decisions inevitably impinge upon other construction contracts and that the solution to the current situation may lie in a review of the drafting of the provisions of the trade contract rather than any dramatic rejection of existing systems.

Introduction

It is not often that two decisions, even at appellate level, could justify the preparation of a conference paper. It is the purpose of this paper to contend that the implications of the cases of *Rosehaugh Stanhope (Broadgate Phase 6) plc and Rosehaugh Stanhope (Broadgate Phase 7) plc* v. *Redpath Dorman Long Ltd*[1] and *Beaufort House Development Ltd* v. *Zimmcor (International) Inc., Zimmcor Co. and Cigna Insurance Co. of Europe SA-NV*[2] are worthy of serious attention both in the context of construction management contract systems and potentially in construction contracting more widely.

---

1 (1990) 50 BLR 69
2 (1990) 50 BLR 91

Background

The *Rosehaugh Stanhope* decisions (as they will be known collectively, except when a distinction is being made between *Rosehaugh Stanhope* v. *Redpath Dorman Long* and *Beaufort House* v. *Zimmcor*) have much in common factually as well as in the contractual framework operated and in the points of law at issue. They concerned very large projects in the City of London. The Broadgate site near Liverpool Street station is almost universally known; the Beaufort House site is at Gravel Lane and Middlesex Street E1. The contract prices for the work in question were similar. Phases 6 and 7 of the Broadgate development were worth some £10,860,000, while the contract sum at Beaufort House was just short of £12,000,000, although it should be noted that the sums claimed against Zimmcor and Cigna by Beaufort House were considerably larger, at nearly £19,000,000, than the £8,300,000 claimed by Rosehaugh Stanhope against Redpath Dorman Long. Both projects were run, crucially, under the construction management system, meaning without a main contractor, the numerous "trade contractors" entering into direct contracts with the employer and working under the direction of the employer's construction managers, employed as agreed "to administer and manage the execution by others of the Project". The construction managers at Beaufort House were Bovis Construction and at Broadgate a Bovis/Schal Joint Venture. The parts of the projects in question were running over the period 1987-89 and both over-ran their completion dates, with the date of actual completion being disputed between the parties. It is salutary to note that, although it was not of consequence in the litigation, neither contract in Broadgate Phases 6 and 7 had been executed at the time of the scheduled contractual completion.

The consequence of the delayed completion was that the respective clients, Rosehaugh Stanhope and Beaufort House, claimed the sums referred to above against the respective contractors Redpath Dorman Long (suppliers and erectors of structural steel) and Zimmcor (manufacturers and installers of external cladding). They sought summary judgment against the contractors under Order 14 of the Rules of the Supreme Court.

The substance of the employers' case was that the contractors had not completed on time and that this entitled them to such loss and damage as was estimated by the construction managers as having been caused by the late completion. The sum claimed included, in the Beaufort House case, financing of capital, loss of rental, provisional claims for consequential delay from other trade contractors, provisional penalties payable to tenants for late completion, increased costs on fitting out and additional professional fees. The employers claimed an entitlement to summary judgment on the basis that the contractors were contractually bound by the construction manager's assessment of the loss and damage suffered.

The first instance decisions

Judge Peter Bowsher QC, hearing Official Referee's business, gave judgment in the *Rosehaugh Stanhope* case on 17th November 1989. He quoted himself with approval importantly in the subsequent first instance decision of the *Beaufort House* case on 12th March 1990.

Judge Bowsher had to deal with the principal issue as to whether the effect of the trade contract was to render binding upon the contractors the construction manager's estimate of the employers' loss. The Beaufort House contract provided in Clause 19 that breach by the Trade Contractor of his obligations to complete stages in the programme on time would entitle the Client to be paid or allowed "forthwith" such sum as the Construction Managers estimated. The contractors took the point that they had not been shown to be in breach, that loss had not been caused and that the Construction Manager had not made a *bona fide* estimate of the damage. Judge Bowsher's interpretation of the contractual provisions was that

> "the whole scheme of Clause 19, read as a whole, is that it gives rise to an obligation to pay a sum estimated by the Construction Manager as an interim payment payable forthwith on the facts as they appear at the time of the estimate ... Reading the contract as a whole, it seems to me that the scheme of the contract is that where the Defendants in the estimation of the Construction Manager failed to complete on time, the Defendants are obliged to pay such sum as the Construction Manager shall estimate. It may be that in the other action brought by the Defendants, a declaration will be granted to the effect that the Trade Contractor is entitled to an extension of time such that he will not be found to be in breach."

This is, of course, the classic view which would be contended for by the proponents of the construction management system of contracting. Judge Bowsher concluded this passage of explanation with the less than illuminating remark that "until an extension of time is granted, he (the Contractor) is in breach". This clearly begs the question as to whether the Contractor was in breach or not. The decision, which was consistent with *Lubenham Fidelities* v. *South Pembrokeshire District Council*[3] was underpinned by the concept that if the Construction Manager had been in error, this could be subsequently corrected, based upon the words of Clause 19 that the estimate was stated to be "binding and conclusive upon the Trade Contractor until such final ascertainment and agreement". It will be recalled that in

3   (1986) 33 BLR 39

Lubenham Fidelities, the architect certifying under a 1963 Joint Contracts Tribunal (JCT) contract, had wrongfully deducted liquidated damages from sums payable to the contractor. This would be effective pending subsequent correction. The employers, South Pembrokeshire, were held not be obliged to pay the full amount owed by them to the contractors' assignees Lubenham due to the premature deductions made at interim certificate stage. Where a certificate is erroneous "the proper remedy available is, in our opinion, to request the architect to make the appropriate adjustment in another certificate or if he declines to do so, to take the dispute to arbitration". The consistency between Judge Bowsher's decisions at first instance and Lubenham Fidelities could however, be regarded as uncertain. Judge Bowsher himself had commented, in dealing with the Lubenham case, that

> "It is always a dangerous thing to rely on a decision based upon the terms of one contract for the purpose of construing the terms of another. It seems to give some assistance by way of an indication of the approach that the courts should adopt. I do not think that it is any more than helpful by way of analogy. There are obvious differences."

In view of this conclusion, Judge Bowsher's reference to "some similarities to the JCT main contract" seems little to the point. Moreover, the view that any assistance rather than none could be derived from other contracts as to the approach which should be adopted may have led the judge to the conclusion that he reached.

The Court of Appeal decisions

When Redpath Dorman Long appealed to the Court of Appeal the principal issue of the interpretation of the role of the Construction Manager was again in contention, meaning in effect the question as to whether the employers were entitled to loss and damage estimated by the Construction Manager as attributable to the Contractor's delay, notwithstanding that the final completion date was not ascertained, but was in dispute. A second issue, not raised in the *Rosehaugh Stanhope* case at first instance was that the contractors were entitled to claim set-off of sums claimed by them against the employer's claim for loss and damage.

Bingham LJ proceeded upon the basis apparently advocated but not clearly followed by Judge Bowsher at first instance. He warned that

> "it would be unsafe to assume that the parties necessarily or even probably intended this form of contract to have the same effect as those standard forms (meaning what he called the 'familiar

forms of construction contract') might have achieved".

The learned Lord Justice fixed upon the question which, it is submitted, had not been satisfactorily answered by Judge Bowsher, namely "are the defendants in breach of any of their obligations under Clause 19(1) if they do not complete within the period stated in the programme, as extended by the Construction Manager?" That this was the crux of the matter arose from the interpretation of the wording of Clause 19(3) of the contract, which enabled the Construction Manager to estimate the extent of the resulting loss if, and only if, "The Trade Contractor is in breach of any of his obligations under sub-clause (1) of this Condition". Whereas Judge Bowsher had held that Clause 19 should be read as a whole so that in ascertaining the extent of the resultant loss or damage the Construction Manager was called upon to decide whether or not there was a breach, Bingham LJ did not so construe Clauses 19(1) and 19(3).

> "The defendants can become subject to no obligation under Clause 19(3) unless they are in breach of an obligation under sub-clause (1). If a breach is admitted or proved or if the defendants can show no arguable grounds for denying a breach, sub-clause (3) may be operated ... But I do not think the two sub-clauses, read together, envisage that the defendants may be in breach for purposes of sub-clause (3) when there is a live and arguable issue whether the Construction Manager has made fair and reasonable extensions to the programmed completion date which, if made, would exonerate the defendants."

Bingham LJ declared that he had "with some hesitation reached a contrary view" to that of Judge Bowsher and that he could "see great force in the plaintiffs' submissions which the judge accepted". He had "not found this an easy question". In the *Beaufort House* case too he described himself as "preferring, although hesitantly, the construction contended for by the trade contractor in *Rosehaugh Stanhope* and the defendants in this".

The policy element

Bingham LJ's doubts have been referred to above. He reasoned why the scale was tipped in favour of the contractors' interpretation of Clause 19 as follows:

> "I incline to this construction the more readily since I cannot believe the parties intended one of them to be subject to a

potentially crippling obligation upon a contingency".

His fellow members of the Court of Appeal shared his view and dissented only in the more forceful language which they used to express it. Stocker LJ agreed with Bingham LJ's interpretation of Clause 19 stating that

> "this construction accords with commercial sense since other-wise the plaintiffs would be in a position to enforce potentially ruinous payments by the defendants in circumstances in which it later is established that they are under no liability to pay".

On an ascending scale of forthrightness, Nourse LJ gave his opinion that

> "on the construction issue there is little more to be said. Believ-ing, as I do, that the answer to it is plain, I need not enlist, although I wholeheartedly endorse, the auxiliary considerations to which Lord Justice Bingham has referred. I absolutely decline, on the wording of this contract, to impute to the parties an intention that the construction manager should have power to impose on the trade contractor a liability which is neither admitted nor proved to exist at the time, which may later be proved never to have existed at all, but which may in the meantime have brought him into bankruptcy, being a power which is not claimed even by the court on an application for interim damages where an arguable defence is shown."

Comment upon this policy basis of the Court of Appeal's reversal of Judge Bowsher's interpretation of Clause 19 of the *Rosehaugh Stanhope* contract will be deferred until the conclusions section of this paper.

Set-off

The contractors were allowed by the Court of Appeal in *Rosehaugh Stanhope* to raise the issue of set-off, even though it had not been argued at first instance. Lord Justice Bingham felt obliged to express his conclusions on the set-off argument in case his finding on the interpretation of Clause 19 was incorrect. His colleagues, who appear to have been more certain that it was not incorrect, merely assented to his findings on set-off without comment. As is mentioned below, the general question of set-off may become more significant in the light of the *Rosehaugh Stanhope* decisions.

The set-off position is relatively clear in construction law generally and the Court of Appeal, despite the argument advanced by John Dyson QC for the employers, found little difficulty in applying it in the specific case of *Rosehaugh Stanhope*.

Most standard forms of building contract contain a mechanism which enables the deduction of specific amounts from sums agreed to be payable. The so-called set-off clause may well contain a clause preventing rights of set-off arising except under the provisions of the contract itself. Thus in the JCT Standard Form of sub-contract, for example, it is provided that "the rights of the parties ... in respect of set-off are fully set out in (the sub-contract) and no other rights whatsoever shall be implied as terms of the sub-contract relating to set-off".

The JCT main form contemplates and specifically provides for deductions for delay under Clause 24:

> "If the Contractor fails to complete the Works by the Date for Completion ... or within any extended time fixed ... and the Architect certifies in writing that in his opinion the same ought reasonably so to have been completed, then the Contractor shall pay or allow to the Employer a sum calculated at the rate stated as Liquidated and Ascertained Damages for the period during which the Works shall remain or have remained incomplete, and the Employer may deduct such sum from any monies due or to become due to the Contractor under this Contract."

It was at one time argued that the only sums which could be deducted or set-off were "liquidated and ascertained sums which are established as admitted to be due". This was Lord Denning's view in *Dawnays Ltd.* v. *F.G. Minter*[4] and this case was regarded as creating the *Dawnays* principle, viz. that there is no such thing as a right to set-off unless expressly provided for in explicit terms: "Payment must not be withheld on account of cross-claims whether good or bad - except so far as the contract specifically provides." Lord Denning was, in the *Dawnays* case, construing the pre-1975 version of Clause 13 of the NFBTE/FASS (Green Form) sub-contract which provided that:

> "The Contractor shall ... be entitled to deduct from or set off against any money due ... any sum or sums which the Sub-Contractor is liable to pay to the Contractor under this Sub-Contract."

Lord Denning construed "is liable" strictly so as to exclude set-off of

4 (1971) 1 BLR 16

unliquidated or undocumented sums.

In the *Rosehaugh Stanhope* case, John Blackburn QC based his argument upon *Gilbert Ash (Northern) Ltd.* v. *Modern Engineering (Bristol) Ltd.*[5] where a majority of the House of Lords disapproved Lord Denning's restrictive view of set-off in the particular context of the JCT forms. Strictly speaking, it may be that these comments should be regarded as obiter, since the *Gilbert Ash* case concerned a special sub-contract with a set-off provision which was decisive in the result, as the claim was detailed and quantified. Nevertheless, Mr. Dyson cited the *Gilbert Ash* case successfully as authority for the proposition that "to deprive a party of his ordinary right of set-off, clear words must be used". This disposes of the so-called *Dawnays* principle and establishes a presumption that neither party intends to abandon any remedies for breach of contract arising by operation of law.

Subsequent case law, while refining and sometimes complicating the *Gilbert Ash* position, has never radically departed from it. *Mottram Consultants* v. *Bernard Sunley*[6], while prima facie differing from it, was consistent with the reasoning in Gilbert Ash. The right to set-off was held to have been successfully excluded by the deletion of one of the crucial parts of the set-off clause, which gave as one of the categories of permissible deductions:

> "Any amount which the employer ... shall be entitled to deduct from or set off against any money due from him to the contractor (including any retention money) in notice of any provisions of the contract of any breach thereof by the contractor."

The deletion of the clause was capable of providing the evidence of the parties' intention to limit the right to set-off which the contract provisions otherwise gave.

The consequence of the following of the *Gilbert Ash* decision was, as Mann LJ expressed it in *A. Cameron Ltd.* v. *John Mowlem and Co.*[7]

> "the application ... could adversely affect cash flows" so "the construction industry redrew its standard forms of contract so as to confine and regulate the exercise of the right of set-off."

Mann LJ was dealing in that case with clauses 23 and 24 of the sub-contract form DOM/1, but the point is of course generally relevant.

---

5   (1974) AC 689
6   (1975) 2 Lloyds Reports 197
7   (1990) CLD Vol. 8 Part 7

Probably the leading statement of the established attitude to set-off is by Lord Salmon in *Aries Tanker Corp.* v. *Total Transport*[8]:

> There can be no doubt that in a claim for the price of work done or goods sold and delivered, any loss caused by the plaintiff's breach of contract under which he sues can generally be set up as a defence. When such a defence is set up, unless its bona fide is assailable or there is some clear provision in the contract to exclude it, there should be no question of the courts giving summary judgment under RSC Order 14 for the amount claimed. The defendant would be entitled to unconditional leave to defend to the extent which his loss caused by the plaintiff's breach of contract diminished or extinguished the amount claimed by the plaintiff under the contract."

Some recent decisions had suggested that there was still potential confusion. This arose from applications for the making of interim payments under Order 29 of the Rules of the Supreme Court, commonly made in conjunction with the applications for summary judgment under Order 14. In the *Beaufort House* case the developers applied for both summary judgment and an interim payment but did not pursue the latter application.

The possible confusion centred upon an apparent conflict between a previous decision on the Broadgate project, namely *Smallman Construction* v. *Redpath Dorman Long*[9] and the subsequent cases of *Shanning International* v. *George Wimpey*[10] and *Ricci Burns* v. *Toole*[11]. The Smallman case occurred as a result of a sub-contract dispute on Phase 4 between Redpath Dorman Long as the steel trade contractors and Smallman Construction as steel erection sub-contractors. Judge Bowsher QC had at first instance ordered Redpath Dorman Long to make an interim payment to Smallman for the balance of their counter-claim against Smallman for late completion. The Court of Appeal reversed this finding on the ground that, although Redpath Dorman Long should not be allowed to set-off its counter-claim, due to non-compliance with Clause 15 of the FASS form (1979 revision) which entitles the contractor to set-off where he

> "has given to the sub-contractor notice in writing specifying his intention to set-off the amount quantified ... and the grounds on

8   (1977) 1 All ER 398
9   (1988) 47 BLR 15
10 (1989) 1 WLR 981
11 (1989) 1 WLR 993

which such set-off is claimed to be made. Such notice shall be given not less than seventeen days before the money from which the amount is to be set off becomes due and payable to the sub-contractor",

nevertheless Smallman should not be entitled to an interim payment since they had not established that they would be entitled to judgment in a substantial sum and it was quite possible that a trial would result in a balance judgment for Redpath Dorman Long. Although Parker LJ gave the principal judgment, Bingham LJ usefully distinguished between the Order 29 interim payment procedure and the Order 14 summary judgment procedure.

"Since the interim payment rules were introduced it has not been uncommon for plaintiffs to combine applications for summary judgment under Order 14 with applications for interim payments under Order 29. This is an understandable and, no doubt, convenient practice, but it should not mask the fact that the two procedures are radically different in intention and operation."

The principal difference which he highlighted was that Order 14 is intended to prevent a defendant with no arguable defence from keeping a plaintiff out of his money. A judgment under Order 14 is a final judgment. Order 29 is to cover situations where no final judgment is possible until full trial but where it is overwhelmingly likely that the plaintiff will win at least a certain sum. This was the point taken in *British and Commonwealth Holdings* v. *Quadrex*[12] where it was remarked that in the absence of a substantial defence, an Order 29 application would be inappropriate and summary judgment could be obtained under Order 14. In the result, in the Smallman case the set-off failed due to the non-compliance with the sub-contract machinery but the sub-contractor failed to satisfy the Court of the overwhelming likelihood of its success in obtaining damages on judgment.

In concluding this summary of the position on set-off, it appears that the basic principle holds good. Summary judgment would be available where there is clear provision in the contract to exclude the right of set-off (such as in the exceptional *Mottram* case) but otherwise it is not appropriate, unless the defence raised is frivolous and vexatious or patently in bad faith.

In the *Rosehaugh Stanhope* case, John Blackburn QC for the contractors contended that such clear provision in the contract as to rebut the presumption of entitlement to set off simply was not present. The contractors' case was that they had arguable claims, both under the contract and for breach of

12 (1989) QB 842

a *Mackay* v. *Dick*[13] implied term, based on the employers' responsibility for the loss suffered by the contractor. The Court of Appeal rejected the existence of a *Mackay* v. *Dick* implied term but held that a court of equity would restrain the employers from exercising their contractual rights without taking account of the claims of the defendants. It was at least arguable that they would do so, and that would be sufficient to prevent the making of an order under Order 14 for summary judgment.

The *Rosehaugh Stanhope* case turned, and was decided, then, upon the interpretation of the trade contract and the finding that an equitable right of set-off could prevent the award of summary judgment upon an Order 14 application. The *Beaufort House* case was also argued upon the construction of similar contractual provisions although with some differences which are worthy of note. In particular, John Uff QC suggested that even if the employers' interpretation could be supported, the construction manager's estimate of loss could be and was capable of challenge if shown to be legally or factually incorrect. The Court of Appeal did not find it necessary to pronounce upon this, since the contractors had already prevailed, save to doubt an analogy proposed between the construction manager's estimate of loss and damage and independent valuation and liquidated damages provisions.

The significance of the Rosehaugh Stanhope decisions

Two days after the Court of Appeal pronounced on the *Rosehaugh Stanhope* decisions, Liam O'Hanlon of Rosehaugh Stanhope's solicitors McKenna & Co. was quoted[14] as saying that it was proposed to appeal to the House of Lords

> "because we believe that the case has serious implications for those who use standard forms of contract. The implications are not just confined to those who use this form of contract. It calls into question the role of the contract administrator and what were hitherto thought to be the effects of his decision."

Ann Minogue, also of McKenna & Co., expressed the view that:

> "The first point that seems to have been missed by some commentators is the fact that the decision is of no more special significance under construction management arrangements than

13 (1881) AC 251
14 "Contractors win Appeal Court fight". *Construction News* 1990, 28th June, p2

under other forms of construction contract. It will have its widest effects in forms of sub-contract. To suggest that it demands a rethink of construction management, as opposed to any other system of contracting, is to miss the point."[15]

These are very definite assimilations of the *Rosehaugh Stanhope* and *Beaufort House* trade contracts with other, possibly all other, major types of construction contracts. It must also be agreed that the *Rosehaugh Stanhope* type contract has been in quite widespread recent and current use.

Although the cases were both subsequently settled, it is seen as desirable to consider the substance of these justifications in order to understand better the significance of the Court of Appeal's judgments.

It is one of the functions of this paper to question whether the assimilation proposed should be automatically made and therefore whether Ann Minogue's implication that any attempt to restrict the effects of the decisions is to miss the point is necessarily correct. In the shorthand notes of the discussion on judgment in the Court of Appeal, Mr. Timothy Elliott, representing Rosehaugh Stanhope, and therefore instructed by McKenna & Co., had expanded the argument that the principle involved other types of contract. He went so far as to state that the case has "ramifications wherever in a construction contract there is an independent third party entrusted with administering the contract". Mr. Elliott referred specifically to the JCT form and to an architect's decision as to delay for the purpose of deduction of liquidated damages, which he compared with the Construction Manager's function under Clause 19(3) of the *Rosehaugh Stanhope* trade contract.

Five observations are offered for consideration in relation to this argument:

   (a) It failed.   John Blackburn QC, appearing for Redpath Dorman Long, accepted that "this is not a one-off contract and that there are other examples of it". Nevertheless, he contended that "it cannot be said to be in extremely widespread use". Lord Justice Nourse, refusing leave, said that if it was to be given the House of Lords would have to grant it. Too much should not be read into this, but it seems fair to say that the learned Lords Justices did not regard the issue as self-evidently of the widest importance.
   (b) Both Judge Bowsher at first instance and the Court of Appeal warned against extrapolating from the provisions of a con-

---

15 "Trade Contractors Victory a double-edged sword". Ann Minogue, *Building* 1990, 20th July

tract form. It will be recalled that Judge Bowsher thought it "always a dangerous thing to rely on a decision based upon the terms of one contract for the purpose of construing another", while Bingham LJ cautioned that "it would be unsafe to assume that the parties necessarily or even probably intended to have the same effect as those standard forms (meaning the 'familiar forms of construction contract') might have achieved".

(c) Mr. Elliott chose the example of JCT contracts with architects deducting liquidated damages as operating "just as in a similar way ... a Construction Manager makes a decision as to an extension of time". Professor Uff, having already succeeded in his principal argument, encountered the scepticism of the Court with a comparable, albeit different, analogy between extension of time and liquidated damages as types of penalty. Bingham LJ declared himself "by no means persuaded that the suggested analogies with valuation and liquidated damages are of assistance in considering the effect of this clause".

(d) Mr. Elliott referred to the *Lubenham Fidelities* case in support of his contention, but did so by virtue of an argument which seems somewhat circular. He submitted that that case was at variance with *Rosehaugh Stanhope*. But that argument is only valid if the contracts are the same. If they are not, it could be quite tenable to say that JCT 1963, as in *Lubenham*, should lead to a difference conclusion from the construction management trade contract, and that difference would constitute no argument at all for a reversal of the Court of Appeal's decision.

(e) Bingham LJ's judgment unequivocally contains an application of the contra proferentum rule. He said, speaking of Clause 19(1) "In any event, I consider these provisions to be ambiguous and so adopt the construction less favourable to the plaintiffs whose document it is". That is a valid way of resolving uncertainty, but would certainly not be automatically extended to an acknowledged negotiated contract where it would be impossible to say that it was the employer's document.

It should be here stated that in questioning the wider implications and applications claimed for the *Rosehaugh Stanhope* decisions, it is not intended to provide an apologia for the conclusions of the Court of Appeal.

Ann Minogue's article gives a valuable perspective which acts as a corrective to some initial reactions within the construction industry, namely that there is nothing in the *Rosehaugh Stanhope* decisions which necessarily "demands a rethink of construction management" in the sense that it must be jettisoned in favour of something obviously superior. The better view is that "more onerous drafting will become commonplace". While it could well be argued that the provisions of Clause 19 were, notwithstanding the opinion of the Court of Appeal, clear enough to evince the intention of the parties, if there is ambiguity, it may be eliminated by drafting. The words of Nourse LJ in *Rosehaugh Stanhope*, although emphatic, appear to be carefully chosen: "I absolutely decline, on the words of this contract, to impute to the parties an intention that the construction manager should have power to impose on the trade contractor a liability which is neither admitted nor proved to exist at the time ..." (emphasis supplied). The crux of the drafting point lies in Clause 19(3) of the *Rosehaugh Stanhope* contract, the wording of which enabled the Construction Manager to estimate the extent of resulting loss, in the view of the Court of Appeal, if and only if, "The Trade Contractor is in breach of any of his obligations under sub-clause (21) of this Condition". While no attempt is made here to resolve a drafting problem which needs to be addressed comprehensively and professionally, the uncertainty which concerned the Court of Appeal undoubtedly consists in the phrase "is in breach". It is questioned whether the message of the Court of Appeal can have been that no formula of wording can be arrived at which would make it possible for the parties to form an enforceable agreement containing the concept of summary judgment. It must be possible to create such an agreement. This is so a fortiori because of the Court of Appeal's somewhat narrow policy view on the merits of the parties. Bingham and Nourse LJJ were especially concerned that the terms of the agreement would bear harshly upon the contractor. But it is not difficult to conceive of an employer who would go into liquidation as forecast for the contractor as a result of being unable to obtain summary judgment for money payable to him. It is submitted that the Court of Appeal said that the agreement before them did not satisfy them as having that effect. They did not say that it could not be achieved. This is related, of course, to the discussion above of the contra proferentum rule. If there is no ambiguity of drafting, the court gives effect to the prima facie intention of the parties. It may be worthy of note here too that Mr. Dyson, as counsel for Beaufort House, did not adopt Judge Bowsher's apparently more extreme finding at first instance, ostensibly in the developer's favour. Mr. Dyson never suggested that the contract empowered the construction manager to determine to his own satisfaction the nature and extent of the contractor's breach. That Judge Bowsher had been understood to hold that this was so made it relatively easy for the appellant contractors to attack the existing formula of wording and for the Court of Appeal to regard it as uncertain.[16] The more modest point contended for on behalf of Beaufort House was that if there is late completion, the construction manager may have granted an extension; if he does not, his decision is effective pending final ascertainment. This may be sustainable in any subsequent litigation, but it is doubted whether Judge Bowsher's decision would be restored upon the grounds which he had been thought to espouse, certainly by the Court of Appeal.

Conclusions

The *Rosehaugh Stanhope* decisions in the Court of Appeal, while serious for the developers concerned, should not be seen as a catastrophe for the construction industry. It is submitted that it is not the case that the decisions will necessarily be applied automatically to other contract systems. This would require not only reconsideration by the House of Lords at some later date, but wide statements of principle which were sedulously avoided by the Court of Appeal and would require the over-ruling at least of *Lubenham Fidelities* in the case of the JCT forms. Nor should it be concluded that the construction management system is fatally flawed. It should be possible for parties to agree on financing arrangements and apportionment of risk in a way that will be enforceable by the courts. The policy argument is by no means as straightforward as might be supposed from a reading of the Court of Appeal judgments which can be characterised (caricatured even) as large wealthy developers entrapping small vulnerable contractors into situations where they are kept out of money owed to them on one hand and obliged to advance money which they may not owe for reasons other than their fault. The potential bankruptcy of contractors if the employers' interpretation prevails could be counterbalanced by potential bankruptcy of developers if the contractors succeed.

The answer to the situation created by the Court of Appeal decisions may well be found in drafting which more perfectly expresses the common intention of the parties and not admitting of the uncertainty which can lead to the invocation of the *contra proferentum* rule.

A more short-term remedy is that identified in Ann Minogue's article. Employers (and contractors in sub-contract situations) may feel more insecure as a result of the decisions about the length of time taken to recover their money, since summary judgment is not readily available. It is fair to

---

16 Judge Bowsher has indicated to the author that this was not his view, and thus his judgment, which does not contain an express statement to this effect, had therefore been misconstrued to that extent. The author is grateful to Judge Bowsher for his comments.

say that it is not necessarily more readily available to contractors seeking payment under certificates. See for example *John Mowlem* v. *Carlton Gate Development Co. Ltd.*[17] where Judge Bowsher held that the Order 14 procedure should not be made available to a contractor, where the appropriateness of set-off was still to be considered as a point of law. Nevertheless, where employers cannot obtain summary judgment, they may well be more anxious to impose set-offs against interim payments. This cannot however, be seen as a comprehensive answer since it will create difficulties and friction as between the parties. The wider use of set-off will only act as an incentive to a more lasting and clearly-defined solution, based upon an accurate reproduction and implementation of the common intention of the parties.

Summary of conclusions

The developers in the *Rosehaugh Stanhope* and *Beaufort House* cases had anticipated being able to recover loss suffered by them as a result of late completion against the trade contractors, based on their construction manager's assessment of cause and extent. The Court of Appeal's view was that the mechanism created did not achieve that result, so that they could not obtain summary judgment. It cannot be that it is impossible to achieve such a result. While the amount of change required may not be great in quantity, a comprehensive re-assessment of the drafting of construction management contracts embodying this mechanism is desirable. Where the common intention of the parties is absolutely clear, or in those situations where the contract cannot be said to be the employer's document, there is no room for the invocation of the contra proferentum rule. The applicability of these decisions to all (or even some) other construction management or other types of contracts is doubted, particularly in view of the care with which the members of the Court of Appeal qualified their statements to discourage analogy. The Rosehaugh *Stanhope* and *Beaufort House* decisions are very important for the significant number of major projects where construction management contracts utilising similar wording have been employed, and may well lead to an increase in reliance upon set-off and thus to disputes about set-off. They should not however be regarded as fatal to the construction management contract system nor as automatically applicable to any other contractual model.

Do Construction Contracts benefit the parties?   6

Richard Winward

Synopsis

The author examines the jurisprudence which lies behind commercial contracts and asks whether construction contracts are beneficial to the industry.

Introduction

I have been studying and practising law for over 25 years during which time I have always believed that an efficient legal system is one of the essential Estates of a civilised society and that competent practitioners are an essential ingredient of an efficient legal system. The title to this paper is pregnant with the suggestion that there is incompatibility between the interests of the construction industry and the interests of the legal profession. I do not agree.

Jurisprudential Justification for Law

An historical analysis of the jurisprudential or philosophical justification for law demonstrates a dependency between the chosen theory of law and the prevailing ethical political social and economic characteristics of the society in which the law is operating. One of the earliest theories of law is Natural Law which subscribes to the view that all laws are subject to overriding immutable truths which are derived from God or a divinity (the idealist school) or from the physical laws of nature (the empirical school).

> "True law is right reason in agreement with nature; it is of universal application, unchanging and everlasting; it summons to duty by its commands, and averts from wrong doing by its prohibitions and it does not lay its commands or prohibitions upon good men in vain, though neither have any effect on the wicked. It is a sin to try and alter this law, nor is it allowable to attempt to repeal any part of it, and it is impossible to abolish it entirely. We cannot be free from its obligations by Senate or

people, and we need not look outside ourselves for an expounder or interpreter of it. There will not be different laws at Rome and at Athens, or different laws now and in the future, but one eternal and unchangeable law will be valid for all nations and all times, and there will be one master and ruler, that is, God, over us all, for he is the author of this law, its promulgator and its enforcing judge. Whoever is disobedient is fleeing from himself and denying his human nature, and by reason of this very fact he will suffer the worse penalties, even if he escapes what is commonly considered punishment."[1]

"The law of nature is the law which nature has taught all animals. This law is not peculiar to the human race, but belongs to all living creatures, birds, beasts and fishes.... The civil law is distinguished from universal law as follows. Every people which is governed by laws and customs uses partly a law peculiar to itself, partly a law common to all mankind. For the law which each people makes for itself is peculiar to itself, and is called the civil law, as being a law peculiar to the community in question. But the law which natural reason has prescribed for all mankind is held in equal observance against all peoples and is called universal law, as being the law which all peoples use. Thus the Roman People uses a law partly peculiar to itself, partly common to all mankind.

The civil law takes its name from the country to which it belongs.... but universal law is common to the whole human race. For under the pressure of use and necessity the peoples of mankind have created for themselves certain rules. Thus, wars arose and captivity and slavery, which are contrary to natural law, for by natural law from the beginning all men were born free. From this universal law almost all contracts are derived, such as sale, hire, partnership, deposit, loan and countless others.

The laws of nature which are observed amongst all people alike, being established by a define providence, remain wed and immutable, but the laws each State makes for itself are frequently changed either by tacit consent of the people, or by a later statute."[2]

The most undiluted statement of the theory of natural law is in Plato's Republic. The replacement of the Greek city state by the Greek super state

1   Cicero: *De Re Publica*
2   Justinian: *Institutes*

with its associated complexities, witnessed natural law becoming influenced by the empirical thought of the stoic philosophers of the Second Century BC. Stoicism became a major influence in Roman philosophy permitting the Roman State to develop a complex system of civil law.

The theory of natural law was sustained by the Medieval views of universal divine law and the subordination of human rights to proprietary rights. However, following the Renaissance, natural law went along the pathway of secular development ending up at the rationalist philosophy of the late 18th Century thereafter being dealt a fatal blow by Hume's empiricism and Rousseau's concept of the "general will". Natural law was perceived as capable of justifying the subordination of proprietary interest to the will of the people. The 19th Century witnessed the evolution of two main jurisprudential justifications for law, the first being based upon Hegel's development "in extremis" of Rousseau's concept to the point of absolutism where the State is the only expression of individual wills and law determines events rather than being governed by events. Secondly the utilitarian philosophy of the Benthamite School emphasising the dichotomy between the laws of man and natural law, the latter being a concern of religion and ethics not law.

> "From whatever side we approach our principle, we reach the same conclusion, that the social compact sets up amongst the citizens and equality of such a kind, that they all bind themselves to observe the same conditions and should therefore all enjoy the same rights."[3]
>
> "When a number of persons (whom we may style subjects) are supposed to be in the habit of paying obedience to a person, or an assemblage of persons, of a known and certain description (whom we may call governor or governors) such persons altogether (subjects and governors) are said to be in a state of political society... A parol expression of will is that which is conveyed by the signs called words... A parol expression of the will of a superior is a command. When a tacit expression of the will of a superior is supposed to have been uttered, it may be styled a fictitious command. Were we at liberty to coin words after the manner of the Roman lawyers we might say a quasi command. Statute law is composed of commands. The common law of quasi commands."[4]
>
> "Law performs certain functions essential to the maintenance of

3   Rousseau: *The Social Contract*
4   Bentham: *A Fragment on Government*

all but the most simple societies. The first is to define relationships among the members of a society, to assert what activities
are permitted and what are ruled out, so as to maintain at least a
minimal integration between the activities of individuals and
groups within the society.
The second is derived from the necessity of taming naked force
and directing force to the maintenance of order. It is the
allocation of authority and the determination of who may
exercise physical cohesion as a socially reorganised privilege
right, along with the selection of the most effective forms of
physical sanction to achieve the social ends that the law serves.
The third is the disposition of trouble cases as they arise.
The fourth is to redefine relations between individuals and
groups as the conditions of life change. It is to maintain adapta-
bility.
Purposive definition of personal relations is a primary law job.
Other aspects of culture likewise worked to this end, and, indeed,
the law derives its work in principles from postulates previously
developed in the non legal spheres of action. However, the law's
important contribution to the basic organisation of society as a
whole is that the law specifically and explicitly defines relations.
It sets the expectancies of man to man and group to groups that
each knows the focus and the limitations of its demand rights on
others, its duties to others, its privileged rights and powers as
against others, and its immunities and liabilities to the contemplated or attempted acts of others... It is the ordering of the
fundamentals of living together.
(Of the third function of law) some troubled cases pose absolutely new problems for solution. In these cases the first and
second functions may predominate. Yet this is not the situation
in the instance of most legal clashes in which the problem is not
the formulation of law to cover a new situation but rather the
application of pre-existing law. These cases are disposed of in
accordance with legal norms already set before the issue in
question arises. The job is to clean the case up, to suppress or
penalise the illegal behaviour and to bring the relations of the
disputants back into balance, so that life may resume its normal
course. This type of law work has frequently been compared to
work of the medical practitioner. It is family doctor stuff,
essentially to keeping a social body on its feet. In more homely
terms, Llewellyn has called it, "garage repair work on the general
order of the group when that general order misses fire, or grinds

gears, or even threatens a total breakdown." It is not ordinarily concerned with grand design, as is the first law job. Nor is it concerned with redesign as is the fourth. It works to clean up all the little social messes (and the occasional big ones) that recurrently arise between the members of the Society from day to day".[5]

The construction industry in this country and indeed in most of the international market, operates within the capitalist system; that system requires profit to be made upon the employment of capital which will necessarily involve risk. If risk is an essential ingredient of the system which generates your profits it is inevitable that there must be a structure for resolving disputes in order to "bring the relations of the disputants back into balance so that life may resume its normal course". Our present society adopts the process of civil law, whether by litigation or arbitration, to resolve disputes. In my considered opinion the efficacy of civil process depends upon the competency of its legal practitioners. This of course has not always been the case.

Prior to the denunciation by Pope Innocent III in 1215, the accepted method of adjudication was trial by the ordeal of hot irons or trial by the ordeal of water; without doubt a system of adjudication which was relatively speedy, inexpensive, certain and not needing the involvement of lawyers! Similarly prior to 1179 there was no right to elect trial by jury as distinct from trial by battle in respect of certain proprietary disputes. Admittedly this was a method of adjudication imposed upon the Anglo-Saxons by the Normans, however, it has to be said that it had the same advantages as trial by ordeal, indeed, the same disadvantages.

Construction Disputes

In my experience disputes fall into one of two broad categories namely (i) disputes as to quality (including structural failure) and (ii) disputes as to price. What are the origins of these types of dispute? Disputes as to quality were considered in some detail by the Building Economic Development Committee in 1987 when they produced a report titled "Achieving Quality on Building Sites".

The key findings of the Report were as follows. (1) Serious quality problems are too common and too often remain unresolved. (2) Realistic and well understood time constraints do not adversely affect the achievement of good quality. (3) Motivation and commitment to producing good

5 Hoebel: *The Functions of Law*

work are essential to the achievement of good quality. (4) Site management
has to spend too much time chasing late drawings and other project
information, which inevitably reduces the time available for quality management. (5) Traditional specifications are often unrelated to the quality
requirements of a particular contract and are therefore rarely referred to. (6)
Specifications based on or similar to the National Building Specification
seemed to produce better results. (7) Contractual arrangements, as such,
have little effect on the quality achieved, but management structures have
considerable influence. (8) Site management is more likely to be successful
in achieving good quality when lines of authority are clearly understood and
site staff have the opportunlty to contribute to and take responsibility for
quality achievement. (9) Where deficiencies in quality are identified,
responsibility and authority to effect remedial action are often unclear. (10)
When project quality is going wrong, clients cannot rely on being informed
of this by any member of the building team. (11) Site Managers often have
to spend a lot of time dealing with technical queries to the detriment of other
aspects of management. (12) Projects exhibiting good quality are characterised by an appropriate level of site management resources, with Managers
who are properly trained and who exercise more authority than usual. (13)
Inadequacies in the quality, completeness and accessibility of the project
information are a major handicap in the achievement of quality. (14)
Meetings between consultants and the contractor and other parties on site are
all too often merely concerned with progress and rarely consider quality.
(15) The Clerk of Works finds it difficult to act as an effective quality
controller because of lack of contractual authority.

The important conclusion of the EDC was that the main causes of quality
failures (and thus quality disputes) were failures in management structures
and breakdowns in human relationships within the industry itself rather than
a consequence of external stimuli. Similarly the Banwell Committee
reporting in 1964 considered that a primary source of price disputes was the
failure of the industry to use Standard Form Contracts. The Banwell Report
stressed

> "the desirability of the widespread use of Standard Forms of Sub-
> Contract in order to foster mutual understanding of rights and
> responsibilities at all points in building operations... unhappily
> however they are not used widely enough, and there is a
> regrettable tendency for some contracting firms to seek to
> impose their own form of sub-contract. We do not like this
> practice and feel strongly that it is does not contribute to
> efficiency and mutual co-operation."

In 1967 the EDC reported:

> "many main contractors have drawn up their own Forms of Sub-Contract and the majority of these have the interest of the main contractors primarily in mind. The Banwell Committee deplored the existence of these forms and so do we."

These are strong words indeed. Whilst I do not necessarily agree that a failure to use a Standard Form Contract is tantamount to a contractual abuse, nevertheless I concur with Banwell that the plethora of individual contracts or individual amendments of Standard Form Contracts leads to greater uncertainty and consequently greater likelihood of dispute and litigation or arbitration. Often it is the case that lawyers are left with clearing up the mess of ill considered contract documents or amendments produced by the industry; sometimes the mess can be caused by the legal profession itself. One of the areas of recent concern has been in the growth of collateral warranties. I refer to the preface in Winward Fearon on Collateral Warranties where the authors state:

> "One of the side effects of the enormous growth in the use of collateral warranties has been the attempts by each of the parties involved to try to have their own interest dominate in the negotiation process. Like all contracts, collateral warranties seek to allocate risk and developers, banks, pension funds, contractors, architects, engineers, quantity surveyors, tenants and purchasers each try to take as little risk as possible and seek to protect their own interest. Inevitably this has produced a plethora of non-standard forms of warranty some as short as one page and some occasionally reaching 40 pages or more. Some have been drafted by commercial conveyancing lawyers who appear to have little understanding of the complex interaction of collateral warranties with the various issues such as the contract at which they are collateral... limitation of action, insurance and the whole basis of professional liability. Many collateral warranties have of course been drafted by lawyers who do understand the issues and of those, some are a sensible commercial compromise between competing vested interest and some are not".[6]

The primary method of determining the legal relationships between the various parties to a construction project is by way of a contract. This is

6 Winward Fearon: *Collateral Warranties* 1990

particularly so with the demise of tortious remedies as a consequence of recent decisions of the House of Lords in *D & F Estates Ltd* v. *The Church Commissioners*[7] and *Murphy* v. *Brentwood District Council*[8]. A contract is[9] "a promise or set of promises which the law will enforce". Save where the law has intervened, in particular statute law for example the Unfair Contract Terms Act 1977 and the Supply of Goods and Services Act 1982, a contract is a matter of private bargain, provided of course the bargain is not illegal nor contrary to public policy. The law of contract was developed during the 19th Century, reflecting the political, social and economic philosophy of *laissez-faire* which emphasised the importance of the legal doctrines of freedom of contract and sanctity of contract.

As a commercial lawyer, as distinct from a consumer lawyer, my goal in drafting contracts is to create certainty not necessarily fairness, although as a personal preference I consider that a fair allocation of risk is more likely to lead to the successful conclusion of a project. Nevertheless clarity subordinates fairness. In the case of *Trollope & Colls Ltd* v. *North West Metropolitan Regional Hospital Board*[10] the contract provided for three phases of work, Phase 1 to be completed by the 30th April 1969 and Phase 3 to commence six months after the date of practical completion of Phase 1 and to be completed on the 30th April 1972 i.e an overall construction period of 30 months for Phase 3. The completion of Phase 1 was delayed by a period of 59 weeks, 47 of which were not the fault of the contractor. Practical completion of Phase 1 was not achieved until the 22nd June 1972 leaving a construction period of only 16 months, rather than the 30 months for the completion of Phase 3. The court took the view that the intention of the parties was perfectly clear from the wording of their contract and accordingly refused to relax the contractor's obligations by implication of a term that the time for completion of Phase 3 should be extended by the same period as the extension of time granted in respect of Phase 1. In other words provided the parties agree nonsense with clarity then nonsense is what they get.

The English legal system is based upon the rule of '*stare decisis*' that is to say the rule of precedent whereby decisions of superior courts bind inferior courts and decisions of coordinate courts are persuasive. It follows that the use of Standard Form Contracts which have been subjected to judicial interpretation leads to greater certainty and permits the parties to the contract to adjust the risk by reference to the pricing mechanism. This is not to say however that all progression in contractual terms should be stultified

7   [1989] AC 177
8   [1990] 2 All ER 908
9   Pollock *Principles of Contract* (13th Edition)
10 [1973] 1 WLR 601

by the law of precedent although I have always been at a loss to understand why contracts should be changed merely for the sake of change rather than for the sake of progress. For example I am sure it would not be disputed that one of the successes of the 'partnership approach' to construction has been the development of superstores by J Sainsbury; whilst they have developed their own form of contract nevertheless in respect of their most recent development, a superstore at Haywards Heath some 6,300 sq. metres of development at a value of £11.7M, they have been happy to proceed on the basis of the JCT Form of Contract 1963 Edition.

The New Engineering Contract

Accompanying the publication of the ICE Sixth Edition has been the launch of the first draft of the New Engineering Contract with the laudable aim of creating flexibility, clarity, simplicity and a stimulus to good management. Dr Martin Barnes[11], a promoter of the new contract, stresses that it is designed to be used with various types of construction management techniques for example design and build, construction management, target or costs reimburseable projects. He also stresses that it has been intentionally written in "straightforward English with few long words and no long sentences".[12] Barnes accepts that the "language used may be strange to (lawyers) but it is intended to be close to the language of builders and other people in the construction industry and professions internationally".

Does the contract succeed? Admittedly the contract is as yet only in draft form. However it seems to me that some fundamental pitfalls have been built into this contract. The desire to move away from "lawyers' jargon" into simple English has the potentiality of moving the contract away from the certainty of precedent into the uncertainty of interpretation. As David Cornes has stated in his criticism of the contract "a desire to have plain English is excellent but this contract goes down that route at the expense of good grammar/syntax and legal certainty. For example, in the drafting the present tense is used almost exclusively - even where the sense of what is being said is in the future or in the past"[13]. Of the arbitration and adjudication clauses Cornes comments "look at arbitration and adjudication (Conditions 90 and 91). It is to be doubted whether an arbitration clause is in law an agreement in writing to refer present or future disputes to arbitrations required by the Arbitration Act 1950. This is because Condition 91 says 'Any party may ... decide to refer the dispute to an Arbitrator'. The word

11 Partner with Coopers & Lybrand Deloitte
12 *New Builder* 31 Jan 1991
13 ibid.

'may' is permissive and does not demonstrate, beyond doubt, an agreement between two parties to refer the disputes to arbitration." By way of riposte Barnes has stated "the intention is to use the word 'may' in the arbitration clause. Is David Cornes 'seriously contemplating' the construction industry accepting that disputes should automatically go to arbitration? Only lawyers would benefit from such a move". It seems to me that this exchange encapsulates the difference between a legal mind and a layman's mind and indeed convinces me that the difference may be irreducible.

The problem as I see it is that the raw material of the law is language. However the finished product is conceptual thinking which happens to be expressed in language:

"Some words, though not equivocal in the sense of having two or more distinct definitions, are yet obviously vague in their meaning, as for example 'about', 'near', 'more or less'. Such words, which ought generally to find no place in legal documents, give considerable trouble when they do occur. What I am concerned to demonstrate in this section is that not merely some but all words are capable of occasioning difficulty in their application...

The difficulty of using such words as these does not press upon the ordinary man because it usually does not matter to him whether, for instance, he calls a number of stones a 'heap' or not. All that matters is that he should make his meaning clear enough for the purpose on hand. Suppose that a housewife is following a cookery book which tells her to add a pinch of mustard to a particular dish. She cannot tell however many grains make a pinch, but she can guess what is meant by a pinch and if she puts too much, or too little, her palate will in due course discover her error.

With law it is different, for in law we make sharp consequences hang upon these words of gradation. The question whether a man is left in freedom or detained in a mental institution depends on whether he is judicially classified as sane or insane, as also does the question whether his dispositions of property are upheld or not. Whether a man is punished or acquitted may turn simply and solely upon whether an attempt to commit a crime was sufficiently 'proximate', or upon whether a statement that he falsely swore was 'material' to a judicial proceeding; and in a murder case it may be literally a question of life or death whether the accused intended to hurt by means of an act 'intrinsically likely to kill'. Well may a convict echo the words of the poet -

'Oh a little more, and how much it is! and the little less, and what worlds away'".[14]

In my view one has to be aware of the dogma of the need for plain English at risk of clarity just as much as one needs to be aware of the dogma of unnecessary legal jargon.

A Chapter of the Broadgate Story

A recent case has provided a useful illustration of the pitfalls of novel drafting. In *Rosehaugh Stanhope (Broadgate Phase 6) Plc and Rosehaugh Stanhope (Broadgate Phase 7) Plc* v. *Redpath Dorman Long Ltd*[15] the Defendants were "trade contractors" for structural steelwork in accordance with bespoke contracts produced by the Developer. The Phase 6 contract sum was £5,152,418 and the Phase 7 contract sum was £5,741,730. Both contracts had a Clause 19 which provided as follows:-

"(1) The works are to be commenced on Site within the period stated in the Programme from the date of the Construction Manager's instruction to proceed on the Site. The Trade Contractor shall complete the works and each part thereof within the periods for completion in relation thereto stated in the Programme, subject only to any instruction issued by the Construction Manager under Clause 19(6)(a) of these Conditions and to such fair and reasonable extensions of time as the Construction Manager may grant in accordance with the provisions of Clause 20 of the Conditions. The Works are to be carried out diligently and in such order, manner and time as the Construction Manager may reasonably direct, so as to ensure completion of the Works and the Project as aforesaid.

(3) If the Trade Contractor is in breach of any of his obligations under sub-clause (1) of this Condition, he shall, without preju- dice to and pending the final ascertainment or agreement be- tween the parties as to the amount of the loss or damage suffered or which may be suffered by the Client in consequence thereof, forthwith pay or allow to the Client such sum as the Construction Manager shall bona fide estimate as the amount of such loss or damage, such estimate to be binding and conclusive upon the

14 Glanville Williams: *Language and the Law*
15 [1990] 50 BLR 69

Trade Contractor until such final ascertainment or agreement. If a Payment Certificate is issued after the date of the Construction Manager's estimate any such amount may be deducted from the amount which would otherwise be stated as due in such a Certificate. Such loss or damage may include, inter alia, any additional professional fees, interest charges or loss of rental income suffered or incurred by the Client and any loss and/or expense suffered or incurred by others engaged by the Client including the Construction Manager for which the Client is or maybe liable under his Contracts with such others."

The contractual completion date for Phase 6 was the 24th October 1987 and for Phase 7 the 6th February 1988. The works were delayed beyond the contractual completion dates and the Construction Manager made an estimate under Clause 19(3) of each trade contract that the Defendant was liable to pay the Plaintiffs £2,228,515 in respect of Phase 6 and £3,140,494 in respect of Phase 7. The Defendants declined to pay and the Plaintiffs issued High Court writs. The Defendants filed notices of intention to defend and the Plaintiffs brought applications for summary judgment which succeeded. Upon appeal the Court of Appeal held that the Defendant could become subject to no obligation under Clause 19(3) unless it was in breach of an obligation under sub-clause (1). If a breach was admitted or proved, or if the Defendant could show no arguable grounds for denying a breach, sub-clause (3) might be operated. The two sub-clauses, read together, did not envisage that the Defendant might be in breach for the purpose of sub-clause (3) when there was a live and arguable issue whether the Construction Manager had made fair and reasonable extensions to the completion date which, if made, would exonerate the Defendant. Although the Construction Manager's bona fide estimates would be binding and conclusive to a final ascertainment, there was no corresponding provision with regard to breach and it could not be argued that a Construction Manager's estimate under the sub-clause was binding.

Per Bingham LJ:
"I cannot believe that parties intended one of them to be subject to a potentially crippling obligation upon a contingency. In any event, I consider these provisions to be ambiguous and so adopt the construction less favourable to the Plaintiffs whose document it is".

Per Nourse LJ:
"I absolutely decline, on the words of this contract, to impute to

the parties an intention that the Construction Manager should have power to impose on the Trade Contractor a liability which is neither admitted nor proved to exist at the time, which may later be proved never to have existed at all, but which may in the meantime have brought him into bankruptcy, being a power which is not claimed even by the court on an application for interim damages where an arguable defence is shown."

Alternative Dispute Resolution

I find it surprising that the New Engineering Contract makes no attempt to incorporate a procedure for conciliation. In my opinion a contract draftsman should be cognisant of the conclusions reached by the ECD in 1987 as to the causes of construction disputes and should provide a mandatory code for conciliation. By doing so the draftsman is not only recognising both the inevitability of disputes and their make-up but also a possible method of resolution.

In my experience disputes have various stages which I would categorise as follows:

(1) origin
(2) discussion and negotiation at site level
(3) discussion and negotiation at management level
(4) conciliation
(5) litigation or arbitration
(6) negotiation
(7) settlement or adjudication

Karl von Clausewitz considered that war was nothing but the continuation of politics by other means; I consider that conciliation, litigation or arbitration should be nothing but the continuation of negotiation by other means.

Alternative dispute resolution is concerned with the process of conciliation. In essence the procedure interposes a mediator, not an adjudicator, to assist the parties in reaching an amicable settlement. This may involve just a conciliator or the executive tribunal or mini-trial procedure or a non-binding arbitration. In the event that a settlement is not achieved neither of the parties' positions will have been prejudiced and indeed the scope of the dispute may well have been reduced. The parties are then free either to litigate or to arbitrate. I am informed by the Centre for Dispute Resolution that approximately $100,000,000 worth of claims are presently being dealt with by their Dispute Resolution Procedure. I would suggest that all construction contracts should provide for conciliation as a condition precedent to the parties bringing formal litigation or arbitration proceedings.

Quality Assurance for Lawyers

Society requires law and thus lawyers. I suspect the real question which flows from this and from the title to this paper is "but at what cost?". Two of the common misconceptions about solicitors' costs are that solicitors simply charge what they like, and what they charge is all profit. In fact, litigation solicitors charge by reference to units of time. They do not earn a profit and a return on overheads by reference to the capital value of the project nor indeed do they use their employers' (i.e clients) capital for the purposes of generating profit. Solicitors' charges are the equivalent of the construction industry's daywork rates where the industry readily accepts uplift on costs of between 150%-200%.

In my experience, in most legal practices the calculation of hourly rates is based upon the Expense of Time calculation prepared by the Law Society's Remuneration Committee. The basic approach of this calculation is that hourly rates are determined by costs levels together with a reasonable return on capital and are not a retrospective calculation from desired profit levels. Solicitors' practices, like any other business, are subject to market forces both as to cost and as to realisable profit. I suggest that the correct test is value rather than simply cost. For example, whilst the hourly rate of a construction specialist may be high, one would expect, if the lawyer is competent, that the total number of hours spent on any particular transaction would be lower than the non-specialist. A rate of £100 an hour may appear reasonable, but not if the multiple is 10 when it should be 5.

I have always been mystified as to why clients are reluctant to discuss costs. In my view a client's exposure to legal costs whether it be the totality of the solicitor and own client cost or the irrecoverable costs (i.e. the difference between solicitor and own client cost and the standard costs which are awarded to a successful litigant) is a matter which should be discussed between solicitor and client in the early stages of a dispute and thereafter kept under regular review. The vehicle used by my Practice is what we call the Costs Risk Analysis. An example of a Cost Risk Analysis is set out in the Appendix to this paper. The use of this analysis should remove or substantially reduce clients' fears as to unquantified cost and at the same time assist in the strategic planning of any proceedings.

Quality assurance also has a role to play in the relationship between solicitor and client. The Law Society has for some time been considering the principles laid down by BS5750. Some of these principles are now set out in Practice Rule 15, being a rule governing the conduct of solicitors, which came into force on the 1st May this year. Essentially this rule, which is known as the client care rule, places obligations on private practitioners to operate in-house complaints and other procedures and also to ensure that clients know certain basic information relating to the solicitors' retainer. On the client side one could always bear in mind the computer terminology of "RIRO" that is to say, "rubbish in rubbish out". As previously stated solicitors charge on a time basis - therefore wasted time arising from unnecessary telephone calls or attendances, inadequate instructions or documentation or half truths is a wasted cost for the client.

In conclusion, therefore, my response to the question posed by the title to this paper is that the construction industry must benefit from the use of clear and unambiguous construction contracts preferably standard form contracts. Furthermore it is in its interest to have an effective legal system operated by a competent, cost effective legal profession.

APPENDIX

The Managing Director
ABC Mechanical Services Plc

Dear Sirs

Cost Risk Analysis
XYZ Management Ltd - Citidal Shopping Centre

Further to our meeting yesterday, as requested, we are writing to set out the Cost Risk Analysis which we discussed at length.

As you are aware ABC are Defendants to High Court proceedings brought by XYZ alleging delays and defective works on the part of ABC in the carrying out of the mechanical sub-contract. ABC counterclaim against XYZ for sums due on the measured account retention and damages for prolongation and disruption. On the face of the pleadings the monied up claims of XYZ and ABC are as follows:-

1. XYZ

(i)	LADs suffered by	£224,000.00
(ii)	Third Party Claims by contractors brought against XYZ	£343,000.00
(iii)	XYZ's own loss and expense	£315,000.00
(iv)	Remedials to boiler installation	£5,000.00
(v)	Interest calculated up to 18th January 1991	£172,442.00
		£1,059,442.00

2. ABC's Counterclaims

(i)	Loss and expense (prolongation)	£352,579.00
(ii)	Loss and expense (disruption)	£278,881.00
(iii)	Interest on items (ii) and (iii)	

	calculated up to 15th June 1990	£188,914.00
(iv)	Measured Account	£448,928.00
(v)	Repayment of LADS	£216,000.00
(vi)	Interest on items (iv) and (v) calculated up to 15th June 1990	£83,105.00
(vii)	Retention (50% moiety)	£14,060.00
(viii)	Interest on item (vii) calculated up to 15th June 1990	£1,627.00
		£1,584,094.00

ABC's and XYZ's claims required to be adjusted as follows:-

1. ABC's Claim

(i)	Interest (calculated as simple interest at a rate of 15% per annum (from the 16th June 1990 to the 15th June 1991)	£237,614.00
(ii)	Interest (15% simple) calculated to end of trial	£239,723.00
(iii)	Retention (50% moiety)	£14,060.00

2. XYZ's Claim

(i)	Interest (15% simple) from 18th January 1991 to the 15th June 1991	£55,445.00
(ii)	Interest (15% simple to end of trial	£133,069.00

As previously stated the above-mentioned figures set out in the monied up figures of the claims on the face of the pleadings and projecting the interest to the end of trial. For the purposes of our cost risk analysis we then made further adjustments to those figures in order to reflect the respective merits of ABC's claims and XYZ's claims. By their amended Statement of Claim served on the 18th April 1991 XYZ appear to be alleging that ABC was not responsible for six weeks delay to practical completion of the main contract works. As practical completion of the sub-contract works was to be the same as that for the main contract works XYZ's pleading would appear to accept that they are responsible for 34/40ths of ABC's claim for prolongation and disruption. Further XYZ have not, to date, made any attempt to plead to ABC's claim on the measured account. Therefore for the purpose of this cost risk analysis we have assumed that all the measured accounts claim will be recovered. As regards XYZ's claim we have substantially discounted those claims on the basis of XYZ's pleadings which do not appear to support sustainable claims. Our main reasons for this discounting are as follows:-

(i)   The alleged deduction of LADs is based upon a defective certificate.

(ii)   All claims in respect of third party trade contractors need to be discounted at least by the fraction of 6/21. Further many of these claims are arbitrary apportionments imposed by XYZ.

(iii)   A substantial part of XYZ's own claim is an attempt to recover on costs after the date of practical completion.

(iv)   XYZ would appear to have settled with its Employer for a sum of £1M on the basis inter alia that the Employer is responsible for rectifying defects to the boiler installation.

Applying the above-mentioned discounts to the claims and counter claims we consider that ABC stands as positive Claimant in the sum of £1,657,000.00

Our projection for ABC's legal costs (estimate) to the end of trial, based on a trial duration of 22 weeks, is as follows:-

1.   Winward Fearon & Co profit costs:-

(i)	Preparation for trial	£250,000.00
(ii)	Attending at trial	£80,000.00

2. Counsel:-

(i)	Brief Fee: Leading Counsel	£80,000.00
(ii)	Brief Fee: Junior Counsel	£48,000.00
(iii)	Refresher: Leading Counsel	£250,000.00
(iv)	Refresher: Junior Counsel	£75,000.00

3. Experts:-

(i)	Quantity Surveyor/Building Surveyor	£24,000.00
(ii)	Mechanical Engineer	£20,000.00

4. Disbursements:-

(i)	Photocopying	£7,500.00
(ii)	Travel and accommodation costs: solicitors, experts and witnesses	£14,000.00
(iii)	Witness expenses (attending trial)	£1,000.00

£749,500.00

In the event that ABC is successful at trial ABC will be entitled to its legal costs and disbursements taxed on a standard basis. In effect this means recovery of all of Counsel's fees, expert fees and disbursements (providing they are not unreasonable) together with approximately 60% of our profit costs. That is to say recovery of approximately £619,000.00. The likely return of £1,657,000.00 must therefore be further discounted by the irrecoverable costs element of say, £130,000.00 giving a net figure for recovery of £1.527M.

Conclusion

Approaching this case from the standpoint of its commercial viability it seems to us that set against a maximum return of some £2,000,000 and a likely return of £1.5M proceeding to trial can be commercially justified. Nevertheless we would advise that negotiations be commenced with XYZ to achieve a settlement in the region of £1.2M to £1.4M.

Yours faithfully

Part II

Tort

Tort and Statutory Duty in English Law 7

Phillip Capper

Synopsis

This paper reviews the development of the law of tort and breach of statutory duty, and the rights afforded in the recovery of loss, with particular reference to recent developments in the courts.

Overview

The English courts began in the mid-80s a new trend of caution, restricting negligence liability outside contract (eg to third parties such as building occupiers) and overruling expansions of the law in the previous decade. Hence, local authorities' liability for building control functions (which exploded in the mid-70s) was first limited to present or imminent threats to health or safety of the occupier, and then in 1990 abolished altogether as a special category[1]. Also, the recovery of purely economic losses not immediately consequential on damage to the person or property of the claimant was also considerably restricted.

This latter restriction is subject to an important exception. There has remained an exceptional category allowing recovery of pure economic loss by third parties not in a contractual relationship with the defendant. However, the House of Lords has also restated the limits on this exception: it is essential to prove, in this category of the tort of negligence, as an essential ingredient of the necessary 'proximity' for a duty of care, that the defendant knew (both in preparing himself for what he said and in saying it) that his statement would be communicated to the plaintiff, either as an individual or as a member of an identifiable class, specifically in connection with a particular transaction or transactions of a particular kind and that the plaintiff would be very likely to rely on it for the purpose of deciding whether or not to enter upon that transaction or upon a transaction of that kind.

The main objection to the recovery of pure economic loss (not immediately consequent on physical damage) is that it opens the floodgates to claims from an indeterminate range of claimants. A further trend emerging

---

1 see *Murphy* v. *Brentwood* [1990] 3 WLR 414

in the case-law of the late 1980s is a renewed emphasis upon the various parties' own contractual framework of risk allocation. Their free assent to such arrangements has not only defined their contractual rights and obligations. The courts have even come to recognise that the contractual structure of risk should also delimit the extent of risk exposure to third parties. Hence liabilities even in tort could be reduced significantly if the extent of reliance were managed by appropriate wording in the contractual terms of engagement and, where relevant and admissible, earlier correspondence. This is as much a matter of positive but realistic portrayal of the limits of the scope of the service intended, as it is perceived in the client's and others' minds, as it is with the language of actual warnings or disclaimers.

The supply of everyday goods and building services typically involves a quality or fitness obligation. Contrast this with the typical duty of professional advisers, engaged for their expertise. They are not normally taken by English law to warrant that the advice will lead to a successful result. They merely have to take reasonable care in the giving of advice. Users who want rights to a certain level of quality or freedom from defects in goods and services (beyond the level that the goods or services must not injure or damage people or other property) must normally get a contract to that effect with whoever they wish to make responsible. If there is a contract, the obligations may be implied, by statute or because a judge would regard them as necessarily implied.

In English law only the parties to a contract are entitled to the rights it creates. Third parties cannot take advantage of the contractual duties. This puts a natural limit on the range of possible claimants who can complain of quality problems. Liability outside contract to third parties (in the tort of negligence) has no natural limits and so has to be restricted in some way to prevent the courts being flooded with claims: the normal mechanism in tort is to allow losses to be recoverable only where these relate to physical harm to person or property. Pure economic losses are not normally recoverable in tort. Contract law does not make this distinction. Between contracting parties all losses (whether physical or wholly financial) are recoverable as damages so long as they arise naturally, according to the usual course of things, from the breach of contract, or were in the contemplation of both parties when the contract was made.

Collateral Warranties

Even though the courts have re-instated fundamental restrictions on negligence liabilities outside contract, a decade or so of expanded liability has left a raised claims consciousness. For example, owners and tenants of buildings have become accustomed to holding builders directly responsible (even if they have no contract with them) for mere defects in the buildings which are not otherwise damaging or dangerous. As tortious negligence liability has receded under a new judicial conservatism, owners and tenants have looked for new forms of legal protection. These are being expressed as "duty of care" letters and deeds, special warranties, and various forms of assignment or novation. They usually attempt to create either a direct additional responsibility in contract from the designer and contractor to the beneficiary, or a transfer of the original clients' rights under the building contact to third party end users.

Torts and Construction

There are many factual contexts in construction which could give rise to tortious liability. These might range across a wide variety of disparate circumstances: examples might include site accidents, injuring employees or passers-by; over-hanging tower cranes; nuisances to neighbouring properties, such as subsidence during the works, or water run-off in later years; and, at the other end of the spectrum, eg, the wrongful use of intellectual property in drawings, or defamation through untruthful comparative advertising.

An interesting recent illustration of construction litigation involving allegations of nuisance and *Rylands* v. *Fletcher*[2] tort arose in *Ryeford Homes Limited & Anr* v. *Sevenoaks D C & Anrs*[3]. However, in order to confine this paper within reasonable bounds, attention will be given only to the tort of negligence, and to certain related instances of statutory duties.

Why will tort liability be asserted by a claimant?

The simplest reason for framing an action in tort is that the claimant has no contract with the defendant. Of necessity all third party claims have to be grounded in tort. The courts may also continue to find a duty in tort even where there is a contract with the defendant (see below).

The advantages of a tort action are that (1) the time limits within which the action could be started may run later in tort, so that it may in some cases still be possible to start a claim on the basis of tortious negligence which would otherwise already be statute-barred; and (2) the basis for calculating damages is potentially different in tort as compared with contract, and this could work to the advantage of the claimant.

2　(1866) LR 3 HL 330
3　[1990] 6 Const. L.J. 170

Essential ingredients of the tort of negligence

A person who has suffered loss or damage may have legal rights to compensation because the person responsible acted in a way which the law regards as wrong (thereby committing a tort). To succeed in the tort of negligence, the claimant has to establish that:

(1) a duty of care is owed to him in respect of the particular kind of damage that has been suffered; this requires a sufficient relationship of proximity between the claimant and the defendant such that it would be just and reasonable that the defendant should owe the claimant a duty to take care to avoid the particular harm that the claimant has suffered - normally justice will require a duty to take reasonable care only to avoid injuring the person or property of people with whom the defendant has such a relationship, but exceptionally the duty in some cases may extend to avoiding causing pure economic loss unrelated to physical harm.

(2) the duty has been broken by carelessness amounting to negligence in law; this requires analysis of what standard of care could be expected of a reasonably competent person in the position of the defendant, in the light of technical knowledge and standards prevailing as the state of the art at the time of the alleged carelessness.

The development of the modern English tort of negligence

The modern English law on the tort of negligence has been developed almost entirely by judges in case law rather than by legislation. The impetus to the development was the decision of the House of Lords in the famous snail case of *Donoghue* v. *Stevenson*[4]. Its major significance was, broadly speaking, that it allowed a short cut for the end user to claim directly against an original manufacturer (if the manufacturer was negligent). This cut out the need to channel claims through the chain of supply contracts from the end user back to the manufacturer. The third quarter of the 20th century saw the limits of this new principle being explored by litigation. Claimants found the courts increasingly indulgent. People in the business of design, manufacture or supply were held responsible for a wider range of risks, so long as it could be established that they had not taken reasonable care.

It was Lord Denning, in the case of *Dutton* v. *Bognor Regis UDC*[5], who first articulated the major new proposition that rules of law applicable to goods and products could equally be applied to buildings. For claimants,

4   [1932] A.C. 562
5   [1972] 1 QB 373

this arose in the fertile context of litigation against local authorities exercising building control functions. The defendants were particularly attractive targets. They were always there and could afford to pay. It was worth taking cases to the House of Lords, and so as a result of the decision in *Anns* v. *Merton LBC*[6] the negligence liabilities not only of local authorities, but also of contractors and consultants in the construction industry, were greatly extended.

A further extension of negligence liability arose by the courts' willingness to recognise that a party could be sued in tort even by his client who had contractual rights against him as well. The allegation of a duty in tort concurrent with obligations in contract between the same parties was normally made by a claimant wanting to take advantage of the longer limitation periods applicable to tort actions under the Limitation Acts. The case of *Batty* v. *Metropolitan Properties*[7] illustrated how tort liabilities could arise alongside contractual obligations to the same claimant.

The late 1980's heralded new limits on the negligence liabilities of ordinary building contractors and designers. In *D & F Estates*[8], Wates won before the House of Lords on the important principle that they owed no duty of care to supervise their independent sub-contractors in relation to claims made by third parties with whom they had no contract. The building owners alleged that Wates were negligent in performing their work under the building contract. Wates denied that they were liable and relied on the fact that defective work had been carried out, not by Wates' own labour, but by an independent plastering sub-contractor. That company no longer existed when proceedings were issued against Wates. The House of Lords agreed that Wates could properly discharge their obligations under the building contract by engaging a sub-contractor to carry out all or part of their contractual obligations providing that they took reasonable steps to ensure that the sub-contractor was apparently competent. The approach of the House of Lords is in line with a series of such restrictive decisions. However, the House of Lords went much further, as is explored further below.

Contractors gained substantial relief from potential liabilities as a result of this decision, but professional advisers, architects and engineers could still be at risk of wide liability to third parties for economic losses because the decision left undisturbed the liabilities arising from the 'reliance' principle (see the line of cases from *Hedley Byrne* v. *Heller*[9] through to

6 [1978] A.C. 728
7 [1978] QB 554
8 [1989] A.C. 177
9 [1964] A.C. 465

Caparo v. *Dickman*[10]).

In *Murphy* v. *Brentwood*[11] the House of Lords decided that *Anns* v. *Merton* was wrongly decided as regards the scope of any private law duty of care resting on local authorities in relation to their function to secure compliance with building byelaws or regulations; and the House overruled *Dutton* and all cases that applied *Dutton* or *Anns*.

Essentially, it appears that the clock has been turned back half a century for ordinary negligence claims against contractors and suppliers (assuming they have no liability under the 'reliance' principle from *Hedley Byrne* v. *Heller*). Restored are the principal limitations of Lord Atkins' neighbour principle in *Donoghue* v. *Stevenson*[12].

The duty relates to a particular kind of damage

For ordinary suppliers of goods and services, the normal requirements of liability in tortious negligence will be actual damage to the plaintiff's person or ('other') property. It will not, it seems, suffice if the only damage occurring is within property which the defendant had negligently designed or produced and such damage is attributable to that negligence. Difficulties will however arise in determining whether the defendant can be said to have caused damage to 'other' property if one part of the product he supplies causes damage to another he supplies with it. (Consider the notion of 'complex structure' mooted in *D & F Estates* v. *Church Commissioners*[13], HL, and clarified in *Murphy* v. *Brentwood*; and see eg *Aswan Engineering Co* v. *Lupdine Ltd*[14] explored further below).

Duty and damage

This fundamental principle of the relationship between the duty of care and the kind of harm which is to be avoided was emphasised by the House of Lords in *Caparo Industries plc* v. *Dickman & others*[15]. Lord Bridge said that it was never sufficient to ask simply whether A owed B a duty of care. It was always necessary to determine the scope of the duty by reference to the kind of damage from which A had to save B harmless. "The question was always whether the defendant was under a duty to avoid or prevent that

10 [1990] 2 A.C. 605
11 [1990] 3 WLR 414
12 [1932] A.C. 562
13 [1989] A.C. 177
14 [1987] 1 WLR 1
15 [1990] 2 A.C. 605

damage, but the actual nature of the damage suffered is relevant to the existence and extent of any duty to avoid or prevent it." (*Sutherland Shire Council* v. *Heyman*[16]). Lord Oliver also adopted those words from Sutherland, adding: "The duty of care was inseparable from the damage suffered. It was not a duty to take care in the abstract but a duty to avoid causing to the particular plaintiff damage of the particular kind sustained".

Plaintiff must have sufficient interest in the property damaged.

This means that in order to be able to claim in respect of damage to property the plaintiff must have had a proprietary or possessory right to it and not a mere contractual right in relation to it (*Candlewood Navigation* v. Mitsui[17]; *Leigh & Sillivan Ltd* v. *Aliakmon Shipping Co Ltd*[18].) The cause of action must have accrued to the plaintiff and not to a previous owner of the damaged property, unless the damage was unknown to the plaintiff who became the owner of the property after 18 September 1986.[19]

Nature of the loss suffered by the claimant

Thus, the law does not proceed from the assumption that just because a product is defective someone must be legally liable. The law will not necessarily hold a defendant liable even if proved to have been 'negligent'. Liability in tort does not exist without proof of a legally recoverable type of loss. So the claimant relying on an allegation of negligence in tort has to complain not of a 'defect', whether in a product or some professional advice, but of a loss; then he must show that that defendant owed an obligation to prevent that loss arising to that party; even if the obligation is owed, it must also be shown to have been broken.

It is vital to distinguish between the different types of losses which the law classifies:
(a) The 'defect' has injured (or, perhaps, may injure) people.
(b) The 'defect' causes (or, perhaps, may cause) damage to other property.
(c) The 'defect' is such that some part of the product itself is damaged.
(d) The 'defect' is merely such that the product is not as 'good' as it might have been. There is a mere diminution in value or quality compared

16 (1985) 60 ALR 1, 48
17 [1986] AC 1
18 [1986] AC 785
19 *Perry* v. *Tendring DC* (1984) 30 BLR 118; and, s.3(1), Latent Damage Act 1986).

with that expected.

This 'hierarchy' of losses is very significant in tort law. Liability is progressively more difficult to establish as one moves from category (a) to category (d). The threshold of liability appeared by virtue of *Junior Books* v. *Veitchi*[20] to drop below category (d). The *D & F* decision moved the threshold back up to draw the line between (b) and (c) in ordinary negligence cases (not involving *Hedley Byrne/Caparo* v. *Dickman* type reliance liability), and that restriction was even more strongly affirmed in *Murphy* v. *Brentwood* (though the 'perhaps' in (b) and (c) arise from dicta of Lord Bridge as to dangers to the highway and neighbouring properties). By contrast, the 'hierarchy' can be irrelevant in contract law. The parties can, by clear drafting of their contract terms, make a designer or builder liable even for the aesthetic defects in category (d), and yet not liable for the apparently more significant losses in categories (a) to (c).

Applying the D & F Estates decision

The House of Lords decision in *D & F Estates* left considerable uncertainty in the law as a result of difficulties presented by their Lordships but not resolved by them. Above all there were apparent inconsistencies between the speeches of Lords Bridge and Oliver even though they said that they agreed! This might be attributable to a failure to clarify whether *Anns* v. *Merton* was being treated as giving rise to a distinct type of duty (based on a threat to health and safety) separate from the ordinary duty flowing from *Donoghue* v. *Stevenson*. Much of the uncertainty has now been removed by their Lordships' decision in *Murphy*. Two aspects of the *D & F* decision caused particular uncertainty.

The 'complex structure' notion.

In *D & F Estates*, Lord Bridge agreed with Lord Brandon's speech in Junior Books to the effect that physical damage to persons or property was an essential ingredient of negligence and for this purpose the property from the defective condition of which damage arose was to be excluded. Lord Bridge had, however, expressed the view that it might "well be arguable in the case of complex structures, as indeed possibly in the case of complex chattels, that one element of the structure should be regarded ... as distinct from another element, so that damage to one part of the structure caused by a hidden defect in another part [might] qualify to be treated as damage to other property." Lord Oliver said: "The proposition that damages are recoverable in tort for negligent manufacture when the only damage sustained is either an initial defect or subsequent injury to the very thing that is manufactured is one which is peculiar to the construction of a building and is, I think, logically explicable on the hypothesis suggested by Lord Bridge".

By what criteria will the courts treat one part of structure as distinct from another for this purpose? Possibilities might include functional interdependence, structural dependence, or sourcing of the different elements from different designers or suppliers. The House of Lords guidance in *Murphy* does not unfortunately resolve the likely difficulties.

Lord Keith observed in *Murphy* that it would be unrealistic to take the view that damage to one part caused by a hidden defect in another part might qualify as damage to 'other property' as regards a building the whole of which had been erected and equipped by the same contractor. In that situation, he said, the whole package provided by the contractor would fall to be regarded as one unit rendered unsound by a defect in a part. On the other hand where, eg., the electric wiring had been installed by a subcontractor and due to a careless defect a fire destroyed the building, "it might not be stretching ordinary principles too far to hold the electrical sub-contractor liable for the damage". However, he concluded, in this regard, that even if Lord Bridge's theory were held acceptable, it would not extend to founding liability on a local authority, as the purposes of the 1936 Act were averting danger to health and safety, not danger or damage to property. Further, it would not cover the situation which might arise through discovery, before damage occurred, of a defect likely to give rise to damage in the future.

Lord Bridge's analysis in *Murphy* was as follows:

"In *D & F Estates*, at p.206G-207H, his Lordship mooted the possibility that in complex structures or chattels one part might, when it caused damage to another part of the same structure or chattel, be regarded in the law of tort as having caused damage to 'other property' for the purpose of *Donoghue* v. *Stevenson*. He had expressed no opinion as to the validity of this theory, but had put it forward as a possible ground on which the facts in Anns might be distinguishable from those in *D & F*... The complex structure theory had, so far as he knew, never been subjected to detailed examination in any English authority. He would not review the numerous authorities in USA jurisdictions... [T]reating each part of the entire structure as a separate item of property seemed quite unrealistic. The reality was that the structural elements in any building formed a single indivisible unit of which the different parts were essentially interdependent. To the extent that there was any defect in one part of the structure it had to a greater or lesser degree necessarily to affect all other parts of the structure. Therefore any defect in the structure was a defect in the quality of the whole and it was quite artificial, in order to impose a legal liability which the law would not otherwise impose, to treat a defect in an integral structure, so far as it weakened the structure, as a dangerous defect liable to cause damage to 'other property'. A critical distinction had here to be drawn between some part of a complex structure which was said to be a 'danger' only because it did not perform its proper function in sustaining the other parts and some distinct item incorporated in the structure which positively malfunctioned so as to inflict positive damage on the structure in which it was incorporated. Thus, if a defective central heating boiler exploded and damaged a house or a defective electrical installation malfunctioned and set the house on fire, his Lordship saw no reason to doubt that the owner of the house, if he could prove that the damage was due to the negligence of the boiler manufacturer or the electrical contractor, could recover damages in tort on *Donoghue* v. *Stevenson* principles. But the position in law was entirely different where, by reason of the inadequacy of the foundations to support the superstructure, differential settlement and consequent cracking occurred. Here, once the first cracks appeared, the structure as a whole was seen to be defective and the nature of the defect was known. Even if, contrary to this view, the initial damage could be regarded as damage to other property caused by a latent defect, once the defect was known the situation of the building owner was analogous to that of the car owner who discovered that the car had faulty brakes. He might have a house which, until repairs were effected, was unfit for habitation, but, subject to the reservation expressed above with respect to ruinous buildings at or near the boundary of the owner's property, the building no longer represented a source of danger and as it deteriorated would only damage itself."

Lord Oliver said in *Murphy* that the 'complex structure theory' had been rightly criticised by academic writers although both Lord Bridge and his Lordship had made it clear in canvassing it in *D & F Estates* that it was not embraced with any enthusiasm but was advanced as the only logically possible explanation of the categorisation of the damage in *Anns* as 'material, physical damage'. Lord Bridge in the present case had amply demonstrated the artificiality of the theory and, for the reasons he gave, it had to be rejected as a viable explanation of the underlying basis for the decision in Anns.

The dicta of Lord Jauncey in *Murphy* take a different line:

"His Lordship agreed with Lord Bridge in this appeal that to apply the complex structure theory to a house so that each part of the entire structure was treated as a separate piece of property was quite unrealistic. A builder who built a house from foundations upwards was creating a single integrated unit of which the individual components were interdependent. To treat the foundations as a piece of property separate from the walls or the floors was a wholly artificial exercise. If foundations were inadequate the whole house was affected. Furthermore, if the complex structure theory was tenable there was no reason in principle why it should not also be applied to chattels consisting of integrated parts such as a ship or a piece of machinery. The consequences of such an application would be far reaching. It seemed that the only context for the complex structure theory in the case of a building would be where one integral component of the structure was built by a separate contractor and where a defect in such a component had caused damage to other parts of the structure, eg a steel frame erected by a specialist contractor which failed to give adequate support to floors or walls. Defects in such ancillary equipment as central heating boilers or electrical installations would be subject to the normal *Donoghue* v. *Stevenson* principle if such defects gave rise to damage to other parts of the building."

Is the cost of averting danger recoverable?

A requirement of normal negligence liability following *Donoghue* v. *Stevenson* is that there must have been no reasonable opportunity for intermediate examination which would have enabled the plaintiff to be aware of the potential for harm before it occurred. So, does discovery of a defect before it causes injury to person or other property normally prevent recovery of the costs of making good the defect? On that basis the costs of averting danger would be recoverable only in three narrow and distinct categories:

(a) where such costs are treated as pure economic loss, but are recoverable because there is exceptional liability for reliance on negligent advice or

information (based on *Hedley Byrne/Caparo* v. *Dickman*, see below); or,
(b) where the costs are inevitable to prevent imminent harm to neighbouring property or users of the highway; or
(c) where the duty alleged is based not on normal *D & F* negligence liability, but was rather a special duty based on *Anns* v. *Merton LBC* (and thus perhaps only in cases of breach of statutory duty by contractors, or negligence in building control by local authorities) as the nature of the duty derives from the purposes of the Building Regulations and is to protect occupiers from present or imminent threat to health and safety.

It appears that the possibility of category (c) has been excluded by the decision in *Murphy* v. *Brentwood*, overruling the line of cases based on *Dutton* and *Anns*.

Category (b) arises from certain dicta of Lord Bridge in Murphy. His Lordship expressed the governing principle, and the qualification, in the following terms:

"The negligent manufacturer of a chattel with a latent dangerous defect would be liable in tort, under *Donoghue* v. *Stevenson*, for injury to persons or damage to property which the chattel causes. But if the chattel was merely defective in quality, even valueless for its intended purpose, the manufacturer's liability at common law arose only under any contract to which he was a party; he had no liability in tort to persons with whom he had no contract who suffer economic loss because of the defect in quality. If a dangerous defect was discovered before it caused any personal injury or damage to property, because the danger was now known and the chattel could not be safely used unless the defect was repaired, the defect became merely one of quality and the loss (repair or scrapping) purely economic. It was recoverable in contract, but not in tort in the absence of a special relationship imposing on the tortfeasor a duty of care to safeguard the plaintiff from economic loss. There was no such special relationship between the manufacturer of a chattel and a remote owner or hirer... These principles were equally applicable to buildings. The only qualification which his Lordship would make was that, if a building stood so close to the boundary of the building owner's land that after discovery of the dangerous defect it remained a potential source of injury to persons or property on neighbouring land or on the highway, the building owner ought, in principle, to be entitled to recover in tort from the negligent builder the cost of obviating the danger, whether by repair or by demolition, so far as that cost was necessarily incurred in order to protect himself from potential liability to third parties."

Lord Oliver expressed some doubts on this qualification: whether, as suggested by Lord Bridge, the builder could be held responsible for the cost necessarily incurred by a building owner in protecting himself from potential liability to third parties was a question on which Lord Oliver preferred to reserve his opinion until the case arose, although he was not at the moment convinced of the basis for making such a distinction.

Dilemmas presented by D & F Estates

The uncertainties and dilemmas presented by the House of Lords decision in *D & F Estates* were well illustrated by the subsequent case of *West Kent Cold Storage Co Ltd* v. *C Hemmings & Co Ltd*[21]. In this case the plaintiff owned cold storage premises and the defendant was a specialist manufacturer of insulating panels for cold stores. The plaintiff contracted with a firm (in liquidation by the time of this dispute) to build extensions to the premises. That firm ordered panels from the defendant manufacturer to form the ceiling and walls of the new stores. The defendant was negligent in manufacture with the result that panels delaminated and sagged. The remedy was to bolt ribs into position to prevent the steel falling from the ceiling and from the walls, thus avoiding any risk of injury to people working in the stores. The plaintiff claimed from the defendant the cost of the necessary remedial work.

The defendant argued that the plaintiff could not succeed because, there being no contractual relationship, as the law stood they could not succeed in tort. In support they relied on Lord Oliver[22]:

"... in no other context has it previously been suggested that a cause of action in tort arises in English law for the defective manufacture of an article which causes no injury other than injury to the defective parts of itself. If I buy a secondhand car to which there has been fitted a pneumatic tyre which, as a result of carelessness in manufacture, is dangerously defective and explodes, causing injury to me or to the car, no doubt the negligent manufacturer is liable in tort on the ordinary application of *Donoghue* v. *Stevenson*. But if the tyre bursts without causing any injury other than to itself or if I discover the defect before a burst occurs, I know of no principle on which I can claim

21 QBD, 7 November 1989, (1990 CILL 547)
22 at p.211G-H in *D & F*

to recover from the manufacturer in tort the cost of making good the defect which, in practice, could only be the cost of supplying and fitting a new tyre. That would be in effect to attach to goods a non-contractual warranty of fitness which would follow the goods into whosoever's hands they came. Such a concept was suggested *obiter* by Lord Denning MR in *Dutton*'s case at p.396, but it was entirely unsupported by any authority and is in my opinion contrary to principle."

H.H. Judge Prosser QC found the best support for tortious liability, to the limit claimed by the plaintiff in this case, in the speech of Lord Bridge, again in *D & F*[23], where he substantially quoted Lord Brandon in *Junior Books Ltd* v. *Veitchi Co Ltd*[24]. Lord Brandon said[25]:

"The actual decision in ... *Donoghue* v. *Stevenson* ... can be summarised in this way: a person who manufactures goods, which he intends to be used or consumed by others, is under a duty to exercise such reasonable care in their manufacture as to ensure that they can be used or consumed in the manner intended without causing physical damage to persons or property... The relevant property was property other than the very property which gave rise to the danger of physical damage concerned."

Later[26], Lord Bridge explained, Lord Brandon said, in relation to *Anns* v. *Merton*:

"an essential ingredient in the cause of action relied on was the existence of danger, or the threat of danger, of physical damage to persons or their property, excluding for this purpose the very piece of property from the defective condition of which such danger, or threat of danger, arises."

H.H. Judge Prosser QC said that in the present case the plaintiff was not claiming as per the example of the tyre but was claiming the cost of averting the threat of danger. His Honour therefore relied on the law as succinctly expressed by Lord Oliver in *D & F*[27]:

23 at p.202
24 [1983] 1 AC 520
25 at p.549
26 at p.550-1
27 at p.216F-H

"... in so far as [*Anns* v. *Merton LBC*] is authority for the proposition that a builder responsible for the construction of a building is liable in tort at common law for damage occurring through his negligence to the very thing which he has constructed, such liability is limited directly to cases where the defect is one which threatens the health or safety of occupants or of third parties and (possibly) other property. In such a case, however, the damages recoverable are limited to expenses necessarily incurred in averting that danger."

That comment had led counsel for the plaintiff to restrict his claim to the sum necessary to make the premises safe. It was necessary to put struts or ribs in to prevent the ceiling and walls from collapsing. As people constantly worked in the cold stores, such a remedy was, his Honour said, surely necessary to cure the defect which undoubtedly, in his Honour's judgment, threatened the safety of the occupants and third parties. His Honour said that it would be absurd to suggest that for the plaintiff to succeed in negligence it was necessary for the plaintiff to wait until damage or injury was actually caused before he could claim. His Honour could see the need to limit the claim in negligence to the expenses necessary to avert the danger, but that was all that this plaintiff was claiming.

In *West Kent Cold Storage Co Ltd* v. *C Hemmings & Co Ltd* the 'complex structure' notion was not raised. This was presumably because the remedial works were described as necessary to prevent injury to people, ie. workers inside the cold store. The problem with the decision is that it perpetuated the confusion as to whether *Donoghue* v. *Stevenson* and *Anns* v. *Merton* together expressed one type of duty or two. It seems more likely that there were actually two quite separate duties. *Donoghue* v. *Stevenson*, affirmed but limited to actual damage to persons or other property by both Lords Bridge and Oliver in *D & F Estates*, was the basis for the more general and normal duty of care in the tort of negligence. By contrast, *Anns* v. *Merton LBC* (so long as it had any continuing significance, which ended with *Murphy* v. *Brentwood*) described a special duty of care arising from carelessness by building control authorities (and perhaps by contractors and others in breach of the Building Regulations) whereby there arose a threat to the health and safety of occupiers.

This latter analysis suggests that the decision in *West Kent Cold Storage Co Ltd* v. *C Hemmings & Co Ltd* was, with respect, wrong to found itself on Lord Oliver's later dicta in *D & F* with regard to *Anns* v. *Merton*. The negligent panel manufacturer was not in breach of a 'building control' duty to protect occupiers from threats to their health and safety. Rather his duty derived from *Donoghue* v. *Stevenson* as interpreted by Lord Bridge and Lord Oliver's earlier dicta in *D & F*. So once the defect in the panels was discovered injury could have been avoided by the simple expedient of excluding workers until the remedial works were carried out. No injury would have been sustained, and so no type of harm protected by the *Donoghue* v. *Stevenson* type of duty would have been suffered. The economic consequences of closing the store and the costs of making good the defect would all have been the consequence of a quality defect which in the absence of a contract would not normally be recoverable as damages in tort. This analysis has since been confirmed by *Murphy* v. *Brentwood*.

Recovery of Cost of making good defects

The cost of remedial works necessary to avert the danger of injury to people was also held recoverable as a matter of principle decided as a preliminary issue in *Portsea Island Mutual Co-Operative Society Ltd* v. *Michael Brashier Associates*[28]. Again (as in the *West Kent Cold Store* case) the basis of the decision is, with respect, not free from difficulty. There is some eliding of *D & F* with *Anns* v. *Merton* (rather than recognition of the two very different duties). Furthermore, it appears that the judge, having concluded that the cost of remedial work was not recoverable under *D & F*, nevertheless regarded it as recoverable as pure economic loss. However, it is not made explicit in the judgment that as economic loss it is recoverable only for reliance on negligent advice or information (based on *Hedley Byrne*). Furthermore, if it was recoverable as economic loss why was it necessary to limit it to costs of removing the danger? The necessary distinctions between *Hedley Byrne* (as since explained in *Caparo* v. *Dickman*), *Anns* v. *Merton* and *D & F Estates* appear more fused than sharpened by the *Portsea Island* case. The *Anns* aspect has now been overruled by *Murphy* v. *Brentwood*.

In the *Portsea Island* case, the defendant architects (Brashiers) were employed by developers to design and supervise the construction, on JCT terms, of a supermarket. In due course, Brashiers issued a certificate of final completion giving the contractor a defence against claims by the developer in contract or in negligence. Since the supermarket was purpose-made both Brashiers and the contractor must have known that Portsea were the intended occupiers, but there was no contract between Brashiers and either the contractor or Portsea. Portsea did not obtain collateral warranties from Brashiers. Portsea said that defects were later discovered: brickslips fell from the walls and others had to be removed to prevent them falling onto

28 (HH Judge John Newey QC, 1989 CILL 520)

staff or members of the public; and there were alleged defects in car park walls, such as lack of mortar at coping level, unsatisfactory pointing and inadequate damp proof courses. Portsea commenced proceedings against Brashiers alleging negligence. They did not allege breach of statutory duty. There were two issues for decision, assuming for the purpose of this preliminary issue that Brashiers were responsible for the defects:

(1) Assuming that the brickslip facing was a potential source of danger, was the cost of replacing all the slips with new ones recoverable as damages in tort against Brashiers?

(2) Assuming that there were defects in the car park walls, which did not involve danger, were the remedial costs recoverable as damages in tort against Brashiers?

Judge Newey said that the major differences between the two issues was that the first involved a risk of personal injuries and of damage to other parts of the building whereas the second did not. Portsea had removed brickslips liable to fall, so any danger from them had been removed. Because of Portsea's repairing obligations under the lease and because they occupied the supermarket, they would have to pay for all necessary repairs and would incur 'pecuniary' or economic loss.

His Honour considered the leading House of Lords judgments:

"In *Junior Books*, Lord Brandon (at p.550) had given as an example of an exceptional case in which a plaintiff would be able to recover pecuniary loss in the absence of physical damage one in which he incurred the loss 'in order to prevent or mitigate imminent danger of damage to the persons or property exposed to that danger'. In *Dutton* v. *Bognor Regis UDC*[29], and *Anns* such 'preventive' expenditure was recoverable as damages for breach of statutory duty. In *DoE* v. *Thomas Bates & Son Ltd*[30], a builder was liable in negligence for the cost of remedying defects in order to avert imminent danger, but not to enable the building to be used to a greater extent than it was being used.[31]

In *D & F Estates*, however, Lord Bridge[32] had said that if a 'hidden danger is discovered before any such damage is caused, there is no longer any room for the application of the *Donoghue* v. *Stevenson* principle' and he did not express a view as to whether there might be a departure from that principle."

29 [1972] 2 QB 373 CA
30 [1989] 1 All ER 1075 CA
31 [cf now House of Lords decision in *DoE* v. *Bates*[1990] 3 WLR 457]
32 (at p.206)

His Honour concluded that Brashiers did owe Portsea a duty to take care. However, the condition of the brickslips rendering them liable to fall could not be relied upon as 'damage'. Indeed, his Honour said, Portsea, by discovering that the brickslips were dangerous and removing them, had effectively prevented any injury or damage from occurring so that there was in Lord Bridge's words in *D & F* 'no room for the application of the *Donoghue* v. *Stevenson* principle'.

Yet it did not seem fair to his Honour that Portsea should be treated as not having suffered 'damage' because they had removed the dangerous brickslips at some expense to themselves but that they would have suffered 'damage' had they left the brickslips to fall on an employer or on a lower part of the building. The escape from that position had, his Honour thought, to be that Portsea could recover their expenditure upon removing the brickslips and any other work necessary in order to make the walls safe, as economic loss. In *Junior Books* Lord Brandon had envisaged that such pecuniary losses might be recoverable and in the breach of statutory duty cases and in *Bates* they had been. Portsea would not be able to recover the cost of re-cladding the wall. The question is whether that result would now be wrong in the light of *Murphy* v. *Brentwood*.

On the second issue, in respect of the car park walls, his Honour concluded that since there was no risk of injury or physical damage, it would not have been just and reasonable that Brashiers should have owed a duty of care to Portsea. Since the defective condition of the walls had not damaged persons or property and there was no danger of their doing so which would warrant expenditure upon them, Portsea had not suffered any damage recoverable in tort.

Economic losses recoverable by third parties

A possible qualification to the above is the House of Lords decision in *Junior Books Ltd* v. *Veitchi Ltd*[33]. A specialist supplier of goods and services was held by a majority of their Lordships to owe a duty to a third party (with whom there was no contract) to take care to avoid the financial losses that would flow from defects in the goods and services provided. However, this was a special case on the facts of a specialist contractor who voluntarily assumed a special responsibility and whose expertise was particularly relied upon by clients (if indeed the case has any significant scope for application after the House of Lords decision in *D & F Estates*). Rather, the dissenting speech of Lord Brandon, denying any duty for such pure economic losses, was a dominant influence in *D & F*.

---

33 [1983] 1 A.C. 520

So, in ordinary negligence cases since *D & F* (ie cases not involving particular and exceptional reliance on negligent advice or information, see below), the courts have to draw an important distinction between:

financial losses which are immediately consequent upon physical damage to people or property (such as loss of profit or disruption occasioned by the physical damage – see *Muirhead* v. *Industrial Tank Specialities Ltd*[34] and *Spartan Steel & Alloys Ltd* v. *Martin & Co (Contractors) Ltd*[35] which are recoverable in ordinary *Donoghue* v. *Stevenson/D & F* cases; and

other claims for financial losses which are wholly unrelated to physical 'damage' in the sense in which this is limited in *D & F*; so this category ranges from the costs of making good quality defects which are not in any way dangerous to neighbouring people or property, to investment losses and diminution in value of assets purchased in reliance on negligent information. See *Caparo* v. *Dickman*[36].

Physical damage is naturally limited in extent and in a sense self extinguishing (except where, eg, there is a catastrophe with the release of harmful replicating organisms, or of nuclear radiation). By contrast, financial losses are conceptual only, with no necessary relationship to the physical world. Thus there are no natural limits to the extent of the financial losses that could flow from a causative negligent event, so far as tortious negligence liability to third parties is concerned. Contractual liabilities are, by contrast, naturally limited in any event to the parties to the contract (the 'privity' principle). Therefore, contract law does not need to distinguish between physical and financial losses. The law of tort does need to impose artificial limits; it is a pragmatic problem – the need to control the unacceptable proliferation of claims: therefore the courts draw an important distinction between financial losses which are consequent upon physical damage and claims which are for purely economic loss unrelated to physical damage.

Economic losses not consequent on physical damage

The ordinary and general duty of care in tortious negligence, epitomised by *Donoghue* v. *Stevenson*, comprising a duty to take reasonable care to avoid causing physical harm to the person or property of others is no longer

34 [1986] QB 507
35 [1973] QB 27
36 [1990] 2 A.C. 605

controversial. However, the problem for the courts since has been to explore the circumstances, if any, in which the *Donoghue* v. *Stevenson* duty might be extended, especially as in *Donoghue* itself Lord Atkin's famous and seminal declaration of the 'neighbour' principle cast the duty of care in wide and general terms, governed principally by the criterion of the foreseeability of the harm that would be likely to arise if reasonable care was not taken.

However, the test of foreseeability proved to be too wide-meshed a sieve. If foreseeability of the harm was the main criterion for identifying losses which were to be compensated by damages in the tort of negligence, then in many instances it was just as foreseeable that third parties would suffer pure economic losses (such as the costs of making good quality defects, or money lost in reliance on negligent information) as it was that they would suffer physical harm. While foreseeability remained the touchstone, the courts would find it increasingly difficult to resist extension of the duty of care from physical harm to economic losses. So the House of Lords in 1963 in *Hedley Byrne* v. *Heller* recognised for the first time that, in appropriate circumstances, the duty could extend to taking care to avoid causing wholly financial loss by negligent information or advice (eg business losses arising from reliance on a negligent banker's reference). But at that stage, the *Hedley Byrne* type duty seemed a special and limited exception to normal requirement of physical harm which had conditioned *Donoghue* v. *Stevenson*. The expansive process, driven by the open-ended nature of the foreseeability criterion, reached its zenith in the House of Lords decisions in *Anns* v. *Merton LBC* and *Junior Books* v. *Veitchi*. First, in *Anns* the foreseeability criterion was explicitly confirmed as the primary necessary ingredient by Lord Wilberforce's now famous 'two-stage' test – dropping the physical harm delimiter assumed in Lord Atkin's 'neighbour' principle in *Donoghue* v. *Stevenson*. Secondly, in *Junior Books* the application of Lord Wilberforce's new test led the majority of the House of Lords to conclude:

> "Though initially there is no doubt that because of Lord Atkin's phraseology in *Donoghue* v. *Stevenson*, "injury to the con- sumer's life or property", it was thought that the duty of care did not extend beyond avoiding physical injury or physical damage to the person or the property of the person to whom the duty of care was owed, that limitation has long since ceased..."

The question which the House of Lords had to decide in *Junior Books* was whether by that time the law 'extends the duty of care beyond a duty to prevent harm being done by faulty work to a duty to avoid such faults being present in the work itself'. It was argued that any remedy of that kind had to lie in contract and not in tort. The expansive attitude of the majority of their Lordships in response was remarkable (but in retrospect short-lived):

"Today the proper control lies not in asking whether the proper remedy should lie in contract or ... in tort, not in somewhat capricious judicial determination whether a particular case falls on one side of the line or the other, not in somewhat artificial distinctions between physical and economic or financial loss... but in... establishing the relevant principles and then in deciding whether the case falls within or without those principles."

So the physical harm limits from *Donoghue* v. *Stevenson*, and the exceptional factual limits on the special 'negligent advice' duty in *Hedley Byrne* v. *Heller*, had been abandoned in favour of single general principle (mainly, foreseeability of loss) as to test whether a duty of care was owed in any factual situation – regardless of whether that situation was already recognised in previous case-law as an established duty-situation or was wholly novel.

This momentous expansion was indeed short-lived. *D & F Estates* (and *Murphy* v. *Brentwood*) restored the *Donoghue* v. *Stevenson* requirement for normal cases – physical injury or physical damage to the person or the property of the person to whom the duty of care was owed. And the exceptional and limited extent of the *Hedley Byrne* principle have been restored by the House of Lords in *Caparo Industries plc* v. *Dickman & others*[37]. This case even questions Lord Atkin's famous 'neighbour test' in *Donoghue* v. *Stevenson* itself to the extent that, as a general principle, it suggested that duty situations would readily be recognised by the courts merely because they fell within the neighbour test. In *Donoghue* v. *Stevenson* Lord MacMillan observed that 'the categories of negligence are never closed'. There must be doubt in the light of *Caparo* v. *Dickman* as to how much force remains in Lord MacMillan's observation.

Return to traditional distinct duty situations

Lord Bridge said that in determining the existence and scope of the duty of care which one person might owe to another in the infinitely varied circumstances of human relationships there had for long been a tension between two different approaches.

37 [1990] 2 A.C. 605

"Traditionally, the law found the existence of the duty in different specific situations each exhibiting its own particular characteristics. In this way the law had identified a wide variety of duty situations, all falling within the ambit of the tort of negligence, but sufficiently distinct to require separate definition of the essential ingredients by which the duty was to be recognised. Lord Atkin, in his seminal speech in *Donoghue* v. *Stevenson*[38], signified the introduction of the more modern approach of seeking a single general principle for all circumstances to determine the existence of a duty of care. Yet Lord Atkin himself sounded an appropriate note of caution[39].

Lord Reid had given a large impetus to the modern approach in *Dorset Yacht Co Ltd* v. *Home Office*[40]. The most comprehensive attempt to articulate a single general principle was reached in the well-known passage from Lord Wilberforce's speech in *Anns* v. *Merton LBC*[41].

But since Anns a series of decisions of the Privy Council and of the House of Lords, notably in judgments by Lord Keith of Kinkel, had emphasised the inability of any single general principle to provide a practical test which could be applied to every situation to determine whether a duty of care was owed and, if so, what was its scope: see *Governors of Peabody Donations Fund* v. *Sir Lindsay Parkinson & Co Ltd*[42]; *Yuen Kun Yeu* v. *AG of Hong Kong*[43]; *Rowling* v. *Takaro Properties Ltd44*; *Hill* v. *Chief Constable of W. Yorks*[45].

What emerged was that, in addition to foreseeability of damage, necessary ingredients in any situation giving rise to a duty of care were a relationship of 'proximity' or 'neighbourhood' and that the court considered it fair, just and reasonable that the law should impose a duty of given scope. But it was implicit in the passages referred to that the concepts of proximity and fairness were not susceptible of any precise definition, necessary to give them utility as practical tests, but amounted to little more than convenient labels for the features of specific situations which, on

38 [1932] AC 562, 579/80
39 (at p.580)
40 [1970] AC 1004, 1026/7
41 [1978] A.C. 728, 751/2
42 [1985] AC 210, 239F-241C
43 [1988] AC 175, 190E-194F
44 [1988] AC 473, 501D-G
45 [1989] AC 53, 60B-D

a detailed examination, the law recognised pragmatically as giving rise to a duty of care of a given scope.

Whilst recognising, of course, the importance of the underlying general principles common to the whole field of negligence, his Lordship thought that the law had now moved in the direction of attaching greater significance to the more traditional categorisation of distinct and recognisable situations as guides to the existence, the scope and the limits of the varied duties of care which the law imposed. We had now to recognise the wisdom of the words of Brennan J in the High Court of Australia in *Sutherland Shire Council* v. *Heyman*[46]:

> 'the law should develop novel categories of negligence incrementally and by analogy with established categories, rather than by a massive extension of a prima facie duty of care restrained only by indefinable "considerations which ought to ... limit... the duty".'

One of the most important distinctions always to be observed lay in the law's essentially different approach to the different kinds of damage suffered by one party in consequence of the acts or omissions of another. It was one thing to owe a duty of care to avoid causing injury to the person or property of others. It was quite another to avoid causing others to suffer purely economic loss. A graphic illustration of the distinction was given in *Elliott Steam Tug Co Ltd* v. *Shipping Controller*[47], deriving from *Cattle* v. *Stockton Waterworks Co*[48], recently re-affirmed in *Candlewood Navigation Corp* v. *Mitsui OSK Lines Ltd*[49] and *Leigh & Sillavan Ltd* v. *Aliakmon Shipping Co Ltd*[50].

Lord Roskill spoke in similar terms of a return to traditional categorisations: Ever since *Hedley Byrne*, in which Denning LJ in *Candler* was held to have stated the law correctly, it was clear that a duty of care could be owed by a professional man to third parties where there was no contractual relationship between them. But subsequent attempts to define both the duty and its scope had created more problems than the decisions had solved.

46 (1985) 60 ALR 1, 43-44
47 [1922] 1 KB 127, 139
48 (1875) LR 10 QB 453
49 [1986] AC 1
50 [1986] AC 785

There was no simple formula or touchstone to provide in every case a ready answer to the questions whether, given certain facts, the law would or would not impose liability for negligence or in cases where such liability could be shown to exist, determine the extent of that liability. Phrases such as 'foreseeability', 'proximity', 'neighbourhood', 'just and reasonable', 'fairness', 'voluntary acceptance of risk', or 'voluntary assumption of responsibility' were not precise definitions. At best they were but labels or phrases descriptive of the very different factual situations which had to be carefully examined in each case before it could be pragmatically determined whether a duty of care existed and, if so, what was the scope and extent of that duty. If this conclusion involved a return to the traditional categorisation of cases as pointing to the existence and scope of any duty of care, as Lord Bridge suggested, his Lordship thought this infinitely preferable to recourse to somewhat wide generalisations which left their practical application matters of difficulty and uncertainty. This conclusion found strong support from Brennan J in *Sutherland*.

Lord Oliver emphasised the same point this way: To search for any single formula as a general test of liability was to pursue a will-o'-the wisp. Once one discarded, as one had to, foreseeability of harm as the single exclusive test – even a prima facie test – of the existence of a duty of care, the attempt to state some general principle served not to clarify the law but merely to bedevil its development: see the penetrating analysis by Brennan J in *Sutherland*[51], and speech of Lord Devlin in *Hedley Byrne*[52].

Negligent statements and economic loss - the governing requirements

In *Caparo* v. *Dickman* the appellant accountants, Touche Ross, were auditors of Fidelity, a public company. The respondent, Caparo, made a successful bid for Fidelity in reliance, it alleged, on Fidelity's accounts. Caparo commenced proceedings against Touche Ross (amongst others) alleging negligence in certifying the accounts. Caparo alleged that Touche Ross owed a duty of care to investors and potential investors, in respect of the audit. This question was tried as a preliminary issue, assuming for this purpose the facts as set out in Caparo's statement of claim. The House of Lords allowed Touche Ross's appeal.

Lord Bridge said that the damage caused by the negligently spoken or written word would normally be confined to economic loss, and so, consistently with the 'traditional' approach (see above), he observed that it was to the authorities[53] and to subsequent decisions directly relevant to this 'relatively narrow corner of the field' that their Lordships should look to determine the essential characteristics for a duty of care to ensure the accuracy of a statement (in the absence of a contractual or fiduciary relationship):

> "The salient feature of all these cases was that the defendant giving advice or information was fully aware of the nature of the transaction which the plaintiff had in contemplation, knew that the advice or information would be communicated to him directly or indirectly and knew that it was very likely that the plaintiff would rely on that advice or information in deciding whether or not to engage in the transaction in contemplation. In these circumstances, the defendant could clearly be expected, subject to any disclaimer, specifically to anticipate that the plaintiff would rely on the advice or information given for the very purpose for which he did rely. So also the plaintiff, subject again to any disclaimer, would in that situation reasonably suppose that he was entitled to rely on the advice or information communicated to him for the very purpose for which he required it.
> The situation was entirely different where a statement was put into more or less general circulation and might foreseeably be relied upon by strangers to the maker of the statement for any one of a variety of different purposes which the maker of the statement had no specific reason to anticipate. To hold the maker of a statement to be under a duty of care in respect of the accuracy of the statement to all and sundry for any purpose for which they might choose to rely on it was not only to subject him, in the classic words of Cardozo CJ to 'liability in an indeterminate amount for an indeterminate time to an indeterminate class': (*Ultramares Corp* v. *Touche*[54]; it was also to confer on the world at large a quite unwarranted entitlement to appropriate for their own purposes the benefit of the expert knowledge or professional expertise attributed to the maker of the statement."

Lord Bridge thus spoke of the necessity to prove that the defendant knew that his statement would be communicated to the plaintiff, either as an

---

53 *Le Lievre* v. *Gould* [1893] 1 QB 491; *Cann* v. *Wilson* 39 ChD 39; *Candler* v. *Crane Christmas & Co* [1951] 2 KB 164, Denning LJ dissenting; and *Hedley Byrne & Co Ltd* v. *Heller Partners Ltd* [1964] AC 465)
54 (1931) 174 NE 441, 444; 255 NY 170

individual or as a member of an identifiable class, specifically in connection with a particular transaction or transactions of a particular kind (eg. in a prospectus inviting investment) and that the plaintiff would be very likely to rely on it for the purpose of deciding whether or not to enter upon that transaction or upon a transaction of that kind.

Lord Oliver said that the significant point was the unanimous approval by the House of Lords in *Hedley Byrne* of Denning LJ's judgment in *Candler* in which he expressed the test of proximity in these words: 'did the accountants know that the accounts were required for submission to the plaintiff and use by him?' This was expanded in *Hedley Byrne*. The respondents there were not aware of the actual identity of the firm for which the credit reference was required nor of its precise purpose. Furthermore, their 'knowledge' embraced not only actual knowledge but also such knowledge as would be attributed to a reasonable person placed as the respondents were.

> "Therefore, the necessary relationship between the maker of a statement or giver of advice ('the adviser') and the recipient who acts in reliance on it ('the advisee') might typically be held to exist where (1) the advice is required for a purpose, whether particularly specified or generally described, which is made known, either actually or inferentially, to the adviser at the time when the advice is given; (2) the adviser knows, either actually or inferentially, that his advice will be communicated to the advisee, either specifically or as a member of an ascertainable class, in order that it should be used by the advisee for that purpose; (3) it is known either actually or inferentially, that the advice so communicated is likely to be acted upon by the advisee for that purpose without independent inquiry; and, (4) it is so acted upon by the advisee to his detriment. That was not, of course, to suggest that these conditions were either conclusive or exclusive, but merely that the actual decision in the case did not warrant any broader propositions.
> *Smith* v. *Bush; Harris* v. *Wyre Forest DC* did not justify any broader proposition, save that an intention that the advice should not be acted upon by anyone other than the immediate recipient could not prevail against actual or presumed knowledge that it was in fact likely to be relied upon in a particular transaction without independent verification. Thus *Smith* v. *Bush*, although establishing beyond doubt that the law might attribute an assumption of responsibility regardless of the expressed intentions of the adviser, provided no support for the proposition that

proximity was to be extended beyond circumstances in which advice was tendered for the purpose of the particular transaction or type of transaction and the adviser knew or ought to have known that it would be relied upon by a particular person or class of persons in connection with that transaction."

Duty of care in relation to negligent information and economic loss

In the ordinary category of the tort of negligence, based on *Donoghue* v. *Stevenson*, the duty is only to take care to avoid physical harm to the person or property of the person to whom the duty is owed. Such a duty of care is found widely and readily to be owed – for the fairly obvious reason that in general everyone is normally entitled to protection from careless invasion of their personal safety or that of their property, whether they have a contract with the careless person or not. Thus, the reasons or purposes for which the defendant was acting are not often relevant to whether the duty is owed in this ordinary category (though they may be relevant to whether the defendant took sufficient care): the duty is presumptively owed in all normal circumstances . However, there may be special circumstances (such as contractual terms) that so limited the defendant's actions or assumption of risks that a court might find that not even a *Donoghue* v. *Stevenson* duty was owed in the circumstances, even though eg negligence may have caused damage to property. See for example *Norwich City Council* v. *Harvey*; and *Briggs Amasco*[55], discussed below.

When exceptional categories of the tort of negligence are being alleged, the question of the purposes for which the defendant was acting becomes crucial. So, the exceptional *Hedley Byrne* duty (in regard to negligent information causing economic loss) was held in *Caparo* v. *Dickman* to depend on the purpose for which the information was given.

In *Caparo* v. *Dickman*, Lord Oliver said that, for a duty of care to exist there, it was not sufficient to ask simply whether there was a 'closeness' between adviser and advisee in the sense that the advisee had a legal entitlement to receive the information or that it was intended to serve his interest or to protect him. One had to go further and ask, in what capacity was his interest to be served and from what was he intended to be protected? Indeed the paradigmatic *Donoghue* v. *Stevenson* case of a manufactured article required, as an essential ingredient of liability, that the article had been used by the consumer in the manner in which it was intended to be used[56]. If the very purpose of providing the information was as the basis for

---

55 [1989] 1 WLR 828
56 *Grant* v. *Australian Knitting Mills Ltd* [1936] AC 85, 104; *Junior Books* v. *Veitchi* [1983] 1 AC 520, 549, 552

making investment decisions or giving investment advice, it was not difficult then to conclude also that the duty imposed upon the adviser extended to protecting the recipient against loss occasioned by an unfortunate investment decision based on carelessly inaccurate information. But that was not the purpose in *Caparo*.

Lord Jauncey also emphasised that the purpose of the audit was simply that of fulfilling the statutory requirements of the Companies Acts. What was the purpose behind the legislative requirement of an annual audit and circulation of the accounts? For whose protection were these provisions enacted? The primary purpose was almost self-evident: the informed exercise by those interested in the property of the company of their proprietary powers. It was argued that there was a wider commercial purpose, of enabling those to whom the accounts were circulated to make informed investment decisions. His Lordship found it difficult to believe, however, that the legislature could have been inspired by consideration for the public at large and investors in the market. The auditors' function was to ensure that the financial information prepared by the directors accurately reflected the company's position, in order to protect the company itself from errors or wrongdoing, and to provide the shareholders with reasonable intelligence for scrutiny of the company's affairs.

Duty of care to avoid pure economic loss

Professional advisers' liability for economic loss has been extended by *Hedley Byrne* and *Caparo* v. *Dickman* beyond their contractual engagements to third parties beyond their immediate client. The clearest applications of this are the many house surveyor and valuer cases from *Yianni* v. *Edwin Evans & Sons*[57] to *Smith* v. *Eric S Bush*[58] where valuers engaged by mortgage lenders were held to owe a duty of care direct to house purchaser in respect of pure economic losses.

Professional advice may be too narrow a definition in this context. Negligent professional acts or omissions, if advisory in nature, may be regarded as breaches of duty leading to recoverable pure economic loss: *Ross* v. *Caunters*[59] (liability of solicitor to a beneficiary under the client's will in respect of the drafting of the will). This could always prove a Trojan horse for duties to warn and other generic liabilities. (See also *Ministry of Housing & Local Govt* v. *Sharp*[60]).

57 [1982] QB 438
58 [1990] 1 A.C. 831
59 [1980] 1 Ch 297
60 [1970] 2 QB 223

A remaining problem is whether the *Hedley Byrne* principle extends beyond the category of undoubted professionals acting in advisory capacity (such as lawyers, accountants, surveyors and valuers) to include other professional and analogous activities. There is even doubt as to whether an architect or consulting engineer owes this form of liability when acting in the traditional way as a consultant on a construction project: consider eg *Pirelli* v. *Oscar Faber & Partners*[61], *London Congregational Union* v. *Harriss*[62], *Pacific Associates Inc.* v. *Baxter*[63] and *Salliss* v. *Calil*[64]. In London Congregation v. Harris, Ralph Gibson LJ said that the ordinary relationship of client and architect, or of client and consulting engineer, was not such that liability for pure economic loss would arise in tort on proof of negligent design or supervision but without proof of damage to property. The concept of negligence was not intended to afford owners of buildings rights equivalent to contract rights.

In two cases since *D & F Estates*, his Honour Judge John Newey QC has however held that designers and contractors may owe duties of care in tort direct to a building owner for pure economic losses not consequent on physical damage (in addition to the Portsea case, discussed above, which might also be interpreted that way).

(1) In *Richard Roberts Holdings Ltd* v. *Douglas Smith Stimpson Partnership*[65] Holdings claimed from their architects economic losses arising from the unsuitability of a lining of an effluent tank, designed by specialists. The contract between Holdings and the architects impliedly included a duty on the part of the architects to take the care to be expected of the ordinary competent architect in carrying out work on behalf of Holdings. His Honour said that the architects no doubt owed a similar duty to Holdings in tort. They should have investigated possible alternatives and have put up possible proposals to their clients, as to effectiveness, cost and expected life of the specialists' design.

(2) In *Frost v. Moody Homes Ltd; Hoskisson v. Donald Moody Ltd*[66] the Hoskissons bought a house on a development by the Moody companies. They alleged that Moodys provided the house with foundations which were not designed to resist heave, failed to connect its water drainage system to the main drainage system and built its first floor

61 [1983] 2 AC 1
62 [1988] 1 All ER 15
63 [1990] 1 QB 993
64 [1988] 4 Const.L.J. 125
65 (1989) 47 BLR 113
66 (1989) CILL 504

joists inadequately. His Honour said that it might be that the first purchaser of a new house from its builder places such reliance upon him to sell him a satisfactory house to his knowledge that the purchaser could, on the basis of *Hedley Byrne & Co Ltd* v. *Heller & Partners Ltd*[67], claim for economic loss as a result of the house being defective. His Honour thought that this was the position between the Hoskissons and Moodys in relation to this house. (Though in *J E Warner & anr* v. *Basildon Development Corporation & anr*[68] his Honour Judge Peter Bowsher QC said that he did not find assistance in the decision in *Frost* v. *Moody* in dealing with the rights of purchasers after the first purchaser.)

Both these decisions were given before *Caparo* v. *Dickman* and so must now be reconsidered in the light of their Lordships' statements in *Caparo*. On the other hand, the province of *Hedley Byrne* is affirmed after *Caparo* by their Lordships in *Murphy*, and *Junior Books* is treated in *Murphy* as an example of the *Hedley Byrne* principle. Hence, for example, in *Murphy* Lord Bridge observed that:

> "There might, of course, be situations where, even in the absence of contract, there was a special relationship of proximity between builder and building owner sufficiently akin to contract to introduce the element of reliance, so that the duty embraced purely economic loss. *Junior Books* v. *Veitchi* could only be understood on that basis."

Caparo refers to negligent advice and information. It appears not to require an actual report or formal tendering of advice, as such, in order for the duty of care to arise. However, it also requires the advice or information to be communicated to the person alleging that the duty is owed to him. This may mean that third party tenants, for example, would in many instances not succeed in asserting a duty of care against an ordinary architect or engineer whose reports, drawings, calculations, warnings, etc, are normally intended to be communicated only to the architect's/engineer's immediate client, and not to the tenant (even though the tenant may in fact rely on such information if it is in fact communicated). By way of contrasting example, a soils investigation report may be commissioned in the explicit knowledge that it will be disclosed to tenderers. If the tenderers are named at the outset, this may prove a likely application of the *Hedley Byrne* duty. If the tenderers are

67 [1964] AC 465
68 (1989) CILL 484

not so named, the crucial question will become whether the tenderers eventually selected were members of a sufficiently ascertainable class (in *Caparo* v. *Dickman* terms) so as to have a duty of care owed them by the soils investigators in respect of economic losses suffered by relying in tendering upon the investigations report.

Duties owed between parties in contract

Since the mid-1970s, the conventional view has been that a tortious basis of action can be chosen by a victim of negligent professional advice, even though the victim also had a contract with the adviser (see *Esso Petroleum Co.* v. *Mardon*[69] (petrol companies advice to a potential tenant), *Batty* v. *Metropolitan Property Realisations*[70] (builder/developer's failure to investigate neighbouring ground conditions before building a house) and *Midland Bank Trust Co.* v. *Hett, Stubbs & Kemp*[71] (solicitors' advice to client)).

However, there are dicta of the Privy Council in *Tai Hing Cotton Mill Ltd* v. *Liu Chong Hing Bank Ltd*[72] which have been interpreted as indicating that their Lordships did not believe there was any advantage for the law's development in searching for liability in tort where the parties were in a contractual relationship. This was said to be particularly so in a commercial relationship. Their Lordships believed it correct in principle and necessary for the avoidance of confusion in the law to adhere to the contractual analysis: on principle because it was a relationship in which the parties had, subject to a few exceptions, the right to determine their obligations to each other, and for the avoidance of confusion because different consequences followed according to whether the liability arose from contract or tort, eg in the limitation of actions.

It is probably wrong to read from these *Tai Hing* dicta any generally applicable stricture on concurrent duties in tort and contract, for the following reasons:

(1) Their Lordships were denying the tort duty in *Tai Hing* in circumstances where the contract contained no obligation of the kind alleged, and so they were not prepared to use the law of tort to provide a remedy which was not even available in the contract. It might be otherwise where there is in the contract already an obligation to take care, analogous to the tort duty being alleged (as in most contracts with

69 [1976] QB 801
70 [1978] QB 554
71 [1979] Ch 384
72 [1986] AC 80

professional advisers, see (3) below).

(2) In *Tai Hing*, no physical harm was involved: the exceptional category of duty, regarding pure economic loss (*Hedley Byrne*), was being alleged. By contrast, it would seem that the ordinary category of duty, to avoid physical harm to person or property (*Donoghue* v. *Stevenson*), would normally be owed even between parties to a contract, unless the contractual framework explicitly displaced such a duty (see eg *Norwich City Council* v. *Harvey*; and *Briggs Amasco*[73]; subject to the Unfair Contract Terms Act 1977).

(3) Even in pure economic loss cases it would seem that a concurrent duty in tort will be found if the contract is for the services of a professional adviser (and does not explicitly displace the tort duty). In this respect, it would seem that *Midland Bank Trust Co.* v. *Hett, Stubbs & Kemp*[74] remains good law. The principle was certainly assumed in *Caparo* v. *Dickman* where Lord Bridge observed that the question what, if any, duty was owed by the maker of a statement to exercise due care to ensure its accuracy arose typically in relation to statements made in the exercise of a calling or profession: 'In advising the client who employs him, the professional man owes a duty to exercise that standard of skill and care appropriate to his professional status and will be liable both in contract and in tort for all losses which his client may suffer by reason of any breach of that duty.' [emphasis added] But the case actually concerned the possibility of a duty of care being owed to third parties with whom the professional man was in no contractual relationship. (However, compare this with the dicta of Ralph Gibson LJ in *London Congregational* v. *Harriss* (above), and see *Richard Roberts Holdings* v. *Douglas Smith Stimpson Partnership* (above)). In *Murphy*, Lord Keith observed that it would seem that in a case such as *Pirelli* where the tortious liability arose out of a contractual relationship with professional people, the duty extended to take reasonable care not to cause economic loss to the client by the advice given. He said that the plaintiffs built the chimney as they did in reliance on that advice, and that the case would accordingly fall within *Hedley* Byrne v. Heller.

However, in *Tai Hing* it was also stated: 'Their Lordships do not, however, accept that the parties' mutual obligations in tort can be any greater than those to be found expressly or by necessary implication in their contract' (having cited as a reason for adhering to the contractual analysis,

73 [1989] 1 WLR 828
74 [1979] Ch 384

and not searching for liability in tort: 'the avoidance of confusion because different consequences do follow according to whether liability arises from contract or tort, eg in the limitation of actions'). Could this mean that even if a duty of care is owed in tort as well as in contract, the extent of the tortious liability (whether as to, eg, damages or limitation period) would be no greater than that in contract? If that was Lord Scarman's intention in *Tai Hing*, it would be consistent with a similar policy which he had articulated in *Parsons (Livestock) Co* v. *Uttley Ingham & Co.*[75]. Such a view would, to be established, require a more explicit recognition and explicit overruling of, eg, *Midland Bank Trust Co.* v. *Hett, Stubbs & Kemp*[76].

The importance of contractual frameworks on duties in tort

The importance of the contractual arrangements between the parties is two-fold. First, there are obvious advantages in terms of the parties being able to control the scope of their duties in framing their relationship in terms of contract rather than leaving matters to the relatively unclear law governing the tort of negligence.

Secondly, if the point is reached where arguments are made as to the existence of duties of care in tort, then the contractual arrangements between the parties may be relevant to displacing a duty of care, particularly in respect of economic loss, which might otherwise be owed (see eg *Pacific Associates Inc.* v. *Baxter* (1989) below). This was the case in *Greater Nottingham Co-op* v. *Cementation Piling & Foundations Ltd*[77] where it was held that a subcontractor owed no tortious duty to the employer and that his obligations to him were limited to those expressed in the warranty agreement executed by them both. That this is not, however, an inflexible rule is clear from cases such as *Abrahams* v. *Nelson Hurst & Marsh Ltd,*[78] where the court recognised the relevance of a contractual chain of liability but in effect reserved its right nonetheless to identify a duty of care where that represented a just and reasonable result.

In *Portsea Island Mutual Co-Operative Society Ltd* v. *Michael Brashier Associates*[79] his Honour Judge John Newey QC said that a consideration tending strongly to negative the existence of a duty in tort owed by a defendant was that at the material time he owed a duty in contract either to the plaintiff or to someone else. In support of this proposition, his Honour outlined the contractual arrangements in *Tai Hing* v. *Liu Chong Hing Bank*

75 [1978] QB 791
76 [1979] Ch 384.
77 [1989] QB 71
78 (1989) CILL 522
79 (1989) CILL 520

Ltd[80]; *Ernst & Whinney* v. *Willard Engineering (Dagenham) Ltd*[81]; *Simaan General Contracting Co* v. *Pilkington Glass Ltd (No 2)*[82]; *Greater Notts Co-Op Society* v. *Cementation Piling & Foundations Ltd*[83]; *D & F Estates* v. *Church Commissioners*[84]; and, *Pacific Associates Inc* v. *Baxter*[85]. Hence, he observed that in *Portsea Island* Brashiers (the defendant architects) were employed by the developers to whom they owed comprehensive duties in contract. Portsea (the tenant) could have invited Brashiers to enter a collateral warranty contract in respect of the superstore; for a suitable consideration they might have agreed to do so. In fact there were no contractual obligations between Portsea and Brashiers yet Portsea were in effect seeking to recover in negligence sums which they might well have been entitled to claim under a collateral agreement. Since there was no risk of injury or physical damage (the car park walls were all free-standing and people and other buildings were not likely to have been directly affected if they had collapsed), it would not have been just and reasonable that Brashiers should have owed a duty of care to Portsea.

In *Norwich City Council* v. *Harvey*; and *Briggs Amasco*[86] the plaintiff employer engaged a main contractor on JCT 63 terms. Roofing works were sub-contracted. A sub-contractor's employee, while using a blow torch, set fire to the existing and the new buildings. The fundamental issue was whether any duty of care otherwise owed by the sub-contractor to the employer had been qualified by the terms of the contracts between the parties, whereby the plaintiff accepted the risk of damage by fire and other perils to their property. May LJ, giving the judgment of the Court of Appeal, said that as between the employer and the main contractor the former accepted the risk of damage by fire to its premises arising out of and in the course of the building works. Further, although there was no privity between the employer and the sub-contractor, it was equally clear from the documents passing between the main contractors and the sub-contractors that the sub-contractors contracted on a like basis. In *Scottish Special Housing Association* v. *Wimpey Construction (UK) Ltd*[87] the House of Lords had to consider whether, as between the employer and main contractors under a contract in precisely the same terms as here, it was intended that the employer should bear the whole risk of damage by fire, even fire caused

---

80 [1986] 1 AC 80
81 (1988) 40 BLR 67
82 [1988] QB 758
83 [1989] QB 71
84 [1989] AC 177
85 [1990] 1 QB 993
86 [1989] 1 WLR 828
87 [1986] 1 WLR 995

by the contractor's negligence. The position of sub-contractors was not strictly in issue in Scottish Housing, but having considered cll.18, 19 and 20C of the same standard form Lord Keith, with whom their Lordships agreed, said[88]:

'I have found it impossible to resist the conclusion that it is intended that the employer should bear the whole risk of damage by fire, including fire caused by the negligence of the contractor or that of sub-contractors.'

May LJ added that a similar conclusion was arrived at in *James Archdale & Co Ltd* v. *Comservices Ltd* (CA) upon the construction of similar clauses. Again the issue only arose as between employer and main contractor, but approaching the question on the basis of what was just and reasonable, the mere fact that there was no strict privity between the employer and the sub-contractor should not prevent the latter from relying upon the clear basis upon which all the parties contracted in relation to damage to the employer's building caused by fire, even when due to the negligence of the contractors or sub-contractors.

In *Pacific Associates Inc & anr* v. *Baxter & anr*[89] Purchas LJ said that the engineer in the context of the contract assumed a responsibility towards the employer to execute his duties in a professional manner. Did the engineer beyond this accept a direct duty towards the contractor? Did the contractor rely upon the due performance of the engineer's duties beyond giving rights to proceed against the employer under the contract? Was an appropriate degree of proximity between the engineer and the contractor beyond the terms of contract established?

From the authorities, many on *Hedley Byrne* or extensions thereto, it was clear that the court had to find it just and reasonable to impose a duty of care. See *Peabody Donation Fund* v. *Sir Lindsay Parkinson & Co Ltd*[90]; and *Greater Notts Co-op Soc Ltd* v. *Cementation Piling and Foundations Ltd*[91], where it was held that no duty of care would be superimposed upon the existing contractual relationship (see p.413G).

The facts of the present case were clearly distinguishable from *Greater Notts Co-op* but from the policy point of view there might be a useful analogy, namely where the parties had come together against a contractual structure which provided for compensation in the event of a failure of one

88 at p.999B
89 [1990] 1 QB 993
90 [1985] AC 210, 241
91 [1989] QB 71

of the parties involved, the court would be slow to superimpose an added duty of care beyond that which was in the contemplation of the parties at the time that they came together.

The contractual structure was substantially provided by the terms of the contract which were part of the background against which the tender was made. By reason of the general conditions the contractor was in a direct relationship with the engineer (eg, GC46, GC56, GC52, GC60, PC60, etc). In other aspects the engineer worked solely as the agent for the employer (eg, the preparation of the invitations to tender and the contract document, bills of quantities, etc, which accompanied it).

There was no simple unqualified answer to the question: 'Does the engineer owe a duty to the contractor in tort to exercise reasonable skill and care?'. This question could only be answered in the context of the factual matrix, especially the contractual structure against which such duty was said to arise. Purchas LJ said that a question mark must reside over the decision in *Michael Salliss & Co Ltd* v. *Calil*[92] [that a contractor had a right to recover damages against an unfair architect]. It apparently overlooked the contractual structure against which any reliance placed by the victim upon the assumption of liability demonstrated by the proposed tortfeasor depended.

If the contractor had required an indemnity or extra contractual protection in respect of defaults by the engineer or insolvency on the part of the employer then it was open to the contractor to have stipulated for such protection. On the contrary, by accepting the invitation to tender upon the terms in the 'Instructions to Tenderers' and the contractual documents he had to be taken to have accepted the role of the engineer as defined in the contract.

PC86 was an important part of the contractual structure against which the contractor accepted the engineer in his role under the contract. The clause provided that 'neither the engineer nor any of his staff shall be in any way personally liable for the acts or obligations under the contract'. Did the protection of this clause extend to the negligent performance of those functions? In this context it was not necessary to establish that the negligence on the part of the person relying on the exclusion clause was the only negligence to which reference could be made as was the case with such a clause in ordinary contracts. The presence of the reservation was given its normal role in the overall consideration of what responsibility was accepted by the proposed tortfeasor. See *Hedley Byrne* v. *Heller,* Lord Reid[93].

Even if PC86 were not included in the contract in this case, the provisions of GC67 would be effective to exclude the creation of any direct duty upon

92 (1988) 4 Const.L.J. 125
93 at p.492

the engineer towards the contractor.

On the question of disclaimer, Lord Brandon in *Leigh & Sillavan Ltd* v. *Aliakmon Ltd*[94], commented upon the speech of Lord Roskill in *Junior Books Ltd* v. *Veitchi* Ltd[95]. There could be no doubt of the force of Lord Brandon's comment as it stood. However, with great respect to the learned and noble Lord, the absence of a direct contractual nexus between A and B did not necessarily exclude the recognition of a clause limiting liability to be imposed on A in a contract between B and C, when the existence of that contract was the basis of the creation of a duty of care asserted to be owed by A to B. The presence of such an exclusion clause whilst not being directly binding between the parties, could not be excluded from a general consideration of the contractual structure against which the contractor demonstrated reliance upon, and the engineer accepted responsibility for, a duty in tort, if any, arising out of the proximity established between them by the existence of that very contract.

His Lordship saw no justification for superimposing upon this contractual structure an additional liability in tort as between the engineer and the contractor.

The propositions established:

1. The engineer remained under contractual obligations to the employer, which gave rise to a duty to exercise skill and care and in appropriate circumstances to act fairly between the employer and the contractor. If the engineer was in breach of this duty he was liable to the employer for economic loss directly flowing from the breach. Whether this action lay in contract or tort or both would only be a relevant question in very exceptional circumstances. Their Lordships did not specifically consider this question in *Sutcliffe* v. *Thackrah*.

2. There was no reason to infer that the contractor was relying on any right to recover damages for economic loss from any breach of duty in (1) above, other than by his remedies against the employer under the contract.

3. There was no reason to infer that the engineer ever appeared to assume a direct responsibility to the contractor for any economic loss to the contractor as a result of any breach of his duty as in (1) above.

4. There was, therefore, no basis upon which a duty of care to prevent economic loss could be imposed upon the engineer in favour of the contractor which would be for all practical purposes co-terminous with the

94 [1986] 1 AC 785, 817G
95 [1983] 1 AC 520, 546

rights to be enjoyed by the contractor under the contract.

The position might well have been otherwise if GC67 or some other provision for arbitration had not been included in the contract. The position of the engineer, if the contract so provided, might well be arbitral or quasi-arbitral (see *Sutcliffe* v. *Thackrah* at p.751G). On the other hand, he might well owe a duty to exercise skill and care to a contractor who relies on his valuations and certificates just as the person operating the weighbridge was found to be liable in *Glanzer* v. *Shepard* or even to be shot at by both sides as envisaged in *Arenson* v. *Arenson*. These were all exceptional cases. It would be rare for a contract for engineering works of any substance in which a consulting engineer was appointed not to have an arbitration clause.

Russell LJ said that the engineers presented the contractors with the contract documents, and the contractors freely chose to enter into the contract with the employers. The contractors were aware that the engineers were not parties to the contract, and that accordingly any complaint that might arise against the engineers at the suit of the contractors would be an extra contractual one which would have to be resolved by a process other than a claim for breach of contract. In the event of non- or under-certification the contractors were entitled to arbitrate under clause 67. The engineers were not able to claim arbitral immunity from suit.

The contractors in reality had their rights adequately protected by the terms of their bilateral contract with the employer. If they had thought not, then they were at liberty to insist upon a tripartite contract before embarking upon the work.

The very existence of clause 67 as drafted was sufficient to dispose of this appeal. The parties having sought to regulate their relationships by a contractual process, the law should be very cautious indeed before grafting on a parasitic duty, unnecessary for the protection of the interests of the parties and, in view of clause 86, contrary to the express declarations of the engineers.

The purpose of clause 86 was, inter alia, to eliminate the possibility of the contractor pursuing a remedy of whatever kind, save fraud, against the engineers. The clause destroyed the duty of the engineers, if duty there ever was. See *Hedley Byrne*[96]. It was effective against the contractors. The clause being present in a contract freely entered into by the contractors, it was not just and reasonable that they should go behind it and take proceedings against the engineers upon the very basis which the clause sought to exclude.

96 at p.492

What degree of care is required to avoid being found negligent?

The normal criterion of negligence liability is pitched by the law at a level of reasonableness consonant with the average competence of the defendant concerned. Furthermore, that competence is to judged by the standards prevailing at the time of the alleged negligence and not with the benefit of hindsight. In other words, defendants are entitled to the benefit of the so-called "defence" of having complied with the "state of the art" applicable at the time. With regard to professional services there are abundant dicta from the courts defining the standard of care required. It has been particularly well explained by Bingham LJ in the Court of Appeal in the *Abbeystead* case (*Eckersley* v. *Binnie & Partners*[97]). Though he was dissenting, and would himself have allowed the engineers' appeal, nevertheless his observations are of general application:

> "The law requires of a professional man that he live up in practice to the standard of the ordinary skilled man exercising and professing to have his special professional skills. He need not possess the highest expert skill; it is enough if he exercises the ordinary skill of an ordinary competent man exercising his particular art. So much is established by *Bolam* v. *Friern Hospital Management Committee*[98] which has been applied and approved time without number. "No matter what profession it may be, the common law does not impose on those who practise it any liability for damage resulting from what in the result turn out to have been errors of judgment, unless the error was such as no reasonable well-informed and competent member of that profession could have made" (*Saif Ali* v. *Sydney Mitchell & Co*[99]).

> From these general statements it follows that a professional man should command the corpus of knowledge which forms part of the professional equipment of the ordinary member of his profession. He should not lag behind other ordinarily assiduous and intelligent members of his profession in knowledge of new advances, discoveries and developments in his field. He should have such awareness as an ordinarily competent practitioner would have of the deficiencies in his knowledge and the limitations on his skill. He should be alert to the hazards and risks inherent in any professional task he undertakes to the extent that

97 (1988) 18 COn LR 1
98 [1957] 1 WLR 582
99 [1980] AC 198 at 220D, per Lord Diplock)

other ordinarily competent members of his profession would be alert. He must bring to any professional task he undertakes no less expertise, skill and care than any other ordinarily competent members of his profession would bring, but need bring no more. The standard is that of the reasonable average. The law does not require of a professional man that he be a paragon, combining the qualities of polymath and prophet.

In deciding whether a professional man has fallen short of the standards observed by ordinarily skilled and competent members of his profession, it is the standards prevailing at the time of acts or omissions which provide the relevant yardstick. He is not ... to be judged by the wisdom of hindsight. This of course means that knowledge of an event which happened later should not be applied when judging acts and/or omissions which took place before that event ...; ... it is necessary, if the defendant's conduct is to be fairly judged, that the making of [any] retrospective assessment should not of itself have the effect of magnifying the significance of the ... risk as it appeared or should reasonably have appeared to ordinarily competent practical man with a job to do at the time."

However, this relatively low standard of care of the ordinarily competent practitioner applies only to obligations involving reasonable skill and care, such as the ordinary negligence responsibility (whether in contract or in tort) of a consulting engineer in respect of design. If a contractor undertakes design along with his building obligations, it does not follow that in respect of that design a contractor will enjoy this low care-based form of liability. For example, a design and build contractor may be held impliedly to have warranted the fitness for purpose of the design: *Viking Grain Storage Ltd* v. *T. H. White Installations Ltd*.[100] The application of the principles governing the required standard of care obviously depends on the particular facts of each case. The relevance of standards current at the time are well illustrated by *Wimpey Construction* v. *Poole*[101] and *Rimmer* v. *Liverpool CC*[102]. Codes of practice, British standards and other advisory documents of a public nature, such as circulars prepared by Government Departments, are of immense importance as indicators of the appropriate standard; but new methods are not in themselves wrong so long as appropriate warnings are given (*Victoria University,. Manchester* v. *Hugh Wilson & Lewis Wom-*

100 (1985) 33 BLR 103
101 [1984] 2 Lloyds Rep 499
102 [1985] QB 1

ersely[103]. One must be careful not to judge the standard with the benefit of hindsight, whether arising from revised CPs and BSs or from the consequences of the 'defect'. The dangers of doing so are particularly great in a field such as construction where the technological advances occur almost daily.

State of the art defence

How will the courts deal with changes in technology and increased knowledge in a particular field? In truth this is not so much a defence but rather the application of the rule that negligence is to be determined by reference to what could reasonably have been expected of the professional at the time of the alleged breach. Where the duty is one of strict contractual performance, the "defence" has no application since, by giving the warranty, the contractor or designer is expressly taking the risk that what he intends to do will turn out to be inadequate.

The decision in *Kimbell* v. *Hart District Council*[104] is illustrative of the operation of the approach adopted in the law of tort. There, the suspect soil did not prove to be unsuitable until the extreme weather conditions made it so. Its vulnerability lay principally in its organic content. His Honour looked to see what warning was available in the early sixties which put or should have put a local authority on notice of possible danger of construction on subsoil of this nature, and to what extent if at all construction founded in such subsoil contravened the By-Laws.

However, the 'state of the art' defence may be unavailable in respect of untried designs if the client is not warned. This is made clear by Judge Newey's decision in *Victoria University, Manchester* v. *Lewis Womersely*[105]

"For the architects to use untried or relatively untried materials or techniques could not in itself be wrong, as otherwise the construction industry could never make any progress. However, architects venturing into the untried or little tried were wise to warn their clients specifically of what they were doing and to obtain their express approval. When the architects mentioned their intention to tile to the plaintiffs, anxiety was displayed which made it all the more incumbent on the architects to be careful. The university wanted a low maintenance building and

103 (1985) 2 Con LR 43
104 (1986) CILL 302
105 (1985) 2 Con LR 43

the architects wrote saying the tiles should last the life of the building. Any doubts about the reliability of the tiles should have been resolved by not using them. Although not obliged to follow the recommendations contained in literature on the subject, the architects should certainly have taken the information into account as opposed to disregarding it. They designed the centre without features to protect from the rain; they used fondu No 1 without waterproof additive and failed to bring about necessary changes in design when the staining began. It also would seem that on no occasion did they discover that the sub-contractors were not doing their work properly. Consequently it was to be inferred that the architects did not inspect properly. Accordingly, the architects acted in breach of contract and were negligent in their design for both phases, in their supervision and failure to review the design."

Duty to warn

It appeared for a while, as a result of the decisions in *EDAC* v. *Moss*[106] and *Victoria University Manchester* v. *Wilson*[107] (in the period when the expansion of tortious negligence liabilities had reached its zenith) that the courts might impose extensive duties to warn on the various parties to the construction process. Hence, in *EDAC* v. *Moss* it was said that a contractor under an ordinary workmanship contract, who had undertaken no design obligation, could nevertheless owe a duty to warn the building owner and the architect of defects in the latter's design. However, these two decisions have been explained in the case of *University of Glasgow* v. *W Whitfield and John Laing Construction Ltd*[108] (affirmed in *Oxford University Press* v. *John Stedman Design Group*[109]) as depending upon a special relationship between the parties. Otherwise, it was said, they could not stand with more recent decisions. Furthermore the reference to a duty to warn the architect was to the architect as agent of the employer. (See also the treatment of duties to warn at first instance and in the Court of Appeal in the *Abbeystead* case).

106   (1984) 1 Const.L.J. 131
107   (1985) 2 Con LR 43
108   (1988) CILL 416
109   (1990) CILL 590

Civil Liability for Breach of the Building Regulations

An action for breach of statutory duty, on the ground that there has been a failure to comply with the Building Regulations, would (if it can be shown to be established in law) remove two of the difficulties associated with actions in negligence in the typical case:

(1)   an action could be brought where there is a recognised threat to health and safety but no actual injury. One consequence of the decision in *Murphy* is to remove the possibility of general recovery in negligence in such circumstances. For, once the threat of injury has been identified, any injury or property damage which is subsequently suffered will be treated as resulting from a failure to take precautions rather than from the threat itself. Recovery under *Donoghue* v. *Stevenson* is then barred because the cost of taking precautions is a purely economic loss.

(2)   there would be no need to establish a 'special relationship' in order to recover the costs of precautions such as is usually required for economic loss.

In *Perry* v. *Tendring D C*[110], His Honour Judge Newey QC summarised the law on liability for breach of statutory duty as follows:

"I think that the effect of the cases is clear. The question of whether an Act creates liability in damages must be decided principally by reference to its wording, but regard may be had to consideration such as the pre-existing law. If an Act makes no provision for penalties or other means of enforcement, the assumption is that an action may be brought for breach of it. If the Act provides sanctions for breach of it, the assumption is that no action will lie. Where, however, the Act is plainly intended to protect an ascertainable class of persons and there are no common law rights upon which they may rely, it may be construed as creating a cause of action for breach of statutory duty.

In *Anns'* case the parties were the lessees of a block of flats and a local authority; no builders were involved. Lord Wilberforce said at p.758:

"The position of the builder. I agree with the majority in the Court of Appeal in thinking that it would be unreasonable to impose liability in respect of defective foundations upon the council, if the builder, whose primary fault it was, should be immune from liability. So it is necessary to consider this point, although it does not directly arise in the present appeal".

Lord Wilberforce next considered whether the builder could be liable for negligence in respect of defective premises and after deciding that he could be, continued:

"In the alternative, since it is the duty of the builder (owner or not) to comply with by-laws, I would be of opinion that an action could be brought against him, in effect, for breach of statutory duty by any person for whose benefit or protection the by-law was made."

Lord Wilberforce's words were, as he himself indicated obiter and they included "in effect", but coming from such a source they obviously carry considerable weight.

In *Eames London Estates Ltd* v. *North Hertfordshire District Council* and Others[111] Judge Fay QC, Official Referee, after quoting Lord Wilberforce, held builders to be liable for breach of by-laws irrespective of negligence. He went on to say that he also held them liable in negligence. In *Worlock* v. *SAWS* Woolf J said obiter that he was satisfied that it would be wrong to regard the Building Regulations (which in 1966 took the place of building by-laws) as giving rise to a statutory duty creating an absolute liability. He said at p.109:

"In my view, when the speeches in the case of *Anns* are considered, which deal in part with the position of the builder, they are inconsistent with any such conclusion...It seems to me very difficult to accept that a person in the position of the plaintiff could establish an absolute duty against a builder by virtue of statute when the contract under which the building work was performed was one which created no such obligation".

In *Taylor Woodrow Construction (Midlands) Ltd* v. *Charcon Structures Ltd & Another*[112] Waller LJ in the Court of Appeal said:

> "Whether or not a breach of [a Building Regulation] would by itself give rise to an action for damages without proof of negligence is to say the least doubtful...I say that the question of proof if negligence is doubtful because the only expression of view which gives any support to any other view was contained in the speech of Lord Wilberforce in *Anns*...Woolf J in *Worlock* came to the conclusion that it was not an absolute statutory duty but a duty which was a duty of care, and without expressing a concluded opinion about it, it seems to me...that a regulation of this kind is very difficult to construe as a regulation imposing an absolute duty in an action for damages".

In view of Waller LJ's and Woolf J's views I feel able not to follow Lord Wilberforce's dictum and Judge Fay's judgment which was based upon it.

In my view the Public Health Act 1936 does not contain any indication that it is intended that by-laws made under powers delegated by it should give rise to claims for damages. The Act provided effective means of enforcement, including injunction. The Act was plainly intended to protect owners and occupiers of buildings, but they were not without remedies at common law, as in respect of almost all matters covered by the by-laws they could bring actions for negligence. Possibly the only exceptions are by-laws dealing with size of windows and space about buildings.

The local authority's liability in *Anns* was not for breach of statutory duty, but for negligence in the exercise of statutory powers. The builders in that case would probably have been liable in negligence.

In my opinion building by-laws did not give rise to liability in damages, but I trust that before long there will be a specific decision of the Court of Appeal on the subject."

In *Kimbell* v. *Hart DC*[113], a breach of statutory duty, under s.64, Public Health Act 1936 was also relied on. However, applying the reasoning of H.H. Judge Newey QC in *Perry* v. *Tendring DC* to a breach of s.64, Judge Smout did not construe s.64 as imposing an absolute duty. Any breach of that statutory duty without proof of negligence did not of itself give rise to a claim in damages. The plaintiffs' claim could lie only in negligence.

The Building Bye-Laws in force in this case dated back to 1953. Bye-Law 16, on clearing turf and other vegetable matter, was not to be read as requiring removal of all organic matter of vegetable origin from the subsoil. Bye-Law 18, on foundations, was directed at such a degree of settlement as impaired stability of any part of the building. Here the stability of the floor was impaired, and the slab was a foundation: see *Worlock* v. *SAWS*[114]. There had thus been on the face of it a breach of the Bye-Law. But as that did not of itself render the local authority negligent, one came back again to the state of the art in 1962.

Were the local authority negligent in failing at that time to reject plans which, as it transpired, did show that the work proposed contravened the Bye-Law? Applying the standard of care of an ordinary competent local authority possessed of the skill and knowledge that such an authority ought to have had at that time, His Honour did not find negligence. Even if the local authority had carried out detailed site investigations which had revealed up to 7% organic content in the subsoil, the local authority would not have been negligent in passing the plans. They were not put on notice at that time that subsoil with such content would be vulnerable. The plaintiffs' claim against the defendants accordingly failed.

Apart from the difficulties raised by the relatively limited scope of the relevant parts of the Building Regulations (set out above), there is therefore considerable uncertainty as to whether builders are liable at all, let alone without proof of fault, for breach of statutory duty for non-compliance with the Building Regulations. The *D & F Estates* decision in the House of Lords could be read as assuming that Lord Wilberforce was right in *Anns* v. *Merton LBC*[115] to regard the builder as under such a duty. Such an assumption seems also to have been made by H.H. Judge Bowsher QC in *Warner* v. *Basildon Development Corpn*[116].

In *Murphy* v. *Brentwood District Council* in the Court of Appeal[117], Nicholls LJ observed that an alternative to *Donoghue* v. *Stevenson* as a possible ground of liability of a builder might be breach of his statutory duty

113   (1986) CILL 302
114   (1983) 22 BLR 66 (Woolf J and CA)
115   [1978] AC 728
116   (1989) CILL 484
117   [1990] 2 WLR 944

to comply with the building regulations. But he added, significantly, that such a claim does not lie had been held by Judge Newey QC in *Perry* v. *Tendring DC*[118], following dicta in *Worlock* v. *SAWS*[119] and *Taylor Woodrow* v. *Charcon*[120]. When it is brought into force, Nicholls LJ said, s.38 of the Building Act 1984 would make a breach of duty imposed by building regulations actionable so far as it caused 'damage'. Whether damage under that section included the onset of a state of imminent danger to health or safety remained, Nicholls LJ said, to be decided.

In the House of Lords in *Murphy* the Lord Chancellor commented in the following terms:

> "It was not suggested that the Public Health Act 1936, in particular Part II, manifested any intention to create statutory rights in favour of owners or occupiers of premises against the local authority with responsibility under the Act. The basis of *Anns* was that the common law would impose a duty. While of course duties at common law might arise in respect of statutory powers or duties his Lordship found difficulty in reconciling a common law duty to take reasonable care that plans should conform with byelaws or regulations with the statute which imposed on the local authority the duty not to pass plans unless they complied with the byelaws or regulations and to pass them if they did."

Lord Bridge also expressed doubts as to a wider action for breach of statutory duty, in these terms:

> "By s.1, Defective Premises Act 1972, Parliament had in fact imposed on builders and others undertaking work in the provision of dwellings the obligations of a transmissible warranty of the quality of their work and of the fitness for habitation of the completed building. But besides being limited to dwellings, liability under the Act was subject to a limitation period of six years from the completion of the work and to the exclusion provided for by s.2. It would be remarkable to find that similar obligations, applicable to all buildings and with none of the limitations or exclusions of the 1972 Act, could be derived from the builder's common law duty of care or from the duty imposed

118   (1984) 30 BLR 118, 139
119   (1981) 260 EG 920, 926
120   (1983) 266 EG 46

by building byelaws or regulations. In *Anns* Lord Wilberforce
said that a builder could be liable for breach of statutory duty for
buildings not complying with the byelaws. But he could not
have meant that the statutory obligation to build in conformity
with the byelaws by itself gave rise to obligations in the nature
of transmissible warranties of quality. Nothing less than clear
express language, such as in s.1 of the 1972 Act, would suffice
to impose such a statutory obligation.

Lord Oliver stressed that it had to be borne in mind that neither in *Anns*
nor in *Dutton* was the local authority's liability based on the proposition that
the 1936 Act gave rise to an action for breach of statutory duty of the type
in *Cutler* v. *Wandsworth Stadium Ltd*[121], a type quite distinct from a claim
in negligence (see *LPTB* v. *Upson*[122]). The duty of the local authority was,
as stressed in *Anns*, p.758, the ordinary common law duty to take reasonable
care. His Lordship was not prepared to find a liability for breach of statutory
duty:

> "If, then, the law imposed on the person primarily responsible for
> a defective building no liability to a remote purchaser for
> expenditure incurred in making good defects which, ex hy-
> pothesi, had injured nobody, upon what principle was liability in
> tort to be imposed on a local authority for failing to exercise its
> regulatory powers so as to prevent conduct which, on this
> hypothesis, was not tortious? The instant case was, to an extent,
> stronger than *Anns*, because there the authority was under no
> duty to carry out an inspection whereas here there was a clear
> statutory duty to withhold approval of the defective design. This,
> however, could make no difference in principle and the reason-
> ing of the majority in *Anns*, which clearly linked the liability of
> the local authority to that of the builder, had equally to apply.
> The only existing principle on which *Anns* liability could be
> based was that in *Dorset Yacht*, ie that the relationship between
> the authority and the plaintiff was such as to give rise to a positive
> duty to prevent another person, the builder, from inflicting
> pecuniary injury. But in a series of subsequent decisions – n
> particular *Curran* and *Hill* – his House had been unable to find
> in the case of other regulatory agencies with powers as wide as
> or wider than those under the Public Health Acts, such a
> relationship between the regulatory authority and members of

121   [1949] AC 398
122   [1949] AC 155, 168

the public for whose protection the statutory powers were conferred (see also *Yuen Kun Yeu*).

His Lordship could see no reason why a local authority, by reason of its statutory powers under the Public Health Acts or its duties under the building regulations, should be any different. Ex hypothesi there was nothing in the purpose of the statutory provisions which supported the creation of a private law right of action for breach of statutory duty. There was equally nothing in the statutory provisions which even suggested that the purpose of the statute was to protect owners of buildings from economic loss. Nor was there any easily discernible reason why the existence of the statutory duties, in contra-distinction to those existing in the case of other regulatory agencies, should be held in the case of a local authority to create a special relationship imposing a private law duty to members of the public to prevent the conduct of another person which was not itself tortious."

It is extraordinary therefore that the matter has already been legislated on by Parliament, yet the relevant provision of the Building Act has yet to be brought into force. Section 38 does not yet apply, even though it states:

"breach of a duty imposed by building regulations, so far as it causes damage, is actionable, except in so far as the regulations provide otherwise, and

... as regards such a duty, building regulations may provide for a prescribed defence to be available in an action for breach of that duty."

Non-compliance with approved documents

The status of approved documents, in liability terms, is made plain by s.7 of the Building Act 1984:

(1) A failure on the part of a person to comply with an approved document does not of itself render him liable to any civil or criminal proceedings; but if, in any proceedings whether civil or criminal, it is alleged that a person has at any time contravened a provision of building regulations-

    (a) a failure to comply with a document that at that time was approved for the purposes of that provision may be relied upon as tending to establish liability, and

(b) proof of compliance with such a document may be
relied on as tending to negative liability.

Burden of Proof

In *Rickards* v. *Kerrier DC*[123], the High Court had to consider for the first
time an important practical point arising in respect of the new 1985 Building
Regulations. It concerned the situation where a local authority had served
a notice under s.36 of the Building Act 1984 (the Act under which the
Regulations were made). The judge held that the burden of proving non-
compliance with the Regulations was on the authority, but if the latter
showed that the works did not comply with the approved document (under
s.6 of the Act) then the burden shifted. The appellant against the notice
would then have to show compliance with the Regulations.

The Defective Premises Act 1972

The principal provisions of the Defective Premises Act 1972 concerning
dwellings were for many years of little significance since they did not apply
to houses covered by the NHBC's predecessor schemes to the Buildmark.
However, houses covered by the NHBC scheme are now governed by the
1972 Act. Furthermore, the restrictive approach to contractors' liability
adopted in the *D & F Estates* and *Murphy* cases adds significance to what
has thereby become the potentially wider liabilities arising under the Act.

Section 1 imposes a duty to build dwellings properly. A person taking
on work for or in connection with the provision of a dwelling (whether the
dwelling is provided by the erection or by the conversion or enlargement of
a building) owes a duty (if the dwelling is provided to the order of any
person) to that person; and to every person who acquires an interest (whether
legal or equitable) in the dwelling. The duty is to see that the work which
he takes on is done in a workmanlike or, as the case may be, professional
manner, with proper materials and so that as regards that work the dwelling
will be fit for habitation when completed.

However, a person who takes on any such work for another on terms that
he is to do it in accordance with instructions given by or on behalf of that
other shall, to the extent to which he does it properly in accordance with
those instructions, be treated as discharging the duty (set out above) except
where he owes a duty to that other to warn him of any defects in the
instructions and fails to discharge that duty. But a person shall not be treated
as having given instructions for the doing of work merely because he has

agreed to the work being done in a specified manner, with specified materials or to a specified design.

A person who in the course of a business of providing dwellings or installations in dwellings (or in the exercise of a statutory power of making such provision) arranges for another to take on work for or in connection with the provision of a dwelling shall be treated as included among the persons who have taken on the work.

The cause of action for breach of the duty is deemed to have accrued at the time when the dwelling was completed, but if after that time a person who has done work for or in connection with the provision of the dwelling does further work to rectify the work he has already done, the cause of action in respect of that further work is deemed to have accrued at the time when the further work was finished.

The duties imposed by the Act are in addition to any duty a person may owe otherwise. Furthermore, any term of an agreement which purports to exclude or restrict, or has the effect of excluding or restricting, the operation of any of the provisions of this Act, or any liability arising by virtue of any such provisions, shall be void.

Liability of local authorities

A great stream of case-law authorities running from *Dutton* and *Anns*, through the *Peabody and Investors in Industry* cases has been swept aside by the House of Lords decision in *Murphy*. In regard to local authorities, perhaps the greatest significance of *Murphy* is the doubt expressed by their Lordships as to whether such building control functions even attract the ordinary *Donoghue* duty in regard to actual damage and physical injury.

Hence the Lord Chancellor cautioned that he expressed no opinion on whether, if personal injury were suffered by an occupier of defective premises as a result of a latent defect, liability in respect of that injury would attach to a local authority for failure properly to carry out its public law duty of supervising compliance with the building byelaws or regulations.

Similarly, Lord Keith expressed doubts:

"The council here did not argue that a local authority owed no duty at all to persons who might suffer injury through a failure to take reasonable care to secure compliance with building byelaws. Counsel was content to accept that such a duty existed but maintained that its scope did not extend beyond injury to person or health and (possibly) damage to property other than the defective building itself. Not having heard argument on the matter, his Lordship preferred to reserve his opinion on whether any duty at all existed. So far as he was aware, there had not yet been any case against a local authority based on injury to person or health through a failure to secure compliance with building byelaws. If such a case arose, that question might require further consideration."

Lord Bridge articulated similar doubts

"The negligent performance of a local authority's statutory function could attract no greater liability than attached to the negligence of the builder. His Lordship was content for present purposes to assume, though by no means satisfied that the assumption was correct, that where the local authority had in fact approved defective plans or inspected defective foundations and negligently failed to discover the defect, their potential liability in tort was coextensive with that of the builder."

Lord Jauncey echoed Lord Keith's doubts

"In *Peabody* Lord Keith pointed out that in each case of alleged negligence the true question was whether the particular defendant owed to the particular plaintiff a duty of care having the scope contended for. In this appeal the appellant defendants had accepted that there was a common law duty of care on them in relation to the passing of the plans and their Lordships were therefore only concerned with the scope of that duty. Like Lord Keith, his Lordship preferred, in the absence of argument, to express no view as to whether the defendants in truth did owe such a duty."

Why are Approved Inspectors' liabilities different?

By virtue of the provisions in the Building Act 1984, building control functions can now be carried out by Approved Inspectors. But, their liabilities are governed by private law and not by the public law considerations which affect local authority liabilities. Hence the Approved Inspector has a contract with the builder or developer whereas the local authority does not, even though it receives fees for building control activities. Having a contract with the Approved Inspector gives some measure of control to the contractor and facilitates clarity as to the allocation of risk. Like local authorities, the Approved Inspector's liability is, by implication from the Building Regulations themselves, limited to what is necessary to secure reasonable standards of health and safety for persons in or about the building and others who may be affected by the failure to comply. However, under the Approved Inspector Regulations an Approved Inspector is required to be satisfied 'within the limits of professional skill and care'. This links the liability to the concept of professional skill and care already well defined by the courts. It implies a potentially more onerous liability for Approved Inspectors than for local authorities, precisely because local authorities have the benefit of the elasticity of discretion available by public law considerations described above.

Statutory product liability

Against this new common law background, it is instructive to recognise the limits of the new statutory regime of product liability. The policy behind *D&F* mirrors much of the statute. Equally, uncertainties raised by *D&F* as to 'other property' and the costs of 'averting danger' could cause problems under the statute.

The European Directive, and the Consumer Protection Act 1987

The European Community Directive on Product Liability has been implemented in the UK by the Consumer Protection Act 1987, Part I, which came into force on 1st March 1988. Broadly, it imposes a liability without fault – 'strict liability'. It is no defence to say that all reasonable care had been taken. It does not displace ordinary negligence liability to third parties but merely adds an alternative, easier access to compensation for the victim.

The claimant must still prove the damage, the defect and the causal relationship between them. Rights of contribution between defendants who have caused the same damage are preserved, as is the principle of contributory negligence (which reduces damages payable in proportion to any blame on the part of the victim).

The Limits on European liability:

Producers and suppliers: Producers are defined as manufacturers, importers, and any person who by using his name or mark in relation to the product holds himself out to be the producer. There is a subsidiary liability on any "supplier" of a product if the supplier does not identify the person who supplied it to him.

"Defect": There has to be a defect in the product. But, this does not mean simply a lack of quality or fitness for purpose. There is a "defect" only if the product is not as safe as persons generally are entitled to expect. Safety includes risk of damage to products within the product, and to other property.

"Damage": The liability arises only if a narrowly defined form of damage is suffered: death or personal injuries; or, damage to any item of property other than the defective product itself (subject to a lower threshold of value of the damage to the property (£275.00), to discourage small claims; and, a requirement that the property was in use by a private consumer). By contrast with *D & F*, "other property" here also excludes any other product in which the defective product is comprised and which was supplied with the defective product. So, the liability will not arise simply because a user has found quality defects in the product itself.

Defences to the European Product Liability

The Act forbids contracting out, or other simple avoidance of the liability, by conventional disclaimers (see Section 7). The emphasis here is on limiting or excluding the liability by terms, notices and other provisions. However, careful attention to the legal implications of this Act can lead to useful devices for controlling the extent to which any product can be said to be defective.

The Act provides certain limited defences. These are set out in Section 4(1):

> "(a)   that the defect is attributable to compliance with any requirement imposed by or under any enactment or with any Community obligation; or
>
> (b)   that the person proceeded against did not at any time supply the product to another; or
>
> (c)   that the supply was not in the course of a business; or
>
> (d)   that the defect did not exist in the product at the time it was first supplied by the producer to another; or
>
> (e)   that the state of scientific and technical knowledge at the relevant time was not such that a producer of products of the same description as the product in question might be expected to have discovered the defects if it had existed in his products while they were under his control; or
>
> (f)   that the defect -
>
> >   (i)   constituted a defect in a product ("the subsequent product") in which the product in question had been comprised; and
> >
> >   (ii)   was wholly attributable to the design of the

> subsequent product or to compliance by the producer
> of the product in question with instructions given by
> the producer of the subsequent product."

The last three of these defences (1) (d), (e) and (f) are likely to prove much more significant in practice than the first three (1)(a), (b) and (c). An important advantage for any potential defendant is the scope for reasonable argument as to the extent of any alleged liability. To that extent, the question whether the defect existed in the product "at the relevant time" (which broadly means the time of original supply) will leave considerable scope for argument.

The "development risk" defence was framed very narrowly in the European Community Directive: "That the state of scientific and technical knowledge at the time when [the producer] put the product into circulation was not such as to enable the existence of the defect to be discovered". This reference in effect to all scientific and technical knowledge makes the defence narrower than the normal "state of the art" defence in ordinary negligence liability actions.

However, the implementation of the "development risk" defence in the UK Act has arguably been framed too liberally for producers. The 1987 Act provides that it shall be a defence "that the state of scientific and technical knowledge at the relevant time was not such that a producer of products of the same description as the product in question might be expected to have discovered the defect if it had existed in his products while they were under his control". This seems much closer to the common law negligence test of "reasonable competence having regard to the scientific and technical knowledge available to the defendant at the relevant time". The UK Act has therefore been challenged by consumer organisations as failing to implement faithfully the European Directive.

The final defence set out in (f) is a very significant line of defence indeed. Here it is clear that careful attention to contractual and other documentation (with a legal eye) could create some solid defences. The vital need is to secure clear definition of the specification or instructions being worked to.

Duration of European product liability

Victims will be able to start an action within three years from the damage, or its discoverability if later. This is directly analogous to the provisions of the Latent Damage Act 1986. However, there will also be a long stop period applicable to product liability claims. This is different to that introduced by the Latent Damage Act 1986 for ordinary negligence claims in three respects: the long stop period is only 10 years; it does not start from breach of duty, but rather from the time the product was supplied; and, it extinguishes the right, rather than merely barring the remedy (this is significan in relation to rights of contribution between defendants).

Tort and economic loss: 8
The rise and fall of the law of negligence

John Powell

Synopsis

The last 25 years have seen major changes in the prevailing orthodoxy as to the test for establishing a duty of care and recovery of economic loss under the tort of negligence. This paper traces the changes through three periods: (1) the pre-Anns orthodoxy 1964-77; (2) the *Anns* orthodoxy 1977-1984; and (3) the new orthodoxy 1984-92, including in particular its most recent reflection in two recent House of Lords decisions.[1]

The Changing Orthodoxies

Pre-*Anns* orthodoxy: 1964-77

Prior to 1977, the test for establishing a duty of care was:

- for negligent acts and omissions: Lord Atkin's proximity test in *Donoghue* v. *Stevenson*;[2] moreover there were particular paradigms wherein it was taken that there was or was not, as the case might be, a duty of care;
- negligent misstatements: the special relationship and assumption of responsibility tests as variously expressed in *Hedley Byrne & Co. Ltd.* v. *Heller & Partners Ltd.*[3]

Under the pre-*Anns* orthodoxy in relation to recovery of economic loss, the position was that:

- such loss consequent on negligent acts and omissions was irrecoverable unless immediately consequent on physical damage: *SCM (United Kingdom) Ltd.* v. *W.J. Whittall and Son Ltd*[4] *Spartan Steel & Alloys*

---

1 The paper substantially updates a lecture delivered to the Society of Construction Law on 4 April 1989 "*The Tort Rollercoaster in a Building Context*".
2 [1932] A.C. 728
3 [1964] A.C. 465
4 [1971] 1 Q.B. 337 (C.A.);

Ltd. v. *Martin & Co (Contractors) Ltd.*[5] (although an inroad on the principle was made in *Dutton* v. *Bognor Regis U.D.C.*[6]

- such loss consequent on negligent misstatements was recoverable given satisfaction of the special relationship and assumption of responsibility tests in *Hedley Byrne & Co. Ltd.* v. *Heller & Partners Ltd.*[7]

- Generally there was no concurrent liability in tort and contract: *Bagot* v. *Stevens Scanlon & Co. Ltd.*[8] (but this was disapproved in *Esso Petroleum Co. Ltd.* v. *Mardon*)[9].

The *Anns* orthodoxy: 1977-1984.

Under this both the test for determining the existence of a duty of care (for acts and omissions as well as statements) and for recovery of economic loss was taken as Lord Wilberforce's two stage test in *Anns* v. *Merton London Borough Council*[10]. The *Anns* orthodoxy is reflected in a large number of building cases including *Batty* v. *Metropolitan Property Realisations Ltd.*[11] and *Junior Books Ltd* v. *Veitchi Co Ltd.*[12] As to negligent statements, see the accountants' negligence case of *Scott Group Ltd.* v. *MacFarlane*[13] and *JEB Fasteners Ltd.* v. *Marks Bloom & Co.*[14]

The new orthodoxy: 1984-92.

The new orthodoxy as reflected in cases subsequent to *Anns* and *Junior Books* entails a considerable narrowing of the test for a duty of care and limitation of the circumstances for recovery of pure economic loss on the basis of the tort of negligence. While *Anns* and *Junior Books* have not been overruled, both must be regarded as consigned to (a Frankensteinesque?) cold storage for the foreseeable future.

In chronological order of the judgments, the cases reflecting the new orthodoxy are:

5 [1973] 1 Q.B. 27 (C.A.)
6 [1972] 1 Q.B. 373 (C.A.))
7 [1964] A.C. 465
8 [1966] 1 Q.B. 197
9 [1976] 1 Q.B. 801 (C.A.)
10 [1978] A.C. 728 (H.L.).
11 [1978] Q.B. 554 (C.A.)
12 [1983] 1 A.C. 520 (H.L.).
13 [1978] 1 N.Z.L.R. 553
14 [1981] 3 ALL E.R. 289 (Woolf J.).

House of Lords/Privy Council:

18.10.84   *Governors of the Peabody Donation Fund* v. *Sir Lindsay Parkinson & Co. Ltd* [1985] A.C. 210 (H.L. (E));

1.7.85   *Candlewood Navigation Corpn* v. *Mitsui O.S.K. Lines Ltd. ("The Mineral Transporter")* [1986] A.C. 1 (P.C.);

3.7.85   *Tai Hing Cotton Mill Ltd.* v. *Liu Chong Hing Bank Ltd* [1986] A.C. 80 (P.C.);

24.4.86   *Leigh and Sillavan Ltd.* v. *Aliakmon Shipping Co. Ltd.* [1986] A.C. 785 (H.L. (E));

8.4.87   *Curran* v. *Northern Ireland Co-ownership Housing Association Ltd.* [1987] A.C. 718 (H.L. (N.I.));

10.6.87   *Yeun Kun Yeu* v. *Attorney-General of Hong Kong* [1988] A.C. 175 (P.C.)

28.4.88   *Hill* v. *Chief Constable of West Yorkshire* [1989] A.C. 53 (H.L.)

14.7.88   *D & F Estates* v. *Church Commissioners* [1989] A.C. 177 H.L.(E));

17.3.89   *Calveley* v. *Chief Constable of Merseyside Police* [1989] 1025 (H.L.)

20.4.89   *Smith* v. *Bush; Harris* v. *Wyre Forest D.C.* [1989] 2 W.L.R. 790 (H.L.)

9.2.90   *Caparo Industries Plc* v. *Dickman* [1990] 2 W.L.R. 358 (H.L.) (see also C.A. judgments on 29.7.88: [1989] 2 W.L.R. 316)

19.7.90   *La Banque Financiere* (formerly *Banque Keyser Ullmann*) v. *Westgate* [1990] 3 W.L.R. 364 (H.L.) (see also C.A. judgment on 28.7.88: [1988] 2 Lloyd's Rep. 513)

5.4.90   *Davis* v. *Radcliffe* [1990] 1 W.L.R. 821 (P.C.)

26.7.90   *Murphy* v. *Brentwood D.C.* [1991] 1 AC 398

26.7.90   *Department of the Environment* v. *Thomas Bates and Son Ltd.* [1991 1 AC 499 (H.L.) (see also C.A. judgment [1989] 1 All E.R. 1075)

Court of Appeal:

31.7.85   *Muirhead* v. *Industrial Tank Specialities Ltd.* [1986] Q.B. 507 (C.A.);

20.12.86   *Investors in Industry Commercial Properties Ltd.* v. *South Bedfordshire D.C.* [1986] Q.B. 1034 (C.A.);

26.11.87   *Jones* v. *Department of Employment* [1989] Q.B. 1 (C.A.);

17.2.88   *Simaan Contracting Co* v. *Pilkington Glass Ltd.* [1988] 2 W.L.R. 761 (C.A.)

23.3.88   *Greater Nottingham Co-operative Society* v. *Cementation Piling and Foundations* [1989] Q.B. 71 (C.A.)

26.2 88   *Al-Khandari* v. *J.R. Brown & Co* [1988] Q.B. 665 (C.A.);
15.12.88   *Pacific Associates Inc* v. *Baxter* [1989] 1 W.L.R. 828 (C.A.)
21.12.88   *Norwich City Council* v. *Harvey* [1989] 1 W.L.R. 828 (C.A.)
22.3.89   *Reid* v. *Rush & Tompkins Plc* [1989] 2 Lloyd's Rep. 167
            (C.A).
22.3.89   *National Bank of Greece S.A.* v. *Pinios Shipping Co. No 1 The
            Maira* [1989] 3 W.L.R. 185 (liability in tort was not dealt with
            on the further appeal to the H.L.: [1989] 3 W.L.R. 1330).

The rest of this paper explores particular aspects of the new orthodoxy. Before doing so, however, particular features of the *Anns* orthodoxy need to be identified.

Features of *Anns*

The unique features of the *Anns* decision related to the formulation of the duty of care and of the nature of the damage which could give rise to a cause of action in negligence to an owner or occupier against a local authority and/ or builder.

Duty of care

Lord Wilberforce expressed what for a while came to be accepted as an apparently universally applicable two stage test for determining whether a duty of care existed on particular facts. The test essentially entailed, at the first stage, a determination of whether there was a relationship of proximity sufficient to give rise to a prima facie duty and, at the second stage, an evaluation of any negativing policy considerations.[15]

From this and an analysis of the Public Health Act 1936 and byelaws made thereunder, there followed the conclusion that a local authority might incur liability in the tort of negligence arising from a negligent exercise of a statutory power and arising from a negligent failure to exercise a statutory power. Owing to the statutory context, a claim in negligence based on *Anns* was sometimes called a statutory cause of action. This was mistaken. Rather (and as recognised by the House of Lords in *Murphy*), *Anns* illustrates the derivation of a common law cause of action from the discharge of statutory functions and not a statutory cause of action.

While the main focus of Lord Wilberforce's speech in *Anns* was on a local authority's duty of care in the performance by its building inspectors of

15 see [1978] A.C. 728 at 752

functions under the 1936 Act, it also extended to the builder's position. The conclusion reached was that both a local authority and a builder might incur liability in the tort of negligence arising from breach of a duty of care arising from the performance of work which did not comply with the statutory requirements of the 1936 Act and byelaws made thereunder.

Nature of damage

The second unique aspect of the *Anns* decision concerned the nature of damage sufficient to give rise to the relevant cause of action. This was analysed by Lord Oliver in *D & F Estates* v. *Church Commissioners*[16] as follows:

"A number of points emerge from this:

1. The damage which gives rise to the action may be damage to the person or to property on the ordinary *Donoghue* v. *Stevenson* principle. But it may be damage to the defective structure itself which has, as yet, caused no injury either to person or to other property, but has merely given rise to a risk of injury.
2. There may not even be "damage" to the structure. It may have been inherently defective and dangerous *ab initio* without any deterioration between the original construction and the perception of risk.
3. The damage to or defect in the structure, if it is to give rise to a cause of action, must be damage of a particular kind, i.e. damage or defect likely to cause injury to health or - possibly - injury to other property (an extension arising only by implication from the approval by this House of the decision of the Court of Appeal in *Dutton* v. *Bognor Regis U.D.C.*[17]
4. The cause of action so arising does not arise on delivery of the defective building or on the occurrence of the damage but upon the damage becoming a "present or imminent risk" to health or (semble) to property and it is for that risk that compensation is to be awarded.
5. The measure of damage is at large, but by implication from the approval of the dissenting judgment in the Canadian case referred to (*Rivtow Marine Ltd.* v. *Washington Iron Works*[18]) it

16 [1989] AC 177
17 [1972] 1 Q.B. 373
18 [1973] 6 W.W.R. 692

must at least include the cost of averting the danger.

These propositions involve a number of entirely novel concepts. In the first place, in no other context has it previously been suggested that a cause of action in tort arises in English law for the defective manufacture of an article which causes no injury other than injury to the defective article itself."[19]

The New Orthodoxy: Existence Of a Duty Of Care

The new orthodoxy has proceeded from:
(1) deprecation of the assumed universality of the *Anns* test: *Peabody, Tai Hing, Aliakmon, Curran, Yeun Kun Yeu; Hill; Murphy*;
to:
(2) emphasis of the importance of other criteria for determining the existence or otherwise of a duty of care:

    (a)   whether it is just and reasonable to impose a duty of care (*Peabody, Curran*);

    (b)   a contractual relationship (*Candlewood, Aliakmon*);

    (c)   a close and direct relationship of proximity (*Yeun Kun Yeu*);

    (d)   voluntary assumption of responsibility (*Simaan, Greater Nottingham, Banque Financiere* but cf. *Smith*);

(3) a composite test involving the three elements of (a) reasonable foresight (b) proximity (embracing assumption of responsibility) and (c) just and reasonable (*Caparo, Smith* v. *Bush*).

Policy is, however, still recognised as sometimes having a role (*Candlewood, Hill, Calveley*).

Particularly influential in the formulation of the new orthodoxy have been judgments delivered by members of the High Court of Australia in *Council of the Shire of Sutherland* v. *Heyman*[20] (a case on almost identical facts to those in *Anns*). The following passage from Brennan J's judgment in that case was quoted with approval by Lord Keith in *Yeun Kun Yeu*:

> "Of course, if foreseeability of injury to another were the exhaustive criterion of a prima facie duty to act to prevent the

19 (ibid. at 390)
20 (1985) 59 A.L.J.R. 564

occurrence of that injury, it would be essential to introduce some kind of restrictive qualification - perhaps a qualification of the kind stated in the second stage of the general proposition in *Anns*. I am unable to accept that approach. It is preferable, in my view, that the law should develop novel categories of negligence incrementally and by analogy with established categories, rather than by a massive extension of a prima facie duty of care restrained by indefinable "considerations which ought to nega-tive, or to reduce or limit the scope of the duty or the class of person to whom it is owed.'"[21]

The composite test as expressed in *Caparo* represents an amalgam of the restrictive criteria variously expressed in recent cases. Identification of the correct test is, however, less important than observation of the general restrictive trend of the new orthodoxy. *Banque Financiere* is noteworthy for the endorsement of the *Hedley Byrne* assumption of responsibility test, in general previously seen as specific to the determination of the existence of a duty of care in the case of negligent misstatements, as applicable also to negligent acts and omissions. However, in view of Lord Griffiths's speech in *Smith* v. *Bush* (a surveyor's negligence case), assumption of responsibil-ity cannot be regarded as a definitive test. He concluded that the composite test was the relevant test.[22]

The New Orthodoxy: Economic Loss

The decision itself in *Anns* also opened the gateway to recovery of pure economic or pecuniary loss for negligent acts or omissions. The major inroad on the pre-*Anns* orthodoxy on the subject was the majority decision of the House of Lords in the Scottish appeal of *Junior Books Ltd* v. *Veitchi Co Ltd*.[23] In retrospect the case proved to be the high water mark of judicial development of *Anns*.

The case concerned a claim in delict by a building employer against a nominated subcontractor to recover the cost of relaying a defective floor laid by the latter. It was not alleged that the floor posed a danger of injury to person or damage to other property. The defenders contended that the employer's pleading disclosed no cause of action. The majority of the House of Lords, however, considered that the pleading did disclose a cause of action on the basis that the duty of care in tort did extend to avoiding pure

21 (1985) 59 A.L.J.R. 564, 588
22 see [1989] 2 W.L.R. 790 at 813
23 [1983] 1 A.C. 520

economic loss consequent upon defects in the work.

To the dissenting judge, Lord Brandon, the absence of an allegation of danger to person or damage to other property was fatal to the success of the claim. In a passage which has become the leitmotif of the new orthodoxy, he said:

> "My Lords, it appears to me clear beyond doubt that, there being no contractual relationship between the respondents and the appellants in the present case, the foundation, and the only foundation, for the existence of a duty of care owed by the defenders to the pursuers, is the principle laid down in the decision of your Lordship's House in *Donoghue* v. *Stevenson* [1932] A.C. 562.
>
> Put shortly, that wider principle is that, when a person can or ought to appreciate that a careless act or omission on his part may result in physical injury to other persons or their property, he owes a duty to all such persons to exercise reasonable care to avoid such careless act or omission.
>
> It is, however, of fundamental importance to observe that the duty of care laid down in *Donoghue* v. *Stevenson* [1932] A.C. 562 was based on the existence of physical injury to persons or their property.... It has further, until the present case, never been doubted, so far as I know, that the relevant property for the purpose on which the decision in *Donoghue* v. *Stevenson* was based, was property other than the very property which gave rise to the danger of physical damage occurred"[24].

The denouement of *Junior Books* and *Anns* and the reversion (almost but not quite) to the pre-*Anns* orthodoxy as to recovery of economic loss can be traced through the following stages:

(1) *Candlewood Navigation Corpn* v. *Mitsui O.S.K. Lines Ltd.*[25]

> "[*Junior Books*] may be regarded as having extended the scope of duty somewhat, but any extension was not in the direction of recognising a title to sue in a party who suffered economic loss because his contract with the victim of the wrong was rendered less profitable or unprofitable. It is therefore not in point here."[26]

(2) Robert Goff L.J.'s analysis of *Junior Books* in *Muirhead* as based on

24 (ibid. at 549)
25 [1986] A.C. 1 (P.C.)
26 (ibid at 24-5).

physical damage or voluntary assumption of responsibility and the actual decision in that case denying recovery of economic loss in a claim against a manufacturer of a defective product.

(3) Application of the principle that in order to enable a person to claim in negligence for loss caused to him by reason of loss of or damage to property, he must have had either the legal ownership of or possessory title to the property concerned at the time when the loss or damage occurred. It is insufficient for him to have had only contractual rights to the property: Candlewood (time charterer) Leigh and Sillavan (c. and f. buyer)

(4) Specific denial of economic loss in cases arising from analogous contexts to those in *Junior Books: Simaan, Greater Nottingham Co-op.*

(5) *D & F Estates* in which the House of Lords:

- dismissed claims in tort against a builder for recovery of economic loss by the plaintiff owner and the plaintiff occupiers;
- treated *Anns* to critical analysis insofar as it affirmed a cause of action based on damage consisting of present or imminent danger to health and safety of owners or occupiers;
- limited scope *Junior Books* to its "unique" facts and to point of virtual inutility as an authority.

Murphy in which a specially constituted 7 man House of Lords decided, in the words of Lord MacKay:

> "to depart from *Anns* in so far as it affirmed a private law duty of care to avoid damage to property which causes present or imminent danger to the health and safety of owners or occupiers, resting upon local authorities in relation to their function of supervising compliance with building byelaws or regulations, that *Dutton* v. *Bognor Regis Urban District Council* should be overruled and that all decisions subsequent to Anns which purported to follow it should be overruled."[27]

The present position as to recovery of economic loss seems as follows:

(1) it may be recovered if immediately consequential upon physical injury or damage;

(2) apart from circumstances in (1), economic loss may be recovered where there is an assumption of responsibility or a special relationship as in *Hedley Byrne*, or deemed assumption of responsibility or under the composite *Caparo* and *Smith* v. *Bush* test;

(3) such a relationship may arise in the contexts involving not only negligent

27 [1991] 1 AC 398

misstatements but also negligent acts and omissions; but in assessing whether such a relationship arises the courts will take into account all the circumstances of the case, including the contractual context if any;
(4) nevertheless, apart from professional relationships,the courts are going to be slow to allow recovery of economic loss other than in the circumstances in (1).

Certain points should be noted in relation to *Murphy*:

-      The emphasis on no reasonable prospect of intermediate (i.e. between the relevant act or omission and consequent physical damage) examination as an essential feature of the species of liability in negligence established by *Donoghue* v. *Stevenson*. Appreciation of an imminent danger indicated an intermediate examination.

-      The anxiety to have consistency of approach as between claims in tort against manufacturers of chattels and claims against builders and others involved in a building operation.

-      Recognition of the limitations of "the complex structure theory" mooted in *D & F Estates* as a basis to explain *Anns*. However, there is some scope for its development. Thus Lord Bridge said:

       "A critical distinction must be drawn here between some part of
       a complex structure which is said to be a 'danger' only because
       it does not perform its proper function in sustaining the other
       parts and some distinct item incorporated in the structure which
       positively malfunctions so as to inflict positive damage on the
       structure in which it is incorporated. Thus, if a defective central
       heating boiler explodes and damages a house or a defective
       electrical installation malfunctions and sets a house on fire, I see
       no reason to doubt that the owner of the house, if he can prove
       the damage was due to the negligence of the boiler manufacturer
       in the one case or the electrical manufacturer on the other, can
       recover damages on *Donoghue* v. Stevenson [1932] A.C. 562
       principles."; see also judgments of Lord Keith, Lord Oliver and
       Lord Jauncey.

-      Lord Bridge allowed one exception to the general principle that economic loss arising from a building defect was irrecoverable in the absence of (as he said) "a special relationship of proximity":

       "if a building stands so close to the boundary of the building
       owner's land that after discovery of the dangerous defect it
       remains a potential source of injury to persons or property on

neighbouring land on the highway, the building owner ought, in principle, to be entitled to recover in tort from the negligent builder the cost of obviating the danger, whether by repair or demolition, so far as that cost is necessarily incurred in order to protect himself from potential liability to third parties."

However, Lord Oliver reserved his view on the point, adding: "although at the moment I am not convinced of the basis of making such a distinction."

Relevance Of Contract

In deciding whether a duty of care is owed by D to P it may be relevant to take into account:
- the terms of a contract between P and D, or between one of them and a third party; or even that
- P and D have had the opportunity by contract or contracts to regulate the relationship giving rise to the alleged duty of care.

Contract between plaintiff and defendant

A development consonant with the *Anns* orthodoxy, although not dealt with in *Anns* itself, was the recognition in several circumstances, in particular professional-client relationships, of a concurrent duty of care in tort owed by one party to a contract to another notwithstanding an equivalent duty in contract. The leading case remains Oliver J.'s decision in *Midland Bank Trust Co. Ltd.* v. *Hett, Stubbs & Kemp*[28]. He held that a solicitor owes to his client not only a contractual duty to exercise reasonable care and skill but also an equivalent duty in tort. The decision led to the still generally accepted view that the same applied to every professional person. Moreover, economic loss is recoverable on the basis of such duty (as recently recognised in *Murphy* per Lord Keith).

From the viewpoint of precedent, Oliver J. was assisted in arriving at his conclusion by *Esso Petroleum* v. *Mardon*[29] in which the Court of Appeal disapproved earlier cases supporting the proposition that a professional person's duty to his client lay in contract only. Among them was *Bagot* v. *Stevens Scanlon & Co. Ltd.*[30]. In that case, on the trial of a preliminary issue of whether the action was barred by limitation, Diplock L.J. held that an

28 [1979] Ch. 384
29 [1976] 1 Q.B. 801
30 [1966] 1 Q.B. 197

architect employed under a contract with the employer to supervise the laying of a drainage system owed him a duty in contract only and not in tort. It followed that since the limitation period for an action based on contract applied, the action was statute barred and was dismissed. Although not formally overruled, it has not in recent years been regarded as good law. Architects' and engineers' negligence cases are generally pleaded both in contract and in tort and have been decided without questioning the availability of the concurrent claim in tort, e.g. *Pirelli General Cable Works Ltd v. Oscar Faber & Partners*[31] (engineers); *London Congregational Union Inc.* v. *Harris and Harris*[32] (architects).

A perhaps underestimated factor favouring the imposition upon a professional person of a concurrent duty of care in tort is its likeness in expression to the duty (although not necessarily the only duty) in contract, namely a duty, implied if not express, to exercise reasonable skill and care. Likeness of expression has enticed an association obtruding on the exclusivity of the contractual analysis which might otherwise have prevailed.

Establishment of a concurrent duty of care is not confined to professional relationships. Thus in several building cases it has been held that a non-professional party to a contract owed a concurrent duty of care to the other party and the latter has recovered economic loss caused by breach of such duty. Examples are *Batty* v. *Metropolitan Property Realisations Ltd.*[33] (developer to purchaser); *Equitable Debenture Assets Corp. Ltd.* v. *William Moss Group Ltd.*[34] (main contractor to employer); *Victoria University of Manchester* v. *Hugh Wilson & Lewis Womersley*[35] (tiling sub-contractor to main contractor); but cf. *Lynch* v. *Thorne*[36]. O'Connor L.J. went further in *Forsikringsaktieselskapet Vesta* v. *Butcher*[37]:

"I regard as a clearly established principle that where under the general law a person owes a duty to another to exercise reasonable care and skill in some activity, a breach of that duty gives rise to a claim in tort notwithstanding the fact that the activity is the subject matter of a contract between them. In such a case the breach of duty will also be a breach of contract." (ibid. at 571).

Relevance: What is the point of raising a concurrent duty of care in tort?

31 [1983] A.C. 1 (H.L.)
32 [1988] 1 All.E.R. 15 (C.A.)
33 [1978] Q.B. 554 (C.A.)
34 (1984) 2 Con. L.R. 1
35 (1984) 2 Con. L.R. 43
36 [1956] 1 W.L.R. 303
37 [1988] 3 W.L.R. 565 (C.A.)

Over the last decade or so, it has proved relevant to do so in the contexts of limitation of actions, contributory negligence and contribution claims in respect of breach of duties arising before 1 January 1979. Only in rare cases has the scope of the concurrent duty in tort been held to extend beyond duties under the relevant contract such as to require more for its discharge than was required under the contract.

Limitation of actions: The availability of a concurrent claim in the tort of negligence has foremost importance in relation to limitation of actions. It may enable a client's claim to succeed, which if founded in contract alone would fail because there would be a good limitation defence. This is a consequence of damage being an essential ingredient of the tort of negligence and the damage may only have occurred within the limitation period applicable to it whereas the relevant breach sufficient to complete the cause of action in contract may have accrued outside the limitation period applicable to it: e.g. *London Congregational Union Inc.* v. *Harris and Harris*[38].

Contributory negligence: Until *Forsikringsaktieselskapet Vesta* v. *Butcher*[39], there was support for the view that the defence of contributory negligence could not be raised to a claim in contract (*A.B. Marintrans* v. *Comet Shipping Co. Ltd.*[40]) and, in any event, could not be raised unless a claim in tort were pleaded (*Victoria University of Manchester* v. *Hugh Wilson & Lewis Womersley*[41]). *Vesta* is now authority for the proposition that a defence of contributory negligence can be raised to a claim in contract except where the defendant's liability arises from some contractual provision which does not depend on negligence on the part of the defendant (e.g. an indemnity as in *Basildon D.C.* v. *J.E. Lesser (Properties) Ltd*[42]).

Contribution: The right to claim contribution under the Law Reform (Married Women and Tortfeasors) Act 1935 only arose between tortfeasors. Unlike the Civil Liability (Contribution) Act 1978, it did not give a right of contribution as between a tortfeasor and a contract breaker or between two contract breakers. The 1935 Act was repealed with effect from the coming into force of the 1978 Act on January 1, 1979. But the 1978 Act preserves the position which prevailed before then. Thus no right of contribution arises against a contract breaker based on his contractual duty where the relevant contractual duty was assumed before then. In such cases, in order to establish a right to contribution it will be necessary to establish a concurrent duty of care in tort.

38 [1988] 1 All.E.R. 15 (C.A.)
39 [1988] 3 W.L.R. 565 (C.A.)
40 [1985] 1 W.L.R. 1270 (C.A.)
41 (1984) 2 Con. L.R. 43
42 [1985] Q.B. 839)

Scope of duty: It is difficult to envisage circumstances in which a concurrent duty of care in tort may be seen as requiring the taking of steps for its discharge extending beyond those required to discharge the duties express or implied in the contract, including in particular the duty to exercise reasonable care and skill. Yet there are rare examples in which it has been so held: see *Kensington and Chelsea AHA* v. *Wettern Composites Ltd.*[43]; *Eckersley* v. *Binnie and Partners*[44] (first instance) but cf. Bingham L.J. on appeal[45]. Nevertheless the overwhelming balance of authority is against imposing a concurrent duty in tort extending wider in scope than the relevant contract.

The minimalist and maximalist positions

Two broad positions are discernible as to imposition of a concurrent duty of care in tort as between parties to a contract, particularly a standard building contract in which the terms are set out in detail. These may be characterised as the minimalist and maximalist positions.

The minimalist position would admit the imposition of such a duty given fulfilment of usual criteria for a duty of care and would not regard the mere existence of a contract as a decisive negativing factor. Nevertheless, the terms of the contract would be regarded as circumscribing the parameters of the duty in tort. In contrast the maximalist position would regard the existence of a contract as allowing no room for a concurrent duty of care in tort. There are several examples in a building context illustrating the minimalist position. The maximalist position is plainly inconsistent with cases in which a concurrent duty of care in tort has been held to exist. Nevertheless it derives support from the trend of recent cases, particularly cases denying the imposition of a duty of care as between particular persons within a matrix of contracts in a building context although not in a contractual relationship with each other. Moreover, there are instances of its specific endorsement.

The minimalist position regards inconsistency as the crucial factor. Inconsistency in result as between application of the contractual analysis and application of the analysis in tort based on a concurrent duty of care will be avoided. It can be avoided by restricting or excluding that duty so as to achieve the result on the contractual analysis. Clearly the terms of the contract will prevail where they expressly exclude liability in tort. However, contractual silence may be enough to produce inconsistency and thus

43 [1985] 1 All. E.R. 346
44 (1987) CILL 332
45 (1988) 18 Con LR, 1.

preclude a wider duty in tort. This is easily rationalised on the basis of contractual opportunity or intention: the parties could have agreed to wider duties under the contract corresponding to the wider duty contended for in tort. The fact that the contract does not, whether expressly or impliedly, incorporate such wider duties is indicative of a contrary intention. To impose a wider duty in tort would be inconsistent with such contrary intention.

The minimalist position is illustrated by two cases in a building context. Both required consideration of the relevance to the employer's claim in tort of a contract, in the first a main contract and in the second a collateral warranty. In the first case, *William Hill Organisation Ltd.* v. *Bernard Sunley & Sons Ltd.*[46], the issue of a final certificate precluded a claim in contract. The plaintiff employers sought to circumvent this difficulty by claiming in tort against the defendant main contractors. Cumming Bruce L.J in a judgment of the court rejecting the claim, said:

> "the plaintiffs pleaded a case in tort. The short answer to this case is that the breaches relied upon arose out of the contract. It was only by reference to the alleged obligations of the defendants under the contract in writing between the parties that the case could be pleaded at all. The allegations of negligence expressly related back to the breaches of contract pleaded in ... the statement of claim. So, on their pleaded case in tort, it was necessary to prove the allegations defined in the contract itself and the alleged failures to comply with the specification, bills of quantities, contractual drawings and the District Surveyor's requirements in relation thereto. There were no pleaded allegations of any fact which added to or modified the contractual duty. The contract itself circumscribed the boundaries of that duty, and defined its content. Clause 24 of the contract set a time limit for complaints relating to the failure to comply with the contractual obligations, and by Clause 24(g) the parties expressly agreed the conditions which alone had the effect of extending the time for relief for breaches of the contract. In these circumstances, it is not open to the plaintiffs in effect to disregard those clauses of the contract which provided for the conclusive effect of the Final Certificate but to claim a remedy for breaches which were only capable of ascertainment by reference to the contract itself.
>
> ... In principle, we can see no reason why, on the facts of this case, the obligations of the parties extended more widely than those

which they had expressly agreed between them. The plaintiffs are not entitled to claim a remedy in tort which is wider than the obligations assumed under their contract."[47]

From the report it does not appear that the maximalist position was argued.

In the second case, *Greater Nottingham Co-operative Society* v. *Cementation Piling and Foundations*[48], the employers sought to recover in tort from piling subcontractors financial loss arising from delay and change in the piling system caused by the subcontractors' negligence in executing the original piling system. The employers failed to recover such loss. There was a direct collateral warranty given by the sub-contractors to the employers whereby the sub-contractors warranted that they would exercise reasonable skill and care in the design of the sub-contract works and the selection of materials and goods therefor. But the warranty was silent as to the manner of execution of the sub-contract works. The silence of the warranty on the point was held by the Court of Appeal to be decisive in negating any concurrent duty of care in tort as to the manner of execution of the works. Purchas L.J. rationalised his conclusion primarily in terms of policy:

"The terms of the direct contractual relationship between the sub-contractors and the employers involve [the particular warranties] and no other obligations imposed upon the sub-contractors by way of a direct duty toward the employers. ... in considering whether there should be a concurrent but more extensive liability in tort as between the two parties arising out of the execution of the contract, it is relevant to bear in mind - (a) the parties had an actual opportunity to define their relationship by means of contract and took it; and (b) that the general contractual structure as between the employers, the main contractors and the sub-contractors as well as the professional advisers provided a channel of claim which was open to the employers ... Although this is new ground, ... I do not believe that it would be in accordance with the present policy to extend *Junior Books Ltd* v. *Veitchi Co Ltd.* [1983] 1 A.C. 520 rather than to restrict it. This does give rise to an apparent inconsistency, namely the effect of enhancing the close relationship upon which Lord Roskill based his duty in tort in *Junior Books Ltd* v. *Veitchi*

47 (ibid. at pp 29-30)
48 [1989] Q.B. 71 (C.A.)

Co. Ltd. by adding a direct contractual relationship does not confirm a duty to avoid economic loss but negatives that liability. But in this compartment of consideration it is not only the proximity of the relationship giving rise to reliance which is critical but also the policy of the law as to whether or not in these circumstances damages for pecuniary loss ought to be recoverable."[49].

He also rationalised his conclusion in terms of the absence of an assumption of responsibility. Woolf L.J. regarded this as the critical issue:

"Did the sub-contractors assume a direct responsibility to the employers for economic loss? Where, as here, the subcontractor has entered into a direct contract and expressly undertaken a direct but limited contractual responsibility to the building owner, I regard the direct contract as being inconsistent with any assumption of responsibility beyond that which has been expressly undertaken. This does not affect the sub-contractor's normal liability in tort but does negative the existence of the exceptional circumstances needed for liability for economic loss".[50]

Mann L.J. concluded that there was no duty both because there was no assumption of responsibility and because it was not just and reasonable to impose such duty:

"However where there is a privity, then in my view the rights and obligations of the parties in regard to economic loss should be solely dependent upon the terms of the privity. I recognise that to breach a contract may also be a delictual act. That is a proposition quite different from asserting that there can be a duty in tort giving rise to a liability to compensation for economic loss in circumstances where the contract between the parties is silent. Contractual silence in my view is adverse to the establishment of a close relationship for the purposes of the law in regard to economic loss.[51]"

The minimalist position is also illustrated by what may collectively be called the fire risk cases. In such cases it has been held that a clause in a

49 (ibid. at 99)
50 (ibid. at 106)
51 (ibid. at 109)

contract requiring one party to insure against the risk of fire, including fire caused by the negligence of the other party. is inconsistent with the imposition on the latter of a duty of care such as to make him liable in negligence for damage caused by the fire. Examples are, in a landlord and tenant context, *Mark Rowlands Ltd.* v. *Berni Inns Ltd.*[52], and, in a building context, *Scottish Special Housing Association* v. *Wimpey Construction UK Ltd.*[53], *Surrey Heath BC* v. *Lovell Construction Ltd and Hayden Young Ltd.*[54]. Note also (though a tort claim does not appear to have been argued) *James Archdale & Co Ltd.* v. *Comservices Ltd*[55]. A clause in the main contract imposing the duty to insure against fire on the employer may also be a decisive factor in negativing a duty of care owed to the employer by the sub-contractor whose negligence causes the fire damage.

The maximalist position is best expressed by Lord Scarman delivering the opinion of the Privy Council in *Tai Hing Cotton Mill Ltd.* v *Liu Chong Hing Bank Ltd*[56]:

> "Their Lordships do not believe that there is anything to the advantage of the law's development in searching for a liability in tort where the parties are in a contractual relationship. Though it is possible as a matter of legal semantics to conduct an analysis of the rights and duties inherent in some contractual relationships including that of banker and customer either as a matter of contract law when the question will be what, if any, terms are to be implied or as a matter of tort law when the task will be to identify a duty arising from the proximity and character of the relationship between the parties, their Lordships believe it to be correct in principle and necessary for the avoidance of confusion in the law to adhere to the contractual analysis: on principle because it is a relationship in which the parties have, subject to a few exceptions, the right to determine their obligations to each other, and for the avoidance of confusion because different consequences do follow according to whether liability arises from contract or tort, e.g. limitation of action."

The strictures thus expressed against searching for a liability in tort where the parties are in a contractual relationship seem as apposite in a building context as in the banking context of that case. There is an example of

52 [1986] 1 Q.B. 211 (C.A.)
53 [1986] 1 W.L.R. 995 (H.L.)
54 (1988) 42 Build L.R. 25 (Judge Fox-Andrews Q.C.,O.R.)
55 [1954] 1 WLR 459 (C.A.)
56 [1986] A.C. 80 (P.C.) at 107

application of the maximalist position in a building context. Judge Bowsher Q.C., O.R. in *University of Glasgow* v. *Whitfield and Laing*[57] adopted it as the alternative basis for his rejection of the plaintiff employer's contention that it was owed a duty of care in tort by the main contractor. The primary basis for rejecting it, however, was that there was no danger to persons or property other than the defective building.

Differences between minimalist and maximalist positions: The main differences pertain to limitation and contribution claims in respect of breach of duties arising before 1 January 1979. Given that the minimalist position allows a concurrent duty in tort, such contribution will be available against other tortfeasors. More importantly, the cause of action will not accrue and hence the limitation period will not start to run until damage is sustained which may be much later than the breach of duty causative of that damage. Also, the Latent Damage Act 1986 may apply to extend the limitation period further. Under the maximalist position, it follows that in the absence of concurrent liability in tort, there is no right to contribution and no limitation period applicable to claims in tort.

No contract between plaintiff and defendant: relevance of other contracts

In deciding whether a duty of care was owed by the defendant to the plaintiff, it may be relevant to take into account the terms of a contract between one of them and a third party. There can be no question of the terms having contractual effect as between the plaintiff and the defendant, since generally a contract binds only the parties thereto. a duty of care in tort, however, is a duty imposed by law having regard to all the relevant circumstances, which may include the terms of such contract.

A simple paradigm serves to illustrate the topic. In relation to a construction project, A may contract with B for B to perform works for A, which B subcontracts to C. As a result of lack of due care by C, damage may be sustained by A or by D, a person not involved in the works at all, e.g. a subsequent purchaser or occupier of the finished building or a visitor or pedestrian. What is the effect as between A or D and C of terms, in particular exclusion of liability clauses, in the main contract between A and B or in the subcontract between B and C?

In this context as previously, a minimalist and maximalist position may be discerned. The minimalist position would not generally regard the imposition of a duty of care as inconsistent with the contractual matrix. It would be a question of examining the particular terms of other contracts and precise relevance of those contracts as between the plaintiff and the defendant. The maximalist position in contrast could generally regard the contractual matrix as indicative of the parties' mutual intentions and the imposition of a duty of care in tort as inconsistent therewith.

The cases reflecting the minimalist position admit of the following analysis. Taking A's position (within the building matrix), a duty of care is unlikely to be imposed upon C so that liability in tort is incurred by him to A, in circumstances where there are terms in the main contract which would preclude a successful claim by A against B whether in contract or tort in respect of the same damage; see *Southern Water Authority* v. *Lewis and Duvivier*[58]; *Junior Books Ltd* v. *Veitchi Co Ltd.*[59]. Also see the fire risk cases: *WHTSO* v. *Haden Young*[60]; *Surrey Heath BC* v. *Lovell Construction Ltd.* and *Haden Young Ltd.*[61] and *Norwich City Council* v. *Harvey*[62].

On the other hand, terms in a sub-contract between B and C which albeit effective to preclude liability whether in contract or in tort in respect of damage caused by C to B, may be ineffective to preclude C being under a duty of care to A in respect of the same damage in the absence of knowledge of, or even consent to, the relevant terms by A: see *Rumbelows Ltd.* v. *A.M.K.*[63]; *Twins Transport Ltd.* v. *Patrick & Brocklehurst*[64].

Similarly taking D's position (outside the building matrix), terms in a main contract between A and B or in a subcontract between B and C are unlikely to preclude C or even B being under a duty of care to D in the absence of knowledge of, or even consent to, the relevant terms by D. On the other hand such contracts are not irrelevant. In the Australian case of *Voli* v. *Inglewood Shire Council*[65], Windeyer J. considered the effect of the contracts made by the architect and the contractor with the employer in determining whether a duty of care was owed to strangers to those contracts:

> ..."neither the terms of the architect's engagement, nor the terms of the building contract, can operate to discharge the architect from a duty of care to persons who are strangers to those contracts. Nor can they directly determine what he must do to satisfy his duty to such persons. That duty is cast upon him by law, not because he made a contract, but because he entered upon the work. Nevertheless his contract is not an irrelevant circum-

---

58 [1985] 2All ER 1077 (Judge Smout Q.C., O.R.)
59 [1983] 1 A.C. 520 (H.L), at 546 per Lord Roskill
60 (1987) 37 BLR 130 Macpherson J.
61 (1988) 42 Build L.R. 25 (Judge Fox-Andrews Q.C., O.R.)
62 (1987) 39 Build L.R. 75 (Garland J.) and [1989] 1 W.L.R. 828 (C.A.)
63 (1980) 19 BLR 25 Judge Fay Q.C., O.R.
64 (1983) 25 BLR 65 Judge Hawser Q.C., O.R.
65 [1963] A.L.R. 657

stance. It determines what was the task upon which he entered. If, for example, it was a design for a stage to bear only some specified weight, he would not be liable for the consequences of someone thereafter negligently permitting a greater weight to be put upon it."[66]

The maximalist position in contrast would hold that, at least in certain circumstances, even the manner of arrangement of contractual relationships may suffice to negative a duty in tort, irrespective of analysis of particular terms with a view to demonstrate inconsistency or anomaly arising from the imposition of such a duty. Thus a chain of contractual relationships may be taken as signifying a particular intention on the part of the parties to the various contracts so to arrange their relationships and the channelling of claims. To impose a duty of care in tort, short-circuiting such chain, would be inconsistent with that apparent intention.

This is illustrated most significantly by *Muirhead* v. *Industrial Tank Specialities Ltd.*[67] albeit in a non-building context. In a building context it is illustrated by *Simaan Contracting Co* v. *Pilkington Glass Ltd.*[68]. In that case the employer withheld payments from the plaintiff main contractor on the ground that glass units were not of a uniform green colour as specified. The glass had been supplied by the defendants pursuant to contract with the plaintiff's curtain walling subcontractor. Thus *qua* the plaintiff contractor the defendant was a sub-sub-supplier. In the present context the following passage from Bingham L.J.'s judgment is relevant:

> "I do not think it just and reasonable to impose on the defendants a duty of care towards the plaintiffs of the scope contended for. (a) Just as equity remedied the inadequacies of the common law, so has the law of torts filled gaps left by other causes of action where the interests of justice so required. I see no gap here, because there is no reason why claims beginning with the [employer] should not be pursued down the contractual chain subject to any short-cut which may be agreed upon, ending up with a contractual claim against the defendants. That is the usual procedure. *It must be what the parties contemplated when they made their contracts. I see no reason for departing from it.* (b) Although the defendants did not sell subject to exempting conditions, I fully share the difficulty which others have envisaged where there were such conditions. Even as it is the defen-

---

66 (ibid. at 662).
67 [1986] Q.B. 507 (C.A.)
68 [1988] 1 Q.B. 758 (C.A.)

dants' sale may well have been subject to the terms and conditions imported by the Sale of Goods Act 1979. Some of those are beneficial to the seller. If such terms are to circumscribe a duty which would be otherwise owed to a party not a party to the contract and unaware of its terms, then that could be unfair to him. But if the duty is unaffected by the conditions on which the seller supplied the goods, it is in my view unfair to him and makes a mockery of contractual negotiation." (emphasis added).

Similarly Dillon L.J.:

"in the present case I can see nothing whatever to justify a finding that the defendants had voluntarily assumed a direct responsibility to the plaintiffs for the colour and quality of the glass panels. On the contrary, all the indications are the other way and show that *a chain of contractual relationships was deliberately arranged the way it was without any direct relationship between the plaintiffs and the defendants"* (emphasis added).

The maximalist position is also reflected in *Pacific Associates* v. *Baxter*[69] where a claim in tort by a contractor against an engineer for undercertification failed. The contractor had a contract with the employer which provided a machinery, arbitration, for challenging the engineer's decisions. Likewise the engineer had a contract with the employer. But there was no contract between the engineer and the contractor. The court regarded the contractual matrix as a crucial factor in denying the imposition upon the engineer of a duty of care in tort in favour of the contractor. But the case cannot be regarded as wholly reflective of the maximalist position since importance was attached to a term in the main contract providing for arbitration. The position might have been otherwise if there had been no arbitration clause.

However, the actual decision and reasoning of the majority of the House of Lords in *Junior Books* stands inconsistently with the maximalist position. In the light of the later passage from his judgment quoted above (para. 6.28), Bingham L.J.'s attempt in *Simaan* to explain *Junior Books* is hesitant and unconvincing, although explicable given that the latter was binding upon him as a decision of the House of Lords:

"Where a specialist sub-contractor is vetted, selected and nominated by a building owner it may be possible to conclude (as in the *Junior Books* case [1983] 1 A.C. 520) that the nominated sub-

69 [1990] QB 993 (C.A.)

contractor has assumed a direct responsibility to the building owner. On that reasoning it may be said that the defendants owed a duty to the Sheikh [the building owner]in tort as well as to Teal [the sub-contractor] in contract."[70].

Simaan marks a further milestone along the road towards the isolation, if not oblivion, to which later cases have sought to consign *Junior Books*.

Apart from analysis of the particular contractual matrix and terms of particular contracts, recent cases also demonstrate the importance of analysing the individual roles of participants in a building project in deciding whether a duty of care is owed by one to another. Such a functional analysis may militate against the imposition of a duty of care on one in favour of another. It is reflected in the conclusions in *Peabody and Investors in Industry* that no duty of care in tort was owed by the local authority to the plaintiff building owner.

Conclusions: contract between plaintiff and defendant

In this case, determining whether the defendant owes to the plaintiff a concurrent duty of care in tort arising out of the same circumstances as covered by the contract, requires due observance of the dichotomy of approach as between contract and tort towards the imposition of duties. In contract it is a matter of ascertaining the intention of the parties as reflected in the terms of the contract, whether express or implied. Consistent with that approach, implication of terms entails minimum interference with the assumed intention. Thus, in general, terms will be implied only if necessary to do so. It is not enough to show that it would be just and reasonable to do so. To do otherwise risks substitution of the intention of the court for that of the parties (see generally on this point, the C.A. decision on 22.3.89 in *The Maira*). In contrast, in tort, imposition of duties is a matter of law, taking into account all the circumstances of the case. In deciding whether on particular facts a duty is to be imposed, it is relevant to consider whether it is just and reasonable to do so.

Contractual silence may present an apparent dilemma. Thus the contractual analysis may preclude imposition of a duty corresponding to the concurrent duty of care claimed as arising on the analysis in tort. Which analysis is to prevail? While the apparent answer is the contractual analysis, the better answer is that both analyses, properly applied, are likely to give a consistent result. Thus the parties' intention is crucial and is generally a determinant factor in negativing the alleged duty in tort as well as that in

70 ibid. at 776

contract.

It may be contended that giving primacy to the parties' intention is unobjectionable where the claimed loss is purely economic loss, but is objectionable where it includes injury to persons or damage to other property. In such a case it may be said that the nature of the harm is such that the parties' intention should not be determinant of the alleged duty on the basis of which the relevant loss is claimed. It is submitted that even then primacy should be given to the parties' intention. The situation, however, is considerably mitigated by the Unfair Contract Terms Act 1977. The Act bans contract terms or notices which seek to exclude or restrict liability for death or personal injury from negligence. In certain other situations terms which seek to exclude or restrict liability or to require an indemnity, must satisfy a criterion of reasonableness. The operation of the Act is relevant in deciding whether a concurrent duty of care should be imposed. It may preclude reliance on contract terms which would otherwise indicate a contractual intention inconsistent with the imposition of a concurrent duty of care in tort. It may thus neutralise such intention to the extent of allowing the imposition of a concurrent duty of care in tort.

Whether there is a contractual intention inconsistent with the imposition of a concurrent duty of care is a question to be determined according to the particular facts of each case. One argument should be mentioned. Where the parties have contracted under seal, it may be contended that that is indicative of the parties having specifically directed their minds to limitation and that the imposition of a duty of care in tort such as would have the effect of a longer limitation period for a claim based on tort arising from particular facts would be inconsistent with such intention. Indeed, having regard to the prevalence of contracts under seal in the construction field, it may even be argued that the fact that a contract is not under seal is also so indicative and thus hostile to the imposition of a concurrent duty of care in tort such as would allow a longer limitation period. Thus it might be said that the parties had the opportunity to make the contract under seal and the fact that they did not do so is indicative of an intention to have the shorter limitation period apposite to contracts not under seal.

Where the imposition of a concurrent duty of care in tort would not be inconsistent with the parties' intention assumed from the relevant contract, should such a duty be imposed? It is in this situation that what have been termed the minimalist and the maximalist positions differ. The former would allow the imposition of such duty whereas the latter would not. Which position is to be preferred? In terms of logic there is no preferred answer. The difference between the two positions is one of judicial preference. Preference for the minimalist position reflects sympathy, hallowed by precedent, for parties who would have been prejudiced if there had not been concurrent liability in tort. Preference for the maximalist position, reflects preference towards the apparent clarity and certainty of the contractual analysis limiting liability to that in contract alone, at least in commercial relationships. It should be mentioned, however, that in *Tai Hing* rejection of the duty of care in tort justified on the basis of the maximalist position, could also have been justified on the basis of the minimalist position.

Conclusions: no contract between plaintiff and defendant: relevance of other contracts

In relation to a building project, the contractual matrix and the terms of contracts within that matrix are relevant in determining whether one participant owes to another a duty of care in tort notwithstanding that neither are in a contractual relationship with each other. Their precise relevance will depend on the particular context and the particular participants involved. The more complex the contractual matrix and the more formal and detailed the contracts, the greater the likelihood of that matrix being taken as signifying a positive intention on the part of the parties to the various contracts so to arrange their relationships and the likelihood of the rejection of a duty of care in tort as inconsistent with that apparent intention. While the particular matrix alone may be insufficient to negate a duty of care in tort, analysis of terms of relevant contracts and the particular functions of the participants in relation to each other may be determinant factors against the imposition of a duty.

Negligence In a Statutory Context

A duty of care and consequent liability in the tort of negligence on the part of public authorities may arise from the performance of statutory functions. The difficulty here is to resolve the relationship between public law powers and duties, the proper exercise and performance of which may cause damage, and the private law concept of a duty of care not to cause harm. Various attempts have been made at arriving at a synthesis. While these attempts have not been entirely satisfactory or wholly consistent, an analysis of the main cases in which the attempts have been made does indicate the broad lines of approach. For present purposes it suffices to take the following cases: *Dorset Yacht, Anns, Curran, Yeun Kun Yeu, Caparo, Davis* v. *Radcliffe* and *Murphy*.

Lord Diplock in *Dorset Yacht* favoured a synthesis based on the public law concept of ultra vires. So long as an exercise of a power (or "discretion"), was intra vires, it was not actionable. If, however, it was ultra vires liability in the tort of negligence might be incurred. Careless exercise of a power alone would not be ultra vires. Nevertheless, there came a stage when a power was exercised so carelessly or unreasonably that there could not be said to be a real exercise of the power conferred, and it was thus ultra vires. Moreover, while a system of control, including its delegation to subordinate officers might itself be intra vires, an act or omission of a subordinate officer employed in the administration of the system might nevertheless be ultra vires if it fell outside the limit of the power delegated to him, including if done contrary to instructions.

Lord Wilberforce in *Anns* also favoured a synthesis based on the public law concept of ultra vires. He rejected an argument that only a statutory duty and not a statutory power could give rise to possible liability. He asserted that both could. He drew a distinction between powers and duties the exercise or discharge of which contained a large area of policy and "operational" powers the exercise or discharge of which amounted essentially to the practical execution of policy decisions. The more operational a power or duty, the easier it was to superimpose upon it a common law duty of care. He further asserted that even the non-exercise of a statutory power could give rise to liability.

It is apparent from both *Curran* and *Yuen Kun Yeu* that the House of Lords and the Privy Council in those cases viewed with some reservation Lord Wilberforce's speech in *Anns* not only in regard to the general two stage test but also in regard to his view that the non-exercise of a statutory power might give rise to liability in negligence. This reservation was clearly motivated by the judgments of the High Court of Australia in *Sutherland Shire Council v. Heyman*[71]. In that case five separate judgments were given. That of Brennan J. is noteworthy in the present context. He proceeded as follows:

- An allegedly negligent act (misfeasance) had to be distinguished from an allegedly negligent omission (non-feasance) i.e. a failure to act to prevent the damage complained of by the plaintiff.
- Generally, an omission did not give rise to a duty of care.
- For a duty to act to prevent damage (and thus for liability to arise in respect of an omission to act) in addition to foreseeability of damage there had also to be either the undertaking of some task which leads another to rely on its being performed, or the ownership, occupation or use of land or chattels to found the duty.
- A distinction had to be made between acts and omissions before one could determine whether a duty of care arose from statutory powers and duties.
- A statutory duty had to be distinguished from a statutory power.

71 [1985] 60 A.L.R. I

- Further the exercise of a statutory power had to be distinguished from its non-exercise.

Generally there was no duty to exercise a statutory power, and thus no liability arose in respect of its non-exercise.

> "Before a repository of a statutory power can be liable in negligence for a failure to exercise it, the statute must (either expressly or by implication) impose a duty to exercise the power and confer a private right of action in damages for a breach of the duty so imposed. The question whether Parliament has conferred a private right of action depends on the interpretation of the statute......[it] is not a matter of judicial policy.....It is a matter of intention".
>
> The exercise of a statutory power might give rise to a duty of care. Liability in negligence would arise from the exercise of a statutory power by a public authority only for the consequence of its acts which could have been avoided by the exercise of reasonable care and skill.

Among the major criticisms directed at Lord Wilberforce's two stage test in *Anns* was that "if [the] first stage is intended to be applied in cases of non-feasance as well as in cases of misfeasance, it elides the distinction between acts and omissions which appears in Lord Atkin's language".

Lord Bridge in *Curran*[72] also made reference to criticisms of *Anns* consisting in "its tendency to obscure the important distinction between misfeasance and non-feasance". Nevertheless he stopped short of stating that *Anns* was wrong on this point but he added the significant caution:

> "But, that said, your Lordships are I think, entitled to be wary of effecting any extension of the principle applied in *Anns* v. *Merton London Borough* whereby, although under no statutory duty, a statutory body may be held to owe a common law duty of care to exercise its statutory powers to control the activities of third parties in such a way as to save harmless those who may be adversely affected by those activities if they are not effectively controlled."[73]

It should be noted that in *Murphy*, it was not argued that a local authority owes no duty at all to persons who might suffer injury through a failure to

72 [1987] A.C. 718
73 (ibid. at 726)

exercise reasonable care to secure compliance with building plans. The case is solely concerned with the scope of the duty. In the absence of argument, no decision was made as to whether any duty was owed at all (see Lord Keith at 525 and Lord Bridge at 439). Lord MacKay said (at 419):

> "While of course I accept that duties at common law may arise in respect of statutory powers or the discharge of statutory duties I find difficulty in reconciling a common law duty to take reasonable care that plans should conform with byelaws or regulation with the statute which has imposed on the local authority the duty not to pass plans unless they comply with byelaws or regulations and to pass them if they do."

Curran, Yuen Kun Yeu, Caparo and *Davis* v. *Radcliffe* are significant in demonstrating that the legislative intention was relevant to the question whether a duty of care arose. Thus in *Curran* the purpose of the statute was interpreted as being to save public money and not the protection of the recipient of the grant and his successors. More significantly in *Yuen Kun Yeu* the absence of a statutory duty was considered of relevance:

> "In these circumstances their Lordships are unable to discern any intention on the part of the legislature that in considering whether to register or deregister a company the commissioner should owe any statutory duty to potential depositors. It would be strange that a common law duty of care should be superimposed on such a statutory framework"[74].

A further factor taken into account in *Curran, Yuen Hun Yeu* and *Davis* v. *Radcliffe* in negativing the defendant public authority's alleged duty of care, was its relative lack of control over the activity which gave rise to the claimed loss. *Curran, Yeun Hun Yeu, Caparo* and *Davis* v. *Radcliffe* demonstrate a more analytical, purposive and circumspect approach to deciding whether a duty of care in private law is to be taken as arising out of the discharge of statutory functions, especially in relation to the exercise of statutory powers.

Some General Conclusions

Since about 1984 the appellate courts have been singing with increasing fervour the anthem of the new orthodoxy as to the role of tort: "Get back to

74 [1988] A.C. 175 at 195

where you once belonged". *Junior Books* and *Anns* must be regarded as relegated to apostasy. The present trend is against broad tests for determining the existence of a duty of care and more in favour of a more analytical approach formulated around particular paradigms.

Nevertheless there is room and a need for a general conception underlying the imposition of a duty of care in all cases even though whether one should be imposed in a particular case can only be determined by reference to particular paradigms and analysis of the particular facts of each case (note Lord Devlin's approach in *Hedley Byrne & Co. Ltd.* v. *Heller & Partners Ltd.* [1964] A.C. 465 at 524). I would suggest the criterion of reasonable expectation.

Penultimately, a plea for explicit recognition of the role of policy. However much the criticism of Lord Wilberforce's two stage test in *Anns*, policy has a role to assist arrival at a conclusion which broad linguistic formulae alone cannot determine. It follows that Lord Keith's statement in *Yuen Kun Yeu*, that the second (policy) stage of Lord Wilberforce's test "is one which will rarely have to be applied" is unrealistic. Judicial minimisation of the role of policy may entail expression of policy factors being suppressed, notwithstanding that such factors clearly contributed to the conclusion in a particular case and notwithstanding that their expression would aid understanding of the case and provide future guidance. Despite recognition of the role of policy, equal recognition must be given to the fact that perception of the correct policy may differ as between judges and may change over the years. Thus, speaking generally, a policy determination is detectable in the reversal by *Peabody and Investors in Industry Ltd.* v. *South Bedfordshire D.C.*[75] of the previous trend which generally favoured liability on the part of local authorities for defective building works negligently inspected by their employed building inspectors. That policy determination would appear to have been motivated in part by adverse and costly claims experienced by local authorities and in part by the private self help climate of the 1980's. A case of judicial privatisation of liability.

Finally, adherents of modern chaos theory will readily find illustration of the "butterfly" phenomenon in judicial variation in the approach to the tort of negligence over the last 25 years. However clear the broad trends may be at present, there can be no prediction of the precise contours of the tort of negligence five years from now. The insignificant obiter dictum of today may spawn the orthodoxy of tomorrow. The roller coaster rolls on – unpredictably.

---

75 [1986] Q.B. 1034

9 Common law developments applicable to construction

Ian Duncan Wallace

Synopsis

This paper examines the impact in the construction field of recent House of Lords' decisions on the law of negligence and the Court of Appeal's decision on a claim for economic loss by a contractor against an Engineer.

Introduction

At the present day cases involving the interpretation of construction contracts are almost invariably the result of poor standard form or other draftsmanship, and rarely illustrate any important principles. In the welter of now specially reported construction cases in almost all jurisdictions I may well have missed an epoch-making decision. One, in the field of quasi-contract, which would certainly merit consideration would be *Pavey and Matthews Pty Limited* v. *Paul*[1]. There are others which I could mention, but in the exercise of my professorial discretion, and at the risk of adding to the groaning burden of preceding "expert" comment both oral and written, I intend to interpret my jurisdiction under the above title as justifying discussion in this paper:

> (a) of the impact in the construction field of *D and F Estates Limited* v. *Church Commissioners for England*[2] and *Murphy* v. *Brentwood D.C.*[3] in the House of Lords, in the broad context of the liability in tort to third persons of all parties to a construction project, including the bylaw authority, for economic loss in the shape of the cost of repair of defects of workmanship or design and
> (b) of the true scope of the Court of Appeal's decision in *Pacific Associates* v. *Baxter*[4], and of its recent application by the British Columbia Court of Appeal in *Edgworth Construction Ltd.* v. *Lea*

1 (1987) 162 CLR 221 (High Court of Australia)
2 [1989] AC 177
3 [1991] AC 177, [1990] 3 WLR 414
4 [1990] 1 QB 993

and Associates[5] in the context of claims in tort for economic loss by contractors against the owner's architect or engineer (A/E).

As it happens, the groaning burden to which I have referred contains articles written by myself on all three of these cases to which, in the interests of brevity, I propose to make reference from time to time in the present paper. These are, on *D and F Estates*, the article *"Confusion Confounded"* and a subsequent Note in LQR[6]; on *Murphy* the article *"Anns Beyond Repair"* also in LQR[7]; and on *Pacific Associates*, the article *"Charter for the Construction Professional"* in the Construction Law Journal[8].

(a) D and F Estates

Shortly, this case made the analysis, (for the first time in England, apart from the original *Dutton* judges and Lord Brandon in *Junior Books* v. *Veitchi*[9]) that, properly understood, the *Dutton/Anns* liability for anticipatory repairs was one of economic loss, in contradistinction to the *Donoghue* v. *Stevenson* liability for personal injuries or damage done by a defective chattel or product to other property. In the *D and F* case the House of Lords, while holding itself bound by its own decision in *Anns* (which had confirmed the liability of bylaw authorities in negligence to subsequent occupiers of property for this type of economic loss) considered that Lord Wilberforce's judgment in *Anns* had been *obiter* only in its comments as to the liability of private defendants, such as builders, architects or developers. Reversing all expectations, the House of Lords, without calling on counsel for the Respondent, then held that no such duty was owed at all by these private defendants (in the particular case by builders to replace plaster which had fallen and larger areas which had not fallen but were still dangerously defective)[10]. Lords Bridge and Oliver left open for future consideration two possible grounds of a continuing liability of private defendants, namely cases where physical damage could be regarded as having been done to "other property", if such damage had occurred to "another part" of the building (the "complex structure" theory); or secondly, in cases where there had been a breach of the bylaws[11]. Both these types of surviving liability,

5 (1991) 7 Const. L.J. P., (1991) 54 BLR 11
6 (1989) 105 LQR 46; (1990) 106 LQR 11
7 (1991) 107 LQR 228
8 (1990) 6 Const. L.J. 207
9 [1983] AC 520
10 See 105 LQR at page 61
11 See generally, 105 LQR at pages 61-62

if they were indeed valid at all, would be applicable on the facts of almost all foundation cases, such as the original *Dutton* and *Anns* cases themselves. It could be (and was) immediately commented about these two possible survivals of liability (a) that the accidental presence of physical damage (superficial cracking etc.) to the "other part" made no sense as a criterion for liability[12], and (b) that virtually all defects in a building would be a breach of one or other of the bylaws as currently drafted (including, as it happened the actual defective plaster in *D and F Estates*)[13].

Murphy v. Brentwood

This case raised directly the liability of the bylaw authority itself to a later owner for economic loss caused by its negligence (through its agents) in approving an inadequate foundation design, as a result of which a purchaser from the original developer subsequently sold at a substantial loss without doing any repairs himself. Put simply, the House of Lords removed the last remaining liability established by *Anns*, namely that of the bylaw authority; interestingly, in the case of *Murphy*, an authority performing its most primary and direct area of statutory duty and not its more incidental exercise of supervisory powers to ensure bylaw compliance as in the *Dutton* and *Anns* cases[14]. In so doing, the House's reasoning not only impliedly disposed of the "bylaw breach" avenue of potential liability against private defendants suggested for consideration by Lord Oliver in the *D and F* case, but all the speeches also expressly disavowed "complex structure" as a possible basis for an *Anns*-type economic loss liability[15]. However, as will be seen, the speeches on complex structure may still have relevance in the quite different area of either personal injury or damage to property under the *Donoghue* v. *Stevenson* principle - for example, if a builder or sub-contractor has negligently caused a collapse or destruction by fire of a building, or a negligent design has caused similar damage.

The obvious and immediate effect of these two cases is to remove any liability, outside contract, for the cost of repairing defects in buildings from architects, engineers, contractors, sub-contractors or developers, or indeed anyone else concerned with their construction, in all cases where no accident or collapse damaging person or other property has as yet occurred. However, there are a number of other consequences, both legal and practical,

---

12 See this submitted and explained in 105 LQR at page 58, and see also Note in 106 LQR 11
13 See 105 LQR at page 76
14 See 107 LQR at page 231
15 See 107 LQR at page 235

which practitioners may need to consider. Three rather peripheral consequences of the *Murphy* speeches which should be mentioned, if only to
dispose of them, are:-

(a) The *Dutton* and *Anns* cases were best justified and supported, in regard
     to the liability of private defendants, by what may be called the
     "dissenting *Rivtow*" principle - namely that if liability would be present
     in the event of a full-scale accident or failure, it would be only logical
     to allow recovery of earlier expenditure designed to avert such an event.
     The speeches indicate very clearly that this principle, whether in the
     field of buildings, or of chattels large or small, or of product liability,
     now appears to be unacceptable as a basis for argument in the English
     Courts in the current judicial climate[16].
(b) While Lord Keith stated at one point that he regarded *Junior Books* v.
     Veitchi as being an application of the *Hedley Byrne* principle, and the
     case was also mentioned by Lord Bridge, that case should not be
     regarded as laying down any useful principle of general application, let
     alone as governing the normal relationships between employers and
     nominated sub-contractors[17].
(c) Lord Bridge mentioned one possible exception (repair of a defect on the
     boundary of a property constituting a threat to persons on adjoining
     property) which might survive the removal of the *Anns* liability. No
     other judge mentioned this, and it seems inconsistent with the express
     rejection of the dissenting *Rivtow* principle in all the *Murphy* speeches,
     including that of Lord Bridge himself[18].

There are, however, a number of perhaps more substantial considerations
arising from the *D and F Estates* and *Murphy* speeches, which may affect
practitioners more directly and merit separate consideration.

Bylaw authorities and bylaw breach

Bylaw authority liability

Having abolished bylaw authorities' liability to the general public, and
in particular to house owners, for any *Anns*-style anticipatory repairs
liability, one might have expected that at least the usual *Donoghue* v.
Stevenson liability of local authorities and their officers for negligently

16 See 107 LQR at page 234-5
17 See the discussion and cases in 107 LQR, pages 240-242
18 See 107 LQR at page 238

caused physical damage to person or property would either remain undis-
cussed, or be expressly left intact. Very surprisingly, however, three of the
four *Murphy* speeches went out of their way expressly to reserve the position
that there might be no liability of a bylaw authority even in such a situation[19].
This would seem to carry concern for the interest of the Exchequer to
considerable lengths.

Bylaw breach by private persons

As stated, the *Murphy* speeches clearly dismiss this, at the very least by
implication, as producing a basis for any *Anns*-type liability of private
persons, such as builders, architects or developers. This was, of course,
initially suggested in only one sentence as a basis for the liability of the
builder by Lord Wilberforce in *Anns* itself[20]. The lack of any reasoned
discussion in *Anns* of how such a statutory duty apparently owed to third
persons would work, coupled with the difficulties thrown up by the peculiar
wording of the bylaws themselves (which on their face appear to suggest a
suitability obligation independent of fault), and a reference to such authorities as exist on the point, was discussed at some length in LQR when
commenting on the *D and F* case[21]. The same point was later made by Ralph
Gibson LJ in the valuable case of *Warner* v. *Basildon Development
Corporation*, published only two days before *Murphy* and after waiting
dutifully for a considerable period since the preceding February: "It is not
easy to work out what the [by-law] liability was which their Lordships in
Anns regarded as capable of being established against the builder in that
case"[22]. However, there is now an express provision on the statute book for
a civil liability for bylaw breach - Section 38 of the Building Act 1984. That
section is (mercifully, perhaps) not yet in force, and would be better left that
way until those in the DOE and the Law Commission have directed their
attention both to its draftsmanship and its intended objective. The wording
has, it would seem, been lifted bodily out of earlier special building
legislation concerned with health and safety at work, and there are other
indications in the wording that it may have been aimed primarily at personal
injury cases. But it does not say so, nor, having regard to the "suitability"
wording of so many of the bylaws, does it indicate clearly whether the
intended duty is strict or one of care[23]. If bylaw enforcement is to be

---

19 see 107 LQR at page 233
20 [1978] AC 728, 759 D
21 105 LQR at pages 72-74
22 (1991) 7 Const. L.J. 146, 152
23 See this discussed in 105 LQR at pages 72-74 and 107 LQR at page 246

improved, incidentally, particularly in cases of defective work and failures of contract compliance, a realistic limitation period beyond the absurdly inadequate six month period from completion for bylaw breach prosecutions is obviously imperative[24].

Complex Structure

As stated above, this clearly will no longer assist in establishing an Anns-type liability against a defendant. But a real question remains, having regard to the *Murphy* speeches, whether the theory may afford a defence, particularly to main contractors, in a *Donoghue* v. *Stevenson* situation where there has been a sudden catastrophic failure or fire which destroys the house or its contents.[25] Some of the statements in the *Murphy* speeches might lead one to suppose that a main contractor whose own employees had put in defective foundations, or some other defective part of the structure, which resulted in collapse or destruction of the building, might have a defence in tort against a later owner, whereas a sub-contractor whose negligent work had done so (e.g. an electrical sub-contractor who had caused a fire) would not. It may be predicted that this will remain a difficult and at present uncharted area, with difficult questions of independent contractor and vicarious liability perhaps also involved, obtaining in the case of major chattels such as ships and aircraft, or even motorcars, as well as of buildings. In the latter case, the new prevalence of subsidence claims and the presence of insurance interests seems likely to bring litigation rapidly to the House of Lords for further elucidation. Looking outside the construction field, will the repairer or supplier of a part of a valuable car later destroyed in an accident as a result of his careless work or defective materials be liable to replace it, whereas a manufacturer or wholesaler negligently supplying the car with an identical defect escape liability in tort for the loss of the car to a subsequent purchaser? Should it make any difference, coming to the construction field, that a faulty electrical or boiler installation is carried out by a main contractor's "in-house" division or staff rather than by a sub-contractor's or repairer's employees[26]?

---

24 See infra para 15.
25 See Note in 106 LQR 11, discussing the *D and F* judgments in this particular light, and see also 107 LQR 228, 235-7, where the *Murphy* speeches in this respect are discussed.
26 See the discussion of these and similar cases and the relevant passages from *Murphy* in 107 LQR at page 235-7.

Independent contractors

The *D and F* and *Murphy* cases both reveal a surprising readiness of the Courts at the present day to allow defendants to avoid liability by delegating the performance of their duties to independent contractors. In *D and F Estates*, there was a finding of fact that the main contractor's supervisors had been either knowing or negligent in permitting plaster work to be carried out with an additional unspecified coat in breach of manufacturer's instructions, and also that the result was a danger to the occupiers, but the Court of Appeal held that the employment of a small firm of presumably self-employed plasterers described as "not worth suing" afforded a defence to substantial main contractors, who had used them on a large residential development, against an *Anns*-type claim by later owners. This provoked an article by the present writer doubting the decision on this point[27], but the House of Lords in the event confirmed the Court of Appeal's view. In *Murphy*, the bylaw authority had employed a private firm of structural engineers to carry out its statutory function of approving or disapproving plans, and though the House eventually found it unnecessary to decide the case on that ground, the course of the argument could have left little doubt in the mind of anyone present that, had it been necessary, they would have upheld that particular defence by the local authority[28].

The Defective Premises Act 1972

Limited to dwelling houses, and with a limitation period restricted to six years from completion, it is nevertheless obvious that there will now be a major re-direction of attention by plaintiffs' advisers to this Act. The (strict?) wording of the primary duty under the Act will no doubt be intensively examined by the Courts. More importantly, perhaps, an extraordinary situation has now apparently been revealed, in that houses built after some (as yet undetermined) date prior to 1988 under the NHBC schemes may no longer enjoy the approved status which would remove them from the operation of the Act.[29]. In *Warner* v. *Basildon D.C.*[30] Ralph Gibson L.J. had been informed by counsel (in February 1990) that 97% of all houses built in any one year were under the NHBC scheme, and so outside the Act. Investigation as to precisely when a house was built, and

---

27 *"The lump and Landlord as Exits from Anns"* (1988) 4 Const. L.J. 100
28 See the discussion in 107 LQR at page 245
29 For the details then currently available about this in early 1991 see 107 LQR pages 242-244.
30 (1991) 7 Const. L.J. 146.

whether at the time the scheme was approved or not, is a task which, while fusion is still averted, the Bar will gratefully leave to their solicitor colleagues.

The Latent Damage Act 1986

This Act was obviously passed to deal with the limitation difficulties created by the new *Anns* liability, with its strong possibilities of unseen breaches and of damage only later emerging (see e.g. Section 3 of the Act, aimed specifically at claims by later property owners, which shows the primary target of the Act). Although the *Anns* liability for buildings has been abolished, its draftsmanship, which by Section 1 applies the Act to any claim for "damages for negligence", ensures that it will continue in being. *Donoghue* v. *Stevenson* situations will rarely involve the use of the Act, since the damage will usually be immediately apparent, but clearly some *Hedley Byrne* economic loss situations (where the cases already indicate difficult questions as to precisely when the original cause of action accrues or damage is as a fact first suffered) will stand to benefit, where the facts are appropriate, from the alternative discoverability periods available under the 1986 Act and the consequentially amended 1980 Limitation Act[31]. On the other hand, it would seem that the 1986 Act will not be available in the case of the statutory liability of fitness for habitation under the Defective Premises Act 1972 (where it will obviously be as appropriate and needed as it was in the case of the Anns liability for which it had been originally designed), since liability under the 1972 Act cannot, it would seem , be regarded as "damages for negligence"[32].

The anomalous limitation position appears to be, therefore, that where the relationship between plaintiff and defendant has reached the stage of a full contract the discoverability extensions under the Act of 1986 are not available (except on the possible basis of concurrent liability in contract and tort), whereas in a *Hedley Byrne* situation (which is akin to but usually short of a full contract) the 1986 Act will be available. *Murphy* therefore suggests the need for a re-appraisal of the limitation legislation so as to eliminate these anomalies, it is submitted[33].

---

31 see 107 LQR pages 244-5
32 See this noted with justified surprise by Ralph Gibson L.J. in *Warner* v. *Basildon D.C.*
    (1991) 7 Const. L.J. 146, 154
33 See further infra paragraph 15 and generally 107 LQR at pages 244-247

The future of Negligence and Economic Loss

One question which has exercised the Courts recently is the extent to which, outside the parameters of a classical *Hedley Byrne* situation with its basic concepts of assumption of responsibility and reliance, there may nevertheless be situations where an "imposed duty" to safeguard the plaintiff against economic loss may not also arise.[34]. Lord Oliver's and Lord Keith's speeches did discuss this possibility, Lord Keith appearing unconvinced when referring to the well-known case of *The Greystoke Castle*[35]. In Lord Oliver's case, there were additional references to *Ministry of Housing and Local Government* v. *Sharp*[36] and *Ross* v. *Caunters*[37]. Neither speech, however, made any serious attempt to define a possible area or the criteria for such a liability, and indeed only Lord Oliver openly accepted it as a possibility[38].

However, the daunting task of suggesting criteria for the future development of economic loss claims in tort has recently been impressively undertaken by Jane Stapleton in LQR[39]. Rightly pointing out that in the light of some of the latest judicial pronouncements in the House of Lords even *Hedley Byrne* might today be expected to be differently decided, she extracts the negative reasoning, as expressly stated in the *Murphy* and *D & F* speeches, for justifying the reversal of *Anns* as being

(a) That it is not a proper exercise of the judicial function to open up large new areas of liability
(b) that matters involving consumer protection are primarily for the legislature
(c) that areas already covered by recent legislation should not be extended by the Courts and
(d) that conferring rights akin to contract should not be encouraged.

However, after a careful analysis of all the developments and cases in tort relating to economic loss since *Donoghue* v. *Stevenson*, and while disapproving the incremental or "pockets" approach to new liabilities for economic loss first enunciated by Brennan J. in the *Shire of Sunderland* case, Stapleton suggests as better founded negative criteria for economic loss liabilities in new situations in negligence:

---

34 See particularly, e.g. per Ralph Gibson L.J. in *Pacific Associates* v. *Baxter* [1990] 1 QB 993, 1026-7, 1030
35 *Morrison Steamship Co.* v. *Greystoke Castle* [1947] AC 265
36 [1970] 2 QB 223
37 [1980] Ch 297
38 See the relevant passages from the *Murphy* speeches and the discussion on this point in 107 LQR at pages 239-240
39 *"Duty of Care and Economic Loss. A Wider Agenda."*, 107 LQR 249

(a) that no "floodgates" involving an indeterminate number of claims should be opened, and only a restricted and ascertainable class of plaintiffs or claims be involved (explaining the *Aliakmon* cases etc.)

(b) that adequate protection for the plaintiff should not be reasonably available by other means, such as contract or insurance (*Smith* v. *Bush, Ross* v. *Caunters* etc.)

(c) that areas should not be invaded where past Parliamentary intervention can be seen as intended to be exhaustive (the Defective Premises Act e.g.) and

(d)   that circumvention of contractual bargains, or of a clear understanding of the parties as to where risks should fall, should not be permitted ("the contract structure" cases etc.).

It will be seen that these various negative criteria take account of many of the "difficult" cases, such as *Ross* v. *Caunters*, and *MHLG* v. *Sharp*, as well as the *Aliakmon* and *Candlewood* and *SCM* v. *Whittall* cases, and much of the reasoning in *Smith* v. *Bush*. Advocates arguing for new areas of liability for economic loss in the appellate courts in need of a supporting rationale should derive assistance from this analysis, it is suggested.[40]

Legislation

The present writer has made a number of suggestions for this in 107 LQR[41]. *Murphy* has undoubtedly left a need at least to reconsider the present extent of statutory intervention with regard to defective buildings. This might involve

(a) reviewing the extent to which purchasers of property should have rights against its original developers, designers and builders. This might or might not involve expanding the 1972 Act to wider classes of new buildings, with a more appropriate limitation period, and perhaps providing for a bonded liability as in the case of the French decennial liability. In this writer's view, recourse to the original wrongdoer by way of subrogation or otherwise should not be discouraged by any compulsory form of insurance. This points to compulsory bonding, both to keep down cost and avoid the protection which would otherwise be afforded to solvent perpetrators of poor design or workmanship

(b) reconsideration of the real objectives of bylaw legislation - primarily, it is submitted, one of initial public restraint preventing unsafe or undesirable

40 See also 107 LQR 242-5.
41 See pages 245-7

design and the subsequent enforcement of proper standards of construction through the deterrent of prosecution when serious bylaw breaches are revealed, rather than by the provision of expensive layers of additional supervision paid for by the taxpayer to ensure contract compliance, which should be the responsibility of the industry. This should involve realistic limitation periods for bylaw prosecutions and heavy fines in serious cases. There may also be a case for licensing the site management of more substantial projects[42]

(c) removing where possible any limitation differences between contract and tort, preferably by extending the Latent Damage Act to selective (if not all) areas of contractual liability. [43]

Professional Liability

One field clearly affected by *Murphy* will be that of professional indemnity insurance, where a very great reduction in long-term risk, in particular to persons other than the client himself, has been effected by the case. This would seem to justify substantial reductions in premiums. The extent to which the Defective Premises Act liabilities will apply to dwelling-houses now being built is, as already explained, uncertain at the moment, however, and professionals with practices in that field may remain at risk to a greater or lesser extent under that Act[44]. Some commentators have suggested that Lord Keith's remarks attributing *Hedley Byrne* as the basis for design and liability in the *Pirelli* case[45] indicate a continuing greater liability of professionals in the design field, but this does not seem justified. The designer is always liable to his client for economic loss in contract and, unless concepts of concurrent liability in tort are ultimately discarded by the Courts[46], no doubt concurrently in tort as well. The reduction in his client's potential liability to later owners, as well as his own, can therefore only be of very real benefit to him. Nor does *Hedley Byrne* liability, as a possible alternative to the *Anns* liability in a typical later purchaser situation, receive any encouragement from the *Murphy* speeches - on the contrary, it is expressly dismissed as a possible basis of claim even in the relatively strong case where, as in *Murphy*, negligent approval by the authority of plans (the design) has taken place.[47] It will take exceptional activities or express

42 See the writer's *"Defective Work. The New Flavours"* (1990) 6 Const. L.J. 87
43 See 107 LQR at pages 246-7
44 See 107 LQR at page 244
45 [1983] 2 AC 1
46 See this touched on in 107 LQR at page 247
47 See 107 LQR at page 238

representations, outside the normal discharge of his duties to his own client, to expose a professional in that way, it is submitted[48].

(b) Pacific Associates v. Baxter

This decision of the Court of Appeal is clearly of outstanding importance in the construction field, in particular in removing an important area of doubt as to the extent of the *Hedley Byrne* liability of the owner's architect or engineer to the contractor. Indeed, it is clear that it is already being cited in the Commonwealth in the wider context of the many tort cases where a defendant sued in negligence seeks to restrict his liability in the light of a contract made by the plaintiff with a third person[49].

Since the emergence of the *Hedley Byrne* doctrine in the Commonwealth, and its U.S. equivalents,[50] contractors' advisers (in particular contractors' sureties' advisers) have for two or three decades now sought to proceed to recover their economic losses under a contract with the owner from the supervising or designing professionals of the owner[51]. There is, of course, no doubt that an architect or an engineer may choose to step outside his normal role and make some specific representation or assurance or take some special action which lies outside the normal performance of his duties and involves a voluntary assumption of responsibility on his part, as a result of which he may find himself liable to a contractor under the *Hedley Byrne* principle - as for example reassurances given to an unpaid sub-contractor who was contemplating ceasing work to the effect that the main contractor would have ample funds due to him under the main contract with which to pay the sub-contractor[52]. The question for discussion, however, is whether an A/E, merely by negligence in performance of one or other of his required functions under the terms of his contract of employment with the owner and of the construction contract itself, with its many possibilities of economic loss to the contractor if negligently performed, owes the latter a duty of care. In many instances, of course, those duties will involve statements or representations or certificates, thus prima facie raising *Hedley Byrne*

---

48 See the writer's "*Construction Contracts: Principles and Policies etc.*" ("CCPP") Chapter 5 generally for this

49 See *London Drugs Limited* v. *Kuhne and Nagel Limited* (1990) 45 BCLR 2nd 1, (British Columbia Court of Appeal) a *Donoghue* v. *Stevenson* case involving the liability of a carrier's employees where the carrier himself enjoyed a limitation of liability, now under appeal to the Supreme Court of Canada

50 See e.g. *Rozny* v. *Marnul* 250 NE 2nd 656 (1969)

51 See the U.S. and two difficult Canadian authorities examined in 1987 in the writer's CCPP paragraphs 5-12 - 28

52 *Day* v. *Ost* [1973] 2 NZLR 385

possibilities. In some more extreme cases (in the U.S. in particular), even affirmative duties have been successfully alleged (at least in principle on a preliminary point of law) - as e.g. a duty to detect and order removal of defective work early when the cost of replacement would be low, or to exercise more strict control over temporary works. Such cases have received short shrift in the U.K. and Commonwealth, however.[53]

Pacific Associates was, of course, a case of negligence alleged by a contractor against an engineer under a FIDIC contract, firstly in rejecting a contractor's applications for interim payment of a clause 12 unforeseeable physical conditions claim, and secondly when reaching his decision adverse to that claim under clause 67 of the Conditions. The plaintiffs started with the advantage of a clear obiter dictum of Lord Salmon, back in the heady earlier days of the development of the *Hedley Byrne* liability, that such an action would indeed lie[54]. Nevertheless, the claim was struck out by H.H. Judge John Davies QC, and the Court of Appeal upheld his decision. No doubt Judge Davies may have been influenced by a distinctly odd "one-off" exemption clause in the Particular Conditions of the Contract purporting to exonerate the engineer, but the Court of Appeal made it crystal clear that their decision would have been the same whether or not the clause had been present.

Broadly, the Court of Appeal considered that neither the "structure" of the construction contract, nor of the consultant's contract of employment, nor considerations of policy, would be consistent with a duty of care owed to the contractor, nor was the element of voluntary assumption of responsibility present to support a *Hedley Byrne* liability. As stated, the case has been analysed in detail by the writer in Const. L.J.[55]. As there pointed out, the headnote in the official Law Reports, (in what so far as this writer is concerned was a very rare lapse in their reports of cases in the construction field), was misleading in placing the emphasis which it did on the exemption clause. For some reason, BLR has not only been dismissive of *Pacific Associates*: "this decision is authority for very little and is best regarded as a decision on its own facts" - but suggests that Bokhary J. in Hong Kong, who had rightly noted "the wide implications of the decision" and who had followed *Pacific Associates* in an architect's certificate case, might have reached a different decision had the House of Lords decision in *Smith* v. *Bush* been available to him at the time[56].

53 Starting with *Clayton* v. *Woodman* [1962] 1 WLR 585 and *Clay* v. *Crump* [1964] 1 QB
   533 in the U.K. including cases where mitigation of damage was claimed, such as *East
   Ham* v. *Bernard Sunley* [1966] AC 406
54 *Arenson* V. *Arenson* [1977] AC 405, 438
55 *"Charter for the Construction Professional"* (1990) 6 Const. L.J. 207
56 (1990) 6 Const. L.J. 207, at pages 213-215

In Construction Law Journal the present writer suggested a much wider interpretation of *Pacific Associates*, and expressly awaited with interest to see if the Courts would adopt it[57]. That interpretation was that, apart from "one-off" cases outside his normal activities, "honest but careless discharge of his required services under the contract will not render an A/E liable for economic loss suffered by the contractor, independently of any remedy available against the owner under the construction contract"[58]. The present writer then suggested that, quite apart from the A/E's certifying or decision roles which were in issue in *Pacific Associates*, the principle of the case would apply equally to his design or general supervision duties, including supply of information and drawings and the condemnation of defective work.

As foreshadowed in Construction Law Journal, *Pacific Associates* has indeed been rapidly followed, and not just in Bokhary J.'s certification case in Hong Kong. Thus in *Edgworth Construction* v. *Lea & Associates in British Columbia*, successful tenderers for a roadworks contract sued a firm of engineers which had been employed by the highway authority to prepare the design and contract documentation, including the specification and provisional quantities, for economic loss caused by their alleged negligence in doing so. The claim was struck out in first instance, and that decision upheld in the Court of Appeal, with *Pacific Associates* as the lynch-pin. The Court considered that the web of relationships in a construction contract were a crucial element in determining proximity. Flaws in design and in the plans and specifications were appropriate subject matter for that contract. The consulting engineers were not compensated on the basis that they would assume risks to prospective bidders or the final contractor. The Court also pointed out that an engineer had no opportunity to define the extent or limits of his own liability by contract with the contractor, whereas, following *Pacific Associates*, the contractor could indicate the extent of his own requirements in regard to the design in his contract with the owner. The case was very obviously fully researched, as in so many Commonwealth jurisdictions at the present day, with some dubious Canadian first instance cases noted but not followed. Lambert J. said: "I know of no case in the Supreme Court of Canada, a provincial Court of Appeal, an Australian or New Zealand Court of Appeal, or a United Kingdom Court of Appeal, where an engineer or architect who did the design work for an owner under a contract with the owner was found liable to a contractor who suffered economic loss in the building of the work because of carelessness in the

57 ibid pages 212 (bottom) -213
58 ibid page 213

design work"[59]. Commenting on three cases in Canada to which he had been referred and which he discussed in detail, Lambert J. added: "the judgment in *Pacific Associates*... is notable in that it decided that the web of contractual relationships in a complex construction project formed a crucial element in the whole context which governed the determination of the question of proximity. That conclusion was adopted in several of the judgments of the members of this Court in *London Drugs* v. *Kuehne and Nagel Limited* and was not rejected in any of those judgments. I regard that point as a decisive factor in this case. It also throws new light on the proximity considerations underlying the three trial decisions in Ontario".

There is no doubt, it is submitted, as to the authority and importance of the *Pacific Associates* case outside as well as inside the construction field. It is also entirely consistent with the prevailing views in the House of Lords, as exemplified by, for example, their subsequent decision in the *Caparo* auditor's liability case. I will conclude this paper with two remarks from *Pacific Associates* itself:-

> "Since ... 1985 there has been an extensive and dramatic reconsideration of the whole area of tortious liability for pecuniary loss arising from negligent mis-statements and the like: see the judgment of Bingham L.J. in *Caparo Industries Plc* v. *Dickman* ..."[60]
>
> "A succession of the cases in the years since *Hedley Byrne* have recognised the necessity to put a brake on these developments relating to the existence of the duty of care..."[61].

It should not be difficult, it is submitted, to distinguish between those actions or representations of an A/E which imply a voluntary assumption of responsibility and lie outside the normal performance of the duties expected of him under the construction contract, so that a *Hedley Byrne* liability can be legitimately established, and the very wide range of matters over which his actions, statements and representations represent no more than a discharge of his required duties, with the result that under the *Pacific Associates* rationale no *Hedley Byrne* liability will attach for a negligent but honest mis-statement or action upon which the contractor may have chosen to rely.

---

59 *Edgeworth Construction Ltd.* v. *Lea and Associates Limited*, CA of British Columbia, February 18th 1991, as yet unreported.
60 [1990] 1 QB 1019 B
61 per Russell L.J. ibid page 1035 G

Part III

Remedies and Sanctions

Legal obligations in construction : 10 remedies and sanctions

John Turnbull

Synopsis

The purpose of this paper is to give a summary of the legal and equitable remedies and sanctions available in relation to construction activities. Other papers in this volume cover contractual, tortious and statutory obligations. This paper seeks to explain how those obligations can be enforced or, if breached, how redress can be obtained.

Introduction

The remedies available under English law are numerous: damages, specific performance, mandatory injunctions, prohibitory injunctions and declarations are but some of the ways in which obligations can be enforced or remedies obtained. Remedies come in many forms and can be classified in different ways: remedies may be compensatory (e.g. damages), punitive (e.g. exemplary damages), specific (e.g. injunctions) or consensual (e.g. liquidated damages).

The principal objective of a remedy is to put right a wrong: it is to compensate the innocent party or to prevent the recurrence of the wrong. The principal objective of a sanction is to deter, or in the case of specific remedies, to prohibit the commission of a wrongful act. The potential scope of an account of the remedies and sanctions available to an English litigant is enormous. In this paper I will confine my comments to an explanation of how damages are quantified where there has been a breach of contract or a tortious act. There are many torts which may be relevant to the construction industry, but space does not permit a full review of the whole field of tortious liability. I will, therefore, confine my comments to negligence, various forms of misrepresentation and nuisance. I will also review how damages for breach of statutory duty are calculated and the basis upon which the courts will grant injunctions and make decrees of specific performance.

Assessment of damages in contract and in tort

The best starting point of any summary of the law of damages is the statement of principle in *Livingstone* v. *Rawyards Coal Company*[1] where Lord Blackburn explained that the proper measure of damages was:

> "That sum of money which will put the party who has been injured, or who has suffered, in the same position as he would have been if he had not sustained the wrong for which he is now getting his compensation or reparation".

This statement of principle is slightly misleading in two ways. First, it refers only to the compensatory nature of damages. Damages can, at least in tort, also include a punitive element. Secondly, a slightly misleading impression is created by the fact that the principle appears to be equally applicable to claims in contract and tort. However, the principle is sufficiently widely expressed to disguise the differences between the measure of damages in contract and the measure of damages in tort.

In tort the plaintiff should be given such money as would put him in the same position as if he had not suffered the wrong. The authorities for this are numerous but in the construction field the principle was recently confirmed in *The Board of Governors of the Hospital for Sick Children* v. *McLaughlin and Harvey plc*.[2] The purpose of the award in tort is restitution: to put the clock back. Conversely, the object of an award of damages for breach of contract is very different. The objective is to turn the clock forward: to give the plaintiff the benefit which would have accrued to him if the contract had been completed. An award of damages in contract ought to secure for the plaintiff the commercial benefit of his bargain. It may be argued that, in truth, this is a distinction without a difference - the principle remains that the plaintiff is put into the same position which he would have been in had the wrong not been committed. However, the key to the distinction lies in the nature of the underlying obligation: in tort the obligation is not to act in such a way as will cause injury or loss. In contract, the obligation is positive: you are required to act in accordance with the terms of the bargain. This is a simple but fundamental distinction which, when properly and pragmatically applied, can solve many of the difficult questions which arise in this field.

1   [1880] 5 AC 25
2   (1990) 19 Con LR 25

Concurrent Causes

A plaintiff suing in contract or in tort must prove that the loss for which he claims compensation was caused by the wrongful act, be it a breach of contract or a breach of a tortious duty. However, it is not always necessary to prove that one or other wrongful act was the exclusive cause of the loss in order to recover the entire loss from one wrongdoer. This is a question which arises with some regularity in our field. A good example arose in *The Victoria University of Manchester* v. *Hugh Wilson and Lewis Womersley*[3]. In this well known case the University sought damages for defects that had occurred in tiled cladding to a building. They joined the architect, the contractors and the nominated sub-contractors as defendants. During the course of the trial the University settled their proceedings against the architect but continued against the other defendants. The issue arose as to whether the remaining defendants could be held liable for the full loss caused by the concurrent breaches of contract by the architect and the remaining defendants. It was held that the University could recover the full amount of damages from the contractors for breaches of contract which they had committed in common with the architect. During the course of his judgment, HH Judge Newey QC adopted the following comment of Devlin J in *Heskell* v. *Continental Express Ltd*[4],

> "Whatever the true rule of causation may be I am satisfied that if a breach of contract is one of two causes, both cooperating and both of equal efficacy....it is sufficient to carry judgment for damages".

Judge Newey concluded as follows:

> "It is surprising that there are not more cases, but I think that the law is clear: if two or more defendants have each committed breaches of the same or different contracts with the plaintiff and as a result of each defendant's breach the plaintiff has suffered the same damage he may recover the whole amount of it from any of the defendants."

There is no reason in principle why this rule should not also apply to concurrent torts or to a breach of contract and a concurrent tort. Indeed, there is some authority to support the proposition: see the comments of Limerick J in *Nowlan* v. *Brunswick Construction Limited*[5]. The ramifications of this

3 (1984) CILL 126
4 [1950] 1 All E.R. 1033
5 (1972) 21 BLR 27

rule can be serious for those involved in multi-party projects. An example will illustrate the potential problem. An architect and a quantity surveyor are retained by, and enter into the appropriate contracts with, the developer. The institution funding the development requires collateral warranties from both architect and quantity surveyor. The architect agrees to enter into a collateral warranty; the quantity surveyor does not. The architect and the quantity surveyor both negligently fail to spot a problem: they are equally blameworthy in a technical sense. The problem causes economic loss to the funding institution which takes over the development when complete. The institution can sue the architect in contract for the whole of the economic loss provided the facts fall within the principle set out in *Victoria University*. However, because of the recent contraction of the law of negligence and, in particular, the law relating to the recovery of economic loss, the institution has no claim against the quantity surveyor. The architect therefore bears the whole of the loss and is unable to seek any contribution from his fellow wrongdoer because the quantity surveyor is not "liable in respect of the same damage" within the meaning of the Civil Liability (Contribution) Act 1978.

Therefore, when considering collateral warranties you should take particular care to identify the extent to which others involved in the project are also prepared to enter into such contractual agreements: a failure by some to execute collateral warranties may well increase the risk taken by others in the event of a "concurrent failure".

Remoteness of Damage

We have discussed, in outline, the first requirement of a claim in contract or tort: causation. The second requirement is that the loss caused by the wrongful act should not be too remote. In the tort of negligence the damage caused by the defendant's breach of duty must be of a type (rather than an amount) which is reasonably foreseeable[6]. In contract the loss will be foreseeable if it arises naturally (according to the usual course of things) from the breach or it is of such a type (again, not amount) which may reasonably be supposed to have been in the contemplation of both parties at the time they made the contract as the probable result of the breach[7].

It was once thought that liability in tort was wider than in contract. This view was largely the result of *Re Polemis*,[8] in which it was held that a defendant was liable in negligence for all loss directly caused whether such

---

6   *The Wagon Mound* [1961] AC 388; *The Wagon Mound (No. 2)* [1967] 1 AC 617 and *Koufos* v. *Czarnwikow Ltd* [1969] 1 AC 350

7   *Hadley* v. *Baxendale* (1854) 9 Ex. 341 [1854] 1843-60 All E.R. 461

8   [1921] 3 KB 560

loss was foreseeable or not. But disapproval of *Re Polemis* by the Privy Council[9] and the House of Lords[10] considerably reduced the practical difference between the two tests of remoteness. Differences do, of course, remain but these appear to be largely semantic: there does not appear to be any significant difference between "reasonably contemplated" (the test in contract) and "reasonably foreseeable" (the test in tort). The residual area of difference, as noted by the editors of *McGregor on Damages* (15th Edition) is that:

> "The contracting parties may contemplate liability on a narrower scale than what is reasonably foreseeable".

This point is highlighted by claims for non-pecuniary loss i.e. mental distress, inconvenience or discomfort. These were for a very long time thought to be heads of loss which were not recoverable in contract; the point being that, whilst it might be reasonably foreseeable that a breach of contract might cause distress or personal inconvenience, it was to be doubted whether such "damage" was within the contemplation of parties to commercially negotiated contracts. This question appears to have been resolved in *Hayes* v. *James and Charles Dodd*[11]. The Court of Appeal held that damages in contract for mental distress and inconvenience should be regarded as a special and restricted head of damage. Such damages should only be awarded where "the contract itself was a contract to provide peace of mind or freedom from distress"[12]. This seems to emphasise the distinction referred to in *McGregor*: whilst such distress might be reasonably foreseeable it is not, in the absence of special circumstances, to be regarded as in the reasonable contemplation of contracting parties.

Mitigation of Damage

A plaintiff must, therefore, establish causation and must also establish that the loss is not too remote. His final hurdle is to mitigate his loss. The extent of damage suffered by a plaintiff can often be considerably reduced by sensible action. In such circumstances the law requires the plaintiff (whether suing in contract or tort) to take all reasonable steps to mitigate the loss caused by the defendant's wrongful act[13]. The question of mitigation

9 *The Wagon Mound* [1961] AC 388
10 *Hughes* v. *Lord Advocate* [1963] AC 837
11 [1990] 2 All ER 815 C.A.
12 see *Bliss* v. *South East Thames Health Authority* [1987] ICR 700
13 see *British Westinghouse Electric and Manufacturing Company* v. *Underground Electric Railways Company of London* [1912] AC 673

gives rise to a great many issues which cannot be explored here in detail. However, one of the most interesting questions is that raised by the issue of betterment. When a builder has built a defective building the employer is entitled, in general terms, to the reasonable cost of the necessary repair works. It is often argued that the remedial measures taken by the plaintiff have resulted in the plaintiff receiving a better building than he was entitled to expect under the terms of the original contract. The clearest explanation of the answer to this problem was given by His Honour Judge Newey QC in *Richard Roberts Holdings Ltd* v. *Douglas Smith Stimson Partnership*[14]:-

> "The law [on betterment] can be shortly summarised. If the only practicable method of overcoming the consequences of a defendant's breach of contract is to build to a higher standard than the contract had required, the plaintiff may recover the cost of building to that higher standard. If, however, a plaintiff needing to carry out works because of the defendant's breach of contract, chooses to build to a higher standard than is strictly necessary the courts will, unless the new works are so different as to break the chain of causation, award him the cost of the works less a credit to the defendant in respect of betterment."

A plaintiff's right to recover may, therefore, be reduced by his failure to mitigate. It may also be reduced by the extent to which his own actions or carelessness have contributed to the loss. The Law Reform (Contributory Negligence) Act 1945 allowed the apportionment of damages in cases where the plaintiff was jointly responsible with the defendant for the damage. In such cases the court was entitled to reduce the award of damages by such sums as it considered just and equitable having regard to the parties' share in the responsibility for the damage. It was long assumed that the 1945 Act was confined to actions for negligence. However, in *Forsikringsaktie-selskapet Vesta* v. *Butcher*[15] the Court of Appeal confirmed that the 1945 Act applied to a case where the defendant's liability in contract was the same as his liability in the tort of negligence independently of the existence of any contract. Accordingly, where a defendant is required by the terms of a contract to exercise reasonable care and the plaintiff has by his carelessness contributed to the loss the award against the defendant may be reduced.

---

14 (1988) 46 BLR 50
15 [1989] AC 852. See also *Basildon* v. *Lesser* [1985] QB 839.

Examples of Damages assessed in contract and tort.

I will consider first breaches of a straightforward two party building contract. A breach of contract by a contractor can take many forms, but I will concentrate on delays and sub-standard work. Where a contractor fails to complete the works contracted for, the ordinary measure of damage is the reasonable cost incurred by the employer in completing the work minus the contract price[16]. There is no reason why, in principle, other consequential costs should not be included in the award provided that they fall within the rules set out in *Hadley* v. *Baxendale*. Where there is a delay in completing the works the proper measure of damage is the value of the use of the building during the period of delay.

Where the contractor's work is defective the basic rule as explained in *East Ham Corporation* v. *Bernard Sunley & Sons Ltd*[17], is the reasonable cost of the repairs (subject to the betterment point) at the date when the defects were discovered. However, in *Cory & Son* v. *Wingate Investments Ltd*[18] the court assessed the damages by reference to the cost of the repairs at the date when the claim was heard. It seems that the courts have, as a matter of policy, adopted a fairly wide discretion in assessing the correct time at which repairs should be undertaken. For example, in *Dodd Properties (Kent) Ltd* v. *Canterbury City Council*[19] Cantley J said that:

> "The appropriate damages are the cost of repairs at the time when it is reasonable to begin repairs".

As mentioned above, a plaintiff is obliged to mitigate his loss. In inflationary times any delay to building work will automatically mean a higher cost. It is not entirely clear what the position will be when a plaintiff cannot raise the money to carry out remedial work as soon as he discovers the defect. There is some authority[20] to suggest that the impecuniosity of the plaintiff is in law too remote a cause of loss to entitle a plaintiff to claim the greater loss he has actually suffered as opposed to the lesser he would have suffered if he were rich. However, this proposition has been the subject of extensive criticism and it seems that the better view is that if remedial work is delayed by reason of the plaintiff's impecuniosity he is still entitled to recover the actual cost provided he has acted reasonably to mitigate his loss insofar as his resources permit.

A further difficulty may arise where the cost of the repairs is wholly

16 (*Mertens* v. *Home Freeholds Company* [1921] 2 KB 526)
17 [1966] AC 406
18 (1980) 17 BLR 104
19 [1979] 2 All E.R. 118
20 (*Dredger Liesbosch (Owners)* v. *S S Edison (Owners)* [1933] AC 449)

disproportionate to the object to be achieved. In such circumstances the award of damages is assessed by measuring the value of the building had it been built as required by the contract less its value as it stands[21]. If, however, the plaintiff sells the property, the correct measure of loss is the value of the building as it should have been less its re-sale value[22]. To this may be added any consequential losses which were in the reasonable contemplation of the parties.

Consequential Loss and Damage

As it is commonly understood in the industry the word "consequential" means, I suspect, all loss other than that directly incurred by way of expenditure by the injured party. That is not, however, the meaning placed upon the word by the English courts. For example, in *Croudace Construction Ltd* v. *Cawoods Concrete Products Ltd*[23] the contract provided that the supplier was "not under any circumstances to be liable for any consequential loss or damage caused or arising by reason of the late supply" of masonry blocks. The plaintiffs alleged that the defendants were in breach of contract because of the late delivery of the blocks. The plaintiffs claimed to be indemnified against a claim which had been made against them by sub-contractors in respect of delay in the sub-contractors' work which was said to have been caused by the absence of the materials which the defendants ought to have delivered. The defendants relied upon the limitation of liability clause and said that they were not liable for the indirect or consequential damage caused by the delayed delivery. The Court of Appeal held that the claim was not a claim for "consequential" damage: it was a direct and natural result of the breach. Accordingly, the defendants were liable to indemnify the plaintiff against the claim made by the sub-contractor.

Loss and Expense Claims

The analysis of direct and consequential damage leads on to claims made by contractors against employers. The issue of what constitutes direct or consequential loss often forms an important part of claims for breach of contract and claims for loss and expense. It should, of course, be remembered that a loss and expense claim is not a claim for breach of contract: it

21 *Applegate* v. *Moss* [1971] 1 QB 406
22 *Rawlings* v. *Rentokil Laboratories* (1972) EG 1947
23 [1978] 2 Lloyds Rep 55

is a claim made in accordance with express terms of the contract. However, the general principles to be applied to loss and expense claims are not (subject, of course, to the precise words of the contract) significantly different to those applied when assessing damages for breach of contract. This proposition is supported by a number of authorities. For example, in *Wraight Ltd* v. *PH & T (Holdings) Ltd*[24] Megaw J said,

> "....there are no grounds for giving the words 'direct loss and/or damage'....any other meaning than that which they have....in a case of breach of contract".

In *F G Minter Ltd* v. *Welsh Health Technical Services Organisation*[25] the Court of Appeal held that the words "direct loss and/or expense" were properly to be interpreted in accordance with the views expressed by Megaw J in *Wraight*. As was noted by the editors of The Building Law Reports in their analysis of *Minter*:

> "The distinction to be drawn is a distinction between losses and expenses which the law regards as 'direct' and those regarded as 'indirect' or 'consequential'. It is the same distinction as that which has to be made wherever common law damages are being considered and a particular item of loss or expense or damage is to be regarded as direct if it can fairly be described as falling within the first limb of the test in *Hadley* v. *Baxendale* as being something which arises naturally and in the ordinary course of things".

As can be seen from *Croudace*, English judges consider the expression "losses which arise naturally and in the ordinary course of things" to cover a very wide range of loss and damage.

In the preceding paragraphs I have commented upon the close relationship between the quantification of consensual remedies (loss and expense claims) and remedies for breach of contract (damages). There appears to be no reason why the rules and principles which govern the formulation (as opposed to the quantification) of loss and expense claims should not also apply to claims for damages. For example, in *J Crosby & Sons Ltd* v. *Portland Urban District Council*[26] Donaldson J accepted the argument that where a claim depends on,

24 (1968) 13 BLR 26
25 (1980) 13 BLR 1
26 (1967) 5 BLR 121

"an extremely complex interaction in the consequences of various denials, suspensions and variations, it may well be difficult
or even impossible to make an accurate apportionment of the
total extra cost between the several causative events".

In such circumstances the courts will accept a "rolled up" claim which
does not differentiate between the different causative events. This is of great
practical assistance to the claimant - provided that the claim is sufficiently
particularised there is no need to seek to unravel the tangled web of causes
and consequences.

This principle was considered and approved by Vinelott J in *London
Borough of Merton* v. *Stanley Hugh Leach Ltd*[27]. The judge did, however,
add a word of caution: he explained that a rolled up claim could only be made
where there was a genuine impossibility of separating the different heads of
claim. The Hong Kong Court of Appeal decision in *Wharf Properties* v.
Eric Cumine Associates[28] may suggest that the courts are, however,
beginning to view rolled up claims with some suspicion.

Damages for Specific Torts

The general measure of damages for negligence has already been
discussed: the plaintiff should be put into the same position he would have
been in had he not suffered the wrong. The courts' attitude to the recovery
of pure economic loss is dealt with in other papers[29] and does not properly
belong in a review of remedies. This is because the question of the
recoverability of such loss is a question of liability rather than quantification. It should, however, be noted that economic loss can be recovered for
negligent misstatement under the principles set out in *Hedley Byrne*[30].

It is curious that economic loss should be recoverable when caused by a
negligent misstatement but not when caused by a negligent act. I do not
argue with the logic of the recent cases which have severely limited the
recoverability of economic loss in negligence: I do, however, suggest that
at bottom these cases were dominated by policy considerations and that
those considerations could have been dealt with in a different way. For
example, if I give negligent advice to a client I am liable for all economic
loss. This will be so whether I am sued for breach of contract or in tort. If
there is a sufficiently close and proximate relationship between me and a
non-client I may also be liable to that non-client for any economic loss which

27 (1985) 32 BLR 51
28 (1988) 45 BLR 72
29 See papers 7 and 8.
30 [1964] A.C. 465

he may suffer when placing reliance upon my advice. The principal objections to allowing recovery for economic loss caused by goods or buildings which have been negligently manufactured or built is the "floodgates" argument (essentially a matter of policy) or the argument that to allow such recovery would require a manufacturer or builder to give, in effect, an indefinitely transmittable warranty of quality. However, both of these potential difficulties also face *Hedley Byrne* type claims: both problems have been resolved not by a blanket refusal to accept claims for economic loss but by a sensible and pragmatic use of the doctrine of proximity. *Junior Books* was, in my view, a pragmatic application of this point: recovery was made subject to very stringent tests of proximity. *Junior Books* is perhaps best regarded as a limb of *Hedley Byrne*[31]. It may, however, be better that we look to the doctrine of collateral contract to produce a just result in cases where there is a very close proximity (but no express contract) between manufacturer and buyer or builder and owner. The doctrine is best explained by reference to the well known case of *Shanklin Pier* v. *Detel Products Limited*[32]. In that case a representation made by a supplier to the owner of a pier that a certain type of paint would last for seven years was held to be actionable and the plaintiff owner recovered pure economic loss although there was no express contract between them. The court held that there was a collateral contract. It is surprising that this doctrine has not been used more frequently. However, the difficulty with collateral contracts is in establishing that the statement was intended to be of contractual effect. This, and other, reservations about collateral contracts were made clear in *Independent Broadcasting Authority* v. *EMI Electronics Ltd*[33].

Other relevant torts which I propose to consider are deceit, misrepresentation and nuisance. In an action in deceit the plaintiff must show that a false representation has been made knowingly, without belief in its truth or recklessly or carelessly as to whether it be true or false: *Derry* v. *Peek*[34]. Proof of damage in consequence of acting upon the representation is required. Damages are limited to the amount of the actual loss suffered by the plaintiff as a result of the deceit[35]. It is not particularly helpful to be told that the damages recoverable are the "actual loss suffered". However, there appears to be little authority on the point. In *Clark* v. *Urquhart*[36] Lord Atkin said that the correct measure of damages was the "actual damage directly

---

31 (see the comments of Lord Keith in *Murphy* v. *Brentwood District Council* [1991] 1 AC 398

32 [1951] 2 KB 854

33 (1980) 14 BLR 1

34 [1889] 14 AC 337

35 *Mahesan s/o Thambiah* v. *Malaysia Government Officers' Co-op* [1979] AC 374

36 [1930] AC 28

flowing from the fraudulent inducement".

The question of the proper measure of damages to be applied in claims for misrepresentation under Section 2(1) of the Misrepresentation Act 1967 has been the subject of much debate. In *Watts* v. *Spence*[37] it was held that the plaintiff was entitled to damages for loss of bargain (i.e. the contractual measure of damages). However, the same issue arose in *Sharneyford Supplies Ltd* v. *Edge*[38] when Mervyn Davies J held that the tortious measure was appropriate and criticised the decision in *Watts* v. *Spence*. The Court of Appeal subsequently reversed the judgment at first instance on different grounds which precluded any consideration of this particular issue. However, Balcombe LJ said that Counsel for the plaintiff was "very wise" not to argue that the proper measure of damages for a Section 2(1) claim was contractual and agreed with the criticisms of *Watts* v. *Spence* made by Mervyn Davies J at first instance. In the recent case of *Royscott Trust* v. *Rogerson and Others*[39] the Court of Appeal held that the correct measure of damages was tortious and, furthermore, that the measure to be applied was that of the tort of deceit. Consequently, even unforeseeable losses are recoverable under Section 2(1).

Nuisance is a tort which is not often the subject of litigation but it can be relevant to the construction industry. Nuisance is a condition or activity which unduly interferes with the use or enjoyment of land. Where a nuisance results in the commission of physical damage to land the damages which are recoverable are those which will compensate the plaintiff for the diminution in the value of the land caused by the nuisance[40]. Where there is no physical damage but the nuisance causes annoyance, inconvenience or discomfort the damages are measured by analogy with personal injury claims rather than those which deal with diminution in property values[41]. Where the nuisance not only interferes with the plaintiff's property but additionally causes some other consequential loss such as a loss of profit then the plaintiff may claim for such additional losses[42].

Damages for Breach of Statutory Duty

The number of statutory duties imposed upon us is immense and grows greater with every day. However, not every breach of statute gives a person

---

37 [1976] Ch 165
38 [1986] Ch 128
39 [1991] 2 QB 297
40 see *Bunclark* v. *Hertfordshire CC* [1977] 243 EG 455
41 See *Halsey* v. *Esso Petroleum Co Ltd* [1961] 2 All E.R. 145 and *Bone* v. *Seale* [1975] 1 WLR 797
42 see *Dodd Properties (Kent) Ltd* v. *Canterbury City Council* [1980] 1 All E.R. 928

who suffers resultant loss a cause of action against the wrongdoer. The purpose of this is to consider how damages are assessed in the event that a breach of statutory duty is actionable at the suit of an individual. The measure of any damages will, of course, depend on the precise wording of the legislation. The damages recoverable are such as are contemplated by the statute and this will probably include damages which are the natural consequence of the breach. However, apart from certain comments in *Cynat Products Limited* v. *Landbuild (Investment and Property) Ltd*[43] there appears to be no modern authority on the question of consequential losses arising as a result of a breach of statutory duty. The difficulties posed by applying the usual test of foreseeability to such actions are great and may, in some circumstances, run counter to the precise wording of the statute. The safest course is to assume that the only damages which will be recoverable will be those necessary to compensate the innocent party for the damage which was caused provided that that damage was of a type which the legislation was passed to prevent.

In summary, the damages recoverable must be contemplated by the statute. Whilst the courts have been ready to infer a right of action for breaches of statutory duties designed to ensure personal safety, particularly of employees, they have been cautious in inferring the existence of such an action where the harm suffered in consequence of the breach of duty is economic loss. However, there is no principle such as that in relation to the tort of negligence which prevents the recovery of economic loss. Where the plaintiff can establish, as in *Rickless* v. *United Artists Corporation*[44] that the purpose of the statute was to safeguard his financial interests he will be entitled to recover economic loss. This was not a construction case but is, nevertheless, instructive lest we come to believe that the recovery of economic loss in any circumstances (save for *Hedley Byrne*) is impossible. The case concerned the Dramatic and Musical Performances Act 1958. The Act, in short, prevented the exploitation of the performance of an actor or a musician by any other person without the consent of the actor or musician in question. The court held that the Act gave rise to a private right of action and that it protected the individual performer's financial interests. Pure financial loss was, therefore, recoverable in the action.

However, following the trend in negligence, the courts will be cautious about inferring such an intention. For example, in the construction field, the higher courts have repeatedly held that statutory powers conferred on local authorities to inspect building works are public health measures. They are not designed to protect developers from economic loss; (see, for example, *Governors of the Peabody Donation Fund* v. *Sir Lindsay Parkinson & Co*

43 [1984] 3 All E.R. 513
44 [1988] QB 40, [1987] 1 All ER 679

Ltd.[45]). The plaintiff in an action for breach of statutory duty can recover only if the damage which he has suffered was caused or materially contributed to by the breach of duty[46]. Whether there is a sufficient causal connection between the breach of duty and the damage is a matter "to be determined by applying common sense to the facts of the case"[47].

In an action for damages for breach of statutory duty the onus of proving that, on the balance of probabilities, the breach caused and materially contributed to the damage to the plaintiff lies on the plaintiff unless that statute expressly or by necessary implication states otherwise.

In relation to European Community law the House of Lords in 1983[48] recognised that breaches of European Community Treaties could give rise to individual rights of action but the principles upon which such a right arises remain far from clear as yet. There is, however, nothing to suggest that the assessment of any damages which might be awarded to an injured party would differ from those set out above in connection with the assessment of damages for breach of statutory duty.

Remedies other than compensation

The remedies considered so far are "substitutional" remedies: the plaintiff does not get what he contracted for nor is he protected from the civil wrong. He is merely compensated, in monetary terms, for the effect of the wrong. I will now consider specific remedies, orders which require a party to comply with his obligations or which prohibit him from taking steps which constitute a breach of his obligations. The basic principles governing the grant of injunctions and the making of orders for specific performance are as follows. As regards injunctions, the High Court has a statutory power to grant an injunction (whether interlocutory or final) in all cases where it appears just and convenient to do so[49]. An injunction can be either prohibitory or mandatory. Whilst the court can grant a mandatory injunction it is a very exceptional form of relief. In order to obtain an interlocutory injunction the plaintiff must establish that he has a good arguable claim that the grant of an injunction is justified on the balance of convenience[50].

The balance of convenience is the critical test. It emphasises the discretionary nature of the relief. In considering this question the court will

45 [1985] AC 210
46 See *Caswell* v. *Powell Duffryn Associated Collieries Limited* [1940] AC 152.
47 *Stapley* v. *Gypsum Mines Limited* [1953] AC 663
48 (*Garden Cottage Foods Ltd* v. *Milk Marketing Board* [1984] AC 130; [1983] 2 All E.R. 770)
49 s.37 Supreme Court Act 1981
50 *American Cyanamid Co* v. *Ethicon Ltd* [1975] AC 396

take all relevant factors into account but will be particularly concerned to determine whether damages would be a sufficient remedy. If so, an injunction will not be granted. Damages are unlikely to be sufficient if the defendant cannot pay them or if the wrong is irreparable or if damages would be very difficult to assess. The balance of convenience test will quite often be a test which is satisfied by the court simply asking itself whether more harm will be done by granting or refusing to grant an injunction. In order to obtain a mandatory injunction the plaintiff must establish that there is a very strong probability that he will suffer grave damage if the injunction is not granted[51]. Furthermore, a plaintiff may be entitled to a *quia timet* injunction (an injunction to stop a threatened wrong) in particular circumstances. Such injunctions will be granted where it is the only way in which to avoid the proven probability of damage to the plaintiff.

Specific performance is a decree of the court which compels the defendant to do what he promised to do. The remedy is an equitable remedy which the court will grant if it is just to do so. No plaintiff is, therefore, entitled to specific performance as of right. The court will grant specific performance instead of damages "only when it can by that means do more perfect and complete justice"[52].

These specific remedies have not readily been accepted into English law - the principal concern of English courts has always been with monetary compensation. The traditional view has been that if there was a sufficient remedy at common law (i.e. damages) then there would be no equitable remedy granted. This is in marked contrast to other jurisdictions. For example, in Scotland many building contracts are specifically enforced. The court simply appoints some suitably qualified person under whose supervision the work is executed[53].

The reluctance by the courts to grant specific remedies has been particularly relevant to the construction industry. The courts in England will not, in general, grant specific performance of a building contract. The principle cannot, however, be formulated in absolute terms. The courts have vacillated. In some cases the courts have declined to issue decrees of specific performance because the effective policing of the order would require the court to supervise, over a long period, successive acts by the contractor[54]. However, in other cases, the courts have accepted that they could order specific performance where the works were specified in a sufficiently definite manner. For example, Megarry J in the well known, and

51 *Redland Bricks Ltd* v. *Morris*[1970] AC 652; [1969] 2 All E.R. 576
52 *Wilson* v. *Nottingham & Banbury Junction Railway Company* [1874] 9 Ch App 279
53 see *Clark* v. *Glasgow Assurance* 1 M'QU 668
54 see *Dowty Bolton Paul Ltd* v. *Wolverhampton Corporation* [1971] 2 AER 277; *Hepburn* v. *Leather* [1884] 50 LT and *Blackett* v. *Bates* [1865] 1 Ch App 117

much criticised, case of *Hounslow LBC* v. *Twickenham GD Limited*[55] suggested that a building contract could be specifically enforced. The case concerned a building contract which contained the usual provision requiring the contractors to proceed regularly and diligently. The architect took the view that the contractors were not proceeding regularly and diligently and the employer purported to determine the contract. The contractor refused to leave the site and the employer sought an injunction requiring the contractor to leave the site. Megarry J refused to grant the injunction because there was, in his view, an implied negative obligation on the employer not to revoke any licence to occupy the premises unless the contract had been validly determined by notice. During the course of argument the question arose as to whether the contract was specifically enforceable. This issue arose because, in effect, a refusal to grant the injunction removing the contractor would have had the result of specifically enforcing the contract. Megarry J said:

> "....I cannot at present see why this contract should not be held to be specifically enforceable by the [employer] against the contractor. The work to be done is sufficiently defined, I do not think that damages would be adequate compensation and the contractor obtained possession of the land under the contract.... however, as I have indicated, I do not consider that this point has to be decided, and I do not do so".

This view has been rightly criticised. It is simply impractical for a court to supervise a building contract which it has decreed shall be specifically enforced. Furthermore, as mentioned above, the refusal of Megarry J to remove the contractor from site had the effect, in real terms, of requiring the contract to be specifically enforced. There was no reason for this: the contractor could be adequately compensated in damages for the wrongful determination. The most cogent criticism of *Hounslow* is made by the authors of *Emdens Building Contracts and Practice* (8th Edition) at page 200 where it is said of the case:

> "....the basic premise is fallacious: the case seems to have been decided on the assumption that the contractor had to go onto site in order to earn his money. In fact the contractor can adequately be compensated by damages, in the same way as an employee who is wrongfully dismissed. No one suggests that a butler who has been dismissed for drunkenness should be allowed to remain

in service and in charge of the wine cellar until his term of employment expires. If he has been wrongfully sacked he is entitled to damages but not to have his job back...."

If *Hounslow* were to be followed it would give contractors a very powerful tactical advantage. They would, in effect, be allowed to keep possession of the site where there was any real doubt as to the lawfulness of the purported determination of the contract by the employer. However, the *Hounslow* case should be considered in the light of the general principles governing the grant of interlocutory injunctions set out in *American Cyanamid Co* v. *Ethicon Ltd* which emphasised that injunctions were discretionary remedies and, at the interlocutory stage, consideration should be given to where the balance of convenience lies. Thus, in a case where a contractor seeks an injunction restraining the employer from re-entering the site or the employer seeks an injunction requiring the contractor to leave the site, the question will usually be determined by reference to the balance of convenience.

In most (but not necessarily all) cases the balance of convenience will lie with removing the contractor from the site. Unless this is done the employer will have no effective means of completing the project and the damage suffered by the contractor can adequately be compensated by an award of damages - there is no need for the contractor to remain on site. This appears to have been the approach adopted by HH Judge Bowsher QC in *Tara Civil Engineering Ltd* v. *Moorfield Developments Ltd*[56]. In that case the plaintiffs were contractors to the defendant developers. The engineer served a notice on the plaintiffs condemning certain works. The plaintiffs failed to rectify the works and the engineer issued a notice under the terms of the conditions informing the plaintiffs of the defendants' intention to expel the plaintiffs from the site. The plaintiffs obtained an *ex parte* injunction restraining the defendants from removing them from site. Judge Bowsher discharged the injunction; he decided that, pending ultimate resolution of the dispute, the court had to decide, on the balance of convenience, whether the engineer's decision should be supported. In his view the balance of convenience was strongly in favour of the court supporting the engineer's decision. He therefore ordered that the plaintiffs should be removed from site. Judge Bowsher considered Megarry J's comments in *Hounslow* but did not follow them. This view seem to accord with the views of the Hong Kong Court of Appeal in *Attorney General of Hong Kong* v. *Ko Hon Mau*[57]. In the light of these developments it seems unlikely that, in the absence of exceptional

56 (1989) 46 BLR 72
57 (1988) 44 BLR 144

circumstances, a contractor will be able to retain possession of a site.

There is a limited exception to the general rule that a building contract will not be specifically enforced. This is where a person has agreed to carry out works in consideration of obtaining possession of land, the proposed works are sufficiently defined and damages will not be an adequate remedy[58].

Conclusion

In this paper I have sought to give a brief review of the way in which damages are assessed in contract, a number of torts and for breaches of statutory duty. I have also sought to give a broad outline of the specific remedies available to those involved in the industry. However, as Professor Bishop states in paper 15, an ounce of prevention is worth a pound of cure.

---

58 see *Carpenters Estates Limited* v. *Davies* [1940] Ch 160

Quantum Meruit 11
as a Quasi-Contractual Remedy

Marshall Levine

Synopsis

This paper gives an overview of the circumstances in which quantum meruit claims can arise, both under valid contracts where no price is fixed or ascertainable and in cases when there is no contract, the latter being the more orthodox application of the term. It is concluded that quantum meruit remains an important principle in construction cases, reflecting the degree of informality which is often found in the drawing up of building contracts.

Introduction

Quasi-contract is best defined by reference to the principle of unjust enrichment, whereby one party is enriched by receipt of a benefit at the other party's expense. At common law quasi-contract formed a significant part of the law of restitution[1] and developed primarily in relation to:

(1) action for money paid where there was a total failure of consideration or where money was paid under a void contract.
(2) action for recompense (quantum meruit) for a benefit (other than a payment of money) conferred on the other party.

Quantum meruit can be used where services have been rendered under contract where the price has not been fixed, or where there is no formal contract but merely an agreement for reasonable payment. Claims under quasi-contract can be brought where a contract does exist, or where it has ceased to exist, or where it never existed. Quasi-contract can therefore be seen as a general term to describe an area of the law of restitution, in relation to the principle of unjust enrichment, where quantum meruit forms one of the principal remedies. Accordingly this paper seeks to focus on quantum meruit as a quasi-contractual remedy.

---

1 (1853) See Goff & Jones "*The Law of Restitution*" 3rd Edition at p12

Definition of Quantum Meruit

Jowitt's dictionary refers to the early history of actions for quantum meruit as genuine actions in the law of contract based on a real promise to pay, although the promise had not necessarily been expressed in words. It appears that the action is now founded in quasi-contract and the court looks at the true facts of the case to ascertain whether or not a promise to pay is to be implied, irrespective of the actual expression of the parties at a time when the work was done or the services rendered.[2]

Winfield has said, quoting *De Benardy* v. *Harding*[3] that the remedy of quantum meruit is available

"where one party has absolutely refused to perform, or has rendered himself incapable of performing, his part of the contract, and puts it in the power of the other party either to sue for breach of it, or to rescind the contract and sue on a quantum meruit for the work actually done."

In the case of *Planche* v. *Colborn*[4] the defendants engaged the plaintiff to write a volume for publication in the defendants' proposed series of books. After the plaintiff had written some of his work the defendants abandoned the whole publication and it was held that the plaintiff would be able to sue to recover the reasonable remuneration for his work already done. Here there was no contract for the work; in fact the plaintiff had not even tendered for it.

The claim on a quantum meruit may be endorsed on a writ as a debt or liquidated demand[5]. An interesting point to note, however, is that an action for quantum meruit cannot be maintained in an action for summary judgment under R.S.C. Order 14, because the courts have no power under the procedural rules to entertain such an action.[6] If a claim for contractual damages fails and a plaintiff is forced to rely upon an alternative pleading for quantum meruit, the plaintiff will have to proceed to full trial to prove its case, which would in certain circumstances provide the defendant with a great bargaining tool. In *Crown House Engineering Ltd* v. *Amec Projects Ltd*, Bingham LJ observed:

"where there were substantial issues of genuine complexity

2   *William Lacey (Hounslow) Ltd* v. *Davis* 1957 1WLR 932
3   (1853) 8 Exch 822
4   (1831) 8 Bing 14
5   RSC Ord 6, r.2.
6   *Crown House Engineering Ltd* v. *AMEC Projects Ltd* (1990) 6 Const LJ 141

[such as issues as to the effect, in an action for quantum meruit, of bad workmanship of the plaintiff and additional losses incurred by the defendant as a consequence] the parties should prepare for trial rather than dissipate their energy and resources on deceptively attractive short cuts".[7]

Quantum Meruit in Construction Contracts

The concept of quantum meruit appears in a disguised form in some standard construction contracts. In the context of termination clauses in, for example, both the JCT Minor Works Contract and the ICE Minor Works Contract, the concept inherent within a claim for quantum meruit appears as follows:

(a) JCT Agreement for Minor Building Works - Clause 3.6:
"the Architect/Contract Administrator may, without invalidating the contract, order an addition to or omission from or other change in the Works or the order or period in which they are to be carried out and any such instructions shall be valued by the Architect/Contract Administrator on a fair and reasonable basis,..."

(b) ICE Minor Works Condition - Clause 6.1:
"if the Contractor carries out additional works or incurs additional cost ... the Engineer shall certify and the Employer shall pay to the Contractor such additional sum as the Engineer after consultation with the Contractor considers fair and reasonable."

It has been noted that these provisions comprise a contractual equivalent of quantum meruit. However, the contract conditions go on to state that the valuing professional, whether architect/contract administrator or engineer, should use the relevant prices in the specification/schedule/schedules of rates agreed in relation to the original basis of contract works, as a guide to evaluating what is "fair and reasonable" in the circumstances. In the absence of contractual provisions to this effect, the courts would in any case take due notice of contractual rates or other surrounding circumstances, to assess the price of works carried on outside the strict wording in a contract, in a claim for quantum meruit.[8]

---

7 See also *British & Commonwealth Holdings PLC* v. *Quadrex Holdings Inc* [1989] 3 WLR 723.
8 See *Way* v. *Latilla* (1937) 3 All E.R. 759

Occasionally, provisions are inserted into contracts for the payment by the employer of "such reasonable remuneration as the contractor shall be entitled to receive". Alternatively, there may be actual reference to the words "quantum meruit" in a clause such as:

> "Upon termination of this appointment ...... the architect shall be entitled to a proportion of its fee calculated on a quantum meruit basis".

Where the term "quantum meruit" expressly appears, the employer may be worse off, because the term imputes a liability to pay a reasonable profit for the work, over and above the rates identified in the contract. In addition, the question arises to what extent the court can take into account the fact that the contractor may have wrongfully determined the contract. In such a case the contractor is in a position to take advantage by claiming for the work done and also for profit. The question is whether the claim for quantum meruit should be reduced on account of the contractor's conduct, or because it has led the employer, for example, to incur further loss and expense as a consequence?[9] The American approach is that the claim for quantum meruit should not be limited in this way, but the point has not been finally settled here.

Claims under contract

As stated above, "quantum meruit" is the right to be paid a reasonable remuneration for work done, which can arise in many circumstances. The following are relevant to claiming "quantum meruit" under a contract:

(1) Where work is carried out at the request of a building owner and no price is stated, the law usually implies a term that a reasonable sum be paid. In particular contracts, the Supply of Goods and Services Act 1982[10] implies into a contract for the supply of a service the promise by the recipient that he will pay a reasonable charge. Though the expression quantum meruit is often applied to this sum, the real basis of its imposition is as an implied term. Strictly speaking, quantum meruit should arise only where the contract has failed.
(2) No action for a reasonable price for work done under a contract can be maintained unless it can be implied that the parties intended that the work should be paid for. The test is whether a reasonable man in the position of

9 See note 7
10 Supply of Goods and Services Act 1982, Section 15

the employer would have believed the person doing the work intended to do it at his own expense. The normal inference is that professionals such as architects or lawyers do not intend to give their services free. The employer or client will be held, by the fact of employment, to have bound himself to pay a reasonable reward for the services rendered.

(3) Where a contract expressly provides for fixed remuneration on specified events, the court cannot award any other remuneration on those events, nor can it award any remuneration if they do not occur.[11] To allow quantum meruit claims in such cases would contradict the agreement reached between the parties, and the courts will do this only if there are special circumstances justifying such a course. This may arise where, for example, one party to a contract starts to perform his duties under the contract but is prevented from completing them by the other party's breach. In such a case he can claim quantum meruit (at the contract rate) for the work done. It may arise also where work is done in partial performance of a contract and is voluntarily accepted by the other party.

(4) Where an agreement contains prices but is silent as to the price to be paid for particular work, for example if varied work has no counterpart in the schedule of rates or bills of quantities, there will be a right to a reasonable sum for the work in question. In *Re Walton-on-the-Naze UDC & Moran*[12] the contract was to construct, inter alia, a "cast iron outlet pipe to low water". The general plan showed the outlet pipe extending to the low water level, but the section showed it as extending 279 feet further into the sea. The bill of quantities stated the length to be the same as that in the section, but there was no price fixed in the bill for pricing underwater works. The court held that the contract was a schedule of prices contract, and as underwater work was not covered by any price in the schedule of prices the contractor was entitled to be paid at a fair valuation. Similarly, in *Constable Hart & Co Ltd v. Peter Lind & Co Ltd*[13] the parties entered into a sub-contract in the FCEC form for the surfacing of a by-pass. It was agreed that the quoted price was to remain fixed until June 1975 and thereafter negotiated. The Court of Appeal held that post-June 1975 rates of work would be reasonable rates, including an element of profit.

Claims where a contract fails

True quantum meruit claims can arise where the contract fails to operate or never exists for various reasons. The first such case is that of an

11 *Gilbert & Partners* v. *Knight* [1968] 2 All E.R. 248
12 (1905) Hudson's BC, Vol 2 p 376
13 (1978) 9 BLR 4.

anticipated contract. This is where work is done in anticipation of a contract, but the negotiations are not ultimately successful. For example, letters of intent normally create no contractual liability. However, in the case of *British Steel Corp* v. *Cleveland Bridge and Engineering Co Ltd*[14] it was held that although no contract had come into existence on the basis of a letter of intent and partial performance, the plaintiff was entitled to be paid upon a quantum meruit. Robert Goff J. said:

"The question of whether in a case such as the present any contract has come into existence must depend on a true construction of the relevant communications which have passed between the parties and the effect (if any) of their actions pursuant to those communications. There can be no hard and fast answer to the question whether a letter of intent will give rise to a binding agreement: everything must depend on the circumstances of the particular case".

And later in his judgment:-

"Both parties confidently expected a formal contract to eventuate. In these circumstances, to expedite performance under that anticipated contract, one requested the other to expedite the contract work, and the other complied with that request. If thereafter, as anticipated, a contract was entered into, the work done as requested will be treated as having been performed under that contract; if contrary to their expectation, no contract was entered into, then the performance of the work is not referable to any contract, the terms of which can be ascertained, and the law simply imposes an obligation on the party who made the request to pay a reasonable sum for such work as has been done pursuant to that request, such an obligation arising in quasi-contract or, as we now say, in restitution".

In the *British Steel* case,[15] Cleveland Bridge were sub-contractors for the fabrication of steel work for the construction of a bank in Saudi Arabia, which incorporated in the design a requirement for cast-steel nodes. British Steel were asked to supply the nodes. After protracted negotiations Cleveland Bridge wrote to British Steel and said that, "it is the intention of Cleveland Bridge to enter into a sub-contract with your company.......We

14 [1984] 1 All ER 504
15 Ibid

request that you proceed immediately with the works pending the preparation and issuing to you of the official form of sub-contract". No formal
contract was ever signed but the steel was delivered. Cleveland Bridge
refused to pay, saying that late delivery had caused them loss and that such
late delivery was a breach of contract. BSC claimed that there could be no
contractual delivery dates as there was no contract. It was held that there was
no contract but that BSC should receive payment on a quantum meruit basis.

A more recent case on an application for a claim for quantum meruit for
preparatory work in pursuance of an anticipated contract is *Marston
Construction Co. Ltd v. Kigass Ltd.*[16] In this case, following *William Lacey
(Hounslow) Ltd* v. *Davis*[17], the plaintiffs tendered for rebuilding the
defendants' factory and it was indicated to them that the contract would be
given to them on the condition that sufficient insurance monies were
forthcoming for the rebuilding. Marston Construction asked that, because
of the large amount of preparatory work it was being asked to do, it could
have assurances that it would get the contract to do the works and that its
costs would be met by Kigass Ltd. It was common ground that it was given
the assurance of being granted the contract, but not the second assurance. On
the facts the Court held that (1) there was no agreement that Marston
Construction should be paid for their preparatory work; (2) there was an
express request to carry out that work and implied request to carry out
preparatory works in general; (3) both requests gave rise to a right of
payment at a reasonable sum in quasi-contract; and (4) there would be a
direction for trial of the quantum meruit assessment of the amount due.

The effect of this is that the party making the request for work to be done
or for services to be provided will be liable to pay for work which he would
not have had to pay for if the anticipated contract had come into existence;
for example, preparatory work which would, if the contract had been made,
have been allowed for in the price of the finished work. The case did reflect
upon some interesting ideas, in that the court considered the subject of
"benefit" in the law of restitution. The old rule was always that, for there
to be recovery for quantum meruit, a plaintiff would have to show that the
defendants (those for whom work or services were performed) received an
actual benefit (in a similar sense to "benefit" and "detriment" in the law of
estoppel) for example cash, paying off creditors, or abatement of a nuisance,
thereby conferring an incontrovertible benefit to the defendant.[18] However,
some doubt has recently been expressed on whether this proposition is
correct.[19]

16 (1989) 46 BLR 109
17 See note 3.
18 See *Craven-Ellis* v. *Canons Ltd* [1936] 2 KB 403 and *Greenwood* v. *Bennett* [1973] 1
    QB 195.
19 See note 17.

Repudiation

Where work is only partly carried out and there is a repudiatory breach by the employer the authorities suggest that a contractor may sue for damages or elect to bring an action in quantum meruit for work done instead.[20] If the plaintiff is unable to complete his duties under a contract except at a loss, he may treat the contract as discharged by the breach and sue on quantum meruit based upon quasi-contractual rights and duties for the entire or partial cost of the work done. As this action does not depend upon the contract it will not necessarily be limited by the contract rate. Where the contractor's rates are highly profitable it is obviously advantageous to claim damages for work done and loss of profit, but if the contract rates are low or uneconomic it may well be that a reasonable price for work done will be more advantageous, especially if a substantial amount of work has been done prior to the employer's repudiation. In addition, and on a purely practical note, the rights of the contracting parties to repudiate or determine the contract should be specifically set down in the contract terms and conditions, and these may include the consequences of repudiation.

The principal authority for the above propositions is *Lodder* v. *Slowey*[21]. In this case a guarantor who had been called upon to complete construction works engaged a builder to do so and left supervision of the contract to the employer. The Privy Council, on appeal from New Zealand, held that in doing so he had made the employer his agent and that, when the employer committed a repudiatory breach by obstructing the builder, the builder was entitled to sue the guarantor on a quantum meruit basis for the actual value of the work, labour and materials he had provided instead of bringing an action for damages for breach of contract i.e. to ignore profitability thereunder. There is, however, doubt as to whether this represents current law on the basis that damages for breach of contract are compensatory and the contractor should recover no more than he could under the contract[22]. In fact the Law Commission[23] recommended that quantum meruit should not be based on the contract price.

A very full consideration was given to quantum meruit in *Morrison-Knudsen Co. Inc.* v. *B.C. Hydro and Power Authority.*[24] The case concerned the construction of a hydroelectric dam during which the employer committed several breaches of contract, including failure to pay for work which had been accelerated, and the court held that these breaches amounted to fundamental breaches. However, the contractor continued to work, com-

20 But see Keating 5th Ed. p.208
21 [1904)]AC 442
22 see Keating ibid
23 Law Comm No 121 at para 2.52
24 (1978) 85 DLR (3d) 186 at pp 224-235

pleted the project and, inter alia, claimed to be entitled to payment on a quantum meruit under the *Lodder* v. *Slowey*[25] principle. The court held that:

(A) Where a repudiatory breach occurs during a contract, a contractor can elect to affirm the breach or to treat it as discharging the contract. In the latter case the contractor can either claim for damages for the breach of contract or can sue under a quantum meruit. If the contractor affirms the contract then he cannot claim under a quantum meruit:

(B) If (a) the breach does not occur until after completion or (b) the contractor does not become aware of the breach until after completion or (c) does not become aware that the breach is fundamental until after completion, then the contractor cannot recover under a quantum meruit. Once he has completed performance his rights are limited to those he is entitled to under the contract as under it he will have an adequate remedy. This remedy is to sue for damages for the breach of contract.

Substantial performance

Substantial performance means performance which is so nearly equivalent to the full performance that was bargained for that it would be unreasonable and unfair to deny the contractor recovery. If the performance rendered is not completely consistent with the terms of the contract, the owner is entitled to an allowance for defects in the work or damages for the contractor's failure to comply with the contract, which will go in diminution of price.[26] Where there has been substantial performance the contractor may in the absence of a contractual price recover for labour and materials, on the basis that the cost of improvement to property should be borne by the owner who benefits.

Refusal of extension of time

An area of building contract law not as yet explored in the United Kingdom arises where extensions of time are refused by the owner's supervising professional. In such circumstances, where the refusal is unjustified, the contractor may be entitled to financial compensation for accelerating progress in order to complete on time. In *Morrison-Knudsen* v. *B.C. Hydro & Power*[27] a British Columbian case, the owner, unbeknown to the contractor, had secretly agreed with a government representative that

25 See note 22.
26 See *Hoenig* v. *Isaacs* [1952] 2 All E.R. 176
27 See note 25.

no extension of time would be granted, in view of the pressing need for electricity by the contract completion date. All requests for an extension of time were refused, and the contractor carried on and finished the project with only slight delay. The Court of Appeal of British Columbia held that the contractor could have rescinded on the basis of a fundamental breach of contract, had he known the real reason for the refusals, and in that event he would have been entitled, on the basis of established case law, to put his claim in quantum meruit and thus escape from the original contract prices. The fact that the contractor had not rescinded, but had completed the project, limited his remedy to the usual one of damages, measured in this case in terms of the additional expense incurred in completing to time (i.e. in accelerating progress).

Partial performance of entire contracts

If part only of a party's obligations under a contract have been performed, that party can normally recover nothing. Since the terms of the contract have not been complied with there is no entitlement to the agreed price, nor is there a right to any smaller sum for the value of its partial performance. The mere acceptance of acts of part performance under contract cannot, taken alone, justify an implied contract to pay on a quantum meruit basis. The common law rule on entire contracts was developed in cases concerning building contracts, or contracts for work and materials, where there was no provision for payment by instalments. Where the builder under such an entire contract fails to perform his obligations fully then, subject to the doctrine of substantial performance as discussed above, he can recover nothing for work completed, despite the fact that the other party may have received a substantial benefit from that work.

If the circumstances justify the inference that the parties have made a fresh contract, under which the original promisee agrees to accept and pay for partial performance of the original promise, he will be liable upon a quantum meruit to pay a reasonable price for the work actually done, or the goods actually supplied. The leading case in this area of law is *Sumpter* v. *Hedges*[28]. Here a builder abandoned the partially completed building on the defendant's land, and the mere fact that the defendant completed the building did not amount to an implied promise by him to pay for the value of the work previously done by the builder. Since the defendant was in possession of his own land and could not be expected to abandon it or to keep the building unfinished, it was not possible to imply a promise to pay. However, the builder had left materials on site and it was held that he could

28 [1898] 1 QB 673.

recover a reasonable sum based on a quantum meruit for the value of those materials which the owner had used to complete the building.

Defendant preventing complete performance

If one party to a contract wrongfully prevents the other party from completing performance, the plaintiff may either recover damages for breach of contract, or alternatively sue upon a quantum meruit to recover a reasonable remuneration for his partial performance.[29] This is an instance in which the contract has failed because of the actions of one party to the contract.

Substituted Contract

Quantum meruit is also used where the parties have not performed the terms of their contract, but where it is possible to infer from their conduct that they have agreed to substitute a new contract for the original one. As the performance is outside the original contract, the contract sum becomes irrelevant and a claim in quantum meruit is possible. For example, in *Steven v. Bromley & Son*[30], Banks L.J. stated that:

> "when the charterers tendered a cargo which was outside the charter party, and for which no rate of freight had been agreed, the inference is justified that they made an offer to the owners to pay a reasonable freight if the cargo were accepted for carriage".

Void Contracts

˒ Where a contract is void, a contractor should be able to recover for any work done on a quantum meruit. This may arise if, for example, the contract is void for mistake. In the case of *Craven-Ellis* v. *Canons Ltd.*[31], the plaintiff was appointed by the defendant company as managing director by an agreement under the company's seal. However, this was void as neither he nor those who appointed him held the necessary qualification shares, so that he could not recover his agreed payment. The Court of Appeal held that he was entitled to a quantum meruit since the company had accepted the benefit of his services, knowing that the services were not intended to be gratuitous.

---

29 see note 5.
30 [1919] 2 KB 722.
31 See note 19.

Where the express contract is a nullity, the argument that the court must not interfere with the bargain between the parties loses much of its force. Liability is not based on any agreement implied from voluntary acceptance by the defendant of the plaintiff's services, since the parties usually think that they are acting under an existing valid contract. In *Craven-Ellis*[32] Greer L.J. said that the liability to pay a quantum meruit:

> "is an inference which a rule of law imposes on the parties where work has been done or goods have been delivered under what purports to be a binding contract but is not so in fact".

This doctrine was upheld recently by the Court of Appeal in *Rover International Ltd* v. *Cannon Film Ltd.*[33] Pursuant to a purported contract in the form of a joint venture between Rover and Cannon for the dubbing and distribution by Rover of certain films supplied by Cannon, Rover claimed for a quantum meruit to cover the costs and reasonable remuneration of the dubbing and distribution that they had undertaken. Unbeknown to the parties, the contract had been void *ab initio* and thus a quantum meruit claim for costs and reimbursement was upheld. Kerr L.J. also ruled against using the terms of the void contract in assessing the quantum meruit. Although remuneration was, under the contract, subject to a ceiling, he did not think that the contention in favour of a "ceiling" was in accordance with general principles. It would involve the application of the provisions of a void contract to the assessment of a quantum meruit which arises only due to the non-existence of the supposed contract. The consequences of relying on the void contract would be far reaching and undesirable and lead to inconsistency, for example, in the case of frustrated contracts, which are governed by the Law Reform (Frustrated Contracts) Act 1943.

Unenforceable Contract

A plaintiff who renders services to a defendant under an unenforceable contract will be entitled to a quantum meruit where the defendant has accepted the benefits arising from the plaintiff's execution of the work. This is, however, subject to the proviso that the restitutionary claim must not undermine the policy of the statute or common law rule rendering the contract unenforceable. In the case of *Pavey & Matthews Pty Ltd* v. *Paul*[34] the builder held a builder's licence under the Builders Licensing Act 1971 (New South Wales). He sued the other party for whom renovation work had

32 see note 19.
33 [1989] 1 WLR 916.
34 (1987) 67 ALJR 151

been carried out under an oral contract for a reasonable sum for work done and materials supplied. The builder made the claim for quantum meruit because non-compliance with Section 45 of the Act precluded recovery by a licensed builder under an oral contact. The contract did not in fact provide for a fixed sum but required the payment of reasonable remuneration for work done to be calculated by reference to prevailing industry rates. The owner of the building relied on Section 45 and contended that an action for quantum meruit amounted to an action to enforce the oral contract and was thereby prohibited by the Act.

The Australian High Court held that the builder could recover the value of work done and materials supplied pursuant to an unenforceable building contract where the other party had accepted the benefit conferred on him by the builder's performance of the unenforceable contract. The Court held that the respondent's interpretation of the Act was too draconian to have been intended and that the restitutionary claim did not undermine the policy of the statute.

Variations

Where the work provided for in the original contract is altered by variations, the change may be such that it can no longer be regarded as work done under the contract. In such circumstances the rule is that the contract has been abandoned as regards the extra work, and the contractor may therefore recover payment for the extra work under a claim for quantum meruit: *Pepper* v. *Burland*.[35] Alternatively it may be possible to claim both for the extra work done and for the original contract work on a quantum meruit basis. In *Thorn* v. *London Corporation*[36] Lord Cairns stated:

> "If it is the kind of additional or varied work contemplated by the contract, [the contractor] must be paid for it, and will be paid for it, according to the prices regulated by the contract. If, on the other hand, it was additional or varied work, so peculiar, so unexpected and so different from what any person reckoned or calculated upon, that it was not within the contract at all; then, it appears to me one of two courses might have been open to him; he might have said: I entirely refuse to go on with the contract ... Or he might have said, I will go on with this, but this is not the kind of extra work contemplated by the contract, and if I do it, I must be paid on a quantum meruit for it".

35 (1792) 1 Peake 139.
36 [1876] 1 App Cas 120 at pp 127-128.

In *Parkinson (Sir Lindsay) & Co. Ltd.* v. *Commissioners of HM Works & Public Buildings*[37] (which is notable as the one case where a quantum meruit was awarded for additional works) a factory was erected according to a varied contract under which the contractors were entitled to recover their costs plus between £150,000 and £300,000 as remuneration, the figures being based on between 3 per cent. and 6 per cent. of the estimated cost which the contractors contemplated to be £5,000,000. The employers ordered extra work which though not different in character from that covered by the varied contract was greatly in excess of the amount contemplated. In fact the value was £6,683,056, and it extended the work by a year. The court held that:

(1) a term could be implied into the varied contract that the employers should not be entitled to require work materially in excess of £5,000,000, as this was the basis of the quantum of work in the varied contract;
(2) as the employers had requested work in excess of £5,000,000 the contractors were entitled to be paid a reasonable remuneration for it, in excess of the £300,000.

However, this decision has been explained in subsequent cases as being decided on the particular facts and the true construction of the deed of variation[38]. A greater degree of variation and delay occurred in *Davis Contractors*[39] where it was held that no quantum meruit applied.

There are various reasons why the doctrine has rarely been held to apply. First, the cost of building work is notoriously difficult to estimate unless one knows the builder's organisation, methods and intentions in detail, and the contractor is in a far better position to estimate the cost than the employer. Secondly, unless the contractor makes a stand or protests it is difficult to contend in building or engineering contracts that the work is so changed as to entitle the contractor to recover other than in accordance with the contract. It was said per Lord Dunedin in *The Olanda*[40] and further approved by the Court of Appeal in *Gilbert & Partners* v. *Knight*[41] that:-

"As regards quantum meruit where there are two parties who are under contract quantum meruit must be a new contract, and in order to have a new contract you must get rid of the old contract".

---

37 [1949] 2 KB 632.
38 See *British Movietones Ltd* v. *London & District Cinemas Ltd* [1952] AC 166.
39 See note 48.
40 [1919] 2 KB 728
41 See note 12.

It will be difficult for the contractor to contend the contract has no application to the work actually done if he receives payment from time to time upon the certificate of the engineer or architect.

In most cases it is not possible to say the original contract work has been entirely abandoned. In the *Morrison-Knudsen Co*[42] case the court considered the law as to quantum meruit, both in this situation and in relation to the doctrine of fundamental breach and severely limited its application in both respects. The respondents contended that the work done under an accelerated programme fundamentally changed the circumstances upon which the original contract was made, and therefore a new contract involving reasonable payment came into existence. The court stated as follows:

(i) The true explanation of the *Parkinson*[43] case was that it fell into the category of cases where a contract existed but contained no provision for payment, where it could not be implied that the work was to be done gratuitously[44]. Therefore the contractors were in that case entitled to reasonable remuneration;

(ii) In order to recover under quantum meruit a contractor must show that the original contract was at an end, e.g. by (a) frustration, (b) express or implied consent, or (c) a repudiatory breach accepted as terminating the contract.

(iii) On the facts and because the contractor had continued to perform, none of these principles applied and the contractor could not recover under a quantum meruit.

Crown House Engineering Ltd v. Amec Projects Ltd

In this case the Court of Appeal[45] discussed issues which bear generally on claims in quantum meruit. The case was an appeal against a judgment refusing to award an interim payment under RSC Order 29 proceedings in respect of interim certificates issued under a building contract. Slade LJ said that on the assessment of a claim for services rendered, based on quantum meruit, it was open to the defendant to assert that the value of such services was to be reduced because of their tardy performance or because of the unsatisfactory manner of their performance, which had exposed him to extra expense or claims by third parties. He added, however, that:

42 See note 25.
43 See note 38.
44 at p.239-40
45 (1990) 6 Const LJ 141.

"the question was not appropriate for determination on an Order
29 or Order 14 application".

Quantum Meruit and Frustration

Where a contract is frustrated a contractor may be able to claim for work
done on a quantum meruit basis. In *Davis Contractors Ltd* v. *Fareham
UDC*[46] Lord Radcliffe described frustration in the following terms:

> "frustration occurs whenever the law recognises that without
> default of either party a contractual obligation has become
> incapable of being performed because the circumstances in
> which performance is called for would render it a thing radically
> different from that which was undertaken by the contract."

In the context of building and engineering contracts, frustration will
normally arise by reason of some supervening event, such as destruction of
the entire site (not merely the works on the site) by fire or flood so that a
resumption of the project is impossible; or the passage of legislation
rendering the work illegal or unnecessary as in *Industrial Overload Ltd* v.
McWatters[47].

In the event of frustration (and in the absence of express provision in the
contract such as ICE Clauses 64 and 65), the financial position between the
parties is governed by the Law Reform (Frustrated Contracts) Act 1943,
which broadly speaking, gives the court a discretion to award reasonable
sums for work done or benefits conferred by the parties to the contract prior
to the frustrating event. The contract rates cease to apply and the obligation
to complete ceases also. If work is recommenced after the frustrating event,
then in the absence of any express agreement to reinstate the contract or to
create a new contract (even though the 1943 Act would not apply), a
contractor would on general principles still be entitled to payment for the
work done on a quantum meruit.

In effect, what the court must decide in such a situation is whether the risk
of what happened was a risk assumed by one of the parties to the contract.
The supervening event must be so unexpected and beyond the contemplation of the parties, even as a possibility, that neither party can be said to have
accepted the risk when contracting. In addition a party cannot rely on what
would otherwise be a frustrating event if it were caused by his own default,
such as delay. For these reasons frustration will be extremely rare in

46 [1956] AC 696 at P729.
47 (1972) 24 DLR (3rd) 231.

building and engineering contracts, since their performance is full of uncertainties and is far more likely to be prevented by physical difficulties than in other types of contract. In general the contractor assumes the risk of most uncertainties and difficulties associated with work in his field. In general it is not a valid excuse for non-performance if the work proves unexpectedly difficult or onerous, and a contractor may still be liable in damages for failing to do something which was impossible at the time of contracting[48].

In *Bush* v. *Trustees of Port and Town of Whitehaven*[49] a contractor tendered in June to lay certain water mains and divert certain streams in Cumberland within four months, on the understanding that work would commence immediately. However, the contractor was not given full possession of the site until October and the contract became a winter one. The court held that the circumstances contemplated by the contract, which gave the contractor no extra money or time extensions unless given by the Engineer, had so changed that the contract ceased to be applicable and the contractor was entitled to be paid on a quantum meruit basis. In effect what was a summer contract became a winter operation.

However, the case was doubted and criticised by the House of Lords in *Davis Contractors Ltd* v. *Fareham UDC*.[50] Viscount Simonds referred to it saying[51]:-

"...I do emphatically say that it cannot, in the light of later authority be used to support the proposition that where, without the default of either party, there has been an unexpected turn of events, which renders the contract more onerous than the parties had contemplated, that is by itself a ground for relieving a party of the obligation he has undertaken."

Following this decision, it may be said that in order for a change in circumstances to give rise to a quantum meruit it must amount to a frustration of the contract. Circumstances which cause the performance of the contract to become more expensive or difficult from that anticipated will not amount to frustration[52].

---

48 See *Jones* v. *St. John's College Oxford* [1870] LR 6 QB 115 and *Smith & Montgomery* v. *Johnson Bros* (1954) 1 BLR 392.
49 (1888) 2 Hudson's BC, 4th Ed, Vol 2, p122.
50 See note 47.
51 at p 716
52 See *Tsakiroglou & Co. Ltd* v. *Noblee & Thorl GmbH* [1961)]2 All ER 179; see also *McAlpine* v. *McDermott* 51 BLR 34 and particularly the judgement of the Court of Appeal.

Ex Gratia Claims

Ex gratia (out of kindness) claims are those claims which an employer has no obligation to meet. They are in effect non-contractual and payment on claims of this nature are made to settle, or compromise a claim rather than go to the expense of contesting it in litigation or arbitration. Such "claims" are recognised under Clause 44(1) of the General Conditions of Government Contracts for Building and Civil Engineering Works (GC Works 1) Edition 2, which gives the employer discretionary power to terminate the contract at any time, upon which event Clause 45(5) provides "if a contractor considers he has suffered hardship by reason of termination, he can make an application for an allowance to the relevant authority whose decision shall be final and conclusive". This provision is of no legal effect, save that it at least obliges the authority to consider the contractor's claim.

Examples outside construction

Quantum meruit is a general legal remedy which is by no means limited to cases involving construction disputes. Claims for reasonable payment are common place in contracts for goods supplied or services rendered as shown in the following examples:

(1) where there is a breach by a party contracting for goods to be carried by sea, land or air, a quasi-contractual claim can be made for a pro-rata amount of the freight remaining;

(2) section 8(2) of the Sale of Goods Act 1979 allows a claim for a reasonable price for goods where the price has not been fixed, or is to be fixed in a manner agreed, or is to be determined given the course of dealing between the parties (known as a quantum valebat);

(3) where wrongful dismissal of an employee leads to discharge of a contract of employment, the employee may bring an action for breach of contract or sue for his wages under the terms of the contract, or he may sue in quasi-contract for services rendered;

(4) like an employee, an agent whose services have been wrongly terminated also has a number of alternative remedies, including suing on a quantum meruit for services rendered;

(5) at common law a shipbroker who receives a commission from a shipowner for effecting the contract will usually receive 5 per cent on the estimated or agreed freight. If this cannot be agreed, and in the absence of a customary rate, he will receive a commission on the basis of reasonable remuneration;

(6) a solicitor who is instructed to carry out professional work is entitled to

reasonable remuneration. This is now a statutory right (not limited to solicitors) under the Supply of Goods and Services Act 1982 which entitles a supplier of services acting in the course of his profession to a reasonable charge.

(7) where there has been a testamentary promise, but in terms too vague to be enforced as a contract, or where a contract is unenforceable but the circumstances indicate that the deceased intended to make a payment, then the promisee is entitled to a reasonable sum from the deceased's estate, quantum meruit being enforced where specific performance is not possible.

Nonetheless, many of the authorities lie in the field of construction law. This reflects the degree of informality in the drawing up of building contracts, including contracts which are not signed or completed by the time the project is completed. Quantum meruit claims are today less frequent than they once were, for example, in regard to employment cases. Many areas of business are becoming more strictly governed by codes, panels, legislation, rules or standardised documentation. Despite similar pressures in the construction industry the number of quantum meruit claims in the building cases still continues to be high.

12 Restitution and property rights

Douglas Close

Synopsis

This paper proposes restitutionary remedies as a solution to disputes as to recovery of money or as to remuneration by way of a quantum meruit or quantum valebat, with particular application to construction disputes. The author seeks to justify the use of restitution in principle and then considers the implications of the proposed model in a series of practical construction situations: first, where substantial preparatory work has been done in anticipation of a contract which does not materialise; second, where money has been paid under a contract which subsequently is held to fail because it is legally incomplete; third, where a sub-contractor is not paid by a main contractor and wishes to proceed against the owner directly; fourth, where an innocent party has supplied goods or services under a contract which is determined by that party for breach and fifth, where a contract is frustrated by some supervening event. The paper concludes by discussing the principles governing valuation of the benefit in the hands of the defendant.

Introduction

The rapidly developing law of restitution has evolved to give justice in situations where, for whatever reason, traditional remedies are unavailable or undesirable. Whilst restitutionary principles are called into play in the law of trusts[1] and, occasionally, tort[2], it is in contractual disputes that their presence is most strongly felt.[3] It may be that services have been rendered under a mistake; that vital terms of the contract remain unresolved; or that a frustrating event prevents further performance. In all these cases, the question of suitable remuneration for work already done or goods already supplied may arise outside the terms of the contract.

---

1 Cf.*Re Diplock* [1948] Ch.253
2 Where a person upon whom a tort has been committed and who brings an action for the benefits received by the tort-feasor "waives" the tort and elects to sue in quasi-contract; *United Australia Ltd* v. *Barclays Bank Ltd.* [1941] AC 1.
3 The law of restitution has developed largely from the common law of quasi-contract involving claims for money had and received and quantum meruit/quantum valebat claims.

In construction disputes, particularly, restitution can be a useful legal tool for the recovery of money or a quantum meruit for services rendered. My first aim in this paper is to justify the use of restitution on the basis of unjust enrichment and, frequently, a bargained-for benefit[4] in the hands of the defendant; I shall then analyse the situations where restitutionary ideas are most helpful, and address the problem of valuing any benefit received to establish just how much restitution is appropriate. As with any work in this area, two sources are invaluable - Goff & Jones,[5] and Birks[6]. This paper owes much to their restitutionary analyses.

Theoretical Justification

"This is indeed by nature fair, that nobody should be made richer through loss to another".

Pomponius, *Digest* 12.6.14

Most mature systems of law have found it necessary to provide, outside the fields of contract and civil wrongs, for the restoration of benefits on grounds of unjust enrichment.[7] Obviously, there are circumstances in which a defendant may find himself in possession of a benefit which he should, in justice, restore to the plaintiff. Clear examples are where A gives money or goods to B under some compulsion or because of some mistake. It is immediately obvious that two distinct elements are required before restoration of such benefits can be justified:[8]

(a)   there must have been an enrichment of the defendant at the plaintiff's expense; and
(b)   an element of injustice requiring the law to intervene and reverse this enrichment.

In construction disputes, arising generally out of contract, the unjust element will rarely, if ever, be a vitiating factor such as mistake or compulsion. More commonly, as we shall see, there will have been a total

4   "*Free Acceptance and the Law of Restitution*" 1988 104 LQR 576 (Burrows).
5   Lord Goff of Chieveley and Gareth Jones, "*The Law of Restitution*", 3rd Ed., London 1986. Hereafter cited as "Goff & Jones".
6   Peter Birks, "*An Introduction to the Law of Restitution*", OUP 1989. Hereafter cited as "Birks".
7   *Fibrosa Spolka Akcyjna* v. *Fairbairn Lawson Combe Barbour* [1943] AC 32, 61, per Lord Wright.
8   In certain circumstances, as will be seen, Goff & Jones and Birks believe that these two elements may both be satisfied by the concept of "free acceptance".

failure of consideration.[9]

Naturally, if A confers a benefit on B under a valid contract, he must seek his remedy under that contract and not in restitution. All the rights and duties of the parties are governed by the contract.[10] This principle has been particularly important in determining claims arising under building contracts. If an architect or a builder agrees to supervise work for a lump sum there is no necessary implication that, if there is extra work, any further payments are due to him.[11] Suppose, however, that I pay you £5000 for work you have agreed to do on my house. If you now refuse to do that work, I can terminate the contract on account of your repudiatory breach, and instead of claiming compensatory damages, I can claim restitution of the £5000 due to your total failure of consideration.[12] The converse is equally true: if I agree to pay for building work, which you subsequently begin, and there is then an anticipatory breach on my part, you may wish to claim a quantum meruit for the work you have already done. Although this failure of consideration manifests itself most commonly where contracts are prematurely discharged by frustration or repudiatory breach, it may occur where there is, for one reason or another, no contract at all.[13]

This failure of consideration is, then, the "unjust" element leading to restitution in construction disputes. The "enrichment" factor is most easily established using the less orthodox restitutionary concept of "bargained-for benefit".[14] Goff & Jones and Birks, however, all support analysis of enrichment primarily in terms of incontrovertible benefit and free acceptance. This latter concept is, indeed, used to explain the unjust element as well - the argument, briefly, is this: If I freely accept goods or services, with the opportunity of rejecting them, and in the belief that the supplier expects payment, it is unjust for me to retain them and refuse to pay. Further, having freely accepted, I am in no position to maintain that I have not been benefited (enriched) by their acquisition. On closer analysis, however, I would submit that neither of these propositions is unassailable: I may be ambivalent in my attitude to the receipt of the goods or services (and, hence, not necessarily

9   cf. Birks, pp 219 et seq.
10 See, for example, *Weston* v. *Downes* [1778] 1 Doug. 23; *Toussaint* v. *Martinant* [1787] 2 TR 100
11 *Webb and Knapp (Canada) Ltd* v. *City of Edmonton* [1969] 3 DLR 123.
12 cf *Ashpitel* v. *Sercombe* [1850] 5 Ex 147.
13 Especially in the case of anticipated contracts which do not materialise; p.8, post
14 Although this concept was only proposed in 1988 (see note 4, supra) Birks already admits that Burrows' picture of restitution in this area, based around bargained-for benefit, is "not unattractive": Birks p.466.

enriched),[15] and I might justifiably argue that the supplier, who does not address the question of payment in advance, takes the risk of my refusing to pay.[16]

Orthodoxy points to the notion of incontrovertible benefit as the alternative method of establishing enrichment.[17] The theory is that the receipt of money or the saving of necessary expenditure[18] are benefits such that no reasonable man could claim he was not enriched. These cases are uncontentious - problems arise, however, where, as in most construction disputes, the plaintiff has delivered to the defendant goods or services. We may ignore the issue of subjective devaluation[19] for these purposes, since, almost inevitably, the defendant will have requested the goods or services from the plaintiff, so he cannot maintain that they are of no value to him. The major problem in this area is that in Birks' view, which is echoed by the cases,[20] the benefit derived by the defendant from the plaintiff's goods or services must have been realised in money before restitution can occur. Clearly this may never happen - an architect's plans may not be sold, for example, even if the project is discontinued. Goff & Jones' alternative, and, with respect, preferable view, that the financial benefit must simply be realisable, but not necessarily realised, has little judicial support[21].

The better view, which eliminates these difficulties, is that the enrichment in construction disputes stems from a bargained-for benefit. If the defendant makes a bargain with the plaintiff for certain goods or services, he cannot subsequently claim that these goods or services are of no benefit to him. We shall see, in the next section, that a bargained-for benefit (the enrichment factor) combined with a total failure of consideration (the unjust factor) will often persuade the courts to grant a restitutionary remedy. Unhappily, however, the judgements are rarely reasoned along these lines.

---

15 Indeed Beatson, in "Benefit, Reliance and the Structure of Unjust Enrichment" (1987) 40 CLP 71-92, argues that pure services which are not incontrovertibly beneficial, but merely freely accepted, can never be enrichments.

16 This argument is less tenable, but further exposition is unwarranted here as the unjust factor leading to restitution in the vast majority of construction disputes is failure of consideration. 17 Goff & Jones, p. 144 et seq and elsewhere; Birks p.116 et seq.

18 *Exall* v. *Partridge* (1799])8 TR 308; *Craven-Ellis* v. *Canons Ltd* [1936] 2 KB 403 (from where it appears that a factual necessity, rather than a legal obligation, is sufficient).

19 That is, that although the goods or services may have a market value, the defendant does not, himself, attach any value to them, and does not consider himself enriched by their receipt.

20 eg. *Stocks* v. *Wilson* [1913] 2 KB 235.

21 Indeed, the only support it receives is an obiter dictum in *Marston Construction Co. Ltd* v. *Kigass Ltd.*: "In appropriate cases, the benefit might consist in a service which gives a realisable, and not necessarily realised gain to the defendant, particularly when.... the service is part of what was impliedly requested;" cf.p26, post.

Restitution in the Courts

In this section I shall examine various common construction disputes to discover how unjust enrichment can, on the above analysis, lead to a satisfactory and fair remedy in restitution - the scheme works equally well where there is no contract (Cases I, II, III) and where a valid contract is prematurely discharged (Cases IV, V).

I Anticipated Contracts which do not materialise[22]

> "In my judgement, the obligation to pay reasonable remuneration for work done when there is no binding contract between the parties is imposed by a rule of law".
>
> Greer L.J.[23]

The leading English cases in this area are undoubtedly *William Lacey (Hounslow) Ltd.* v. *Davis*[24] and *British Steel Corpn.* v. *Cleveland Bridge & Engineering Co. Ltd.*[25] More recently the theory underlying these two decisions has been confirmed in *Marston Construction Co. Ltd.* v. *Kigass Ltd.*[26] In *William Lacey* the plaintiffs submitted a tender for building work and were led by the defendant landowners reasonably to believe that the contract would be theirs. Subsequently, at the defendants' request, the plaintiffs did substantial preparatory work, the cost of which would have been included in the contract price. Unfortunately, however, the contract fell through because the defendant sold the building. Barry J. held that the plaintiffs were entitled to a restitutionary quantum meruit for the work done at the defendants' request. It is easy to use the restitutionary scheme proposed above to support this result: the defendants had requested the plaintiffs' preparatory work as part of the contractual bargain; it is thus a bargained-for benefit, and they are therefore obliged to accept the "enrichment" element. Equally, the failure of the expected payment through the main contract can be seen as a failure of consideration - and the "unjust" element is satisfied. Birks is, himself, prepared to admit that a free acceptance approach is less than satisfactory in this case.[27]

In the *British Steel* case, Robert Goff J. relied on *William Lacey*, though outside the construction sphere, and held that the plaintiffs were again

---

22 Cf. 104 LQR 595-8 (Burrows).
23 *Craven-Ellis* v. *Canons Ltd* [1936] 2 KB 403, 412
24 [1957] 1 WLR 932
25 [1984] 1 All ER 504.
26 (1989) 46 BLR 109
27 Birks, pp 273-4.

entitled to a quantum meruit for the reasonable value[28] of work carried out at the request of the defendants and in anticipation of a contract which failed. Once again, Burrows' bargained-for benefit meets the case.

In *Marston* v. *Kigass* the facts were similar in kind to those of *William Lacey*. The defendants' factory was destroyed by fire, and the plaintiffs tendered for a design and build contract to replace it. The plaintiffs were given an assurance that the contract was theirs, providing the insurers paid enough to cover the costs of rebuilding to local authority standards. They did not. As nothing was said to the plaintiffs to indicate that preparatory work up to that point was to be at their own risk, and as the defendants were held to know such work was necessary, if the plaintiffs were to be ready for the stipulated start date, the judge found that the defendants impliedly requested the plaintiffs to carry out the preparatory works. The judge cited Robert Goff J., in *British Steel*:

> "If [in these circumstances], no contract [is] entered into,.... then the law simply imposes an obligation on the party who made the request, to pay a reasonable sum for such work as has been done pursuant to that request, such an obligation sounding in quasi-contract, or, as we now say, in restitution."[29]

Although this view is undoubtedly correct, the case for restitution in *Marston* may seem slightly less strong than that in *William Lacey*. In the latter case, the failure of the contract was directly attributable to the defendant; in the former, on the other hand, it was the fault of the third-party insurer. Furthermore, whilst there was a direct request that the plaintiffs begin preparatory work in *William Lacey*, this request was only implicit in *Marston*. It is foolish to presume that the courts take no notice of such factors. Nevertheless, a quantum meruit was allowed in *Marston* v. *Kigass* on the basis of a realisable benefit in the hands of the defendant.[30] Once again, however, the answer is clearer on the basis of a bargained-for benefit and total failure of consideration under the anticipated contract.

The law in this area is complex and very new – it is therefore unsurprising that the courts find it difficult to articulate clearly the rationale behind any restitutionary remedy they give. Certainly, none has been analysed directly

---

28 The contentious issue of valuing a benefit for restitutionary purposes is dealt with post, p.20.

29 Note 25, supra: p.511.

30 Some designs and working drawings together with an implied (limited) licence to build to those drawings. Whether the defendants decided ultimately to build a factory or to sell the land, they had a benefit which was realisable; cf note 21, supra.

along the lines of the scheme proposed above[31]. It is submitted, however, that when an anticipated contract does not materialise, the concepts of bargained-for benefit and total failure of consideration show the way forward for the courts.

II Incomplete Contracts

In this area, too, the concepts are valuable. Where there is held to be no contract, because of some unresolved ambiguity in, or incompleteness of, the contractual terms, and money has been paid under the supposed contract, it can be recovered provided the consideration for the payment has totally failed.[32] The principal English case is *Way* v. *Latilla*[33]. The plaintiff had, at the defendant's request, obtained for him gold-mining concessions in Africa. The plaintiff claimed that his services were rendered pursuant to a contract by which the defendant had agreed to give him a share in the concessions, and to pay him for the information supplied. They paid him nothing, and the House of Lords held that there was no concluded agreement as to the amount of the share which the plaintiff was to receive. They did, however, award him £5000 quantum meruit, justifying the decision on an artificial contract of employment.

Goff & Jones and Birks analyse the decision in terms of free acceptance.[34] This is the strongest case for free acceptance I have come across,[35] but it fits equally easily into the scheme of this paper. The unjust factor can be regarded as the total failure of consideration, in that the plaintiff did not receive the share in the concession which he had been led to expect; and the defendant was benefited by the work for which he had bargained.[36] Although this case is not in the construction field, it serves to illustrate the approach in all contracts which are missing a vital term, or are ambiguous; hence, its relevance extends across all types of contract-based obligations.

31 Although support for the concepts is found in a few cases, notably *Craven-Ellis* v. *Canons Ltd* (supra, note 18) and *William Lacey*.
32 Cf. *Re Vince* [1892] 2 QB 478 (void contract of loan); and, in America *Turner* v. *Webster* 24 Kan.38 (1880).
33 [1937] 3 All ER 759
34 Goff & Jones, p.382; Birks, p.272.
35 Dicta in the case also support this analysis: Lord Wright, p. 765.
36 It is also true, though only Burrows seems to recognise this, that the defendant was incontrovertibly benefited by the realisation in money (subsequent sale) of the concessions: 104 LQR 595, n. 99.

III Sub-Contractors

Problems inevitably arise where a sub-contractor contracts with the main contractor to do work on the owner's building, and the contractor is unable to pay him.[37] At present, English courts will deny the sub-contractor any restitutionary claim against the owner. The only current exception to this principle is when the landowner is contractually bound to make payments to the head-contractor for the sub-contractor's services. It is said that to allow the sub-contractor a direct claim against the landowner may result in the sub-contractor gaining priority over the contractor's general creditors in the event of insolvency. It is far from clear that this would be an undesirable result; furthermore, if there is no insolvency, and the owner has not paid the main contractor, there is no just reason to deny the sub-contractor's claim.[38] The owner has indirectly received a bargained-for benefit, or is, alternatively, incontrovertibly benefited, and should be liable for a quantum meruit to the sub-contractor. The development of a generalised right to restitution may lead a court in the future to grant relief in such a case.[39]

IV Contracts discharged by breach

(a) The Innocent party:

If the innocent party has supplied goods or rendered services under a contract determined by him because of the other party's breach, he may claim a quantum valebat or quantum meruit rather than sue for damages under the contract.[40] Again, a bargained-for benefit/failure of consideration approach may be used to justify this result. The Californian case of *Boomer* v. *Muir*[41] illustrates how, in the construction field, claiming a quantum meruit can produce substantially greater rewards than simply suing on the contract - particularly where the innocent party has entered into a loss-making contract. In *Boomer* v. *Muir*, the innocent constructor of a dam was awarded $258,000, even though only $20,000 was still due under the contract. The rationale is that

"a defendant cannot refuse to abide by his contract [i.e. breach]

37 *Hampton* v. *Glamorgan C.C.* [1917] AC 13
38 Cf. *Costanzo* v. *Stewart*, 453 P 2d 526 [1969].
39 Cf. *Klug & Klug* v. *Perkin* [1932] CPD 401 (a South African decision in which restitution was allowed on similar principles).
40 Unless the innocent party has fully or substantially performed, in which case his action will lie in contract.
41 24 P 2d 570 [1933]

and at the same time claim its protection when the other party is not in default."[42]

The unjust element is clear, and the enrichment is established on the basis of the original contractual bargain.

(b) The Party in Breach:

As far as the party in breach is concerned, if the contract is divisible he can recover payment under the contract for any divisible part of services rendered or goods supplied - at the contract rate, or failing that, on a quantum meruit/quantum valebat basis.[43] If, on the other hand, the contract is entire, the party in breach can generally obtain no recompense for work done. Thus, in *Sumpter* v. *Hedges*[44] Sumpter contracted with the defendant to do work on the latter's land. He did something over half the work and received part payment of the price, before he became insolvent and was unable to complete. The defendant finished the building using materials which the plaintiff had left behind. Sumpter was allowed a quantum valebat for the materials left on the site, but nothing more. The defendant had no choice whether to accept or reject the materials which had already been incorporated into the building on his land and this factor outweighed any restitutionary claim by the party in breach, with respect to those materials.

It should be noted that there are exceptional cases in restitution where a party in breach can obtain recompense for benefits conferred, even under an entire contract. In *Sumpter* v. *Hedges*, for instance, the innocent party was required to pay for the materials left on the site, on the basis that, having the opportunity to reject, he accepted (and used) the materials instead.[45] Equally, under an entire contract for the sale of goods, where a seller delivers less than the quantity contracted for, and the purchaser accepts the goods so delivered, he will be liable to pay a reasonable sum for them.[46] In these circumstances, the innocent party is not prejudiced - he has had the opportunity to accept or reject the part performance, and, having accepted, should pay its reasonable value. The courts, rightly, recognise this.

42 Restatement of Contracts, 2d; Williston
43 *Hoenig* v. *Isaacs* [1952] 2 All ER 176
44 [1898] 1 QB 673
45 Indeed, this principle was accepted as early as 1808 - *Christy* v. *Row* [1808] 1 Taunt. 300.
46 *Steven* v. *Bromley & Son* [1919] 2 KB 722; the common law rule has been adopted in s.30(1) of the Sale of Goods Act 1979.

V Contracts discharged by frustration

"Unjust enrichment provides no easy formula for the solution to
the question whether parties should restore to each other benefits
conferred under a contract thereafter frustrated."

Goff & Jones, p.484

Despite this tentative beginning, Goff & Jones are prepared to accept that
in this area it is the principle of unjust enrichment which has guided both the
courts and Parliament to a just (if not easy) solution to the problem. If the
benefit conferred by the plaintiff, before the frustrating event, takes the form
of money, the defendant is incontrovertibly benefited. In this case, the loss
suffered by the plaintiff is generally equal to the defendant's gain, so that no
difficulty arises concerning the amount to be paid.[47] If, on the other hand,
the defendant receives a benefit other than money, for example goods or
services, the matter becomes more complicated. Historically, the plaintiff's
claim is for a quantum valebat/quantum meruit, though, following the Law
Reform (Frustrated Contracts) Act 1943, the basis of this claim is the actual
benefit gained by the defendant. It is, however, rare for the courts to apply
the 1943 Act for two reasons.[48] The first is found in s.2(3) of the Act itself,
which provides that the contract terms will govern, if, on a true construction,
they were intended to apply in the situation which has occurred. The second
reason is that the courts are traditionally loath to hold a contract frustrated
except where the subject matter is destroyed, or performance, as contemplated by the contract, is literally impossible.

In the construction field, this reluctance is clearly demonstrated by *Davis
Contractors* v. *Fareham UDC*[49], where the House of Lords rejected the
claim that the contract had been frustrated. Contractors agreed to build 78
houses for a local authority in eight months for £94,000. Because of labour
shortages, the work took 22 months, and cost the contractors £115,000.
They claimed that the contract had been frustrated, and that they were
entitled to extra remuneration on a quantum meruit basis. The House of
Lords' view was that the events which caused the delays were within the
ordinary range of commercial probability and had not brought about a
fundamental change of circumstances. This approach seems strict, particularly in the light of the recent decision of the Court of Appeal in *Williams*
v. *Roffey Bros Ltd.*[50] In that case, the plaintiffs entered into a subcontract
with the defendants to carry out carpentry work in a block of flats for an

---

47 *BP Exploration Co.(Libya) Ltd.* v. *Hunt (No.2)* [1983] 2 AC 352
48 *BP* v. *Hunt*, in 1979, was the first case to utilise the Act's provisions.
49 [1956] AC 696
50 [1990] 2 WLR 1153.

agreed price. The plaintiff got into financial difficulties because this price was too low for him to operate satisfactorily and at a profit. The defendants consequently agreed to pay him an additional sum for each completed flat. This they failed to do, however, and the plaintiff sued for the additional sums. The Court of Appeal held that the discharge of existing contractual obligations could amount in law to good consideration for the promise of additional money, and upheld the claim. Although *Williams* v. *Roffey* concerns neither frustration nor restitution directly, it does, I would submit, enable us to reconsider the principles underlying the decision in *Davis* v. *Fareham*. In *Davis*, commercial necessity was valued below the sanctity of the original contract; in *Williams* v. *Roffey*, the opposite was apparently true.[51] This is an example of the courts adopting a more pragmatic and desirable approach to contractual problems - an approach which could usefully be extended into the realms of "economic" frustration, to provide plaintiffs, in the position of the contractors in *Davis*, with a successful restitutionary claim.

Until such avenues are explored by the courts or Parliament, a plaintiff seeking restitution of benefits other than money must look to s.1(3) of the 1943 Act. He may then receive any sum, not exceeding the value of the benefit to the defendant[52], as the court considers just, having regard, in particular, to expenses incurred by the defendant before the frustrating event, and the effect of the frustrating event on the benefit received. Once again it is clear that the unjust element leading to restitution is the failure of consideration under the frustrated contract; and the enrichment is established on the basis of a bargained-for benefit.

Valuing the Benefit

Where a money benefit is concerned, valuation will present the court with few difficulties - the defendant will simply be required to restore to the plaintiff a sum equal to that received. Restitutionary claims for services rendered or goods received are, however, more problematic. A general principle, nevertheless, guides the courts even here: a plaintiff will recover the "reasonable value" of the services or goods at the date they were rendered or delivered. This value will include the plaintiff's margin[53], and, although based on an objective value for the goods or services, will take account of the "special position" of the parties.[54] This method of valuing the benefit

---

51 The court was prepared to accept what is, in effect, a variation of the original contract, supported by no new consideration, partly because of the overwhelming economic factors; Cf. Purchas LJ, pp 1171-2.
52 For valuation of benefits, see p.20, post.
53 *Lodder* v. *Slowey* [1904] AC 442
54 *Seager* v. *Copydex* (No.2) [1969] 1 WLR 809, 814 per Winn LJ

received leads to two results already noted - in cases like *Boomer* v. *Muir* the plaintiff may recover a reasonable sum even though he made a losing contract; and, in cases like *William Lacey*, he may recover, despite being unable to sue on the original agreement because it was unenforceable.

The problem of valuing a benefit has recently been considered in *Crown House Engineering Ltd.* v. *AMEC Projects Ltd.*[55], albeit obiter. On a quantum meruit claim by the plaintiffs, the question arose whether the levels of cost incurred by the defendants, as a result of the timing and manner in which the plaintiffs undertook the work, could be relevant in calculating the objective value of services rendered. Slade LJ considered that the answer was uncertain, and might depend on the facts of particular cases; he did, however, suggest that an unqualified "no" would be an unsatisfactory answer, and could lead to manifest injustice. Bingham LJ agreed, though less forcefully, and Stocker LJ expressed no view. All three Lords Justices did, however, feel that the question was unsuitable for determination in *Crown* v. *AMEC* itself. There is no authority on this point[56], but, in my submission, the rational answer is clear. The law of restitution is designed to prevent unjust enrichment. The defendant, as we have seen, is only enriched by the objective value of the benefit, taking into account the special position of the parties. Consequently, if, due to the plaintiff's late or unsatisfactory performance, the defendant has been exposed to extra expense, the value of his benefit is reduced - and the plaintiff's claim in unjust enrichment should be similarly reduced. Otherwise, as Slade LJ points out, there would result injustice of a nature which the whole law of restitution was intended to avoid. It should be noted that where a contract is frustrated, statutory provisions govern the valuation of a benefit received: s.1(2),(3) Law Reform (Frustrated Contracts) Act, 1943.

Conclusion

It would be easy to conclude that, in construction disputes, where the contract has failed, restitutionary remedies will be granted on the basis of a total failure of consideration, and Burrows' "bargained-for benefit" view of enrichment. If a plaintiff can establish these two factors, in the absence of any overriding defences, the courts will award him a quantum meruit for work done. However, such a conclusion would not do justice to the complex law of restitution. The central concept is that of unjust enrichment, and the courts will strive to intervene in any case they feel they should. In

---

55 (1989) 6 Const LJ 141

56 The trial judge sought to use *British Steel* to support his view, but Slade LJ considered that this case was distinguishable.

consequence, it is impossible to lay down a strict set of rules defining the circumstances in which the courts will grant a remedy. All I have attempted here is an analysis of the existing law, and a discussion of how the courts may proceed in the future. The law of restitution has developed rapidly to give justice in situations where traditional remedies are unavailable or undesirable - unfortunately, this development has been somewhat haphazard. Nevertheless, the case law to date has laid solid foundations, upon which the judiciary, or, perhaps, Parliament, should now start to build.

Economic loss: Sub-bailment 13
and other remedies in quasi contract

Elizabeth Jones

Synopsis

This paper examines the possible ways in which the common law may develop post *Murphy*. Parties endeavouring to establish claims against those with whom they are not in contract will be driven, it is suggested, to look again at the doctrines of quasi contract, developed in the days before *Junior Books* et al took tort into new areas of liability.

Introduction

This paper is intended not to be an exhaustive review of these issues, but to throw out ideas which ought to be considered. After the judgments in *Murphy* v. *Brentwood*[1] and *DoE* v. *Bates*[2] disapproving the decision in *Anns*,[3] recovery of economic loss in tortious negligence can be said to be restricted to the following categories:

(a) where there is loss as a result of reliance (which was or might reasonably have been anticipated) on a negligent misstatement (*Hedley Byrne*[4]) and

(b) an indeterminate and miscellaneous category which includes cases where solicitors' negligence has led to pecuniary loss being suffered by third parties (*Ross* v. *Caunters*)[5]

We also have a clear indication of what amounts to economic loss for these purposes (to be disallowed except in the two categories above.) It is, apparently, any financial loss which is not the cost of repair of other property (pace the complex structure theory as re-enunciated by Lord Bridge in *Murphy*[6]) which has suffered damage, or the compensation payable for injury to a person, as a result of a latent defect in the article or building,

---

1 [1990] 2 All ER 908
2 [1990] 2 All ER 943
3 *Anns* v. *London Borough of Merton* [1978] AC 758
4 *Hedley Byrne* v. *Heller & Partners* [1964] AC 465
5 [1980] Ch 297
6 Transcript P21

produced or constructed by the defendant. Presumably the proximity rules will now be the subject of much close scrutiny in view of the dicta, again from Lord Bridge[7] in *Murphy*) that

> "There may of course be situations where, even in the absence of contract, there is a special relationship of proximity between builder and building owner which is sufficiently akin to contract to introduce the element of reliance so that the scope of the duty of care owed by the builder to the owner is wide enough to embrace purely economic loss".

He goes on to give *Junior Books*[8] as an example.

Now that it is clear that the Courts will look with disfavour upon attempts to recover economic loss in tort what can be expected to develop? One view seems to be that there will be a return to claims in quasi-contract; perhaps renewed attempts to breach the privity principle by building on cases such as *Beswick*;[9] a new look at the quasi-contractual warranty cases such as *Shanklin Pier*;[10] and perhaps excursions into the realms of concepts such as sub-bailment, trusts, and agency.

The law of trusts

In *Beswick* (where specific performance of a contract to pay an annuity was ordered even though no trust was found to exist) the view was advanced that "any person for whose benefit the contract is made can enforce it even if no consideration has moved from him"[11], Snell rather unhelpfully adds that "The inquiry plainly involves the construction of the contract and the special circumstances in which it is entered into, but on the authorities as they stand there is little more that can usefully be said"[12]. Equity will recognise a trust of the benefit of a contract, and a party can contract as trustee so that a third party is entitled to the benefit of the contract *ab initio*. The courts do not, however, readily find that this is the case.

The use of a constructive trust in enforcing contracts has been recognised since 1753;[13] but to quote Cheshire and Fifoot[14] "despite its promising

7 Transcript P26
8 *Junior Books Ltd.* v. *Veitchi Co.Ltd.* [1983] 1 AC 520
9 *Beswick* v. *Beswick* [1968] AC 53
10 *Shanklin Pier Ltd* v. *Detel Products Ltd* [1951] 2 KB 854
11 Snell's *Principles of Equity* 26th Edition p103
12 Snell's *Principles of Equity* 29th Ed at p96
13 *Tomlinson* v. *Gill* [1756] Amb 330
14 Law of Contract 10th Edition p 410

appearance and the positive terms in which it has occasionally been acclaimed, the device has, in practice, proved a disappointing and unreliable instrument". Reasons for this included the "feeling that a trust was a "cumbrous fiction"[15]. The decision in *Beswick* was subsequently applied in a case dealing with a claim against the Motor Insurers Bureau, which is enforceable by the Minister by application for specific performance, but not by the injured person[16]. The Court of Appeal (Lord Denning presiding) held that if the Minister obtained specific performance, the injured person could enforce the order for his own benefit.

The *Beswick* line of cases were concerned with specific performance and although the use of trusts generally is not unknown in building law – covenants to exercise rights in a building contract for the benefit of purchasers or tenants, and transfers of the benefit of collateral warranties to management companies set up in multiple occupation blocks are some of the speculative devices I have seen being tried out - the courts are in their present restrictive mood perhaps unlikely to be susceptible to argument along these lines.

In any event, attempts to enforce, by the device of a trust, performance of a contract which benefits the plaintiff does not assist the claimant wishing to establish a right of action in damages against a third party, except in so far as it indicates that in certain circumstances the Courts will, albeit reluctantly, relax the doctrine of privity[17]. This essentially, (for non-lawyers), restricts enforcement of rights under a contract to the parties thereto and is the reason why the actions by building owners, tenants and others against builders and building professionals are, or have been, so often brought in tort; simply because there has been no obvious relationship in contract. In an earlier case in contract, *Scruttons* v. *Midland Silicones*[18] the House of Lords had held that a defendant could not take advantage of a term which might operate to limit his liability in a contract to which he was not a party - and there are dicta which go much further:

> "a stranger to a contract cannot in a question with either of the contracting parties take advantage of provisions of the contract

15 Ibid quoting Lord Wright 55 LQR 189 at 208

16 *Gartner* v. *Circuit* [1968] 2QB 587

17 In a Consultation paper recently published, - *Privity of Contract : Contracts for the Benefit of Third Parties*; Paper 121 - the Law Commission make a number of provisional recommendations designed to extend the Beswick principle and "allow third parties to enforce contractual provisions made in their favour". If these become law the situation described in this paper will change drastically, although not perhaps for the better in terms of legal certainty, since much litigation will undoubtedly be necessary to establish the precise parameters of the new rights.

18 [1962] AC 446

even where it is clear from the contract that some provision in it
was intended to benefit him"[19].

Other means of avoiding the privity rule

Besides *Beswick* and the implied trust, what other possible routes are
there for a third party to claim the benefit of a contract to which he is not a
party? - the obverse of the claim in tort that a duty of care exists so to build
the building or manufacture the article that the third party, in addition to the
purchaser of the goods or services, suffers no harm. Section 56 of the Law
of Property Act 1925 provides that "a person may take an immediate or other
interest in land or other property, or the benefit of any condition right of
entry covenant or agreement over or respecting land or other property,
although he may not be named as a party to the conveyance or other
instrument". Lord Denning picked this up in an obscure case called *Drive
Yourself Hire Co (London) Ltd* v. *Strutt*[20], a case relating to assignment of
a sub-lease. According to Cheshire and Fifoot "Denning LJ's observations,
though they command great respect were .... unnecessary to the decision".
The dicta, which must therefore be considered obiter, are as follows:

> "Section 56(1) applies to any instrument of agreement, and it
> applies not only to land, but to any property real or personal. It
> says that: a person may take.......the benefit of any..... agreement
> .... respecting .... property, although he may not be named as a
> party to the.......instrument."

He adds that these words effectively allow the Courts, "in cases respecting property, to go back to the old common law whereby a third party can
sue on a contract expressly for his benefit".

Cheshire and Fifoot add that the old common law cases to which Denning
referred[21] may "like other cases of the period, represent judicial opinion
when the dependence of contract upon bargain had been shaken and had not
yet been restored".[22] The learned editors do however go on to say that the
language of the section is in itself sufficient to support this interpretation,
but in subsequent cases the courts have shown themselves unwilling to
apply the principle, identifying perhaps another set of floodgates. Indeed in

19 Ld Reid Ibid at p473
20 [1954] 1 QB 250. See *Smith & Snipes Hall Farm Ltd* v. *River Douglas Catchment Board*
   [1949] 2 KB 500
21 *Dutton* v. *Poole* [1678] 1 Lev 210 and *Martyn* v. *Hind* [1779] 1 Comp 437
22 Op cit p309

the final round of the *Beswick* case which reached the Lords in 1968[23] they considered the significance of Section 56 and held unanimously that it had not abolished privity of contract and that a person could not sue on a contract merely because he would benefit by its performance. Three of the Lords gave it as their view that the section applies only to real property and not to personal property. Two Law Lords, one "obiter and tentative"[24] stated that the application of the section is confined to documents under seal and made inter partes, where someone covenants with or makes a grant to someone not a party to the contract or deed. (The restriction to property may not be of concern where the terms of an agreement for lease are expressed to become part of a lease and the interest which needs to be enforced is a warranty relating to the quality of construction of, for example, the shell and core of a building).

Lastly, with regard to privity, the Law Commission recommended as long ago as 1937 that a third party who benefits under a contract should have the right to sue in his own name -

> "Where a contract by its express terms purports to confer a benefit directly on a third party it shall be enforceable by the third party in his own name subject to any defences that would have been valid between the contracting parties. Unless the contract otherwise provides it may be cancelled by the mutual consent of the contracting parties at any time before the third party has adopted it either expressly or by conduct"[25].

This would not in point of fact assist our householder with defective foundations or tenant with defective cladding, because of the use of the words "express" and "directly" and the reference to cancellation of the contract might prove tempting for developers and contractors who might otherwise be besieged by claimants. Nevertheless, it is another straw in the wind and in *Woodar Investment Developments Ltd* v. *Wimpey Construction (UK) Ltd*[26] Lord Scarman urged the desirability of the House of Lords reconsidering the rule.

The Shanklin Pier case

Another fringe area of contract which might now be the subject of renewed attention is that of the collateral or implied contract, a theory which

23 AC 58
24 Ld Upjohn at 106
25 Sixth Interim Report para 50 (9)
26 [1980] 1 All ER 571 and 590

caused much comment in the early 1950s but which has not been developed because the decisions were very much 'representation' decisions and the combination of the *Hedley Byrne* decision and the introduction of statutory remedies for misrepresentation may have directed attention away from them. The leading case is *Shanklin Pier Ltd* v. *Detel Products Ltd*[(10)] where the plaintiffs entered into a contract to have their pier repainted with the right to specify the paint. The defendants made certain representations as to the quality of the paint and the plaintiffs' contractors used it. It was not suitable and the plaintiffs sued and won.

There were other cases which followed, all during the fifties. The Misrepresentation Act will obviously have dealt with the specifics of some of them but the principle, that a contract can be implied where there is none, is presumably still available to be exploited, though the *Hedley Byrne* "reliance" and the "proximity" and "special relationship" requirements spelled out in *Murphy* may, in effect be a development of the same strand of remedy, albeit clothed in tort rather than contract. The term "collateral" is also liable to cause confusion with the ubiquitous collateral warranty. Implied contract is probably a better term and, apart from the misrepresentation cases, there seem to be very few implied contracts recognised other than those implied by a course of action - entering a race and agreeing to abide by club rules have both been held to create a contract between competitors.

Sub-bailment

The third category of possible and somewhat circuitous routes to recovery of economic loss outside a contract is the sub-bailment analogy. It posits that an Employer and sub-contractor are in the same position as a bailor and sub-bailee where (according to Denning MR's dissenting judgment in *Morris* v. *C W Martin Sons Limited*[27]) "the owner is bound by the conditions of the sub-bailment if he has expressly or impliedly consented to the bailee making a sub-bailment containing those conditions" ie. that the Employer could be bound by the terms of a sub-contract to which he was not a party. There has been some doubt (Garland J in *Norwich City Council* v. *Harvey*[28]) cast over whether the principle operated so that a Plaintiff's contract could define his rights of action in tort towards a Defendant with whom he was contractually unrelated i.e. whether the principle operated to provide a right of action rather than a defence only.

He distinguished the sub-bailment analogy on the ground that the

27 [1966] 1QB 716 and 729
28 unreported 2nd November 1987

authorities involved a defendant at the end of a chain of contracts who sought to argue that his own immediate contract qualified his responsibility towards a plaintiff at the head of the chain. They were, he said, merely authorities on the question whether the defendant's contract could define his obligations in tort towards a contractually-unrelated plaintiff; they cast no light on the question whether a plaintiff's contract could define his rights of action in tort towards a defendant with whom he was contractually unrelated.

In a later case called *Rumbelow* v. *AMK*[29] Judge Fay QC said "if the Plaintiffs had not only known of but assented to the second Defendant's conditions (as between themselves and the first Defendant) then having regard to *Morris* v. *Martin* I think the implied term (of good workmanship and sound materials) as between the Plaintiffs and the first Defendant would indeed have been modified so as to limit the first Defendant's liability to conform with the limits on the second Defendant's liability." However, Garland J in the *Norwich* case pointed out that a sub-bailee owes a duty at common law to the bailor independent of contract and that both the recent authorities on bailment – *Morris* v. *Martin* and *Johnson Matthey* v. *Constantine*[30] – were decided before "the great expansion of tort in the late seventies and early eighties which made the Sub-Contractor a potential tortfeasor qua the employer and nearly analogous to a bailee".

The *Norwich* decision was confirmed on appeal[31] when the Court of Appeal held that though "there was no question of the main contractor acting either as the agent or trustee for the sub-contractors"[32] and though the situation was not one akin to bailment, it was nonetheless "just and reasonable" to allow the sub-contractors the protection of the relevant term of the contract. Having created an anomaly by excluding either agency (another possible device for circumventing privity) or trust they went on in addition to exclude any duty of care on the ground that the relationship was not close enough.

Taking advantage of an exclusion clause in someone else's contract is one thing, but acquiring a right to one is another. It remains to be seen to what extent (if at all) sub-bailment will be developed together with the other pre-seventies doctrines referred to above. The Courts are extremely jealous of the doctrine of privity and a more fruitful line of development might be the proximity or special relationship referred to in *Murphy* or even Lord Bridge's anomalous approval of a possible right of action in a *Bates*-type

---

29 *Rumbelows Ltd* v. *AMK (a firm) and Firesnow Sprinkler Installations Ltd* (1980) 19 BLR 25
30 [1976] 1 Lloyd's Rep 215
31 [1989] 1 All ER 1180
32 Ibid at 1183-84

situation, again in Murphy. It is appropriate to conclude with this observation from Lord Templeman, in a case called *CBS Songs Ltd* v. *Amstrad Consumer Electronics plc*[33] in 1988.

> "The pleading assumes that we are all neighbours now, Pharisees and Samaritans alike, that foreseeability is a reflection of hindsight and that for every mischance in an accident-prone world someone solvent must be liable in damages".

33 [1988] AC 1013 and 1059

Quality Management - 14
Remedy or sanction

John Barber

Synopsis

This paper is based on a research project entitled "Quality Management in Construction - Contractual Aspects", being undertaken by the author for CIRIA (Construction Industry Research and Information Association). The paper describes the background to and the present attitudes to Quality Management, and seeks to define its objectives. The problems of placing Quality Management within the Contractual framework are discussed and proposals advanced.

Introduction

That success and profitability in business should be pursued through commitment to ensuring purchaser satisfaction is not a new idea; it might even be described as old-fashioned. Nor is there much new about the formalisation of management systems, or the pre-planning and documentation of work and inspection procedures. Yet the combination of the three ideas, together with a few other ingredients, under the title "Quality Management", "Quality Systems" or even "Quality Management Systems", has brought marked improvements to some manufacturing industries in recent years. It is now poised to bring similar widespread benefits to construction.

The spread of Quality Management is partly purchaser-led, partly driven by supplier initiative; but it is also partly due to the publication of BS 5750 - "Quality Systems". The growing acceptance of Quality Management amongst suppliers can be traced to realization that the pursuit of profitability alone, without regard to purchaser satisfaction, is a short-sighted policy and that long-term success requires more responsible attitudes. In a competitive market-place, however, where competition tends to be based on promises rather than performance, there must be common ground rules for such attitudes to survive. The publication in 1979 of BS 5750 - "Quality Systems", provided such common ground rules, particularly where used as a basis for prequalification of potential suppliers. A substantial boost came with the adoption of that publication in 1987 (subject to a few minor amendments) as an international standard. BS 5750 has been re-issued to correspond to the international version.

Other British Standards are also relevant. BS 4778: Part 1: 1987 - "Quality vocabulary, international terms" is an international standard. Others, including BS 4891: 1972 - "A guide to quality assurance" and BS 4778: Part 2: 1979 - "Quality vocabulary, national terms", have national status.

There are questions how far BS 5750, written for manufacturing industries, can be applied to construction, but it provides a starting point. It has been supplemented by a substantial amount of work on the application of Quality Assurance and Quality Management to construction, carried out under the auspices of CIRIA. The first two CIRIA publications on the subject appeared in 1985, and work is continuing apace with several research projects in progress or about to start.

Satisfaction of the purchaser's requirements has, of course, always been a legal obligation imposed by the standard forms of contract and consultancy agreements in construction. Is that not enough? There may be reluctance in some quarters to admit the limited capacity of legal obligations and forms of contract to ensure purchaser satisfaction but, as pointed out by Cole[1], while quality itself concerns things, products or services, its achievement concerns people and depends how they work and how well they communicate. Quality has to start with the producer. Directing and controlling the work of people is a function of management.

Other factors also affect quality, including knowledge and understanding, and sufficiency of time, money and resources. Management is not a substitute for these - there is a serious danger of creating an impression that it is - but management can contribute in various ways, by avoiding or, perhaps, focusing attention on deficiencies in these areas. The improvements available are not limited to increased purchaser satisfaction or even supplier profitability. Other interests converge to the same solution. For a supplier, the reduction of defects by the introduction of Quality Management Systems is probably the most effective means of reducing the threat of legal proceedings. Avoiding involvement in legal proceedings, with its attendant cost, uncertainty and diversion of effort, can be as significant as the ability to resist liability or obtain an indemnity at the conclusion of such proceedings. Traditionally in construction, purchasers have relied on supervision by their own agents to ensure satisfactory performance by contractors and reduce the need to bring legal proceedings for the recovery of compensation. If a purchaser can invoke the implementation of an adequate Quality Management System by his supplier, it might prove to be a more effective means of achieving those purposes. The crucial question arises and remains

1   W. Cole, 21st Quality Assurance Conference, Oxford 1982.

to be resolved, how the two approaches of purchaser supervision and supplier Quality Management should coexist.

In relation to design services, invoking a Quality Management System can bring a degree of formal quality assurance where none was demanded before. It also provides a means of assuring quality with other forms of contractual arrangement, such as design and build, management contract or construction management. The words "purchaser", "supplier" and "product" are used in this paper, as in BS 5750, to cover all types of commercial relationship and product or service.

Faced with enthusiastic assertions of the merits of Quality Management, it is essential still to keep feet firmly on the ground. As has been remarked by Robbie Burns, the best laid plans o' mice and men - Quality Management is all about best laid plans - aft gang a-gley. Practitioners in the arts of Quality Management are apt to deny this with their motto "Right first time every time", but as Lord Wright once observed in relation to tests on some itchy underwear[2]:

"The significance of this experiment seems to be that, however well designed the manufacturer's proved system may be to eliminate deleterious substances, it may not invariably work according to plan. Some employee may blunder."

Quality Management will reduce defects; it will never entirely eliminate them. Therefore, the adoption of Quality Management does not eliminate the need for legally binding obligations, nor the need for insurance. With these two or three approaches to assuring quality working alongside each other[3], the possibility then arises of interaction between them. In particular, legal obligations and management systems may be complementary and consistent, or there may be incompatibility and conflict between them. Finally, the invocation of Quality Management Systems by a purchaser as a legal obligation raises difficult problems of legal enforceability in relation to construction projects. The purchaser's intention may be to promote the performance of primary obligations by the imposition of ancillary ones, but are the remedies available at common law effective in the event of a breach of the ancillary obligations? What self-help remedies (such as powers to withhold or deduct monies due) can be stipulated in the contract, and will they be upheld by the courts? On the other hand, will the threat of oppressive legal remedies have the effect not of deterring breaches, but of deterring the

---

2 *Grant* v. *Australian Knitting Mills* [1936] AC 85

3 Despite the now familiar use of the word "assurance" as part of Quality Assurance, the dictionary recognises that confidence may be assured not only by actions, but also by promises (corresponding to contracts) and insurance.

adoption of Quality Management Systems?

Quality Assurance and Quality Management

Quality Assurance is the totality of "planned and systematic actions" to ensure that "a product or service will satisfy given requirements for quality". The actions may be undertaken by the supplier, the purchaser, a third party or a combination of all three. Delving into history, the approach of the Quality Assurance movement, that actions to ensure purchaser satisfaction should be planned and systematic, was first adopted in relation to NATO defence procurement with the publication in 1968 of two documents, AQAP-1 and AQAP-2, setting out NATO quality control system requirements. The term "Quality Assurance" appeared in the title of BS 4891, "A guide to quality assurance", in 1972. In the same year the Institute of Quality Assurance adopted that name, having previously been called for some fifty years the Institute of Engineering Inspection.

Quality Management can be explained as an offshoot of Quality Assurance, a branch that may blossom and bear fruit for both parties, because Quality Management has grafted on the self-interest of the supplier in achieving cost-effectiveness and long-term profitability. Quality Assurance can exist without Quality Management, but it may be less fruitful. With either approach, maximum benefit depends on regular pruning to prevent excessive growth of bureaucracy.

The distinction between Quality Assurance and Quality Management is explained in the National foreword to BS 4778: Part 1: 1987 that,

> "the terms "quality management" and "quality control" are considered to be a manufacturer/supplier (or 1st party) responsibility. "Quality assurance" on the other hand has both internal and external aspects which in many instances are shared between the manufacturer/supplier (1st party), purchaser/customer (2nd party) and any regulatory/certification body (3rd party) that may be involved."

The distinction between "external quality assurance" and "internal quality assurance" is explained in BS 5750[4], that the former covers activities aimed at providing confidence to the purchaser, the latter is aimed at providing confidence to the management of the supplier organization. The internal aims of a Quality Management System are, however, not limited to achieving quality; in particular a supplier needs to ensure that the system is

---

4 BS 5750 Part O Section 0.1 Notes to Figure - Relationship of Concepts

cost effective. Quality at any cost is not the aim.

The distinction between internal and external aims is also made clear by the separate parts of BS 5750. Parts 1, 2 and 3 of BS 5750 are to be "used for external quality assurance purposes in contractual situations"[5]. Guidance on internal quality assurance aspects is contained in BS 5750: Part 0 Section 0.2[6]. The possibility of placing greater emphasis on the supplier's own planned and systematic efforts to ensure quality, coupled with assessment of his quality organization and procedures, was canvassed in BS 4891: 1972 under the heading "Purchasing control", as follows:

"8.3.2 There is, in many fields, a trend away from placing sole reliance on incoming inspection towards a more rigorous assessment of the supplier's ability to satisfy the purchaser's needs. This cannot be derived solely from the check inspection of a small sample from a product batch, but involves also continuing surveillance of the supplier's quality organization and procedures. Alternatively, such evaluation and surveillance might be carried out by an independent third party in the form of certification schemes which can be particularly advantageous where standardized products (both in the national and international sense) are involved....

"8.4 Receiving (incoming) inspection. In determining the amount and nature of inspection applied to delivered products, consideration should be given to the controls exercised at source and the objective evidence provided. If a supplier or vendor has an effective quality control system, the purchaser may reduce his goods-inward inspection. It should be apparent, however, that the purchaser's knowledge of a supplier's or vendor's quality stems primarily from proven performance, the records the supplier/vendor furnishes and any previous assessment. Receiving inspection should thus complement and supplement source quality control, rather than ignore it, or duplicate it unnecessarily."

These ideas were developed in BS 5750, with several innovatory features, including "audits" to examine the efficacy of the system and check it has been implemented, and the requirement of a management representative with specified functions in relation to the system. Audits are carried

---

5 BS 5750 Part O Section 0.1 Clause 6
6 BS 5750: Part O Section 0.2 is misleadingly entitled "Guide to quality management and quality system elements". It is doubly misleading by being part of Part O "Principal Concepts and Applications", instead of a separate standard as in the international enumeration.

both by the management representative or his assistants internally, and by second or third party assessors as external auditors. Third party assessment is generally carried by Government accredited bodies for "certification".

Reliance on the supplier is commonplace in regard to the supply of construction design services, but external supervision and inspection by the purchaser's representative is still the norm for the physical work of construction on site. This arrangement has yet to be adjusted in response to the introduction of suppliers' Quality Systems. Adjustment involves a degree of mutual trust for which there is limited precedent in past relationships. It demands changes in attitudes on both sides as well as the introduction of appropriate systems and procedures. A chicken-and-egg situation arises. The supplier is put off assuming responsibilities for quality assurance while his efforts would be duplicated or even overridden by the purchaser's representative, but the purchaser is unwilling to relax control until the supplier has demonstrated "quality function maturity". This is not to suggest that the purchaser's representative becomes wholly redundant, but that his role requires modification.

There are signs, however, of willingness to take the bold step. For example, in the nuclear power plant industry, where QA has been practised for a considerable time, several speakers at a Workshop in 1983[7] spoke out in favour of greater reliance on the supplier. M A Rheanne described experience on a project in Canada:

> "The control and inspection of all contractors' activities were performed entirely by the Resident Engineer's group ... We have proof that it did work ... but it was not the most efficient way of achieving that assurance. Furthermore 100% inspection by a group not responsible for performing the work caused other problems, such as
>
> - decreased motivation of the construction personnel
> - poor co-ordination of the planning of control activities with respect to performance activities
> - need for more inspection personnel, which resulted in greater control-related costs
> - reduction in both efficiency and optimization of resources."

Rheanne concluded that his employers, Hydro Quebec, would restructure

---

7 *"Quality Assurance in Nuclear Power Plants"* edited by Ron Matfield. Proceedings of a Workshop held at the Joint Research Centre, Ispra (Italy) 20-23 June 1983

arrangements for future projects to increase the contractor's motivation and responsibilities.

There is limited evidence yet on which to assess the record of success where such restructuring has been implemented. Most experience of Quality Systems as a contractual requirement relates to projects with a nuclear element. On such projects extensive requirements and controls are commonly superimposed on the supplier's Quality System. A high degree of traceability is demanded, which can generate copious quantities of documentary records. Multiple layers of supervision and checking are applied, based on a high degree of risk aversion and a need to satisfy the Nuclear Inspectorate, rather than any intention of cost- effectiveness. Even in the offshore and process plant industries, where Quality Systems have also been established for some time, the economics of avoiding failure are rather different from most building and civil engineering construction.

There are, however, some examples where Quality Systems have been adopted with the aim of cost-effectiveness, and there are some encouraging signs of success. There are also discouraging examples which demonstrate the need for fresh attitudes and commitment on all sides in order to achieve success.

For legal purposes, a clear distinction should be drawn between an individual organization's company quality system, which is usually the basis of certification and prequalification. and its project-specific quality systems as expressed, typically, in project quality plans. Although the project-specific quality system may incorporate parts of the company system, it is better considered as an offspring with a separate existence. Any contractual requirement should only attach to the project-specific system. Arguably there is also a need on construction projects where several organizations are employed independently, for a project-wide system embracing all the organizations involved.

Quality

Bringing Quality Systems into the contractual framework makes it essential to reconsider carefully the definitions used in specifying the objectives and requirements of a System. Books and papers on Quality Assurance and Quality Management often start by exploring dictionary definitions and popular connotations of the word "quality". They conclude, correctly, that the quality to be assured is not the popular connotation of a specially high standard, but only the consistent achievement of the standard intended. Such publications have tended, however, to disregard the pronouncements of judges relating to quality, relying instead on the definition in the British Standards as if that alone were conclusive of the matter.

In his paper, "The Control of Quality in Construction", presented to the 1988 Conference at King's, Donald Keating QC commented[8]: "It is to be observed that the British Standards Quality Assurance Documents use the term "quality" in the sense of fitness for purpose". This conclusion was based on the definition in BS 4778: Part 1, which applies for the purposes of BS 5750, that "quality" is

> "The totality of features and characteristics of a product or service that bear on its ability to satisfy stated or implied needs."

BS 4778: Part 2 (which does not apply for the purposes of BS 5750) goes on to state

> "Within the context of this standard and in accordance with established usage in the quality assurance field the word "quality" is used in the "fitness for purpose" sense as defined in 4.1.1."

This interpretation is reinforced by the Institute of Quality Assurance literature which describes Quality Assurance shortly as "achieving fitness for purpose at an economic cost".

Yet, as stated powerfully in *Arcos* v. *Ronaasen*[9], the achievement of fitness for purpose does not of itself satisfy other contractual requirements, such as stipulated dimensions. Indeed fitness for purpose may not even be a requirement of the contract. It is apparent that, if quality is concerned with satisfying contractual requirements, then "stated or implied needs" in the BS definition cannot be interpreted as synonymous with fitness for purpose.

The words "implied needs" are open to a very wide range of interpretations, which can cause difficulties in a contractual situation. The parties may start to argue about what they expected. Yet the law is quite clear that mere expectations do not create legal obligations[10]. As Scrutton LJ stated: "A defendant is not liable in damages for not doing that which he is not bound to do".

The meaning of "quality" is of fundamental importance, as under BS 5750 the objective of a Quality System is to ensure quality, as defined. This can be traced through a sequence of interdependent definitions ("quality system", "quality management", "quality policy" and "quality") set out in

8 In *"Construction Contract Policy - Improved Practices and Procedures"* ed Uff and Capper, 139 at p 141
9 *Arcos* v. *Ronaasen* [1933] AC 470
10 *Abrahams* v. *Reiach* [1922] 1 KB 477

BS 4778: Part 1, and repeated in BS 5750: Part O Section 0.1. Some assistance in establishing the meaning of "quality" is obtained by comparing Clause 4.2 of BS 5750 Parts 1 and 2[11], as this gives an alternative statement of the objective of a Quality System:

> "The supplier shall establish and maintain a documented quality system as a means of ensuring that product conforms to specified requirements."

This implies that quality is equivalent to conformance with specified requirements. It might be inferred that specified requirements are those set out in the specification, which is defined in BS 4778: Part 1 Clause 3.22, as "the document that prescribes the requirements with which the product or service has to conform", but this would presume that the specification lays down requirements in explicit, exhaustive and exclusive detail. Requirements may also be implied.

A further attempt to clear up the point has been made in the new national guidance document, BS 5750: Part 4 : 1990, which, as stated in its Clause O, "attempts to redress some of the residual ambiguity of BS 5750 Parts 1, 2 and 3". Clause 3.1 gives a new definition of "specified requirements" as follows:

> "Either of the following applies
> a)   Requirements prescribed by the purchaser and agreed by the supplier in a contract for products or services
> b)   Requirements prescribed by the supplier which are perceived as satisfying a market need."

This illustrates a source of difficulty in BS 5750, that it provides for Quality Systems where there is no contract in existence as well as the situation where there is such a contract. Note 2 to the definition of quality in BS 4778: Part 1 states that

> "In a contractual environment, needs are specified, whereas in other environments, implied needs should be identified and defined."

It may be argued on the basis of that Note that "or" in the definition of "quality" is to be interpreted disjunctively, so that in a contractual context

---

11 This clause is identical in Parts 1 and 2. Clause 4.5 of Part 3 refers similarly to "conformance of product to the specified requirements".

only stated needs apply. This would make BS 4887: Part 1 almost consistent with the nuclear standard BS 5882: 1990 where "quality" is defined for nuclear installations as

> "The totality of features and characteristics of a product, service or activity that bear on its ability to satisfy a defined requirement."

On the other hand, Note 7 to the definition of "quality" in BS 4778: Part 1 states

> "In some reference sources, quality is referred to as "fitness for use" or "fitness for purpose" or "customer satisfaction" or "conformance to the requirements". Since these represent only certain facets of quality, fuller explanations are usually required that eventually lead to the concept defined above".

The difficulty remains that stated or defined requirements or needs may not describe adequately the full extent of the supplier's obligations under the contract. As intimated in the original BS definition of quality, there may also be implied needs or requirements, although the definition itself does not indicate how the implied needs are to be ascertained with certainty.

The confusion and uncertainty can only be overcome by acknowledging that

- a contract, which may either be in existence or be anticipated in the future, fixes requirements by a combination of its express terms and the terms implied by law;
- additional requirements may be imposed by law through statute or common law outside of contract (for example, by the Defective Premises Act 1972);
- the nature and extent of the implied requirements can only be reliably ascertained by reference to the law;
- the proper objective of a Quality System in a contractual situation is to satisfy the requirements stipulated by the contract or imposed by law: no more, no less.

A new definition of "Quality Systems" (or "Quality Management Systems", to adopt a new name) is proposed accordingly for project-specific systems in a contractual situation, as follows:

> documented management systems, established by or under the

authority of top management of an organization, for ensuring the proper fulfilment of its primary duties or obligations undertaken expressly or by implication under a contract, or otherwise imposed by law.

In the definition, the objective of the management system is stated as the fulfilment of primary duties and obligations; it is aimed at avoiding, (though not evading) secondary obligations, such as paying compensation for defects, which arise if the primary duties and obligations are not fulfilled. Such secondary obligations are the province of the contract, possibly in conjunction with insurance arrangements.

In a non-contractual situation, including the general company quality system, it may make sense to treat quality management as the pursuit of excellence or some other objective, but in a contractual situation, any definition of quality which is not congruent with legal obligations will result in either over- or under-provision. Nevertheless, fitness for purpose remains relevant to certain questions, for example, resolving non-conformance events. It also remains the underlying or ultimate objective of any contract for design services, although the legal obligation is only to exercise due skill and care.

Legal Obligations relevant to Quality

Legal obligations relevant to quality can be divided into four categories:

a)   fitness for purpose - this category includes requirements as to "quality" or "merchantable quality";

b)   conformance to description - the description may have been stipulated by either the supplier or the purchaser, and may include detailed specification requirements;

c)   conformance to sample - again, the sample may have been provided by the supplier or the purchaser;

d)   exercise of due skill and care, or compliance with stipulated procedures.

The first three categories correspond to sections of the Sale of Goods Act. They are all examples of end-product obligations, which are satisfied only if the end-product conforms to the requirement, irrespective of the method used to attain the result. The fourth category, on the other hand, does not stipulate an end result and, in principle, does not depend on the achievement of an end result, although the end result is the underlying purpose. The obligation is in theory not even discharged by achievement of an end-result if a stipulated procedure has not been followed.

The essential legal point is that legal obligations may comprise one or more obligations in any number of the four categories. Such obligations will be concurrent and may be wholly or partially independent. Each of the legal obligations must be satisfied separately; the discharge of one will not be accepted as discharging another. Difficulties arise if the obligations are not compatible[12].

On the other hand, where a contract clearly stipulates the agreed intentions of the parties as to their respective obligations, the Courts will not imply additional obligations as part of the contract or in tort[13]; but where a contract drafted by one party is silent as to that party's obligations, obligations may be implied on the basis of reasonableness and what is necessary[14].

Thus, in *Greaves* v. *Baynham Meikle*[15] the Court of Appeal held there could be concurrent obligations to exercise due skill and care, and to provide a building fit for purpose. In *Arcos* v. *Ronaasen*[16], the House of Lords held that the purchaser was entitled to reject timber for breach of description as to dimensions, despite a finding by the arbitrator that the timber was of merchantable quality for the intended purpose. In *Grant* v. *Australian Knitting Mills*[17] the Privy Council held that the question whether due skill and care had been exercised was irrelevant to the question whether the supplier was liable for breach of contract in regard to merchantable quality. The meanings of the legal terms "quality" and "merchantable quality" were considered by the House of Lords in *Young & Marten* v. *McManus Childs*[18]. It was held that a requirement of merchantable quality could exist independently of a requirement of fitness for a specific purpose as in that case where a product for incorporation in building works had been specified by name. The Sale of Goods Act 1979 s14(6) has since[19] clarified that "merchantable quality" is a degree of fitness for purpose. The term is defined as :

12 In *Thorn* v. *London Corporation* [1876] 1 App Cas 120, the House of Lords held that the purchaser did not even impliedly warrant that the works could be constructed in accordance with the contract drawings.

13 *Greater Nottingham Co-op* v. *Cementation* [1988] 2 All ER 971. The decision of the Court of Appeal was actually limited to the issue of liability in tort; counsel conceded that the claim could not succeed in contract.

14 *Liverpool City Council* v. *Irwin* [1977] AC 239

15 *Greaves* v. *Baynham Meikle* [1975] 3 All ER 99

16 *Arcos* v. *Ronaasen* [1933] AC 470

17 *Grant* v. *Australian Knitting Mills* [1936] AC 85

18 *Young and Marten* v. *McManus Childs* [1968] 2 All ER 1169

19 The definition was first inserted by the Supply of Goods (Implied Terms) Act 1973 s7(2)

"fit for the purpose or purposes for which goods of that kind are commonly bought as it is reasonable to expect having regard to any description applied to them, the price (if relevant) and all other relevant circumstances".

Note that this definition introduces an interdependence between quality and description.

Fitness for purpose depends in any event on the purpose made known by the purchaser at the time of contract, not the actual purpose to which the product is applied[20] The scope of the warranty may also be qualified by instructions as to use[21]. It is submitted that Quality as the objective of a Quality System embraces all legal obligations within the first three end-product categories (not merely legal "quality") insofar as stipulated by the contract or implied by law.

Where the legal or contractual obligation is the exercise of due skill and care, the position is rather different. The aim of due skill and care is fitness for purpose of the product, but fitness for purpose is not warranted. This apparent dichotomy is resolved once it it is appreciated that the legal obligation of due skill and care corresponds to adherence to the procedures of a Quality System, not the attainment of the objective. The Quality objective in such situations is fitness with the aim of fitness for purpose.

In contracts for design services the position is further complicated as there are a number of "products" to be considered. There is the immediate product of drawings and documentation setting out the design. These are the "deliverables", as are the acts of attendance at meetings and visiting the site. The second product is the subsequent realization of the design in bricks and mortar and plant. There is even a third product - the operation of the constructed item, for example, the water produced by a treatment plant. A designer is concerned with the quality of all these products and his Quality System needs to address them all with the aim of fitness for purpose.

It is suggested that, particularly in construction, the objectives of Quality Systems should also be extended to include legal obligations as to time or rate of performance. Quality procedures ought to be planned with regard to adequacy of resources. There may, however, be conflicts between time and quality, which involve some compromise.

Others have suggested a still broader interpretation of the BS definition of Quality, as including price, on the grounds that an implied need of the customer is a competitive and/or reduced price: these are stated as potential benefits to the customer in BS 5750: Part O Section 0.2, clauses 0.1 and

20 *Aswan Engineering Establishment Co.* v. *Lupidine (Thurgar Bolle, third party)* [1987] 1 All ER 135
21 *Wormell* v. *RHM Agriculture East Ltd.* [1986] 1 All ER 769, [1987] 3 All ER 75

0.4.4.2. This may be valid for an organization's company Quality System, but it is submitted that, for a project-specific system in a contractual situation, such a view must be rejected. Price and provisions for adjustment of price are stipulated in a contract as part of the bargain. The price, once fixed, does not vary with cost (except insofar as the parties may have agreed that it should). The obligation to pay the price belongs to the purchaser; it is not an obligation of the supplier. The aim of the supplier as regards saving or optimizing costs is of no concern to the purchaser: the cost of discharging legal obligations is no defence in the event of failure to do so.

The aim of a Quality System is still to be cost-effective in achieving Quality. The point is that cost or price are not part of Quality in a contractual situation except in particular cases, for example, the economics of the ultimate product in a design services contract.

Assumption of Additional Obligations

It is a potential danger for a supplier that by adopting a Quality Management System he may assume additional legal obligations. Two dangers arise from the present wording of BS 5750. One is that addressed earlier, that "implied needs" in the British Standard definition of "quality" may be interpreted more widely than the needs implied by law. Clarification of the Standard is required to avoid this. There is also a danger that the introduction in BS 5750: Part O Section 0.2 of additional considerations such as environmental protection, safety and energy saving, could inadvertently impose additional liabilities in tort.

In the case of a contract where the legal obligation, whether express or implied, is to exercise due skill, care and diligence, the procedures documented by a Quality Management System may well be taken as defining what constitutes due skill, care and diligence, particularly if the customer is aware of, or has even approved, the procedures. Certification of a System may also be relevant. This aspect of definition may have positive or negative effects. Dugdale and Stanton comment[22]

> "While it may be difficult for a plaintiff to establish a negligence claim when matters of professional judgement are at issue, it is only too easy to do if damage can be shown to have been caused by a failure of management or procedure on the part of the professional person. Such cases are important not only because they almost certainly constitute the majority of professional negligence claims, but also because failures to adopt correct

22 Dugdale and Stanton "*Professional Negligence*" 2nd ed. 1989 pp 248 and 249

procedures and work practices are examples of negligence situations which are simple to avoid given adequate precautions...

The cases also illustrate the importance of ensuring that systems of work are correctly followed by staff. Failure to operate a system designed to secure the client's protection will be strong evidence of negligence."

A Quality Management System can be beneficial in helping to ensure compliance with procedures, and in providing records as evidence of compliance. It should also help ensure the existence of appropriate procedures, but there is a risk that the supplier may create a rod for his own back by adopting documented procedures which are either too enthusiastic or inadequately defined. The crucial lesson is that quality procedures should be written for practical application, not to impress clients or prospective clients. A supplier should not commit itself in any quality procedure to taking steps which it does not consider essential; and procedures should be written so that compliance can clearly be demonstrated.

In the case of contracts for the physical work of construction the position is more complex. Most specifications are end-result specifications. The legal obligations imposed are not discharged by showing that a procedure intended to produce that result has been followed. Therefore Quality Management only assists if it succeeds in producing the required end result. The possibility exists that compliance with the quality procedures may become an additional legal obligation, independent of achieving the end result, and that there may be independent breaches.

Contractors may wish to believe that their adoption of quality procedures is to provide confidence at a comfort level only without assuming any additional legal obligations, while customers may be keen not only to incorporate the implementation of a Quality System as a legal obligation, but also to see compliance with adopted quality procedures as a specific binding obligation. The risk of presuming that the courts will interpret the position one way or the other, if the contract does not make the position clear, is apparent in *Malaysia Mining Corp* v. *Kleinwort Benson*[23] Hirst J, at first instance, was prepared to hold that "Letters of Comfort" were contractually binding, although the decision was reversed by the Court of Appeal on the facts[24]. The parties need to agree on a common intention, and state it clearly in their contract.

There is also a possibility that a pre-contract statement that a Quality Management System is operated could give rise to liability under the

23 *Malaysia Mining Corp* v. *Kleinwort Benson* [1988] 1 All ER 714
24 *Malaysia Mining Corp* v. *Kleinwort Benson* [1989] 1 All ER 785 (CA)

Misrepresentation Act 1967, if the statement was not true up to the time of contract.

Appraisal and Verification

The old name of the IQA, the Institute of Engineering Inspection, serves as a reminder of an aspect where lawyers have shown their own lack of appreciation and understanding. Assessment to determine whether quality requirements have been satisfied is not the straightforward subject sometimes contemplated by the greatest of lawyers. Problems are posed as to accuracy of measurement, reliability of measuring devices, and representativeness of samples. Tests are required which will assess significant qualities reliably, economically, within a reasonable time and without destroying the product; tests do not always measure the required quality directly, but may do so indirectly relying on empirical relationships. At a more fundamental level, there is a need to understand what qualities are significant in a particular situation before suitable tests can be specified or devised.

There is also a distinction between appraisal, which is testing for the purpose of feedback to control the production process, and verification, where the test is intended merely to answer whether there is conformance to specification or not. The nature of the tests applied, as well as the reporting and use of the data obtained, may be different for the two purposes.

Lawyers have tended to ignore such subtleties, as can be seen in two leading cases, both involving the Russian timber importers, Arcos. In *Arcos* v. *Ronaasen*[25] Lord Atkin expressed his opinion as follows:

> "It was contended that in all commercial contracts the question was whether there was a "substantial" compliance with the contract: there always must be some margin: and it is for the tribunal of fact to determine whether the margin is exceeded or not. I cannot agree. If the contract specifies conditions of weight, measurement and the like, those conditions must be complied with. A ton does not mean about a ton, or a yard about a yard. Still less when you descend to minute measurements does 2" inch mean about 2" inch. If the seller wants a margin he must and in practice does stipulate for it. Of course by recognised trade usage ... there may be even incorporated a definite margin more or less: but there is no evidence or finding of such a usage in the present case.

25 *Arcos* v. *Ronaasen* [1933] AC 470

No doubt there may be microscopic deviations which business-men and therefore lawyers will ignore ...But apart from this consideration the right view is that the conditions of the contract must be strictly performed. If a condition is not performed the buyer has a right to reject. I do not myself think that there is any difference between business men and lawyers on this matter."

In *Hillas* v. *Arcos*[26], also before the House of Lords, a different question arose, whether an agreement for the supply of timber of "fair"merchantable quality" was sufficiently certain to constitute a binding contract. Lord Tomlin, with whom Lord Warrington and Lord Macmillan concurred, stated as follows:

"Reading the document of the 21st May 1930 as a whole and having regard to the admissible evidence as to the course of the trade, I think that upon their true construction the words "of fair specification over the season, 1930," used in connection with the 22,000 standards, mean that the 22,000 standards are to be satisfied in goods distributed over kinds, qualities, and sizes in the fair proportions having regard to the output of the season 1930, and the classifications of that output in respect of kinds, qualities, and sizes. That is something which if the parties fail to agree can be ascertained just as much as the fair value of a property."

The possible procedure for dealing with any questions which might arise was elaborated by Lord Wright[27] as follows:

"Hence the 100,000 standards are to be of Russian softwood goods of fair specification. In practice, under such a description, the parties will work out the necessary adjustments by a process of give and take in order to arrive at an equitable or reasonable apportionment but if they fail to do so, the law can be invoked to determine what is reasonable in the way of specification, and thus the machinery is always available to give the necessary certainty. As a matter of strict procedure, the sellers would make a tender as being of fair specification, the buyers would reject it, and the court or an arbitrator decide whether it was or was not a good tender. It is, however, said that in the present case the

---

26 *Hillas* v. *Arcos* (1932) 147 LT 509
27 Ibid at p516

contract quantity is too large, and the range of descriptions, qualities and sizes is too complicated to admit of this being done. But I see no reason in principle to think that such an operation is beyond the powers of an expert tribunal, or of a judge of fact assisted by expert witnesses."

The two cases demonstrate a degree of unpredictability as to when conformance will be treated by the courts as a matter of opinion. The unpredictability needs to be avoided in practice by stipulation of objective standards and defined tolerances.

Acceptance and Right of Rejection

The existence of a legal obligation is of limited significance unless there is an effective legal remedy where the obligation is breached. In Sale of Goods, the availability of legal remedies is subject to the doctrine of "acceptance". Thus, most legal obligations relevant to quality under the Sale of Goods Act are treated initially on delivery of the goods as "conditions", the breach of which entitles the innocent party to reject the goods, repudiate the contract (i.e. refuse to carry out any further obligations under the contract), and recover monies already paid on the basis of failure of consideration. The right to treat a breach as a breach of condition is curtailed, however, either by actual acceptance of the goods or by deemed acceptance if the buyer does not reject the goods. Deemed acceptance is inferred within a reasonable time after delivery, subject to reasonable opportunity for examination of the goods[28]. Thus, in *Bernstein* v. *Pamson Motors (Golders Green) Ltd*[29] 3 weeks and 140 miles was held longer than a reasonable time or reasonable opportunity for rejection of a defective Nissan car.

Once the goods are accepted, section 11(4) of the Act provides:

"the breach of a condition to be fulfilled by the seller can only be treated as a breach of warranty, and not as a ground for rejecting the goods and treating the contract as repudiated, unless there is an express or implied term to that effect."

In other words, if a buyer discovers a breach after acceptance, he cannot reject the goods, he can only recover damages; but damages are only recoverable for actual loss and damage suffered. The practical effect of this

28 See Sections 34 and 35(1) of the Sale of Goods Act 1979.
29 *Bernstein* v. *Pamson Motors (Golders Green) Ltd.* [1987] 2 All ER 220

can be to commute a right to total rejection to no right at all. For example, if the buyer in *Arcos* v. *Ronaasen*[30] had not rejected the timber immediately, he would have had no remedy since the timber was of merchantable quality for the purpose required and therefore there was no actual loss.

While the Sale of Goods Act does not apply directly to construction work, standard forms of contract employ similar concepts. For example, under the ICE Conditions, Clause 38 reserves the opportunity to inspect work before it is covered up. Clause 39 confers powers to reject work not in conformance with the contract. The powers under Clause 39 endure "during the progress of the Works", and Sub-clause 39(3) stipulates that the right to disapprove is not to be prejudiced by earlier failure to do so. Thereafter, during the Period of Maintenance, Clause 49(2) provides power to order "repair amendment reconstruction rectification and making good of defects imperfections shrinkages or other faults". If fresh defects are found after the Period of Maintenance has expired, the Employer is relegated to recovery of damages at law.

Postponement of acceptance or deemed acceptance by a purchaser, which might arise out of the adoption of Quality Management Systems as part of contractual arrangements, is not in the interests of the supplier. Prompt decisions on acceptance or rejection are desirable for commercial certainty. On the other hand, Quality Management Systems can help to bring forward decisions on acceptance through the procedures for reporting of "non-conformances" by the supplier, and for "control and disposition of non-conforming product". BS 5750: Part 1 Clause 4.13.1 contemplates alternative courses of action in the event of non-conformance, including acceptance with or without repair by concession, or rejection. It is essential, however, that such actions should be within the contract. It is also desirable that the contract should require that decisions be made promptly and on sound engineering grounds; otherwise, the willingness of suppliers to notify non-conformances will be inhibited.

Compatibility with Contracts

It is the intention of BS 5750 that Parts 1, 2 and 3 should be used in contractual situations and that the procedures implemented are to ensure that the requirements of the contract are met. For end-product contractual requirements, this entails the conversion of the requirements into procedures and methods. At a practical level this requires feedback and perhaps research and development to ensure that the procedures and methods adopted will reliably produce the end result required.

30 *Arcos* v. *Ronaasen* [1933] AC 470

It is also a feature of Quality Management that compliance with the procedures and methods should be full and faithful. This has major implications in the construction industry for specifications written by or on behalf of the purchaser. It is vital that

a) end results specified should be realistic and practicable, particularly in regard to tolerances, and should reflect the needs of the user[31];
b) end result requirements should be capable of assessment by the supplier himself - this requires objective definitions;
c) specifications should be standardised so that suppliers can develop their procedures with confidence[32].

This will entail a great deal of effort and thought by specifiers, and a marked change in attitudes. It will require constructive criticism of specifications by suppliers. The use of phrases such as "to the satisfaction of the Architect, Engineer or SO" as a means of specifying end product requirements will have to be replaced by objective requirements. (This is separate from providing that the decision of the Architect, Engineer or SO shall be conclusive as to compliance - that is a matter of acceptance.)

It may even be necessary to allow suppliers contractually to require changes to the specification, and to make decisions about existing materials on site, (for example, to require the removal of soft material in trenches), where the supplier considers end quality will be affected. Obviously such moves would have payment implications.

The introduction of Quality Management does not eliminate the need for the purchaser to stipulate adequate powers in reserve. The powerful provisions contained in standard forms of contract to deal with defects can still be incorporated. It is also essential that any powers which are required, such as access for inspection, taking samples and testing, should be reserved in the contract.

Purchaser Supervision and Control

The most controversial question over the introduction of Quality Management Systems in construction is likely to concern the role of the Architect/Engineer and his site representative, the Clerk of Works, Resident

31 BS 4778: Part 1 Clause 3.6 notes: "Unless given requirements fully reflect the needs of the user, quality assurance will not be complete".
32 This point was made strongly by Michael Pepper in his paper "Safeguards and Sanctions" published in *Construction Contract Policy, Improved Procedures and Practice*, ed Uff and Capper (1989) p179

Engineer or Supervising Officer. New roles need to be defined.

The need for a designer to inspect during the course of construction remains. He needs to check whether his design intentions are being carried through, whether any problems have arisen or become apparent, and whether changes are required for any other reason. If the designer is himself operating a Quality Management System, the need for changes due to unsystematic design should, however, be reduced.

On the other hand, excessive involvement of a purchaser's representative in the supplier's Quality Management System is, arguably, not conducive to the improvements in efficiency and attitude intended. Requirements for submission of quality procedures for approval on each project are contrary to the idea that the constructor should develop his own procedures to achieve and ensure the end result required. The use of "hold points" to allow inspection may be valuable, but they should be considered as part of an acceptance function.

The purchaser may also wish to reserve the right to step in if it becomes apparent that the system is not being operated correctly or otherwise cannot be relied upon. This implies a need to monitor both the operation of the Quality System and its efficacy in assuring quality. Third party certification is a valuable aid in relation to prequalification, but a much higher level of assessment and monitoring is needed during construction on site.

A further possibility may be considered, that verification and appraisal functions involving acceptance should be undertaken by an independent agency, who would report both to purchaser and supplier. This would also overcome the present unsatisfactory position in conventional arrangements where the contractor is not entitled to feedback from the purchaser's supervision. It would release the contractor from condemning his own work, promote early acceptance or rejection by the purchaser, and probably generate a higher degree of confidence with the purchaser. It is submitted that the advent of documented procedures and records should overcome previous reasons for objection to shared verification.

Analogy between Quality Management and Legal Systems

The introduction of documented procedures as part of Quality Management invites some resistance on the grounds that they make work and stifle initiative. The key benefit, which proponents would argue outweighs the disadvantages, is explained by John Ashford[33], that documenting a management system renders it amenable to management control.

On examining the structure which has evolved for documentation of a

---

33 John Ashford, *"The Management of Quality in Construction"* (1989)

Quality Management System lawyers may recognise a striking resemblance to legal systems, save that a legal system applies within the jurisdiction of a state, while a Quality Management System applies within the confines of an organization. Whereas, for example, a legal system operates by the authority of the constitutional sovereign, a Quality Management System operates under the warrant of the Chief Executive acting with the authority of the Board of Directors.

The rules of the System are laid down in a hierarchy of documents, corresponding to statutes, subsidiary legislation, autonomous legislation, and so on. The sanctions and incentives available to enforce the rules are available by the authority of the Chief Executive, possibly circumscribed by the law on unfair dismissal.

BS 5750 requires clear allocation of responsibilities and authorities related to work affecting quality, and it has introduced a new creature, a management representative responsible for ensuring that the requirements of the Standard are implemented and maintained[34]. As with a legal system, the rules in a Quality Management System are manmade. Whether the rules are obeyed depends partly on effective policing, but also on the respect of those subject to the rules.

Documentation

A large part of Quality Management is concerned with documentation. Firstly quality plans and procedures should be documented. Secondly documents should be controlled to avoid mistakes due to working to outdated drawings or other documents. Thirdly records of quality activities should be fully documented, to demonstrate their implementation and the results of inspections and tests; traceability is an important aim, particularly where later access to work is difficult, as in nuclear installations.

The existence of such documentation will be of great practical significance in any contractual or legal dispute. In the event of a dispute taken to arbitration or litigation under English Law, all the relevant documents will become available to both parties under the doctrine of Discovery. It may be equally significant to a purchaser, however, to have the records available earlier; any such arrangements should be stipulated in the contract[35].

The documents would be significant evidence as contemporaneous documents in a commercial case, but section 4 of the Civil Evidence Act 1968 may lend additional significance. This concerns the admissibility of documents as evidence of the facts stated therein where the document has

---

34 BS 5750 Parts 1, 2 and 3 Clause 4.1.2.3
35 This is stated in BS 5750 Part 1 Clause 4.16; Part 2 Clause 4.15; and Part 3 Clause 4.10.

been compiled by a person acting under a duty. The section applies to arbitration as well as litigation.

Documents related to quality procedures and records should therefore be retained as potential evidence, having regard to the provisions of the Limitation Act 1980 and Latent Damage Act 1986. This need for retention runs counter to the requirements of document control to destroy superseded documents; it is essential that record copies of superseded documents should be archived. There may well be issues such as, what were the current procedures or documents at a particular time.

The time required for the production of documentation, particularly quality procedures, is a significant factor in practice. It is submitted that it is inappropriate to require complete ad hoc documentation for each project; it is, in any event, unrealistic to require production of complete ad hoc documentation within a week or two of starting a project. Quality procedures, or at least the basic elements, need to be developed over a period of months. Their development should essentially be a matter for the supplier, respecting his primary responsibility for quality.

The development of documentation which is efficacious in assuring quality cost-effectively, and which is readily accessible and avoids unnecessary proliferation of paper, is the fundamental aim of Quality Management. The requirement to document procedures is likely to exacerbate the disruptive effect of changes to the specification. Where suppliers are working in languages other than English, there can be problems over translation. If English versions of quality procedures are required, there are time and cost implications.

Reciprocity and Total Project Quality Assurance

An organization can implement a quality management system solely for its own internal benefit; it appears that some effective and successful systems have originated from such internal motivation. In a contractual situation, however, external quality assurance is regarded as assurance in one direction only, from the supplier to the purchaser. In construction, when design is separated from construction, such one-way assurance is only a partial solution. A constructor has a proper interest that the architect, engineer and quantity surveyor operate Quality Systems. Equally, the subcontractor has an interest vis-a-vis the main contractor, the works contractor vis-a-vis the management contractor. There may even be a proper interest that the purchaser himself operates a Quality System, or at least fulfils his role in the Quality System of others, for example, in defining the brief. These interests have two aspects: a long term interest that the total quality of the product is assured, and a short-term interest in being able to perform cost-effectively.

A further step is a total quality assurance programme for the project. On nuclear installations where the statutory responsibility for quality starts with the owner, BS 5882: 1990 provides a specification for such a programme. It is submitted that a similar approach is needed on construction projects where several independent parties are involved. The law of contract is about mutual obligations. There is no obvious reason, other than reluctance on the part of those involved, why obligations to implement Quality Systems should not be mutual or interlinked. Such obligations could be incorporated in standard forms of contract.

Legal Enforceability of Quality Management Systems

The implementation of a Quality Management System may be required contractually by a purchaser, after prequalification of prospective suppliers as to whether they have a Quality Management System. Prequalification will relate to the organization's company system, possibly based on certification of the system by an accredited body. The contractual requirement will relate to a project-specific system, expressed by a Project Quality Plan, derived from the company system.

The purchaser will wish to ensure legally that the project-specific system is implemented and operated as promised. In manufacturing, where there is a contract for the supply of batches of product, the means of legal enforcement is straightforward. Operation of the system is made a condition of the contract. If it becomes apparent that the system is not being operated, the customer may reject goods which he has not accepted and, if he wishes, treat the contract as repudiated; it would not be necessary to demonstrate physical defects in the product.

A similar approach may be workable in relation to contracts for design services prior to construction, but with construction work on site the position is less simple. The right to reject recently-completed work for non-compliance with quality procedures can be stipulated, but it will rarely be a practical solution to treat the whole contract as repudiated, that is to determine the contract, except as a last resort in extreme circumstances. The product is attached to the purchaser's land. Bringing in a new constructor is fraught with problems of delay and cost. There would be questions about the work already executed and the liability for any defects which appeared later.

On the other hand, simple damages do not provide an adequate remedy for non-compliance with quality procedures, since there will generally be no loss flowing from a non-compliance unless a physical non-conformance can be shown to have resulted. Exemplary damages are not recoverable. It might be argued that non-compliance with the Quality Management System throws the integrity of the product into question, and thereby reduces its value. But as few customers are yet willing to accept that the value of the product in construction is enhanced by the implementation of Quality Management, it is difficult to put a value on the diminution of value, if any, resulting from non-implementation.

Self-help measures may be stipulated in the contract, such as powers to withhold or deduct monies in the event of non-compliance with quality procedures: the right to withhold payment in respect of defective work in construction was upheld by the House of Lords in *Gilbert Ash* v. *Modern Engineering*[36]. But a contractual provision stipulating the right to withhold or deduct specified sums of money for non-fulfilment of a contractual obligation falls within the doctrine on penalties[37]. It is submitted that a provision whereby the amount to be withheld does not relate to the magnitude of the non-compliance and does not reflect the likely financial consequences, might be treated as a penalty and therefore unenforceable.

Even if the law did not treat such a provision as a penalty, the practical impact must be considered. The spread of Quality Management Systems depends on the willingness of suppliers to undertake the additional burden. Such willingness will soon evaporate if the undertaking is seen to be used as an instrument of oppression.

Specific Performance would not be available as a remedy, since it would involve supervision by the courts. One approach to avoid these problems would be based on a realistic practical response: firstly to require that prospective suppliers enter a sum in the tender or contract in respect of implementing a Quality Management System, as a specified percentage of the total contract value, payable in instalments. The percentage would be fixed by reference to the cost to the purchaser in resurrecting full supervision, assuming that the level of representation had been reduced to take advantage of the Quality Management System, rather than the cost to the supplier of implementing the system. It would then be stipulated that in the event of non-implementation becoming apparent, the purchaser would be entitled forthwith to cease payment of further instalments and bring in full external supervision, which would be paid for from the instalments withheld. It would be appropriate for the purchaser also to reserve the power to investigate work already completed where there was doubt as to its quality resulting from the non-compliance, such investigation to be at the supplier's

---

36 *Gilbert Ash* v. *Modern Engineering* (1974) AC 689
37 *Public Works Commissioners* v. *Hills* [1906] AC 368; *Jobson* v. *Johnson* [1989] 1 All ER 621; and see *Bridge* v. *Campbell Discount* [1962] A.C. 600 and *Coneco* v. *Foxboro UK* (1992) CA (unrep). 24.2.92.

expense.

Insurance

The adoption and implementation of Quality Management Systems should have the effect of reducing latent defects, but owners, future owners and tenants will still require security against such defects as do occur. Reliance on insurance effected by others and sympathy from the courts, though fashionable and apparently free, is a short-sighted approach. It should come as no surprise if the security has faded from the picture when the hour of need eventually comes. It is an elementary principle that insurance cannot be effected retrospectively.

Latent Defects Insurance, though not free, provides a much greater degree of reliability. Following the excellent report by Professor Bishop's NEDO committee[38], it is gaining in popularity. The question raised but not fully answered by that report, however, is the means by which insurers offering such policies should satisfy themselves as to the quality of design and construction. It might be feasible for verification by insurers to tie in with any Quality Management System. Indeed, it might be made a condition of such insurance that Quality Management Systems are operated by all those involved in design and construction.

The spread of Latent Defects Insurance could also bring enormous practical benefits as regards quality. Many quality defects now encountered could have been avoided but for two factors:

a)   the lack of funding for disseminated research
b)   the imposition of secrecy on the substantial amount of investigation into
     defects, already carried out in connection with litigation and arbitration.

The secrecy surrounding such investigations would become greatly reduced, if not eliminated, by the spread of Latent Defects Insurance, since insurers would be liable on the basis of defects occurring rather than proof of fault. The amount of investigation for each defect might be reduced without the forensic incentive, but the Latent Defects Insurers would surely begin to fund research into problems encountered and ensure that the results were widely disseminated.

38 BUILD: Building Users' Insurance against Latent defects, NEDO 1987

Conclusions

HG Wells wrote[39]

"Most of the great controversies of the world... arise from this: from differences in (men's) way of thinking. Men imagine they stand on the same ground and mean the same thing by the same words, whereas they stand on slightly different grounds, use different terms for the same thing and express the same thing in different words. Logomachies, conflict about words - into such death-traps of effort do ardent spirits run and perish"

If Quality Management is to form part of the arrangements for the implementation of construction projects, the first step is that lawyers and construction folk should understand each other and reconcile their concepts and their terminology.

The successful integration of Quality Systems into contractual arrangements will require adjustment to the standard forms of contract, but it will also entail considerable efforts by all parties involved to eliminate obstacles, and the exercise of restraint to avoid burial in paper. The fulfilment of primary obligations in construction can be promoted by the contractual requirement of Quality Management Systems; but a careful balance is needed in framing any sanctions, so as to deter noncompliance without deterring the common acceptance of Quality Management principles.

The author is grateful to the Director of CIRIA for permission to publish this paper, and to the Research Manager and the Steering Group under its Chairman, John Ashford, for their comments during the project. The opinions expressed in this paper are, however, those of the author and do not necessarily reflect the views of CIRIA or the Steering Group.

---

39 H.G. Wells, *"First and Last Things"* (1929)

15 Legal Obligation in Construction. Responsibility, Liability and Redress. Is anybody there?

Donald Bishop

Synopsis

This paper examines the conditions which are necessary or conducive to the achievement of a successful construction project. It recalls and comments on the findings of the Professional Liability Review committee and the earlier Insurance Feasibility Steering committee, both of which were chaired by the author; and discusses subsequent developments including the EC harmonisation proposals.

Introduction

Shortly after he had joined the then Ministry of Public Buildings and Works as its Permanent Secretary, I asked Sir Michael Cary for his impression of the construction industry. His reply was both to the point and germane to this paper: "When I ask those who are carrying out a particular major project to identify themselves, everybody stands up; when I further ask who is responsible, they all sit down". An independent observer might conclude from the list of the subjects in this volume that the setting and the avoidance of traps are central to the construction process. Of course they are not. The business of construction is the realisation of affordable and reliable projects on time. This end is served best if clients can be confident that responsibilities are grasped and that there is a reliable route to redress should the risks that they have not accepted materialise. That is, clients need to be assured that somebody is there.

In a world characterised by adversarial attitudes, it is not a matter for astonishment that legal devices are accepted as the effective way of reducing the uncertainties implicit in construction and to ensure, as far as is possible, that redress can be obtained from an adequately resourced participant or one with adequate liability insurance. But this paper challenges that assumption.

Legal advisers should pay more attention to tactics that will encourage the commitment and cooperation of all concerned with a project. Some important risks are best managed by clients, who alone can make the important decisions which set the context in which others will function. This does not imply that conditions of engagement and contracts should not be well drawn. Clarity reduces uncertainty and the risk of misunderstanding. But it is not an end in itself.

This paper draws on two reports: Professional Liability; Report of the Study Teams[1] and Building Users Insurance against Latent Defects[2]. Their executive summaries are at Annexes A and B respectively. As with the great majority of national reports, publication does not automatically lead to implementation without a great amount of effort by all concerned. This will be outlined. Fortunately much that needs to be done can now be done by developers[3] acting in their own interest.

Are Construction Processes reliably predictable?

Developers alone are able to set a context for a project. This is done, ideally, only after the developer has the results of a thorough study to demonstrate that a project is feasible in its management, engineering and financial aspects. Many of the crucially important decisions are then made by this developer. They include scope and scale, the time available, technical complexity, quality and a realistic budget. At one extreme the conditions specified could be achieved by the majority of competent producers[4]; at the other the client would have only a handful of suitably experienced producers to choose from. Also, throughout design and construction, effective co-ordination of the many producers depends on their willingness to be co-ordinated, and often on their mutual respect of one another's competence. Therefore the selection of the "right" team is of crucial importance and is a matter not to be left to the chance outcome of open competition.

Surely, one might ask, if the context of a project and its appointments and contracts are correctly thought through, then responsibility and liability can be determined? In theory possibly, but if and only if the boundaries of responsibilities are immutable and the tasks within each boundary are self-contained. This may be possible if what is required is specified strictly in

---

1 Professional Liability: Report of the Study Teams (HMSO 1989).

2 Building Users Insurance against Latent Defects (BUILD). National Economic Development Office 1988.

3 Developers: All who initiate and bring building projects to completion, whether operating in the public or private sectors or building on their own account.

4 Producers: A conglomerate term including designers, other professional consultants, main contractors, subcontractors and, in certain circumstances regulatory authorities under the Building Regulations, but not including manufacturers and suppliers of building materials and components.

performance terms, the liability made the responsibility of one producer, and without any intervention by the developer until commissioning. This is not the way most projects are procured. Given the normal allocation of tasks in conventional procurement arrangements, it is probably impossible exactly to describe responsibilities. Even were this initially possible for each of the responsibilities of the many principal producers, these inevitably change both as a project progresses and as phases of a project are reiterated to overcome problems encountered, especially during the design stage.

Moreover the great majority of tasks are not self-contained, ie the boundaries of the various groups of responsibilities are not independent. To a greater or lesser degree every task can be made more simple or much more complicated by the work of others. Mistakes and late completion of design lead to hasty corrections as other elements of the design are changed: in turn these impinge on the work of others, and the risk of error is sharply increased. Similarly, during construction each specialist will have assumed that the workplaces they will occupy will be ready, correctly prepared and conveniently accessed. If these conditions are not met the tempo of work will falter and claims will follow. That is even if no major client's changes are made, boundaries of responsibilities are essentially fuzzy and good relationships between the producers make heavy demands on understanding and tolerance.

Matters are usually more complicated. Although good planning and co-ordination may result in many potential problems being anticipated, few projects are brought to completion without changes in developers' requirements, technical mistakes being discovered and put right, substitute materials being specified, disputes about, eg, standards achieved, programme slippage, payments due and, inevitably, personality clashes. Each upset subtly alters the "transaction" negotiated when responsibilities were accepted and payments agreed. Often these changes are accepted as part of construction's give and take. This reserve of goodwill can become exhausted by a succession of events all of which distract site management from getting on with their proper job progress. Also, as has been shown by extended BRE studies, a worrying proportion of "quality related events" are never resolved.

Occasionally a single event, a major change in a client's requirements or a partial collapse, is an obvious indication that the majority of the agreements, and the compromises embedded in them, made when engagements or contracts were negotiated need to be re-thought. A succession of less traumatic events have much the same but less obvious effects. In practice these system effects are often ignored. Projects then limp to completion using irrelevant protocols which may be accompanied by increasingly acerbic relationships. The Australian Royal Commission's report on the collapse of the Westgate Bridge is salutary reading.

Construction law and construction management practice assume that construction processes and construction projects are reliably predictable. It follows that, if the intended results are not realised, somebody must be at fault and that retribution should be exacted from those who are to blame. It is questionable whether this basic assumption accords with reality. Almost certainly construction processes are non-linear and recursive.

They are non-linear in that changes in one variable need not produce proportional changes in another. For instance materials shortages may be absorbed as long as there is float on the affected activities; subsequently when this freedom to redeploy resources is exhausted the effects may bite on many unrelated activities. Recursiveness follows from the fact that the starting point of an event is the position created by the previous event. In other mainly scientific fields - turbulent dynamics for example - it is known that such systems behave unpredictably if forced sufficiently far from their steady state. This may happen with projects which encounter multiple problems. Then it is not easy to predict either what will next happen or where the liabilities rest for what has happened. This is not the place to pursue this analogy too far.

Many, possibly most, construction projects are brought to a successful conclusion by the commitment of all concerned, by sound judgment and by good luck. Despite this, unforeseeable problems generate repercussions, can lead to the chaos outlined above and, importantly to a hardening of attitudes and, ultimately, confrontation. The industry's well attested uncertainties include:

- the uniqueness of projects, large and small;
- technical uncertainties arising from the many ways in which materials have to be brought together in a design;
- technical uncertainties arising from innovation, whether involuntary (using substitutes for materials that are no longer available) or deliberate;
- management uncertainties because the various producers are normally mobilised ad hoc with no prior experience of working together and therefore with different expectations and procedures;
- communication uncertainties which change as projects progress
- control uncertainties because some of the producers will be fully committed to a project's success, others will be distracted by other calls on their resources, whilst to others 'this' project will be only one amongst many;
- financial uncertainties, perhaps stemming from the original feasibility study which may have assumed reliable resources that do not material-

    ise or may have underestimated the budget; and
-   uncertain law.

    If construction is not reliably predictable then the assumptions implicit
in the current arrangements are almost certainly mistaken. Whilst it may be
right to assign responsibilities and liability carefully at the outset it may be
quite wrong to assume that these arrangements reflect what needs to be done
as projects progress. Clearly defined boundaries between the tasks of the
various producers may become distinctly fuzzy as the project management
attempts to maintain progress by diverting resources from one task to the
next, bruised relationships may blind managers to opportunities for sharing
tasks and responsibilities. This suggests that there would be advantage if the
parties were not held apart by their contractual obligations and that an
adaptable style of management may better safeguard clients' interests than
conflict.

DTI/DOE Review of the Construction Professions

    In October 1987, following representations to the Department of Trade
and Industry (DTI) by a number of professions, the then Minister for
Consumer and Corporate Affairs announced three fact-finding reviews of
the liability of three professional groups; auditors, non-construction surveyors and the six construction professions. Each team was asked to establish
the facts about the extent of professional liability for negligence, the cost and
availability of professional indemnity (PI) insurance and the way in which
it and the law operates. They were also asked to report how these matters
influenced the services of their profession and, where appropriate, to
suggest possible reforms. The Study Teams were appointed in May 1988,
they reported in May 1989, their reports were published in October 1989 (1).
The following paragraphs are derived from the report of the Study Team
responsible for the review of the liability of architects, building surveyors,
civil engineers and quantity surveyors (referred to as "the review" in the
remainder of this paper). Subsequently the scope of the review was
broadened to include contractors offering design services.

Study Method

    The construction review invited the relevant professional institutions and
associations and others to state their understanding of the problem and their
priorities for reform. About fifty significant responses were received and
were considered as conjectures which were challenged by the review's

questionnaire surveys (addressed separately to the professions, clients, small clients, contractors, insurers and brokers); brainstorming sessions to explore specific topics; visits to Scotland and to DoE's regional offices to meet groups of clients and consultants; a survey of the records of the Official Referees Court, and by a substantial number of face-to-face interviews.

The general thrust of the professions' concerns was confirmed; they are now more exposed because construction is more complex and problematic, some (but not all) clients are highly risk averse and set out to transfer to others risks that they, the clients, are best able to control; litigation is chancy, costly and protracted; PI insurance is now amongst the most costly of a consultant's overheads; and trust and confidence is being eroded to the disadvantage of all concerned. There were, however, important differences relevant to the argument of this paper between the public's perception of construction and between the assertions of the institutions and the associations and the findings of the review.

Interdependence

On the evidence of the review interdependence is the operational characteristic of construction. This has several consequences: uncertainty; changing roles, responsibilities and liabilities as projects progress; a very complex web of liability and reliance on the work of others.

Risk is inevitable. From the standpoint of this paper, the important issue is whether the current practice for assigning responsibilities and liability together with the context of law and of insurance is conducive to good management. Let us first dispose of the meaning of good management in this paper, which is the "allocation of risks to those best able to control them and the sharing of risks that do not uniquely fall to any single party". Good management obviously implies much else e.g. the efficient pursuit of a client's objectives, quality management, and the containment and prompt settlement of disputes.

In former times, the practical consequences of interwoven responsibilities were less important, projects were less complex with fewer specialisms, materials and components. More work was under the direct control of the main contractor who resolved much detail by good trade practice. Nowadays more precise design methods lead to solutions that are inherently less robust. The general pursuit of value-for-money, often in terms of reduced fees and lower capital costs rather than with a proper regard to life cycle costs, can lead to lower standards and adversarial attitudes. No one factor is of decisive importance. Taken together, they make construction much more problematic. All have brought risk management and defensive tactics to the fore and have encouraged risk shedding.

Attempts to define liability precisely must fail. Roles, responsibilities and liability change as projects progress, partly reflecting operational necessities and partly action taken to maintain the momentum of a project should matters go awry. Also less than adequate performance by one participant can create additional tasks for others and management can become overwhelmed by the work entailed in resolving uncertainties and correcting mistakes. Most consultants would accept liability for their own activities. In practice, their liability is much affected by the acts or omissions of others.

Quality

A considerable effort was made to elicit clients' perception of the quality of the industry's professional services. Those contacted ranged from major clients with continuous workloads, to occasional clients, to domestic clients. Rather unexpectedly the response was that the great majority of clients were either satisfied or more than satisfied with the professional services they receive. They were rather less satisfied with the final projects but this is only to be expected because projects must necessarily reflect any shortcomings in the quality of materials, components and workmanship.

Clients' role

It is not too much to assert that good construction projects start - or very often start - with good clients. Alone of all the construction team, developers have the power to decide priorities, make compromises between funding and their ideal requirements, appoint the principal actors and to monitor progress and intervene to anticipate problems or to nip them in the bud. The evidence of the review is that some clients, often commercial developers with good reputations to uphold, and some public sector clients, are good clients in this sense. They are committed to their projects' success, accept risks that properly fall to them and invest resources in project management.

Other clients fall far, far short of fulfilling their role. Some are inexperienced and do not buy in project management skills; some set out to commission larger or more elaborate projects than they can afford, some appoint consultants and place contracts with those lacking the necessary skills and experience. All of these make failure more likely. Mistaken pursuit of "the bottom line" or, in the public sector, of some aspects of "public accountability" leads to risk aversion and to attempts to transfer all risks to others. This undermines trust and confidence and encourages further attempts to transfer risks down the line.

Consultants' role

Many of the responses of the Study Team dealt at length with the consultants' role, emphasising the essential ingredients of informed judgement. Less was made than might have been made of the efforts now being made to systematise and improve quality management. This sometimes involved defensive design (which is not necessarily a bad thing). Conversely, both clients and experienced consultants identified over-reaching as the single most important factor leading to poor consultant performance. This may be in terms of experience, or resources, or the availability of seniors to lead or supervise design. An influx of new staff puts a consultant at risk because they will be of unknown competence and will not be able to make full use of their firm's informal peer reviews and advice.

Consultants were greatly concerned that successive changes in construction practice had reduced their ability to control events without reducing their liability. Many commercial buildings are essentially an assembly of components designed by specialist sub-contractors or by specialist manufacturers. Inevitably some of the advanced design skills and methods of testing are the intellectual property of these specialists. This is a far cry from times past when the lead consultant together with a few specialist consultants would have designed virtually the whole of each project. Yet the widespread use of performance specifications, which are often problematic, draws these consultants into the liability net and, once enmeshed, the law of joint liability can make them wholly liable for damages and costs almost irrespective of their actual culpability.

This discrepancy between imputed liability and consultants' ability to control events emerges clearly with inspection (often referred to as supervision). Alleged lapses in workmanship often are accompanied by alleged lax professional supervision. In reality consultants' ability positively to supervise construction is limited. Their powers are restricted compared with those they enjoyed two or three decades ago, their relationship with sub-contractors and sub-sub-contractors is at arms length, and they do not have the resources to duplicate contractors' first line supervision. Also much completed construction is necessarily quickly concealed by succeeding work. Despite this, poor supervision of construction accounted for 25 per cent of the alleged faults reported to the Study Team.

Finally consultants believed that many conditions of engagement were imposed rather than being the outcome of negotiations between two equal partners. They instanced fee competitions that had blatantly disregarded good practice, attempts to impose extremely onerous collateral warranties, conditions that would have novated a warranty every time a property changed hands. There was substance in these allegations. With the recent fall in new orders it is likely that consultants are now even less well placed to resist conditions that may vitiate their professional indemnity (PI) insurance.

Technology

Several of the responses explained the risks posed by modern technology and by more exacting performance requirements. On the evidence of the review, such innovative projects are no more prone to failure than are traditional projects, always providing they are tackled by technically competent and experienced designers sufficiently funded to carry out the necessary research or development. However any failure can be costly, because overt innovation is more likely to feature in large projects.

Attitudes

Several of the responses received made much of the damaging effects of a continued erosion of trust and confidence between client and consultant. Initially somewhat sceptical, the Study Team accepted that this was the fundamental issue and the one that justifies action now if defensive tactics and risk shedding are not to become accepted practice, impeding change and reducing efficiency and competitiveness. Events since the Study Team reported have reinforced this conclusion and made the implementation of their recommendations more urgent in the combined interest of the industry and their clients.

Developments since October 1989

When the Professional Liability Report was drafted the expectation was that DGIII of the European Community would shortly consult member states about the desirable scope of the harmonisation of construction liability and practice in the Community. On the basis of a report prepared for DGIII by Claude Mathurin, a senior French technical civil servant, it was believed that the Commission's proposals would be radical and wide-ranging. In the event DGIII's working document emerged only in August 1990. It carries the argument that harmonisation involving legislation might be restricted to housing in the first instance and that any wider harmonisation should be obtained by voluntary convergence of current practice.

The Construction Industry Council (CIC), representing all professions and some of the associations of the industry, will be pressing DoE and DGIII to pursue across-the-board construction harmonisation generally. It may be remembered that the CIC responded positively to Claude Mathurin's report with its own set of proposals which included mandatory material damage and PI insurance, time limitation and joint liability restricted to a defendant's adjudged share of blame.

However, even should DGIII and other member states accept the need for broadly based harmonisation on these lines, some years would pass before the new arrangements could be implemented. Should DGIII stand its ground many years will elapse before another opportunity occurs. Does this imply that nothing can be done to take advantage of the recommendations of the report of the DTI/DoE Study Team until the UK government can be persuaded to legislate? Fortunately the emphatic answer is No.

The Construction Industry Council has unanimously endorsed the Study Team's recommendations and the individual institutions have undertaken to press ahead with numerous recommendations addressed to them. Second, the CIC set up the Liability Task Force (LTF) initially charged with devising responses to EC initiatives and with preparing a costed programme for placing the Study Team's recommendations on the statute book. LTF is engaged in the first task and has the second in hand. There is every likelihood that there will be a long haul ahead.

This is not all the action that should and can be taken. At the heart of the recommendations was the thought that much can be done to improve quality management and this would greatly reduce the chance of serious latent defects. The corollary is that developers and their successors should have an assured route to redress for the most serious of those risks. The action needed to achieve these objects can be taken only by developers in the early stages of projects and the burden of this paper is that solicitors have a responsibility to advise developer clients so to act in their own interests.

The review's survey of clients and of consultants produced a composite assessment of the attitudes and attributes that could be expected to lead to reliable quality. This was all the more convincing because the separate assessments of "good" clients and "good" consultants were substantially similar. This does not imply that good clients were soft clients: quite the converse. The majority were highly successful commercial developers whose experience had demonstrated that quality and profitability went hand-in-hand. Similarly the good consultants were not wedded to narrow commercial practice in this country: they had international reputations and were frequent winners of design awards for a variety of project types.

Obtaining projects of more reliable Quality

The action needed is to advise – positively to encourage – developer clients to be good clients in whatever sector and in whatever scale they operate. Good clients were distinguished by their commitment to the success of their projects and were actively involved from start to finish, intervening as required to nip problems in the bud. This was done despite their recognition of the fact that their involvement might reduce the chance of successful litigation - a rare event in their experience. In their view what mattered was that they were judged to be capable of putting prestigious buildings of good quality on the market. Litigation was irrelevant except for the very occasional catastrophe.

To this end the good clients:
- commit management resources to brief development and verification;
- appoint a project manager (Bloomfield uses the term "project chief executive");
- set a realistic budget;
- carefully select consultants from a small pool shown by experience to be competent to handle their work (new blood is introduced cautiously);
- agree sensible fees: none indulged in fee competition;
- appoint the contractor after a highly selective competition amongst contractors of proven ability;
- closely monitor progress, sometimes to the extent of seconding professional staff to a design team; and
- ensure that their management can react promptly and decisively when answers to questions are sought.

All − or nearly all − employed the policy of settling disagreements quickly and decisively rather than allowing them to fester. Should matters go awry financial contributions were sought all round − and usually obtained, such was their power in the market place. All the good clients interviewed asserted that the selection of the construction team was the most important client function. No commercial developer practised fee competition as this made it impossible for the developer personally to select the members of a well-balanced team. Without exception they thought that fee competition was counter-productive, mere candle-ending. If consultant selection was so important what were the criteria? Interestingly they differed little from consultants' own yardsticks.

As a group the consultants with a high reputation and virtually clear track record employed no unusual or no advanced management device, rather they relied on a total commitment to high standards and on unremitting attention to detail.[5] The yardsticks were:

5　The review was undertaken at a very early stage in the promotion of quality assurance for consultants. Some of those interviewed were either contemplating or in the process of being quality assured. Whilst few thought they would have radically to revise their

- partner (or the senior equivalent in incorporated consultancies) involvement (not merely keeping in touch) with every project: in practice this implied a partner: qualified professional ratio of roughly 1 : 10 to 1 : 15;
- maintenance of a stable core of experienced staff perhaps accounting for 75 per cent of the firm's maximum size;
- never over-reaching, i.e. undertaking projects which would either entail substantial and rapid recruitment or tackling very much more complex subjects than previously experienced, or both. That is a consultancy should manage its growth in size and technical range;
- innovation undertaken only with a client's knowledgeable agreement and then only when there are sufficient funds and time to undertake the essential development and testing;
- quality management is accepted as an integral part of design and management, employing peer reviews to subject proposals to the criticisms of peers knowing nothing of the compromises made during design; and
- experience is shared with in-house training events to keep all professionals and technicians abreast of developments.

Such firms had, as a matter of course, adequate technical libraries, a librarian/information officer and the larger had systematic training and development programmes. If clients can be persuaded to act as good clients and to invest sufficient management resources in selecting and appointing their construction team, the evidence was that they can be confident of being rewarded by reliable quality. This does not imply that mistakes are never made or that latent damages are never discovered. Whatever the cause, reliance on litigation is not an efficient way of obtaining redress. Multi-party proceedings – the norm – are inevitably costly and normally long-drawn. Preparation for a hearing makes heavy demands on all involved and this is especially damaging to small clients and consultancies. Moreover, if the plaintiff is to rely on damages being met by professional indemnity insurance, then the potential loss must be at once mitigated if the cost of the resultant damage is to be met in full by the insurers. The current arrangements do not serve clients' needs to have certain and reasonably quick restitution.

Obtaining more reliable restitution

The Insurance Feasibility Steering Committee (IFSC) appointed by the

quality management, all expected the method to become widely adopted in response to clients' demands.

then Economic Development Committee for Building considered three possibilities for reform against the criteria of:

(1) compensation not depending upon the chance of a producer being in business many years after the completion of a project, or on one or other of the producers having maintained professional indemnity insurance, or on proof of fault;

(2) settlements should be certain and speedy and avoid adversarial procedures; and

(3) reforms giving effect to (1) and (2) should make a significant contribution to reducing the incidence of building defects.

Reform of professional liability (PI) insurance included the possibilities of changing from a claims made to an occurrence basis (that is the liable insurer would be the one whose policy was valid when the breach occurred). Experience elsewhere, in France especially, had pointed to the difficulties encountered with occurrence policies. These included the task of identifying when a breach occurred and of ensuring the continuing existence of the insurer many years after the event. This option was not pursued.

Another possibility was project-based PI insurance. This, if available, would assure clients that every aspect of a project had some PI cover for the term of the policy. Such policies would have to be kept in force to satisfy 'claims made' conditions, which would be difficult to ensure with the passage of years. One possibility would be for developers to pay the premiums and one such policy is now available for sums in excess of the sum of the limits of PI indemnity of the individual consultants. However, all such policies would inherit the prime characteristic of PI insurance, which is to safeguard the interests of the insured not those of their clients. Indeed reformed PI insurance might lead to more robust and better coordinated defence which may not be to the advantage of claimants.

The same considerations apply to the burgeoning practice of clients extracting collateral warranties, normally from only some of the producers thus enforcing risk transfer to them. There is the assumption that the conditions imposed by collateral warranties will be acceptable to the consultants' insurers when a claim is made. This is by no means certain. What is even less certain is whether clients' interests will be properly safeguarded by a patchwork of different undertakings by the various producers, some backed by insurance, some not. The only certainty will be greater uncertainty.

First party material damage insurance was seen to go to the heart of the matter, which is to put right the insured defects and damage without the need to prove breach of contract or negligence by producers. This led to the

IFSC's recommendation for Building Users' Insurance against Latent Defects (BUILD), a non-cancellable material damage insurance for a fixed period, negotiated by the developers and assignable to others, paid by a single premium, possibly in two instalments. The IFSC were satisfied that this form of insurance met – or very nearly met – the criteria.

Principal features of BUILD

The Committee examined the principal features to be negotiated by the insurer and insured. Our understanding was that the practice of UK insurers is to launch a new policy cautiously, concentrating on the features thought to be of primary concern to their potential customers, then allowing policies to evolve in the light of experience and in the face of competition. With this in mind the IFSC set out to outline a framework which insurers could adapt as needs and opportunities dictate, concentrating on five features: cover, term of years, commencement of cover, subrogation rights and quality.

Cover

The IFSC thought that the minimum cover likely to be attractive to developers would be for the structure and weathershield. Clearly wider cover would be more attractive and engineering services and occupational costs, albeit with conditions, are now offered by the latest entrants to the market.

Terms and commencement

Developers and consultants would prefer the term of cover to run for at least twelve years, and possibly fifteen years, from the date of practical completion. In the IFSC's understanding ten years, which is accepted practice in much of the EC, was then the longest period that insurers were currently willing to contemplate. It was accepted on pragmatic grounds, which also dictated the starting point, the date of practical completion, staged if necessary, as the most certain of the other events that might have been used for this purpose.

Subrogation rights

In the normal course of events, material damage insurers would have full subrogation rights against any party responsible for the defect or damage.

In this event, the PI insurers could launch multi-party actions against the defendants who would then face a well-resourced and vastly experienced claimant. In practice it is unlikely that relatively small claims – the great majority – would provoke subrogation litigation, because insurers are well aware of the risks and costs entailed. However the possibility of second round litigation for more sizeable claims would not reduce the uncertainty, apprehension and defensive tactics of consultants, contractors and other producers. Therefore, after protracted debate, the IFSC recommended that insurers should waive subrogation rights in the expectation that the direct loss to them would be small and that this would be offset by better co-operation between producers, a management style known to lead to improved quality and, hence, to reduced risks.

Quality

The IFSC was determined that a BUILD policy should not be seen as avoiding responsibility or commitment by any of the producers and recommended that each policy should entail a 1–2 per cent deductible that the principal producers would be committed to meet. Additionally the majority of insurers will insist on risk assessment and verification, a form of third party inspection, throughout design development and construction. Experience indicates that this does not cause delay except in the comparatively few cases when material issues are discovered and have to be put right - which must be in the developer's interest. This requirement is now being relaxed when the insurers have confidence in the competence of all involved in a project.

The developer's standpoint

When advised to negotiate a BUILD policy, a developer's first question must be the cost and availability of these policies. Cost is especially sensitive because the direct benefit of a BUILD policy would normally accrue to a successive owner or tenant although the developer will have reaped the immediate benefit of a more easily negotiated sale or lease. Premium rates depend, of course, on the terms of the policy but now are in the region of 0.8 of the rebuilding cost plus the cost of risk assessment and verification which turns on its intensity, the size of a project and its location. One comparatively painless solution for developer and tenant would be for BUILD premiums to be recovered from rents paid during the first five years of occupation. This would increase a tenant's occupation costs by between 1.5 and 2.5 per cent – an estimate involving heroic assumptions – an increase well within normal negotiating limits.

The penultimate paragraph of the BUILD report reads: "any of the changes above (factors affecting demand) could trigger a surge in demand and, perhaps, the entry of one major UK insurer to the market". Much more quickly than expected, and in ways that could not be foreseen, those changes have taken place including the House of Lords decisions greatly reducing the grounds for tortious claims, uncertainties about the reliability of many collateral warranties, and in many areas the end of the long sustained sellers' market.

The three insurers – Allianz, Norman and SCOR – who pioneered the market continue to write BUILD-type policies. Several of the larger composite insurers have been testing the temperature of the water. At least one Lloyd's syndicate is writing or is prepared to write BUILD policies. Sun Alliance and Commercial Union, both with extensive property insurance portfolios, are in the market as is the mutual insurer WREN for its own members. Finally a group of established developers have negotiated their own version of a BUILD policy with an insurer. Your clients can be assured that supply exists.

Coda

The implementation of the recommendations of the DTI/DoE Study Team will take time in whatever way it is achieved. Harmonisation of construction practice and liability in the European Community will take time, again in whatever way that is achieved. There is no need to wait for Godot. Developers can be advised - persuaded - to safeguard their own interests by being good clients in the sense outlined in this paper and by negotiating a BUILD type policy to safeguard a project within the cover period.

Acknowledgment

All the many contributions of members of NEDO's Insurance Feasibility Steering Committee, the DTI/DoE Construction Review Study Team, and the Construction Industry Council's Task Force and of the institutions and associations and individuals consulted are warmly acknowledged.

Annex A

Professional Liability : Report of the Construction Professionals Study Team. Executive summary

Background

"In the light of current concern about the cost and availability of professional indemnity insurance and the extent of professional civil liability for negligence", the Secretary of State for Trade and Industry announced the appointment of three fact-finding study teams in May 1988. The selected professions were auditors, non-construction surveyors and the construction professions; the last were architects, building surveyors, civil engineers, services engineers, structural engineers and quantity surveyors, to which were added contractors offering design services.

The chairmen of the three study teams formed a Steering Group under the chairmanship of Professor Andrew Likierman. The reports of the Steering Group and of the three Study Teams were published as a single report at the end of October 1989 (Professional Liability HMSO 1989 ISBN 0 11 515205 9 £14.95).

The report of the Construction Professionals Study Team is prefaced by an Executive Summary which is attached. The report's ten sections closely follow the terms of reference:

- the nature of the services provided;
- standard and reliability of professional services;
- professional indemnity insurance;
- the law and law reform;
- routes to redress, claims and litigation;
- international comparisons and trends;
- priorities for reform;
- the case for action now; and
- recommendations.

Apart from the notes of personal interviews and the brainstorming sessions, the evidence collected during the review has been made available in a set of annexes. These are prefaced by a review of the current legal background (by Professor Phillip Capper and Professor John Uff QC) and include a report of the detailed evidence about professional indemnity insurance, analyses of the formal submissions by the Institutions and

Associations, analyses of the questionnaire surveys, an analysis of sample records of the Official Referees Court and international comparisons (based on a survey by Peter Madge).

The set of annexes is available on request from the Construction Directorate, Department of the Environment, Room P1/115, 2 Marsham Street, London, SW1B 2EB.

Professional Liability is subject to Crown copyright. HMSO has agreed to waive its copyright with respect to the Executive Summary and this is gratefully acknowledged.

Annex B

Building Users Insurance against Latent Defects (BUILD) NEDO 1980
Executive Summary

Background

The Study Team was appointed in May 1988 to examine the effect on the
construction professions of the way the law and insurance operates in
providing remedies for those who suffer loss as a result of a professional
person's duties. The professions reviewed were architects, building services engineers, building surveyors, civil engineers, structural engineers and
quantity surveyors. Before stating the Study Teams' principal conclusions
and recommendations, two matters must be emphasised.

Firstly, although some of the services of construction professionals are
between one consultant and one client, the great majority are an integral part
of an industrial process which is unique in that clients commission temporary coalitions of, on the one hand, consultants and, on the other, contractors, specialist subcontractors and suppliers for the purposes of single
projects. Clearly, these arrangements pose problems that are not faced by
other professions.

Secondly, construction practice is changing rapidly. During the course
of the review, the Study Team was told of the very much reduced role of
scale fees in negotiating commissions, of the extent of component construction and the growing involvement of specialist sub-contractors in design and
of the increased demands now being placed on contractors offering design
services. Each has an influence on professional roles and on clients'
prospects of redress. Taken together, and if the current direction of change
is maintained, they will materially affect the deployment, roles and liabilities of consultants. Moreover, legal practice and the law have not stood still.
The use of collateral warranties imposed on consultants has become more
widespread, the scope for actions in tort has been reduced and the validity
of disclaimers has been addressed by recent decision of the House of Lords.

The Principal Findings

The Professions

The activities of construction professionals range from the highly
specialised to the very general. Moreover, their services are offered in very
different ways, by, for example, sole specialists, consultants employing

1,000 professional staff or more and working at the leading edge of technology, small local practices and public service organisations. The study made no attempt to enumerate or classify these activities. Rather, an attempt was made to understand and forecast the implications for professional liability of the many changes that have taken place or are in train.

Interdependence

Interdependence is one of the dominant characteristics of construction. In building, interdependence has grown as contractors' and specialists' responsibilities for design have developed and as component building has replaced much of the conventional construction. Although it is less important in civil engineering, because there are fewer parties and the main contractor is likely to execute much of the works, the contributions of client, consultants and contractor are nevertheless intertwined.

Typically, the many parties-perhaps more than 100 for a major project-will have different formal conditions of engagement, contract or supply, often with intermediate parties having different liabilities to, for example, the main contractor or the client. Moreover, roles and responsibilities change as projects progress and the work of others. Many specialists are able to impose their own conditions of engagement on contractors, which may or may not marry with those of others.

Attitudes

Clients' attitudes are now more commercial than they were, with private sector clients insistent on completion on time and within budget and with public sector clients concerned more with value-for-money in the short term rather than with the whole life cost. Professionals believe they now fact a more hostile world. Their experience is that many clients set out to impose onerous conditions and to transfer risks to them which they are not able to control and that they are now more likely to be joined in multi-party litigation.

Technology

Construction is now more demanding because performance requirements are more exacting. On average, projects are larger and many are technically complex. Some innovation is deliberate. Much is involuntary, to meet new situations or to find substitutes for materials that are no longer available. There are three effects. Professional roles and tasks are changing, some advanced design skills now reside with specialists and the task of co-ordination is more demanding.

Professional Services

The evidence of the review is that these arrangements, complex as they are, work well enough when experienced clients play their proper role and take care to appoint experienced and adequately resourced consultants and contractors. Co-ordination is then less difficult and problems are more easily anticipated. Moreover, such clients normally have realistic expectations and use their market strength to achieve negotiated settlements, turning to litigation only as a last resort.

Other less expert or less good clients may be unwilling or unable to fulfil a client's role, thus throwing more responsibilities on their consultants. They may also have unreasonable expectations. When matters go awry, they are less able to negotiate, either because they lack the experience or because their management finds it too difficult to make the unpalatable decisions that are often needed to achieve a negotiated settlement.

Fault-free professional services cannot be guaranteed. Informed professional judgement may be mistaken or contradicted by events which neither a client nor a consultant can control. Lapses and mistakes happen and of course, some consultants are less committed or less competent than others. Nevertheless, the evidence is that the great majority of clients responding to this review were content with the quality and reliability of professional services. they were less satisfied with the quality of projects which is, of course, the outcome of a range of inputs, any of which are beyond any consultant's control.

Do the Current Arrangements for Appointing Consultants, Allocating Risk, Settling Disputes and Making Redress...

... generate trust?

In an increasingly commercial world and in their search for certainty and risk limitation, clients and consultants are adopting defensive tactics as a matter of course. These may be advantageous when they lead to greater clarity. They are damaging when co-operation is stifled and risks are transferred to those who cannot control them.

...promote quality?

Fear of litigation, reinforced by well publicised cases, has made many consultants acutely aware of the advantages of systematic quality management. Informal procedures have been codified, there is greater commitment to continued professional development and more consultants are considering applying for Quality Assurance (QA) certification.

...promote efficiency and competitiveness?

Roles in construction are inevitably intertwined. Experience suggests and research has demonstrated that cooperation and a participative style of management lead to increased efficiency and few mistakes. As trust evaporates, cooperation and participation are less likely and both may be further impeded by defensive tactics. Almost certainly, efficiency and competitiveness are reduced when commitment to a project's success has been eroded by cost cutting and risk transfer.

...encourage innovation?

Much innovation is imposed by the necessity to meet a client's brief, to comply with new statutory requirements or to substitute for materials that are no longer available. Current apprehensions and uncertainty about liability have caused both clients and consultants to be wary of innovation, which is now attempted only if time and resources permit searching investigations. Also consultants are – or should be – now alerted to their duty to advise clients when a necessary innovation entails unusual risks.

...influence the management of projects?

Conditions of engagement are increasingly taking more time to negotiate, since many are peppered with non-standard conditions devised by individual clients. More clients now set out to impose increasingly onerous conditions, including indemnities. There is a dramatic growth of demands for collateral warranties, some of which greatly enlarge professional liability. When these much amended standard conditions have been accepted, consultants may be accepting risks which they are not able to manage. The result is likely to be a further increase in litigation. Doubt breeds doubt. Risk transfer by clients is countered by consultants' defensive design and by further risk transfer. The strong impression is that these attitudes now characterise much of construction and contribute nothing to efficiency, competitiveness and quality.

...influence consultants' management?

Coerced by their clients' insistence on tighter control of time and budgets and reduced fee income arising from fee competition and negotiation, consultants have responded by investigating few options, adopting simpler design solutions and transferring more detailed design to specialist subcontractors. It has, however, not been shown that these trends have either reduced or increased their liability. Some large practices have become incorporated. A variety of reasons are advanced; for example, financial and taxation advantages, tighter management control and a reduction of partners' personal liability for the activities of other partners. Retired directors are also less vulnerable to claims against their personal assets or estates than are retired partners. As far as can be discerned, clients are not disadvantaged.

...constrain the development of the industry?

As has been explained, many factors are now influencing the way in which clients obtain the industry's services and the roles of consultants and contractors are changing. In practice, there is no barrier to entry. However, all new arrangements pose risks. When the law and the likelihood of redress are both highly uncertain, these additional risks may inhibit developments that are needed for the industry to be fully effective.

...create an efficient framework for containing and settling disputes?

Formal litigation is viewed with abhorrence by clients and consultants. It diverts senior management's attention, incurs irrecoverable costs and is protracted and uncertain. Fear of the consequences of becoming enmeshed in litigation encourages the parties to settle before writs are served. In particular, experienced clients use their market strength to negotiate settlements, reserving litigation for large claims (in excess of £½ m in the case of one major developer). Less experienced clients may blunder into litigation which cannot be justified by the outcome. More use should be made of conciliation. A short arbitration system for claims of up to £50,000 would provide a better response to the needs of occasional and domestic clients.

...lead to an intolerable volume of litigation?

Despite the widespread apprehensions of clients and consultants and the number of claims notified to insurers, the risk of a writ being served in respect of any project is small and the risk of a court hearing is very small. Evidence about the probable volume of litigation in the foreseeable future points to increasing litigation, partly because of all the uncertainties that now operate and partly because of the potential for litigation created by much amended conditions of engagement and onerous collateral warranties.

...lead to fair settlements?

Clients may be affronted when they discover either that no producer is liable for damage suffered, that the action is time barred or that defendants lack funds. Consultants strongly believe that they are often made responsible for the liabilities of others and that the combination of unlimited liability, high levels of Professional Indemnity (PI) insurance cover and the law regarding joint liability and contribution encourages claims against them. This, they believe, obliges them and their insurers to pay for an unreasonable share of negotiated settlements and awards.

...protect consultants' interests?

On the evidence of this study, PI insurance effectively protects consultants' interests. However, the increases in premiums have resulted in PI insurance being the most costly overhead for about 50 per cent of the consultants responding to the review and the second most costly overhead for a further 30 per cent. The PI insurance market is now softer; when next it hardens, PI insurance could become even less affordable for many consultants, unless higher deductibles are accepted. This puts them at risk when one project is the subject of several distinct claims. Finally, insurance capacity, although not now a problem, could quickly become one were insurers and re-insurers to withdraw again from the PI insurance market.

...protect clients' interest?

PI insurance is not in place to protect clients' interests. If they cannot accept the risk of not being able to obtain timely redress, they should directly insure their own risks. This is important because, as has been emphasised, the current arrangements do not ensure that clients have a certain route to redress, even if all the possible defendants are available and have adequate funds to meet their potential liabilities.

The Problem

Risk allocation

With all development and production, risk is inevitable. In manufacturing industry, all production functions and the risks entailed normally fall to the management of a single organisation. They include decisions about what is to be produced, design, quality, production methods and quality control. In construction, these functions are widely distributed. Clients, consultants, contractors and a myriad of sub-contractors, specialists and suppliers all operate in situations that do not repeat. It is little wonder that risk allocation and the attendant liabilities and rights of redress are major problems and that clients and consultants are apprehensive and uncertain.

Ideally, risks are best allocated to those best able to control them. Indeed, this fairly describes the attitudes of the experienced 'good' clients who contributed to the review and of the consultants and contractors they regularly employ. Repeated experience engenders trust. Together they create confidence and certainty.

The search for certainty

In normal circumstances, the search for certainty bears differently on clients and consultants. Consultants need to be sure of the responsibilities they have undertaken and the liabilities they incur. This is not impossible when one consultant provides a service. It is much more difficult when there are several consultants, with interwoven tasks, whose designs are brought to fruition by contractors, sub-contractors and specialists with whom they may have little contact and over whom they can exercise no effective control. Established practice, aided by cooperation and common sense, normally makes these risks manageable.

Clients need to be certain of their route to redress should contracts run late, overspend, be of unacceptable quality or develop latent defects. Such certainty is not possible. The many producers will be liable in different ways and will have different relationships, actual and implied. Some causes of damage may involve either an external agency or no breach of duty. Thus, even when clients have taken the greatest care to safeguard their interest, redress is far from certain. This is the crux of their problem.

In their search for certainty, clients are now creating unprecedented contractual liabilities for consultants to an array of third parties. In particular, collateral warranties often set out to create a new category of potential plaintiffs who were not party to the construction process and will know nothing of its circumstances. It is clear that the full effects of such liabilities have yet to be felt and that their implications are not yet generally understood by consultants or by their insurers. Therefore, consultants cannot be certain of effective PI insurance cover when these new liabilities materialise.

When matters go awry, clients, again in search of certainty, will join all producers who may have been liable, unless there is a producer with ample funds or insurance who is clearly to blame. A selected defendant will almost certainly join other potential defendants in third party proceedings, because this will be cheaper and less time consuming than separate contribution proceedings. Whatever the route, the effect is the same: those who can, pay. Often, those paying will be consultants, who are more likely to have a continuing existence and the near certainty of PI insurance. In this way, consultants and, to a lesser extent, contractors of substance pay for the faults of others.

The basis for reform

The interwoven responsibilities and liabilities of those engaged in construction are such that reform based on the liability of construction professionals alone cannot resolve every problem. If it is accepted that the combination of unlimited professional liability, high levels of PI insurance cover, and the law relating to joint liability and contribution has the effect of making consultants prime targets for litigation, and that the effect is counter productive to clients' interests, a comprehensive solution to professional liability would entail legislation to ensure:

- capped liability;
- mandatory PI insurance;
- equitable risk sharing;
- more certain time limitation; and
- that defendants in commercial cases not involving personal injury should only be responsible to the plaintiff for damages equivalent to that part of the plaintiff's loss fairly attributable to the breach.

The Study Team accepts the desirability of comprehensive reform, which would lead to more efficient risk sharing, but draws back, mainly because legislation to cap the liability of construction professionals would raise complex issues of public policy, probably requiring a review of the liability of other professions, which could be a major remit for the Law Commission. This could postpone any reform for several years. Moreover, the current negotiations leading to the Single European Market may eventually involve legislation which would impinge on that needed to achieve a comprehensive solution in the United Kingdom for the construction professions alone.

The Study Team makes two complementary groups of recommendations: action by the professions and their clients and legislation. Recommendations for better practice, which can be implemented by professional institutions and consultants' associations in collaboration with their clients, will go a long way to creating the confidence and greater certainty sought by clients and consultants alike. The legislation recommended below is essential if the current erosion of trust and confidence is to be stopped and the benefits of better practice are to be fully realised.

The Study Team's Principal Recommendations

(i)   Improved Quality and Risk Management

The objectives of improved quality and risk management, clarity of responsibilities and greater certainty in law can be pursued immediately, through initiatives by the institutions and associations representing clients, the professions, consultants and insurers. The recommendations invite them to, *inter alia*:

- establish a trans-professional short arbitration procedure which would mainly serve the interests of occasional and domestic clients;
- devise reformed and unified consultants' conditions of engagement;
- work with others to align the consultants' conditions of engagement and the standard conditions of contract;
- review the arrangements for regulating the standards of professional competence of members;
- consult about the possibility of devising guidelines:
- for limiting the liability of professionals, commission-by-commission, by agreement with their clients;
  and
- for limiting the liability of a defendant to a plaintiff to a just and equitable proportion of the damages suffered, when there is more than one defendant and they have not acted jointly:
  and
- play a more active role in providing quality management and risk management advice.

(ii) Time Limitation

The Study Team recommends that serious consideration be given to alterations in the law to make the time limitation on liability certain. This proposal is supported by all the institutions and associations and by the

British Property Federation.

The proposal is:

> To amend in English law the Limitation Act 1980 and thus the provisions introduced into the 1980 Act by the Latent Damage Act 1986, and in Scotland the Prescription and Limitation (Scotland) Act 1973, to achieve the following:
> - a limitation (prescriptive in Scotland) period of ten years from the date of practical completion or effective occupation (staged if necessary) for negligent actions in tort (delict in Scotland) and in contract (whether or not under seal);
> - the ten years limitation period acting as a longstop extinguishing the right;
> - redefinition of the term "deliberate concealment" so that ordinary construction processes would not lead to an exception to the longstop.

These statutory provisions, although part of general law, are crucial to construction litigation because of the importance of latent defects. The principle of a decennial limitation period is already part of English statute law. This was established by the Consumer Protection Act 1987 which itself was a consequence of European Community legislation. If Ministers accept this recommendation, amending legislation could be deferred until negotiations preparing for completion of the Single European Market are well advanced, since these themselves may lead to legislation which will affect liability in the construction industry.

(iii) Joint Liability

The Study Team recommends that serious consideration be given to the alteration of the law in commercial cases, not involving personal injury, where the plaintiff's claim exceeds, say £50,000. In such cases, a defendant whose actions are partly the cause of damage to the plaintiff, but were not carried out jointly with another defendant, should be responsible to the plaintiff only for damages equivalent to that part of the plaintiff's loss fairly attributable to his or her breach.

This recommendation is strongly supported by the professional institutions and consultants' associations. The British Property Federation accepts that the current law can be unfair to consultants. Clearly, this recommendation, of crucial importance to the construction professions, raises issues of public policy which may need to be considered by the Law

Commission.

Crown Copyright. Reproduced with the permission of the Controller HMSO

Part IV

Comparative Law

Aspects of comparative law 16

Christopher Thomas

Synopsis

The author explores the Roman law origins of key construction law concepts in civil jurisdictions, specifically Italy, France and Germany. The different forms of locatio, obligatio and culpa are traced into the modern Civil Codes of these countries. Special reference is made to the requirement of acceptance in relation to a defective product and the position is compared with entirety as modified by the doctrine of substantial performance under English law.

Introduction

The themes of conferences of the Centre for Construction Law have highlighted and elucidated problem areas, whether extant or future, for the practitioner. Some papers have given us an insight into approaches adopted outside England. I have been asked to assist in the continuation of this study but with reference to a wider context of comparison that may be applied when individual features of construction law across the Channel fall to be considered.

It seems that the appropriate starting point for comparison between English law of building contracts and that pertaining in Europe is through the notion of work on goods in order to distinguish it from sales. When the result of the work includes the supply of goods, the key element in making the distinction is that the operation of labour forms an essential part. In England we know of the distinction historically from *Lee* v. *Griffin* (1861)[1] and the need for classification remained and was probably enhanced by the enactment of the Sale of Goods Act 1893 with formal requirements for enforcing contracts of sale.[2] Even if the approach is to pose the question whether the main purpose of the transaction is the supply of a complete

---

1 *Lee* v. *Griffin* (1861) 1 B&S p.272. Agreement by dentist to make a denture regarded as a sale of a chattel rather than a contract for work and labour.
2 *Robinson* v. *Graves* [1935] 1 KB 579 (C.A.). Agreement to paint a portrait regarded as outside Sale of Goods Act (and so enforceable in the case); paint and canvas ancillary to the skill and labour.

article, it is suggested that the nature of the article may act as a determining feature.[3]

The necessity to distinguish a building contract from a contract of sale may not arise in England, having regard to implications of similar warranties in the former, but there can be a practical significance in the distinction in civil law systems, particularly in connection with remedies available in respect of defects. It seems that under Italian law it is only in the case of a contract for work and labour that rectification of defects may be required, whereas in a contract of sale reduction of the price or cancellation of the contract are the ordinary remedies. [The Italian Civil Code Article 1662 gives the right to demand that the contractor conforms to the conditions of contract and after a period of time fixed for the purpose the contract is terminated upon the failure to remedy defects].[4] For the purposes of the distinction where materials supplied are merely instrumental and accessory (meramente strumentale ed accessoria) as against the skill and labour to be engaged in the production of the article, the Courts, it appears, tend to assume a contract for work and labour (appalto) rather than a sale (vendita). Both objective and subjective criteria are applied and the fact that the value of materials exceeds the value of work done is not, taken alone, decisive.[5]

In France it appears that the classification lies ordinarily in favour of a contract of sale (simple vente à livrer) whenever the supply of materials dominates, as compared with the work to be done, and in favour of a contract for work and labour (contract d'entreprise) when the converse applies. Such considerations apply to work on movables, but there is a different view if the obligation concerns the delivery of movables to be incorporated into immoveables when the sales element becomes absorbed by the building contract (marche d'entreprise). [A practical consequence of such latter characterization under French law is that the provisions of the Code Civil Article 1641 governing the seller's warranty against hidden defects will not apply, although clauses attempting to limit the seller's warranty (garantie du

---

3   *Clark* v. *Bulmer* (1843) 11 M & W 243

4   Italian Civil Code. Article 1662.
    "... When in the course of the work, it is ascertained that performance is not proceeding in accordance with the conditions established by the contract and according to the standards of the trade, the customer can establish a suitable time limit within which the contractor must conform to such conditions. If such time limit expires without results, the contract is terminated without prejudice to the right of the customer to be compensated for damages." Trans. Beltramo, Longo & Merryman. Oceana Publications Inc.

5   Cass. 8th October 1983. No. 2528. Common intention of parties important in deciding whether obligation is to do something (fare) or to give (sell) something (dare).

vendeur) will also be ignored as not pertaining to the work to be done.][6]

Under German law legislation expressly covers borderline cases on the line between sales law and the law relating to work and labour, for Article 651 of the BGB covers a situation where a workman supplies the materials from which the work is to be made (contract for the delivery of work - Werklieferungsvertrag) and it is treated as if it were a contract of sale except in those cases where the product cannot be replaced by a simple purchase of another (nicht vertretbare Sache) in which case Article 651 provides a number of applicable rules. In this way the warranty against defects of quality under sales law is effectively replaced by specialised rules prevailing in the area of contracts for work and labour.[7]

The roots of the civil law systems for work on goods and building contracts assists in appreciating their distinction from contracts of sale, but more importantly they assist in an understanding of the principles possibly unfamiliar to the common lawyer concerned with construction which will inevitably lie behind any approaches to future regulation or harmonisation.

A comparative study may well refresh the study of one's national law and promote a more positive criticism of, or search for, broad principles that might otherwise remain hidden by small points of procedural doctrine. Bare rules may mislead where one is looking for functional equivalents just as the distinctive mode of legal thinking in the different legal families may affect the identification of those principles, and the approach of English lawyers may require change in order to assist in the debate with those from the Germanic and Romanic families. For present purposes a brief glimpse of some of the characteristics that have moulded the principles of law and legal thinking of our neighbours is offered.

---

6 French Civil Code. De la garantie des défauts de la chose vendue. Article 1641. "Le vendeur est teau de la garantie à raison des défauts cachés de la chose vendue qui la rendent impropre à l'usage auquel on la destine, au qui diminuent tellement cet usage, qui l'acheteur ne l'aurait pas acquise, ou n'en aurait donné qu'un moindre, s'il les avait connus."

7 Burgerliches Gesetzbuch (BGB). Article 651. (Contract for delivery of work).

(1) If the contractor binds himself to produce the work from material provided by him, he shall deliver the thing produced to the customer and convey ownership in the thing. The provisions applicable to sale apply to such a contract; if a non-fungible thing is to be produced, the provisions relating to a contract for work, with the exception of *647, 648, take the place of *433, 336 (1)-1, and of *447, 459, 460, 462 to 464, 477 to 479.

(2) If the contractor binds himself only to provide additives or other accessories, the provisions relating to a contract for work apply exclusively.

Trans. Forrester, Goren, Ilgen. North Holland Publishing Co.

Roman Law Origins of the Civil Law Systems[8]

The contract "locatio conductio" was a letting and hiring - a contract whereby one person agreed to give to another the use or the use and enjoyment of a thing or his services or his labour in return for remuneration. Whilst in terms of rules closely resembling a contract of sale, it was legally distinct and referable to a hiring. Like a contract of sale it was complete by the agreement of the parties and equally produced only personal obligations not real rights. The contract of letting and hiring approaches very nearly to that of sale and is governed by the same rules of law. As the contract of sale is formed as soon as a price is fixed, so a contract of letting and hire is formed as soon as the amount to be paid for the hiring has been agreed on; and the "letter" has an action locati, and the hirer an action conducti.[9]

The "locatio conductio" took on three forms:

(a)   the hire of a thing (locatio conductio rei);
(b)   the hire of services (locatio conductio operarum); and
(c)   the hire of a piece of work (locatio conductio operis).

Different meanings became attached to the word "locare" and its derivations such that in the first two cases the person who supplies the thing or the services is the "locator" and the person who pays is the "conductor". Conversely in the third case, the "locatio conductio operis", the person giving the order is the "locator" (he "places" the order) and the person who executes the work or provides for its execution is the "conductor". This was because the Roman jurists generally looked at the work itself that was to be done, and spoke of the person who contracted for its performance i.e. gave it out as the "locator" and the person who engaged to perform or execute it, or "took it in", as "conductor".

Whilst the concept of labour producing or creating a piece of work originated in the category of hiring, the distinction shown by the different meanings that became attached to the same work illustrates that under Roman law the contract for work or building contract outgrew its origins. This would follow from the limitations on the contract of hire where in the earliest forms there was always something "placed":

(a)   I place a thing at your disposal.
(b)   I place myself or my slave at your disposal.

8   The body of Roman Law is taken from the Digests, including the Institutes of Justinian. References are to Mommsen's edition of the Digests in "Corpus Iuris Civilis" published in 1880, with identification of relevant articles.
9   Institute 3-24 from Digest XIV. 2.2 and Proemium -15. Trans. Sandar, the Institutes of Justinian.

(c)   I place in your hands something on which you are to expend your labour e.g. material to construct a house.

That the locatio conductio operis grew distinct and should outgrow the terminology is understandable when there was a need to cater for the placing of an order e.g. to construct a building (insulam aedificandum loco). Paulus considered the placing of the order made a contract of hire, but Sabinus provided a different reason, that the principal thing comes from "me" namely that the building accedes to "my" soil.[10]

This may well have derived from the more formalistic thinking of the Sabinian school for despite difficulties of application and some inconsistencies the point of the building acceding to the soil was a reflection of the law relating to acquisition by occupation and other methods. "Accessio" might be the addition or accrual to property previously belonging to the owner, for instance by the gradual deposit of alluvial soil on the bank of a river[11] but a person who used materials might either give them new form or make something from them, different from the materials themselves, a nova species, so that a person who has made wine with another's grapes was considered the owner. This mode of acquisition by conversion of another's materials into a new form or "species" was recognised and termed "specificatio", and was expressly viewed by the Sabinians as a kind of "accessio."[12]

The principles were that "accessio" could not affect the right to things that kept their independent existence but only those which lost it when combined in other things; so that when in the latter case a new thing was formed which was a whole by itself it absorbed the other irrespective of the relative values, for example materials in a building.[13] The point arose as to who could claim the resultant thing by a real action. An owner of a thing which came into the possession of another could ordinarily bring an action called "ad exhibendum" to make the person, in whose possession it was, produce or exhibit it, so that the owner, if he could establish his claim to the thing by vindication, could be sure it was not made away with,[14] but the distinct nature of buildings gave rise to specific exceptions even to the extent that:

"If a man builds upon his own ground with the materials of another, he is considered the proprietor of the building, because

---

10 Digests 19-2.22 (2) and Digests 18-1.20.
11 Institutes 2-1.20.
12 Institutes 2-1.25.
13 Gaius 2-79.
14 Institutes 2-1.26.

Comparative Law

everything built on the soil accedes to it."[15]

and the paragraph of the Institutes continued with this exception even where the materials had been stolen from a third person, although provision for recompense was made.

Locatio Conductio Rei

The duties of he who hired out a thing (locator rei) were to procure to the hirer its use and enjoyment for the purpose contemplated by the contract during the time agreed upon, unless prevented by impossibility arising from no fault of his own, (in which case he could not demand the hire money (merces)); to keep it in repair (except that the hirer was responsible for trifling repairs); and to compensate the hirer for necessary and "useful" expenses.[16] Necessary expenses were such as were required to preserve the property from destruction or depreciation. Useful expenses increased the value of the property, though their omission did not render it less valuable.

The first obligation was to deliver the thing free from defects so as to be fit for its purpose (for example the supply of wine vats that leak is not the supply of that to which I am entitled); and it was a liability based on the status of the contract (ex locato) and not on fault. So that in the case of the locatio conductio operis, and appreciating the mutation within the terms, the contractor (the conductor) was thus similarly liable[17] (for example when the fuller or cleaner loses cloth given to him to clean or allows mice to gnaw it) without question of fault.

Locatio Conductio Operarum

The hiring of services, locatio conductio operarum, gave rise to the obligation on the hirer or receiver of the services (the conductio in that case) to pay the wages or price for the full term agreed upon if the person hired was ready to render the services, whether the services were used by the hirer or not.[18] The price of or consideration for the letting was generally called "merces".

Prevention from doing the work by some cause extrinsic to the person hired did not disentitle the workman from his wages, (unless he had succeeded in getting other work) but failure to deliver the services did so

15 Institutes 2-1.9. Trans. Sandar.
16 Digests 19-2.9, 2.55 and 3.4.
17 Digests 13-1.6.
18 Digests 19-2.14 and 2.25.

disentitle him. As to the remuneration itself this had to consist of money. It had to be certain or ascertainable and provision for the fixing of the remuneration by a third person came within these requirements so as to constitute the contract of hire, provided the third person actually fixed the amount.[19] The Institute recorded: "What we have said above of a sale in which the price is to be..." The person hiring himself out had to be competent for the work he undertook and negligence or fault made him liable for the consequences.[20]

Just as the "conductor"/hirer was at risk in a hiring of services (when an extrinsic cause intervened to prevent the locator providing his service) so it became in the locatio conductio operis. The work was at the risk of the "conductor"/contractor so that the price would not be due if it was destroyed whilst in the contractor's hands. If, however, the work was destroyed due to a defect in the material supplied by the "locator"/employer, then there was no such liability[21] on the contractor without fault on his part. The standard of care that had to be applied by the "conductor" was high, being:

> "as great care on the safe custody of the thing he hires, as the most careful father of a family bestows on the custody of his own property (qualem diligentissimus paterfamilias suis rebus adhibet)".

However:

> "If he bestows such care, but loses the thing through some accident, he is not bound to restore it."[22]

As the risk was on the contractor so also the burden of showing the defect in the material fell on him.

Locatio Conductio Operis

What was contemplated by the locatio conductio operis was an engagement for a particular piece of work and, practically, with a physical subject matter. There was the familiar difficulty over the dividing line with contracts of sale where the goldsmith was to make rings, himself supplying the material and where it was ultimately decided that this was a sale, not hire,

19 Institutes 3-24.1
20 Digests 19-2.19
21 c.f. French Civil Code Articles 1787 to 1790.
22 Institutes 3-24.5. Trans. Sandar.

nor as Cassius had determined, sale of the materials and hire of the goldsmith's labour.[23] One who had contracted to build a house finding the materials himself was clearly "conductor operis"; whether because of the point that the site was part of the finished product so that he only provided part of the material or because the result of the work merged in the land and had no separate existence.

The locatio conductio operis was said to be made "per aversioneum" if the agreement was to do the whole job at a sum absolutely fixed, as distinct from so much per diem, or so much for each portion completed. The conductor operis had to execute and deliver the "opus" according to the specifications, and was answerable for all defects, whether due to his own want of skill or that of his workmen and subordinates. Acceptance or approval of the work by the locator had the important effect of extinguishing this liability except where there had been "dolus" (wilful injury) on the part of the "conductor".

For the locatio conductio operis the same rules as to remuneration as in the locatio conductio rei applied and the price fixed might well be a lump sum or so much for each part of the work. This did not prevent a claim by the employer for bad work at completion of the whole, unless it was arranged that the work should be approved at each stage.[24] The locator had to pay the merces agreed provided the work was satisfactorily executed, but he was permitted to withdraw from the contract if the ultimate cost exceeded the estimate given by the conductor.[25]

The civil law approach to approval, as under Roman Law, depended critically on the question of risk and its transfer. When the work was to be done subject to the locator's approval as a whole (aversione locatum), it remained at the risk of the contractor until approved, and equally if the work was to be done by the measure or section then the risk in respect of that measure remained until reached and approved. Agreement that work was to be completed so as to satisfy the locator or "Subject to the locator's approval" was interpreted to mean subject to a reasonable, not an arbitrary approval[26].

The approval could be that of a nominee of the "locator" but reasonable approval still applied and it was of that which ought to satisfy the approver: the judgment had to be that of a "bonus vir". This doubtless derived from the standard of obligation imposed on the "conductor" in relation to the contract of locatio conductio under which:

23 Gaius 3-147; Institutes 3-24.4.
24 Digests 10-2.51.
25 Digests 17-2.77.
26 Digests 19-2.60

"The "conductor" ought to do everything according to the terms of his hiring, and if anything has been omitted in these terms, he ought to supply it according to the rules of equity (id ex bono et aequo debet praetare) ..."[27]

Approval obtained by fraud was void so that there could still be a claim for defects "fraudulently concealed" even after the work had been approved[28]. Whilst rational, there is some doubt as to the clarity with which this aspect was approached.[29]

The time of any approval to which work was subject was important as it bore on the question of risks. Approval had to be made within a reasonable time of demand and the risk was on the "locator" so that he had to pay the "merces" whatever happened to the work, so far as it had been approved, or if approval had been delayed (mora) such as ought to have been approved[30]. Further, the conductor was entitled to payment so far as he had gone if the work was accidentally destroyed before completion. The work was and remained at the risk of the employer in the event of destruction by "vis major" but fault on the part of the contractor was not excused by this.[31]

Obligation and Culpa

Consideration was given to whether obligations fell to be included under things (res) or actions (actiones). Gaius, from whom the Institutes derived the point, preferred to consider obligations by reference to their ultimate result (res) rather than with reference to the mode by which the law secured this result (actio). From this may come the link, from the thing itself to the obligation attaching to it (the example of the wine vats carrying the obligation of producing non-leaking vats), albeit that without the ability to enforce an obligation by action it would have little practical effect.

Whether a right of action was on a contract or in delict, the right which the action was designed to enforce was in personam, and it was the obligation that was of primary importance for a promise without an obligation was in law non-existent, whereas an obligation had independent legal status. This explains the Roman law consideration of contracts under the head of obligations. It also helps to explain the emphasis on the obligation arising out of legal relations rather than on the terms of the

27 Institutes 3-2.45. Trans. Sandar.
28 Digests 19-2.24, Proemium 51.1.
29 Albertario: L'arbitrarium bonis viri del debitere, 14; does not accept that the proposition was clear law.
30 Digests 19-2.136, 37, 59, 62.
31 Digests 14-2.10.

promise. This is not to diminish agreement as an act or event giving rise to an "obligatio" but to show the context in which agreement was considered. Obligations could arise equally without an agreement or delict and these were referred to as "quasi ex contractu" or "quasi ex delicto"[32].

The possible duties an obligation could create were thought to be "dare" to give the absolute ownership of a thing; "facere" to do, or not do, some act; or "praestare" to provide or furnish some advantage or thing, the yielding of which could not be included in "dare". The "obligatio" was a special tie between two or more particular people but it also expressed the right gained, the duty thus owed, and also the mode of creation of the tie, the latter being used as equivalent to "contractus".[33]

If one person who was bound to another by contract, designedly subjected him to harm or loss (damnum) with respect to anything included in the contract, the wrongdoer in inflicting such wilful injury, was said to be guilty of "dolus"); if he was the means of an injury being inflicted, but not by design, then unless the "damnum" was the result of unavoidable accident, he was said to be guilty of "culpa". This "culpa" admitted of degrees. The fault might have been such that any man in his senses would not have committed and it was then termed "late culpa" ("late culpa est nimia negligentia, id est, non intelligere quod omnes intelligunt"[34]) or it might consist in falling short of the highest standard of carefulness to avoid injury that could be found, such as the care in the management of affairs by a "bonus paterfamilias", and then the "culpa" was termed levis or levissima. Further it might be a falling short of the care which the person guilty of "culpa" was accustomed to bestow on his own affairs and in this case the measure was not by an absolute standard but a relative one, "culpa levis in concreto", being measured by the particular individual as opposed to the "culpa levis in abstracto" estimated by an absolute standard.

The "late culpa" was treated on the same footing as "dolus", as there was always something of the wilful in extreme negligence, with "crassa negligentia" characterising the "late culpa". The technical term for the responsibility for malicious injury or fault was "dolman, culpam praestare" and an agreement excluding it was void.[35] In terms of time, where a person bound by a contract delayed in its execution and such delay ("mora") was of a kind that culpa could be attributed then more than the necessity of fulfilling the contract was exacted and he was liable to pay interest ("usurae").[36]

---

32 Digests 2-13.2.
33 Digests 12-2.9; 50-16.21; 5-1.20.
34 Digests 16-213.2.
35 Digests 2-14.27.
36 Digests 22.1.

Each of these facets of Roman law to a greater or lesser extent finds its way into the principles applicable to construction law in France and in other European countries. The special difficulties relating to construction work on land were addressed but were not separately or clearly resolved and this may be seen as the reason why so few specific rules relating to building contracts were to be found in the civil codes based on Roman law.

In France the revolutionary events were naturally critically important for the Code and its formulation but there was an absorption of the results of a long historical development of the ancient droit and the influence of Pothier (1699-1772). Whilst the Code was founded on the creed of the Enlightenment and the law of reason that social life could be put into a rational order if only the rules of law were restructured according to a comprehensive plan, the influence of the droit coutumier evolved in the century before the Revolution bore its mark, as did the droit écrit. Historically the droit coutumier had been more prevalent in the north and influenced by Germanic - Frankish customary law, while the droit écrit as developed in the southern areas was heavily influenced by Roman Law, albeit there was an overlap. The Coutume de Paris became generally accepted as applicable and the influential work of Bourjon (1720) had the significant title "Le Droit commun de la France à la coutume de Paris reduit en principles."

The Commission of four appointed by Napoleon to draft the Code were experienced practitioners: Tronchet, President of the Cour de Cassation, and Bigot de Preameneu had both been advocates at the Parliament of Paris and represented the droit coutumier while Portalis a high administrative official, and Maleville, a Judge of the Cour de Cassation, represented the droit écrit. Napoleon's significant contribution included achieving clarity of expression and language in relation to the realities of life and the ideas incorporated in the Code. The original Code Civil was the law book of the third estate, the bourgeoisie, so that the concept in the minds of the draftsmen was not the artisan or day labourer; rather the man of property, judgment and reason who would depend on guaranteed personal freedom especially to engage in economic activities, free from the dominance of the feudal groups of the ancien regime.

Consistent with the social aims of the introduction of the Code Civil, forced execution of obligations was not possible where the obligation was to "do" and the Code did not provide regulation of the "astreinte" as it was termed, the legal mechanism for enforcing orders for performance subsequently developed by the Courts. "Every obligation to do resolves itself into damages in case of inexecution"[37], and restriction on payment of damages for breach of contract devolves on the ability to escape upon proof that a

---

37 From Planiol: Traite Elementaire de Droit Civil

"cause étrangère qui ne peut lui être imputée" was the reason for non-performance or in the event of "force majeure" or "cas fortuit"[38], deriving from the Roman law concept of relief from the performance of the obligation to which it attached in circumstances of the intervention of an extrinsic cause.

The secondary effect of such intervention, the inability of the party prevented to claim payment for the services or compensation is equally carried forward, albeit that one can find as in Italy special rules relating to construction that permit recovery of payment on termination for impossibility[39]. Essentially the obligation in construction is one of producing the result (une obligation de résultat) and some of the provisions of the Code reflecting the aspects that have been referred to above are identified elsewhere in this volume[40].

One such provision was Article 1792-6, of which the first part provides:

"La réception est l'acte par lequel le maître de l'ouvrage déclare accepter l'ouvrage avec ou sans reserves. Elle intervient à la demande de la partie la plus diligente, soit à l'amiable, soit a défaut judiciairement. Elle est, en tout état de cause, prononcée contradictoirement."[41]

This Article,[42] with the expressed effects in Articles 1792- 6, 1792-3 and 2269 of bringing about the commencement of the periods for repairing defects notified or reserved matters and the two and ten year liabilities respectively, does not reduce the need to appreciate the previous operational rules which have derived from and moulded the Roman law concept of acceptance. Equally an understanding of the prescribed regime for la réception within the frequently used standard form (Norme française, NF/

---

38 Civil Codes Article 1147 and 1148.
39 Italian Civil Code: Articles 1218 and 1483 (general rules),
   Article 1672: If the contract is terminated because performance of the work or service has become impossible due to causes which cannot be imputed to either party, the customer must pay for that part of the work which has already been completed, to the extent that the work is useful to him, in proportion to the price agreed upon for the whole work. Trans. Beltramo, Longo and Merryman.
40 J.B. Winter: Civil Law Solutions to Common Law Tort Problems. Paper 17
41 Article 1792-6, first part:
   Acceptance is the act by which the employer registers his acceptance of the work, with or without reservation. It takes place on the application of either party, either amicably or in default by judicial intervention. It may be ordered at any stage of an adversarial proceeding.
42 Introduced on 4th January 1978. In force from 1st January 1979.

P 03.001 April 1989) benefits from an appreciation of its roots[43]. Belgium had not introduced the equivalent 1978 laws and so retained the original text of Article 1792, and the procedures for and effects of "la réception" are again much considered on questions of form and timing, provisional and tacit acceptance, and on the necessity for single or multiple acceptances[44].

In Germany, the traditional and diverse laws of the various peoples and cities with the weakening of imperial power made easier the reception of Roman Law which offered concepts and rational methods of thinking. With the Age of Reason it gave a system of principles and logical deduction. The General Land Law for the Prussian States was introduced in 1794 with its authoritarian regulation by the state of the details of life with a mass of rules. From about 1814 under Savigny and Thibaut the Historical School of Law concentrated on the historical development of the law and turned to Roman Law. There developed the Pandectist School, with its aim being the systematic and almost dogmatic study of Roman material. This was a technical process that was remote and theorising, without questioning its practical application or social justification. The first moves to codification were made around the mid 19th century with the General German Commercial Code in 1861; the draft law of obligations (Dresdner Entwurt) in 1865, and the Courts system and civil procedure (Reichsjustisgesetz) in 1879. In 1890 the second draft code came into force, the Burgerlicke Gesetzbuch (BGB), where the typical citizen was not the artisan but the monied entrepreneur or landed proprietor, with business experience, capable of succeeding in society with freedom of contract and able to take steps to protect himself from harm.

The BGB, being aimed at the man of property and not the ordinary citizen, displays abstract conceptual language alongside precision and rigour of thought. This display of technical merit and powerful thought has to be contrasted with the haphazard, almost off the cuff, development of English Law without the guidance from careful theorising over concepts.

The general principle of the law of contract is that contracting parties are formally free and equal, and few rules seek to give protection to those for whom "freedom" of contract is illusory, being economically inferior or dependent on the other party. Thus by BGB Para. 138 a contract is void if it is contra bonos mores or if one party has exploited the plight and inexperience or lack of judgment of the other; or by BGB Para. 343 penalties can be modified by the Court if too high. The liberal principles have been

---

43 Y. Gaudemet, La réception de l'ouvrage dans la loi reformant l'assurance construction, Moniteur des Travaux Publics, 16th and 23rd April 1979. G. Liet-Veaux, le Droit de la Construction, 9th edition 1989.
44 M-A. & P. Flamme, Le Droit des Constructeurs, 1984.

modified by laws on specific subject matters outside the Code, but there remain the principles of the law of contract. By BGB Para. 242, in general terms everyone must perform his contract in the manner required by good faith ("treu und glauben"). The individual's liberty in the original contract law has been qualified by devices developed by the Courts; the collapse of the basis of the transaction "clausula revus sic stantibus", the improper exercise of rights "venire contra factum proprium", and the forfeiture of rights especially by laches "verwickung". Of interest is the use of BGB Para. 242 to control the content of general conditions of business, so as to invalidate standard terms excluding or limiting liability as being inconsistent with the obligation of good faith if "they are inequitable on a balancing of the interests of those who typically enter such transactions."

In Germany, the law of obligations is dealt with in Book Two of the Civil Code BGB and is not simply subdivided into contract, tort and sundries as an English Code might be. It is presented as a self-contained body of law revolving around the central action of an obligational relationship. Within this Book is the section on the Contract of services (Werkvertrag) with certain specially applicable rules including Para. 640 which provides for acceptance in terms of a duty of the client[45].

When governed by Article 640 of the BGB and whether the contract is for work or for architect's services, acceptance may be written or inferred, again from taking possession, but reservations are essential because of the

---

45 Acceptance
  1. If a contractor requests acceptance after construction work has been completed the client shall have 12 working days in which to effect this. Any other period may be agreed.
  2. Special acceptance may be given for the following, on request:
  (a) isolated parts forming a whole;
  (b) parts on which the continuance of the work is dependent.
  3. In the event of a substantial defect acceptance may be refused until repairs are made.
  4. Formal acceptance shall take place when one of the contracting parties requires it. Each party may then have recourse to an expert at his own expense. The expert's report is put in writing after joint negotiation. The report records any reservations relating to known defects and to penalties, and any objections by the contractor. Each party receives a copy.
  5. When one of the contracting parties is freed from his obligations with respect of paragraphs 2, 3 or 4 above, this discharge shall also apply to their legal representatives and their subcontractors, except where the latter have acted with intentional or gross negligence.
  6. If a third party claims against one of the contracting parties for any loss for which the second contracting party is responsible by virtue of paragraphs 2, 3 or 4, the former may request that the later release him from his obligations with regard to third parties. He must not accept or satisfy claims by third parties without first providing the other party with an opportunity of being represented.

four-fold impact of acceptance whereby:

- risks are transferred from the contractor to the owner;
- the "burden of proof" in the event of defects in the work is reversed from the contractor to the owner;
- the end date of the "warranty" period which the law provides for the owner is by reference to the date of acceptance;
- the contractor is given the right to receive all contractual remuneration.

Acceptance by the client is therefore equated with conformity by the contractor with the contract and taking possession within the contract is regarded as tacit acceptance so that even early possession forced on an owner requires explicit rejection of acceptance. Bad work in the context of acceptance relates to known not hidden defects so that it is regarded as a conscious act of the owner and, without reservation, gives rise to loss of the rights to secure the repair of the defects (Nachbesserung) or a reduction in the price (Munderung), but not to the right to damages (Schadenersatz). It seems that reservations by the owner must be made at the time of acceptance, not before or afterwards, but whilst this may appear to require a positive approach of the owner, the initiative to achieve acceptance rests firmly with the contractor.

These special rules of the BGB may be amended by agreement in particular where general conditions of supply (allgemeine Lieferbedin-gungen) have been accepted, and with contracts for construction work of the type known as the VOB (Verdingungsordnung fur Bauleistungen - the conditions applicable to construction work which were negotiated with the building industry and which are compulsory for government contracts and frequently incorporated into private contracts) there are specific provisions that constitute such amendments to the BGB code including provisions as to acceptance of the work. Thus acceptance may be governed by Article 640 of the BGB or Article 12 of the VOB.

The text of Article 12 of the VOB is set out in the notes[45] and acceptance is more onerous for the owner than would be the case under Article 640 of the BGB, for, unless otherwise agreed, it is deemed to take place within 12 days following written notification of completion of the work. Additionally it seems that taking possession gives rise to acceptance at the expiration of 6 days. The VOB contract is used in the vast majority of cases and with the propensity towards the use of many contracts between owner and various contractors engaged in a project, as opposed to one contract with a main contractor, successive acceptance of parts is usual.

As a function of closing down the obligations of a contractor to perform under the contract, the Civil Law concept of acceptance is, at its base, recognisable in English Law in the principle of substantial performance and without the necessity for recourse to particular standard conditions of contract providing for certification and its consequences. Without action by the Employer, substantial performance impacts on the parties so as to:

- transfer risks in and from the works from the contractor to the employer;
- give rise to the right of the contractor to receive his contractual remuneration;
- start time running in ordinary circumstances for the purposes of the Limitation Acts;
- place the burden on the Employer to identify and prove deficiencies in the work by way of breaches of contract for the purposes of recovery of damages.

The traditional concept of an entire contract in English Law[46], under which complete performance is a condition precedent to payment, is mollified particularly in the construction field by the application of the concept of substantial completion equating to substantial performance. Only the clearest of language would be permitted to deprive the contractor of any payment until completion of every minor detail, but undoubtedly parties are at liberty to contract on those terms[47]. The ordinary lump sum contract for building work provides the best comparison with the civil law elements of acceptance for it is clear that the employer cannot refuse to pay the price merely because of the existence of minor defects and omissions. The root of this principle is in the ability of the employer to recover damages as set out in the judgment in 1779 of Lord Mansfield:

> "... where mutual covenants go to the whole of the consideration
> on both sides, they are mutual conditions, the one precedent to
> the other. But where they go only to a part, where a breach may
> be paid in damages, there the defendant has his remedy on his
> covenant, and shall not plead it as a condition precedent."[48]

The principle became muddied with questions of set-offs and cross-actions and in 1841[49] the differences were re-stated in these terms:

> "In the one case, the performance of the warranty not being a

46 *Cutter* v. *Powell* (1795) 6 Term. Rep. 320
47 *Appleby* v. *Myers* (1867) LR 2 CP 651.
48 *Boon* v. *Eyre* (1779) 1 Hy. Bl. 273.
49 *Mondel* v. *Steel* (1841) 8 M&W 858.

condition precedent to the payment of the price, the defendant, who had received the chattel warranted, has thereby the property vested in him indefeasibly, and is incapable of returning it back; he has all that he stipulated for as a condition of paying the price, and therefore it was held that he ought to pay it, and seek his remedy on the plaintiffs contract of warranty.

"In the other case, the law appears to have construed the contract as not importing that the performance of every portion of the work should be a condition precedent to the payment of the stipulated price, otherwise the least deviation would have deprived the plaintiff of the whole price; and therefore the defendant was obliged to pay it, and recover for any breach of contract on the other side."

In *Boon* v. *Eyre* possession had been taken of the plantation the subject of the action and in *Mondel* v. *Steel* the ship, built under the contract, had been used on a voyage from London to Australia. It is suggested that these factors equate to acceptance or inferred acceptance in the civil law to the like extent of depriving the employer of the ability to refuse payment, but casting on him the right to recover, upon proof, a claim for damages.

The possession taken by the employer was a significant consideration in *H. Dakin & Co. Limited* v. *Lee*[50], where the Plaintiff builders had lost their claim for the price of the work by failing to fulfil specification provisions. In the Divisional Court the builders succeeded:

" ... where a building or repairing contract has been substantially completed, although not absolutely, the person who gets the benefit of the work which has been done under the contract must pay for that benefit."[49]

with the argument, that no promise to pay could be implied from the fact that the defendant occupied the house because the work was carried out on the employer's land and therefore could not be rejected, being described as fallacious in circumstances where the work had been substantially completed, though not entirely in the manner provided for in the contract. The result was the same in the Court of Appeal.:

"The work was finished ... I cannot think of a better word to use ... Take a contract for lump sum to decorate a house; the contract provides that there shall be three coats of paint, but in one of the

---

50 [1916] 1 KB 566 per Ridley J. at 569.

rooms only two coats of paint are put on. Can anybody seriously say that under these circumstances the building owner could go and occupy the house and take the benefit of all the decorations which had been done in the other rooms without paying a penny for all the work ..."[51]

The test of the work being "finished" or "done" though in some respects not in accordance with the contract inevitably is linked with possession, use, or benefit of the work in considering substantial performance and is frequently likely to be determinative and identical to acceptance in the civil law jurisdictions, at least to the extent of the release of the contractor from further obligations of performance under the contract and to payment. In this way acceptance is reflected again in English Law in waiver so as to give rise to the like result:

"Even if entire performance was a condition precedent, nevertheless the result would be the same, because I think the condition was waived. It is always open to a party to waive a condition which is inserted for his benefit. What amounts to a waiver depends on the circumstances. If this was an entire contract, then, when the Plaintiff tendered the work to the Defendant as being a fulfilment of the contract, the Defendant could have refused to accept it until the defects were made good, in which case he would not have been liable for the balance of the price until they were made good. But he did not refuse to accept the work. On the contrary, he entered into possession of the flat and used the furniture as his own, including the defective items. That was a clear waiver of the condition precedent. Just as in a sale of goods the buyer who accepts the goods can no longer treat a breach of condition as giving a right to reject but only a right to damages, so also in a contract for work and labour an employer who takes the benefit of the work can no longer treat entire performance as a condition precedent, but only as a term giving rise to damages. The case becomes then an ordinary lump sum contract governed by the principles laid down in *Mondel* v. *Steel* and *H. Dakin & Co. Limited* v. *Lee*. The employer must, therefore, pay the contract price subject to a deduction for defects or omissions."[52]

Acceptance in this sense by occupying or using the work does not

51 per Lord Cozens-Hardy M.R. at 578 and 579.
52 *Hoenig* v. *Isaacs* [1952] 2 All ER 176, per Lord Denning, M.R. at 181.

however deprive an employer of his right to seek damages for defects and this is true also where the employer pays the contractor even in full under judgment; for, on the hypothesis that the builder seeking his price is in default in some respects that do not negate substantial performance, the basis for his action is usually immediate and relatively straightforward, whilst the extent to which there is a breach of contract and monetary consequences will usually not be capable of ascertainment or even discovery until some time after the date for payment has arrived. On these grounds, the fact that the employer had the ability to utilise the existence of breaches in diminution of the price claimed and recovered even by action was not held to deprive the employer of the right to recover damages[53].

It is suggested that comparison of civil law acceptance with substantial performance indicates that possession of or benefit from work which may be regarded in civil law as critical to acceptance of the work in reality goes no further than in English Law. Possession as such does not prevent a determination that substantial performance or completion has not been achieved, which is illustrated by *Sumpter* v. *Hedges*[54] where the Plaintiff builder, having left unfinished his contract to build two houses, recovered nothing for his part finished work although the Defendant carried on and completed the works. The abandonment by the Plaintiff was critical to the decision that nothing could be recovered, and an inference of a new contract to pay for the work done on a quantum meruit could not be drawn from the mere fact of the owner being in possession of what he could not help keeping.

This is not, it is believed, contrary to the principle of "acceptance" as that presupposes purported completion, whether "a building built" within Article 1792 of the Civil Code, or a notification of completion within the German VOB conditions, but it does highlight a potential, even if unlikely, dissimilar result stemming from enforced possession without reservation[55].

The structure of construction law in civil law countries may be found to

53 *Davis* v. *Hedges* [1871] LR 6 QB 687.
54 [1898] 1 QB 673 (CA).
55 The Italian Civil Code expressly links the right of the contractor to payment with acceptance and embodies the owner's right and his obligation to check completed works as provided in Article 1665:
Verification and payment for the works. The Owner, before receiving delivery of the works, has the right to verify the completed works. The verification must be made by the Owner as soon as the contractor makes it possible for him to proceed with it.
If, notwithstanding the installation of the contractor, the Owner delays his verification without justifiable grounds, or does not communicate within a short period of time his findings, the works are considered accepted. If the Owner takes delivery of the works without reservation, this is considered as an acceptance even if verification has not taken place. Unless otherwise agreed, or by contrary custom, the contractor has the right to payment of the consideration when the work is accepted by the Owner.

be broadly the same, with the Civil Codes containing some Articles of principle but with a growth in a body of standard forms to guide the practices deriving from the parties themselves having been left to develop their own rules for the operation of building contracts. The strength of the professions and associations or groups within the building and engineering industries has given rise to almost standard self-made rules, or norms within the industry. The German term is "selbstgeschaffenes Recht de Wirtschaft" - self-made law of industry. Such rules may be regarded as "law" in the sense that the thing done becomes the done thing.

The development of such standard provisions by or on behalf of economic or social/professional groups has brought in its wake legislative control impinging on freedom of contract, for example, the Unfair Contract Terms Act 1977, and the proposal of the Commission of the European Communities for a Council Directive on unfair terms in consumer contracts. In this sense legislative control is endorsing standard provisions, provided such standard provisions conform with the impositions of the legislature, but whatever course is taken with regard to comparison of terms and procedures under standard forms, a brief view of the roots of concepts which such terms may seek to apply or adopt may prove of assistance.

Summary of conclusions

This paper highlights the benefits of comparative study of law as a means of better understanding one's own system. France, Italy and Germany all have Civil Codes whose construction law provisions are consistent with the rules of Roman Law governing locatio and obligations. Much of this derivation has had positive effects, with a coherent and precise development of rules, such as in the German BGB, comparing favourably with the piecemeal growth of English law, as a self-contained body of law based upon obligation. Acceptance by the client is the key to the problems which English law has sought to tackle through the concept of entire contracts and modifications by substantial performance. Movement towards harmonisation in Europe of control of consumer contracts (inter alia) renders explorations of this kind particularly necessary.

Civil law solutions to 17
common law tort problems

Jeremy Winter

Synopsis

The purpose of this paper is to examine the law of tort under civil law
systems, principally as applied in France, to see whether it suffers from the
same ailments as are apparent in the UK; and if this is so, whether the law
of tort is perceived as the disease or the cure. To the extent that the civil
law system avoids the problems experienced under the common law, the
reasons are examined.

Basic Principles

The writer is not a French lawyer, and does not claim any special skill in
comparative law. It has therefore been necessary to start with basics,
examining every concept to see whether there was an equivalent in the
foreign law being studied, and if there were apparently similar concepts,
checking that they were truly comparable.

First, what is the common law tort problem? It might appear from reading
the decision in the *Murphy* case[1] that construction law in the UK is now rid
of some creeping cancer from which it had been suffering since 1972, which
spread from limb to limb until by 1980, nearly the whole body was infected;
but on which, since then, various life- saving operations have been performed, until a final (and very drawn-out) operation was carried out to
remove the last vestiges. The worst thing about this disease was that it was
deliberately introduced into the body in an attempt to cure existing deficiencies in construction law, but like some untested wonder drug, the cure was
seen as having wholly undesirable side-effects.

The two foundation stones of relationships in English law are contract
and tort. The first question in this comparative exercise is to ask whether
they exist in civil law. The answer, fortunately, is yes. One of the most
interesting features of researching this paper was to find how often,
sometimes linguistically and sometimes conceptually, words, expressions
and terms of art that UK construction lawyers are familiar with have exact
parallels in both English and French law. This is perhaps not surprising

1   *Murphy* v. *Brentwood District Council* [1990] 3 WLR 414

when one realises the fact that situations that have led to the development of the law in this country have had their exact equivalents in other countries. As to contract, of course the concept is recognised in civil law. But as every potential comparative lawyer knows, it does not have all the same elements as English law. The civil law finds no need for consideration, but has rules to deal with bargains, rules as to how they should be performed and as to what happens when they are not. It has been said that:

> "This codified civil law was the heart of the private law and the dominant concepts of the code were individual private property and individual freedom of contract"[2]

As to the law of tort, here too the common lawyer is relieved to find a body of law apparently similar to his own. But he should not be surprised, as every civilised system of law must provide a remedy to those injured by the acts of others. "Responsabilité civile" covers liability in both tort and contract, and this is sub-divided in tort into "responsabilité delictuelle/ delit", meaning intentional harm and "quasi-delit", unintentional harm. Some of the detail of the law in this area will be considered later. This section is intended to set the scene.

Structure of the construction industry

In order to see where the law of tort (or delict, to adopt the familiar Scots term) might be relevant, one needs to look at the structure of construction contracts used under a civil law system, to see where any gaps are, and whether they have to be filled by tort, or whether there is anything else that performs the role occupied by tort in the UK. First the parties under a civil law contract are as follows: the employer/client is the "maître d'ouvrage"; the main contractor is the "entrepreneur principal", the sub-contractor is the "sous-traitant" and the project manager or contract administrator is the "maître d'oeuvre". These terms are reassuringly familiar and easily translatable. The only one that is not quite straightforward is the "maître d'oeuvre" as his role is not directly comparable to that of the architect/ engineer deciding on extensions of time etc. under the UK system.

As to how contracts are structured, the CIRIA report[3] entitled "The French construction industry - a guide for UK professionals" gives an admirable and accurate guide to this. As it is readily available and in English, it would be unnecessary duplication to give more than an overview

2 Merryman, *The Civil Law Tradition*, p100
3 CIRIA Special Publication 66, 1989

of the contract structure in this paper. The types of structure used are:

(a) "lots séparés", where the employer lets a separate contract direct to individual trade contractors, or groups of trade contractors, one of whom may be the "pilote" or co-ordinator of the trade contractors. Overall project supervision is undertaken by the maître d'oeuvre. This is the traditional method used.

(b) main contracting. This is the same structure that we are familiar with in the UK. While the CIRIA report is no doubt correct in saying that main contracting is still not widely used in France, our understanding is that it is becoming much more popular, certainly among the biggest contractors. This is borne out by the facts of the cases that will be discussed below.

(c) "groupement solidaire" and "groupement conjoint". This where contractors group together to do work. Where it is "solidaire" the members of the group are jointly responsible for all parts of the work. Where it is "conjoint" each contractor is responsible for a particular piece of work, but the group tenders together in one tender.

The average UK construction lawyer will have two perceptions about French construction law:

- that there is no need for lengthy contracts like the JCT form, because the Code Civil provides all the answers, and
- that there is no need for any litigation in construction contracts, as decennial insurance provides a solution to every dispute.

Both of these are, at least in part, misconceptions. French "standard form" contracts have many clauses, and the legal reports contain a good number of decisions of the Cour de cassation on construction cases. The genesis of these two perceptions is Art.1792 of the Code Civil[4]. This reads in (very literal) translation:

> "Every constructor of a work is fully legally responsible to the employer or purchaser for damages, even resulting from a defect in the ground, which compromises the solidity of the works or which, affecting one of its constituent elements or one of its elements of equipment, renders it unfit for its purpose. Such responsibility does not apply if the constructor proves that the damage was caused by an outside cause."

4 Dalloz edition 1989-90

Art.1792-1 goes on to provide that "constructor" includes:

"1.   Every architect, contractor, technician or other person
          bound to the employer by a contract of works.
2.   Every person who sells after completion works that he
          has constructed or had constructed.
3.   Every person who, while acting in the capacity of agent
          of the employer, accomplishes a mission similar to that
          of an employer."

Art.1792-2 provides that the presumption of liability (for ten years) extends to damage affecting elements of equipment in a building, but only when they are inextricably a part of the works of viability, foundations, framework, enclosure or roof (i.e. when their replacement cannot be carried out without damaging the substance of the works).

Art.1792-3 provides that other elements of equipment in the building are subject to a guarantee of proper performance for a period of two years from the acceptance of the works.

Art.1792-4 provides that a manufacturer of a work, part of a work or an element of equipment "purpose-built" for the works is jointly liable under the remainder of the parts of Art.1792 where the article is incorporated unmodified and in accordance with the manufacturer's instructions. Where the item is imported, the importer takes the responsibility of the manufacturer. [Note that this is not a full translation of this article]

Art.1792-5 provides that any attempt to exclude or limit these liabilities is void.

Art.1792-6 deals with acceptance of the works and a one year "defects liability" period.

As to the duration of the warranty under Art.1792, Art.2270 of the Code Civil provides:

"Every person, physical or moral, who can be held responsible
by virtue of Arts.1792 to 1792-4 of this Code is discharged from
the responsibilities and guarantees imposed on it by the application of Arts.1792 to 1792-2 after ten years, counting from the
acceptance of the works, or, by the application of Art.1792-3, on
the expiration of the period envisaged by that article" [i.e. two
years].

Note that the expiry of the ten or two year period is not an absolute bar to recovery, but an end to the presumption of liability i.e. the employer may still prove liability against the constructor in tort.

Art.1646-1 provides that the vendor of a new property is bound to the purchaser and his successors by the same obligations that 'constructors' have under Art.1792 et seq.

The French civil code, therefore, contains a thorough regime to deal with defects arising after completion of the construction of works: a ten year warranty from all those involved in the construction process,that the works will be fit for their purpose, the liability being joint and several by law in some cases: see Article 1792-4 above. The onus of proof is therefore on the constructor to prove that the cause of a defect was not his responsibility, which in practice means only force majeure. In common law language this is strict liability. The warranty extends to equipment inextricably incorporated into the structure; where it is not so incorporated, a two year warranty applies.

All of the above were inserted into the Code Civil by amending legislation passed in 1978. The original version of Art.1792 simply read:

"If a building perishes in whole or in part because of a defect in construction, including a defect in the ground, architects, contractors and other persons bound to the employer by a contract of works are responsible for them for ten years."

Claude Mathurin remarked, when summarising these superseded provisions, that they had "the merit of simplicity"[5]. They were also however the subject of very considerable criticism (see e.g. Fossereau[6]).

In its old form or its new, Art.1792 is the main solution of the civil law to the tort law problems suffered by all sides of the construction industry in the UK (equivalents or similar articles are found in many other codes e.g. Art.1792 of the Belgian Code which is still in a form very similar to the old French form and Article 1591 of the Spanish Civil Code). Ignoring the insurance aspects for the moment (they will be dealt with below), it is a solution not in the sense that it limits liability: on the contrary, the solution is to provide a regime where almost everyone is liable, but they are aware of their responsibilities, as they are written down in an accessible form. It is also a solution in the sense that it provides many targets for the employer to shoot at for the same problem. For example, when settlement of foundations occurs, the architect/structural engineer cannot say that it was a defect in the workmanship not the design, and that the contractor has ceased to exist, which (prior to Murphy at least) would have caused the

---

5 Mathurin, *Controls, Contracts, Liability and Insurance in the construction industry in the European Community*, pF33, 271

6 *'Le "clair-obscur" de la responsibilité des constructeurs'* by Joele Fossereau, Recueil Dalloz Sirey 3e Cahier 1977, p13

employer to look to the local authority with his claim. There is no equivalent in France of Building Regulations inspection which could give rise to a Murphy-type claim.

Note that where the constructors are not jointly and severally liable by law - except under Art.1792-4 - in the case of defects caused by several constructors not contractually related to each other resulting in the same damage, French Courts would hold them jointly and severally liable towards the employer. This liability regime created by French case law is called "Responsabilité in Solidum". The liability of the defendant sued by the employer would, however, be apportioned by the court between the other defendants who are liable, at a further stage.

Importantly, Art.1792 is a solution to the large void now left in the UK by the Murphy decision, namely the position of subsequent owners who suffer from defects in the building they have purchased, but who find themselves barred from any claim against the builder because of the Murphy definition of physical damage. While the original version of Art.1792 gave a remedy only to the original employer, the 1978 version gives the same remedy to a purchaser from the employer, whereupon the vendor employer himself becomes liable by virtue of Art.1792-1, para 2. and Art.1646-1.

It is also a solution to the ridiculous chasing of limitation periods that is found in cases such as *Pirelli* v. *Oscar Faber*[7], where the employer's contractual remedy is barred but his tort limitation period starts later. It is a solution because it provides a lengthy period, not because it is the only applicable limitation period. Two limitation periods under French law have already been referred to, and there is a third which will be dealt with later.

It should not be forgotten that the Defective Premises Act 1972 made similar efforts to resolve the problems arising from seeking a liability in tort. It too imposes a duty to ensure a result (a dwelling fit for habitation) on a potentially wide number of parties (the obligation is on "a person taking on work"). The benefit is also automatically transferred to subsequent owners[8]. It too cannot be excluded[9]. The problem with the act is the well known one that it has not applied to houses built under the NHBC scheme, and has therefore been subject to very little analysis in the court.

The insurance regime

Overlying the regime of liability under Art.1792 of the Code Civil is a scheme of compulsory insurance introduced at the same time as the

---

7 *Pirelli General Cable Works Ltd* v. *Oscar Faber & Partners* [1983] 2 AC 1
8 Section 3(1)
9 Section 6(3)

amendments to the Code i.e. 1978.[10] Contained in a separate insurance code are the following:

Art.L.241-1: "Every person, physical or moral, who can be held responsible on the basis of the presumption established by Articles 1792 et seq. of the Code Civil in relation to building works must be covered by insurance".

Further, Art.L.242-1 provides:

"Every person, physical or moral who, acting in the capacity of employer of works, seller or agent of the proprietor of the works causes building works to be carried out, must subscribe, before the opening up of the site, for his own benefit and for his successive owners, insurance guaranteeing, without investigation of responsibility, payment of the totality of the works of repair of defects of the nature of those for which constructors are responsible under Art.1792-1, and manufacturers and importers or the technical controller on the basis of Art.1792 of the Civil Code.

Art.L 243-2 provides that anyone contravening these provisions will be punished with imprisonment for ten days to six months and to a fine of between 2,000 and 500,000 French francs or one of these two penalties only.

Art.L 243-7 provides that those who have suffered loss as foreseen by this law can act directly against the insurer of the party responsible for the said losses if the latter is in judicial control or in liquidation.

In summary these provisions provide for a two-tier compulsory (on pain of severe penalties) insurance protection against the cost of repairing the kind of defects covered by Art.1792, one to be obtained by the employer for his own benefit and for the benefit of his successors in title (to use the English term), and the other to be obtained by anyone falling within the definition of constructor under Art.1792 et seq, to cover his own liability under that article, and giving a direct right against the insurer in the event of insolvency. It is interesting to note at this point that the primary insurance legislation was introduced in 1978, the same year as *Anns*[11]. The insurance legislation is interventionist and avowedly for the protection of the employer who was perceived as being less able to protect his interests, whether by negotiation of contractual terms, obtaining insurance, or by simple

---

10 Law no. 78-12 of 4 Jan 1978 (the 'Spinetta' Law)
11 *Anns* v. *Merton London Borough Council* [1978] AC 728

financial muscle. The legislature clearly had in mind the individual who builds a home for himself (or perhaps more so a small syndicate building a block of apartments). This was a sign of the rather more caring 1970's, in stark contract to the laissez-faire 1980's and '90's both generally and as judicially epitomised in the House of Lords' decision in *Murphy*.

Following secondary legislation introduced in 1982[12] the idea of the "single work-site insurance policy" ("police unique de chantier" or PUC) was introduced with the objective of saving half of the total insurance cost by having the employer and the maître d'oeuvre subscribe to the same insurance company for their insurance under the 1978 law. It is easy to see how this represents at least a large part of a solution to the problems of tort law in the UK, in that it minimises the extent to which tort law would need to be relied on - the employer's own insurance should reduce to a minimum the number of litigation cases over defects, and the second layer makes it unlikely that any of the primarily (and contractually) responsible parties will be unable to meet their liabilities through lack of funds.

How effective has the new insurance regime been? Statistics post-dating the legislation are not generally available, although the records show that before its introduction not more than 50% of those potentially liable under Art.1792 were insured, the size of insurance losses was constantly increasing by an average rate of 15% per year between 1965 and 1971, while the time taken to obtain compensation (when there was insurance) was often exceeding 8 years and could take as long as 20 years. The situation has radically improved so that times of payment have decreased considerably, and the amount of litigation overall has been reduced. Mathurin comments[13] that "after compensation the insurers try to act quickly. Damage insurers have recently concluded an agreement designed to ease the settlement between themselves of losses not exceeding 100,000 ecus." This sounds remarkably like a "knock-for-knock" system.

The impression the writer has received from contacts with those in the construction industry in France is that the system functions well, so that when claims arise they tend to be resolved between insurers without too much trouble or delay. The PUC has not however significantly reduced the total cost of insurance, for reasons no doubt connected with subrogation. Subrogation rights of insurers are similar under French law, except that they can sue in their own name (see Art.1249 et seq of the Code Civil). Allowing rights of subrogation is a weakness, because it allows a perpetuation of litigation, whereas a very bold legislature would have stopped this by abolishing subrogation. As in the UK insurance industry, this was no doubt opposed by the French insurance industry as being too expensive. On the

12 Law of 28 June 1982
13 Ibid, p246, 284

other hand, subrogation does in theory mean that those responsible for defects pay for them, either directly or in the form of increased premiums. It is an interesting thought whether Murphy is a ruling against subrogation by the "back door", given that the effective plaintiff in the case was an insurance company.

Despite this extensive legislation, the reports of the decisions of the appeal courts in France, particularly the Cour de cassation, the ultimate appeal court, contain a not insignificant number of reports of cases where the law of tort has been used to claim against a party other than the contractual party most obviously liable. This defendant is more often than not a sub-contractor, reminiscent of the English case of *Junior Books*[14]. Why should this be so, when:

(a) Art.1972 provides for strict liability on the part of a wide variety of defined "constructors" and
(b) that liability must generally be insured?

The answers are many and various. The following are some of them, but there are no doubt more:

1. As indicated above, the compulsory insurance regime for employers applies only to damage suffered falling within Art.1792 and Art.1792-2: reference in the code to Art.1792 applies only to that clause and not to Art.1792-1 et seq; in other words these subsequent clauses have an identity of their own and are not simply sub-paragraphs as in a UK statute. It is not therefore obligatory for the employer to have insurance to cover losses under Art.1792-3, the warranty of proper operation of moveable equipment, or under Art.1792- 6, the warranty given by the contractor that he will repair defects notified to him within a year from the taking over of the works. This explains how the employer can, in the circumstances of some kinds of defects, be looking to a party other than his own insurer for compensation.
2. Despite the compulsion and the penalties, not all those who should subscribe to or maintain compulsory insurance do so. It is in the nature of things that these are the parties who are going to be insolvent when claims start to arise. Indeed, the indications are that the very companies that this legislation was designed to deal with (typically small home-building companies) are the least likely to have the required insurance cover. The employer (or his insurer, who has rights of subrogation very similar to those in the UK, as described above) will in this situation have to look to other parties for compensation, and the law of tort may provide the only remedy.

14 *Junior Books Co Ltd* v. *Veitchi Co* [1983] AC 520

3. The insurance cover required to be obtained by both the employer and the contractor is only for the cost of repair of the damage to the works. It does not therefore provide cover for other losses consequential upon the damage. The injured party may therefore have to look for other avenues and other parties to recover these losses.

4. The insurance cover is only for the declared value of works. It is possible, therefore, to find oneself under-insured. Further, the insurance cover is only required for the original works; thus if repair works are carried out, there is no requirement that these works be insured.

5. French law operates a fairly rigid principle of "non cumul des actions"; in other words, where a party has a contractual relationship with another, his only remedy will be in contract and not both contract and tort as in the UK and in Germany[15]. This is what Lord Scarman advocated in *Tai Hing*[16] and seems likely to be one of the next major areas of law that the English courts will look at (one wonders whether they will take account of the debate that France has undergone on this topic). Thus if there is a contract, but contractual relief for one reason or another is not available (for limitation or other reasons), the claimant cannot turn to tort against the same party (so no *Pirelli*[17] situations can arise). This may force the claimant again to look at other parties and other remedies.

Tort

The basic elements of the law of tort in France will now be considered, before an examination of cases where tort has been applied against parties other than those liable under the decennial or biennial responsibility regime under Art.1792 et seq. The starting point is Art.1382 of the Code Civil. It reads in translation as follows:

> "Any act whatsoever by a person which causes damage to others obliges he by whose fault it is caused to make it good".

This is supplemented by Art.1383 and 1384 paragraph 1, as follows:

> "Every one is responsible for damage that he has caused not only by his act, but also by his negligence or by his imprudence".
> "One is responsible not only for damage which one causes by

---

15 See Lawson & Markesinis, *Tortious Liability for unintentional harm in the Common Law and the Civil Law* Cambridge University Press, 1982
16 *Tai Hing Cotton Mill* v. *Liu Chong Hing Bank Ltd* [1986] AC 801
17 Ibid

one's own act, but also for that caused by the act of persons for whom one is responsible, or things which one has under one's guard".

These short articles are the foundation of the law of tort in France and are obviously the subject of an enormous amount of debate, just as the law of tort in this country has been. It is beyond the scope of this paper to delve into the fascinating world of the development of the law of tort in France other than superficially and by examples from the cases on construction liability. An excellent illustration of how the courts in France (a) legislate in just the same way that they are not supposed to here, and (b) are subject to and influenced by their perception of how public opinion dictates that they should deal with a particular situation is given by Professor André Tunc in an essay entitled "It is wise not to take the Civil Codes too seriously"[18]. In it he describes how Art.1384, paragraph 1 (quoted above) came to be used as providing a remedy of strict liability that was clearly never intended by the draftsman. A statement made in the course of this raging debate demonstrates the "legislative powers" of the Cour de cassation; in the case of *Chemins de fer de l'Ouest* v. *Marcault*[19], it said:

> "The presumption of fault, established by paragraph 1 of Art.1384, on the part of the person who has under his guard the inanimate object causing the damage, can be rebutted only by the proof of a cas fortuit, a force majeure or a cause étrangère that cannot be imputed to him; it is not sufficient to prove that he did not commit any fault or that the cause of this damage has not been determined."

Prof. Tunc asks sardonically: "In which provision of the Civil Code did the Cour de cassation find this elaborated principle?"[20] He then makes the comment that forms the title of his essay. The title applies particularly in the sense that one cannot necessarily take at face value what is found in the bare wording of an article in the Code. Depending on one's viewpoint, judicial legislation is arguably even more reprehensible in a codified system than it is under common law, as in the former the court is more likely to be interfering with legislation than in the latter where the court may simply be modifying case law which was judge-made in the first place.

Another problem is that the very distilled and formal decisions given by

18 In *Essays in Memory of Professor F.H. Lawson*, ed Wallington and Merkin, Butterworths 1986
19 Referred to in Tunc's essay, ibid p74
20 Ibid, p74

the Cour de cassation often give no clear indication of any policy factors that might have influenced them; that has to be derived from "breaking the code" of the decisions, a skill acquired only after some years of reading them, and reading the influential commentaries on the decisions which are generally given by respected academics often directly involved in the case. Also helpful are the annual reports of the Cour de cassation submitted to the "Garde des Sceaux" in showing how policy factors are influencing their thinking.

It will be seen from Art.1382 that French tort law differs significantly from English law in that there is no apparent necessity for a duty of care to be established as one of the elements of a successful tort claim. Predictably this is not as simple as it might appear, as elements of establishing a 'duty situation' come into establishing whether there has been fault. French law students have had the same discussion as English ones about various knotty problems that have troubled the English as duty of care problems, but under a different heading i.e. the concept of fault. This is again (to lawyers) a fascinating topic but is beyond the scope of this paper. In summary, however, the three requirements are fault, damage and a causative link between the two; and the test of whether a tort has been committed is whether the defendant has acted as "bon père de famille", that is, how a good father would have behaved in a given situation. It is analogous to the English reasonable man test.

The main differences between liability in tort and in contract in the field of construction are summarised in the following paragraphs with examples which are taken from claims by the employer against a sub-contractor:

1. Fault is required to be proved in tort whereas it is not in contract under Art.1792. To elaborate on this, it is necessary for a claim under Art.1382 of the Civil Code that the employer proves fault on the part of the sub-contractor, tortious liability under Art.1382 being a regime of proven fault. In contrast, if the liability of the sub-contractor towards the employer was contractual, the sole fact that the obligation had not been carried out leads to a presumption, unless proved to the contrary by the defendant (the sub-contractor here), that the defendant is at fault. (see Art.1792 above.)

2. The same point, put rather differently, is that the responsibility of the main contractor under Art.1792 et seq. is that of fitness for purpose (obligation de résultat), whereas the obligation towards the employer of anyone who does not have a contract with him (so as to be liable only in tort) is to act as "bon père de famille", i.e. with reasonable care.

3. Liability under Art.1792 is, as already stated, a contractual remedy, and thus not available to an employer against a sub-contractor. Art.1792 does not apply between these two parties. Nor does it apply as between the main

contractor and the sub-contractor, and a sub-contractor is not required by the insurance law of 1978 to insure his liability to the main contractor. The apparent logic behind this is that main contractors can look after their own interests and insurance, and do not need the compulsion of law (it can of course be and often is a term of a sub-contract that the sub-contractor should insure, as the case is in the UK). Note, however, that sub-contractors do have an "obligation de résultat" vis-à-vis the main contractor, and will be liable for breach of contract under Art.1147 of the Code Civil if their work or materials do not prove fit for their purpose.

4. The limitation periods are different: ten or two years under Art.1792 et seq/Art.2270, as described above (note that the common contractual liability is 30 years - see Art. 2262 of the Code Civil), and ten years in the case of tort: see Art.2270-1 of the Code Civil.

Items 1 and 2 above have in recent years given rise to a significant amount of litigation which has in turn given rise to decisions of the Cour de cassation. For a long time the traditional doctrine followed was that since the sub-contractor is not bound by contract to the employer, the employer's only remedy against him was in tort (with all the difficulties that that involves of proving fault). Then, around 1979 there arose a great debate as to whether, in the case of a group or chain of contracts for the sale of goods, the remedy of the ultimate purchaser against a sub-vendor was in tort or in contract. Supporters of the contract theory argued that it was undesirable to have different regimes governing the responsibilities of each of the multiple parties towards the others, so that the purchaser's remedy against the sub-vendor must be in contract. The other school followed the traditional line of: no contract, no contractual remedy. The latter had in their favour Art.1165 of the Code Civil, which says that agreements have effect only between the contracting parties; they do not prejudice a third party, and they do not benefit him except in the situation foreseen in Art.1121. The latter allows in some circumstances clauses to be inserted in contracts for the benefit of others.

Unfortunately, each of these two different schools of thought was adopted by a different chamber of the Court de cassation, the first and the third. For example in 1984, the two chambers gave totally contradictory decisions in two cases on very similar facts (defective roof tiles - claim by employer against manufacturer) and on dates within less than a month of each other[21]. The first chamber took the contract route and the third the tort route. Commenting on both cases, Professor Bénabent referred to the "open

---

21 Decision of 1st Chamber on 29 May 1984 and of 3rd Chamber on 19 June 1984 in Recueil Dalloz Sirey, 1985 17e Cahier p 213

crisis", but ultimately came down in favour of the contract theory, saying that "it was justifiable to conclude that the presence of a contractual group (more so if it is a group of simultaneous or successive contracts relating to the same object) justifies unity of actions which are brought within its domain and condemns the use of an action of a delictual nature. Even between the extremes of the chain, it is therefore exclusively in the domain of contract that one assesses the elements of responsibility in the same sense".[22]

In 1986 the Cour de cassation was given an opportunity to try to resolve the conflict, by sitting as a full assembly, which it does generally to resolve conflict between two chambers and/or where an important question of principle is involved. In a decision of 7 February 1986[23] in a case which was again a sale of goods claim, but in a construction context (a product applied as insulation to pipework caused corrosion of the pipes), the court came down in favour of the contract theory, saying that the employer, as the sub-purchaser, enjoyed all the rights and actions which belonged to its author, and that there was therefore a direct contractual action against the manufacturer based on the non-conformity of the product delivered.

In a decision of 17 February 1987[24] the commercial chamber of the Cour de cassation gave judgment in a case which was not a simple chain of contracts. It concerned the partial sub- contracting of the construction of a ship and a claim arising from an undefined hidden defect. This was not a construction case strictly; but the similarity between the two types of project is clear. As the Cour de cassation (in its usual fashion) gave no indication of its reasons for holding there to be no delictual remedy, it was left to the commentator to guess that what the court had in mind was that the employer had a contractual remedy against the sub-contractor and therefore because of the non-cumulation rule it could not have a tort remedy. The guess of the commentator was that the court had in mind the previous decisions dictating that contract should apply in such situations, but had not alluded to this thought process as none of the parties had invoked the question of contractual responsibility. On this he commented that to come to this conclusion, the court needed to have fully examined the question of contractual responsibility because to fail to do so was to ignore the chance that a contract claim might be impossible (because the sub-contract was void, for example). He concluded that if the decision did not involve the recognition of a contractual remedy, it constituted a regrettable diminution in the rights

22 Ibid, p214
23 Recueil Dalloz Sirey, 1986, 24e Cahier p293
24 Recueil Dalloz Sirey, 1987, 36e Cahier p543

of the employer[25].

In a decision of 8 March 1988[26], the first chamber predictably followed the contract line in a non-construction case where the plaintiff gave some photographic slides to a company for enlargements to be made. This company passed the slides on to another company, which then lost them. The plaintiff sued the sub-contractor. As in the ship case, this was a true sub-contract for work, rather than just a chain of sales. Interestingly, it was the sub-contractor in this case that stood to benefit from the claim being held to be contractual, as it wished to benefit from an exclusion clause in the main contract. The court held that it could do so, and therefore created a new "double limit" rule, i.e that the plaintiff's rights were limited both by what was contained in the main contract and by the extent of the obligations of the "substituted defendant", that is, the sub-contractor.

Despite the guidance given to it by the full assembly in the decision of 7 February 1986, the third chamber has as recently as 22 June 1988[27] refused to follow what, by then, had become the orthodox line, in a case where plaintiff home-owners claimed against a carpenter sub-contractor (the main contractor being in liquidation) for repair of defects. The third chamber held firmly to their long-held view that such an action should be in tort (the plaintiffs were unable to succeed in tort, as they were unable to prove fault on the part of the sub-contractor: there is no explanation as to why this was not an Art.1792 insurance case.)

On the very same day the first chamber gave their decision in another sub-contract case[28] and followed the contract line. Confirming the view that this was now the orthodoxy, the commentator on both cases said that the solution of the third chamber seemed like "islands of resistance to the phenomenon of contractualisation[29].

Does this contractualisation doctrine offer any possible solutions in the UK to injured parties left without remedy by the combination of an insolvent main contractor and *Murphy/D&F Estates*[30]? Almost certainly not, because of the difficulties of privity and consideration. It is however surely not impossible that in the future a new Lord Denning might take such a route. After all, if the highest French court can so comprehensively ignore its own privity rule (Art.1165 above), why should not an English court? The open warfare between the two chambers of the Cour de cassation does no credit to that court, and makes the House of Lords, even when reversing its own

25 Ibid, commentary of Prof. Jourdain at p545
26 La Semaine Juridique, Ed.G, No.40 21070
27 La Semaine Juridique, Ed.g, No.47 21125
28 Ibid (in same report)
29 Ibid, commentary of Prof. Jourdain
30 Ibid and *D & F Estates* v. *Church Commissioners* [1988] 3 WLR 368

decision in *Anns*[31] 12 years later, look extremely stable. It must, however, be understood that the motivation behind controversial decisions of the French courts is often to put pressure on the legislature to amend the law, where the courts feel that the pace of legislative change has not been fast enough. The situation here, at least as far as the first chamber is concerned, is an example of that judicial lobbying.

Pure economic loss

Turning briefly to the subject of pure economic loss, French law does not find any particular problem here. Indeed, some of the cases discussed above would have been pure economic loss cases as now defined by the House of Lords. It will be recalled that Art.1382 says simply that:

"Any act whatsoever of a person, which causes damage to others, obliges he by whose fault it is caused to make it good."

Whether the damage is to the person of the plaintiff or his property does not in theory influence the right of recovery or the quantum. It is "in theory" because of course there are other elements in establishing liability in tort which can influence the outcome of a claim, and meet the court's perception of what is deserving and what is not. French law does not therefore have any difficulty with cases such as the cable cutting, as in *Spartan Steel*[32] (every country seems to have had a similar occurrence).

Under German law, by contrast, negligently inflicted economic loss is not, in principle, recoverable in tort, and can be compensated only in contract: see para 823 of the Buergerliches Gesetzbuch (BGB), or civil code. Interestingly, the German courts have also indulged in "contractualisation" in pure economic loss situations which have seemed to them to require a remedy which the BGB does not apparently permit. Thus, in accountant-type situations (like *Caparo*[33]), para 676 of the BGB provides that a person who gives advice or a recommendation to another is generally not bound to compensate for any damage arising from following the advice or recommendation, without prejudice to his responsibility resulting from a contract or delict. Despite this, accountants have been found liable to those whom they knew would read and rely on their reports, on the basis that good faith, and the special position which accountants occupy in society, put them under a special duty of care when making such statements. Their liability

31 Ibid, 9
32 *Spartan Steel & Alloys Ltd* v. *Martin & Co* [1973] QB 27
33 *Caparo Industries plc* v. *Dickman* [1990] 2 WLR 358

has been held to be contractual in nature. An essential requirement is that the maker of the statement should know the person who will rely on it[34]. One wonders whether an architect would be similarly liable under German law, to a person acquiring a building from the party with whom the architect is in contract, where pure economic loss results.

Despite the difficulties alluded to above, it is inevitable in English law that efforts will be made to create contracts where none was previously thought to exist. Examples of this are already evident, in cases such as *Blackpool and Fylde Aero Club* and *Williams* v. *Roffey Bros*[35].

Sub-contractors' rights

Recent cases of substantial main contractors in the UK going into liquidation leaving large unpaid debts to sub-contractors will add particular interest to the last feature of civil law to be considered in this paper. This is law no. 75-1334 of 31 December 1975 (note the decade again, the French legislature apparently feeling that the sub-contractor as well as the employer needed protecting) under which, depending on the type of contract, the sub-contractor either has a right to immediate payment direct from the employer, or a right of indemnity in the event that the main contractor does not pay. To avoid the likelihood of the employer having to pay twice, it is provided that he is obliged to pay only what he has not paid to the main contractor at the date of the sub-contractor's demand.

Furthermore, the main contractor is obliged to have each sub-contractor and his conditions of payment approved by the employer. If he does not, the main contractor cannot invoke the terms of the sub-contract against the sub-contractor. It is unlikely that legislation of this kind will ever find its way onto the UK statute books, unless imposed by the EC. But similar measures have been enacted in Spain (Art.1597 of the Civil Code) and in Belgium, where Art.1798 of the Civil Code was modified as recently as February 1990[36] to facilitate direct claims against the employer.

Conclusions

The conclusions that might be drawn from this brief overview of the law in France and other civil law jurisdictions are that:

---

34 For further detail on this, see Lawson and Markesinis, ibid, p 82
35 *Blackpool and Fylde Aero Club* v. *Blackpool District Council* [1990] 1 WLR 1195 and *Lester Williams* v. *Roffey Bros and Nicholls* (1990) CILL 552
36 See Moniteur Belge 24.3.90 p5561

(a) Much construction litigation must have been avoided by the combination of liability without fault under Art.1792 et seq and the two-tier insurance system;

(b) But Art.1792 and the insurance regime might seem excessively protective of the interests of the employer, and unrealistic in regarding him as more in need of legislative protection than other parties to the construction process;

(c) permitting subrogation claims by insurers perpetuates litigation over defects where the injured party has been compensated, but does theoretically help to ensure that losses fall where they ought to;

(d) tort litigation survives and even flourishes, seemingly against all odds: the "contractualisation" theory strikes English ears (and some French ones) as unsound, and the continuing disagreement between different chambers of the Cour de cassation is unappealing in a system where, even though there is no doctrine of precedent, it is desirable that there be some consistency emerging from the country's highest court;

(e) legislation to protect sub-contractors is likely to be attractive to their UK cousins, but unlikely to be the subject of legislation here. The interesting question is what is likely to emerge from the European Commission following the Mathurin report. This topic is dealt with in other papers in this volume.

Postscript

The debate on the relationship between an employer and sub-contractor has continued since the presentation of this paper. Theoretically, the debate was put to an end on 12 July 1991, when the full assembly of the Cour de cassation rendered a decision concluding that since agreements only have effect between the contracting parties (article 1165 of the Civil Code) "the sub-contractor has no contractual relationship with the employer".

The full assembly has therefore come back to the initial traditional doctrine which used to apply before 1979 that the liability of a contractor towards a third party is necessarily a tort liability.

This will have wider impact than just in the construction field. The difficulty remains that this decision apparently does not affect the decisions rendered in 1979 and 1986 concerning the contractual nature of the action brought by the employer against a manufacturer of materials purchased and used (by the main contractor) for the construction. In the latter case it was held that the contractual right of the employer to sue the manufacturer directly was literally transferred by the main contractor to the employer upon the transfer of property of the structure incorporating the defective materials. The test therefore is whether property in materials is transferred to the employer. As the 1991 decision concerned defective plumbing one would imagine, the transfer of materials) there seems still to be some scope for confusion.

Meanwhile, in the UK, if the proposals of the Law Commission in Consultation Paper No. 121 are adopted, the full rigours of the English doctrine of privity may be relaxed, and an employer may be able to make a claim direct against a sub-contractor of supplier.

The author gratefully acknowledges assistance received from Eric Pomonti and Robert Silvey from Baker & McKenzie Paris, Valerie de Gendre and Dr Karsten Schmidt O.B.E. from Baker & McKenzie London, Peter Bogaert from Baker & McKenzie Brussels and Alvaro Espinos from Baker & McKenzie Barcelona, and from other members of the firm's European construction practice group.

18 Economic loss under the law of tort in the U.S.

Charles Lewis

Synopsis

In this paper the author, a practising US lawyer, describes the ways in which US courts have approached the development of the law of tort where the relationship of the parties is also influenced by contracts. A process of attenuation has led to what is termed "tortification" of contract and the effective re-defining of contractual rights, a development which the author criticises. The recovery of economic loss in the context of construction is used to illustrate these principles.

Introduction

Contract and tort law have historically and theoretically served to protect and promote different individual and societal interests. Contract law has developed in the United States to recognize and enforce the efficiency of the free market, ensuring that each contracting party receives the benefit and burden of his bargain. Tort law, on the other hand, has evolved from the concept that society has the right to impose on all of its members a duty of "due care," the breach of which will entitle another to recovery, without regard to any lack of privity between the injured party and the tortfeasor. These important yet diverse interests collide when inventive litigants attempt to impose tort duties in a commercial setting.

Lawyers representing dissatisfied construction industry clients are increasingly attempting to turn every breach of contract into a tort."[1] This "tortification" of construction contract law occurs for many reasons. First, tortification seeks to substitute a better bargain for the deal originally negotiated quite simply to avoid the language of the contract. True breach of contract claims necessarily begin with the language of the contract as the basis for determining the rights and liabilities of the parties. Construction contracts often contain provisions which limit or preclude recovery, such as a "no damage for delay" clause. A contractor bringing suit against an owner in tort for delay or disruption, however, can often avoid this type of express

---

1 W. Prosser & W. Keeton, *The Law of Torts*, Section 92 at 658 (5th ed. 1984)

contractual limitation. Tortification can change the implied terms of the original deal, as well as the express terms. The longstanding rule of *Hadley v. Baxendale*[2] has limited contract recovery to the damages reasonably within the parties' contemplation at the time of contracting. Consequential damages have not been favoured. Tortification substitutes the ambiguous tort limitation of proximately caused damages, and creates the potential for punitive damages, with their *in terrorem* effect.

The second greatest reason for tortification is the desire to redefine the contract measures of performance that one party may seek to avoid. Defined expectations are the essence of a consensual bargain. Tortification often seeks to avoid reference to plans and specifications and to substitute reliance on a battle of experts over terms like due care and reasonableness. Although a contractor's work may be in conformance with the plans and specifications, a plaintiff will argue that the work was nevertheless defective in that it did not conform to "good construction practice." Consequently, a plaintiff, relying on common law negligence principles, unfettered by the punctilio of the contract, is able to redefine what others should have done on the project in the hope of maximizing his recovery.

Third, tortification makes privity a non-issue and affords a plaintiff access to an array of defendants other than the one with whom he contracted. Many consequences may result. Access may be obtained to a more solvent defendant. The total number of defendants may be increased with a resulting increase in the value of even a nuisance settlement based only on cost of defense. A party may be reached who has a liability insurance policy that responds to the negligence allegations. Or, if the tortification cannot, in a particular jurisdiction, totally override a restrictive contract clause, such as "no damages for delay," it may give the plaintiff an entirely different defendant with whom no such contract has been made.

A judicial willingness to expand traditional tort remedies in combination with increasingly frequent attempts to turn every breach of contract into a negligence claim have lead some experts to contend that contract law is dead in the United States.[3] The elimination of the privity requirement in personal injury lawsuits was both understandable and consistent with expressed public policy interests. A less compelling argument was also made for the elimination of the privity requirement in property damage cases, i e., claims for damage to property other than the property purchased from the defendant. Further judicial expansion of tort law, however, to create an

---

2 9 Exch. 341, 156 Rep. 145 (1854).
3 See, G. Gilmore, *The Death of Contract* (1974).

alternative to contract enforcement in economic loss[4] cases undermines the risk/benefit analysis that is the essence of consensual relationships. This evisceration of contract law is, in this author's opinion, detrimental to the free market policy which is the very basis of the American economic system and construction contract negotiation.

In discussing the tortification of construction contract law, I will focus on the historical antecedents, the current state of the law and offer an opinion as to what the future should bring.

Historical background

The legal principles governing the liability of architects, engineers, owners and construction contractors for damages to parties with whom they are not in privity of contract derived from the principles governing the liability of manufacturers.[5] In order to appreciate fully the present state of the law in the construction industry as it relates to tort recovery for economic loss, we should begin with a brief history of the development of products liability law from which the economic loss doctrine[6] arose.

The 1842 English common-law decision of *Winterbottom* v. *Wright*[7] provided the early precedent in the United States for the non-liability of a party not in privity of contract with the plaintiff. Lord Abinger, in holding that the breach of contract to maintain a coach gave no tort remedy to an injured passenger when the coach collapsed, emphasized that abandonment of the privity doctrine would lead to "the most absurd and dangerous consequences, to which [he could] see no limit."[8] Only those parties in contractual privity had any claim on the contract and the parties' rights were defined by the contract alone.

In attempting to follow the precedent of Winterbottom, the early American courts unfortunately began to speak in terms of an implied warranty of merchantability in personal injury or property damage lawsuits. The courts reasoned that the sale of goods was accompanied by an implied warranty of merchantability, requiring that a product be manufactured in such a manner

---

4 "Economic loss," as the term is used in this article, includes damages for inadequate value, repair, replacement costs, lost profits and the increased cost of performing or completing the work as a result of delays or disruptions. For a discussion of the term, see the Illinois case of *Moorman Mfg. Co.* v. *National Tank Co.*, 91 Ill. 2d 69, 435 N.E. 2d 443 (1982).

5 See, ALR Annotation, *Contractor - Liability to Third Person.*

6 The "economic loss doctrine", as the term is used in this article, refers to that rule of law that prohibits the recovery of economic loss in tort.

7 152 Eng. Rep. 402 (1842).

8 Id. at 405.

as to not cause personal injury or property damage from normal use.[9] The difficulty with the implied warranty approach was that this had many tort as well as contract aspects. Indeed, Dean Prosser spoke of the "peculiar and uncertain nature and character of warranty, a freak hybrid born of the illicit intercourse of tort and contract.[10]

In 1916, the landmark decision of *MacPherson* v. *Buick Motor Co.*,[11] put an end to any clear distinction between contract and tort. While courts had applied a significant exception to the general rule, providing that a third party could recover if the product was inherently or eminently dangerous, Judge Cardozo's opinion in *MacPherson* redefined the term "dangerous" to the degree that repudiation of the privity doctrine was imminent. Judge Cardozo expressed the view that a plaintiff could recover in negligence, despite the fact that he was not in privity with the defendant, if the product was "reasonably certain to place life and limb in peril when negligently made ..."[12] The effect of this holding was the virtual abandonment of the *Winterbottom* rule in those instances where an allegedly defective product caused personal injury.

By 1966, every jurisdiction in the U.S. had accepted the *MacPherson* view that one who negligently manufacturers a product was liable for any personal injuries proximately caused by the defect.[13] Furthermore, most courts began to allow tort recovery for any resulting property damage from a negligently manufactured product.[14] For this reason, many courts began to abandon the language of "implied warranty" in favour of recovery in strict tort liability.[15] The adoption of this approach was the beginning of modern-day products liability law in the United States.

After the adoption of the *MacPherson* rule for personal injuries and its extension to property damage, a debate soon began as to whether economic loss could be recovered in tort. While *MacPherson* addressed only the threat of personal injuries and property damage posed by a defective product, it was inevitable that litigants would attempt to extend the doctrine to disputes involving economic losses. In addressing whether a plaintiff who suffered only economic harm could recover in tort, a sharp division developed

---

9 See, Gilliam, Products Liability in a Nut Shell, 37 Ore. L. Rev. 119, 153-155; Prosser, *"The Assault upon the Citadel"*, 69 Yale L.J. 1099, 1126.

10 Prosser, *The Assault on the Citadel*, 69 Yale L.J. 1099, 1126 (1960).

11 217 N.Y. 382, 111 N.E. 1050 (1916).

12 MacPherson, 111 N.E. at 1053.

13 See, Restatement of Torts (Second), Section 395.

14 See, Keeton, Prosser, Keeton & Owen, *Prosser & Keeton on Torts*, (5th Edition, 1984).

15 This trend began with the California decision *Greenman* v. *Yuba Power Products, Inc.*, 59 Cal. 2d 57, 27 Cal. Reptr. 697, 377 P. 2D 897 (Cal. 1963).

among the courts.[16]

While the first court in the United States to confront this issue held that economic loss should be recoverable,[17] this decision was squarely rejected by a different jurisdiction the same year (1965).[18] In the years which followed, a majority of courts refused the recovery of economic loss in tort, adopting what became known as the economic loss doctrine.[19] Today, the overwhelming majority of courts deny recovery in negligence and strict product liability for economic losses to the buyer of a defective product.[20] While there is still some authority to the contrary,[21] many of the cases permitting liability in tort for economic losses are no longer authoritative or are subject to serious question.[22] Unfortunately, this virtual unanimity is limited to the products liability area.

The Economic Loss Doctrine in the Construction Industry

While the economic loss doctrine is now well-settled law in the area of products liability, its application to the construction industry is still the subject of considerable debate. As courts adopted the economic loss doctrine in the products liability context, the first reaction was to apply the same standard in the construction context. Application of the economic loss doctrine to the construction setting had a rather significant impact. An aggrieved plaintiff was limited to a claim for breach of contract and this claim was limited to parties in privity with the claimant. Because this rule often left aggrieved parties without any recourse, several courts began to limit the doctrine's applicability.

The context in which this deviation first occurred was the architect-contractor relationship. While contractors generally perform their work under the direction of, and in accordance with plans and specifications prepared by an architect or engineer, only the owner is in contractual privity with the architect. Nonetheless, a contractor can sustain significant economic loss due to defective plans and specifications or other actions of the

---

16 See, Schneier, "*Recovery of Economic Loss Damages in Strict Liability*", 7 Construction Litigation Reporter 702 (1986).

17 *Santor* v. *A & M Karagheusian, Inc.*, 44 NJ 53, 66-67, 207 A. 2D 305, 312-13 (1965).

18 *Seely* v. *White Motor Company*, 45 Cal. Rptr. 17, 403 P. 2d 145 (Cal. 1965).

19 See, Schneier, "*Recovery of Economic Loss Damages in Strict Liability*", 7 Construction Litigation Reporter 702 (1986).

20 See, Jones, *Product Defects causing Comercial Loss: The Ascendancy of Contract over Tort*, 44 U. Miami L.R. 731, 799-803 (1990) (citing all jurisdictions, supporting this theory).

21 Id. at 803-804 (citing all relevant cases).

22 Id at 804-805 (citing all relevant cases and statutes).

architect. As professionals, the courts imposed upon architects and engineers the independent duty to exercise that degree of care, technical skill and diligence as are ordinarily required of architects or engineers in the course of their plans, specifications and supervision during construction.[23] In the absence of this standard appearing in the contract, the court nevertheless implied its existence. As a result, various courts began to speak of an architects' negligent breach of contract in reference to their failure to use reasonable care.[24]

Accordingly, courts began to recognize a cause of action sounding in tort, for breach of this duty, thereby permitting non-privity plaintiffs to recover for economic losses.[25] Today, a majority of jurisdictions allow the recovery of foreseeable damages, including economic losses, in negligence actions against design professionals.[26] There are only a few jurisdictions which do

23 See, e.g. Surf *Realty Corporation* v. *Standing*, 195 Va. 421, 78 S.E. 2d 901 (1953); Miller v. DeWitt, 59 Ill, App. 2d 38, 208 N.E. 2d 249 (1965), affirmed in part and reversed in part, 37 Ill. 2d 273, 226 N.E. 2d 630 (1967); Architects' Handbook of Professional Practice (AIA, 1982).

24 See, Cohen and Bain, *"Negligence Claims in Construction Litigation"*, 8 The Construction Lawyer 3, 3-4 (1988).

25 Jackson, *"The Role of Contract Architectural and Engineering Malpractice"*, Insurance Counsel Journal, 517, 519 (Oct.1984).

26 See, *Mattingly* v. *Sheldon Jackson College*, 743 P. 2d 356, 360 (Alaska 1987) (judicial reluctance to allow recovery for pure economic losses [in a construction case] is discordant with contemporary tort doctrine); *Forte Bros.* v. *National Amusements Inc.*, 525 A. 2d 1301, 1303 (Rhode Island 1987) (an emerging majority of jurisdictions [which] have taken the position that a contractor can maintain a negligence action against an architect without direct privity of contract between the parties); *Magnolia Construction Co.* v. *Mississippi Gulf South Engineers, Inc.*, 518 S. 2d 1194, 1204 (Mississippi 1988) (because of the contractual obligation to the owner, the architect owes a further duty, sounding in tort, to the contractor who relies upon the design to his economic detriment) (citations omitted); *Conforti v. Eisel, Inc.* v. *The John C. Morris Associates*, 418 A. 2d 1290 (New Jersey Super 1980); *Bacco Construction Co.* v. *American Colloid Co.*, 384 N.W. 2d 427 (Mich. App. 1986); *Connelly Construction Co.* v. *Oberg/Hunt/Gillelland*, 677 P. 2d 1292 (Arizona 1984); *Gurtler, Herbert & Co. Inc.* v. *Weyland Machine Shop, Inc.*, 405 Southern 2d 660 (LA App. 1981); *Waldor Pump & Equipment Co.* v. *Orr-Schellen-Mayerson & Son Associates*, 385 N.W. 2d 375 (Minn. App. 1986); *Doran-Main, Inc.* v. *American Engineering & Testing, Inc.*, 608 Fed. Sup. 609 (D.C. ME 1985); *American Fidelity Fire Insurance Co.* v. *Pavia Birne Engineering Corp.*, 393 Southern 2d 830 (LA App. 1981); *AR Moyer, Inc.* v. *Glam*, 285 Southern 2d 397 (Florida 1973); *Edmond* v. *Pyler Building & Construction Co. Inc.*, 483 Southern 2d 681 (LA App. 1983); *E.C. Ernst, Inc.* v. *Manhattan Construction Company of Texas*, 551 F. 2d 1026 (5th Circuit 1977); *Shoffner Industries, Inc.* v. *W.B. Lloyd Construction Company* 257 Southeast 2d 50 (N.C. App. 1979); *A.E. Investment Corporation* v. *Link Buildings, Inc.*, 214 N.W. 2d 764 (Wisconsin 1974); *Mayor and City Council of City of Columbus* v. *Clark Dietz & Associates-Engineers, Inc.*, 550 F. Supp. 610 (N.D. Miss. 1982); *Berkel & Co. Contractors* v. *Providence Hospital* 454

not allow negligence actions against design professionals.[27]

With the development of tort recovery against design professionals for economic loss, courts began to explore tort recovery by subcontractors against owners. Unlike architects, however, owners are not "professionals," and therefore the exception to the economic loss doctrine applicable to architects and engineers did not easily lend itself to the owner-subcontractor relationship. Nevertheless, subcontractors in privity of contract with the general contractor began to assert tort liability directly against the owners for nonpayment, delay, and disruption.

The initial response of many U.S. courts was to deny tort recovery for economic losses in cases not involving the design professional.[28] Several

Southern 2d 496 (Pal. 1984); *Davidson & Jones* v. *County of New Hanover*, 255 Southeast 2d 580 (N.C. App. 1979); *Peter Kiewit Sons Co.* v. *Iowa Southern Utilities Co.*, 355 F. Supp. 376 (S.D. Iowa 1973); *Detweiler Bros., Inc.* v. *John Graham & Co.*, 412 F. Supp. 416 (E.D. Wash 1976); *Owen* v. *Dodd*, 431 F. Supp. 1239 (N.D. Miss. 1977); *Mikropul Corporation* v. *Desinone & Chaplin-Airtch, Inc.* 599 F. Supp. 940 (S.D. N.Y. 1984); *Peerless Ins. Co.* v. *Cerny & Associates, Inc.*, 199 F. Supp. 1951 (D. Minn. 1961); *Aetna Insurance Company* v. *Hellmuth, Obata & Kassabaum, Inc.* 392 F. 2d 472 (8th Circuit 1968); *Westerhold* v. *Carol*, 419 Southwest 2d 780 (11th Circuit 1986); *Wayne* v. *Geiger-Berger Associates*, P.C., 608 F. 2d 1148 (8th Circuit 1979); *United States Ex rel. Los Angeles Testing Laboratory* v. *Rogers & Rogers*, 161 F. Supp. 1332.

27 *2314 Lincoln Park West Condominium Association* v. *Mann, Gin, Ebel & Frazier*, 136 Ill. 2d 302, 310, 555 N.E. 2d 346 352 (Ill. 1990); *Blake Construction Company, Inc.* v. *Milton M. Alley, et al.*, 233 Va. 31, 353 S.E. 2d 724 (Va. 1987); Hercules & Company, Ltd. v. Shama Restaurant Corporation, et al. 556 A. 2d 31 (D.C. Ct. App. 1989); *Jordan* v. *Talaga*, 532 N.E. 2d 1174 (Ind. Ct. App. 1989).

28 *Employers Insurance of Warsaw* v. *Suwanee River Spa Lines, Inc.*, 866 F. 2d 752 (5th Circuit 1989) (the construction of ships, applying federal admiralty law); *Pierce Associates, Inc.* v. *Federal Insurance Co.*, 865 F. 2d 530 (3rd Circuit) (applying Delaware law); *Hercules & Company, Ltd.* v. *Shama Restaurant Corporation*, 566 A. 2d 31 (D.C. App. 1989); *Tusch Enterprises* v. *Coffin*, 113 Idaho 37, 740 P. 2d 1022 (1987); *Moorman Manufacturing Co.* v. *National Truck Co.* 91 Ill. 2d 69, 435 N.E. 2d 443 (Ill. 1982); *Sanco, Inc.* v. *Ford Motor Company*, 579 F. Supp. 893 (S.D. Ind. 1984) (applying Indiana law); *Hinz* v. *Elanco Products Co.*, U.S. Dist LEXIS 10433 (1988) (applying Kansas Law); *Bryant* v. *Murray-Jones-Murray, Inc.*, 653 F. Supp. 1015 (E.D. Mo. 1985) (applying Missouri law); *Minneapolis Society of Fine Arts* v. *Parker-Klein Associates Architects, Inc.*, 354 N.E. 2d 816 (Minn. 1984); *Local Joint Executive Board of Las Vegas* v. *Stern*, 98 Nev. 409, 651 P. 2d 637 (Nev. 1982); *Public Service Company of New Hampshire* v. *Westinghouse Electric Corporation*, 658 F. Supp. 1281 (D.C.N.H. 1988) (applying New Hampshire law); *Hammermill Paper Co.* v. *C.T. Main Construction, Inc.*, 662 F. Supp. 816 (W.D. Penn. 1987) (applying South Dakota law to a products liability case); *Arkwright-Boston Manufacturers Mutual Insurance CO.* v. *Westinghouse Electric Corp.*, 844 F. 2d 1174 (5th Cir. 1988) (applying Texas law); *Sensebrenner* v. *Rust, Orling & Neale Architects, Inc. and KDI Sylvan Pods, Inc.*, 236 Va. 419, 374 S.E. 2d 55 (Va. 1988); *Stuart* v. *Coldwell Banker Commercial Group*, 109 Wash. 2d 406, 745 P. 2d 1284 (Wash. 1987); *Basham, et al* v. *General Shale*, 377 S.E. 2d 830 (W.Va. 1989) (applying doctrine to a products liability case).

courts found the economic loss doctrine distasteful, applying instead a "reasonably foreseeable" test which essentially amounted to a complete abandonment of the doctrine.[29] Finally, those courts which were uncomfortable applying the doctrine yet felt compelled to recognize its existence permitted tort recovery for economic losses in varying circumstances.

Several jurisdictions, for example, allow recovery only when there is no privity of contract between the plaintiff and any of the defendants.[30] The rationale for this approach is that an aggrieved party should have a right of action against a tortfeasor if there is no claim in contract. If a contract exists, however, the bargained for terms will provide the means of recovery. Another court has held the contrary, finding privity must exist in order to establish a duty to use reasonable care.[31] The rationale for this approach is that without privity, no duty exists, and thus, an action cannot be maintained in negligence. The damages in such cases have been limited by the contract remedy.[32] Other courts have allowed recovery for economic losses in negligence only when there is a parallel tort, such as personal injury or property damage.[33] The justification for this approach seems to be administrative convenience.

Finally, some jurisdictions have found relationships, such as multiple prime contractors, establish a third- party beneficiary right of action in contract, limited to contractual remedies.[34] While this variation is not an

29 *J'Aire Corporation* v. *Gregory*, 86 Cal. App. 3d 499, 150 Cal. Rptr. 329 (Cal. Ct. App. 1978); *Jardel Enterprises, Inc.* v. *Triconsultants, Inc.* 770 P. 2d 1301 (Colo. Ct. App. 1989); *Cosmopolitan Homes, Inc.* v. *Weller*, 663 P. 2d 1041 (Colo. 1983); *People Express Airlines, Inc.* v. *Consolidated Rail Corporation*, 100 N.J. 246, 495 A. 2d 107 (N.J. 1985); *Morse/Diesel, Inc.* v. *Trinity Industries, Inc.*, 664 F. Supp. 91 (S.D.N.Y. 1988) (applying New York law; however, the New York Supreme Court has taken a more narrow approach, see infra.); *Oates* v. *Jaq, Inc.*, 314 N.C 276, 333 S.E. 2d 222 (N.C. 1985); *Floor Craft Floor Coverings, Inc.* v. *Parma Community General Hospital Associates, et. al.*, Ohio App. LEXIS 1007 (Ohio Ct. App. 1989).

30 *Drexel Properties,Inc.* v. *Bay Colony Club Condominium*, 406 So. 2d 515 (Fla. Ct. App. 1981); *Kennedy* v. *Columbia Lumber and Manufacturing Company*, 299 S.C. 335, 384 S.E. 2d 730 (S.C. 1989).

31 See, e.g. *State of Alaska* v. *Tyorek Timber, Inc.*, 680 P. 2d 1148 (Alaska 1984).

32 Id. at 1154.

33 See, e.g. *Strickland-Collins Construction* v. *Barnett Bank of Naples*, 545 So. 2d 476 (Fla. 1989); *Oliver B. Cannon & Sons, Inc.* v. *Dorr-Oliver, Inc.*, 336 A. 2d 211 (Del. 1975); *Seiler* v. *Levitz Furniture Company*, 367 A. 2d 999 (Del. 1976).

34 *Flintkote Company* v. *Drano Corporation*, 678 F. 2d 942 (11th Circuit 1982) (applying Georgia law); *Malta Construction Co.* v. *Henningson, Durham & Richardson, Inc.*, 694 F. Supp. 902 (N.D. Ga. 1988); *Moore Construction Co.* v. *Clarksville Dept. of Electricity*(Tenn. App. 1985), 707 S.W. 2d 1, aff'd (1986); *Visintine & Co.* v. *New York, Chicago & St. Louis R. Co.* (1959), 169 Ohio St. 505, 160 N.E. 2d 311; *J. Lewis Crum Corporation Co.* v. *Alfred Lindgren, Inc.* (1978), 564 S.W. 2d 544; *Thomas G. Snavely*

exception to the economic loss doctrine, many American courts have seized upon this alternative in order to avoid a frontal attack on the doctrine. The Restatement (Second) of Contracts expresses the view adopted by most American jurisdictions that a third party may recover if he falls into the class of intended beneficiaries.[35] For a third party to be an intended beneficiary, the parties must have expressed the intent in the contract to confer upon third party rights thereunder.[36] It has generally been held that simply bestowing a benefit of the contract on the third party was insufficient to create the status of third party beneficiary.[37] The Second Restatement of Contracts, Section 302, provides that such a third party beneficiary status exists: (1) if the beneficiary would be reasonable in relying on the contract; (2) if the performance is to run directly from the promisor to the third-party; and (3) the parties to the contract intended that the third party was to be a beneficiary.[38]

In determining whether or not a plaintiff is a third party beneficiary of a contract in the construction context, American courts looked to the following factors:

(1) the construction contracts amongst the various parties contain substantially the same language;
(2) all contracts provide that time is of the essence;
(3) all the contracts provide for prompt performance and completion;
(4) each contract recognizes the other contractor's right to performance;
(5) each contract contains a non-interference provision; and
(6) each contract obligates the contractor to pay for the damage it may cause to the work, materials, or equipment of other contractors working on the project.[39]

The foregoing contractual provisions appear frequently in multi-prime construction projects. Consequently, courts can recognize the standing of

Co. v. *Brown Construction Co.* (1968), 16 Ohio Misc. 50, 239 N.E. 2d 759; *M.T. Reed Construction Co.* v. *Virginia Metal Products Corp.* 213 F. 2d 337 (5th Circuit 1954) (applying Mississippi law); *Hanberg Corporation* v. *State Building Commission,* 390 So. 2d 277 (Miss. 1980); *Knight & Jillson Co.* v. *Castle et al,* 87 N.E. 2d 976 (Ind. 1909); *Fiat Distributors, Inc.* v. *Hidbrader,* 381 N.E. 2d 1069 (Ind. App. Ct. 1978); *Broadway Maintenance Corp.* v. *Rutgers,* 434 A. 2d 1125 (N.J. Sup. Ct. 1981); *Shea-S & M Ball* v. *Massman-Kiewit-Early,* 606 F. 2d 1245 (D.C. App. Ct. 1979).

35 Restatement (Second of Contracts, Section 301(1).
36 Restatement (Second of Contracts, Section 302(1).
37 Restatement (Second of Contracts, Section 302(1).
38 Restatement (Second of Contracts, Section 302.
39 See, e.g. *Moore Construction Company* v. *Clarksville Department of Electricity,* 707 S.W. 2d 1 (Tenn. App. 1985).

a plaintiff to sue as a third party beneficiary without directly undermining the economic loss doctrine.

The diverse positions taken by American courts naturally create uncertainty and confusion as to what legal standard will be applied in a construction contract dispute. This problem is exacerbated when a large contractor or subcontractor performs work in numerous jurisdictions. It is virtually impossible for such a national contractor to research thoroughly the law of every jurisdiction before entering into a construction contract. The need for consistency is manifest.

The Case against the Economic Loss doctrine.

As previously noted, the extension of negligence principles to the construction context began in connection with the actions against design professionals. As the courts began to reject the economic loss doctrine as a defence asserted by architects, the courts reasoned that the next logical step was to eliminate this defence in other third-party actions. Even where the economic loss doctrine was followed, various exceptions to the rule of non-recovery existed. The critics argue that these exceptions expose the hopeless artificiality of the doctrine.

The most common argument for eliminating the economic loss doctrine is the seemingly arbitrary distinction between economic loss and loss from personal injury or property damage. As the Supreme Court of one state noted:

> "The contention that a distinction should be drawn between mere economic loss and personal injury is without merit. Why there should be a difference between an economic loss resulting from [defects] in property and an economic loss resulting from personal injury has not been revealed to us. When one is personally injured from a defect, he recovers mainly for his economic loss. Similarly, if a wife loses a husband because of injury resulting from a defect in construction, the measure of damages is totally economic loss. We fail to see any rational reason for such a distinction.[40]"

The difficulty with the case against the economic loss doctrine is that it fails to recognize that tort and contract law are intended to protect different interests.

---

40 *Barnes* v. *Mac Brown & Company,* 264 Ind. 227, 342 N.E. 2d 619, 621 (Ind. 1976).

The Case for the Economic Loss doctrine

Despite the emerging trend which allows negligence claims for economic losses in the construction context, the majority of courts still follow the economic loss doctrine in construction cases. While this trend of extending modern negligence theories to contractual relationships has a certain superficial appeal, the theoretical justifications for the economic loss doctrine remain persuasive.

In *East River Steamship Corp.* v. *Transamerica Delaval. Inc.*[41], the United States Supreme Court articulated those considerations which attend a determination of whether a cause of action in tort is stated when a defective product purchased in a commercial transaction malfunctioned, injuring only the product itself and causing purely economic loss. The plaintiffs in East River alleged that defendants were negligent in the design, manufacture and supervision of the installation of turbines on certain steamship tankers. Transamerica Delaval designed, manufactured and supervised the installation of the turbine and turbine valves under contract with the ship builder, who in turn had a contract with the ship owner. Plaintiffs, East River Steamship Corporation, chartered the ships from a trustee of the owner. The plaintiff apparently could not recover from the owners on their contract because each charter assumed responsibility for the cost of any repairs to the ships. Consequently, the charters sued the designer and manufacturer in tort. In holding that the plaintiffs' claim was one for breach of contract, not negligence, the United States Supreme Court stated:

> Contract law, and the law of warranty in particular, is well suited to commercial controversies of the sort involved in this case because the parties may set the terms of their own agreements. The manufacturer can restrict its liability, within limits, by disclaiming warranties or limiting remedies. See UCC 2-316, 2-19. In exchange, the purchaser pays less for the product.
> A warranty action also has a built-in limitation on liability, whereas a tort action could subject the manufacturer to damages of an indefinite amount. The limitation in a contract action comes from the agreement of the parties and the requirement that consequential damages, such as lost profits, be a foreseeable result of the breach. See *Hadley* v. *Baxendale*, 9 Ex. 341, 156 Eng. Rep. 145 (1854). In a warranty action where the loss is purely economic, the limitation derives from the requirements of foreseeability and of privity, which is still generally enforced for such claims in a commercial setting. See UCC 2-715; White &

41 476 U.S. 857 (1985) (applying admiralty law).

Summers, supra, at 389, 396, 406-410.

In products liability law, where there is a duty to the public generally, foreseeability is an inadequate brake. Permitting recovery for all foreseeable claims for purely economic loss could make a manufacturer liable for vast sums. It would be difficult for a manufacturer to take into account the expectations of persons downstream who may encounter its products. In this case, for example, if the charterers - already one step removed from the transaction - were permitted to recover their economic losses, then the companies that subchartered the ships might claim their economic losses from their economic losses, and so on. "The law does not spread its protection so far." *Robins Dry Dock & Repair Co.* v. *Flint*, 275 U.S. 303, 309 (1927).[42]

While it can be argued that the United States Supreme Court was simply recognizing on a federal level what the state courts had previously recognized with respect to recovery of economic losses in the product liability context, the ratiocination of America's highest court is cogent argument for the broader implementation of the economic loss doctrine. The conceptual and practical differences between tort and contract were underscored:

> The distinction that the law has drawn between tort recovery for physical injuries and warranty for recovery for the economic loss is not arbitrary and does not rest on the 'luck' of one plaintiff having an accident causing injury. The distinction rests, rather, on the nature of the responsibility a manufacturer must undertake in distributing his products. When a product injures only itself the reasons for imposing a tort duty are weak and those for leaving the party to its contractual remedies are strong.[43]

Finally, the court's statement that "[s]ociety need not presume that a customer needs special protection"[44] is the clarion call for freedom of contract.

Conclusion

From a philosophical viewpoint, the tortification of construction contract law is troubling for a number of reasons. The willingness of courts to

42 Id. at 871-873.
43 Id. at 872.
44 Id. at 872.

substitute their own sense of public policy for voluntary contractual arrangements strikes at the heart of the American free enterprise system. It is also symptomatic of a more insidious disease - the belief that the judicial system is better equipped to define the rights and liabilities of the parties to a commercial transaction than the parties themselves. The recent tendency of judges to transform contract claims into torts is yet another example of governmental meddling, which is not any less suspect because the governmental officials happen to wear robes.

From a practical viewpoint, the tendency of contract disputes to metamorphosize into tort claims deprives the individual of the right to rely on his or her assessment of the benefits and burdens of a contract. Bargained for clauses in the contract are judicially disregarded, not because the clauses are unconscionable, but simply because the contract no longer is the basis of liability. This author respectfully suggests that it is time to reaffirm that there is indeed a principled distinction between a tort and a breach of contract. It is this author's hope and belief that the courts will indeed recognize this distinction and apply it consistently in the future.

Jeremy Winter

Synopsis

This paper reviews the authorities under English law relating to the existence and nature of a duty on a contractor to warn of defects in the design furnished to him. The paper considers liability in contracts and in tort. The position in other European countries and in USA is reviewed and it is concluded that there is general recognition that such a duty must exist.

Introduction

It might be thought that the existence of a contractor's "duty to warn" disappeared with the demise of pure economic loss in tort. That this is not so is confirmed in the new edition of *Keating on Building Contracts*[1] which states that "...contractors generally have an obligation to warn of defects in design which they believe exist." The issue with which this paper is concerned is whether or not a building or engineering contractor owes to his employer a duty, either by way of implied contract term or in tort, to warn the employer of defects in the design (prepared by others) which the contractor is to erect. There are variations on this theme; for example, whether the contractor owes a duty to the architect and whether a subcontractor might owe the same duty to the employer. The paper will then consider how this same issue has been approached in other countries.

Background History

Apart from a fleeting reference in 1820, the idea of a duty to warn had apparently not been successfully argued in England before the case of *Equitable Debenture Assets Corporation Ltd* v. *William Moss and Others*[2] in 1984. In that case EDAC engaged Morgan as architect and Moss as contractor in the construction of a new office block in Ashford, Kent. A subcontractor designed, supplied and fixed curtain walling to the building,

1   5th Edition, 1991, p.56
2   (1984) 2 Con LR 1

which it transpired was defective. The contract was the JCT Standard Form of Contract 1963 edition. The design by the subcontractor must have been part of the contract drawings, to which Moss had to complete the works to comply with clause 1(1) of the contract, which read as follows:

> "The contractor shall upon and subject to these conditions carry out and complete the works shown upon the Contract Drawings and described by or referred to in the Contract Bills and in the Articles of Agreement and these Conditions (which Drawings, Bills, Articles of Agreement and Conditions are hereinafter called "the Contract Documents") in compliance therewith..."

The contract did not contain an express condition requiring the contractor to warn either the architect or the employer of defects in the drawings. But the contract also made no attempt to exclude implied terms eg, by stating that this was the entire agreement.

The only English authority cited by counsel for the employer was the 1820 decision of *Duncan* v. *Blundell*[3]. He also relied on a decision of the Canadian Supreme Court in *Brunswick Construction Ltd* v. *Nowlan*[4]. In the latter case, an owner employed an experienced contractor to erect a house for him in accordance with plans prepared by an engineer, but without supervision. The plans turned out to be defective. Ritchie J on behalf of the Supreme Court said:

> "In my opinion a contractor of this experience should recognise the defects in the plans, which were so obvious to the architect subsequently employed by the [owner] and knowing the reliance which was being placed upon it, I think the [contractor] was under a duty to warn the [owner] of the danger inherent in executing the plans."

Judge Newey in *EDAC* v. *Moss* considered that both *Duncan* v. *Blundell* and *Brunswick Construction Ltd* v. *Nowlan* were based on implied contractual terms. Relying on the normal *Moorcock*[5] principles that for a term to be implied into a contract it must be necessary to give the contract business efficacy and/or to make it work, the judge concluded as follows:

> "I think that if on examining the drawings or as a result of

3   (1820) 3 Stark. 6
4   (1974) 21 BLR 27
5   (1889) 14 PD 64

experience on site, Moss formed the opinion that in some respect the design would not work, or would not work satisfactorily, it would have been absurd for them to have carried on implementing it just the same. In my view, if the directors of EDAC and of Moss had been asked at the time when the contract was made what Moss should do in those circumstances, they would have agreed at once that Moss should communicate their opinion to Morgan. I think therefore, that in order to give efficacy to the contract, the term requiring Moss to warn of design defects as soon as they came to believe that they existed was to be implied in the contract."

The Judge concluded that there was an implied contractual duty to warn. Without further analysis, he went on to conclude that Moss also owed EDAC and Morgan a duty of care in negligence to inform the architect of design defects known to them.

Later that year, Judge Newey gave judgment in the case of *Victoria University of Manchester* v. *Hugh Wilson & Lewis Womersley*[6]. In that case, there were defects in the design of tiled cladding to buildings. The contractor was again employed on the JCT Standard Form of Contract (1963 edition), and again the employer employed an architect. The judge simply followed his decision in *EDAC* v. *Moss* and concluded that:

"In this case, I think that a term was to be implied in each contract requiring the contractors to warn the architects as the university's agents of defects in design, which they believed to exist. Belief that there were defects required more than mere doubt as to the correctness of the design, but less than actual knowledge of errors."

EDAC v. *Moss* and *Victoria University of Manchester* v. *Wilson* both predated the radical changes in the law of tort culminating in the decision in *Murphy* v. *Brentwood District Council*[7]. The next time the duty to warn came to be considered was in 1988, when these developments had begun (the decision postdates *Muirhead* v. *Industrial Tank Specialities*[8] and *Simaan General Contracting Company* v. *Pilkington Glass Ltd*[9]), but not yet concluded (the decision predates *D&F Estates* v. *Church Commission-*

---

6 (1984) 2 Con LR 43
7 [1990] 3 WLR 414
8 [1986] QB 507
9 [1987] 1 WLR 516

ers[10]). The decision is *The University Court of the University of Glasgow v. William Whitfield & John Laing (Construction) Ltd (Third Party)*[11]. The University employed Whitfield as architect and John Laing as contractor, again on the JCT 1963 Standard Form. The design defect in this case led to leaks of water and condensation. The contractor, John Laing, was only a third party and not a defendant. Thus the University did not itself make any claim against the contractor for breach of a contractual or tortious duty to warn of defects in the design. Such a claim was, however, made by the architect in third party proceedings, claiming contribution based on the Civil Liability (Contribution) Act 1978. Section 1(l) of this Act provides:

> "Subject to the following provisions of this section, any person liable in respect of any damage suffered by another person may recover contribution from any other person liable in respect of the same damage (whether jointly with him or otherwise)."

The difficulty faced by the architect under the 1978 Act was that under the transitional provisions in the Act, no person was entitled to recover contribution by reference to any liability based on breach of an obligation assumed by him before the date on which the Act came into force. The contractor's obligations were assumed well before 1 January 1979, when the Act came into force, and therefore the architect was unable to claim any contribution from the contractor based on any alleged breach of contract between the contractor and the employer.

Based on decisions in *Tai Hing Cotton Mill* v. *Liu Chong Hing Bank*[12] and *Lynch* v. *Thorne*[13], Judge Bowsher concluded that:

> "...there was no room for the implication in the contract of an implied duty to warn the building owner of defects in the architect's design..."

The judge relied on the following passage in *Lynch* v. *Thorne*:

> "...where there is a written contract expressly setting forth the bargain between the parties, it is, as a general rule, also well established that you only imply terms under the necessity of some compulsion."[14]

---

10 [1989] AC 177
11 (1988) 42 BLR 66
12 (1986) AC 80
13 [1956] 1 WLR 303
14 Page 306

The finding on contractual liability was crucial, because of the judge's subsequent conclusion that there should be no wider duty in tort than there was in contract. The authority was the well-known dictum of Lord Scarman in *Tai Hing*, in which he says:

> "Their lordships do not, however, accept that the parties' mutual obligations in tort can be any greater than those to be found expressly or by necessary implication in their contract."[15]

Judge Bowsher distinguished this case from *EDAC* v. *Moss* and *Victoria University of Manchester* v. *Wilson* by suggesting that the judge in those cases had in mind the situation where the contractor knew that the owner placed reliance on him in the matter of design. He went on to say:

> "It seems to me that the decisions in *EDAC* v. *Moss and Victoria University of Manchester* can stand with more recent decisions if they are read as cases where there was a special relationship between the parties, but not otherwise..."

Analysis of Contract Position

As already stated, the editor of *Keating on Building Contracts* seems to consider the earlier decisions on duty to warn correct. The basis for distinguishing the University of Glasgow case from the earlier two seems doubtful as, although in the Canadian case relied on by Judge Newey there may have been a high degree of reliance by the owner on the contractor in relation to design, in each of *EDAC*, *Victoria University* and *University of Glasgow* there was a JCT 1963 Standard Form Contract, design responsibility on the part of the architect, and the normal supervision/inspection carried out by the architect. While in the *University of Glasgow* decision, the judge sets out the legal principles as to implied terms, he does not explain why it would not have been just as absurd for Laing to have carried on implementing a defective design, once they became aware of this, as it was for Moss to do so in the *EDAC* case.

A number of other terms are generally implied into any building or engineering contract. Subject to express terms to the contrary such terms may be implied regardless of the length and detail of the contract. Examples of these are:

---

15 Page 107

On the Part of the Employer:
- to do all that is necessary on his part to bring about completion of the contract;
- particularly, to give possession of the site within a reasonable time;
- not to interfere with the proper performance by the certifier (architect or engineer) of the duties imposed by the contract;
- not to prevent the contractor from performing his obligations.

On the Part of the Contractor:
- to do the work with all proper skill and care
- to warrant[16] that materials supplied are:
  - reasonably fit for the purpose for which they are intended; and
  - of good quality.

In all of these cases, the *Moorcock* test must be satisfied, such that if the absence of these clauses had been pointed out at the time of entering into the contract, both parties would have agreed that they would apply. Stated in the way expressed in *EDAC* v. *Moss*, it is hard to disagree with Judge Newey's view that in order to give efficacy to the contract, a term requiring the contractor to warn of design defects as soon as they become apparent would generally be implied into a contract.

On the other hand, if so obvious, why is it that the Standard Forms (where there is commonly a division of responsibility between design and construction) do not incorporate such a term? There is no such term in the JCT Standard Form of Building Contract 1980 edition, nor is there in the ICE Conditions, 5th or 6th Edition, nor the FIDIC Contract Conditions. On the contrary, the ICE based forms all contain an express provision which might be thought likely to override the implication of a duty to warn. For example, the ICE 5th edition states in clause 8(2) as follows:

> "The Contractor shall take full responsibility for the adequacy, stability and safety of all site operations and methods of construction, provided that the Contractor shall not be responsible for the design or specification of the Permanent Works (except as may be expressly provided in the Contract) or of any Temporary Works designed by the Engineer."

Does this mean that if, for example, the contractor sees that the Engineer's design of a temporary cofferdam is bound to fail, he is obliged to go

---

16 These warranties are very much the same as but exist independently of, the warranties under the Sale of Goods Act 1979 and the Supply of Goods and Services Act 1982: See *Keating on Building Contracts*, page 48 and onwards

ahead with the work, and has no contractual obligation to warn the client, or the Engineer as his agent, of the danger? Again, put this way the proposition is absurd. There must remain considerable scope for argument that there is an implied contractual duty on the contractor to warn the employer, or the architect/engineer as his agent, of defects in the design, even where there is wording similar to that in the ICE forms placing responsibility for design on others. The primary responsibility remains where the contract places it, but an underlying duty to warn may remain.

What would be the wording of an appropriate implied term were the parties notionally to consider the question of a duty to warn? There are many different options, but an analysis of the following alternatives will indicate that this is not quite as straightforward as it might seem:

(a)   The contractor shall warn the employer of defects in design which he believes to exist.

(b)   If the contractor fails to notify the employer of defects of which he ought reasonably to have become aware, he shall be liable to the employer for the additional loss and expense suffered by the employers as a result of the failure to warn.

This wording could be improved upon (as it is in the Dutch clause referred to below), but it will serve to illustrate the point. The first version is entirely subjective, whereas the second is objective in terms of when the contractor ought to have become aware of the defect. The parties would no doubt be more likely to pick the first version as being far simpler (it reflects the wording of the decisions in *EDAC* v. *Moss* and *Victoria University of Manchester* v. *Wilson*). The problem with that version is this: if the contractor is so incompetent that he fails to notice that the design is defective until after the building has been completed, he will never be in breach of his duty to warn, because he never acquires the knowledge necessary to give the warning. In this way a more competent contractor is treated less favourably than a less competent one.

The second version attempts to deal with that apparent unfairness, but adds a degree of complexity which would be unlikely to pass the Moorcock test. Therefore, despite its problems, the implied term would probably be that in (a) rather than that in (b). That conclusion is strengthened when one appreciates that the obvious fault that the term is seeking to legislate against is the failure to do anything once the design defect is noticed, rather than a failure to notice it in the first place.

In the light of the above, it is instructive to consider when, in the cases cited, the duty to warn was said to arise. The *EDAC* v. *Moss* and *Victoria University* cases are not reported in full in the Construction Law Journal and little is revealed on this point from the abbreviated reports. The full decisions are however available on Lexis and the picture becomes clearer from these. In *EDAC* v. *Moss* that the judge concluded that:

> "Moss's staff must have become aware of the difficulty of applying sealants in accordance with Alpine [the subcontractor]'s drawings; in other words they must have come to know of the lack of buildability in the design.[17]"

In other words, the contractor was deemed to have actual knowledge of the defect, and they failed to do anything about it. The issue of when the duty to warn arose is dealt with more briefly in the *Victoria University* case. The judge said this:

> "I think that the contractor's obligation to warn arose when, in the light of their general knowledge and practical experience, they came to believe that an aspect of the design was wrong. As they had no previous experience of external tiling, it is not surprising that they did not discover defects in the tiling design.[18]"

In other words, although the judge found that the contract contained the implied term, he found that the contractor was not in breach. In the *University of Glasgow* case (where there is a full judgment in the Building Law Reports) there is no indication that the question whether and if so when the contractor became aware of the defect was considered.

An issue not considered in any of the cases is that of timing. If the contractor notices a defect (but does not warn of it) at a time when the construction is already so far advanced that it will have to be totally re-done to remove the defect, will he be liable? I suggest not, because the employer in this case will suffer no further loss as a result of the failure to warn. The employer's loss will still be recoverable from the designer.

In dealing with the contract position I have not dealt with the situations where the contractor has a primary responsibility to ensure that the works are fit for their purpose. As is stated in Keating[19]:

> "Where the employer makes known to the contractor the particular purpose for which the work is to be done and the work is of a kind which the contractor holds himself out as performing, and

17 LEXIS transcript, page 28
18 LEXIS transcript, page 34
19 at Page 55

the circumstances show that the employer relied on the contractor's skill and judgment in the matter, there is an implied warranty that the work as completed will be reasonably fit for the particular purpose ... Where a contractor had expressly warranted the fitness of the works, it was held that such warranty overrode the duty to comply with the detailed specification..."

In that situation, there would be no need to rely on a duty to warn of defects in the design. The transcripts of the decisions in *EDAC* v. *Moss* and *Victoria University* reveal that the contractor in each case was found liable to the owner on other grounds, essentially responsibility for the work of his sub-contractor.

Since this paper was presented, His Honour Judge Newey has held there to be a duty to warn in a further decision, *Lindenberg* v. *Canning* (unreported 6 January 1992). In that case the defendant builder removed walls from a basement in accordance with instructions on a plan provided to him by the employer's building surveyor (Mr. Carlish). It turned out that these walls were load-bearing, and Acro props had to be installed very quickly, but some damage was caused. The Judge held that:

"Mr. Canning should I think have proceeded with the very greatest caution. At the very least he should have raised with Mr. Carlish doubts as to his plan and asked whether Mr. Carlish was sure that the 9" walls were not load bearing. Even if Mr. Carlish had given assurances Mr. Canning would I think have been prudent to have put up temporary propping, but in the absence of such assurance he should undoubtedly have done so. Instead, without taking any precautions whatsoever Mr. Canning proceeded to demolish the walls. I think that he behaved with much less care than was to be expected of the ordinary competent builder and that he therefore acted in breach of contract."

There was no formal building contract, so to that extent the case was analogous to *Brunswick Construction* v. *Nolan*. Because the builder had no actual knowledge of the problem, this case supports the proposition that the implied duty to warn is an objective one, not dependent on actual knowledge. There was however little or no analysis of this issue in the judgement.

Analysis of Tort Position

The law currently appears still to recognise concurrent liability in contract and in tort: see Batty v. *Metropolitan Property*[20] and *Midland Bank* v. *Hett Stubbs & Kemp*[21]. As stated above, *Tai Hing* suggests that obligations in tort cannot be any greater than those to be found expressly or by necessary implication in the contract. The case of *William Hill Organisation Limited* v. *Bernard Sunley Limited*[22] demonstrates that a claim in tort cannot be used to get round the effect of contract provisions: the plaintiff was prevented from relying on a tort argument in order to escape the effect of a final certificate under JCT 1963. However, there are limits to the principle: the fact that a contract claim will be time barred does not bar a similar action in tort during the potentially longer limitation period: see *Pirelli* v. *Oscar Faber*[23]. Indeed, the purpose of many tort claims is to avoid limitation problems.

In the traditional form of contract where the architect designs and the contractor constructs, it will be rare for there to be the necessary degree of reliance by the employer for liability in tort to arise in relation to matters of design. As stated above, this was the way in which Judge Bowsher distinguished his *University of Glasgow* case from its predecessors.

Pure Economic Loss

Assuming that there is sufficient reliance, what is the contractor's position? I deal first with pure economic loss. The decision in *Murphy* v. *Brentwood District Council*[24] has severely restricted the recoverability in tort of such loss. The decision, however, affirmed the recoverability of pure economic loss where there is a sufficient relationship of proximity to bring into play the *Hedley Byrne*[25] principle of recoverability for negligent misstatement. In *Murphy* it was said that the relationship between a sub-contractor and his employer could still give rise to a *Hedley Byrne* liability. Lord Keith said (admittedly *obiter*):

> "It would seem that in a case such as Pirelli, where the tortious liability arose out of a contractual relationship with professional people, the duty extended to take reasonable care not to cause economic loss to the client by the advice given ...I regard *Junior Books* ... as being an application of that principle."

20 [1978] QB 554
21 [1978] 3 WLR 167; and see also paper 7
22 [1983] 22 BLR 1
23 [1983] 2 AC 1
24 [1990] 3 WLR 414
25 [1964] AC 465

If *Hedley Byrne* can apply as between sub-contractor and employer, then a fortiori it can apply as between main contractor and employer. It appeared at one stage that *Hedley Byrne* liability was restricted to "professionals", and would therefore exclude contractors. It is now clear that the liability is not so restricted: see above and *Morgan Crucible Co* v. *Hill Samuel Bank*[26]. The only requirement is that the person making the representation professes some special knowledge or expertise.

On the basis that the contractor's liability to the employer in tort for pure economic loss is limited to liability under the *Hedley Byrne* principle, there will be problems in finding a duty to warn. This is because *Hedley Byrne* cases have generally required a positive act in the nature of providing advice, a failure to perform an act which ought to have been carried out not being sufficient. Paper 7 of this volume makes the following comment in relation to this issue:

> "Professional advice may be too narrow a definition in this context. Negligent professional acts or omissions, if advisory in nature, may be regarded as breaches of duty leading to recoverable pure economic loss: *Ross* v. *Caunters*[27]. This could always prove a Trojan Horse for duties to warn and other generic liabilities...."

It is to be doubted that the Trojan Horse principle would extend to holding a contractor in breach of duty in tort for simple failure to warn of a defect in design. It is therefore doubted that a contractor has any liability in tort for pure economic loss if he fails to give such a warning.

Physical Loss

What is the position if physical loss (that is, physical damage to person or property other than the works themselves) results from a defect in design which the contractor has failed to warn of? In the few cases where there is reliance, as noted above, the contractor will be liable in tort to the employer, not under *Hedley Byrne*, but under the general *Donoghue* v. *Stephenson*[28] duty, which includes a duty to take reasonable care to avoid omissions (as well as acts) which can reasonably be foreseen as likely to injure. The contractor will also be liable in tort, on the same basis, to others suffering physical loss or injury[29].

26 [1991] 1 All ER 148
27 [1980] 1 Ch 297
28 [1932] AC 562
29 see inter alia *Clay* v. *Crump* [1964] 1 QB 533

Sub-Species of duty to warn:

(1)   Contractor's duty to warn the architect in his own capacity not as an agent of the employer

This contention was correctly rejected in *University of Glasgow* v. *Whitfield and Laing*, where Judge Bowsher refused to find that Laing was responsible to the architect, Whitfield, and stated :

> "The damage which the defendant [Whitfield] alleges the third party [Laing] should have guarded him against was the defendant being found liable to pay damages to the plaintiffs [the University] as a result of the defendant's defective design. That is pure economic loss and is irrecoverable, because no duty is owed to the plaintiff in respect of it."

(2)   Subcontractor's duty to warn the Architect or the Employer

A number of the judgments in *Murphy* v. *Brentwood* interpreted *Junior Books Limited* v. *Veitchi Co Limited*[30] as a *Hedley Byrne* case. The effect of this is open to considerable debate. It will be rare, however, that a sufficient degree of proximity exists for a duty to arise. The same problem will exist as with the contractor's duty to warn, ie, that *Hedley Byrne* does not generally extend to omissions, but is limited to advice or representations given.

(3)   Engineer's or Architect's Duty to the Contractor

This question is dealt with in the following statement in Professor Abrahamson's Engineering Law and the ICE Contracts[31] which has been validated by the decision in *Pacific Associates* v. *Baxter*[32].

> "It is worth emphasising that the engineer has no duty to the contractor as such to detect or prevent faults in temporary works (or the permanent works). The engineer is appointed to protect the employer, not the contractor. The argument often put forward in practice that it is somehow an excuse for faults in workmanship or materials that they were not objected to by the engineer or resident, is to imply that the employer is in a worse position if he engages engineers to supervise the contractor than if he does not."

30 [1983] AC 520
31 4th Edition, at page 53
32 [1990]QB 1993

(4) The Designer's duty after the completion of the works

In the first instance decision in the *Abbeystead* case[33] the judge dealt with the consulting engineers, who were responsible for the design of the pumping system which exploded as a result of the ignition of the methane present in the system. He said that

> "they were to some degree negligent in not keeping abreast with, passing on to the Third Defendants [North West Water, who owned the plant] and considering, in relation to design, developing knowledge about methane between handover and 1984".

In the Court of Appeal decision on this case[34] Bingham LJ at the end of a very long judgement dealt in passing (and obiter) with this statement. I quote in full what he said on this issue:

> "We were told that this finding had caused some concern among professional indemnity underwriters. I am not surprised. It has never to my knowledge been held that a professional man who advising on a tax scheme or on draft trading conditions, is thereafter bound to advise his client if within a period of years the statutory provisions or the relevant authorities change. Nor has it ever to my knowledge been suggested that a retired practitioner is bound during his retirement to keep in touch with developments in his profession in this way. These would be novel and burdensome obligations. On the other hand, counsel for the Plaintiffs was able to advance persuasive examples, involving dangers to life and health, where some responses by a professional might well be called for.
>
> What is plain is that if any such duty at all is to be imposed, the nature, scope and limits of such a duty require to be very carefully and cautiously defined. The developments of the law on this point, if it ever occurs, will be gradual and analogical. But this is not a suitable case in which to launch or embark on the process of development because no facts have been found to support a conclusion that ordinarily competent engineers in the position of the First Defendants would by May 1984 have been alerted to any risk of which they were reasonably unaware at the time of handover. There was in my view no evidence to support such a conclusion. That being so, I prefer to express no opinion on this

33 (1988) 18 Con Law Rep p. 3-44
34 (1988) 18 Con Law Rep p. 44-151

potentially important legal question".

This summary raises as many questions as it answers. Since the decision there has not been (to my knowledge) a case in which there has been any of the gradual and analogical development referred to, and it will be very interesting to see whether there will be any such development in the future. On the one hand, to hold that the continuing duty exists would represent an increase in the scope of the duty of care and change significantly the concept of foreseeability. On the other hand, one can imagine situations where a court might find that there was a continuing duty: for example, if a new construction material was later found to be carcinogenic, would the designer not have a duty to warn the owner or occupier of any building in which the material was used? Similar questions arise to those discussed above as to whether actual knowledge is required, or whether it is sufficient that a reasonable designer would have learned about this problem.

If there was such a duty, how does it square with the "state of the art" or "development risks" defence to the otherwise strict liability for damaging products under the Consumer Protection Act 1987[35]. There seems to be no reason why a consulting engineer or architect should be in a worse position than, say, a pharmaceutical company. If there is a continuing duty, is this likely to be an implied term of the contract, rather than arising from the law or tort? Answers to some of these questions will no doubt be provided when a case on the point arises[36].

(5)   The Contractor's duty to warn under the Defective Premises Act

Section 1 (2) of the Defective Premises Act 1972 states that a person who takes on work for another on terms that he is to do it in accordance with instructions given by that other shall, to the extent to which he does it in accordance with those instructions, be treated as having discharged the duty imposed on him by Section 1 (1) except where he owes a duty to that other to warn him of any defects in the instructions and fails to discharge that duty. The statute does not state when such a duty arises and there seems to be no case on the point. The duty is said to be in addition to any duties owed apart from those owed under Section I of the Act.

Duty to warn under Foreign Law

The paper now turns to consider how some other countries approach these

---

35 see Section 4(1)(d) of the Act
36 *E. Hobbs (Farms) Ltd.* v. *The Baxenden Chemical Co. Ltd.* [1992] 1 Lloyd's Rep.54

problems.

The Netherlands

The Dutch Civil Code has only a limited number of provisions relating to the contracting of work. It does not of itself impose upon the contractor any duty to warn of defects in the architect's design. However, the basic rule of the law of obligations is that contracts must be performed in good faith. For a contract for the performance of works of any size at all, the parties will nearly always stipulate that the 1989 Uniform Administrative Conditions (the "UAV") are to apply to the contract. The UAV conditions are often mandatory for building projects subsidised by the government. They are a comprehensive set of rules for the construction process, dealing with aspects such as:

- representation of the parties;
- general obligations of the employer and contractor;
- completion;
- termination in an unfinished state;
- suspension;
- the site, materials, execution of the work, etc.

The UAV Conditions thus constitute a complete code of the kind that we are familiar with from standard forms in the UK. The underlying presumption of the UAV conditions is that, as between the employer and the contractor, the employer is responsible for the design which is carried out by the architect or, for example, by special technical advisers in the case of any special structures or technical installations. The contractor is responsible for correct and proper performance of the building work. However, without prejudice to the architect's liability for his design, the UAV conditions impose upon the contractor a duty to warn of any defects in the design. Section 6.14 of the UAV conditions reads:

"If the construction, construction methods, instructions and directions referred to in Clause 5, Paragraph 2, or the materials or ancillary plant and equipment as referred to in Clause 5, Paragraph 3, evidently contain or show such faults or defects that the contractor would be in breach of good faith if he were to proceed to execute the part of the works concerned without notifying the Employer's Agents of such faults or defects, he shall be liable for any prejudicial consequences caused by his failure to so notify the Employer's Agent. The provisions of this

> paragraph shall apply mutatis mutandis to the cases referred to
> in Clause 5, Paragraphs 4 and 5."

This duty to warn does not imply that the contractor should carry out an in-depth investigation into the design or re-do it. However, as an expert and because of his position, a responsible and conscientious contractor may be expected to point out any defects in the design when performing the work and report them to the employer (or the architect). The more expert advice that the employer gets from elsewhere, the more restricted will be the contractor's responsibility. Also relevant is the size, expertise and specialisation of the contractor's business. Where a large company is involved with a very expert technical staff, it will more readily be assumed that they have failed to comply with the duty to warn, than in the case of a small and non-specialised contractor.

The question has arisen how to divide the responsibility for defects in design as between the architect and the contractor. There is an argument that where both the architect and the contractor are at fault, their respective liability should be assessed in proportion to the extent that each of them is in default. However, decisions by the Court of Arbitration for the Construction Industry in the Netherlands point in a different direction. It has been held[37] that where the contractor has failed to warn, he is responsible for the entire damage because it is his failure that has led to the entire damage. The issue of distribution of liability is all the more important because the general conditions that usually govern the employer/architect relationship (SR 1988 Standard Conditions) impose only very limited liability on the architect as opposed to the unlimited liability of the contractor.

Comparing this with the English situation, it will be seen that the construction industry in the Netherlands apparently has no difficulty in accepting an express contractual duty to warn of defects in the design. This may be because of the overriding obligation under Dutch law to conduct contracts in good faith; or it may be because it is seen to be common sense. The way in which the duty is expressed is such that actual knowledge is not required, and liability can arise from failure to notice as well as failure to warn after noticing a defect. However, the reference to good faith relates only to the obligation to warn and not the obligation to discover a defect.

Italy

The general rules on defect liability are laid down in Articles 1667 and 1669 of the Civil Code, which read in translation as follows:

37 R v A 7 October 1983, No. 11.380

"Article 1667 Non-conformity or defects in work: The independent contractor is bound to warrant the customer against non-conformity or defects in the work. The warranty does not apply if the customer has accepted the work and the changes or defects were known to him or were detectable, provided that such defects were not passed over in silence by the contractor in bad faith. The customer shall, under penalty of forfeiture, notify the contractor of the nonconformity or defects within sixty days from the discovery thereof. The notice is not necessary if the contractor acknowledged such non-conformity or defects or concealed them.

The action against the contractor shall be prescribed (2934 ff.) in two years from the date of delivery of the work. A customer who is sued for payment can always enforce the warranty, provided that the notice of the non-conformity or defects was given within sixty days from discovery thereof and within two years from delivery."

"Article 1669 Destruction of and defects in immovables: In the case of buildings and other immovables intended by their nature to last for a long period of time, if within ten years from completion, the work is totally or partially destroyed by reason of defects in the soil or in construction, or if such work appears to be in evident danger of destruction or reveals serious deficiencies, the contractor is liable vis-a-vis the customer and his assignees and successors, provided that notice of said destruction or defects has been given within one year of their discovery."

Both case law and legal commentators have considered that design defects that may adversely affect the structure place the contractor under an obligation (within the limits of what may reasonably be required under the circumstances) to warn the employer of such defects and depart from the design specification in order to build a safe structure[38]. Only to the extent that the employer disregards the contractor's advice, instructing him to comply with the original design, may the contractor be relieved of liability for damages deriving from design defects[39]. The reasoning behind relief from liability in these circumstances is that the contractor then becomes a "nudus minister", i.e. a mere performer of the employer's decisions, unable to avoid complying with the specific instructions of the same.

38 See Supreme Court decisions nos. 4204 of May 6 1987 and no. 821 of January 29 1983.
39 See Supreme Court decisons nos. 3092 of March 31 1987, no. 4352 of July 25 1984, and no. 4697 of November 7 1984.

The architect or engineer who prepares the design for the employer has a general duty to perform with due diligence the professional contract entered into with the employer, and he is liable to the employer for any breach of such duty of diligence[40]. As to the problem of sharing the liability between the contractor with a duty to warn and the architect or engineer with a duty of diligence, the Italian Supreme Court has held that the architect and contractor are jointly liable where the architect is employed by the employer[41], but not jointly liable where the architect is employed by the contractor[42].

It will be seen from Arts 1667 and 1669 that the contractor has a primary responsibility for defects, whether they are caused by design or faults or defective workmanship. This is similar to the position in France, which is dealt with in my paper "Civil Law solutions to Common Law Tort problems"[43]. The duty to warn is merely a gloss on that responsibility. To this extent the position is similar to those situations in England where the contractor does have some degree of responsibility to ensure that the product is fit for its purpose (see above). The Italian courts have been faced with the same issue of joint liability, and in the classical situation where the architect is employed by the employer, have reached the same conclusion as the Dutch, that liability ought to be joint.

Germany

In a typical German construction project there is the same division of initial responsibility between design and construction. The contract between the employer and the architect is a "contract to manufacture"[44] (in contrast to an employment contract) which means that the architect is obliged to produce to the owner a final product, being the design. The architect is solely responsible for his product[45] and cannot pass responsibility on to the contractor by asking him to review it. The contracts between the employer and the contractors (there are often more than one) are also contracts to manufacture. The contractors must deliver to the owner the part of the building which their contract requires them to construct. As well as their express duties to construct, the contractors also have implied notification duties. When they recognise severe faults or errors in the design of the architect, they must communicate those faults to the owner and also to the

40 See Article 1176 of the Italian Civil Code.
41 Supreme Court decision no. 1114 of Feburary 24 1986
42 Supreme Court decision no. 4531 of July 12 1986
43 Paper 17 above
44 Para. 631 BGB
45 BGHZ 43, 227

architect himself.

The responsibilities of the architect and the contractors towards the owner have to be divided into two categories. Each of them is responsible for the fulfilment of their contractual obligations to produce a product, because each has different duties[46]. However, if any damage occurs to the building and the owner suffers loss, each of them (the architect and the contractors) is jointly and severally liable to the owner[47]. The purpose of this is that the employers should be able to recover his full loss from a defendant or defendants of his choice. As to the division of responsibility amongst the joint defendants, in general they will all pay an equal amount. However, those equal shares can be altered to reflect the individual degree of negligence of the particular defendant. If one defendant is solely responsible he will not be able to get an indemnity from the others. Here again, the duty to warn is only a gloss on the primary responsibility of the contractor to produce a final product which is fit for its purpose.

Spain

In Spain, responsibility for design rests with an architect and for construction with a contractor. The architect also directs the execution of the works with the help of another professional called the "aparejador", whose role is overseeing the execution of the works.

Article 1591 of the Spanish Civil Code states:

> "The contractor of a building that collapses due to defects of construction is liable for damages if the collapse occurs within ten years from the termination of the construction; the architect who directs the construction will incur the same liability and for the same period if the collapse is due to a defect of the land base or to the management. If the cause is the non-compliance by the contractor to the agreement conditions, then the action for liability will have a duration of fifteen years."

The courts have given a very broad interpretation to the word "collapse", comprising any important defects that may be considered as likely to lead to "incipient collapse" or that exceed "the usual imperfections". The architect is liable for defects in the management; the courts usually consider that this term includes the conception of the project, and the actual supervision of the works. In cases where the cause of the collapse cannot

46 BGHZ 43, 230
47 BGHZ 51, 275

be clearly identified, the courts usually impose joint liability on the architect, the aparejador and the contractor.

As to the duty to warn, a decision of the Supreme Court on 19th April 1977 is relevant. In that case it was held that the contractor was liable for the incipient collapse of the structure due to the lack of protective painting on some tubes supplied by a third party. The court stated that the contractor ought to have known of the necessity of protecting the tubes and should have warned the owner, even where he did not supply or procure the supply of the tubes, but simply incorporated them in the structure. The tubes had been supplied by a third party who contracted directly with the owner. The basis of the court's decision was Article 1258 of the Civil Code which requires the performance of contracts in accordance with good faith, custom and law. As the contractor was bound by his obligation of good faith, he was committed to inform the owners of the defect.

From this it will be seen that liability under Spanish law is not dependent on actual knowledge: it is sufficient that the contractor ought to have noticed and reported the defect. Such an extension of the scope of the duty to warn is made easier by the existence of the wide primary liability under Article 1591.

USA

Many construction contracts in the USA contain a provision requiring the contractor to review plans and specifications and report errors or omissions that he discovers. For example, the American Institute of Architects Form, para 2.3.1, provides:

> "The contractor shall carefully study and compare the Contract Documents with each other and with information furnished by the Owner pursuant to subparagraph 2.2.2, and shall at once report to the architect errors, inconsistencies or omissions discovered. The Contractor shall not be liable to the Owner or Architect for damage resulting from errors, inconsistencies or omissions in the contract documents unless the contractor recognised such error, inconsistency or omission and knowingly failed to report it to the architect."

This clause is in similar terms to the typical clause found in English contracts to deal with discrepancies in, or divergence between, individual contract documents (see e.g. clause 2.3 of JCT 80 and clause 5 of the ICE 5th Edition). It does of course have the added sting of imposing on the contractor the obligation to study the documents. The second sentence of the clause makes clear, however, that the contractor is liable only for failing to report in the case of actual knowledge, and is not subject to any wider liability on the basis of what a "reasonable" contractor ought to have noticed.

Given the clear contractual responsibility, the duty under the law of tort is unlikely to be very relevant. As is well known, the American courts have had a somewhat relaxed approach (by current English standards) to the recoverability of pure economic loss in the absence of privity of contract. For example, architects have been held liable in tort to contractors, and owners liable to subcontractors, and vice versa[48]. It does not seem impossible that liability in tort for failure to warn could exist even where the contract does not contain a clause of the kind set out above.

Conclusion

It will be apparent from this cursory examination of the situation in a number of different countries, from both a civil and common law background, that while there are some major differences in the structure of contracts and liability regimes, there are similarities between them. Each country has faced and tackled the same issue and with really quite small differences has come to the same conclusion: that contractors are under some obligation to warn employers of defects in design. If there is a lesson to be learnt from this in England, it is that there is a need to imply such a term into most contracts, but one where liability is triggered by actual knowledge. The bodies responsible for drafting the standard contracts could resolve the issue once and for all by including a term considered fair to all parties.

Acknowledgement

I acknowledge with thanks assistance received from the following lawyers in the following offices of Baker & McKenzie: Frank van Buuren, Amsterdam; Alberto Feliciani, Rome; Carola Hildenbrand, London; Alvaro Espinos, Barcelona; Charles Lewis, Chicago.

48 Refer to paper 18

20 Construction law practice in Socialist countries

George MacIlwaine

Synopsis

A significant market for construction activity is developing in socialist countries. This paper seeks to evaluate the risks and benefits of participation in this activity by looking at the provisions of socialist legal systems, and having regard to economic activity generally. Note is taken of the points of difference between these provisions and the precepts of the common law upon which those of an anglo- saxon tradition base their views of risk in construction contracts. The socialist system chosen for this review is that of the Peoples' Republic of China (PRC).

Introduction

Three principal factors affected the choice of the PRC as the basis for this paper. Firstly, the PRC is probably the "purest" of socialist legal systems from the point of view of political dogma. The legal system of China before the Long March was not something given to precise definition and was completely swept away upon the triumph of the communist faction. Secondly, it is the socialist legal system with the clearest provisions for economic activity within its jurisdiction by foreign nationals. Thirdly, it is a well entrenched system which may not be as likely as certain other socialist systems to experience substantial change in the near future.

Some Key Legislative Provisions

The Overall Picture

The PRC is a socialist state which by its constitution is declared to be "under the people's democratic dictatorship led by the working class and based on the alliance of workers and peasants, which is in essence the dictatorship of the proletariat." When engaging in economic activity in a socialist country one must always remember that the base line by reference to which property rights are defined is rather different from the capitalist equivalent.

The Detailed Legislation

For years, international companies have complained about the lack of a detailed legal regime for undertaking business with China. Now, at least for some types of business, the detailed legal structure is at hand. China has experienced both continuity and change in contract practice. In the most common purchase and sales contracts, standard-form contracts prepared by Chinese parties are accepted by foreigners. The more interesting and complex licensing, compensation trade, and joint venture contracts are more flexible and creative and have been drafted relatively recently. If China's policy continues on encouraging foreign trade and investment, more complex contracts between foreign participants and Chinese entities to be performed in China should become relatively more common. The Foreign Economic Contract Law has institutionalized China's open policy and laid a foundation for the further development of Chinese contract law in line with international practice. It seems likely that foreign companies and firms will keep on facing many of the issues that they have faced in the past and will continue to try to resolve them by negotiating appropriate provisions in their contracts; and where this does not succeed by reference to mediation, arbitration, or even litigation.

The Foreign Economic Contract Law

This law was passed in 1985 by the Standing Committee of the National People's Congress, and covers almost all types of contract that foreign firms sign with Chinese entities. It covers the most common type of contracts (purchase or sales contracts, insurance contracts, credit contracts, licensing and compensation trade Contracts) and the less common joint venture contracts. International transportation contracts are excluded. This is an indication that the PRC authorities have decided upon greater foreign trade investment than in the pre 1985 period.

The Foreign Economic Contract Law is a result of this new policy, and is used to promote it. In drafting the Foreign Economic Contract Law, the Chinese authorities were trying to facilitate China's economic contacts with the rest of the world. The Foreign Economic Contract Law confirms certain contract principles already established in practice, and lays a foundation for further development in the direction of international practice.

As noted above, the Foreign Economic Contract Law covers most types of contract between Chinese entities and foreign firms. This has two implications: first, foreign entities will be subject to the Foreign Economic Contract Law in business activity in China. Second, the Foreign Economic Contract Law, because it covers most types of contract, by necessity sets forth general principles only. The Foreign Economic Contract Law became effective on the 1st of July 1985. It is applicable to all contracts signed after that date. Contracts effective before that date may apply the Foreign Economic Contract law by agreement of the parties. It is not clear whether or not this is true in the case of an extension of a contract effective before that date.

The Foreign Economic Contract Law is not a long and complex statute. It consists of 43 Articles divided into seven chapters. The central chapters (the second, third, and fifth) relate to the formation of contracts, performance and liability for breach, amendment and cancellation, and termination of contracts.

Application and Applicable Law

The Foreign Economic Contract Law applies to economic contracts which are agreements "concluded in accordance with the principles of equality and mutual benefit" between legal entities that specify their mutual rights and obligations for the purpose of realizing certain economic goals. Such contracts should take consideration of the PRC's laws and should not violate public policy. Chinese law allows the contracting in parties to choose the applicable law for settling a dispute. If the parties have not stipulated, the law of the country with the closest connection to the contract applies. Chinese Law generally does not contain a "minimum connection" requirement. The draft of the Foreign Economic Contract Law proposed by the Ministry of Foreign Economic Relations and Trade included a provision requiring the parties to choose the law of a country with an actual connection to the contract, such as the law of the place where the contract was made, the law of the place of performance, or even the law of the place where the subject matter of the contract is located.

The choice of law provisions in the Foreign Economic Contract Law can be viewed in a variety of ways. Article 5 states that "the parties to a contract may choose the law to be applied to the handling of contract disputes." Under a narrow interpretation, the law chosen by the parties applies only to the procedures for settling relevant contract disputes. A broader interpretation would allow application of the chosen law to all areas relevant to dispute settlement, including substantive areas such as the capacity of the parties and the appropriateness and applicability of damages.

For certain transactions Chinese law limits the contracting parties' choice of law. Under article 40 of the Foreign Economic Contract Law, Chinese law is the governing law for contracts involving Sino-foreign equity or contractual joint ventures and contracts for natural resource exploration and development. If Chinese law contains no pertinent provisions, international custom and practice may apply. Generally when parties to a contract do not stipulate the applicable law, Chinese courts will apply the law of the country most closely related to the contract. This rule ordinarily results in the application of the law of the place where the contract is made or the law of the place of performance.

Basic Contract Rules

A contract is made when the parties have concluded an agreement in writing and have signed it. But where the contract needs approval by Chinese authorities, the contract is considered effective upon approval. Contracts that violate the laws of the PRC or public policy are considered void or not valid.

Each party has rights and obligations to fulfil. If one party does not perform its obligations under the terms of the signed contract, the other party has the right to claim remedies and compensation. The party in breach is liable for the damage caused to the other party. The extent of the liabilities of the parties to the contract shall be those foreseeable at the time that the contract is concluded and may be agreed between the parties at the time of contract. Damages may be provided for in a contract, but the parties can always go to a judicial or arbitral body in order to decrease or increase them. In the case of force majeure a party is excused from its contractual responsibilities. Causes of force majeure should be stated in the contract but may include only occurrences which are unforeseeable at the time of making the contract. Strikes, failure to obtain export licences or foreign government actions may only be included by agreement with the Chinese party to the contract and are generally viewed as being avoidable or foreseeable.

The consent of the other Party is required when an assignment is made. If the original contract required governmental approval, the assignment will also be subject to such approval. Parties may amend a contract by agreement, but only under certain circumstances. Either party has the right to cancel the contract. A contract is terminated by certain events such as mutual agreement of the parties, or the order of a judicial or arbitral body. There are certain contractual rights and obligations that survive cancellation or termination of contract.

Disputes may be settled through mediation or consultation with a third Party chosen the contracting Parties. The parties may submit their dispute to an arbitral body, such as the Chinese Arbitration Agency, if the contract provides to that effect or if the parties so agree. Otherwise the parties are left with their litigation rights.

The statute of limitations for commencing contractual proceedings concerning the sale or purchase of goods sets a limiting period of four years from the breach. Case law is sparse on this subject.

UN Convention on International Sales

The Foreign Economic Contract Law is influenced by the earlier Economic Contracts Law of the PRC passed by the National People's Congress on 13 December 1981, and by the United Nations Convention on Contracts for the International Sales of Goods completed on 11 April 1980. The Economic Contracts Law of the PRC is the basis of the Foreign Economic Contract Law, while the United Nations Convention is the source for the provisions which deal with the foreign aspects and international practice.

Both the Economic Contracts Law and the Foreign Economic Contract Law include sections concerning the principles, formation, and performance of contracts, the liability for breach, the amendment and termination of contracts, and the settlement of disputes through mediation, consultation, or arbitration. The articles which state that contracts made according to law are legally binding, and are to be performed by the parties, and that neither party has the right unilaterally to alter or cancel the contract for example are similarly expressed in each text. Article 3 of the Foreign Economic Contract Law treats the principles of equality, mutual benefit, and responsibility for breach, and provides that a contract is made when both parties reach an agreement, that a contract should be in writing, that contracts should conform with the law and that certain contracts are considered void clearly reflects the intention and content of the Economic Contracts Law. Both laws have similar provisions concerning dispute resolution and the alteration or termination of a contract. The Foreign Economic Contract Law differs from the Economic Contracts law, however, in treating questions of liquidated damages, limitation on liability, and suspension of performance.

The Foreign Economic Contract Law differs from the Economic Contracts Law in its purpose. The purpose of the Foreign Economic Contract Law is to safeguard the lawful rights and interests of the Parties to foreign economic contracts and to promote the development of the foreign economic relations of China. The purpose of the Economic Contracts Law is to protect the lawful rights and interests of the parties to economic contracts, to safeguard social and economic order, to improve economic results, to guarantee the implementation of the state plans and promote the progress of socialist modernization. China being a planned economy, economic contracts between Chinese entities must serve the government economic plan. Such contracts are more like administrative orders than voluntary contracts. Article 4 of the Economic Contracts Law states that contracts must be made in accordance with laws and the 'state policy and plans'. If such is not the case, the contract will be considered void. Only the administrative authorities have the right to supervise and inspect an economic contract through credit control and settlement control, and the right to cancel the contract signed by the parties. The Foreign Economic Contract Law does not contain any such provision concerning administrative control, even though foreign contracts are part of the state economic plans. The Foreign Economic Contract Law contains provisions concerning the choice of law and the effect of international treaties on contracts.

Both the United Nations Convention and the Foreign Economic Contract Law refer to international practice as a source of law. As in the United Nations Convention, the Foreign Economic Contract Law limits the damages obtainable for the breach of a contract to those foreseeable at the time of the formation of the contract. Both the United Nations Convention and the Foreign Economic Contract Law contain almost identical articles concerning the obligation of the breaching party to pay damages, the payment of interest, and the excuse for non performance of force majeure.

Although there are many similarities between the United Nations Convention and the Foreign Economic Contract Law, there are many differences. For example, the Foreign Economic Contract Law does not provide specific performance as a remedy, whereas the United Nations Convention does. The Foreign Economic Contract Law implies that a seller is to be afforded additional time for performance after failure to meet a delivery date, while the Convention stipulates that such a grace period is at the option of the buyer.

While the Convention deals only with sales of goods, the Foreign Economic Contract Law deals with a wider range of types of contract. Not all sales transactions are covered by the Convention. Article 2 Specifically excludes Six categories: goods bought for personal, family, or household use, goods bought by auction, sales on execution or otherwise by authority of law, sales of Stocks and bonds, sales of Ships, vessels, hovercraft, or aircraft, and sales of electricity. Unlike the Foreign Economic Contract Law, the Convention does not apply to contracts for labour or services.

The Foreign Economic Contract Law is more general and less complex than the Convention. The Convention provisions relating to contract formation include specific rules regarding when an offer becomes effective, when it may be revoked, when an acceptance of an offer becomes effective, and when an offer or an acceptance may be withdrawn. The United Nations Convention goes on to deal with other details such as the offer and the acceptance, and the rights and obligations of each party. The seller, for example, has to deliver his goods in conformity with the contract, whereas the buyer has to make the payment for these goods.

Comparative Law

Formation of contracts

In an effort to resolve "battle of forms" situations, the Convention provides that when a reply to an offer purports to be an acceptance but contains additions, limitations, or other modifications, it is a rejection of the offer and constitutes a counter-offer except when the changes or additions contained in the reply are not material. In such a situation, the offeror would have to object to the change or addition, and his failure to do so would mean that the terms of the contract are the terms of the offer, with the modifications as contained in the acceptance.

In order to limit problems which may arise from this formulation, the Convention defines material changes or additions as those "relating, among other things, to the price, payment, quality and quantity of the goods, place and time of delivery, extent of one party's liability to the other or the settlement of disputes." The Convention does not require signed writing for the formation of a sales contract. China has made a reservation to the Convention waiver of writing requirement, in accordance with article 96 of the Convention. The reservation is consistent with a provision of the Foreign Economic Contract Law that allows a contract to be established only when the parties reach an agreement on its articles in writing and sign their names. Because of this reservation many of the Convention articles that relate to the formation of a contract, such as those discussed above, probably will not come into full play.

Although the Foreign Economic Contract Law plays an important role in clarifying the legal basis for contracts between Chinese entities and foreign parties, it leaves unclarified matters and unanswered questions. For example, the scope of application of the Law is not clarified because there is no definition of the word 'enterprise' or 'economic organization'.

Organisation of Labour

As noted above the Foreign Economic Contract Law has a different purpose to the domestic Economic Contracts Law. The following scenario sets out how a domestic contract for a major work of construction would be fixed.

(a) The client authority would probably be the provincial division of a central government ministry, for example the Ministry of Electricity and Water for Guangdong province. Such a client authority has a number of direct labour organizations which act as the executive arm of the client authority in performing works for the client authority. These direct labour organisations tend to be highly specialised and perform the works in that specialisation throughout the province or area administered by the client authority.

(b) Standards have been established for productivity throughout most areas of industry in the PRC and construction is no exception. Thus if works as defined call for (say) 200 000 square metres of formwork to be erected and there are 200 working days available for such works, if the standard for production of formwork is 2 square metres per man per day then the formwork specialist direct labour organisation of the client authority will make 500 formwork carpenters available.

(c) Responsibility for providing materials, drawings, plant, equipment, etc. rests with the client authority. The direct labour organisation merely makes available the resources calculated as necessary to meet the programme and performs as instructed.

This is of course a highly flexible way of working. Should the client authority wish to vary the works, or vary the tempo of the works then he can do so. Quality control, liability, programme, scope of works - everything pertinent to the execution of the works is entirely in the hands of the owner, through his agent, the client authority.

It is also a highly inefficient way of working. The total freedom to vary and redefine the scope of works during the construction militates against the production of near definitive information pre-contract. Chinese construction projects are littered with the debris of inadequately conceived works with consequent cost and time over-runs.

Foreign contractors working in China

The leopard does not change his spots. A Chinese client authority when calling for participation in construction in China by international contractors will be hoping to eliminate the faults inherent in the contracting system described in greatly simplified terms above.

But the same client authority will wish to retain his freedom to vary and redefine the scope of works and the programme to take due account of his contemporaneous particular requirements. The same client authority will not always be ready to recognise the consequences of the exercise of such freedom upon the rights of an international contractor.

This is not of course a problem which is in any way peculiar to China or any other socialist country, although custom in China has added an almost magical authority to the way in which this freedom is exercised there. It is extremely rare to find international contractors carrying out major works on their own in China. Client authorities are reluctant to fund the foreign exchange element of foreign participation unless that participation is quite necessary for one reason or another.

Would-be international participants are introduced to specialist direct labour organisations of the client authority prior to the contract with a view to minimising the foreign exchange exposure of an individual project. The formation of joint ventures is enthusiastically encouraged.

Joint venture arrangements

Joint ventures are essentially a method of combining the efforts, resources and skills of a group of people or entities in order to achieve a common commercial objective. In China, this may be achieved either by the parties entering into an agreement whereby they agree to join forces but which does not involve setting up a new entity, or by the parties entering into a partnership or a limited company.

The most common method, however, is for the parties to invest in a new private limited company which then engages in the new business. This has the advantage over the other two arrangements of separating the activities of the joint venture from the participators' other business interests. In addition, because the parties are investing in a limited company, their liability is limited and therefore so is their risk. The division of the profits of the new company can be arranged so as to reflect the original investment. The disadvantage is that decision making becomes potentially more difficult where the ownership is shared. A mechanism should be provided for unravelling the joint venture company if it should fail or otherwise cease to be desirable.

Where the participators form a partnership, the normal rules of partnership liability will apply. Each participator's liability will normally be joint and several and not limited to its capital share. Limited partnerships have, in the past, rarely been used but are now beginning to enjoy some popularity. At least one partner must have unlimited liability but the others (the limited partners) may limit their liability to the extent of their capital contribution. Limited partnerships must be registered at the Companies Registry, but do not need to file accounts or hold annual general meetings. A limited partner may not participate in the management of the partnership but he does have the right to inspect books and advise on the state and prospects of the partnership business.

A limited company is a more appropriate vehicle for a joint venture than a partnership or a limited partnership where (as in many major construction projects) there is to be major investment by several investors, or where the intention is to obtain investment from the public by selling shares. Under English law a company is relatively easier and cheaper to establish than a limited partnership, assuming that a full partnership deed is drawn up and there is no reason to suppose that in China things are very different. In the long term, continuity can be more readily maintained through a company than through a partnership and, in addition, a company is less difficult to unscramble. A company, but not a partnership, may create a floating charge over its assets as security for borrowing. The liability of all members of a company is limited to the assets of the company.

Foreign Exchange problems

For several years in China, the foreign parties in a production joint venture have been required to export a predetermined percentage of production. Further, Chinese law provides that a joint venture shall in general keep a balance between its foreign exchange receipts and expenditures. The purpose of these provisions is to protect China's foreign exchange reserves. Without these provisions foreigners could monopolize China's huge domestic market and deplete the nation of its foreign currency reserves.

The Overview of the Chinese Authorities

At the same time, China needs to attract foreign investment and technology. Without incentives, primarily the ability to repatriate legitimately earned profits, China will be unable to attract this foreign investment. Article I of the Regulations of the State Council concerning the Balance of Foreign Exchange Income and Expenditure by Sino-foreign Joint Equity Ventures clearly states that:

> "These Regulations are formulated for the purpose of encouraging foreign joint ventures to establish in China Sino-foreign joint equity ventures involving Chinese and foreign exchange income and expenditure, to the advantage both of production management and the repatriation of legally earned profits by the foreign joint venture."

This straightforward language indicates that Chinese policy makers are acutely aware of China's need to encourage more Sino-foreign ventures and the joint venture's need for assistance in balancing its foreign exchange account by allowing for repatriation of excess foreign exchange.

The articles that follow are far less succinct and conclusive. The drafters leave room for bureaucratic manoeuvring, often requiring the joint venture to seek approval at several layers of authority as the condition to trigger the provisions allowing repatriation. Further, the drafters do not specify which authority, within the complex Chinese bureaucratic apparatus, has the power to grant these approvals. In other words, the Chinese have built into the new law a discretionary authority in order to determine which joint ventures may take advantage of the provisions. The law proposes several creative and deceivingly complex methods to facilitate the repatriation of profits.

The Chinese have reintroduced the ancient method of bartering. This ancient method of transacting business and of repatriating profits is incorporated in Article 6:

> "In order to achieve a balance of foreign exchange income and expenditure, Sino-foreign joint equity ventures may, with the approval of the Ministry of Foreign Economic Relations and Trade, utilise the sales connections of the foreign joint venturer to promote the sale of Domestic Chinese goods on the export market."

The Law stipulates that a foreign party may purchase goods in China for local currency and resell it on the international market for foreign exchange. In effect, the local currency profits are used to purchase goods for export sale to obtain foreign exchange. This new law grants a joint venture the power to barter its goods for others. This grant of power is indeed unique and, if practical, would afford the investor a relatively painless method of earning foreign exchange.

A closer look at the provision, however, indicates that subtle limitations may work to hinder any positive effect the drafters might have envisioned. The right to barter is conditioned upon receiving prior approval from Ministry of Foreign Economic Relations and Trade (MOFERT). The process is relatively new, and many joint ventures in the PRC may attempt to capitalize upon it. Because of this, MOFERT will most likely restrict trade in Chinese domestic goods solely to those joint ventures with a foreign exchange imbalance. Without express approval from MOFERT the investor will not be granted authority to barter.

Parallel Legislation

(a) The Regulations for the Implementation of the Law of the PRC on Joint Ventures Using Chinese and Foreign Investment cover all types of joint venture between Chinese entities and foreign ones. This law consists of 118 Articles divided into sixteen chapters. Joint venture contracts are agreements "concluded with the principles of equality and mutual benefit" between legal entities that specify their mutual rights and obligations for the purpose of promoting the development of China's economy, and the raising of scientific and technological levels for the benefit of socialist modernization. Article 3 of the Regulations for the Implementation of the Law of the PRC on Joint Ventures Using Chinese and Foreign Investment states that the permitted joint ventures must be in the following industries:

(1) Energy development, the building material, chemical and metallurgical industries;
(2) Machine manufacturing, instrument and meter industries and offshore oil exploitation equipment manufacturing;
(3) Electronics and computer industries, and communication equipment manufacturing;
(4) Lighting, textiles, foodstuffs, medicine, medical apparatus and packing industries;
(5) Agriculture, animal husbandry and aquiculture;
(6) Tourism and service trades.

(b) All joint ventures must take into consideration the PRC's laws and regulations. Joint ventures should not violate Chinese public policy. The parties to a joint venture will not be granted approval if the projects involve (1) Detriment to China's sovereignty;(2) Violation of Chinese law; (3) Nonconformity with the requirements of the development of China's national economy; (4) Environmental pollution; (5) Obvious inequity in the agreements, contracts and articles of association signed, impairing the rights and interests of one party.

At the same time, joint ventures using Chinese and foreign investment established within China's territory in accordance with the law on Chinese-Foreign Joint Ventures may be Chinese legal persons and thus become subject to the jurisdiction and protection of Chinese law. The government department in charge of the Chinese participant will be the department in charge of the joint venture. The department in charge is responsible for guidance, assistance, and supervision of the joint venture.

An equity joint venture must be approved by MOFERT and registered with the General Administration for Industry and Commerce before it can conduct business under licence. MOFERT has the power to examine and to approve or reject the application within three months. Article 8 of the Regulations provides that the establishment of joint ventures has to comply with the following conditions:

"(1)   The total amount of investment is within the limit set by the State Council and the source of capital of the Chinese participants has been ascertained;

(2)   No additional allocations of raw materials by the state are
       required and do not affect the national balance of fuel,
       power, transportation, and foreign trade export quotas."

A joint venture contract, as defined in the 1983 Joint Venture Implementing Regulations, is a legally binding document signed by the joint venture
partners that spells out the rights and obligations of each partner. The
Chinese entity must submit a project proposal and a preliminary feasibility
study to its department in charge for a provisional clearance . A carefully
prepared feasibility study covering all the major issues of concern to the
partners should conform to the framework of the contract, leaving only the
precise wording to be negotiated and worked out.

After preliminary approval is obtained, the proposed participants may
further negotiate and sign a joint venture agreement incorporating the main
terms and conditions of their cooperation while they conduct a more detailed
feasibility study. After the findings of the feasibility study are analysed and
if considered acceptable, the parties may negotiate on the final points of their
cooperation and proceed to sign a formal joint venture contract.

The experience of many companies suggests that, in drawing up the
contract, it is advisable to follow the sample joint venture contract published
by MOFERT as closely as possible. Clauses that are not entirely agreeable
to one of the partners can be tempered with provisions that clarify the
partner's position. When MOFERT officials review a contract that follows
a format familiar to them, they are likely to raise fewer questions, and the
contract is likely to be approved more readily. Wherever possible, foreign
companies should build into the contract balanced and equal provisions that
protect both parties, rather than one sided demands.

Other types of agreement

A joint venture contract is often confused with a joint venture "agreement" - a separate document occasionally drawn up by the partners to a joint
venture. According to the Implementing Regulations, the "agreement"
formalizes the main points and principles governing the venture rather than
the rights and obligations of the partners, and is usually drawn up before the
contract. Of the two documents, the contract is clearly the more important
since its terms prevail if a conflict occurs between the two documents. If the
partners agree, they may forego the "agreement" and conclude only a joint
venture contract. In practice, very few companies have opted to sign a joint
venture "agreement" in addition to the contract.

There may also be other types of agreements drawn up to govern specific
aspects of the joint venture not covered in the main contract for the transfer

of technology, or a technical assistance contract. These can be negotiated separately, but should be submitted for approval together with the joint venture contracts. The Implementing Regulations specify in Article 9 the documents that must be submitted for examination to the approval authority:

(a) Application for the establishment of a joint venture;
(b) The feasibility study report jointly prepared by the parties to the venture;
(c) Joint venture agreement, contract and articles of association signed by representatives authorized by the parties to the venture;
(d) List of candidates for chairman, vice-chairman and directors appointed by the parties to the venture;
(e) Written opinions of the department in charge and the people's government of the province, autonomous region or municipality directly under the central government where the joint venture is located with regard to the establishment of the joint venture.

The documents cited above must be in Chinese. Documents (b), (c), and (d) may be written simultaneously in another language agreed upon by the entities to the joint venture. Both versions must be legally notarized. After submitting all of these documents to the local People's Government entrusted by MOFERT for approval, the local People's Government will review the application in the light of the written report of the department in charge of the proposed Chinese joint venture partner and also by reference to the published guidelines on approving joint ventures.

Within one month of being granted final approval, a joint venture must register with the provincial Bureau of the State Administration of Industry and Commerce which will issue an operation licence. This process is outlined in and governed by both the Joint Venture Implementing Regulations and the Regulations on the Registration of Joint Ventures. It may be useful to notify the local administration of industry and commerce early on during project negotiations. In one case in which the partners did not do so, an otherwise uncomplicated process of final joint venture approval met with unexpected delays of many months. The date of issue of the operation licence is the date of formal establishment of the joint venture. The joint venture parties may not commence business operations before the operation licence is issued.

Operation of Joint Venture

A joint venture is a separate legal entity distinct from the participants

(Chinese and foreign) who constitute the joint venture. It often takes the form of a limited liability company which has a registered capital. The parties to a joint venture share the profits, risks, and losses of the joint venture in proportion to their contribution to the registered capital.

The registered capital of a joint venture refers to the total amount of investment registered at the registration and administration office for the establishment of the joint venture. The parties to the joint venture must agree on presenting their registered capital in local currency or in any foreign currency. During the term of the joint venture, this registered capital may not be reduced. On the other hand it can be increased with the approval of the board of directors and the concerned authority. Any changes have to be dealt with at the original registration and administration office.

The law requires a foreign input of capital to be at least 25 percent of the total. Although no upper limit has been set, it is unlikely that the Chinese government will encourage foreign ownership of more than 50 percent of the joint venture. Each party to a joint venture may contribute cash, buildings, premises, equipment, materials, industrial property, or know-how. Where a contribution is not cash, its value must be mutually agreed and assessed by the parties concerned, or by a third party agreed upon the parties to a joint venture. Such assessment must be reasonable and realistic; it is subject to approval by a Chinese registered accountant who will verify the participants' contributions and if considered proper, issue a certificate of verification in accordance with which the joint venture will issue to each of the joint venture parties a Certificate of Investment.

In the event that the contribution by a foreign party is cash which has to be converted into local currency, it will be converted according to the exchange rate announced by the State Administration of Foreign Exchange Control of the PRC on the day of submission of funds. The same will be applied to a Chinese participant converting his contributed cash to foreign currency.

The machinery, materials, and equipment contributed by a foreign participant have to meet specific conditions. They have to be indispensable to the activities of the joint venture. For example, it must be shown that China is unable to manufacture the items, or manufactures them at a high price, or that technical performance or time of delivery of items from China cannot meet the joint venture's requirements. Their fixed price cannot be higher than the current international market price for similar products.

The industrial property, or know-how contributed by the foreign participant has to be (1) Capable of manufacturing new products urgently needed in China or products suitable for export; (2) Capable of improving markedly the performance quality of existing products and raising productivity; (3) Capable of notable savings in raw materials, fuel, or power. These contributions are specified in the joint venture agreement and the articles of association. The most common contributions from the Chinese partners are land, factory, labour, raw materials, and to a limited extent, cash. The ways of contributing investment have to be examined and approved by the department in charge of the Chinese participant and then submitted to the examination and approval authority for approval.

The duration of a Joint Venture, stipulated in the agreement, contract, and articles of association, is to be decided upon through consultation of all parties to the joint venture according to the actual circumstances of the particular lines of business and projects. The duration of a joint venture is normally from 10 to 30 years. The duration of joint ventures requiring a large amount of investment, long construction periods, and low interest rate on funds can exceed 30 years. The duration begins from the day when the joint venture is issued a business licence, and can be extended upon the approval of all parties six months before the date of expiry of the duration. The extension can be obtained only with a written approval of the examination and approval authority.

Dissolution

On the other hand, Article 102 of the Regulations states that a joint venture may be dissolved in the following situations:

(1) Termination of duration;
(2) Inability to continue operations due to heavy losses;
(3) Inability to continue operations due to the failure of one of the contracting parties to fulfil the obligations prescribed by the agreement, contract, and articles of associations;
(4) Inability to continue operations due to heavy losses caused by force majeure such as natural calamities and wars, etc.;
(5) Inability to obtain the desired objectives of the operation and at the same time to see a future for development;
(6) Occurrence of other reasons for dissolution prescribed by the contract and articles of association.

In cases described in (2), (3), (4), (5), and (6), the board of directors has to submit an application for dissolution to the examination and approval authority. In a situation where one of the contracting parties fails to fulfil obligations prescribed by the agreement, contract, and articles of association, that party shall be liable for any losses caused.

Upon the disestablishment of a joint venture, its board of directors carry out the liquidation by nominating candidates for the liquidation committee, who are usually selected from among the directors. In the event that the directors cannot perform such a task, the liquidation committee may be formed of lawyers and accountants registered in China. The liquidation committee formulates a liquidation plan and represents the joint venture to sue and be sued. After dissolution of the joint venture, its accounting books and documents are left in the care of the Chinese participant.

Dispute Resolution in Joint Venture

Disputes arising over the interpretation or execution of the agreement are to be settled through friendly negotiation, consultation, or mediation. If such disputes cannot be settled promptly by any one of the above mentioned means, the parties to a dispute may have recourse to arbitration for settlement in accordance with provisions specified in their contracts or other agreements to submit to arbitration. Such arbitration may be conducted by the Foreign Economic and Trade Commission of the China Council for the promotion of International Trade, by an arbitration agency in the country where the defendant is located, or by another agency in a third country in accordance with the arbitration agency's procedures. If the contract has no provision for arbitration, a party has to file a suit to a court, the Chinese People's Court.

A joint venture contract, as defined in the 1983 Joint Venture Implement-ing Regulations, is a legally binding document signed by the joint venture partners that spells out the rights and the obligations of each partner. The operations of joint venture are governed by the Law of the PRC on Joint Ventures Using Chinese and Foreign Investment and the Regulations for the Implementation of the Law of the PRC on Joint Ventures Using Chinese and Foreign Investment.

Equity Joint Venture

The basic forms of joint venture which are active today in the PRC are equity joint venture, contractual joint venture, and hybrid joint venture. The equity joint venture is the most widespread in the PRC. The term 'joint venture' has been widely used in many different contexts to refer to different business transactions in the PRC. However, an equity joint venture has a special meaning. The pure equity joint venture is the most popular among many Chinese organisations and multinational corporations. There seems to be a tendency to assume that creating an equity joint venture is the only proper way for significant companies to do business in China. This may not be true depending upon the goals of the foreign party - particularly if a speedy negotiation process is one of the objectives. The key characteristic of an equity joint venture is that it is a limited liability company incorporated and registered in the PRC. Being such, it is subject to Chinese laws and administrative procedures. This can have both advantages and disadvantages. It may mean that the joint venture company has better access to the domestic supply of goods or retail markets. It may also mean, however, that one encounters further bureaucratic delays in the organisation of the joint venture.

The percentage of ownership of the foreign party in a joint venture varies, but the joint ventures of today are either 50/50 or 51/49 joint ventures. Two years ago, most of the joint ventures provided for Chinese control through at least a 51/49 ownership structure. Occasionally, foreign parties will request an even greater equity ownership. While this is, of course, permitted by law, some foreign companies do not wish to increase their equity ownership beyond 50 per cent insofar as it exposes them to additional liability for future capital contributions or expenses should the joint venture have difficulties during its early years. Nevertheless, some corporations, as a matter of policy, require that they avoid joint ventures in foreign countries and push to retain as high a percentage of ownership as possible on the assumption that they will control the joint venture company. The mere contribution of an increased percentage of equity will not significantly increase the control by the foreign party, either over the joint venture company or its technology.

Contractual Joint Venture

The second type of joint venture is the contractual joint venture. As its name suggests, this type of joint venture results from a contract. There is no separate, legal entity formed by the foreign and Chinese parties. Instead, the parties agree through a contract to undertake a particular type of joint activity. Typically the contract will begin by reciting that the foreign parties agree to join forces to work on a particular project. It may also then recite which items of cash, expertise, technology, buildings, or land may be contributed by each party. The contract will also provide for a division of the profits by both parties. With regard to control, this matter is always a subject for negotiation between the parties and may be resolved through the appointment by the foreign party of the general manager of the particular project; such as a hotel, construction site, factory, etc.

The foreign party should avoid confusing types of joint ventures when it comes to management. Many joint ventures whose precise nature is unclear provide for a board of directors. While this may be a useful means of resolving disputes, a different term should be used for the board, such as management committee, unless the parties intend to create an equity joint venture. Confusion as to the type of joint venture created causes problems when the time comes to decide what tax treatment the joint venture will receive, as it may be unclear whether it is equity or contractual in nature.

Hybrid Joint Venture

The third type of joint venture is the hybrid joint venture. This type of joint venture is generally similar to a contractual joint venture, except that labour and utilities may be contributed by the Chinese party as equity. As the tax treatment for a hybrid joint venture is significantly different from that of a contractual joint venture, it is important to identify this type of joint venture in the documentation as clearly as possible in order to avoid confusion.

There are many ways to set up a joint venture to operate in the PRC. Each has its advantages and disadvantages having regard, for example, to protection from liability for the joint venture partners, speed of establishment, degree of access to local market, tax considerations, etc. Foreign parties wishing to set up a joint venture in China will have to consider carefully each of these aspects before deciding which form of joint venture is most suitable for them.

Practical applications

From the above it should be clear to all but the most innocent that the international contractor participating in construction in China is almost certain to find himself bound to perform in tandem with an organisation who at the very least is steeped in the traditions of the client authority, if indeed his interests are not entirely coincident with those of the client authority.

Whilst less than desirable (at least from a traditional anglo-saxon adversarial contracting viewpoint) such a contractual relationship is not necessarily fatal to the interests of the international participant. But it does entail that the performance contract should be extremely clear as to the responsibility for the definition of the scope of the works, the power to amend and vary the scope of works and the programme and the mechanisms to adjust the terms of the contract to take due account of any such amendments and variations and as to the enforceability of such mechanisms.

Dispute resolution in China

It is a marked feature of Chinese commercial practice that there is a great unwillingness to admit to the existence of disputes. Joint venture agreements, for example, as a matter of form carry expressions of mutual trust and esteem which tend to arouse suspicion in even the least cynical of minds. China has however, accepted the need to define a framework to allow for the settlement of disputes arising from international commercial activity.

For somewhat specious reasons, the Chinese have been extremely reluctant to engage in any agreement involving the International Chamber of Commerce. It is not because of any dissatisfaction with the rules themselves or because of the high cost of ICC arbitration, but because Taiwan is still a member. Politics is the only reason why Chinese entities do not call either for ICC arbitration in their contracts or for the ICC rules of procedure. When an international contractor succeeds in inserting a clause providing for dispute resolution by international arbitration the preferred venue and forum of the Chinese is Stockholm and the rules of the Stockholm Chamber of Commerce. (The Swedes find themselves pushed towards Switzerland).

China's new policy of seeking a broad foreign economic cooperation has brought to the fore the entire question of dispute resolution, and of arbitration in particular. Foreign governments concerned with providing adequate dispute resolution facilities for their nationals engaged in the China trade have sought to negotiate assurances with China. The most elaborate provision thus far concluded is Article VIII of the Sino-American trade agreement of 7 July 1979, which states:

"A. The contracting Parties encourage the prompt and adequate settlement of any disputes arising from or in relation to contracts between their respective firms, companies and corporations, and trading organizations, through friendly consultations, conciliation or other mutually acceptable means.

B. If such disputes cannot be settled promptly by any one of the above mentioned means, the parties to the disputes may have recourse to arbitration for settlement in accordance with provisions specified in their contracts or other agreements to submit to arbitration. Such arbitration may be conducted by an arbitration institution in the PRC, the United States of America, or a third country. The arbitration rules of procedure of the relevant arbitration institution are applicable and the arbitration rules of the United Nations Commission on International Trade Law recommended by the United Nations, or other international arbitration rules, may also be used where accept-

               able to the parties to the disputes and to the arbitration
               institution.

C.   Each Contracting Party shall seek to ensure that arbitra-
           tion awards are recognized and enforced by their compe-
           tent authorities where enforcement is sought, in accor-
           dance with applicable laws and regulations."

This leaves it to the parties to each contract to decide how to deal with arbitration. In agreements with certain other governments China has been more specific, stipulating that in commercial disputes between entities of the two countries any necessary arbitration shall take place in the country of the defendant.

Legislative provisions

The question of the resolution of disputes between Chinese and foreign-ers has now been dealt with in a number of parts of China's legislation. For example Article 14 of the Law of the PRC on Joint Ventures Using Chinese and Foreign Investment states:

"Disputes arising between the parties to a joint venture that the board of directors cannot settle through conciliation may be settled through conciliation or arbitration by a Chinese arbitra-tion agency or through arbitration by another arbitration agency agreed upon by the parties to the venture."

Thus, Article 14 clearly states that it is up to the parties to the transaction to decide, if consultation fails, whether to resort to conciliation prior to arbitration. The parties may also decide whether arbitration is to take place in China or abroad.

Foreign Economic Contract Law provides in relation to all contracts between Chinese and foreign economic enterprise bodies, that if consulta-tion and mediation between the parties are unsuccessful the parties may submit the dispute between them to a Chinese arbitral body or another arbitral body for arbitration, in accordance with the arbitration provisions in the contract or a subsequent written arbitration agreement. In the situation where the parties do not include an arbitration clause in the contract and do not subsequently conclude an arbitration agreement, they are entitled to sue in the People's Courts.

Conciliation

Although China has begun to pay more attention to litigation and arbitration than in the past, it continues to put more emphasis on the desire to settle disputes through conciliation. In recent years Chinese tribunals have continued their previous practice of making an award only when the dispute cannot be settled through conciliation. If either party insists on avoiding conciliation and going directly to arbitration, although this is not recommended, it is permissible unless it violates a compulsory conciliation clause in the contract. Chinese arbitration specialists make it clear that consultation, conciliation, and arbitration are three successive stages, and their hope is that disputes can be settled at the first or second stage.

Article 7 of the Civil Procedure Code for Trial Implementation provides that:

> "If a civil action which has been accepted by a people's court is able to be resolved through mediation, the court shall conduct mediation on the basis of investigation and examination of the facts and the distinguishing of right from wrong, and shall persuade the parties to understand each other's positions and to arrive at an agreement of settlement."

Although the Code further provides that "If no agreement can be reached through mediation, or if one of the parties changes his mind before the written mediation statement is served, the people's court shall proceed with trial and adjudication and shall not prolong mediation without resolution." So strong is the preference for informal settlement that the Code even authorizes further conciliation at the conclusion of the trial following the final arguments of the parties and prior to judgment, and allows for conciliation during any appeal against the judgment.

If read literally, the Joint Venture Law suggests that while arbitration of disputes may be concluded in China or abroad, conciliation may only be conducted by a Chinese arbitration institution. But in fact, as Chinese specialists have explained, conciliation under these laws may take place in any location and be conducted by non-Chinese as well as Chinese.

In order to meet the concern for "equality and mutual benefit" the China Council for the Promotion of International Trade (CCPIT) and the American Arbitration Association (AAA) began a joint conciliation for resolving disputes in Sino-American trade. Under this arrangement each organisation appoints a conciliator and the two cooperate in helping the parties to find a solution. Joint conciliation has already been successful in the trade area, and can be expected to operate in joint ventures and other forms of cooperation. CCPIT decided to use joint conciliation to resolve disputes arising under

Chinese commercial contracts. It refers a dispute to a commission of two to six persons, composed of equal numbers from the CCPIT and an approved sponsoring Organisation from the country of the other party. Joint conciliation can take the form of the very informal ad hoc cooperation of two or more persons representing the respective parties.

Very few contracts have referred to joint conciliation. The failure of contracts to provide for this new technique is not remarkable, however, in view of the fact that many contracts make no reference to conciliation in any form, despite its prominence in China trade. Rather, they often give the impression that the parties will or should proceed directly from consultation between themselves to arbitration. Nevertheless, an increasing number of investment contracts contain a conciliation clause. Some joint venture contracts, for example, simply provide for the CCPIT's Foreign Economic and Trade Arbitration Commission (FETAC) to conciliate any dispute that the Board of Directors cannot settle. Another example is a contract that authorizes conciliation by either the FETAC or an ad hoc panel composed of one conciliator appointed by each of the two parties and a third appointed by the first two conciliators. At the same time, these contracts make it clear that arbitration is to occur only if conciliation fails.

It is very unlikely, though, for a foreign entity to object to conciliation as a matter of principle. In fact, conciliation can settle a large number of disputes and possesses distinct virtues. No one is eager to submit to arbitration or litigation. Yet, as the Civil Procedure Code recognizes, an objection arises if conciliation drags on to the point of denying one or both of the parties a desired opportunity to conclude the dispute through a determination on the merits of the case. This is why some foreign companies have persuaded their Chinese counterparts to insert time-limits into the dispute resolution clauses of their contracts. For example, the parties can prescribe in their contract that if the conciliation process proves ineffective ninety days after it has been invoked, either party may initiate arbitration proceedings.

Disputes involving foreign interests

The PRC, its domestic legislation and its international agreements authorize Chinese entities to conclude contracts that call for the arbitration of disputes in China and abroad. Naturally, the Chinese prefer that arbitration take place at home, whereas foreign parties prefer that the arbitration takes place outside China, especially in the present circumstances. Thus, in general, the arbitration takes place in a third country.

The Chinese party, when confronted with a foreign party's request for third-country arbitration, usually responds with two suggestions. The first one is arbitration where the defendant is domiciled. The second Chinese alternative is to suggest that the contract provide for arbitration in China unless the parties, at the time a dispute occurs, agree upon arbitration outside the PRC.

Foreign investors tend to reject both of the alternatives mentioned above as too similar in effect to a provision that calls for arbitration in China. The foreign party believes that, in most cases, the Chinese entity would be the defendant, and therefore they believe that the provision that states arbitration in the defendant's domicile calls indirectly for the arbitration in China. Such provision leads the parties to a dispute to manipulate their relationship in an effort to emerge as the defendant. Foreign parties consider the second alternative as a pious hope that if a dispute should occur, the Chinese party might agree to substitute third-country arbitration for submission in China even though it refuses to do so while the contract is being negotiated, when negotiations are still unmarred by a dispute.

The result of this bargaining has thus far been that China accepts third-country arbitration in investment and loan contracts as well as in contracts for the purchase of capital goods and for the licensing of technology. What future policy will be is uncertain. If at the outset of every negotiation China is prepared to accept Stockholm or other third-country arbitration, the parties will be able to spend a good deal of time negotiating other issues of the contract. China Council for the Promotion of International Trade (CCPIT) have stated that China generally agrees to Stockholm arbitration in foreign trade contracts. Yet foreign companies are still finding it hard negotiating this subject matter.

There might be advantages to China in selecting a single foreign jurisdiction and arbitration institution for the settlement of most disputes outside China, especially since China is still new to the actualities of international commercial arbitration. It would be difficult for the officials of any country in such a situation to become familiar with the variety of places and foreign arbitration organizations as well as the relevant legal environment in each jurisdiction. Concentrating on one place and one organisation should simplify the matter. China's general preference for Stockholm as a place and, for the Arbitration Institute of the Stockholm Chamber of Commerce as an organization, appears to be grounded in careful analysis based on continuing close contacts with the officials of this arbitral body.

There are organizations other than the Institute of the Stockholm Chamber of Commerce which seem to be less distant from China, and may be less expensive For a time Tokyo seemed to be gaining favour in China, not only because of geographic propinquity but also of the belief that Japanese arbitrators might be more capable of understanding China's circumstances and attitudes toward law and contracts than would Europeans. Hong Kong has more recently established itself as an arbitration centre for the Asian region and hopes to create conditions that will make it an attractive site for the settlement of China-related disputes. Hong Kong is geographically contiguous to China and relations between it and China are increasingly cordial in the lead up to 1997. Hong Kong has strong linguistic, cultural, and economic bonds with China, and China has a great many government offices and companies operating there. Thus considerations of convenience would appear to favour Hong Kong arbitration. On the other hand, the China Council for the Promotion of International Trade (CCPIT) has established a branch of the Foreign Economic and Trade Arbitration Commission (FETAC) in the Shenzhen area in order to facilitate on the spot resolution of disputes. Initially political sensitivity and competitive considerations appeared to lead Chinese arbitration experts to promote the Shenzhen organisation while remaining unenthusiastic about Hong Kong as a forum for arbitration. In fact, with the restoration of China's sovereignty over Hong Kong in 1997, China seems willing to cooperate in promoting Hong Kong as an arbitral forum. Indeed, several Chinese-owned institutions, including the Bank of China, have made financial donations towards the establishment of the Hong Kong International Arbitration Centre. CCPIT officials have also begun to support the idea of arbitration in Hong Kong and to co-operate with the Centre. If Hong Kong has indeed won the support of China as an arbitral forum, the interesting question is whether Hong Kong will also be able to win the support of foreign countries and more specifically of foreign parties, so that it may emerge as the leading arbitral forum in China business matters.

Arbitration Rules and Procedure

Under Chinese practice, the parties to a contract are free to choose the rules of procedure applicable to arbitration and the place of arbitration. Chinese contracts provide for the rules of procedure of the named arbitral body. Although contracts that provide for arbitration in China generally state that it shall be governed by the rules of procedure of the relevant institution, the Chinese do not believe that this provision is a necessary one. Chinese contracts which refer to arbitration in the defendant's domicile generally do not mention anything about the rules of procedure. If the contract refers to a third-country arbitration, the rules of procedure are specified, and they are usually those of the named arbitral body. A contract, for example, may provide that "In the event that conciliation cannot resolve the dispute, the matter shall be brought for arbitration before the Arbitration Institute of the Stockholm Chamber of Commerce, Sweden, and shall proceed according to the arbitration regulations and procedures of that arbitration organization, The decision of the arbitration shall be final and will be binding on both parties". Sometimes, however, the contract only provides that "In the event that conciliation cannot resolve the dispute, the matter shall be brought for arbitration before the Arbitration Institute of the Stockholm Chamber of Commerce, Sweden. The decision of the arbitration shall be final and will be binding on both parties," In other cases, the clause designates the place of arbitration and at other times it omits any reference to the place.

Even when the contract refers to third-country arbitration and specifies that the rules of procedure are those of the named arbitration organization, Chinese contracts may single out certain of those rules for emphasis or stipulate details about those rules or modify the rules in some respect, For example, providing that the tribunal shall consist of three arbitrators, one chosen by each party and the third by the institute of arbitration; that the tribunal shall state in writing the reasons for its decision; or that the language of the Proceedings shall be in English, The foreign parties, who are concerned that the rules of procedure might be altered in unacceptable ways, usually insert a provision stating that the rules of procedure to be applied are those of the named Organisation that are in effect on the date the contract is signed.

As the Sino-American trade agreement indicates, Chinese are willing to prescribe other international rules of procedure instead of the ones of the named organization, such as using the UNICITRAL Arbitration rules under the administration of the Arbitration Institute of the Stockholm Chamber of Commerce.

China has been considering whether to revise the rules of procedure of its own arbitration institutions. The State Council did approve a change of name for the Foreign Trade Arbitration Commission which is now known as the Foreign Economic and Trade Arbitration Commission (FETAC). The new name is meant to symbolize the anticipated expansion of the Commission's work as it prepares to take cognizance of the disputes arising from the implementation of agreements and contracts in utilizing foreign funds, joint ventures, foreign technology, co-production by Chinese and foreign firms and compensation trade.

Although the language of the FETAC's rules of procedure, like its original name, is broad enough to encompass these transactions, some Chinese experts think that it may be appropriate to change the rules to take account specifically of China's recent participation in such transactions. It is also reported that the Commission will be enlarged in proportion to the expansion of its business scope.

Whether significant changes are made in the Commission's rules and practice remains unclear. One change that Chinese officials have considered would be to permit non-Chinese to serve as members of the arbitration tribunal body to be constituted under the FETAC. Foreign parties nonetheless prefer third-country arbitration because the rules have required that all arbitrators be chosen among the members of the Commission who are Chinese. Although FETAC is said to be opposed to national egoism in making use of arbitration to favour the party of their own nationality, foreigners would have more confidence in China if membership in the tribunal body was more broadly based.

Even if the rules of these Chinese institutions are not changed to allow foreign arbitrators, the contracting parties could provide for foreign representation on an arbitration tribunal, with the arbitration still being conducted in China, by inserting into their contract a clause that calls for UNICITRAL arbitration to take place in China.

Finality of Awards and Enforcement

Although Chinese contracts usually state that the arbitration award shall be final and binding upon the parties, they often make no provision for enforcement. China has concluded a number of bilateral trade agreements and navigation treaties that, like the Sino-American trade agreement, obligate the participating governments to strive to ensure that the arbitration awards are recognized and enforced by their competent authorities in accordance with applicable laws and regulations. Yet such provisions are general expressions that lack specific assurances and procedures. China hesitated for many years before deciding to join any of the international conventions for the enforcement of foreign arbitral awards. In 1986, China agreed to adhere to the United Nations Convention on the Recognition and Enforcement of Foreign Arbitral Awards, the so called New York Convention of 1958.

There has been little experience of arbitration awards in China trade. Although a number of contracts with Chinese companies have provided for arbitration in Stockholm, as of 31 December 1989 no award had ever been made by a Stockholm panel relating to any such contract. Moreover the number of FETAC awards each year, although increasing, is still very small. There is even less experience with respect to the enforcement of such awards. Chinese officials have asserted that, since the founding of the PRC, there has not been a single case in which China's courts have decreed the enforcement of an award involving foreign interests. This is said to be because Chinese foreign trade and maritime entities are state-owned enterprises that recognize that a Chinese arbitration award has the force of law and must be executed by the parties within the time prescribed. Thus there has been no need to seek court enforcement. Even before the promulgation of the Civil Procedure Code, Chinese officials claimed that, should a Chinese enterprise fail to respect a Chinese award, the people's courts would accept a petition from the other party for enforcement. Indeed the governmental decisions establishing China's two principal arbitration commissions state that their awards are to be final, that neither party shall bring an appeal for revision before a court of law or any other organization, and that Chinese courts shall, upon the request of a party, enforce the award of these commissions in accordance with the law.

Article 195 of the new Code provides and confirms this arrangement.

"When one of the parties concerned fails to comply with an award made by a foreign arbitration organisation of the PRC, the other party may request that the award be enforced in accordance with the provisions of this Code by the intermediate people's court in the place where the arbitration organisation is located or where the property is located."

How the courts will carry out this mandate (for example, what the scope of their review awards will be in an enforcement proceeding) is a matter of considerable interest to foreign companies.

Because the new forms of economic co-operation between China and the industrialized nations generally provide for arbitration outside China, the recognition and enforcement of foreign awards in China is a topic of even greater concern to foreigners. Chinese officials have long offered assurances that "Chinese corporations and enterprises will, in fact, execute foreign arbitral awards so long as they are fair and not in violation of the Chinese laws and policies." In the event of the non-execution of awards, foreigners have been advised in the past by the China Council for the Promotion of International Trade (CCPIT) not only to petition the Chinese government department concerned but also to request the assistance of the CCPIT in persuading the Chinese party to carry out the award, or to seek enforcement through the people's courts.

China's adherence to the New York Convention has become effective, and foreign awards covered by the Convention should be enforced upon presentation of the authenticated original award or a certified copy, and the original agreement with respect to arbitration, in addition to a certified Chinese translation of both documents. The Convention states that each contracting State shall recognize arbitral awards as binding and enforce them in accordance with the rules of procedure of the territory where the award is relied upon, subject to the conditions laid down in the Convention. For example, there shall not be imposed substantially more onerous conditions or higher fees or charges on the recognition or enforcement of arbitral awards to which the Convention applies than are imposed on the recognition or enforcement of domestic arbitral awards. Therefore, under the New York Convention, the conditions on enforcing a foreign award should not be more onerous than those provided in Article 195 of the Civil Procedure Code.

However when enforcement of an award is sought in court, the New York Convention does provide for certain defences on the basis of which the request for enforcement may be refused. These defences deal with specific legal issues such as incapacity of the parties, invalidity of the agreement, lack of notice, lack of opportunity to present one's case, rendering of an award outside the scope of the arbitral agreement, invalidity of the arbitral authority or procedure in light of the parties' agreement or the law of the country in which the award was made, and lack of binding force of the award. The other two more general issues are stated in the Convention:

(a) The subject matter of the difference is not capable of settlement by arbitration under the law of that country; or

(b) The recognition or enforcement of the award would be contrary to the public policy of that country.

Sub-paragraph (a) should not present an obstacle to the enforcement of arbitral awards, especially when the Chinese Civil Procedure Code provides for the enforcement by courts of arbitral awards with respect to disputes involving foreign nationals and contemplates arbitration as a means of settling disputes arising from foreign economic relations, trade, transportation, or even maritime affairs. On the other hand, sub-paragraph (b) of the Convention might be a problem for the enforcement of awards in China. The concept of public policy is notoriously flexible in China and occurs throughout Chinese law as an exception to various legal requirements.

There are still other arbitral awards which are not covered by the Convention, and their legal situation continues to be unclear. Even if a contract provides for enforcement of a foreign award "by any court of competent jurisdiction" or "in any ordinary court of law", it does not make clear the prerequisite judicial enforcement, and it cannot control the standards prescribed in the Civil Procedure Code for enforcement by Chinese courts. The Civil Procedure Code appears to preclude direct judicial enforcement of a foreign award. Article 195 only authorizes direct enforcement of an award made by a foreign arbitration organisation of the PRC.

The possibility of enforcing a foreign arbitral award on the basis of Chinese law apart from the Convention must be considered in connection with chapter 22, entitled "Judicial Assistance". This chapter is concerned with legal actions that Chinese courts and foreign courts may entrust each other to take on behalf of the other. Article 202 authorizes a Chinese court to reject a case entrusted to the court if it violates the sovereignty and security of the PRC.

> "In dealing with a judgment or award that has already been confirmed and that a foreign court has entrusted a people's court of the PRC to enforce, the people's court shall examine the judgment or award on the basis of an international treaty concluded or participated in by the PRC or in accordance with the principles of reciprocity and shall determine to recognize the legal effect of such judgment or award and enforce the same according to procedures prescribed by this Code if the court believes that such a judgment or award does not violate the basic principles of the laws of the PRC or the interests of our country's state and society. Otherwise the matter shall be returned to the foreign court." (Art. 205 of the Civil Procedure Code)

The structure appears to require that the enforcement of a foreign award not covered by the New York Convention be requested by a foreign court and suggests that the participation in that award by a foreign court is a prerequisite to enforcement in China. The court does not have to be necessarily the court of the jurisdiction in which the award was made. Moreover, it is not known what kind of awards are deemed to violate the basic principles of Chinese law or the interests of the Chinese society and state. These criteria give great latitude to the courts that may interpret these standards along the lines of the public policy exception applied by other countries in order to ensure maximum international judicial cooperation.

If seeking initial confirmation by a foreign court seems too burdensome or if a foreign court will not request enforcement, perhaps the only alternative open to the party seeking satisfaction of the award would be to initiate a regular civil suit in China and to rely on the award as evidence in support of its claim. In general, the Code stresses both international custom and reciprocity, and the ease with which foreign awards will be enforced in China even apart from the New York Convention will probably depend considerably on the treatment afforded to Chinese awards in the courts of foreign states.

Choice of Law

With the enactment of the Foreign Economic Contract Law, the parties had the right to choose the law applicable to the contract.

> "The parties to a contract may choose the governing law for the
> settlement of the disputes arising from the contract. In case no
> governing law is chosen by the parties, the law of the country
> which is most closely connected with the contract applies.
> The Chinese Foreign equity or contractual joint venture con-
> tracts and the contracts of Chinese Foreign cooperative exploi-
> tation and development of natural resources which are performed
> within the territory of the PRC shall be governed by the law of
> the PRC.
> The international practice may apply in case no rules are pro-
> vided for by the law of the PRC." (Art.5)

It is obvious that the intention behind this Article is to allow the parties
the autonomy to choose the governing law of the contract except under
certain circumstances listed in the Foreign Economic Contract Law or other
Chinese laws. The breadth of the principle is significantly limited in Article
5 itself, and by Articles 4 and 9 of the Foreign Economic Contract Law.
Article 4 of this law states that "Contracts must be made in accordance with
the law of the PRC and without prejudice to the public interests of the PRC."
Meanwhile, Article 9 provides that contracts that violate the laws of the PRC
or contravene the social or public interest are void.

The relationship of Article 5 to Articles 4 and 9 of the Foreign Economic
Contract Law is not clear. If Article 5 is interpreted so as to permit the parties
to a contract to choose their own law, the provisions of the Foreign
Economic Contract Law should cease to apply to that contract if the parties
choose to be governed by a foreign law. In practice, however, the principle
of autonomy of choice of law is never unrestricted in any country. Wherever
a contractual dispute is litigated or arbitrated, the forum will have its own
conflict rules regarding the proper law to be applied in relation to such
matters as formal validity and the capacity of the parties. It will also be
constrained by its own domestic laws in relation to the permissible subject-
matter and the provisions to a contract. Most jurisdictions will not apply a
foreign law where the application would be contrary to the public policy of
the forum. Similarly, the court of a forum may be constrained by its
domestic law to apply a particular rule of that domestic law in relation to a
contract, whether or not the contract is governed by foreign law.

In the context of China, this gives rise to two significant problems, the
first one being the scope of the public policy exception, and the second one
being the extent to which Chinese courts will consider that a contract is
governed by Chinese law. These problems become relevant when a contract

dispute is being heard in China, or when the enforcement of an award or judgment is sought in China. If the parties have chosen foreign law to be the governing law of the contract, it seems unlikely that a Chinese arbitral or judicial body will resolve the disputes by ignoring the Foreign Economic Contract Law and the Chinese laws. Chinese law will probably be applied, to some extent, (for example, determining whether a contract that is required to be approved by the state has been formally concluded prior to the grant of that approval) regardless of the parties' choice, although there is as yet relatively little information on which to anticipate the approach that the Chinese bodies will take or the conceptual basis that they will apply.

The failure of contracts to specify the applicability of Chinese law does not seem to trouble Chinese negotiators who are generally content if the contract does not mention anything about the governing law. This is especially true if the contracts call for arbitration in China for the settlement of disputes. The Chinese parties seem confident that Chinese arbitrators will apply private international law principles to any of the disputes that might come before them in a way that they will ensure due regard for the application of Chinese law.

It has been difficult for the Chinese parties to do without a Chinese governing law clause when negotiating with foreigners, especially in the construction field, whether by equity joint venture, a cooperative venture, or some other investment-type arrangement. Foreign entities consider the Chinese legal system as deficient in various respects in relation to contract disputes with foreigners. The Foreign Economic Contract Law, the Civil Law, and many other Chinese laws aimed at regulating and protecting the interests of foreigners have created an atmosphere of somewhat greater certainty. China lacks other laws and the application of the existing laws is still uncertain, in comparison with countries with a complete and well established legal structure such as France and Germany. Moreover, China does not systematically publish its judicial and arbitral decisions, and in any event it will be decades before the Chinese courts and arbitration tribunals have authoritatively interpreted the many important provisions of the evolving legislative framework.

In non-investment contracts, if no choice of law is made, much depends on the domestic law rules to which the arbitrators consider themselves subject. In the absence of a clear choice of law, the arbitrators will determine the proper law in the light of all the circumstances and their own conflict rules. If the arbitral tribunal is Chinese, it is clear that depending on the provisions of the Chinese law, they will choose the law of the country that has the closest connection to the contract. There is no simple answer to this question, but some factors like the origin of the parties, the place of performance, of signature, and of negotiation are relevant. Both the Foreign

Economic Contract Law and the Civil law state, however, that the tribunal should decide on the law of a particular country; the tribunal is not free to apply any principles it may think appropriate. Nevertheless, in both investment and non-investment contract disputes, if Chinese law is deemed to be applicable, the tribunal may resort to its understanding of "international practice" to the extent that it determines that Chinese law lacks relevant provisions.

Use of Arbitration in Practice

In China, as in any other socialist state based on Marxism- Leninism, international commercial arbitration is the creature of a government bureaucracy and the servant of a planned economy. Nevertheless, as part of its new policy of welcoming foreign investment, loans, and other forms of cooperation with business firms that generally are privately owned, the PRC has taken several steps to improve the facilities for resolving the disputes that will inevitably arise in the course of these developing relationships.

Consistent with its traditional preference for conciliation rather than arbitration in those cases where the parties cannot resolve a dispute by themselves, China has adopted the innovation of joint conciliation as a means of expanding conciliation's acceptability and efficacy. And in line with its long-standing preference for arbitration rather than litigation in those cases where conciliation is unsuccessful, China, in order to make arbitration more attractive to foreign business men, has usually agreed to arbitrate in third countries under the procedural rules of designated foreign institutions, even though China would prefer that arbitration take place in China or in the country of the defendant. Moreover, at least until China enacts a full set of commercial laws, it does not always insist that its non-investment contracts with foreign business partners prescribe Chinese law as the governing law but is often willing to leave the problem of applicable law to the arbitrators of any dispute. Chinese courts are now available to enforce arbitral awards in the case of Chinese awards and foreign awards enforceable under the New York Convention.

Such a reasonable and flexible system for dispute settlement can be expected to stimulate the economic transactions that China desires with the capitalist world.

Part V

EEC Law and Practice

Public procurement and 21 harmonisation

Laurence Gormley

Synopsis

This paper explains EC measures designed to address the problems created by the tendency of Member States to discriminate in favour of their own contractors and suppliers in the award of contracts. Reforms in public works contracts and public supplies contracts by EC Directives are analysed, and the respective attitudes of the Commission and The European Court of Justice to the operation of regional preferences following those reforms are examined. The paper also notes the extension of procurement regulation to the utilities and the proposals relating to the coverage of services. It further considers harmonisation of mechanisms for review and enforcement.

Introduction

Whilst harmonisation of laws is most often discussed, in many textbooks and elsewhere, in the context of the elimination of barriers to trade between Member States as a practical means of putting flesh on the bones of the four freedoms it should not be forgotten that it also has competition policy implications, seeking to ensure equal conditions of competition throughout the single domestic market which characterises the Community system.[1]

Public procurement has long been a byword for discrimination in favour of national products. If a salary review or increment were on offer for every time that the phrase "We've bought British as much as possible" was used in the public procurement field then Community lawyers would be rich men and women. Indeed some of them already are. Already in 1985 the White Paper on Completing the Internal Market[2] noted the widespread tendency of national authorities to keep their purchases and contracts within their own

---

1 For a discussion of how harmonisation of laws supplements the working out of the four freedoms see Kaptyen & VerLoren van Themaat: *Introduction to the Law of the European Communities* (2nd. ed., Kluwer, Deventer/Graham & Trotman, London, 1989) 467-469. In this work harmonisation of laws appears in the chapter on competition, rather than as an adjunct to the four freedoms. The competition point becomes clearer if Articles 101 & 102 EEC are also taken into account.

2 COM (85) 310 final.

country. The market partitioning in this sector is naturally incompatible
with the free movement of goods and services demanded by the EEC Treaty.
Standing practice of the Commission and a line of cases before the Court
show a firm attitude, particularly in relation to non-agricultural products.[3]

Characteristic problems in the field of public procurement include
ensuring adequate advertising; the transparency of procedures, and the
prohibition of the use of discriminatory standards. In future, the desirability
of standard Community-wide model contracts will also have to be addressed.

Initial harmonisation in the field of public procurement concentrated on
public works contracts and public supplies contracts and in particular on
three specific aspects:

- Compulsory advertising by tender notices in the Supplement to the
  Official Journal of the European Communities for tenders above
  certain thresholds
- The prohibition of discriminatory standards and technical requirements
- Transparency in selection and award procedures.

Reforms in Public Works Contracts

By the mid 1980s Directive 71/305[4] on award procedures for public
works contracts was in need of substantial adaptation for three main reasons:
various Member States had not properly transposed the Directive into their
national legal systems (and there must at the very least be a question about
the United Kingdom's use of circulars in this respect); sometimes Member
States did not advertise contracts when they were supposed to (not always
deliberately - initial estimates in respect of negotiated procedures could
prove to be too low after all), and at the international level developments
within the GATT brought about the need for adaptation of the existing
machinery.

Major changes to Directive 71/305 were made by Directive 89/440[5]
which had to be implemented by July 19, 1990, save by Spain, Portugal and
Greece which had until March 1, 1992. The definition of public works
contracts in Article 1(a) embraces contracts in writing, for pecuniary
interest," which have as their object either the execution, or both the

---

3 For a brief general overview see 52 Halsbury's Laws of England (4th. ed., London,
   1986) paras. 12.68-12.69 & 12.80).
4 O.J. English Special Edition 1971 (II), p. 682.
5 O.J. 1989 L 210/1. For the proposal for consolidation see O.J. 1992 C 46; SEC (91) 2360
   final.

execution and design of works ... [as defined] ... or a work ... [as defined] ..., or the execution by whatever means of a work corresponding to the requirements specified by the contracting authority". The definition of "a work" relates to the functional whole and thus Article 1(c) embraces "the outcome of building or civil engineering works taken as a whole that is sufficient of itself to fulfil an economic and technical function". Contracting authorities are also more precisely defined; direct subsidies by a contracting authority (as defined in the Directive) to bodies which fall outside the definition of a contracting authority, will bring the awarding body within the scope of the Directive for the purpose of the contract concerned.

The threshold of application has been raised from 1 million ECU to 5 million ECU, reflecting in part the legitimate view that trans-national contracts below a certain amount are not economically attractive (at least in most cases). The threshold cannot be got around by dividing into lots: if the aggregate value of the lots is at or above the threshold then the advertisement of each lot is required, except for lots valued at less than 1 million ECU as long as the total value of all such exempted lots is no greater than 20% of the total value of all the lots. Furthermore, the Directive now makes stricter provision in respect of negotiated procedures; prescribes more generous time-limits for the receipt of requests to participate in award procedures and for the delivery of tenders, and requires prior and retrospective advertising. The use of the TED data base should improve access to advertisements for prospective tenderers.

Finally, the Directive now also includes strengthened provisions on technical specifications. European standards and technical approvals or common technical specifications must now be used where they exist. The importance of preventing the discriminatory use of standards had, of course, been recognised in the original text of Directive 71/305 but the new text represents a considerable improvement on the old. More generally, in the field of public procurement but outside the scope of Directive 71/305, the application of Article 30 EEC to strike down blatant discrimination in the use of standards can be seen in Case 45/87 *Commission* v. *Ireland*[6] (the Dundalk case) in which the Court found that the refusal to examine or accept products conforming to national or international standards recognised in other Member States which offered equivalent guarantees of safety and suitability to those offered by the Irish standard concerned was incompatible with Article 30 EEC and incapable of any justification in Community law. A particular aggravating circumstance (although the infringement was committed by the exclusive specification of the standard in any event) was that only one company - by pure chance, of course, an Irish company - was

6 [1988] ECR 4929.

certified as supplying pipes of the diameter involved to the standard concerned.

The list of bodies covered by the scope of the Directive has just been revised by Decision 90/380.[7]

Reforms in relation to Public Supplies Contracts

Just as Directive 71/305 had to be revised, the Community provisions on the award of public supplies contracts, contained in Directive 77/62[8] have also been the subject of adaptation, not least because of the Community's international obligations in the GATT, by Directive 88/295.[9] This had to be implemented in most Member States by the beginning of 1989 (Spain, Portugal and Greece had until March 1, 1992).

Again, the definition of contracts covered is strengthened, so that Article 1 (a) embraces contracts in writing, for pecuniary interest, "involving the purchase, lease, rental or hire purchase, with or without an option to buy, of products .... The delivery of such products may include siting and installation operations." The definition of contracting authorities is unchanged, save for the bodies corresponding to those covered by the general definition; here Annex I has been updated. Whilst the threshold of 200,000 ECU is maintained, for bodies covered by the GATT procurement arrangements the threshold is set at 130,000 ECU. Again, there are provisions relating to open, restricted and negotiated award procedures. Particularly in relation to the use of restricted procedures there are certain substantial differences from the regime governing public works contracts. There are also differences in the advance advertising requirements in cases covered by the GATT procurement arrangements, with advance indication of the total contracts estimated at a value of 750,000 ECU or over, which the authorities covered by the GATT arrangements intend to offer during their financial year. This information is broken down by product and industry. Again, there are firmer provisions relating to the use of standards and technical specifications. The importance of European standards, technical approvals and common technical specifications in the field of supplies as well as works is self-evident. Again, the use of the TED data base is expected to improve access for prospective tenderers.

7   O.J. 1990 L 187/55.
8   O.J. 1977 L 13/1.
9   O.J. 1988 L 127/1. For the draft proposal for consolidation see the Advisory Committee documents CCO/92/35; CC/92/35, Brussels 1 April 1992.

Regional Preferences

In both the works and the supplies directives there are now specific provisions relating to contracts which have as their objective "the reduction of regional disparities and the promotion of job creation in regions whose development is lagging behind and in declining industrial regions."[10] However, this derogation lasts only until the end of 1992 and the provisions concerned must in any event be compatible with the Treaty and with the Community's international obligations. The Commission's thinking, at least on internal aspects, in this area is set out in its Communication on the regional and social aspects of public procurement.[11]

However, several important judgments relating to regional preferences have recently been handed down by the Court of Justice. Preference for tenderers offering to take people from the lists of the long-term unemployed was considered, before the modification of Directive 71/305 by Directive 89/440 and before the Commission's Communication, in Case 31/87 *Gebroeders Beentjes B.V.* v. *Staat der Nederlanden.*[12] The Court accepted that it was permissible to include a condition in an invitation to tender about employment of people registered at a local office as long as there was no discrimination on the ground of nationality involved (i.e. anyone of any Community nationality there registered must be eligible).

In Case C-113/89 *Rush Portugesa Lda* v. *Office National d'Immigration*[13] the Court dealt with an attempt to penalise a Portuguese firm for bringing its own labour force from Portugal to perform a contract in the West of France. According to French law only the Office National d'Immigration was allowed to recruit nationals of third countries in France. In virtually all sectors (save for those covered by Article 221 of the Act of Spanish and Portuguese Accession) the freedom to provide services between Portugal and the other Member States applies since accession. The free movement of workers was, however, subject to a transitional regime. The Court had little difficulty in concluding that the right at issue was the right of the firm to provide services, not the right of free movement of workers. Accordingly, it upheld the right of the firm to use its own workforce (it being clear that the case concerned a genuine workforce, not a firm which had recruited temporary workers in an attempt to circumvent the restrictions on the free movement of workers laid down in the Act of Spanish and Portuguese Accession).

10 (Art.29a of Dir. 71/305 as amended by Dir. 89/440; Art. 26 of Dir. 77/62 as amended by Dir. 88/295.)
11 COM (89) 400 final, O.J. 1989 C 311/7.
12 [1988] ECR 4635.
13 [1990] ECR I1417.

The final contribution of the Court on the question of regional preferences is contained in Case C-21/88 *Du Pont de Nemours Italiana SpA* v. *Unità Sanitaria Locale no. 2 di Carrara.*[14] Italian legislation obliged local authorities to obtain at least 30% of their supplies requirements from companies established in the Mezzogiorno. The Court found such a condition to be incompatible with Article 30 EEC and incapable of justification under the rule of reason or Article 36 EEC. There was no doubt that products from other Member States were the victims of discrimination (which is, it will be remembered, a sufficient, but not necessary criterion for the infringement of Article 30 EEC). The argument that Italian companies in other regions were also hit, was advanced to no avail. The Court also observed that even if the preference system could be considered to be a state aid that did not save it from being caught by Article 30 EEC.

The whole question of regional preferences in public procurement is acutely sensitive in political terms and more so in the light of the commitment to economic and social cohesion introduced into the EEC Treaty by the Single European Act and now further developed in the Treaty on European Union. Yet the Court's message is plain: the fundamental principles of the Treaty cannot be overridden willy-nilly by national measures. Existing case-law[15] also makes it clear that the Community is bound by those principles, save in so far as expressly or impliedly authorised by the Treaty. It remains to be seen how the Court will view in due course the necessary compromises which may be made between these fundamental principles and measures taken to promote economic and social cohesion.

Coverage of the utilities

The Council has now adopted Directive 90/531[16] which regulates the procurement of works and supplies by the utilities.[17] A particularly controversial point in Directive 90/531 is the provision dealing with third country tenderers.[18] Its aim is clearly to provide an incentive to third countries to enter into bilateral or multilateral arrangements with the Community to

---

14 [1990] ECR I-889.
15 E.g. Cases 80 & 81/77 *Société Les Commissionnaires Réunis Sàri et al.* v. *Receveur des Douanes* [1978] ECR 927; Case 37/83 *Rewe-Zentral AG* v. *Direktor der Landwirtschaftskammer Rheinland* [1984] ECR 1229 and Case 218/82 *Commission* v. *Council* [1983] ECR 4063.
16 O.J. 1990 L 297/1. See for attached commentary Trepte 1 Utilities Law Review 158.
17 This Directive applies from 1 January 1993, although greece and Portugal have until 1 January 1998 and Spain until 1 January 1996.
18 Art. 29. A proposal for an extension of Directive 90/531 to embrace contracts for the provision of services has been presented by the Commission, see COM(91)347 final.

ensure comparable and effective access for Community undertakings to the markets of third countries. The preference for tenders using products originating in the Community thus operates, within certain limits, against tenderers from countries which have not reached an access agreement with the Community. The working of the provision is to be kept under annual review and modifications may be made by the Council, acting on the basis of a qualified majority on a proposal from the Commission, in the light of developments.[19]

Coverage of Services

The next item on the Commission's harmonisation programme in this field is the procurement of services, both generally and in the sectors of the utilities. A draft proposal on the general procurement of services is at an advanced stage and is likely to be adopted by the Council in the near future;[20] the question of services and the utilities is now under discussion in the Council[21]. Procurement of services in the public sector amounts to a significant proportion of all public procurement (about 5% of the Community's GDP) and the same tendency to reserve services procurement to national providers applies here just as it has applied in respect of works and supplies. The proposal faced particular drafting problems, because the range of service sectors to be covered is so broad and the range of interests involved is extremely diverse. Moreover, as has frequently happened in relation to mutual recognition of qualifications, intra-professional wrangling is as much a problem as inter-profession wrangling.

Harmonisation of remedies in national law

Despite the fact that the EEC Treaty provides the Commission with supervisory tools, it has become apparent that adequate means of redress for breach of Community law - or indeed national law implementing that law - needs to be guaranteed in all the Member States. It is with this in mind that the Council adopted Directive 89/665 on remedies relating to the award of public works and supplies contracts.[22] It applies to the fields covered by Directives 71/305 and 77/62 and had to be implemented by 21 December 1991. Member States are obliged to ensure that decisions relating to contract

19 Art. 29(b).
20 A common position was adopted by the Council on 25 February 1992.
21 See note 18, supra.
22 O.J. 1989 L 395/33.

award procedures covered by these two directives can be reviewed effectively and as rapidly as possible for infringements of Community law in the
field or national provisions implementing that law. There must be no
discrimination between undertakings claiming injury in an award procedure
as a result of the distinction made in the directive between national law
implementing Community law and other national rules. This copes with
arguments that particular national rules were not intended to give effect to
the directive.

Review procedures are open, subject to detailed national rules, "at least
to any person having or having had an interest in obtaining a particular
public supply or public works contract and who risks being harmed by an
alleged infringement." The person may be required to have previously
notified the contracting authority of the alleged infringement and of his
intention to seek review. Remedies which must be available include
damages; interim measures to correct the alleged infringement or prevent
further damage to the interests concerned, including measures to suspend
the award procedure or the implementation of a contracting authority's
decision, and the setting aside of unlawful decisions (such as discriminatory
specifications in tender documents). The review procedures themselves
need not automatically suspend the award procedure. The review body is to
be independent and may be judicial in character; if it is not judicial then
appeal must lie to a body capable of making references for preliminary
rulings under Article 177 EEC and reasons for the review body's decisions
must be given in writing. Review bodies may have regard to the balance of
convenience and in particular the public interest. Thus if the negative effects
of interim measures would outweigh the benefits, they may refuse to grant
the measures. Any decision on interim measures is of course without
prejudice to any final decision on the merits of a complaint.

Directive 89/665 also establishes a corrective mechanism whereby the
Commission can intervene in cases, prior to the award of the contract, in
which it believes that a clear and manifest infringement of Community
provisions in the field has been committed. It notifies the Member State and
- for the first time - the contracting authority of its reasons and the Member
State is then obliged to notify the Commission within 21 days that the
infringement has been terminated, or provide reasons why it has not, or that
the award procedure has been suspended either by the contracting authority
on its own initiative or as a result of an order of a review body. Reasons for
not suspending may include pending judicial or other review. If the award
procedure is suspended, any reactivation or new award procedure relating
in whole or in part to the same matter must be notified to the Commission.

Given that the utilities are now coming within the scope of Community
rules, the Council has just adopted Directive 92/13 which deals with

remedies relating to procurement by the utilities[23]. Broadly this follows the general remedies structure set out above. A new feature, however, relates to certain types of claims for damages. If a claim is made for damages representing the costs of preparing a bid or taking part in an award procedure, the claimant has to prove the infringement of Community law in the procurement field or of national rules implementing that law; the claimant also has to prove that he would have had a real chance of winning the contract and that, as a consequence of that infringement that chance was adversely affected. The claimant would not have to prove that in the absence of the infringement he would have been awarded the contract. On this point Directive 89/665 is silent. In the Commission's proposal the amount of such costs was deemed to be 1% of the value of the contract unless the claimant proves that his costs were higher. This proposal to fix a deemed amount was not, however, accepted[24].

Another innovation in Directive 92/13 is the system of attestation as a means of ensuring compliance. This was introduced not least because of difficulties in certain legal orders of applying public law remedies to private law bodies - various utilities are public operations in one form or another in some member states whereas in others they are entirely private. Given the industrial and public service character of the utilities and the requirement that a continuous service to the public be provided it was felt that classic remedies would not always be appropriate. Particular examples are suspension of contract award procedures and the setting aside of decisions.

The attestation system as originally conceived by the Commission meant, briefly, that Member States could decide to depart from the classic remedies scheme as regards suspension and the setting aside of decisions for any category of undertakings objectively defined, provided that the entities concerned were subject to at least annual attestation of their procurement procedures and practices by an independent qualified and recognised person and, in addition, effective interlocutory remedies were still available. A review body faced with a claim involving an entity subject to attestation would have been able to declare in interlocutory proceedings at any stage that an infringement has been or risks being committed. However, the entity concerned would be left to decide whether it corrects the infringement or pays a financial penalty instead. This idea is partially based on the dwangsom concept well-known in particular in Belgium and Holland. It differs from that concept, though, because the financial penalty is a fixed sum, not a periodic penalty and would extinguish any further claim to recovery of costs taken into account by the review body when the order was

---

23 O.J. 1992 L 76/14. This Directive applies from the same dates as the Utilities Directive (see Note 17, supra).
24 For the proposal see COM (90) 297 final.

made. A review body would have been able to make payment of the penalty conditional upon a final decision being reached that the infringement has indeed been committed. Here too, the financial penalty was designed to be dissuasive and cover at least any bid costs or costs of participating in the procedure incurred by the person seeking review. The amount of costs was deemed to be 1% of the value of the contract unless proof were adduced that the costs were greater.

Directive 92/13 still makes provision for an attestation procedure and for measures other than suspension or set aside but the automatic link between attestation and the remedies available has not been accepted. Thus contracting entities may have recourse to the system of attestation but there are no consequences set out in the Directive as to the remedies available. Given, though, that Member States have the choice of using suspension and set aside or the dwangsom concept (as a particular sum rather than a periodic penalty; the proposal that the sum be fixed at 1% was, as with the damages for loss of chance, not accepted) it will be possible for them to provide for a separate regime for contracting entities which opt for the attestation system. In an event, whichever set of remedies the Member State chooses, it must be possible for persons injured by the infringement to be awarded damages.

Directive 92/13 also establishes a conciliation procedure, using the good offices of a conciliator drawn from a list of independent persons accredited for that purpose drawn up by the Commission, following consultation with the appropriate Advisory Committee, to seek a non-litigious means of dispute settlement. The procedure is filtered, though, to avoid requests for conciliation becoming a source of abuse. A request for conciliation must be made to the Commission or the competent authority of a Member State; in the latter case the request is then forwarded to the Commission as soon as possible. The procedure is voluntary and the parties designate additional conciliators who may invite experts acceptable to the parties to work with them. The conciliation procedure is without prejudice to the Commission's right to take infringement proceedings or to invoke the corrective mechanism provided for in Chapter 3 of Directive 92/13. It is also without prejudice to the rights of the persons requesting the conciliation procedure, of the contracting entity, or of any other person.

The availability of appropriate remedies in the Member States has had to be guaranteed by legislation, not least because of the unsatisfactory state of affairs in various Member States (including the United Kingdom) about obtaining damages for breach of Community law. However, the directives do not affect the right of the Commission or a Member State, under Articles 169 and 170 EEC respectively, to bring infringement procedures for breach of Community law.

Conclusions

The Community's activities in the field of public procurement have undergone a transformation in recent years, designed to ensure greater compliance with Community law and open up the Member States' activities in this important sector of the economy. Those efforts are to be welcomed as improving the competitive chances of Community industry as a whole and as an important and useful step in eliminating obstacles to market interpenetration within the Community and cosy arrangements which mean that the taxpayer does not get best value for money in procurement.

Of course it must be remembered that the scheme of coverage of procurement practice is as yet not complete. Indeed in some ways it never will be complete as there is no intention to remove all discretion for Member States in this field. In such circumstances contracting entities are free, provided that they remain within the limits imposed by Community law, to apply their own evaluation and even criteria - as was demonstrated in *Beentjes* although they must be transparent in so doing. The Community's harmonisation activities have established a partial harmonisation and co-ordination but are a long way from occupying the whole field in the sense of depriving contracting entities of all freedom of action. In particular, proper commercial and suitability judgments remain in the hands of contracting entities. Areas such as common standard contracts, too, remain untouched by specific secondary Community law. However, as the Dundalk case shows, the general and specific rules of the EEC Treaty must be respected, even in areas in which the Community legislator has not acted.

Much of the success of the harmonisation programme in this field will depend on proper compliance[25] and as the legislative programme goes into its final phase (with the important questions of developments in the GATT outstanding in particular) the balance of resources will need to shift in due course from policy to enforcement. Given the considerable achievements of the public procurement directorate originally under the leadership of Robert Coleman, fine building blocks are available on which the two units, now in a directorate with wider responsibilities under different leadership, can complete their edifice and maintain its well-being.

Conclusions and proposals

While this paper discusses particular aspects of procurement and competition issues, several more general observations may be included in the conclusions section.

25 See, generally, the Reports of the 14th. FIDE Congress, Madrid, 1990, Vol. I.

First, there is a perception amongst some of those present that the 1992 programme is nothing more than a marketing exercise for the Commission. This is somewhat wide of the mark. If you talk to old Brussels hands you will find that they frequently refer to a golden age, when Hallstein was President of the Commission, in which the Commission was dynamic, pro-active and the motor behind integration in the Community. The White Paper of 1985 with its political deadline of December 31, 1992 appeared - at least in the late Eighties - to recreate something of that golden age. The 1992 programme was certainly not perceived inside the Commission as a PR exercise; rather it was (and is) seen as a political, economic and socially-orientated programme addressing most of the remaining obstacles to the completion of the establishment of the common market required by Article 2 EEC. I say "most of the remaining obstacles" because the emphasis in the White Paper is on the elimination of barriers to trade within the Community, characteristic of the definition of the internal market subsequently incorporated as Article 8A into the EEC Treaty, rather than on the equalisation of conditions of competition which is the additional requirement of a common market.[26] The White Paper was seen as a remotivating and reinvigorating cure for Eurosclerosis but certainly not as mere window-dressing. David Marks[27] and I accordingly part company on that point.

Let me turn to some points more specifically relevant for construction. Will the U.K. market find more foreign participants? I was interested to hear that whilst some local authorities have had no response from abroad in years to invitations to tender published in the Official Journal, there have been instances of Dutch companies being awarded care and maintenance contracts for municipal parks and gardens. Transfrontier procurement in the public sector and concerning the utilities may be expected to increase substantially in the next few years. Some people will undoubtedly seek to get around national preference by establishing joint ventures or subsidiaries. In other cases assistance in opening up markets will have to be sought by complaints to the Commission. So far in the procurement field the tendency to prefer national goods, supplies and services has been particularly marked - as a close look at the activities of the Offshore Supplies Office over the years will demonstrate. On many occasions the Commission has taken action against the United Kingdom and other Member States to seek the revocation of conscious or unconscious policies or practices. In the Ninth Round of offshore licensing the UK was forced to remove criteria such as the contribution to the development of the UK economy and the extent to

---

26 Kapteyn & VerLoren van Themaat *Introduction to the Law of the European Communities* (2nd. ed., Kluwer Law & Taxation, Deventer/Graham & Trotman, London, 1989, 78).

27 Paper 22.

which UK goods and services would be or had been used.[28] Local authorities tried to "do their bit" to support UK industry by giving car loans on preferential terms to their employees who bought British cars. This too was incompatible with Community law and the Government had to carry the can, although the Commission withdrew infringement proceedings once the last of the Councils backed down.

In Community law matters, local interests, sensitivities and political pressures are often to the fore, as various of the cases mentioned above demonstrate. Two of these cases have implications for movement of labour.[29] In *Beentjes*, you will recall, the Court accepted a special condition in the invitation to tender that a certain percentage of the workforce had to be recruited from the long-term unemployed registered at a particular local unemployment office. That is, when all is said and done, preference for a local labour force. The Court's view that this was acceptable as long as there was no infringement of Article 7 EEC (discrimination on grounds of nationality) may be realistic in Belgium, Holland, parts of Germany, Denmark, Italy and France or in border regions of Ireland and Northern Ireland, border regions where substantial transfrontier labour movements may be expected; in somewhere like mainland UK or in the heart of Poitiers (well-known for the video clearance saga) or Saxony such a policy amounts to little more than a local grab measure of the worst sort. The importance of *Rush Portugesa* has already been dealt with above. A further example of the Court striking down a long-standing local grab measure can be seen in Case C-21/88 *Du Pont de Nemours Italiana SpA* v. *Unità Sanitarià Locale no. 2 di Carrara*.[30]

As the Dundalk water pipeline case[31] shows, local authorities and procurement entities in general will have to be particularly careful in drafting contracts and invitations to tender, all the more so as bidders become more aware of their rights under Community law and the remedies directive (and the directive on remedies for the utilities) take effect. The use of standards as a weapon of protectionism within the Community is clearly now off limits for the public sector even on the basis of Article 30 EEC alone and will be off limits on the basis of Community procurement law for the utilities.

28 See Hailsham of St. Marylebone (ed.) 52 Halsbury's Laws of England (4th ed., London, 1986) para. 12.80; Commission Press Release IP (85) 303; Financial Times, July 8, 1985, p. 2.

29 Case 31/87 *Gebroeders Beentjes BV* v. *Staat der Nederlanden* [1988] ECR 4635 and Case C-113/89 *Rush Portugesa Lda* v. *Office national d'immigration* [1990] ECR I-1418.

30 [1990] ECR I-889.

31 Case 45/87 *Commission* v. *Ireland* [1988] ECR 4939, see Gormley (1989) 14 EL Rev. 156.

The adoption of the proposal on the procurement of services and the consolidation of existing Directives will complete the legislative programme (save for any amendments resulting from the GATT procurement negotiations) envisaged in the White Paper for procurement. Thereafter the emphasis will shift to enforcement and it is to be hoped that enforcement will maintain the momentum of recent years rather than return to the doldrums occasioned by lack of political resolution in the years prior to 1986.

Public procurement rules 22
and their effect in the
UK construction industry

David Marks

Synopsis

Having outlined current UK practice on public contracts, the paper sets out the principal EC directives affecting public procurement, namely works, supplies, utilities and services, and the mechanisms for their enforcement. The author examines potential implications for the principal parties in the UK industry: contractors, suppliers, construction professionals and contracting authorities.

Introduction

The purpose of this paper is to consider aspects of public procurement from a number of perspectives. The first of these is from the perspective of UK law and practice: as will be seen there is little or no UK public procurement law. The second is from the viewpoint of EC law and the nature of the various EC directives actual or contemplated on works, services and supplies, the utilities sectors, as well as their enforcement. This is a much more extensive task as the legislation is voluminous and detailed. The third is to assess how the UK construction industry will be affected by all this and to balance what might be described as the great expectations of the EC on the one hand and industry scepticism on the other.

That the EC has legislated so prolifically on procurement indicates the importance it attaches to an open public procurement sector in realising a single market. Considerable emphasis was placed on public procurement in the 1985 White Paper which outlined the single market programme[1]. For those interested in some statistics the figures involved are truly immense. According to EC studies[2] public procurement could be worth over 500bn. ECUs (about 15% of EC GNP) annually and is thought to exceed the value of all trade between member states in the EC. Furthermore the loss of economies of scale resulting from national preference is thought to be costing around 20bn. ECUs per annum. National preference is considered to be responsible for low import penetration levels of under 0.2%.

---

1 *Completing the Internal Market.* White Paper from the Commission to the European Council, June 1985.
2 Paolo Cecchini, *The European Challenge 1992 - The Benefits of a Single Market,* 1988.

The EC argues that low import/export activity in procurement is due to national preference. The sceptics believe that this may only be part of the picture and that legislation designed to remove national preference and win business opportunities in the public sector across the EC is optimistic.

Current UK law and practice

Leaving aside the effect of the various EC directives on UK practice, there is little general law on public contracts. This is a great contrast with many continental legal systems, some of which have extensive codes on the subject and indeed have a strong and separate tradition of administrative or public as opposed to private law.

Competitive tender has increasingly been addressed in local government legislation. There is a statutory requirement that local authorities should set out formal contracting procedures which would usually involve competitive tender[3]. Some local government legislation expressly requires authorities to give reasons for their procurement decisions and prohibits contract awards based on certain non-commercial grounds[4]. Indeed local authority activities in the procurement area have increasingly been the subject of judicial review[5]. At central government level the value for money principle is overseen informally by the Treasury where competitive tendering is encouraged as a general concept. However, there is little to say about how it should be conducted. Nonetheless, the question of procedures has been addressed by the National Joint Consultative Committee for Building (NJCC) which brings together many interested parties in the UK contracting sector. In conjunction with the Department of the Environment the NJCC has drawn up various Codes of Procedure on procurement arrangements[6]. These are widely used but are no more than codes of practice.

The NJCC Code of Procedure for Single Selective Tendering illustrates the approach. It recommends the use of "selective" (in EC parlance "restricted") tendering to reduce contractors' exposure to lost tender costs and to decrease the administrative burden on the contracting authority. This is based on approved contractor lists. Generally there should be no more than six contractors involved. Then usually the successful candidate is the lowest bid. It is recognised that post tender negotiation is often appropriate

---

3   Local Government Act 1972, s.135.
4   Local Government Act 1988, s.20.
5   eg R v. Enfield LBC ex parte T.F. Unwin (Roydon) Ltd. (1989) 46 BLR 1; R v. Islington LBC ex parte Building Employers Federation (1989) 45 BLR 45.
6   NJCC Codes of Procedure Single Stage Selective Tendering: Two Stage Selective Tendering; Selective Tendering for Design and Build.

and similarly that the lowest bidder should not always receive the award. Whilst these are rules of guidance they do not generally help a disappointed contractor learn why he did not obtain a contract or provide him with recompense where discrimination has occurred.

In contrast with this loose domestic law framework the EC directives provide a detailed procedural code to be followed in those cases where they apply. This represented an innovation for UK law and practice on the UK's accession to the EC in 1973. Directive 71/305[7] required competitive tendering by publication in the Official Journal of the European Community of public works with a value of over 1m. ECUs (£700,000 approx.) and this became a Community obligation in the UK from 1st July 1973 and was implemented by ministerial circular[8]. Subsequently Directive 77/62[9] applied to supplies of goods as opposed to works with a qualifying value threshold of 200,000 ECUs (£140,000 approx.). These rules left out the water, energy and transport sectors for supplies and works and the telecommunications sector for supplies. Services were altogether untouched and there were no specific enforcement rules or remedies.

What kind of impact did these rules have on bringing EC competition into public procurement in the UK? The answer is likely to be very little judging from the experience of the Property Services Agency (PSA) over this period:

> "...it must also be said that in 1987, for example, there were 7000 works projects advertised in the Official Journal. It may be that the true figure ought to have been larger. Nevertheless, those 7000 advertisements provided 7000 opportunities for non-national contractors to tender.
>
> The evidence is that few did so. PSA's own experience certainly bears this out. Despite the scale of the PSA's operations, the number of non-British contractors who have responded to Official Journal advertisements can be counted on the fingers of both if not one hand. Of course, the fact that an advertisement has been placed does not itself guarantee that there is not discrimination, either within its terms or at subsequent stages. But this evidence suggests that the factors which govern the frequency of cross-border contracting in construction works go much deeper than the superficial issue of compliance with the procedural rules of the Works and Supplies Directives."[10]

7 OJ L185/5, 16.8.71.
8 eg Joint Circular Department of the Environment 59.73 and Welsh Office 109/73, 11.5.73 concerning Directive 71/305.
9 OJ L13/1 15.1.77.
10 Michael Wanstall, *The Public Procurement Directives - a procurer's view.* Building Technical File No.29 April 1990 p.37.

It is therefore reasonable to summarise the position by saying that there is, first, little UK law on public procurement; and second, initial EC rules on the subject apparently did little to encourage bids in the UK from non-UK firms.

The EC Directives

Introduction

Before outlining the provisions in the main directives it may be helpful to summarise what subjects are to be covered and where individual measures currently stand. This is set out in the following table:

	General Sectors	Water, Energy Transport and Telecom
Works	Basic text: Directive 71/305[11] Last amended by Directive 89/440[12] to have been implemented by 19.7.90	Directive adopted 17.9.90
Supplies	Basic text: Directive 77/62[13]. Last amended by Directive 88/295[14] to have been implemented 1.1.89	Implementation by member states end 1992 (covers both works and supplies)
Services	Official Commission proposal announced September 1990	Official Commission expected by end 1990
Enforcement	Directive 89/665[15] to be implemented by 1.12.91	Official Commission proposal July 1990[16]

11 Ibid n.7 supra.
12 OJ L210/1 21.7.89.
13 Ibid n. 9 supra.
14 OJ L127/1 20.5.88
15 OJ L395/33 30.12.89
16 COM (90) 297 final 30.7.90

The basic texts on works, supplies and services all have a number of common factors including:

- the reiteration of the basic principle in Article 7 of the EEC Treaty prohibiting discrimination against other EC nationals;
- a qualifying value threshold for contracts above which contracts are to be advertised by specific procedures;
- a distinction between open, restricted and negotiated (i.e. single tender) procedures;
- the publication of tender notices in the Official Journal of the European Communities in a prescribed form;
- the promotion of EC as opposed to national standards;
- the imposition of time limits for publication and response
- the publication of award notices;
- selection on the basis of lowest price or the most economically advantageous tender; and
- the preservation of compliance records by the contracting authority.

A number of distinctions need to be understood when working through the various directives. First, there is the sector: does it concern certain utility functions or not (i.e. in water, energy, transport or telecommunications?). Second, there is the nature of the contract: does it concern works, supplies (goods) or services? Third, some directives lay down rules on how tendering procedures should operate; others deal with methods of enforcing their compliance. These different aspects will be examined briefly in turn.

General Sectors

Works

Directive 71/305[17] on works contracts was last amended by Directive 89/440[18] with an implementation date of 19th July, 1990 for a majority of member states. The qualifying threshold is currently 5m. ECUs (£3.5m. approx)[19]. There are provisions preventing contracts being split to bring them below the threshold[20]. A wide variety of works contracts are caught[21] and there are specific provisions dealing with public works concessions[22].

17 Ibid n. 7 supra
18 Ibid n.12 supra
19 Directive 71/305 as amended Article 4a.
20 Ibid Article 4a.
21 Ibid Article 1(a).
22 Ibid Article 1b.

Significantly, certain projects part funded by the public sector to the extent of more than 50% are also covered[23].

Contracting entities are now required to publish an indicative notice giving the essential characteristics of qualifying works contracts following decisions to approve the planning of the works[24]. When inviting tenders negotiated procedures may only be used in exceptional circumstances[25]. The choice is essentially between open and restricted procedures[26]. In a restricted procedure, between 5 and 20 contractors should normally be invited[27].

Time limits for receipt of tenders are 52 days from despatch of the notice to the Official Journal of the European Communities in the case of open procedures[28] and in the case of restricted procedures expressions of interest are to be made within 37 days of despatch with a further 40 days to tender from the issue of the invitation to participate[29]. There are strict provisions on technical standards requiring the use of European standards. When this is not possible and national standards are used, the words "or equivalent" must appear and they must not be employed in a discriminatory fashion[30]. It is possible for an unsuccessful contractor to obtain reasons for rejection of a tender within 15 days of request to the contracting authority[31] and the contracting authority is required to prepare a report to be available for Commission inspection on the award of each contract to include reasons for decisions taken[32]. Post tender negotiations between candidates and the contracting authorities are prohibited[33].

Supplies

Directive 77/62[34] on supplies was last amended by Directive 88/295[35] and was to be implemented by 1st January 1989.

The qualifying threshold is currently at 200,000 ECUs (£140,000 approx), but is set at 134,000 ECUs (£93,800 approx) for supplies to

23 Ibid Article 1a.
24 Ibid Article 12.1
25 Ibid Article 5.3.
26 Ibid Article 5.1 and 5.2.
27 Ibid Article 22.2.
28 Ibid Article 13.1.
29 Ibid Article 14.
30 Ibid Article 10
31 Ibid Article 5a.1.
32 Ibid Article 5a.3.
33 Ibid Article 5.4 and annexed Statement of Council and Commission.
34 Ibid n.9 supra.
35 Ibid n.14 supra.

specified central government authorities under GATT requirements[36]. Again, negotiated procedures are the exception[37], time limits for open and restricted procedures are the same as for works[38] and European standards are to be preferred[39].

Services

So far there are no rules on the procurement of services, although a formal Commission proposal has just been announced[40]. The latest Commission working draft available at the time of writing categorises services into two lists: those in Annex 1A and 1B respectively[41]. Where a contract consists predominantly of services under Annex 1A, these are subject to the proposal's full tendering procedures, whereas if the contract concerns mainly Annex 1B services these are only covered by general requirements on standards and on contract award notices[42]. Value thresholds are set at 200,000 ECUs (£140,000 approx) but at 400,000 ECUs (£280,000 approx) in the case of construction related services, i.e., architectural, engineering, planning and similar technical services, all of which fall in Annex 1A[43]. There are also specific rules for design contests where the execution of the project concerned would be over 5m. ECUs[44].

As with the works and supplies directives, open or restricted procedures will be the usual tender method and negotiated procedures will be the exception[45].

1.2 Utilities sectors

A number of utility sectors were left outside the scope of the earlier works and supplies directives principally because the entities running these utilities did not have a common legal form[46]. These sectors might be run by

---

36 Directive 77/62 as amended Article 5.1(a). The GATT threshold was modified for the period 1.1.90 - 31.12.91 by OJ C 18.3 25.1.90.
37 Ibid Article 6.
38 Ibid Articles 10 and 11.
39 Ibid Article 7.
40 Announced 19.9.90. Most recent available Commission working draft CCO/90/31. 17.4.90.
41 Ibid Article 9.
42 Ibid Article 10.
43 Ibid Article 8.
44 Ibid Article 15.
45 Article 13.3.
46 Directive 71/305 as amended Article 4, Directive 77/62 as amended Article 2.2.

public companies in some member states and by the state itself in others. A fresh mechanism was needed to deal with this type of situation.

The mechanism adopted was to clarify specific activities which are either state-run or which are somehow licensed to operate by the state. The precise legal form of the contracting entity therefore ceases to be relevant.

1.2.1 Works and Supplies

A directive dealing simultaneously with works and supplies in the utilities area was adopted on 17th September 1990 and implementing legislation was required to be in place in the member states by 1st July, 1992[47].

The thresholds are 5m. ECUs (£3.5m. approx) in the case of all works and 400,000 ECUs (£280,000 approx) for supplies, save in the case of telecommunications supplies where the higher 600,000 ECUs (£420,000 approx) applies[48]. The principal difference with the rules in the general sectors is a more flexible procedure. Contracting entities can choose calls for competition in three main ways: by a periodic indicative notice, by a list qualification system or by the publication of invitations to tender under the usual open or restrictive procedures[49]. There are specific provisions dealing with tenders of non-EC origin. These will be tenders where more than 50% of the value of the tender is manufactured outside the EC. There is positive discrimination in favour of EC tenders where the EC bid is up to 3% higher. The application of these rules to particular countries will be linked to reciprocal access of EC tenderers to that country's markets[50].

1.2.2 Services

The Commission is at the time of writing preparing proposals on utilities services anticipated by the end of 1990. They are expected to draw upon the principles established in the utilities works and supplies proposal and in the general services proposal[51].

47 Text unavailable at the time of writing. It is understood to differ little from the re-examined proposal on the procurement procedures of entities operating in the water, energy, transport and telecommunication sectors. COM (90) 301 final - 12.7.90.
48 Ibid Article 12.
49 Ibid Article 16.
50 Ibid Article 29.
51 Discussion paper CCO/90/28 23.4.90.

1.3 Enforcement

There has been general difficulty in enforcing public procurement rules because many breaches simply pass undetected. Also the procedure for enforcement by the Commission against the infringing member state before the European Court is very unwieldy. That some provisions in the directives can be directly relied upon by disappointed tenderers before national courts has now been confirmed by the European Court[52]. The Commission has also shown that an interlocutory injunctive remedy is available from the European Court to prevent a contract procedure progressing to the award stage in violation of the correct EC procedure[53]. It seems unlikely that the European Court would be prepared to go a step further and order a contract to be suspended or to be set aside once awarded[54]. Specific measures were needed to make remedies more effective and accessible.

1.3.1 General Sectors

A remedies directive for the general sectors has now been adopted[55] and is to be implemented by 1st December 1991. This directive requires member states to create a cause of action before national authorities or courts providing injunctive and compensatory relief in case of infringement of the substantive public procurement rules[56]. There is also a procedure for the Commission to request and obtain within 21 days a reaction from member states on alleged infringements of the substantive public procurement rules[57]. This greatly accelerates the Commission's remedy available under Article 169 EEC Treaty by which proceedings for infringement can be commenced against a member state but only following the statement of reasoned submissions by the Commission. Nonetheless it falls short of a direct power temporarily to suspend a contract procedure which the Commission had originally been seeking[58].

---

52 eg Case 31/87 *Gebroeders Beentjes BV* v. *Netherlands* [1988] ECR 4635.
53 Case 194/88R *Commission* v. *Italy* [1988] ECR 5647.
54 Case 243/89R *Commission* v. *Denmark* - statement in open court by Denmark acknowledging fault. This case concerned the Commission's attempt to use interim measures to require the retendering of contracts for the Western Great Belt Bridge, Denmark. The interim measures application was withdrawn following Denmark's statement in open court.
55 Ibid n. 15 supra. The remedies issue was examined in detail by the House of Lords Select Committee on the European Communities Session 1987-88 12th Report.
56 Ibid Article 2.
57 Ibid Article 3.
58 eg initial draft OJ C 230/6 28.8.87 Article 3.

1.3.2 Utilities Sectors

The Commission only recently adopted a proposal on enforcement in the utilities sector[59]. This will now go through the EC legislative machinery. The target date for adoption of implementing legislation is 1st July, 1992 but the taking effect of such legislation will be linked to the basic utilities directive[60].

The aim is to provide remedies substantially similar to those available in the general sectors[61]. Yet just as the substantive rules in the utilities sectors show greater flexibility so too do the remedies rules. Where damages are claimed for tender costs it will not be necessary to prove that the applicant would have won the contract; it will be sufficient to establish that an infringement of the rules occurred and that the infringement adversely affected his chance of success. Normally the damages will be 1% of the contract value unless the applicant can establish that his costs were higher[62]. Member states are not required to adopt a legislative, judicial style remedy. As an alternative they may instead adopt an audit procedure by which reports on the conformity with the procurement rules would be drawn up and be made available to interested parties and to the Commission[63]. Linked to this alternative is a review procedure for fixing a financial penalty in the event that an identified infringement is not discontinued. Again the sum will normally be 1% of the contract value unless the applicant can establish that his costs were greater[64].

There are provisions similar to those in the general sector directive whereby the Commission can require urgent explanations of alleged infringements from member states[65]. Finally, interested persons can invoke a rapid conciliation procedure involving EC advisory committees on public procurement which will attempt to reach an appropriate solution[66].

2. Consequences for the UK construction industry

Works and supplies in the general sectors have been covered by procurement rules since the 1970s. Thus the extension of procurement legislation to the utilities sector, to services in all sectors and the introduction of specific

59 Ibid n. 16.
60 Ibid Article 17.
61 See 3.4.1 supra.
62 Ibid n. 16 Article 2(7).
63 Ibid Articles 3 - 11.
64 Ibid Article 11.
65 Ibid Article 12.
66 Ibid Articles 13 - 15.

enforcement measures all represent considerable innovations. How will the various changes affect the players in the UK construction industry? Distinctions can usefully be made between contractors, suppliers, construction professionals and the contracting authorities themselves. Some general conclusions might then be drawn.

2.1 Contractors

The consequences for contractors will depend on their size. Small and medium sized contractors generally serve local or regional markets and are likely to lack the financial standing or resource to bid elsewhere. The UK's island geography (with the exception of Northern Ireland) means there are limited local cross-border opportunities.

Generally the most attractive commercial opportunities will go to the larger rather than the smaller contractors. The advertising threshold in the works contracts is now 5m ECUs (£3.5m approx.). Where a project is a traditional building contract and bidding is linked to bills of quantities, there is often little opportunity for healthy margins. Thus commercial reasons alone could deter medium sized firms from operating in a market further from home. Design and build contracts and other more sophisticated contract structures with possibly better margins tend to come in at above the £15m value level. This will in many cases take a project beyond the reach of the medium sized contractor and into the hands of the larger ones.

The larger contractors in any event are in a better position to overcome national preference on large projects by forming consortia with major local contractors. Joint venturing of this nature has proliferated in recent years. If large contractors can overcome barriers to entry in this way, the erosion of barriers to market entry becomes of less practical importance.

If anything, there is a changing attitude which makes contractors more prepared to link internationally either on a project by project basis or more formally by acquisition or through long term strategic alliances. There is thus an increased tendency toward concentration in the upper reaches of the industry for which any demise of national preference may be incidental.

Project by project some impact will be felt. Specialist contractors in the utilities sectors can expect to face increased competition. Also, the rules requiring contracts to be tendered where they are more than 50% part-funded by public authorities could well act as a disincentive to private promotion initiatives. This might also be true in the utilities sectors where a contractor might be part of a consortium to promote, say, an energy generation project, the construction work for which may one day have to be let by competitive tender.

2.2 Suppliers

The nature of construction materials is almost infinitely varied. Basic commodity materials such as aggregates will have naturally local markets and national preference will not be an issue with them. This is not the case for higher value added products which might be exported worldwide.

Where works projects are let by public authorities, construction materials purchases are separate subcontracts by the successful private contractor and are not in themselves public procurement supplies. Thus suppliers will only be affected where products are bought in by public bodies for in-house construction and maintenance.

The main impact on suppliers is likely to be on the suppliers of capital goods such as power generators who perform turnkey contracts. The utilities directive considers that where the value of the product including the installation cost exceeds the value of other related services, the project will be a supply[67]. It has been seen that lower value thresholds are applicable to supplies and hence this type of contract will more readily be caught. National preference in this type of sector might have been particularly strong and hence might be the more susceptible to change.

2.3 Construction Professionals

According to the general services proposals advertisement of tenders is required in the Official Journal of the European Communities for a number of construction related services including architectural, engineering, urban planning, landscape architectural and related technical and testing services[68]. Although competitive tendering in these circumstances is already common, the geographic net will of necessity become wider.

2.4 Contracting Authorities

The directives are addressed to the member states. The member states therefore need to ensure that contracting bodies at all levels implement this increasingly complex body of rules. One main consequence for contracting bodies is to place a heavier compliance burden on them. The more decentralised the procurement process, the more difficult it may be to ensure that every contracting body is well versed in the correct procedures. This burden will be particularly great for the utilities sectors. They will be covered for the first time and will have to adjust their procedures and retrain

---

67 Ibid n. 16 Article 1(3).
68 Ibid n. 40 Article 9 and Annex 1A.

their procurement officers.

Contracting entities will for the first time be subject to a clearly defined code of enforcement in public contracting. Whilst this will not be new for a number of member states with codified systems and a separate branch of public or administrative law, it will be an innovation for the UK. The need to keep records for audit and to provide reasons for actions is only one aspect. The prospect of injunctive and compensatory remedies from unsuccessful tenderers could make the area considerably more litigious. It may be particularly attractive for contractors to recover flat rate tender costs at 1% of the contract price. It is unclear whether contractors will be prepared to go to law or otherwise use the available procedures in these circumstances, particularly if they fear discrimination on future opportunities.

2.5 General Conclusions

The introduction of extensive regulation in the procurement area will, in theory, create wider opportunities. The main imponderable is whether market players will avail themselves of those opportunities. Judging from the experience of the PSA already noted[69] the existence of a more open tendering structure seems to be no guarantee of greater interest from non-nationals. There is no compelling reason why the introduction of more rules in this area should be a major engine for change. It seems to be the experience of the large contractors that those who want to go into the market place indeed do so, despite perceived local impediments, by teaming locally. Any additional advantages resulting from a change in the rules might have little practical effect to encourage this further.Perhaps the last word should be left for the procurement authorities. They, after all, have to implement the rules and have to find the money to pay successful claimants when they get it wrong. In a recent article by the director of contracts at the PSA the following view was expressed:

> "...there is no question that a fundamental need does exist for enforceable rules to secure transparency - that is a knowledge of opportunities - and to end technical or other forms of clear discrimination. These are both essential to the development of a genuine single market in construction. The rules within which procurement authorities have to operate, and the monitoring mechanisms in Brussels and elsewhere, need to recognise this fact. Those procedural rules must to some extent inhibit the freedom of the individual procurement authority. What we must

69 See 2 supra.

avoid is procedural restrictions which, based on the possibility of misuse, unnecessarily and unjustifiably restrict the legitimate pursuit of value-for-money by procurement authorities."[70]

Developments in liability 23
under European Community law

Phillip Capper

Synopsis

This paper considers the EC Directive on Product liability and the Consumer Protection Act 1987 passed to implement it in the UK. It examines implications for producers, "branders" and importers, particularly the extent of their liability and possible defences. The author asks if the House of Lords' decision in *Murphy* v. *Brentwood* will increase attention upon statutory rememdies. There is exploration of the horizontal Services Directive and of EC Directives specifically targetted at the construction industry including the Construction Products Directive.

Introduction

The European Community Directive on Product Liability was implemented in the UK by the Consumer Protection Act 1987, Part I, which came into force on 1st March 1988. Broadly, it imposes a liability without fault or "strict liability". It is no defence to say that all reasonable care had been taken. It does not displace ordinary negligence liability to third parties but merely adds an alternative, easier access to compensation for the victim. The claimant must still prove the damage, the defect and the causal relationship between them. Rights of contribution between defendants who have caused the same damage are preserved, as is the principle of contributory negligence (which reduces damages payable in proportion to any blame on the part of the victim).

"Producers" are defined as manufacturers, importers, and any person who by using his name or mark in relation to the product holds himself out to be the producer. There is a subsidiary liability on any "supplier" of a product if the supplier does not identify the person who supplied it to him. There has to be a defect in the product. This does not mean simply a lack of quality or fitness for purpose. There is a "defect" only if the product is not as safe as persons generally are entitled to expect. Safety includes risk of damage to products within the product, and to other property.

The liability arises only if a narrowly defined form of damage is suffered: death or personal injuries; or, damage to any item of property other than the defective product itself (subject to a lower threshold of value of the damage to the property (£275.00), to discourage small claims; and, a requirement that the property was in use by a private consumer). By contrast with the common law position, 'other property' here also excludes any other product in which the defective product is comprised and which was supplied with the defective product. So, the liability will not arise simply because a user has found quality defects in the product itself. There are limits on the liability by way of defences, which are covered in detail later in the paper.

Victims will be able to start an action within three years from the damage, or its discoverability if later. This is directly analogous to the provisions of the Latent Damage Act 1986. However, there will also be a long stop period applicable to product liability claims. This is different to that introduced by the Latent Damage Act 1986 for ordinary negligence claims in three respects: the long stop period is only 10 years; it does not start from breach of duty, but rather from the time the product was supplied; and it extinguishes the right, rather than merely barring the remedy (this is significant in relation to rights of contribution between defendants).

Statutory Product liability

"1. (1) This Part shall have effect for the purpose of making such provision as is necessary in order to comply with the product liability Directive and shall be construed accordingly."

The essence of the liability is stated in Section 2(1):

"2 (1) Subject to the following provisions of this Part, where any damage is caused wholly or partly by a defect in a product, every person to whom subsection (2) below applies shall be liable for the damage."

This is put differently in Article 1 of the Directive:

"The producer shall be liable for damage caused by a defect in his product"

There are four vital elements in this short provision:
- damage
- caused by
- a defect
- in a product

The principal liability imposed applies, by virtue of subsection (2) to three categories of person:
- Producers
- "Branders"
- Importers

The Act actually expresses this in the following terms:

"2.(2) This subsection applies to -
(a) the producer of the product;
(b) any person who, by putting his name on the product or using a trade mark or other distinguishing mark in relation to the product, has held himself out to be the producer of the product;
(c) any person who has imported the product into a member State from a place outside the member States in order, in the course of any business of his, to supply it to another."

However, a secondary liability is also imposed by Section 2 upon a further category of person: suppliers. This is, as we shall see later, a much more limited liability with clear reliefs for potential defendants.

The main liability therefore is a concern for those whom the Act defines as "producers". The definition is contained in Section 1(2):

"producer", in relation to a product, means -
(a) the person who manufactured it;
(b) in the case of a substance which has not been manufactured but has been won or abstracted, the person who won or abstracted it;
(c) in the case of a product which has not been manufactured, won or abstracted but essential characteristics of which are attributable to an industrial or other process having been carried out (for example, in relation to agricultural produce), the person who carried out that process;"

These attempts at definition in the legislation perhaps raise as many questions as they answer. The main defensive position will be to assert that the relevant defendant does not fall within these phrases. There are evident difficulties. Consider for example the potential application of the phrase "industrial or other process" in (c) above.

More fundamental is the difficulty of defining who is the "manufacturer". What is the "it" which is being manufactured? There is obviously an identity in component materials, parts and systems. What identity does the construction process add? What, overall, is the product? What relation and proportion does the component element bear to the thing which is the "product" in terms of the legislative definition?

Note the form of the definition of producer in the Directive:

> "Article 3 : "Producer"   means the manufacturer of a finished product, the producer of any raw material or the manufacturer of a component part and any person who, by putting his name, trade mark or other distinguishing feature on the product presents himself as its product."

What is a product? The definition itself is contained in Section 1(2) and is as follows:

> " "product" means any goods or electricity and (subject to subsection (3) below) includes a product which is comprised in another product, whether by virtue of being a component part or raw material or otherwise."

Further definitions are found in s.45 of the Act:

> " "goods" includes substances, growing crops and things comprised in land by virtue of being attached to it and any ship, aircraft or vehicle;
>
> "substance" means any natural or artificial substance, whether in solid, liquid or gaseous form or in the form of a vapour, and includes substances that are comprised in or mixed with other goods;
>
> "supply" and cognate expressions shall be construed in accordance with section 46 below;"

But when we look at the qualification referred to, set out in subsection (3) of Section 1, we find that the notion "product" may be rather a chameleon. Subsection (3) states:

> "1.... (3) For the purposes of this Part a person who supplies any product in which products are comprised, whether by virtue of being component parts or raw materials or otherwise, shall not be treated by reason only of his supply of that product as supplying any of the products so comprised."

What constitutes a product for any particular instance of supply may depend upon the context of that supply. The Directive was apparently clearer in its potential application to the construction industry:

"Article 2 : For the purpose of this Directive 'product' means all movables, with the exception of primary agricultural products and game, even though incorporated into another movable or into an immovable..."

Who is a supplier? A fundamental notion common to both Part I of the 1987 Act (on product liability) and Part II (on criminal liability in respect of safety requirement) is the meaning of "supply". This is a central question in relation to the application of the statutory product liability provisions to the construction industry. All turns on the rather peculiar provisions tucked away in s.46 of the Act:

"46. (1) Subject to the following provisions of this section, references in this Act to supplying goods shall be construed as references to doing any of the following, whether as principal or agent, that is to say-
(a) selling, hiring out or lending the goods;
(b) entering into a hire-purchase agreement to furnish the goods;
(c) the performance of any contract for work and materials to furnish the goods;
(d) providing the goods in exchange for any consideration (including trading stamps) other than money;
(e) providing the goods in or in connection with the performance of any statutory function; or
(f) giving the goods as a prize or otherwise making a gift of the goods;
and in relation to gas or water, those references shall be construed as including references to providing the service by which the gas or water is made available for use.
(2)
(3) Subject to subsection (4) below, the performance of any contract by the erection of any building or structure on any land or by the carrying out of any other building works shall be treated for the purposes of this Act as a supply of goods in so far as, but only in so far as, it involves the provision of any goods to any person by means of their incorporation into the building, structure or works.
(4) Except for the purposes of, and in relation to, notices to warn or any provision made by or under Part III of this Act, references

in this Act to supplying goods shall not include references to supplying goods comprised in land where the supply is effected by the creation or disposal of an interest in the land.

(5) Except in Part I of this Act references in this Act to a person's supplying goods shall be confined to references to that person's supplying goods in the course of a business of his, but for the purposes of this subsection it shall be immaterial whether the business is a business or dealing in the goods."

Controlling expectations as to safety

An attractive first line of defence occasionally available will be to demonstrate that the relevant alleged defendant is not a producer or supplier of the relevant product. Obviously there is scope also for further argument as to the potential application of the "brander" provision in Section 2(2)(b). As regards the main line of defence let us assume that we have an identified product and the party alleged to be responsible for it comes within the terms creating liability in Section 2. Significant scope for a defence arises from the provisions defining the meaning of "defect". These are contained in Section 3:

"3.   (1) Subject to the following provisions of this section, there is a defect in a product for the purposes of this Part if the safety of the product is not such as persons generally are entitled to expect; and for those purposes "safety", in relation to a product, shall include safety with respect to products comprised in that product and safety in the context of risks of damage to property, as well as in the context of risks of death or personal injury.

(2) In determining for the purposes of subsection (1) above what persons generally are entitled to expect in relation to a product all the circumstances shall be taken into account, including -

(a) the manner in which, and purposes for which, the product has been marketed, its get-up, the use of any mark in relation to the product and any instructions for, or warnings with respect to, doing or refraining from doing anything with or in relation to the product;

(b) what might reasonably be expected to be done with or in relation to the product; and

(c) the time when the product was supplied by its producer to another; and nothing in this section shall require a defect to be inferred from the fact alone that the safety of a product which is supplied after that time is greater than the safety of the product in question."

A curious complexity arising here is that safety includes safety with respect to products comprised in the defective product. However, compare the content of Section 5(2) by virtue of which the liability does not extend to damage to any product within which the defective product has been supplied.

The main thrust, however, of the notion of "defect" depends on general expectation, with the addition of a form of "state of the art" relief. This is in the sense of permitting no hindsight, by virtue of the proviso at the end of Section 3. Given the detail contained in Section 3(2)(a)-(c) attention needs to be focussed on methods of keeping within reasonable limits the expectations of those likely to be affected by the product.

It seems that the UK implementation may include contemplated mis-use as relevant to safety. This was not intended apparently in the Directive, as one of the Recitals declares:

"whereas, to protect the physical well-being and property of the consumer, the defectiveness of the product should be determined by reference not to its fitness for use but to the lack of the safety which the public at large is entitled to expect; whereas the safety is assessed by excluding any misuse of the product not reasonable under the circumstances;"

See also therefore Article 6 of the Directive:

"1. A product is defective when it does not provide the safety which a person is entitled to expect, taking all circumstances into account, including:
(a) the presentation of the product;
(b) the use to which it could reasonably be expected that the product would be put;
(c) the time when the product was put into circulation.

Defence against certain forms of damage

It is important to realise the limited scope of the "damage" which gives rise to this form of product liability. The legislative definition is contained in Section 5:

"5.   (1) Subject to the following provisions of this section in this Part "damage" means death or personal injury or any loss of or damage to any property (including land).

(2) A person shall not be liable under section 2 above in respect of any defect in a product for the loss of or any damage to the product itself or for the loss of or any damage to the whole or any part of any product which has been supplied with the product in question comprised in it.

(3) A person shall not be liable under section 2 above for any loss of or damage to any property which, at the time it is lost or damaged, is not -

(a) of a description of property ordinarily intended for private use, occupation or consumption; and

(b) intended by the person suffering the loss or damage mainly for his own private use, occupation or consumption.

(4) No damages shall be awarded to any person by virtue of this Part in respect of any loss of or damage to any property if the amount which would fall to be so awarded to that person, apart from this subsection and any liability for interest, does not exceed £275.

(5) In determining for the purposes of this Part who has suffered any loss of or damage to property and when any such loss or damage occurred, the loss or damage shall be regarded as having occurred at the earliest time at which a person with an interest in the property had knowledge of the material facts about the loss or damage.

(6) For the purposes of subsection (5) above the material facts about any loss of or damage to any property are such facts about the loss or damage as would lead a reasonable person with an interest in the property to consider the loss or damage sufficiently serious to justify his instituting proceedings for damages against a defendant who did not dispute liability and was able to satisfy a judgment.

(7) For the purposes of subsection (5) above a person's knowledge includes knowledge which he might reasonably have been expected to acquire -

(a) from facts observable or ascertainable by him; or .

(b) from facts ascertainable by him with the help of appropriate expert advice which it is reasonable for him to seek; but a person shall not be taken by virtue of this subsection to have knowledge of a fact ascertainable by him only with the help of expert advice unless he has failed to take all reasonable steps to obtain (and, where appropriate, to act on) that advice.

(8) Subsections (5) to (7) above shall not extend to Scotland."

The claims threshold of £275 for property damage will screen out many mere quality complaints. However there will be more scope for quality arguments, albeit over the threshold of value, if one part of a product can be said to have caused damage to another part. It is for this reason that the rather peculiar wording of Section 5(2) could give rise to doubt and difficulty. Can it seriously be read as meaning that the liability can arise where a defective product causes damage to products comprised within that product? Compare Article 9(b) of the Directive:

"Article 9

For the purpose of Article 1, damage means:

(b) damage to, or destruction of, any item of property other than the defective product itself, with a lower threshold of 500 ECU, provided that the item of property:

(i) is of a type ordinarily intended for private use or consumption, and

(ii) was used by the injured person mainly for his own private use or consumption.

There will also of course be scope for arguing that the statutory liability does not arise because the relevant property damaged is not "consumer" property within the meaning of Section 5(3).

If a death or personal injury has occurred, there will presumably be little room for argument about that, though it should be noted that by Section 45(1):

" "Personal Injury" includes any disease and any other impairment of a person's physical or mental condition."

In these cases, the defensive line will be not so much to contradict the allegation that the unfortunate death or injury has occurred, but rather to investigate whether the defect caused the death or injury. The legal concept of causation introduces into this regime of liability an important defensive mechanism.

The provisions contained in subsection (5) through (7) of Section 5 are rather odd. They link the occurrence of the damage, in terms of time, to the time of its reasonable discoverability. The provisions concerned reflect a fairly standard approach to what might be called reasonable discoverability, in the context of the Limitation Act 1980, as amended by the Latent Damage Act 1986. However it is odd that in the new provisions added to the Limitation Act 1980 by Schedule 1 Part I of the Consumer Protection Act 1987, a distinction is drawn between the date on which the cause of action accrued and the date of knowledge of the plaintiff (see the new Section 11A(4) in Schedule 1, Part I). More curiously still, it should be noted that subsections (5)-(7) do not apply to cases of personal injury (or of course death).

The explicit defences

We have seen so far that a mechanism for a potential defendant to limit or avoid the risk of liability arising under the Consumer Protection Act 1987 in regard to product liability is by reference to the legislative definitions of the central elements in the liability: producer, supplier, product, defect, causation, and damage.

Careful attention to those central elements does indeed allow scope for management of the liability. This is all the more important since the Act forbids contracting out, or other simple avoidance of the liability, by conventional disclaimers. See Section 7:

> "7. The liability of a person by virtue of this Part to a person who has suffered damage caused wholly or partly by a defect in a product, or to a dependant or relative of such a person, shall not be limited or excluded by any contract term, by any notice or by any other provision."

The emphasis here is on limiting or excluding the liability by terms, notices and other provisions. It must be recognised however that careful attention to the legal implications of this Act can lead to useful devices for controlling the extent to which any product can be said to be defective.

The 1987 Act itself provides certain limited defences. These are set out in Section 4:

> "4. (1) In any civil proceedings by virtue of this Part against any person ("the person proceeded against") in respect of a defect in a product it shall be a defence for him to show -
> (a) that the defect is attributable to compliance with any requirement imposed by or under any enactment or with any Community obligation; or
> (b) that the person proceeded against did not at any time supply

the product to another; or

(c) that the following conditions are satisfied, that is to say -

(i) that the only supply of the product to another by the person proceeded against was otherwise than in the course of business of that person's; and

(ii) that section 2(2) above does not apply to that person or applies to him by virtue only of things done otherwise than with a view to profit; or

(d) that the defect did not exist in the product at the relevant time; or

(e) that the state of scientific and technical knowledge at the relevant time was not such that a producer of products of the same description as the product in question might be expected to have discovered the defects if it had existed in his products while they were under his control; or

(f) that the defect -

(i) constituted a defect in a product ("the subsequent product") in which the product in question had been comprised; and

(ii) was wholly attributable to the design of the subsequent product or to compliance by the producer of the product in question with instructions given by the producer of the subsequent product.

(2) In this section "the relevant time", in relation to electricity, means the time at which it was generated, being a time before it was transmitted or distributed, and in relation to any other product, means -

(a) if the person proceeded against is a person to whom subsection (2) of section 2 above applies in relation to the product, the time when he supplied the product to another;

(b) if that subsection does not apply to that person in relation to the product, the time when the product was last supplied by a person to whom that subsection does apply in relation to the product."

The last three of these defences (1) (d), (e) and (f) are likely to prove much more significant in practice than the first three (1) (a), (b) and (c). An important advantage for any potential defendant is the scope for reasonable argument as to the extent of any alleged liability. To that extent, the question whether the defect existed in the product "at the relevant time" (which broadly means the time when the actual product was last supplied by a producer/brander/importer) will leave considerable scope for argument.

The "development risk" defence was framed very narrowly in the European Community Directive: "That the state of scientific and technical knowledge at the time when [the producer] put the product into circulation was not such as to enable the existence of the defect to be discovered". This reference in effect to all scientific and technical knowledge makes the defence narrower than the normal "state of the art" defence in ordinary negligence liability actions.

However, the implementation of the "development risk" defence in the UK Act has arguably been framed too liberally for producers. The 1987 Act provides that it shall be a defence "that the state of scientific and technical knowledge at the relevant time was not such that a producer of products of the same description as the product in question might be expected to have discovered the defect if it had existed in his products while they were under his control". This seems much closer to the common law negligence test of "reasonable competence having regard to the scientific and technical knowledge available to the defendant at the relevant time". The UK Act has therefore been challenged by consumer organisations as failing to implement faithfully the European Directive.

For the construction industry in particular the final defence set out in (f) is a very significant line of defence indeed. Here it is clear that careful attention to contractual and other documentation (with a legal eye) could create some solid defences. All will depend on when a product is being supplied within a product. This makes crucial the extent to which a building can itself be said to be a product. If this defensive provision is applicable to construction, the vital need will be to secure clear definition of the specification.

The defences in the Directive are expressed as follows:

"Article 7
      The producer shall not be liable as a result of this Directive if he proves:
      (a) that he did not put the product into circulation; or
      (b) that, having regard to the circumstances, it is probably that the defect which caused the damage did not exist at the time when the product was put into circulation by him or that this defect came into being afterwards; or
      (c) that the product was neither manufactured by him for sale or any form of distribution for economic purpose nor manufactured or distributed by him in the course of his business; or
      (d) that the defect is due to compliance of the product with mandatory regulations issued by the public authorities; or

(e) that the state of scientific and technical knowledge at the time when he put the product into circulation was not such as to enable the existence of the defect to be discovered; or

(f) in the case of a manufacturer of a component, that the defect is attributable to the design of the product in which the component has been fitted or to the instructions given by the manufacturer of the product."

Defences for suppliers

The liability of a supplier which is not itself a producer, brander, or importer, is only secondary. Hence the 1987 Act provides ready relief for any supplier who maintains careful records and is thus able to comply with the relatively easily invoked defence set out in Section 2(3):

"2... (3) Subject as aforesaid, where any damage is caused wholly or partly by a defect in a product, any person who supplied the product (whether to the person who suffered the damage, to the producer of any product in which the product in question is comprised or to any other person shall be liable for the damage if -

(a) the person who suffered the damage requests the supplier to identify one or more of the persons (whether still in existence or not) to whom subsection (2) above applies in relation to the product;

(b) that request is made within a reasonable period after the damage occurs and at a time when it is not reasonably practicable for the person making the request to identify all those persons; and

(c) the supplier fails, within a reasonable period after receiving the request, either to comply with the request or to identify the person who supplied the product to him."

We have also already seen that a further defence for a person who is only a supplier arises by virtue of the wording of Section 1(3):

"For the purposes of this Part a person who supplies any product in which products are comprised, whether by virtue of being component parts or raw materials or otherwise, shall not be treated by reason only of his supply of that product as supplying any of the products so comprised."

Barring of stale claims

There is a final refuge. This is the limitation defence: that the claim asserted by the victim is statute barred because it has been commenced too late. However, unless the plaintiff is extraordinarily dilatory, these provisions (set out in Sched.1 Part I) are likely to be of significance only in the context of latent defects causing damage many years later.

Victims will be able to start an action within three years from the damage, or its discoverability if later. This is directly analogous to the provisions of the Latent Damage Act 1986. However, there will also be a long stop period applicable to product liability claims. This is different from that introduced by the Latent Damage Act 1986 for ordinary negligence claims in three respects: the long stop period is only 10 years; it does not start from breach of duty, but rather from the time the actual product was last supplied by a producer/brander/importer; and it extinguishes the right, rather than merely barring the remedy (this is significant in relation to rights of contribution between defendants). The timing of this longstop provision could therefore be manipulated by appropriate legal dispositions if the building was likely to remain unoccupied for some time after completion.

Passing the buck

Although these are strictly not defences there are other important principles within the product liability legislation which give some measure of relief to the potential defendant. We have already noted above the opportunity to argue the question of causation. This is part of a general principle in law that he who asserts must prove. The burden of proof is therefore on the victim. The victim must prove all the important elements set out above, such as that the damage has occurred, and that it was caused by a defect in what is, for the purposes of this legislation, a product. Of course, the burden of proving any defence is on the defendant.

However the Act goes even further in giving some measure of protection to the potential defendant. It preserves the principle of contributory negligence. See Section 6(4):

> "Where any damage is caused partly by a defect in a product and partly by the fault of the person suffering the damage, the Law Reform (Contributory Negligence) Act 1945 and section 5 of the Fatal Accidents Act 1976 (contributory negligence) shall have effect as if the defect were the fault of every person liable by virtue of this Part for the damage caused by the defect."

Two other provisions of significance to the defendant are tucked away at the end of Section 2. These are Section 2(5) and Section 2(6):

"(5) Where two or more persons are liable by virtue of this Part for the same damage, their liability shall be joint and several.
(6) This section shall be without prejudice to any liability arising otherwise than by virtue of this Part.

Notice that the liability is "joint and several". Also other liabilities are left in place. Therefore a person found liable under the Act has the opportunity to claim a contribution from some other person who was also partly responsible for the same damage. The main problem, however, with joint and several liability is that each defendant is potentially liable to the plaintiff for the whole amount of the damage (with a right of recovery against the other defendants, who may not be solvent). It is not the case that each defendant has to bear only their proportion of the responsibility vis a vis the plaintiff.

Effect of *Murphy* v. *Brentwood*

The English courts began in the mid-1980s a new trend of caution, restricting negligence liability outside contract (eg to third parties such as building occupiers) and overruling expansions of the law in the previous decade. Hence, local authorities' liability for building control functions (which exploded in the mid-70s) was first limited to present or imminent threats to health or safety of the occupier, and then in 1990 abolished altogether as a special category:[1]. Also, the recovery of purely economic losses not immediately consequential on damage to the person or property of the claimant was also considerably restricted.

This latter restriction is subject to an important exception. There has remained an exceptional category allowing recovery of pure economic loss by third parties not in a contractual relationship with the defendant. However, the House of Lords has also restated the limits on this exception: it is essential to prove, in this category of the tort of negligence, as an essential ingredient of the necessary 'proximity' for a duty of care, that the defendant knew (both in preparing himself for what he said and in saying it) that his statement would be communicated to the plaintiff, either as an individual or as a member of an identifiable class, specifically in connection with a particular transaction or transactions of a particular kind and that the plaintiff would be very likely to rely on it for the purpose of deciding

1   see *Murphy* v. *Brentwood* (1990) 3 WLR 414

whether or not to enter upon that transaction or upon a transaction of that kind.

The main objection to the recovery of pure economic loss (not immediately consequent on physical damage) is that it opens the floodgates to claims from an indeterminate range of claimants. A further trend emerging in the case-law of the late 1980s is a renewed emphasis upon the various parties' own contractual framework of risk allocation. Their free assent to such arrangements has not only defined their contractual rights and obligations. The courts have even come to recognise that the contractual structure of risk should also delimit the extent of risk exposure to third parties. Hence liabilities even in tort could be reduced significantly if the extent of reliance were managed by appropriate wording in the contractual terms of engagement and, where relevant and admissible, earlier correspondence. This is as much a matter of positive but realistic portrayal of the limits of the scope of the service intended, as it is perceived in the client's and others' minds, as it is with the language of actual warnings or disclaimers.

The supply of everyday goods and building services typically involves a quality or fitness obligation. Contrast this with the typical duty of professional advisers, engaged for their expertise. They are not normally taken by English law to warrant that the advice will lead to a successful result. They merely have to take reasonable care in the giving of advice.

Users who want rights to a certain level of quality or freedom from defects in goods and services (beyond the level that the goods or services must not injure or damage people or other property) must normally get a contract to that effect with whoever they wish to make responsible. If there is a contract, the obligations may be implied, by statute or because a judge would regard them as necessarily implied.

In English law only the parties to a contract are entitled to the rights it creates. Third parties cannot take advantage of the contractual duties. This puts a natural limit on the range of possible claimants who can complain of quality problems. Liability outside contract to third parties (in the tort of negligence) has no natural limits and so has to be restricted in some way to prevent the courts being flooded with claims: the normal mechanism in tort is to allow losses to be recoverable only where these relate to physical harm to person or property. Pure economic losses are not normally recoverable in tort. Contract law does not make this distinction. Between contracting parties all losses (whether physical or wholly financial) are recoverable as damages so long as they arise naturally, according to the usual course of things, from the breach of contract, or were in the contemplation of both parties when the contract was made.

For ordinary suppliers of goods and services, the normal requirements of liability in tortious negligence will be actual damage to the plaintiff's person or ("other") property. It will not, it seems, suffice if the only damage occurring is within property which the defendant had negligently designed or produced and such damage is attributable to that negligence. Difficulties will however arise in determining whether the defendant can be said to have caused damage to "other" property if one part of the product he supplies causes damage to another he supplies with it.

Progress of the Services Directive

Legislative protection for the consumer of a defective product used in a construction process raises many issues, some of which are far from being resolved. Granting similar protection for harm caused by the poor provision of services raises even more numerous, and more complex, issues. Claude Mathurin grappled with them for years without being able to produce a solution acceptable to the Commission or Member States. Whilst he was compiling his report, in September 1989, Directorate General XI (which has responsibility for Consumer Protection matters) announced a draft directive on the liability of a supplier of defective services. The original proposal was intended to cover the Construction industry. To say that this proposal took construction industry professionals (and Directorate General III) by surprise is something of an understatement.

DG XI originally saw the wisdom of excluding the construction industry (along with the legal and medical professions) from the scope of the proposed directive. However, it has done so only on the assumption that industry specific directives concerning the services provided in these sectors will be implemented before 1992. Given the developments that had taken place in regard to the the Mathurin report, that seemed for a short while no longer a realistic prospect for the construction industry. Now, however, there seems little doubt that professionals providing a service within the industry will be affected by an E.E.C directive at some time within the next three years or so. What is unknown is whether the Community authorities will finally approach this task from a rather narrow consumer protection point of view, or from a wider consideration of liability of providers of construction services. It is important to understand the approach of DG XI, especially as the proposal was created according to the power granted by Article 100a of the Treaty, paragraph three of which provides:

"The Commission, in its proposals ...concerning... consumer protection, will take as a base a high level of protection".

Rationale behind the "horizontal" services proposal

The Commission advance several reasons why a directive relating to defective services should be implemented:

- There are disparities found between Member States in the system of liability of the suppliers of services: these disparities cover matters such as varying burdens of proof, causative requirements, and the levels of injury sustained by consumers;
- It appears to be anomalous for consumers to have a legislative remedy against a supplier of a defective product, but not the designer of that product or the person who put that product in situ.

Although the medical, legal and construction services sectors were, in the early draft, to be given exemptions by specific directives for those services, all other providers of professional services were to be affected, and the published draft does not contain the exemptions. The Commission maintains that all services have certain characteristics in common which make it appropriate to promulgate one horizontal, rather than sector specific, legislative act. The characteristics in common are said to be the technical nature of the services to be provided, absence of written contracts, and the disappearance of the cause of damage during the provision of the service. Only time will tell whether this approach is too simplistic. It may well be that a whole series of similar rules will need to be published, in order to cover different sectors satisfactorily.

Essential contents of the services proposal

The draft seeks to establish the liability of a supplier of services for direct damage caused to persons or their property. It is designed to apply to any transaction carried out on a commercial basis or by a public body which does not have as its direct and exclusive object the manufacture of goods or the transfer of rights in rem or intellectual property rights. Salient points to note are that:

- The draft concerns the safety of private persons or private property. Thus only physical damage to property or persons is covered; it is not the intention to compensate for pure economic loss.
- Liability is to be joint and several in respect of the damage caused; where a service is provided by a participant in a franchise agreement, the franchisor will also be held liable for any loss caused.
- The draft does not provide for limits on the amount of compensation

for direct damage suffered by injured persons.
- There are limitation periods within which time a person who suffers injury must bring an action.
- The burden of proof has shifted in favour of the injured person. It is for the supplier of the service to prove that he did not commit a fault, rather than for the injured party to prove that the supplier did.

The draft horizontal Services Directive

The draft Services Directive was originally to have no impact at all on the construction industry. The published draft then included construction. Now, at the time of writing this paper, it seems likely (as a matter of speculation) that construction will be excluded from the eventually enacted horizontal Services Directive. However this particular topic is probably the most uncertain area of liability yet considered by the Community authorities. There is little reason to doubt that providers of services in the construction industry will be affected by harmonization rules within the near future. Considerable doubt surrounds the extent of those rules. Considering other Community provisions, such as those relating to defective and unsafe products, one can be confident that if the suppliers of services are to be affected by a Community wide rule, they can expect the burden of proof to be reversed in favour of the person injured.

The Commission's explanatory background

The Commission considered that this initiative should take the form of a proposal for a Directive on the liability of suppliers of defective services to establish clear standard principles at European level for the compensation of persons injured by those services. The proposal, which applies across the board, should, in the Commission's opinion, avoid excessive regulation and have the effect both of repairing any damage which does occur and, indirectly, helping to prevent its occurrence in the first place.

Initially, the Commission's consumer policy department envisaged a Directive designed to establish a standard system of no-fault liability in respect of damage offsetting the "physical" integrity of persons and property. The principle underlying this proposal was that damage is a risk to society and that the cost of repairing it should be distributed fairly between all those concerned.

However, since (a) some of the interest groups concerned had misgivings about such a Directive, (b) most national systems are still - except in certain specific areas - based on the principle that the supplier is at fault, although this principle is often interpreted very broadly, and (c) there was a certain reluctance to change this situation too radically at present, the Commission decided to propose a Directive based not on a system of objective liability but on a uniform system of liability based on reversal of the burden of proof to the advantage of the injured person. The principal aim being safety, it is confined to physical damage to persons and to consumers' property.

The proposal is based on the premise that it is extremely difficult for an injured person to prove that the supplier of a service is at fault in the case of damage resulting from a defective service whereas the trader, with the technical knowledge at his disposal, can provide proof to the contrary much more easily. In general, case law is tending more and more to grant injured persons compensation for damages caused by defective services, on the basis of the principle that the burden of proof lies with the supplier of the service.

Fault is an infinitely variable concept which is changing all the time. Increasingly courts are tending to interpret it very broadly. It relates to the behaviour of the supplier, which includes the means he uses to provide his service. In order to take account of these developments, distinctions made by national courts between obligation regarding the end and obligation regarding the means, any agreed limitations placed on the service, and third party status, the proposal refers to the concept of the legitimate expectations of the consumer in respect of the safety of the service. Hence it is possible in any given case to assess the fault in terms of the safety aspect.

This proposal will therefore mean that the person suffering damage will have to prove only that damage occurred and that there was a causal relationship between the damage and the supply of the service. The supplier will be exonerated only if he can prove that there was no fault on his part, this fault being interpreted very broadly in terms of the legitimate expectations of consumers as regards the safety of services. For example, he may disclaim liability by invoking force majeure or compliance with binding regulations, which would enable him to overturn the presumption of liability incumbent upon him.

Links with other Community legislation

The proposal for a Directive applies across the board and lays down basic points of general application when there are no more specific provisions. There are more specific Community legal provisions which apply to package holidays and waste. Services in these sectors are thus excluded from the scope of this Directive.

It was necessary to propose a general Directive on liability for suppliers of services because there is no current legislation in the very important area of service safety. Because of the wide variety of different services, it is difficult to take effective action at Community level in the form of a Directive establishing a general principle of safety, as the Commission did with products. On the other hand, it is possible to take a posteriori action by guaranteeing compensation for victims of services, whatever the service concerned.

There is already a general Directive covering the liability of manufacturers of defective products. So that consumers can take advantage not only of the internal market in products but also of the internal market in services under the best possible conditions, it is necessary to have a similar Directive on liability of suppliers of services.

There is obviously some duplication between the Directive on liability for products and the Directive on liability for suppliers of services. This is inevitable because in many cases services involve the use of products. This duplication is acceptable and necessary if liability is to be covered in full. It is important to note that the proposed Directive in no way affects the rights of the victims of defective products.

Legal Basis

This proposal is based on Article 100A because it is related to completion of the single market. The proposal is also designed to provide consumers with better protection and takes account of the Council Resolution of 9 November 1989 on future priorities for relaunching consumer protection policy. The principal draft provisions of the horizontal services Directive are set out below.

Article 1 - Principle

1. The supplier of a service shall be liable for damage to the health and physical integrity of persons or the physical integrity of movable or immovable property, including the persons or property which were the object of the service, caused by a fault committed by him in the performance of the service;

2. The burden of proving the absence of fault shall fall upon the supplier of the service.

3. In assessing the fault, account shall be taken of the behaviour of the supplier of the service, who, in normal and reasonably foreseeable conditions, shall ensure the safety which may reasonably be expected.

4. Whereas the mere fact that a better service existed or might have existed at the moment of performance or subsequently shall not constitute a fault.

Article 2 - Definition of Service

For the purpose of this Directive, "service" means any transaction carried out on a commercial basis or by way of a public service and in an independent manner, whether or not in return for payment, which does not have as its direct and exclusive object the manufacture of movable property or the transfer of rights in rem or intellectual property rights.

This Directive shall not apply to public services intended to maintain public safety. It shall not apply to package travel or to waste services.

Article 4 - Definition of Damage

The term "damage" means:

(a)   death or any other direct damage to the health or physical integrity of persons;

(b)   any direct damage to the physical integrity of movable or immovable property, including animals, provided that this property

      (i)   is of a type normally intended for private use or consumption, and

      (ii)   was intended for or used by the injured person, principally for his private use or consumption;

(c)   any financial material damage resulting directly from the damage referred to at (a) and (b).

Article 5 - Proof

The injured person shall be required to provide proof of the damage and the causal relationship between the performance of the service and the damage.

Article 6 - Third parties and joint liability

1. The liability of the supplier of the service shall not be reduced where the damage is caused jointly by a fault on his part and by the intervention of a third party.

2. The liability of the supplier of the service may be reduced, or even waived, where the damage is caused jointly by a fault on his part and by the fault of the injured person, or a person for whom the injured person is responsible.

Article 7 - Exclusion of liability

The supplier of a service may not, in relation to the injured person, limit or exclude his liability under this Directive.

Article 9 - Extinction of rights

The Member States shall provide in their legislation that the rights conferred upon the injured person pursuant to this Directive shall be extinguished upon the expiry of a period of five years from the date on which the supplier of services provided the service which caused the damage, unless in the meantime the injured person has instituted legal, administrative or arbitration proceedings against that person.

However, this period shall be extended to 20 years where the service relates to the design or construction of immovable property.

Article 10 - Limitation period

1. Member States shall provide in their legislation that a limitation period of three years shall apply to proceedings for the recovery of damages as provided for in this Directive, beginning on the day on which the plaintiff became aware or should reasonably have become aware of the damage, the service and the identity of the supplier of the service.

However, this period shall be extended to 10 years where the service relates to the design or construction of immovable property.

2. The laws of Member States regulating suspension or interruption of the limitation period shall not be affected by this Directive.

Article 12 - Implementing provisions

1. Member States shall adopt the laws, regulations and administrative provisions necessary to comply with this Directive by 31 December 1992.

The proposal for a "vertical" construction-specific Directive

As the Services Directive is a horizontal one and in view of the complexity of the construction sector, the Commission also decided on the same day as its decision on the horizontal Directive that it was necessary to elaborate a specific Directive for the construction sector in relation to the design and construction of buildings. This specific directive is regarded as necessary in order to adapt the general concepts and provisions of the horizontal directive to the particular features of the construction sector (involving as it does some sub-sectors, such as professions, suppliers, etc) and for which it is impossible to have the same regulation as, for example, for mechanical repairers.

The Commission's DGIII, through Mr Renato Caronna, is now engaged on the formulation of drafts for a proposal for harmonisation in close cooperation with the relevant European Associations. Four working groups have been constituted:

- taking-over
- liability
- legal guarantee
- financial coverage of the legal guarantee

to consider in addition to the substantive aspects, also relevant aspects to terminology. Each of these groups is composed of experts nominated by European Associations: Group 1 by CEBI/CEDIC the European Committee of Engineers- Counsellors; Group 2 by the European Union of Developers and Constructors; Group 3 by the European Committee of Social Housing; and, Group 4 by the European Committee of Insurance. FIEC, the European Federation of Construction Industry will coordinate work of the four groups, but the whole responsibility of work and of all the activity is headed by the Commission.

The mandate of each group is as follows:

for taking-over:
- to define the legal significance, consequences and forms of "acceptance" (or, handover)

for liability, legal guarantee and financial coverage of the legal guarantee:
- to define systems based on uniform criteria in respect of duration, scope, reliability and simplicity in order to strike a fair balance between the various national systems and to satisfy the different parties involved in the act of construction (building owners, designers, contractors, developers, subcontractors, suppliers), as well as the end-users who acquire the products resulting from the act of construction.

In addition, under the topic of financial coverage of legal guarantee, it is intended to allow parties concerned to be free to choose the most suitable formula from among those available (for example: insurance, bank guarantee, bonds, deposits, joint and several guarantee by the interested parties in question). Each group has been asked to finish work before the end of

October 1992 in order to have the time to prepare the proposal of a specific directive to submit it to the Commission and after approval, to the Council, the European Parliament and the Economic and Social Committee. At present, as a matter of priority, the work will only concern the design and the construction of residential and non-residential public and private buildings.

Implementation of EC Directive on Construction Products

Introduction

The EC Directive on Construction Products (89/106/EEC) was adopted unanimously in December 1988. The main purpose of the Construction Products Directive (CPD) is to achieve free movement of construction products throughout the Community, mainly by removing technical barriers to trade between member states. The CPD is one of the family of "new approach" directives which set out in general terms "essential requirements" (eg for safety) that must be met for products of various kinds to be fit to be sold both in the domestic and the Community market. The United Kingdom (UK) is required to adapt its laws to give effect to the Directive by 27 June 1991.

The CPD is to be implemented within the UK by means of Regulations made under the European Communities Act 1972. Most helpful explanatory documents are available from the UK Government, such as that from the DTI entitled "The Single Market: STANDARDS: construction products", which summarises the principal provisions as follows:

Essential requirements

The essential requirements apply to construction works, not to construction products as such, but they will influence the technical characteristics of those products. Construction products must be suitable for construction works which (as a whole and in their separate parts) are fit for their intended use, account being taken of economy, and which satisfy the essential requirements where the works are subject to regulations containing such requirements. The essential requirements relate to mechanical resistance and stability; safety in case of fire; hygiene, health and the environment; safety in use; protection against noise; and energy economy and heat retention. These requirements must, subject to normal maintenance, be satisfied for an economically reasonable working life, and generally concern actions which are foreseeable. The essential requirements are set out in full in Annex A.

The essential requirements may give rise to the establishment of classes of a construction product corresponding to different performance levels, to take account of possible differences in geographical or climatic conditions or in ways of life as well as different levels of protection that may prevail at national, regional or local level. Member States may require performance levels to be observed in their territory only within the classification thus established.

The essential requirements will be given concrete form in interpretative documents, which will create the necessary links between those requirements and, for example, the mandates to draw up European standards for particular construction products. The European Commission are to draw up, and update, a list of construction products which play a minor part with respect to health and safety, which need only to be manufactured in accordance with the "acknowledged rule of technology".

Methods of satisfying the essential requirements

In practice the primary methods will be:

(a) manufacture in compliance with specified harmonised European standards, which will be published in the United Kingdom as identically worded British Standards; or

(b) manufacture in compliance with a European technical approval.

The reference numbers of the harmonised European standards will be published in the Official Journal of the European Communities. The reference numbers of the British Standards are to be published.

The interpretative documents will harmonise the technology and the technical bases, and indicate classes or levels for each requirement where necessary and where the state of scientific and technical knowledge so permits. They will indicate methods of correlating these classes or levels of requirement with standards or technical approvals, for example through methods of calculation and of proof, or through technical rules for project design. The interpretative documents will be published in the Official Journal of the European Communities.

A European technical approval is a favourable technical assessment of the fitness for use of a construction product, based on fulfilment of the essential requirements for construction works for which the product is intended to be used. Such approvals are to be issued by bodies authorised by a Member State, generally for five years and on the basis of the relevant interpretative documents and common guidelines. They may be issued for, broadly, products for which there are no specified harmonised European standards or approved national standards or for products which differ significantly from such standards.

Transitional arrangements

In the absence of relevant specified harmonised European standards and European technical approvals:

(a) national standards and other technical specifications that have been approved by the Standing Committee may be used. Their reference numbers will be published in the Official Journal of the European Communities and by the Member States.

(b) Member States shall allow construction products to be placed on the market in their territory if they satisfy national provisions consistent with the Treaty. The Member State of destination shall, on request in individual cases, consider a product to be in conformity with the national provisions in force if it has satisfied tests and inspections carried out by an approved body in the producing Member State according to the methods in force in the Member State of destination or recognised as equivalent by that Member State.

The principal provisions of the Construction Products Directive are as follows:

Article 1

1. This Directive shall apply to construction products in so far as the essential requirements in respect of construction works under Article 3 (1) relate to them.

2. For the purposes of this Directive, 'construction product' means any product which is produced for incorporation in a permanent manner in construction works, including both buildings and civil engineering works. 'Construction products' are hereinafter referred to as 'products'; construction works including both buildings and civil engineering works are hereinafter referred to as 'works'.

Article 2

1. Member States shall take all necessary measures to ensure that the products referred to in Article 1, which are intended for use in works, may be placed on the market only if they are fit for this intended use, that is to

say they have such characteristics that the works in which they are to be incorporated, assembled, applied or installed, can, if properly designed and built, satisfy the essential requirements referred to in Article 3 when and where such works are subject to regulations containing such requirements.
2. When products are subject to other Community directives with regard to other aspects, the EC conformity mark, hereinafter referred to as the 'EC mark', referred to in Article 4(2) shall indicate in these cases that the requirements of those other directives have also been complied with.

Article 3

1. The essential requirements applicable to works which may influence the technical characteristics of a product are set out in terms of objectives in Annex 1. One, some or all of these requirements may apply, they shall be satisfied during an economically reasonable working life.
2. In order to take account of possible differences in geographical or climatic conditions or in ways of life as well as different levels of protection that may prevail at national, regional or local level, each essential requirement may give rise to the establishment of classes in the documents referred to in paragraph 3 and the technical specifications referred to in Article 4 for the requirement to be respected.
3. The essential requirements shall be given concrete form in documents (interpretative documents) for the creation of the necessary links between the essential requirements laid down in paragraph 1 and the standardization mandates, mandates for guidelines for European technical approval or the recognition of other technical specification within the meaning of Articles 4 and 5.

Chapter II

Harmonized standards

Article 7

1. In order to ensure the quality of harmonized standards for products, the standards shall be established by the European standards organizations on the basis of mandates given by the Commission in accordance with the procedure laid down in Directive 83/189/EEC and, after consulting the committee referred to in Article 19, in accordance with the general provisions concerning cooperation between the Commission and these bodies signed on 13 November 1984.
2. The resulting standards shall be expressed as far as practicable in product

performance terms, having regard to the interpretative documents.

3. Once the standards have been established by the European standards organizations, the Commission shall publish the references of the standards in the 'C' series of the Official Journal of the European Communities.

Chapter III

European technical approval

Article 8

1. European technical approval is a favourable technical assessment of the fitness for use of a product for an intended use, based on fulfilment of the essential requirements for building works for which the product is used.

Chapter IV

Interpretative documents

Article 12

1. The Commission shall, after consulting the committee referred to in Article 19, instruct technical committees in which the Member States participate to draw up the interpretative documents referred to in Article 3(3).

2.   The interpretative documents shall:

(a)   give concrete form to the essential requirements laid down in Article 3 and in Annex 1 by harmonizing the terminology and the technical bases and indicating classes or levels for each requirement where necessary and where the state of scientific and technical knowledge so permits;

(b)   indicate methods of correlating these classes or levels of requirement with the technical specifications referred to in Article 4, for example, methods of calculation and of proof, technical rules for project design etc;

(c)   serve as a reference for the establishment of harmonized standards and guidelines for European technical approval and for recognition of national technical specifications in accordance with Article 4(3).

3. The Commission shall publish the interpretative documents in the 'C' series of the Official Journal of the European Communities after soliciting the opinion of the Committee referred to in Article 19.

Chapter VIII

Standing Committee on Construction

Article 19

1. A Standing Committee on Construction is hereby set up.
2. The Committee shall be made up of representatives appointed by the Member States. It shall be chaired by a representative of the Commission. Each Member State shall appoint two representatives. The representatives may be accompanied by experts.
3. The Committee shall draw up its own rules of procedure.

The General Product Safety Directive

As a means of complementing Directive 85/374 on Product Liability, the Commission has proposed a Directive concerning general product safety [Proposal for a Council Directive concering general product safety, COM(89) final, OJC 193/1 1989]. It should be made clear that the Product Safety Directive is at a very early stage of drafting. There are many points of uncertainty contained in the Directive (some of which will be highlighted below) and there will probably be significant changes to the text by the time the Directive reaches its final form.

Obviously as part of the harmonization drive towards 1992, the Community authorities wish to have in place a standard procedure for ensuring that all products placed on the internal market are safe. Once again the Community authorities are prepared to enact a "horizontal" measure affecting all products put into free circulation, rather than a series of "vertical" measures which would be sector specific in their application.

According to this measure, Member States must ensure that products which are put into free circulation are "safe". Article 2(a), which defines products, says that they may consist of "movables incorporated into immovables". Thus, the draft will apply to construction products. Article 2(c) goes on to say that a "safe product" is one that:

> "...does not present, in particular in respect of its design, composition, execution, functioning, wrapping, conditions of assembly, maintenance or disposal, instructions for handling and use, or any of its other properties an unacceptable risk for the safety and health of persons, either directly or indirectly, in particular through its effect upon other products or its combination therewith."

An acceptable risk is to be evaluated in the light of a product's normal use, under normal circumstances, during the foreseeable lifetime of the product in question.

Member States are under a duty to ensure that only safe products are placed on the market. They must do this by creating (or nominating) 'appropriate authorities' which will have the task of monitoring markets and production centres to ensure the directive is complied with. Such monitoring will be aided by the duty placed on suppliers to 'make appropriate arrangements for permanent monitoring' of their output. If a product is deemed to be unsafe, then it will be withdrawn from free circulation upon notice to that effect. On the other hand, a product which 'presents a significant risk which is acceptable as such' must have clear warnings informing users of the potential risk.

In the UK we already have a set of rules intended to ensure that only safe products are placed on the market, Part II of the Consumer Protection Act 1987. For present purposes it is most useful to concentrate on comparing the basic points of the directive with the Consumer Protection Act (for a discussion of this topic, see eg *"Product Safety: The E.E.C Follows UK Lead"*, by J.R. Bradgate, Trading Law, Vol 7, p.2) a

nd considering how the proposal is likely to affect the construction industry (including other EC rules which have been passed or are shortly to be passed).

The Product Safety proposal and Part II of the Consumer Protection Act 1987 compared

As a preliminary point, there may be some confusion relating to the scope of the Product Safety Directive and the Product Liability Directive (implemented in Part I of the Consumer Protection Act): after all, a product which is unsafe is likely to be 'defective' and so give rise to liability under the Act. In fact, product liability and product safety, although related, are distinct. Generally, the former notion carries with it the idea that in a batch of generally safe products there may be a few, perhaps because of poor quality control, which are defective and cause the consumer harm. Arguably product safety covers situations where the product may have been produced in the way it was intended to be produced, but there is an inherent defect in design, rendering the product unsafe.

Under Part II of the Consumer Protection Act it is now a criminal offence to supply, offer or agree to supply or expose or possess for supply consumer goods which do not satisfy the "general safety requirement", as defined in the Act. The proposed Directive is not intended to impose criminal liability on the suppliers of unsafe products; it is to be an administrative measure.

Thus, although the aim of the two legislative measures are ostensibly the same, ie eliminating unsafe products from the marketplace, the means of achieving it are different. That said, the enforcement mechanism under the Act is not solely criminal in nature: the general regulatory powers of the Secretary of State and the relevant authorities may be invoked whenever appropriate.

Part II of the Consumer Protection Act applies to consumer goods which are ordinarily supplied for private use or consumption (although there are limited exceptions to this where certain products are covered by specific regulatory schemes). As indicated above, the ambit of the proposed directive is much wider. Reconditioned products, components of finished products and agricultural produce all qualify as products for the purpose of the Directive.

Under both existing and proposed pieces of legislation, there is no "absolute" standard of safety - assuming that such a standard can ever be achieved. In fact both the Directive and the Consumer Protection Act appear to judge the safety of goods in comparison with the state of the art, compliance with published safety standards and seem to involve some sort of cost-benefit equation.

The requirement that a supplier must monitor the safety of the products he places into free circulation is a noteworthy departure from any other legislative enactments in this area of law. Under the directive, "supplier" is defined as:

- the manufacturer of a product,
- the importer into the Community from a third country,
- distributors and other professionals in the supply chain insofar as their activities may affect the safety properties of a marketed product.

Manufacturers and importers must already be following similar procedures in order to comply with the product liability provisions in Part I of the Consumer Protection Act. Suppliers, however, need only keep administrative records which will allow them to identify their own supplier if need be. The obligations contained in the draft directive would have the effect of considerably extending the administrative burden of suppliers.

The draft Product Safety Directive and the construction industry

Article 5 of the draft Directive states that products manufactured in accordance with specific Community rules will be deemed to be safe. Thus, provided that manufacturers comply with sector specific product standards, they will be unaffected by the rules and procedures contained in the Product

Safety Directive. Furthermore, in the absence of any specific legislative standards, manufacturers can rely on the "state of the art" defence.

In this respect it is worth distinguishing the intended effect of the Construction Products Directive [Council Directive on the approximation of laws, regulations and administrative provisions on the Member States relating to construction products, Directive 89/106, OJL 40/12 1989]. Under that directive products must be manufactured so that they satisfy the "essential requirements". Annex 1 of the Directive defines "essential requirements" in terms of products being used in construction works. Thus, provided that products are "fit for their intended use" in construction works, they will satisfy the requirements of the Construction Products Directive. Once in place however, a construction product may be unsafe in relation to end consumers - in which case the product safety rules would come into play. The Essential Requirements are printed below:

Essential Requirements

The products must be suitable for construction works which (as a whole and in their separate parts) are fit for their intended use, account being taken of economy, and in this connection satisfy the following essential requirements where the works are subject to regulations containing such requirements. Such requirements must, subject to normal maintenance, be satisfied for an economically reasonable working life. The requirements generally concern actions which are foreseeable.

1. Mechanical resistance and stability

The construction works must be designed and built in such a way that the loadings that are liable to act on it during its construction and use will not lead to any of the following:
(a)   collapse of the whole or part of the work;
(b)   major deformations to an inadmissible degree;
(c)   damage to other parts of the works or to fittings or installed equipment as a result of major deformation of the load-bearing construction;
(d)   damage by an event to an extent disproportionate to the original cause.

2. Safety in case of fire

The construction works must be designed and built in such a way that in the event of an outbreak of fire:
-     the load-bearing capacity of the construction can be assumed for a

specific period of time,
- the generation and spread of fire and smoke within the works are limited,
- the spread of the fire to neighbouring construction works is limited,
- occupants can leave the works or be rescued by other means,
- the safety of rescue teams is taken into consideration.

3. Hygiene health and the environment

The construction work must be designed and built in such a way that it will not be a threat to the hygiene or health of the occupants or neighbours, in particular as a result of any of the following:
- the giving-off of toxic gas,
- the presence of dangerous particles or gases in the air,
- the emission of dangerous radiation,
- pollution or poisoning of the water or soil,
- faulty elimination of waste water, smoke, solid or liquid wastes,
- the presence of damp in parts of the works or on surfaces within the works.

4. Safety in use

The construction work must be designed and built in such a way that it does not present unacceptable risks of accident in service or in operation such as slipping, falling, collision, burns, electrocution, injury from explosion.

5. Protection against noise

The construction works must be designed and built in such a way that noise perceived by the occupants or people nearby is kept down to a level that will not threaten their health and will allow them to sleep, rest and work in satisfactory conditions.

6. Energy economy and heat retention

The construction works and its heating, cooling and ventilation installations must be designed and built in such a way that the amount of energy required in use shall be low, having regard to the climatic conditions of the location and the occupants.

Summary of Conclusions

The author identifies "expectations" (as to safety) as the key to the concept of defect and thus to defences against liabiilty under EC Product Liabiity legislation, with the addition of the "state of the art" relief. The latter has been criticised by consumers in its UK manifestation as too generous to producers and is a promising line of defence in the construction industry. The author concludes from a review of the common law position in the UK that consumers may be compelled to look for statutory protection in the light of restrictions to recovery in contract and tort. The EC is moving to fill the void; some overlap is observed between Directives, notably Product Liability and Services.

24 Competition law within the EEC and its impact upon construction

Michael Bowsher

Synopsis

In this paper the author considers why the competition law of the European Community has had only limited direct impact on the construction industry and how competition law may affect the industry to a considerably greater extent in the near future. He reviews, in particular, the consequences of the interaction and division of jurisdiction between national and Community competition laws. The paper is brought up to date by a postscript describing the EC Commission's decision in the Dutch construction cartel case adopted in February 1992. This postscript was written before the text of the decision became publicly available and is based primarily on the Commission's public statements.

Introduction

This paper considers the current and potential effect of EEC competition law in the construction sector. Although its subject is described as competition law in the EEC, no attempt is made to compare comprehensively each system of national competition law in the Community. However, the paper does consider the important interrelationship between national and Community law in this field. The scope of this paper is also limited to the market for the goods and services commonly supplied by contractors and subcontractors. References to the construction industry should be regarded as being limited in this way. Only incidental reference is made to the important subject of anti-competitive agreements in markets for construction materials and components and professional services in the construction industry.

The object of competition law

EEC competition law operates to promote certain policy goals which the drafters of the Treaty of Rome regarded as important. It operates in addition to, and sometimes in place of, existing national law regulating the conduct of business activities. EEC competition law pursues two primary goals. The first and often most important goal is the prevention of any restrictive practices which interfere with the integration of the markets of the separate Member States into a single market. Throughout their history, the Commission and the Court of Justice have acted vigorously to prevent the compartmentalisation of geographical markets in the Community. This element of competition policy is, therefore, closely linked to the Community's general objective to integrate the markets of the Member States.

The second goal of EEC competition law is the protection and promotion of "competition" itself. The concept of a competitive market is necessarily rather loose and the precise objective of Community law may, therefore, differ from the similar goals of the various national systems of competition law. The Commission and national authorities may also differ as to the extent to which other goals may counterbalance the interests of competition. For instance, the provisions of the Treaty of Rome and the U.K. Restrictive Trade Practices legislation, which may both apply to particular behaviour of any business operating in the United Kingdom, operate and have significantly different effects on that behaviour.

Thus, while community law considers the effects of any agreement so as to prohibit any agreement which has or is intended to have an anti-competitive impact, the U.K. Restrictive Trade Practices legislation looks at the form rather than the effect of the agreement. The statute requires that agreements which incorporate a specific type of restriction be registered in certain circumstances. Failure to register when required leads to invalidity of the registrable agreement. If an agreement is registrable, it may nevertheless be justifiable on condition that it fulfils the complex public interest criteria in the Restrictive Trade Practices Act 1976. The public interest justification based on a number of different legislative 'gateways', tends to lead to inconsistent assessments of the effect of any agreement by the Restrictive Practices Court. This makes it hard to draw firm conclusions as to a provision's validity. The system thereby discourages analysis of the substantive nature of a restriction but encourages the development of sophisticated drafting techniques designed to avoid the need for registration.[1] Competition law under the Treaty of Rome is more clearly intended to pursue pro-competitive policy goals as it looks at the impact of any conduct rather than the formal nature of an agreement. The Commission's competition policy pursuing the twin goals described above forms an essential tool in integrating the various national markets of the Community into a thriving single market. It thus promotes the general liberalisation of economic conditions.

1 Douglass Klein, "*Cooperation and the per se debate: evidence from the United Kingdom*", The Antitrust Bulletin, Fall 1989, page 517.

The basic provisions of EEC competition law

The two primary provisions of EEC competition law are Articles 85 and 86 of the Treaty of Rome. Article 85(1) prohibits all agreements between undertakings and concerted practices which may affect trade between Member States and which have as their object or effect the prevention, restriction or distortion of competition within the common market. Any prohibited agreement is automatically void and, therefore, unenforceable by virtue of Article 85(2). Article 85(3) provides, however, that an agreement may benefit from an exemption from the prohibition if it has specific positive effects and a fair share of the benefits of these effects is passed on to the ultimate consumers. Only the Commission may grant such an exemption so that a national court cannot enforce any contract or contractual provision which it is satisfied is in breach of Article 85(1), even if it thinks the agreement merits exemption. It can only adjourn while the Commission takes its time to decide whether to grant an Article 85(3) exemption. In addition to notifying the Commission of an agreement so that it may consider whether the agreement should be granted an exemption, parties may also apply to the Commission for a decision that the agreement does not fall within Article 85(1). This decision is called a negative clearance.

Article 86 has been found to apply to a number of suppliers of construction materials which enjoy what is described as a dominant position in respect of specific geographic and product markets[2]. Article 86 prohibits "abuse" of "a dominant position" in a "substantial part" of the EEC. A number of examples of abuse are given in the Treaty. The market for the services of contractors is highly fragmented and it does not seem likely that any European contractor would be found to enjoy a dominant position, except possibly in respect of a particularly specialised, separate construction market. However, a number of agreements which are commonly entered into in the construction industry may fall within Article 85's definition of a prohibited agreement. The effect of Article 85 on agreements and in particular "cartels", agreements on standard conditions of contract or tender, and joint ventures is considered below.

National and Community Jurisdiction

Community competition law does not apply to all business activities within the Community. Articles 85 and 86 only apply if the jurisdictional requirement that the agreement or concerted practice may affect trade between Member States is satisfied. This is of particular importance in the

2   e.g. BPB Industries ~1c OJ No L 10, 13th January 1989, p. 50; *Italian Flat Glass*, OJ No L 33, 4th February 1989, p. 44.

construction sector. It is this test of effect upon inter-State trade which draws a line between the field of application of EEC law and that in which national law is exclusively applicable. One of the early cases in the European Court of Justice discussing this requirement related to a price-fixing cartel in the cement industry in the Netherlands.[3] The Court interpreted this test widely and decided that a potential effect on trade could be found to exist when the conduct in question may deflect trade from the cross-border channels that it might otherwise follow, even though the conduct complained of took place only in one Member State. A national cartel may well have such effect, and was found to have that effect in that case.

While there is substantial inter-State trade for materials in the construction industry there is, for a number of reasons, much less well developed trade in contractors' services. In some sectors there may be no significant work carried out by contractors from another Member State. As a result of this jurisdiction test a large part of activity in the construction sector is likely only to be subject to national law. It is important, therefore to compare the approach of national authorities with those of the Commission. The approaches are not always consistent and in some Member States there is little effective competition law. The issue of jurisdiction may, therefore, be of great importance in determining the substantive evaluation of particular behaviour or the availability of appropriate remedies.

Trade between Member States

The case-law of the Court of Justice in Luxembourg has consistently stated that for a restriction to have an effect upon trade between Member States for the purposes of the Articles of the Treaty it must be possible to foresee with a sufficient degree of probability that, on the basis of all the objective factors of law or of fact, the restriction may have a direct or indirect influence, whether actual or potential, on the pattern of trade between Member States in such a way that it might hinder the attainment of the objectives of a single market in the Community. Any restriction must therefore be analysed in light of the objective, factual or legal circumstances in order to establish whether it appears to be capable of having an appreciable effect on trade between Member States. In a number of cases this test has required a complex analysis of the facts of the case.

In the *Cementhandelaren* case, already referred to, the members of a cement price fixing cartel in the Netherlands sought to argue that their agreement could not affect trade between Member States because it was a "purely national cartel" limited to the territory of the Netherlands which did

3   *Cementhandelaren* v. *Commission*, case 8/72 [1972] ECR 977.

not apply to inter-State trade. The Court of Justice stated that an agreement extending over the whole territory of a Member State by its very nature reinforced the compartmentalisation of national markets and therefore impeded the aims of the Treaty of Rome. In *Salonia* v. *Poidomani and Gialio*,[4] the Court held that a "closed circuit" distribution system applying to most sales outlets for newspapers and periodicals in Italy might have repercussions on the distribution of newspapers and periodicals from other Member States.

One may contrast these cases with the position in *Hugin* v. *Commission*.[5] A Swedish manufacturer of cash registers refused to supply Liptons with the necessary spare parts for Liptons to offer a maintenance service for Hugin cash registers. This service would have been largely confined to the London area as such services could not be operated profitably beyond a certain distance from the business. Liptons had tried to obtain spare parts from other Member States, but the Court said that this was an exceptional occurrence and that the abuse of dominant position complained of did not affect any inter-State trade in spare parts, since there was no indication of the existence, whether actual or potential, of a normal pattern of trade between the Member States in these spare parts. The Court held that the spare parts were "not such as to constitute a commodity of commercial interest in trade between Member States".

A number of factors are likely to affect the existence or otherwise of any actual or potential trade between Member States in a particular product market. The ratio of profit to cost in making such trade is of primary importance. The need for rapid response to customer orders, the need for geographical proximity to the customer for goods which are perishable or which like ready mixed concrete do not lend themselves to long distance transport, and cultural factors can all affect the development of inter-State trade. Finally, the legal and regulatory conditions of a product market in a particular Member State may prevent or restrict the development of such trade. Insofar as the Community is able to break down any of these barriers it may create the necessary conditions for such inter-State trade where none existed before. The Commission's programme of integration will likely extend the scope of its own competition law.

Indeed, as the progressive integration of markets develops in the Community the likelihood will be that anti-competitive restrictions in one geographical area will need to have an ever-wider geographical effect upon trade between Member States if they are to be effective. As potential cross-border trade develops for a specific product or for a particular service an anti-competitive practice in a local market will be rendered irrelevant by freely

4   case 126/80 [1981] ECR 1563.
5   case 22/78 [1979] ECR 1869.

competing importers, unless those importers also take part in the restraint, or are in some way excluded from reaping the benefit of their competitive advantage.

Buildings do not cross borders and historically construction and engineering in Western European markets has been carried out by local contractors. Government bodies have, in particular adopted chauvinist attitudes. There has, therefore, been little inter-State trade in the goods and services supplied by contractors. The Commission is, however, actively seeking to break down the barriers to this trade and, in particular, to prohibit nationalistic procurement policies. Private clients have also shown a tendency to contract primarily with local contractors. There are a number of reasons for this. A local contractor may be more economic, he may have greater familiarity with local conditions and materials, and the design of the building may have been drawn up in such a way that it would be inappropriate to use contractors from elsewhere in the Community.

It is clear, however, that substantial trade in contractors' services is now developing between Member States. This is not the place for a detailed analysis of the volume and growth in cross-border trade in the construction sector. By way of illustration I would refer to John Bellhouse's paper at this conference in 1988 in which he provided statistics indicating an almost two-fold increase from 1986 to 1987 in the value of contracts obtained by U.K. contractors in the Community.[6]

As the scope and volume of inter-State patterns of trade increase, Community competition law will have a progressively greater effect upon contractors.

National approaches to restrictive trade practices

Contractors may be subject to Community law or national control (or both), depending on the sector of the industry and the area of the Community under consideration. Commercial behaviour can therefore only be planned by reference to both national and Community competition laws. Some Member States have little or no effective control of competition. Of those which do, Germany, the United Kingdom and France have taken a consistently hard line with any attempt by contractors or suppliers in the construction industry to fix prices, or to agree to share markets or tender for contracts on any other agreed basis. Such agreements are regarded as violations of the law which can rarely, if ever, be justified.

For example in West Germany, in 1983 the Bundeskartellamt fined 80

6 Bellhouse, "UK Construction Abroad" in *"Construction Contract Policy - Improved Procedures and Practice"* ed. Uff & Capper. See also Knechtel & Wiegand *"1992: The Internal E.C. Construction market Data - Facts - Commentaries"*, [1989] I.C.L.R. 4.

building contractors a total of DM 56 million after investigations had established that for some years they had been rigging tendering, establishing quotas and sharing markets. In 1988 fines amounting to DM 7 million were imposed on the companies Bilfinger & Berger, Dyckerhoff & Widmann and Philipp Holzmann and their directors. However, some of these fines were reduced on appeal.

In France, in 1989 the Conseil de la Concurrence imposed fines of FF 166 million on 71 public works contractors for rigging 80 separate tenders for road building and repairs between 1984 and 1986. The companies involved included eight companies in the Bouygues group and a subsidiary of GTM-Entrepose/Dumez. when announcing its decision the Conseil de la Concurrence observed that since 1977 there have been at least three cases every year of rigged public works tenders for roads, buildings or procurement. This year the Conseil de la Concurrence has fined 43 electrical contractors a total of FF 128 million for rigging bids on electrical installation and maintenance contracts. The effect of the relevant French legislation in the construction industry has recently reached the front page of "Le Monde" as a result of a complaint made by the leading Italian contractor Condotte d'Acqua to the Conseil de la Concurrence.[7] The complainant has alleged that French competitors (including Dumez) have conspired with the agent letting a contract for a motorway tunnel to prevent Condotte d'Acqua winning that contract.

The competition law of the United Kingdom is currently in rather a confused state as the provisions of the Restrictive Trade Practices Act, the Competition Act, the Fair Trading Act and even the common law may apply to the competitive practices of construction companies. In the past, agreements such as the agreement in *Re Birmingham Association of Building Trades Employers' Agreement* [1963] 1 WLR 484 that the members of the association should press for the use of the R.I.B.A. standard form of contract, and the agreement between seven electrical contractors not to tender considered in *Re Electrical Installations Agreement* [1970] 1 WLR 1391 have been found to be registrable.[8]

Many different markets for construction supplies in the U.K. have also been the subject of intense investigation by the Director General for Fair Trading. In 1989 the Director General for Fair Trading expressed his particular concern about collusive behaviour in the construction sector which he suggested was having a substantial effect on the costs of construc-

7 "Italian building group accuses French of cartel", Financial Times, September 24, 1990, and "Une société italienne dénonce des 'ententes' en France", Le Monde, September 22, 1990.
8 See also *Re Building Employers Confederation's Application* [1985] ICR 167.

tion projects.

These attitudes may be contrasted with the attitude in the Netherlands to concertation in the construction industry. A Royal Decree of 29th December 1986 prohibits a number of categories of restrictive agreement including price fixing and market sharing arrangements, with the exception of arrangements provided for by certain private agreements. It is thought that in the construction industry not all forms of concertation between contractors should be considered detrimental to competition. The view is taken that a general prohibition of all forms of concertation would be violated so extensively that it is better to allow certain forms of controlled concertation. The arrangements which are excepted by the Royal Decree are those made on the basis of the rules of various contractors' associations, in particular the Dutch Building Trade Price-regulating Association. These rules provide for a degree of formalised concertation between contractors prior to the submission of a tender. The concertation takes place in formal meetings. The meetings are presided over by an official employed by one of the limited liability companies which operate the contractors' associations. The rules allow contractors to compare the prices submitted by them so that any one of them can withdraw its tender before presenting the price submitted in the meeting as a binding and irrevocable offer to the employer. The rules also allow contractors to add a sum to the price submitted so as to cover the calculation costs of the other participants to a tender. The Royal Decree sets maximum levels for these additional sums in proportion to the type and the value of the construction work, the extent to which the plans have been specified, and the extent to which the risk in respect of error is shifted to the contractor.[9]

In March 1989 the Commissioner responsible for competition, Sir Leon Brittan, stated that the Commission was investigating the compatibility of these rules with the competition rules of the Community, and in particular to determine whether and in what circumstances these arrangements may noticeably affect trade between Member States.[10] At that point the Commission was bringing proceedings against the Netherlands under Article 169 of the Treaty of Rome for failure to fulfil its treaty obligations by permitting such concertation. The outcome of this investigation is discussed in the postscript below.

A similar example of the tension between the competition policy and other priorities of national government is supplied by recent Italian legislation. A law has recently been enacted which limits the proportion of any public works contract which may be subcontracted, establishes a minimum for the subcontract price and limits the subcontractors which may carry out

9 Glazener, Pijnacker, Hordrijk & van der Riet, SEW 4 (1990) p. 194.
10 OJ No C 174, 10th July 1989, p. 37.

such work. This would seem to conflict with Article 85 and the compatibility of the law with the Treaty of Rome has been raised in the European Parliament.[11] The Commission has asked the Italian government for its comments. The law, however, had a clearly expressed purpose to reduce the number of sub-contracts let to companies with links to the Mafia or Camorra.[12] These and other aspects of competition in Italy are likely to develop as a result of the enactment on 27th September 1990 of an Italian competition statute in language similar to that of Article 85 and 86.

Implementation of Community Law in national courts

EEC competition law may affect undertakings in two ways. First, an undertaking may become the subject of Commission competition proceedings. The more common effect of EEC competition law is that it may alter or render invalid parties' contractual obligations. By virtue of section 2(1) of the European Communities Act 1972, Articles 85 and 86 of the Treaty of Rome have, in the parlance of Community law, "direct effect" and create individual rights enforceable in national courts. Thus if national law does not grant an adequate remedy a national court may apply Community competition law and any party to a contract may go to a national court and seek a declaration that the contract or a part of it is void. EEC law provides that void provisions may be severable and that domestic law applies in determining whether a particular provision may be severed.[13] The conventional English law rules apply.

The procedure becomes more complicated if one of the parties applies to the Commission for an exemption pursuant to Article 85(3) in respect of the agreement. As explained above, Article 85(3) provides that an agreement may be exempted from the prohibition when it has specific positive effects and a fair share of the benefits of these effects is passed on to consumers. While any court can decide whether or not an agreement is prohibited by Article 85(1) and is therefore void, only the Commission can grant an exemption and it may be necessary to adjourn the national proceedings while the Commission considers the matter. However, in *BRT* v. *SABAM*[14] the European Court of Justice made it clear that while a national court may adjourn its proceedings while the Commission considers the matter the national court should generally allow proceedings before it to continue if it decides either that the behaviour in question is clearly incapable of having any appreciable effect on competition on trade between Member States, or

---

11 OJ No C 207, 20th August 1990, p. 10.
12 See "Breaking the grip of the Mafia", Financial Times, 8th October 1990.
13 *Chemidus Wavin* v. *TERI* [1978] 3 C.M.L.R. 514 (C.A.).
14 case 127/73, [1974] ECR 51 & 313.

that it is clearly in breach of Article 85(1) and incapable of exemption.[15]

It seems likely, although it has not been finally decided, that Articles 85 and 86 give rise to a cause of action in damages or for an injunction at the suit of a party injured by the abusive conduct of a dominant undertaking or the operation of a prohibited agreement. Two English decisions are now taken to indicate that, in principle, a right of action for damages exists in English law under Article 86 on the basis of breach of statutory duty.[16] It would seem that Article 85(l) should also, therefore, give rise to an action in damages even though this would lead to the anomalous result that conduct of a kind which would rarely be actionable in damages under United Kingdom domestic law would be actionable in damages under Community law. The right to damages would, as a consequence, turn on whether some actual or potential effect on inter-State trade could be demonstrated. An injunction should also be available to prevent the continuation of a breach of Article 85(l) or Article 86 at the suit of an individual injured by that breach, on the basis of the normal principles relating to injunctions.

The existence, or otherwise, of a pattern of inter-State trade may in certain circumstances be open to interpretation. A national court which is keen to grant a remedy on the basis of Community law where the applicability of Community law is open to question may adopt a liberal approach in applying the inter-State trade test. It seems that Sir Neil Lawson did just that in *Cutsforth* v. *Mansfield Inns*[17] in granting an interim injunction to the suppliers of amusement machines on the basis of Article 85(l) and subsidiary Community legislation restraining brewery companies from excluding suppliers from their tied houses. Sir Neil Lawson was asked to grant interim relief to prevent the brewery from ordering the removal of the plaintiff's gaming machines from all the pubs owned by the defendant brewery. Specific Community legislation grants a block exemption to all leases which comply with the provisions of the legislation.[18] Such leases are thereby exempted from the prohibition of Article 85(l). Leases which do not comply with the Regulation must be the subject of an individual application if they are to be granted an exemption. The judge found that it was arguable that the provisions of the lease which the brewery sought to rely on in excluding the plaintiff's machines did not benefit from the block exemption.

---

15 On the approach of English courts see Kerse, "EEC Antitrust Procedure" (2nd ed.), paragraph 10.14.
16 *Garden Cottage Foods* v. *Milk Marketing Board* [1984] A.C. 10 (H.L.), which was only an interlocutory decision, and *Bourgouin* v. *Ministry of Agriculture* [1986] Q.B. 716 (C.A.), which was primarily a decision on Article 30 of the Treaty of Rome; see Collins, "European Community Law in the United Kingdom" (4th ed.), p. 103 et seq.
17 [1986] I WLR 558.
18 Commission Regulation No 1984/83 on the application of Article 85(3) to categories of exclusive purchasing agreements, OJ No L 173, 30th June 1983, p. 5.

However, in finding that the system of brewery leases operated by this relatively small brewery might affect trade between Member States and that Article 85 was applicable, the judge sought to distinguish the Hugin case, mentioned above, on two rather surprising grounds. He observed that Hugin was not a Community person and therefore not subject to the Treaty of Rome and that in Hugin the question of spares for cash register repairs was not bound up with other, prohibited, transactions. The first basis for distinguishing this case is without any basis in Community Law. The second is puzzling as it does not appear to relate to the issue of effect upon trade between Member States. Hugin could more appropriately have been distinguished on the basis that the supplies of the spare parts would have come from the Member State affected (the U.K.) or from outside the Community (Hugin in Sweden). There was no pattern of trade between Member States. If Hugin had supplied the U.K. from another Member State there would have been such a pattern of trade and there would have been an impact on trade between Member States.

Nevertheless, the enthusiasm of national courts to apply Community law remedies is important for the development and enforcement of Community competition law. The Commission's competition directorate-general encourages parties to seek remedies available under EEC competition law in national courts. The Commission's staff are not able to cope with the increasing volume of work and are keen for complainants to seek their Community law remedies without their involvement whenever possible. In the 17th Report on Competition Policy the Commission said that it was seeking to increase awareness within the Member States of the possibilities afforded by the direct effect of Articles 85 and 86. The Commission reiterated this in a press release issued at the end of 1989 when it announced that it had required a German manufacturer of machinery for making a building material to terminate a violation of Article 86. The Commission observed that a national court could have terminated the violation by means of an injunction and would also have had the power to award damages, which the Commission does not have.

As already mentioned, there is no conclusive English authority for this proposition put forward by the Commission - however, it is likely that English courts will adopt this position. It seems, therefore, that damages may be recovered in respect of any loss suffered by virtue of any action by contractors which violates Articles 85(1) or Article 86 and which also affects inter-State trade.

Categories of Agreement falling within Article 85(1)

Article 85 lists a number of categories of agreement or concerted practice which are treated as anti-competitive and which fall within the scope of the Article if they satisfy the jurisdiction requirement of effect upon inter-State trade. However, this list is not exhaustive, nor is it in any sense definitive of the type of restriction which may be regarded as falling within the scope of the prohibition.

In the context of commercial activity in the construction sector a number of types of agreement may fall within the scope of Article 85. Some of these categories of restriction are almost invariably regarded as prohibited anti-competitive agreements. Some of these agreements may have certain positive characteristics and may therefore qualify for exemption for a period of time pursuant to Article 85(3). The categories of agreement described below illustrate the effect of Article 85.

Collusive tendering

For these purposes collusive tendering is defined as any agreement, understanding or practice among a group of tenderers which is designed to distort the process of competitive tendering. Collusive tendering is the clearest example of an agreement or concerted practice falling within Article 85(1) which might be encountered in the construction industry. Collusive tendering may take a number of forms. It may be analogous to a simple price-fixing cartel in a commodities market or of the kind which the Commission commonly finds in markets for particular building components, as in recent cases such as *Belgian Roofing Felt*[19] and *Welded Steel Mesh*[20]. It may also be a more sophisticated arrangement to arrange for contracts to be apportioned amongst a group of contractors or sub-contractors.

Any collusive tendering agreement in the construction industry which came to the attention of the Commission would almost certainly be regarded as an intentional and therefore automatic violation of Article 85(1) of the Treaty of Rome. There would be no need for the Commission to prove that the agreement had any anti-competitive effect. There remains only the possibility that in special circumstances such an agreement might benefit from an exemption under Article 85(3) because of some wider beneficial effect.

The rules of the Dutch Building Trade Price-regulating Association discussed enable the Association to operate such a collusive tendering agreement. The Commission clearly regards this agreement as anti-competitive. The wording of the statement on this subject by Sir Leon Brittan which were referred to above suggests that the only question which

19 OJ No. L 232, 19th August 1986, p. 15; Decision of the Court of Justice, case 246/86 dated 11th July 1989 (unpublished)
20 OJ No. L 260, 6th September 1989, p. 1

the Commission regarded as open to question was whether the inter-State trade requirement was satisfied so that the agreement was subject to the jurisdiction of Community law. The Commission seemed to assume that if the agreements were subject to Community jurisdiction then they would fall within Article 85. The compatibility of such government approved agreements is, however, the subject of debate.[21]

Standard conditions

An agreement among contractors or sub-contractors to provide goods and services only on certain standard conditions may fall within Article 85. Article 85(1) expressly states that agreements which directly or indirectly fix trading conditions are to be regarded as anti-competitive agreements within the terms of the Article.

The Commission's approach is demonstrated by the approach it took in a case in 1988 in which it chose not to take any action in respect of an agreement between the International European Construction Federation (FIEC) and the Comité Européen des Equipements Techniques du Bâtiment which standardised tender procedures for the supply of specialised technical equipment to the building sector. This agreement included measures tending to favour the consultation of a limited number of firms, especially sub-contractors, for the supply of the equipment to which the agreement related, and established a system of compensation for unsuccessful valid tenders, where tendering costs are high. The Commission stated in its 18th Report on Competition Policy[22] that this cooperation should help to promote, or in any event maintain, market access for small and medium-sized enterprises.

The Commission had previously published a public communication[23] in which it stated that amendments had been made to the agreement at its request so that main contractors were merely advised, but no longer obliged, to consult three to five or five to ten subcontractors, depending on the complexity of the work to be performed. The agreement in its final form also advised but did not require contractors to announce the number of subcontractors consulted and to incorporate in the invitations to tender the arrangements for the indemnification of the unsuccessful valid tenders. Before amendment, the Agreement had provided that indemnification was automatically triggered by either of two thresholds relating to the number of subcontractors consulted and to the tender costs incurred. The Commis-

---

21 See, for example, Joliet, "National Anti-Competitive legislation and Community law" (1989) 12 Fordham Intl L.J. 163.

22 para. 60.

23 OJ No C 52, 24th February 1988, p. 2.

sion's requirement that mandatory thresholds be removed from the Agreement reflected its strict view of interference with the price formation system. Automatic indemnification would have eliminated one area in which tenderers compete in making their bids.

The Agreement contained several provisions relating to payment guarantees designed to ensure transparency of payments between the principal, the contractor and the subcontractors. The Agreement requires that the forwarding of such payments be covered by contractual provisions and time limits. The contractor and the subcontractor may supplement these payment guarantees by other measures allowed by the law.

The Agreement also provided that the main contractor must inform the subcontractors consulted of the identity of the successful tenderers. In that respect, the Commission requested that the parties amend the Agreement to provide that the main contractor not be required to provide the subcontractors with a list of the subcontractors consulted and the amount of the bids. This requirement is evidence that the Commission will permit exchange of information within a trade association only if that information does not give the parties access to individualised data on the competitive situation of the others.

The Commission published no legal analysis of this agreement, but the notice published and the amendments which the Commission requested illustrate the Commission's concern to prevent unnecessary restraints on price competition even when taking steps to encourage small and medium-sized enterprises to compete with larger businesses.

Information agreements

Even pure information agreements are regarded by the Commission as falling within Article 85(1) in certain markets. The evaluation of the effect of these agreements depends on analysis of the economic structure of the market. The view taken by the Commission has been that the risk of anti-competitive effect is greater in oligopolistic markets for homogeneous products and one would not normally categorise the market for completed construction works as a homogeneous market. However, the Commission has brought proceedings against manufacturers and importers of agricultural tractors in the United Kingdom. Agricultural tractors are not homogeneous products. The Commission has not taken its final decision in this case, but if the Commission decided to pursue this approach in the tractors case it is at least conceivable that information agreements in parts of the housing market might, on the same basis, be regarded as anti-competitive as the information gleaned from such an agreement might form the basis for a sophisticated form of collusive tendering.

Joint ventures and other forms of cooperation

It is now increasingly common for contractors to enter into arrangements with other contractors either for the purposes of work on one particular contract, or in order to cooperate in a particular market[24]. Some of these arrangements may be called joint ventures, and would more likely be characterised as a form of cooperative arrangement.[25] Others may be mergers or "concentrations" within the meaning of the merger control regulation, Regulation 4064/89.[26]

A joint venture of this type presents three specific anti-competitive risks. First, it may become the foundation for collusive agreements between the parents. Second, as a result of the creation of the joint venture the parents will be discouraged from making any separate entry into the market in which the joint venture operates. Insofar as they were both potential entrants into this market the existence of the joint venture will have eliminated potential competition. Third, the joint venture may be used by the parents as a means of excluding others from competing in the market. On the other hand the joint venture may also give rise to substantial benefits. A useful, though dated, statement of Commission policy is set forth in its 6th Report on Competition Policy.[27]

The Commission generally considers cooperative joint ventures to be within the prohibition of Article 85(1) if they are between actual or potential competitors or if collaboration with respect to the joint venture is likely to affect competition between the parties in other areas. However, the Commission regularly exempts joint ventures between competitors. Indeed, recent cases suggest that a small but growing category of joint ventures or cooperative arrangements may fall outside Article 85(1) altogether.[28] In analysing joint operations the Commission distinguishes between the "concentrative" joint ventures, which are treated as mergers under the merger control regulation, Regulation 4064/89, which came into effect on

24 For present purposes one may adopt the definition of a joint venture given by Professor Brodley in "Joint Ventures and Antitrust Policy" (1982) 95 Harvard LR 1523 as:
"An integration of operations between two or more separate firms in which the following conditions are present: (i) the JV is under the joint control of the parent firms, which are not present; (ii) each parent makes a substantial contribution to the JV; (iii) the JV exists as a business entity separate from its parents; (iv) the JV creates significant new enterprise capability in terms of new productive capacity, new technology, a new product or entry into a new market."

25 See "Joint ventures become more popular", Financial Times, 20th November 1989, "Builders put their European houses in order", Financial Times, 18th June 1990 and "Builders take their partners for Europe", The Economist, 14th July 1990.

26 OJ No L 257, 21st September 1990, p. 14.

27 p.38

28 *Elopak/Metalbox-Odin* OJ No. L 209, 5th August 1990, p. 15; *Konsortium* ECR 900 OJ No. L 228, 22nd August 1990, p. 31.

21st September 1990, and "cooperative" joint ventures, which are analysed under Article 85(1) or Article 86. Both the Court of Justice and the Commission consider minority shareholdings in competitors to be violations of Article 85(l) where they allow the investor to exercise influence over the competitor or where they provide for commercial cooperation or create a structure likely to be used for such cooperation.[29]

Consortia for specific projects

Contractors commonly create a consortium in order to tender for and execute particularly large or technically challenging works. In principle such a consortium of competitors may be regarded as restricting competition. However, the Commission granted a negative clearance to the construction contract between Eurotunnel and the eight contractors for the Channel Tunnel.[30] The Commission referred to its Notice on Cooperation[31] and stated that agreements setting up a consortium for the purpose of carrying out works which each of the members of the consortium could not carry out themselves do not restrict competition. They would not therefore fall within Article 85(1). This would even be the case where the consortium was made up of enterprises which normally compete with each other.

Long-term joint ventures

As already indicated, joint ventures fall into two categories, "cooperative" and "concentrative" joint ventures. Article 3(2) of the merger control regulation, Regulation 4064/89 provides that:

"The creation of a joint venture performing on a lasting basis all the functions of an autonomous economic entity, which does not give rise to coordination of the competitive behaviour of the parties amongst themselves or between them and the joint venture, shall constitute a concentration."

A concentrative joint venture will be subject to Community or national merger control depending on its size, rather than subject to Article 85. It is important to note that, on the basis of the "Commission's notice regarding

29 *Philip Morris/Rembrandt/Rothmans*, Joined Cases 142 and 156/84 [1987] ECR 4487.
30 *Eurotunnel*, OJ No L 311, 17th November 1988, p.36.
31 Notice concerning agreements, decisions and concerted practices in the field of cooperation between undertakings - OJ No C 75, 29th July 1968 p.3, corrected in OJ No C 84, 28th August 1968, p.14.

the concentrative and cooperative operations under Council Regulation 4064/89 of 21 December 1989 on the control of concentrations between undertakings"[32] if either parent of the joint venture parents carries on a business similar to that of the joint venture anywhere in the Community, the Commission is likely to regard the joint venture as being cooperative in nature and falling under Article 85. It appears, however, that this position is being reexamined within the Commission.

Joint ventures between contractors operating for more than one contract or project will almost certainly be regarded as falling within Article 85(1) and it will be necessary to apply for an exemption pursuant to Article 85(3). Such exemption will not be forthcoming if the joint venture merely operates a business related to that of the parents' without presenting some economic or technological benefit. In the field of satellite technology the Commission granted an exemption in respect of a cooperative agreement between Alcatel and ANT until the end of 1996.[33] The Commission regarded this agreement as likely to give rise to coordination of the type seen in a joint venture. The agreement covers a broad range of commercial activities. It is intended to provide a framework for joint research and development, joint exploitation and joint marketing of electronic equipment in the field of civil radio communications and broadcasting satellites or space vehicles throughout the world. This is however an unusual market. A joint venture, cooperative arrangement or consortium between construction or engineering contractors would have to be rather special to benefit from this type of treatment.

As contractors become more involved in this country in the operation as well as the construction of roads, bridges and other public works, they may become involved in joint ventures or cooperative agreements relating to the operation of such public works after their completion. It may be possible to obtain an exemption for such an arrangement if the transport benefits are sufficiently great. The Commission has allowed one three-year exemption to be granted by default[34] in respect of the agreements between SNCF, British Rail and Eurotunnel for the use of the Channel Tunnel. The Commission has recently indicated that it will grant a further limited exemption.[35] It appears from the press release the Commission issued on 20th February 1989 that it allowed the previous exemption to be granted because of the improvement in cross-channel transport which the Commission expects will flow from the operation of the Channel Tunnel. It may be that contractors which have been permitted to collaborate on the construc-

32 OJ No C 203, 14th August 1990, p. 10.
33 *Alcatel*, OJ No L 32, 3rd February 1990, p.19.
34 by virtue of a provision applicable to the transport sector, Council Regulation No 1017/68, OJ No L 175, 23rd July 1968, p. 1.
35 OJ No C 176, 17th July 1990, p. 2.

tion of a project will also be permitted to collaborate on the operation of the finished works.

The Future

EEC competition law has not had a great effect upon contractors since 1957, or 1973. This is likely to change for a number of reasons. The integration of the single market and the development of cross-border activities of contractors will extend the scope of Community law. When the construction sector was merely a set of national markets for the fabrication of fixed structures it would have been contrived to talk of an effect on trade between Member States. This is no longer the case.

The coming into effect of the merger control regulation may bring a few large mergers in the construction sector to the attention of the Commission thus exciting their interest in the industry's behaviour. There is also a steady increase in the number of cross-border cross-shareholdings which may be reviewed under Article 85(l)..While the operation of merger control may stretch the resources of the Commission, issues of EEC competition law are likely to litigated in national courts. The English courts for their part seem to be willing to adopt an active and intelligent approach to applications for relief based on EEC law. The primary weakness of this system will be that although the High Court could award damages in respect of a violation of Article 85(1), it may in a number of circumstances have to adjourn the matter while the defendants' application for exemption under Article 85(3) is dealt with by the Commission.

It has for sometime been government policy to reform U.K. competition law. This policy is described in the White Paper *"Opening Markets: New Policy on Restrictive Trade Practices"*.[36] The effect of this proposal if it were to be made law would be to repeal the existing restrictive practices legislation and replace it with a system of law modelled on Article 85 of the Treaty. The wording of the main sections of the legislation would have almost the same effect as those of Article 85, subject to certain minor or technical modifications.

Most importantly there would be no requirement that anti-competitive behaviour affect trade between Member States for the legislation to bite. The vigorous, effects-based system evolved under the Treaty of Rome would therefore bite on any significant restrictive practice in the industry, however local its effect may be. It seems unlikely, however, that any such amendment will be made in the near future.

In conclusion, the inter-State trade requirement has substantially limited the scope of application of EEC competition law in the construction industry and the application of that law has been insignificant in comparison with the constant influence it has had in sectors such as chemicals, pharmaceuticals, branded food products or the market for the supply of construction materials. An increasing part of the construction market does now fall within the scope of EEC competition law by virtue of the erosion of the borders of national markets. At the national level the requirement may also be removed altogether as the new competition legislation will likely be a replica of the EEC law having its effects without any limitation save that of a de minimis rule. It seems, therefore, that the effect of EEC competition law on the construction industry is set to grow.

Postscript

There have been a number of important developments in competition law since this paper was delivered. Most important for the construction industry was the adoption by the Commission of its first ever decision finding that a cartel in the construction industry infringes Article 85 on 5th February 1992.

The Commission imposed a fine of 22.5 million ECU (about £16 million) to be paid by 28 associations of Dutch construction companies and their joint federation, the Vereniging van Samenwerkende Prijsregelende Organisaties in de Bouwnijverheid (commonly called the "SPO") for operating a cartel in the Dutch construction industry. The cartel's intention was found by the EC Commission to be the co-ordination of the competitive conduct of building and construction companies in responding to invitations to tender for contracts to be let by public authorities or private companies or individuals. The 28 associations which are the subject of the decision represent over 4000 Dutch builders including all the large and most of the medium-sized companies and the SPO's regulations are binding on all these companies. Another 3000 companies participate in the arrangements on a case-by-case basis.

The turnover of the Dutch construction industry in 1988 was in the region of 14 billion ECU (about £10 billion) and the cartel's activities affected about 30,000 contracts in that year with a total value of about 5.2 billion ECU (about £3.7 billion). The EC Commission's inquiry related to activities after 1980 when the SPO adopted uniform regulations on prices and competition and from 1986 when the Uniform Price-Regulating Rules (Uniforme Prijsregelende Reglementen) were adopted to arrange for the employer to pay for the tendering costs incurred by all contractors competing for a particular bid. As described above, each member of the cartel was required to notify the SPO of its intention to submit a bid for a particular contract. All companies that had expressed an interest in bidding for a particular contract were to be summoned to a meeting of all prospective tenderers at SPO. At these meetings the prospective tenderers would (i) decide to designate one tenderer as the "entitled bidder" which would have the exclusive right to negotiate the terms of the contract after the bids were submitted; (ii) compare costs of the contract and exchange technical and economic information; and (iii) submit to the chairman of the meeting their tender prices which could be communicated to other participants in the tender. At this meeting each tenderer could ask for its tender to be given preference or withdraw its offer. The rules of the cartel prevented tenderers from undercutting each other. The cartel members also agreed that the costs of unsuccessful bids and the costs of operating the cartel could be added to the tender price of all tenderers so that the client would bear these costs in the price paid. The tenderer which the cartel members agreed would be the entitled bidder for a project would be protected from any attempt by the employer to bargain over the price or terms of the contract as all other tenderers would be forbidden to have any contact with the employer after the bids were submitted. The rules of the cartel could be waived if contractors which did not participate in the cartel sought to tender for a contract, but otherwise breaches of the cartel rules were punishable by fines of up to 15% of the estimated value of the project in question.

The EC Commission decided to reduce the fine imposed in light of the involvement of the Dutch government, the fact that the cartel was not clandestine and that the members of the cartel had cooperated with the Commission during its enquiries.

A number of relevant articles have been published since the delivery of this paper. In particular: Kodwo Bentil : "*Applicability of EEC Economic Competition Law for the Regulation of Restrictive Practices within the Construction Industry*" (1991) 7 Const. L.J. 167; Lloyd-Schut "*Construction Joint Ventures: EEC Competition Aspects*" (1992) 9 I.C.L.R. 3; and Ainsworth, L. "*Competition Law Enforcement in the Construction Industry*", Centre of Construction Law, King's College London, 1991, published in this volume.

Select Bibliography

Bellamy & Child,	"*Common Market Law of Competition*" (1987)
Goyder,	"*EEC Competition Law*" (1988)
Green,	"*Commercial Agreements and Competition Law: Practice and Procedure in the UK and EEC*"

(1986)

Korah,   *"An Introductory Guide to EEC Competition Law and Practice"* (1990)

Competition Law Enforcement 25
in the Construction Industry

Lesley Ainsworth

Synopsis

This paper compares competition law under the EEC with UK domestic legislation, which is significantly different in its approach. The means of enforcement and penalties are described. Particular applications to the construction industry, some of which are of long standing, are reviewed.

Introduction

The EEC Treaty gives rise to rights and obligations that affect businesses operating in the UK no less directly than UK domestic legislation. For the EEC competition rules to apply it is necessary for an agreement or practice to have an actual or potential effect on trade between EEC Member States. The notion of trade between Member States is given a fairly broad interpretation and domestic agreements may, in consequence, be subject to the EEC competition rules. There are significant differences between the competition laws of the EEC and the UK. These differences are not merely technical but reflect the policy objectives of, and circumstances surrounding, the development of competition policy.

Competition law

Competition policy in the EEC plays a major role in achieving the goal of the creation of a single market and has been profoundly affected by it. The fundamental task of the Community is described in Article 2 of the EEC Treaty:-

> "The Community shall have as its task, by establishing a common market and progressively approximating the economic policies of Member States, to promote through the Community a harmonious development of economic activities, a continuous and balanced expansion, an increase in stability, and accelerated raising of the standard of living and closer relations between the States belonging to it."

One of the principle activities of the Community in pursuing that goal is contained in Article 3(f) of the EEC Treaty as follows:

"the institution of a system ensuring that competition in the common market is not distorted."

In developing the "system" referred to in Article 3(f), the EEC has always had in view the goal described in Article 2. This has had two practical results for the enforcement of competition policy:

- (1) the EEC competition authorities are particularly concerned by any activities which tend to reinforce the barriers between markets. Export bans, market sharing or other activities tending to isolate markets will be punished severely;
- (2) the EEC competition authorities will regard more favourably those agreements which, while potentially caught by the EEC competition rules, have a beneficial effect on cross border integration and encourage interstate trade: e.g. horizontal or vertical collaboration between companies in different Member States.

By contrast, the development of competition law and policy in the UK has been piecemeal. This is reflected in the volume and variety of approach in the legislation. In the UK there has been no single objective pursued through competition policy.

Enforcement

Enforcement embraces three concepts, the structure of the laws, the investigatory process and the possible penalties for infringement. By way of example, this section indicates some types of conduct which may be of particular concern for the construction industry.

(a)   Structure of the laws

EEC competition law

EEC competition law, in its most basic form, has the advantage of brevity. It is contained in two Articles of the EEC Treaty.

Article 85:

"1. The following shall be prohibited as incompatible with the common market: all agreements between undertakings, decisions by associations of undertakings and concerted practices which may affect trade between Member States and which have as their object or effect the prevention, restriction or distortion of competition within the common market....

2. Any agreements or decisions prohibited pursuant to this Article shall be automatically void."

Article 86:

"Any abuse by one or more undertakings of a dominant position within the common market or in a substantial part of it shall be prohibited as incompatible with the common market insofar as it may affect trade between Member States."

Article 85 deals with anti-competitive agreements between two or more undertakings while Article 86 controls the abuse of market power by the unilateral conduct of businesses with strong market positions. Both Articles contain examples of the types of behaviour that may be caught. Those examples are merely illustrative.

Article 85(3) provides for the exemption of agreements or practices falling within the scope of Article 85(1) but which have benefits outweighing their anti-competitive effects and which fulfil the conditions set out in Article 85(3). There is no exemption procedure for conduct contrary to Article 86.

UK competition law

As mentioned above, UK competition legislation is complex and contained in a number of sources. A brief description of each is given below:

The Restrictive Trade Practices Act 1976.

The purpose of this act is to control restrictive agreements between independent undertakings which could be injurious to the public interest. If an agreement falls within the scope of the legislation particulars must be filed with the Office of Fair Trading and the parties may be called upon to justify the restrictions in the agreement.

Essentially four categories of agreement may be registrable under the Act:

-      restrictive agreements as to goods;
-      information agreements as to goods;
-      restrictive agreements as to services;
-      information agreements as to services.

The Competition Act 1980.

This act provides for the control of anti-competitive practices. A person engages in such a practice pursuant to Section 2 of the Competition Act 1980 if:

> "in the course of a business that person pursues a course of conduct which of itself or when taken with a course of conduct pursued by persons associated with him is or is intended to have or is likely to have the effect of restricting, distorting or preventing competition in connection with the production, supply or acquisition of goods in the United Kingdom or any part of it or the supply or securing of services in the United Kingdom or any part of it". (Section 2 Competition Act.)

The Act provides for investigation initially by the Office of Fair Trading and, where necessary, by the Monopolies and Mergers Commission.

The Fair Trading Act 1973.

This act contains detailed provisions dealing with the control of monopolies and provides for the referral of "monopoly situations" to the Monopolies and Mergers Commission ("MMC") for investigation. Monopoly situations may be either "scale" or "complex". A scale monopoly exists where at least one quarter of the goods (or services) of any description supplied in the United Kingdom are supplied by or to one and the same person or by or to two or more companies which are part of a single economic unit. A complex monopoly exists where at least one quarter of the goods (or services) of any description supplied in the United Kingdom are supplied by or to:

> "..any two or more persons .. who whether voluntarily or not, and whether by agreement or not, so conduct their respective affairs as in any way to prevent, restrict or distort competition in connection with the production or supply of goods [..or services] of that description, whether or not they themselves are affected

by that competition and whether the competition is between persons interested as producers or suppliers or between persons interested as customers or producers or suppliers". (Section 6(2), Fair Trading Act.

Essentially a complex monopoly situation is defined by reference to the ways in which firms behave.

The division between EEC and UK competition law

Because of the differences in substance, approach, investigatory powers and penalties, it is necessary to establish whether a particular course of conduct falls under the EEC rules, the UK rules or both. In order for a course of conduct to fall within the jurisdiction of the Commission, and thus within Article 85 or 86, it is necessary for it to have an effect (actual or potential) on trade between Member States. If a course of conduct will affect trade between Member States it falls to be dealt with at Community level.

The Commission generally has not required very substantial evidence of an effect on trade between Member States before asserting its jurisdiction. The best known definition is:

> "it must be possible to foresee with a sufficient degree of probability on the basis of a set of objectives factors of law or of fact that the agreement in question may have an influence, direct or indirect, actual or potential, on the pattern of trade between Member States."[1]

This gives great scope for an assertion of jurisdiction by the Commission even where the agreements in question all take place within one Member State[2]. The anticipated effect on trade may be merely a potential effect as long as the possible consequences of the agreement may reasonably be expected to affect interstate trade[3]. It must be remembered that for an agreement to fall within Article 85 or Article 86 there must be an appreciable effect on trade between Member States and on competition, i.e. it must not be de minimis. It should also be noted that the European Court has held that sufficient effect on interstate trade will be present if there is likely to be any alteration in the structure of competition in the Common Market. This test is more likely to be used in relation to Article 86 but has also been applied

1 *Société Technique Minière* v. *Maschinenbau Ulm* [1966] ECR 235
2 *Cutsforth* v. *Mansfield Inns* [1988] AER577; *Vereeniging van Cementhandelaren* v. *Commission* [1972] ECR 977
3 *Vacuum Interrupters* v. *Commission* [1983] ECR 315

under Article 85[4].

(b)   The Investigatory process

EEC competition law

EEC competition law is enforced, in the first instance, by the EC Commission in Brussels. The EC Commission has wide ranging powers of investigation and enforcement which are contained in Regulation 17 of 1962. The Commission may, acting on a complaint or on its own initiative, take action against behaviour which appears to infringe the competition rules by:

-    requesting information;
-    carrying out "on-the-spot" investigations;
-    imposing periodic penalty fines on companies which do not co-operate in the investigatory process;
-    requiring the parties to cease the offending conduct or agreement;
-    imposing fines - which can amount to 10% of world-wide group turnover.

The largest fine to date was for ECU 75m (around £50m) imposed on Tetra Pak in July 1991.

UK competition law

The Office of Fair Trading ("OFT"), led by the Director General of Fair Trading, is involved in the policing of UK competition legislation. The powers of the OFT are, however, limited and nowhere near as far reaching as those available to the EC Commission. Generally the OFT is confined to investigating conduct and making recommendations whether for further review by the Monopolies and Mergers Commission ("MMC") or the Restrictive Practices Court ("RPC").

The Office of Fair Trading has limited resources to devote to investigations and therefore relies heavily on the public for assistance in identifying the existence of cartels. The Office of Fair Trading is trying to encourage more complaints and has just published two booklets entitled "Cartels - Detection and Remedies". One is addressed specifically to local authorities, which as major purchasers of a number of materials are potential victims of cartels. These booklets give examples of clues to the possible existence of

---

4   *Commercial Solvents* v. *Commission* [1974] ECR 223;
      Polypropylene OJ [1986] L230/1

a collusive tendering arrangement, namely:-

- fewer competitors than usual submitting bids;
- obvious rotation of successful bidders;
- the same bidder winning in a single area but never winning bids in another area;
- a high margin between the winning bid and the other bids;
- higher prices for no obvious reason in a particular area;
- a high proportion of sub-contracting of orders by the successful bidder to its competitors.

The MMC investigates alleged monopoly situations under the Fair Trading Act 1973 and alleged anticompetitive practices under the Competition Act 1980 to determine whether they are likely to operate against the public interest. The RPC considers the effects of agreements registered under the Restrictive Trade Practices Act and has powers to make orders in relation to such agreements. The Secretary of State for Trade and Industry has particular responsibility for competition matters and has duties or powers under the Fair Trading Act, the Competition Act and the Restrictive Trade Practices Act.

Methods of Investigation

Written requests: Both the UK and EEC authorities can write to businesses to ask for information. Both sets of authorities have the power to impose penalties for failure to reply and for giving misleading or inaccurate answers. Under the EEC rules fines for providing inaccurate or misleading information can be up to a maximum of 5,000 ECU (approximately £3,500) coupled with a daily fine of 1,000 ECU (approximately £700) for each day that the information is withheld. The power to impose a daily fine is a particularly powerful sanction. Under the UK domestic legislation fines can also be imposed but also with the threat of imprisonment if misleading information is given. In addition in the UK, the RPC has the power to examine witnesses under oath in order to obtain information.

Power of search : The EC Commission is entitled to go into business premises anywhere in the EEC and examine and take copies of business records. That means that they can go through not only the companies official documents such as accounting records and board minutes, but also correspondence between the company and its customers and suppliers and internal company correspondence. The effectiveness of the EC Commission's investigatory powers and in particular their power to go into premises and take copies of documents has led to regular requests from the Director

General of Fair Trading for greater investigatory powers for the UK competition authorities. In a White Paper in July 1989 the wholesale reform of the Restrictive Trade Practices legislation was proposed and it was suggested that the Office of Fair Trading should have investigatory powers similar to those of the EC Commission. It appears that the government does not intend to implement the proposals of that White Paper.

(c)   Remedies and Penalties

There are three remedies for breaches of EEC competition law.

(1)   Power to fine : The EC Commission has the power to impose fines of up to 10% of group worldwide turnover and it has proved itself willing to use this power. In the UK, by contrast, the Director General of Fair Trading has no power to impose fines for breaches of the UK competition law.

(2)   Injunction to stop a cartel: Both the UK and EEC authorities can order the parties to cease operating their restrictive arrangements - once they have established that the cartel exists. Both the UK and EEC authorities also have the power to act by issuing an interim order requiring the parties to cease their allegedly anti-competitive behaviour pending the outcome of the full investigation.

(3) Unenforceability of agreement: One consequence of entering into a restrictive agreement is that the restriction is unenforceable. This is true under both UK and EEC competition law. However, in the context of cartels, the fact that the cartel arrangement may be unenforceable hardly constitutes a sanction that is likely to weigh heavily in the minds of the participants. Parties to cartel arrangements are not in the habit of launching litigation before the courts against their fellow cartel members in order to enforce the cartel agreement. Consequently, although the risk of the restrictive agreement being unenforceable may be a significant concern in the context of other types of restrictive agreements, the mere risk of the agreement being unenforceable does not provide a meaningful sanction in the context of cartel arrangements.

Third parties who have suffered loss flowing from a breach of Article 85 or Article 86 may seek to recover that loss in the national court. The Commission has no power to award damages. Under both UK and EEC law, a third party who has suffered loss as a result of the anti-competitive agreement can claim damages from the parties to the agreement.

The Office of Fair Trading and the EC Commission are not, however, permitted to share information with the victims of a cartel. Consequently until such time as either the UK or the EEC competition authorities conclusively establish that a cartel exists, claimants are unable to benefit from the information that the enforcement authorities may have obtained - and then they only see the information that goes on the public register of restrictive agreements or that is disclosed in a Commission decision.

In the US the possibility of recovering three times the loss has provided a considerable incentive to private enforcement of competition rules. Neither UK law nor EEC law provides the possibility of litigants claiming treble damages. In the absence of this possibility, private actions to enforce competition rules play only a minor role in competition law enforcement in both the UK and the EEC and the burden of enforcing the competition rules rests with the regulatory authorities.

Remedies under UK competition law

Under the Fair Trading Act the Secretary of State has power, following an MMC investigation, to take action to remedy any adverse effects flowing from a monopoly. This may include orders to terminate agreements or prohibit courses of conduct. Under the Restrictive Trade Practices Act an agreement which is registrable under the Act but is not registered, will be void: anyone harmed by the operation of that agreement will have a cause of action. If an agreement is registered under this Act and is referred to the RPC, the Court may require the agreement to be abandoned and require the parties to undertake not to participate in similar agreements or practices.

If a company gives an undertaking to the Court, or is subject to a Court order which it subsequently breaches, it will be in contempt of court and may be fined. The penalties that can be imposed for contempt of court are:

- fines;
- imprisonment;
- sequestration of assets.

Although the power to fine is unlimited, in practice the level of fines tends to be fairly low.

A recent case in the Court of Appeal (July 1991) has highlighted what Counsel for the Director General of Fair Trading called "a gaping hole in the Director General's powers". The judgment of the Court of Appeal casts doubt on the effectiveness of the UK authorities' powers to act even when there has been a repeated breach of the UK competition rules. The case arose out of investigations in the late 1970's which revealed that a number of cartels existed in the ready mixed concrete industry in the UK. Orders were made against a number of companies prohibiting them from operating price fixing and market sharing cartels relating to ready mixed concrete. However, a number of the cartels were re-established. The re-establishment of these cartels came to light and the Director General of Fair Trading brought contempt proceedings against various concrete companies including one called Smiths Concrete Limited, together with one of its employees, a Mr. Hayter.

The Director General's action was based on Mr. Hayter's participation in price fixing and market sharing arrangements with representatives of other ready mixed concrete suppliers. The Restrictive Practices Court accepted the Director General's arguments that as a result of Mr. Hayter's action, Smiths, his employer, had breached the order made against them some years previously and in addition Mr. Hayter himself was guilty of aiding and abetting the contempt of court by his employers. However, the Court of Appeal quashed the Restrictive Practices Court judgment on the ground that although Mr.Hayter was involved in the subsequent cartel arrangements his behaviour could not be imputed to his employers. The Court of Appeal reached this conclusion on the basis of evidence that Smiths had specifically told Mr. Hayter not to get involved in cartel arrangements and had apparently taken reasonable steps to ensure that he did not become involved in such arrangements. On this basis the Court of Appeal said that Smiths was not vicariously responsible for Mr. Hayter's action.

Since the original order had been made against Smiths (rather than against Mr. Hayter) and since Mr. Hayter's action was not attributable to Smiths, there was no breach by Smiths of the original order made against it and therefore no contempt of court by Smiths. If Smiths were not guilty of contempt of court then Mr. Hayter could not be guilty of aiding and abetting a contempt of court by Smiths. This judgment has the effect of removing any incentive for senior management to check the activities of their employees. Provided an employer tells its staff not to participate in cartel agreements and makes some gesture towards checking that they comply with this, it is arguable that the company cannot be held responsible for any action that employees may subsequently take. The individual employees involved in the breaches may be fined and may be imprisoned for up to two years. No individual has yet been imprisoned for conduct under the Restrictive Trade Practices Act. As already noted, it is possible for third parties to sue for damages under section 35(2) of the Restrictive Trade Practices Act.

Finally, under the Competition Act there is a two stage investigation. The first is carried out by the OFT which, if it finds that an anti-competitive practice exists and if no satisfactory undertakings are given by the parties under investigation, may ask the MMC to investigate further to determine whether the conduct in question is likely to operate contrary to the public interest. Following the MMC investigation, orders may be made by, or undertakings given to, the Secretary of State.

Particular Issues of concern to construction

What types of agreement or practice are most likely to have competition law implications for the construction industry under either EEC or UK competition law?

(i) Cartels

Cartel activities i.e. agreements or restrictive practices between competitors, restricting their ability to act freely on the market will be prohibited under both UK and EC law. Activities undertaken by cartels, and prohibited by the competition authorities, include:

- price fixing;
- quota agreements;
- market sharing arrangements;
- information exchanges.

A working definition of a cartel would be that it is co-ordinated action by competitors (or businesses that should be operating as competitors) in respect of their sales activities (sometimes in respect of their purchases) which results in a reduction or elimination of competition. There have been a number of instances of companies involved in construction products being investigated by the EC Commission, for example, Cimbel-Belgian Cement Industry[5], Belgian Roofing Felt[6] and Italian Flat Glass[7].

The UK competition authorities have been no less busy with cartels in the construction industry and Sir Gordon Borrie, the Director General of Fair Trading, has characterised the construction industry as having the worst record of cartelisation of any industry. The construction industry is prone to cartelisation for a number of reasons.

- Small number of suppliers to the market (and therefore inevitably the various suppliers become known to each other);
- A relatively "low tech" product - where it does not matter much to the customer from whom he buys the product, there is a greater risk of

---

5 [1972] L13/14
6 OJ [1986] L348.50; [1991] 4 CMLR 96
7 No.1 OJ [1981] L326/32; No.2 OJ [1989] IL33/44

cartel. By contrast, in "high tech" industries where the attributes of a particular supplier's product are critical to the customer, cartels are rarely, if ever, seen.

- Low relative price - cartels are much more prevalent in the supply of raw materials which are used in a high added value manufacturing process. If the raw material is only a small component of the finished product, the customer will be less concerned about raw material prices.
- Demand not affected by price - constant demand for the product concerned;
- Large number of buyers - who are therefore less able to get together and compare notes than the suppliers;
- Products where the buyers are able to pass on the price of their raw materials to their customers.

The construction products industry has all of these ingredients and this is reflected in the number of cartel arrangements that have been found to exist in the industry. Recent OFT investigations have concentrated on the market for supplies of glass and of ready mixed concrete. See for example, the OFT press release of 21st August 1990 on the Steel Roofing Purlins Cartel, the recent (13th August 1991) comments in the Times on the cartel for the Supply of Glass and the OFT press release of 21st February 1991 on Ready Mixed Concrete.

The construction industry has been a focus of attention for a number of years. In the 1981 Annual Report the Director General of Fair Trading referred to 11 producers of processed steel reinforcing bars agreeing to abide by a common rebate scheme and minimum prices. In 1986 the Report refers to proceedings involving concrete manhole covers, concrete pipes, polythene pipes, steel tubes and steel lintels. In 1987 the Report refers to a price fixing agreement being discovered affecting black-top (roadmaking material).

Collusive tendering i.e. the practice of collaborating in response to invitations to tender for the supply of goods or services is always likely to infringe Article 85: European Sugar Cartel[8]. In the construction industry, where so many contracts are awarded on a competitive tendering basis, collusive tendering between suppliers is of particular concern to customers. There has been a recent example in the UK industry where evidence was discovered of an arrangement under which a number of ready mixed concrete suppliers had entered into a collusive tendering agreement. They all tendered for contracts but they had previously agreed amongst themselves who should be successful. They adjusted their tender prices to control

8   OJ [1973] L140/17 and [1975] ECR 1663

where the contracts were awarded. The nominated supplier would bid below the agreed price and the remainder of the cartel group would bid at higher prices.

Collusive tendering is also likely to be prohibited under UK law and may, indeed, amount to the criminal offence of conspiracy to defraud: *Scott v. Metropolitan Police Cmr*[9]. Of particular interest to the construction industry may be an early (1954) report by the Monopolies Commission under the Monopoly and Restrictive Practices (Inquiry and Control) Act 1948 in relation to the supply of buildings in the Greater London Area[10]. The Commission found that, contrary to the arguments of members of the London Building Conference, collusive tendering did not enable members to maintain standards of workmanship.

Collective Boycotts i.e. an agreement not to deal with a particular firm of groups or businesses, are likely to be prohibited under both EC and UK legislation. For example, see the Commission's decision in *Belgian Central Heating*[11] .

As well as obvious price fixing or market sharing cartels, other forms of horizontal co-operation between competitors may fall within the ambit of UK and EEC competition rules. Information Exchanges are likely to be prohibited under Article 85(1): see European Glass Manufacturer case[12]. Under the Restrictive Trade Practices Act parties are required to register agreements to exchange information. The MMC has also condemned an exchange of pricing information, see its report on White Salt[13].

(ii) Abuse of market power

As well as cartel-type arrangements, the abuse of market power in the construction industry and related industries has been attacked under both EC and UK legislation. For example, BPB Industries plc was fined over £2 million in 1988 for abusing its dominant position in the market for plasterboard. Also in 1988 Hilti, a manufacturer of tools for use in the construction industry, was fined over £4 million for abusing its dominant position in an attempt to damage the business of small competitors[14]. In the UK, there have been monopoly investigations into, for example, the supply of roofing tiles and the supply of plasterboard (twice).

The construction industry itself is generally sufficiently fragmented to

9   [1975] AC 819,1039
10 (1954) Cmnd 264
11 OJ [1972] L264/22
12 [1974] L160/1 GISA O] [1972] L303/45
13 1986 Cmnd 9778
14 *Hilti* - OJ [1988] L65/19; *BPB Industries Plc* OJ [1989] L10/50

make it unlikely that any single construction company would have a sufficient degree of market power to enjoy a dominant position under Article 86 but firms should be aware of the provisions relating to "complex monopoly situations" under the Fair Trading Act and the possibility that the EC Commission might find a joint dominant position under Article 86.

(iii) Joint ventures

Joint ventures comprise an area in which the dividing line between cooperation which is permissible and that which is not is particularly blurred. Joint ventures can give rise to benefits which outweigh potential adverse effects on competition. Neither the EEC nor the UK competition authorities have found it possible to formulate clear guidelines on the treatment of joint ventures.

The Commission has recognised that joint ventures can be pro-competitive and may contribute to the general objective of achieving a single market:

> "The joint venture is a flexible instrument of industrial co-operation which will enable many undertakings to adapt to the new conditions of the single market. However, it is also essential that effective competition should be maintained throughout the common market."[15]

There is no clear definition of what constitutes a "joint venture" as opposed to an informal co-operation, a consortium or a partial merger. Indeed, except for those joint ventures which are `concentrative' and which may, therefore, fall within the Merger Regulation, the legal form of a joint venture is irrelevant when considering the applicability of Article 85. The EC Commission has been very ready to find that joint ventures fall within Article 85 because of the inherent probability of an effect on competition arising from a cooperation agreement between competitors. However, recognising the potential benefits of joint ventures, the Commission has been relatively liberal in exempting joint venture agreements particularly of recent years: *Optical Fibres*[16] (exemption) and *Eurotunnel*[17] (held not to apply).

The nature of UK competition legislation does not permit a clear policy approach to joint ventures. This problem is exacerbated by the multiplicity

---

15 17th Report on Competition Policy
16 OJ [1986] L236/30
17 OJ [1988] 1311/36 Article 85(1)

of forms which may be taken by a joint venture. Joint venture agreements will often be registrable under the Restrictive Trade Practices Act, although restrictions contained in such agreements may be exempt. They may also be the subject of an investigation under the Competition Act.

26 European harmonisation in the field of construction

John Uff and Nerys Jefford

Synopsis

In this paper the authors discuss the need for unification in the construction field. A number of specific problems are addressed and proposals made for achieving harmonisation. It is concluded that a European form of contract offers a solution in many areas, but legislation is needed in others. In relation to disputes it is concluded that a strong case exists for the creation of a European Court of Arbitration.

Introduction

The European Commission has been aware of the potential problems of creating a single market in construction for some time. In 1987 a comparative study was commissioned into the variety of national systems applying to construction.[1] In October 1988 the European Parliament adopted a resolution that a Community strategy for the construction industry should be adopted which, while allowing for local peculiarities, would provide for a more unified market.[2]

After extensive consultation on the study, the Commission produced a number of draft proposals for achieving unified remedies and liabilities. The future progress of these proposals, however, remains doubtful. One thing that is evident is the immense complexity of harmonisation by legislative action. This complexity stems from the nature of the construction process and of the construction industry, each project typically involving many different parties performing a variety of tasks over a long period of time, and under an array of legal arrangements. The addition of an international dimension does not mean, as is usually the case in a typical commercial transaction, that the laws and practices of two different countries have to be considered; but rather that many different nationalities may be involved, different parts of the project may have a close connection with different states, and the predominant national influence may change several times during the course of the work.

1 Undertaken by M.Claude Mathurin and published in two parts in 1988 and 1989.
2 Resolution 13.10.1988.

In these circumstances, some form of harmonisation is highly desirable. Fortunately, harmonisation of technical standards and of rules governing professionals is well advanced. There is, therefore, no reason to suppose that buildings and other works cannot be constructed satisfactorily by teams drawn from all parts of the Community. It is only when a dispute arises in relation to performance of the work that it becomes necessary to consider the effect of different national systems of law. This paper, therefore, addresses the problems of harmonisation specifically in relation to the obligations and liabilities of parties to construction disputes, and to the procedures which govern the resolution of those disputes. This paper does not aim to deal comprehensively with all problems that can arise; and it is written specifically from the viewpoint of English law.

Available Solutions

Consideration by the European Commission has been limited to the possibility of Community directives or regulations to achieve harmonisation. Undoubtedly there are areas where this is an appropriate approach. Other problems may be susceptible to other solutions[3]. In relation to disputes, a measure which would obviously be beneficial is the adoption of uniform contract documentation, so drafted as to achieve, so far as possible, a uniform effect throughout the Community. In the following sections we seek to indicate which areas ought in principle to be susceptible to which solution. Harmonisation through contract is thought to have a clear advantage in many areas, inter alia, because it offers the opportunity for appropriately qualified professionals to participate in the drafting process, and offers much more flexibility than the process of regulation by statute. Contracts can be kept regularly under review and drafting bodies can react swiftly when the need for change is apparent. The construction professions within the United Kingdom have considerable experience in these processes.

The overall aims of harmonisation are to promote free trade within a common construction market. The specific aims which are addressed here are the need to promote fair dealing between contracting parties, including the consumer, the producers and the professionals. To achieve this we suggest that a useful objective is to ensure, so far as possible, that contracts will have the same meaning and effect in whatever jurisdiction they may be enforced, and that no material advantage is to be gained by appealing to one particular national jurisdiction in comparison to others.

It should be remembered that international contracts will continue to be

---

3 M. Mathurin, since completion of his report for the Commission, has been advocating a European Construction Agency.

subject to a "proper law" either by express or implied choice. We do not contend for the equivalent of a *lex mercatoria*[4] in construction. Our approach is that a Community law of construction applying in every member state can be built up, in effect, principally by the use of some degree of legal harmonisation, coupled with effectively harmonised contracts.

This paper now proceeds to consider individual areas in which we suggest harmonisation needs to be considered. Our review is necessarily broad rather than deep, since the primary object is to identify the nature of the problems which are likely to exist in the future and the feasibility of possible solutions.

Liability

Definition of Terms

All parties in a construction project will undertake obligations defined by contract. It is clear, therefore, that the terms used in such contracts should have the same meaning wherever they are construed or enforced. This principle is more easily stated than achieved: English law has long grappled with the meaning of a variety of important terms: consider, for example, the meaning of "completion"[5] or "consequential loss"[6] The solution to these difficulties, both in national and trans-national law, is to adopt precise (and if necessary lengthy) definitions of those terms which are susceptible to different interpretations. Some problems will exist in relation to defining terms in a manner contrary to definitions laid down in legislation or legal decisions. It is not thought, however, that this should pose insuperable problems.

A specific area particularly suitable to definition is the right to recover damages for breach, or conversely the restriction of such damages. The traditional approach of lawyers, particularly when negotiating contracts, is to seek to restrict recovery as much as possible or alternatively to preserve the right to recover all damages permitted by the law, depending on which party the lawyer represents. The matter is then left to the Courts to construe and give meaning to. It is the opposite of this process that is now suggested: that the parties should find in their contract a complete definition of what is recoverable on a claim for damages. Such an enterprise should not cause alarm. Construction contracts usually seek to define, sometimes with precision, what the contractor is entitled to recover on a claim for additional

---

4 See Schmitthof: Export Trade at p.601.
5 See *Westminster CC* v. *Jarvis* [1970] 1 WLR 637.
6 *Croudace* v. *Cawoods* (1978) 2 Ll. Rep. 55 and see *McGregor on Damages* 15th Ed. Ch.1.

payment[7]. Thus, instead of seeking to exclude "consequential" loss, the contract should define what is to be recovered. At the same time, it may be that the draftsman of a European form of contract may wish to dispense with "damages" claims and provide specifically all the remedies that are to be available to the parties in the event of non-performance.

A further case for clear definition, already mentioned, is the concept of "completion". This is partly a question of selecting appropriate administrative machinery[8]. The nature of the problem can be expressed as a question: does the contract supervisor have power to accept the works as complete when there is some outstanding or patently defective work? Different contracts provide a variety of answers. The solution needed is a clear definition.

Limitation

One area which is of great significance and more obviously susceptible to being dealt with by harmonising legislation is that of limitation (or prescription) of causes of action. Different jurisdictions may treat matters of limitation and prescription as variously procedural or substantive. Consequently, the national court or other tribunal with jurisdiction over a dispute may well apply its own laws of limitation or prescription[9]. Further in some countries, such as France and Belgium, the limitation period for "serious" defects cannot be restricted by the parties by contract and applies even when the proper law of the contract is other than Belgian or French law[10]. This is certain to promote forum shopping.

Where European Community legislation itself provides for the creation of some cause of action, it can and should at the same time deal with the questions of when a cause of action arises and the limitation of the period during which proceedings may be commenced in respect of that cause of action. A good example is the product liability directive[11]. The directive did not address, however, the difference between national laws of limitation which bar the remedy (eg. England and Wales) and of prescription which extinguish the right (eg. Scotland). The Mathurin Report gave no or little emphasis to this distinction. Yet the distinction may be of real importance, for example, an English Court might refuse a late amendment to plead a limitation defence but could hardly do so if the right sued on had been

7 See e.g. ICE Conditions of Contract clause 1 (5) defining "cost".
8 See e.g. ICE Conditions of Contract clause 48.
9 But in England, see the Foreign Limitation Periods Act 1984.
10 See Van Houtte *"Professional Liability in Construction Before and After 1992"*, International Business Lawyer May 1990.
11 Council Directive 85/374, Art. 10; the Consumer Protection Act 1987

extinguished. In practical terms what also really matters is how different national laws permit limitation/prescriptive periods to be extended by reference to concepts such as deliberate or fraudulent concealment.

One of the most difficult problems in English law has always been to fix the date at which time starts to run for the purposes of limitation. In relation to Standard Form Building Contracts, time is normally said to run from "practical completion" but, as discussed above, this term itself is undefined. Whilst such a term could effectively be defined by contract, if such a date is to be the starting point for a limitation period, we would consider it preferable for there to be a legislative definition. One further issue of particular importance to the construction industry must be to define when time starts to run under contracts of indemnity[12].

Many standard forms of contract (like charterparties for example) have in effect provided their own limitation periods by conclusive evidence clauses and clauses limiting the time at which arbitration may be commenced[13]. In English law provision exists for the Courts to extend the time for commencing arbitration. We consider that such legislation could and should be relatively easy to standardise (see below). It is important to note that the 1968 Brussels Convention on Jurisdiction and the Enforcement of Judgments in Civil and Commercial Matters expressly does not apply to arbitration so that again there may be wider scope for forum shopping[14].

Right to Payment

This is an issue of fundamental importance under any commercial contract, particularly where cash-flow can affect the ability of the contractor to continue performance of the contract. Under English law, the authorities leave a number of important questions open to doubt, such as the ability to challenge an interim certificate, or the right to recover payment without a certificate[15]. Likewise, the employer's rights of set-off against sums otherwise due still give rise to dispute[16]. It is now common for rights of set-off at least to be dealt with expressly in contract forms, particularly sub-

---

12 *Telfair Shipping Corp.* v. *Inersea Carriers, 'The Caroline P'*, [1985] 1 W.L.R. 553

13 eg. cl. 30 (7) of the JCT Standard Form, 1963 ed.

14 Art. 1, but see also papers in Arbitration International 1991 v7 No.3 and *Marc Rich & Co. A.G.* v. *Societa Italiana Impianti* P.A. Case No. 190/89, giving a wide interpretation to this exclusion.

15 See *Modern Engineering* v. *Gilbert-Ash* [1974] AC 689, *Panamena* v. *Leyland* [1947] AC 428 and cf. *Lubenham* v. *S. Pembrokeshire DC* (1986) 33 BLR 46.

16 See *Modern Engineering* (ibid), and see also *Dole Dried Fruit* v. *Trustin* (1990) CILL 594, *John Mowlem* v. *Carlton Gate* (1990) CILL 584, *Beaufort House* v. *Zimmcor* (1990) 50 BLR 91.

contracts[17].

It is inherently undesirable that uncertainty should exist as to whether a contractual debt is due, particularly where there may be uncertainty as to which (if any) national Court has jurisdiction; and, where the matter has to be referred to arbitration, as to whether the arbitrators will have effective powers to resolve such disputes speedily. We suggest that these matters are eminently suitable for detailed contractual provision. It is particularly important that co-ordination and consistency should be achieved between related contracts, not simply between main contracts and sub-contracts, but also between these contracts and the terms of appointment of the relevant professionals who are to issue certificates and adjudicate upon the matters which give rise to the certificates.

Effect of Exclusion Clauses

These are common in construction contracts and related commercial arrangements. They exist in many forms, and are not always identified as exclusion clauses. For example, provisions rendering an Architect's decision final in specified circumstances can operate as an exclusion of the liability which would otherwise exist. Similarly, provisions requiring notice as a condition precedent have the effect of excluding liability which would otherwise exist. English law has traditionally adopted a restrictive if not hostile attitude towards such provisions, requiring, for example, clear drafting[18] appropriate notice[19] and in some cases, fairness[20]. Clauses which do not satisfy the appropriate requirements, however finely balanced the judgment may be, are struck down and the contract applied as though the clause were absent. Attempts at statutory regulation have probably produced greater, rather than less uncertainty[21].

The approach of civil law jurisdictions is more in terms of seeking to apply principles of good faith, for example in restricting the type of breach which may be governed by an exclusion clause[22]. There are many potential situations in which exclusion clauses will be given different effect in different countries ranging from, being fully enforced at one extreme, to

17 See notably DOM/1, NSC4 and NAM/SC, published by the JCT.
18 See *Photo Productions* v. *Securicor* [1980] AC 827, *George Mitchell* v. *Finney Lock* [1983] QB 284 (CA) [1983] 2 AC 803) (HL).
19 *Interfoto* v. *Stiletto* [1989] QB 433.
20 Unfair Contract Terms Act 1977. C.50.
21 See *George Mitchell* v. *Finney Lock* [1983] QB 284, *Phillips* v. *Hyland* [1987] 1 WLR 659, *Smith* v. *Eric Bush* [1988] 1 QB 743 (CA) [1989] 2 WLR 790 (HL).
22 See e.g. Greek Civil Code Art. 332, which prevents reliance on an exclusion clause where the breach is intentional or in gross disregard of the contract.

being disregarded at the other. It is plainly desirable that uniformity, and certainly predictability, should be available to those involved in the construction process. This is not a matter capable of being dealt with other than by unifying legal rules which will transcend the national legal principles otherwise applicable.

Finality of Certificates

This is related to the question of exclusion clauses in terms of enforceability, but it poses a separate problem in that there are wide varieties of practice as to the applicable contract provisions governing such finality. The question also involves the rights of Third Parties, i.e. persons not party to the contract in question, who may nevertheless seek to place reliance on the binding effect of a certificate under a related contract, for example, a certificate under the head contracts to the effect that the work had been completed in accordance with the specification[23].

We suggest that, since the effect of and ability to challenge certificates is of such fundamental importance to the ability to pursue disputes, there needs to be uniformity both in the practice of giving certificates which have or may have a binding effect, and as to their interpretation. This issue is capable of being regulated by the terms of the construction contract, provided that the governing law recognises and will enforce contractually binding certificates[24]. The effect of certificates given under the head contract upon subcontracts is similarly a matter which in principle can be dealt with in the subcontracts themselves, provided proper account is taken of problems of privity[25].

Liquidated Damages and Extensions of Time

The reasons for providing liquidated damages under construction contracts are well appreciated by all sides of the industry. They provide a ready means of recovery for the employer without the attendant difficulty and cost of proof, while from the contractor's viewpoint, they give advance notice of the consequences of breach, and frequently represent a material limitation on liability[26]. Despite these obvious mutual advantages, English law had

---

23 There are conflicting decisions under English law: see e.g. *Leigh & Sillavan* v. *Aliakmon* [1986] AC 785, 817 per Lord Brandon

24 See under English law, *Kaye* v. *Hosier & Dickinson* [1972] 1 WLR 146.

25 See e.g. *Southern Water Authority* v. *Lewis* (1984) 27 BLR 116, *New Zealand Shipping* v. *Satterthwaite* [1975] AC 154. See also Law Commission Consultation paper No. 121 on Privity of Contract.

26 See *Suisse Atlantique* v. *Rotterdamsche Kolen* [1967] 1 AC 361.

adopted an extreme approach, derived from commercial practice in the 19th century, which has the effect of striking down the whole clause where there is any material uncertainty in its application even at the risk of exposing the contractor to claims for general damages for delay[27].

Conversely, in many civil law jurisdictions, there is a useful and undeniably reasonable provision for liquidated damages to be reduced but nevertheless enforced[28] in circumstances where the English Courts would leave the parties to pursue the remedies that they would have had without the clause. It is suggested that in this respect, English law is plainly out of step with the requirements of commerce. The notion of pre-fixed damages is of such importance in relation to curtailing or restricting the dispute process, that it is suggested that a unifying regulation would be justified to secure the general enforceability of such clauses, notwithstanding any technical objection.

As regards extensions of time, it is thought that this is a matter which should essentially be dealt with under the contract. However, one matter of principle needs to be highlighted, namely the appropriate time for exercising the power to grant (or withhold) extension, and the effect of not complying. To express the matter in more practical terms, if the architect, for whatever reason, has failed to grant an extension of time, but the contractor has put forward an arguable case for such entitlement, is the contractor to be regarded as in breach (as though he is not entitled to an extension) or in some other transient state, which will not be resolved until final decisions are rendered, possibly by an Arbitrator, on the question of extensions. There is little jurisprudence on this question[29]. One possibility is to adopt Lord Diplock's label of "temporary disconformity"[30]. The problem is essentially a product of the construction process, where decisions inevitably follow events at what may turn out to be a significant distance in time, and the parties have to continue to perform their mutual obligations on the basis of some obligation. Clarification of these issues would clearly be desirable.

Duties existing outside Contract

As far as we are aware all common law and civil jurisdictions recognise some form of tortious/delictual liability. Restitutionary claims are also recognised[31]. Extra-contractual duties and liability for breach of them may

27 *Peak* v. *McKinney* (1970) 69 LGR 1, 1 BLR 111.
28 See e.g. Greek Civil Code Arts. 281, 300, 401.
29 It was argued but not resolved by the Court of Appeal in *Rosehaugh Stanhope* v. *RDL* and *Beaufort House* v. *Zimmcor* (1990) 50 BLR 69, 91
30 *Kaye* v. *Hosier* ibid.
31 See the paper by Douglas Close.

be imposed by legislation, including harmonising legislation[32].

The 1968 Brussels Convention addresses the jurisdiction of national courts over claims in tort[33], but not the issue of the proper law of the tort; nor apparently does it give any additional basis of jurisdiction over statutory liability (unless this could be "quasi delict"). Thus if a German architect prepares plans for a housing development in England, can subsequent purchasers of those houses sue him under the Defective Premises Act 1972 in England or elsewhere? Although the task seems daunting, the only effective way of dealing with such problems must be some form of harmonising legislation in respect of fault or non-fault based liability[34] backed perhaps by compulsory insurance.

Unless and until such arrangements exist, and perhaps, ex abundante cautela, even afterwards, those involved in construction projects will seek to protect themselves by direct assignable warranties taken from contractors and professionals. How effectively an assignee can enforce an assigned warranty must, it is submitted, be a question for the proper law of the warranty (or, quaere, of the assignment). A comparatively easy, if partial, solution to the problems discussed above would, therefore, be the harmonisation within the European Community of the law relating to assignments. It is worth noting that the Mathurin Report canvassed a system of a "minimum Community guarantee of 5 years of satisfactory completion and durability attached to all new or renovated building or civil engineering works".

We are not aware that there is any uniformity within the European Community as to rights of contribution and third party proceedings. The 1968 Brussels Convention by Article 6 expressly provides an additional basis of jurisdiction namely that:

"A person domiciled in a Contracting State may also be sued:

(2) as a third party in an action on a warranty or guarantee or in any other third party proceedings, in the Court seized of the original proceedings, unless these were instituted solely with the object of removing him from the jurisdiction of the Court which will be competent in his case".

The Schlosser Report on the Convention explains that the term "third party proceedings" relates to a legal institution which is common to the legal systems of all the original member states, with the exception of Germany.

32 eg. the Product Liability Directive 85/374
33 Arts. 2 and 5 (3).
34 The Mathurin Report proposes just such a model code.

Since the Convention in no way addresses the question of when a third party may be joined into proceedings, the Report concludes that:

"....the provisions already existing in, or which may in future be introduced into, the legal systems of the new member states with reference to the joining of third parties and legal proceedings, remain unaffected by the 1968 Convention." (para. 135)

In effect, national courts are left to apply national laws. This is an area not capable of standardisation by contractual means and one which must therefore be dealt with by legislation.

Disputes

Role and jurisdiction of the adjudicator

One of the particular features of the FIDIC form of contract, which is widely known throughout the European community, is the provision for disputes first to be referred to the Engineer as an adjudicator, and for the subsequent arbitration to be an appeal from his decision. The decision of the engineer is therefore a condition precedent to arbitration. The time limits and other requirements governing submission to arbitration may have a barring effect if not properly operated[35]. The effect of these provisions is of such potential importance that a uniform approach is highly desirable. For example, the question of when a party should be entitled to an extension of time for reference to arbitration: there could be a dispute as to which national Court had jurisdiction over this question and as to what law should apply. Further, the machinery of clause 67 of the FIDIC form of contract, while undoubtedly serving a useful purpose, is not thought to be appropriate for general adoption in European Community Projects[36]. The EC has recently published its own conditions for European Development Fund contracts overseas[37], which contains no such provision.

It may be that a uniform code for submission of disputes could be achieved through forms of contract, but the question of challenge and enforcement necessarily requires consideration to be given to questions of jurisdiction and applicable law[38].

---

35 See generally I.N.D. Wallace, *Construction Contract Policy* Ch.18.
36 It is understood that a material proportion of disputes under the FIDIC form referred to the ICC include issues of compliance with clause 67.
37 O.J. L40 v.35, 15th Feb. 1992
38 Refer generally to Freshfields Lecture at Queen Mary Coll. Prof. A. Van den Berg, May 1992 (to be published)

Exclusivity of Arbitration

This is a question which is presently governed in English law by a single Court of Appeal authority, the particular decision not being essential to the case in question[39], but having been treated as binding by the English Courts ever since. Before this decision, Arbitration had not been regarded as exclusive, and there was a widespread practice of permitting parties to choose to litigate or arbitrate, arbitration being enforced only if requested. However, whether the decision is sound or not, English practice has had some eight years experience of arbitration being regarded as an exclusive remedy, the role of the Courts being limited to deciding whether or not the parties are performing their primary obligations and, to a limited extent, supplying a remedy where the agreed machinery has "broken down". Curiously, English law is out of step in the opposite direction in terms of enforcing Arbitration Agreements, treating this as a matter of discretion[40] as compared to the mandatory effect in International cases[41].

The problem faced by parties to construction disputes, is that there are often two or more related disputes which need to be determined, if not simultaneously, at least conformably. In purely domestic disputes, the particular problems arising from the foregoing principles, are that the Court represents the only practical means of bringing all appropriate parties before the same Tribunal. Where one or more of the disputes is governed by an Arbitration Clause, however, the Courts will not regard themselves as capable of exercising the necessary powers to resolve those disputes. The parties therefore have the unenviable choice of having their disputes decided by separate Tribunals or having one Tribunal without the power to resolve all the disputes. Assuming that the Courts are not able to offer an appropriate solution, the problem would appear to be capable of solution only by reinforcing the Arbitration process to ensure that related disputes can be dealt with at least with consistency.

When the International dimension is added to this problem, the difficulties of parties to disputes become immense. One has the prospect of a variety of different national Courts which may accept jurisdiction in general, but which might take a variety of views about their particular jurisdiction over matters within the Arbitration Clause. Under English law, the parties are now permitted to agree to vest the Court with jurisdiction[42] but other states may plainly take a different position. It is suggested that the introduction

---

39 *Northern RHA* v. *Derek Crouch* [1984] QB 644, *Finnegan* v. *Sheffield CC* (1988) 43 BLR 124.
40 Arbitration Act 1950, section 4 (1).
41 Arbitration Act 1975 section 1.
42 Courts and Legal Services Act section 100, inserting section 43A of Supreme Court Act 1981.

of an International element makes the Court system in general even less appropriate as a primary forum for resolution of construction disputes, and that the only viable solution is an enhanced arbitration system which is effectively enforceable in any jurisdiction. A necessary or highly desirable part of this system would be the achievement of a uniform code governing arbitration in order to avoid procedural variation in different states. The UNCITRAL model law cannot be regarded as a solution since it does not attempt to cover the particular matters under discussion, and in any event will not be adopted uniformly throughout the European Community[43].

What is needed to solve these serious and financially significant problems is a set of arbitration rules applying specially to construction throughout the European Community.

National Courts and Supervisory Jurisdiction

If the European Community achieves a common market in construction without any further or specific measures governing the dispute process, then disputes will continue to be dealt with as under current International construction contracts, i.e. with Arbitration being prescribed under the Rules of one of the major International centres such as the ICC or the London Court of International Arbitration. Under the current system, each arbitration will have a "seat" which will determine prima facie the national Court having, at least in theory, a supervisory jurisdiction. The major problems of the current system are the following:

(a) Many arbitrations are truly international in the sense of having no obvious venue, so that the selection of one particular state, by whatever system of rules the selection is made, is somewhat artificial and may cause one party at least to feel disadvantaged.

(b) In many cases, the national Court can offer little in terms of supervision: the English Courts in particular are likely to regard the chosen arbitration rules as intended to be comprehensive[44].

(c) It may not be possible to restrict the supervisory jurisdiction to one national Court, and there are well-known differences of approach in different states[45] leading to uncertainty.

(d) There are instances in which it would be appropriate for the arbitration administering body itself to render decisions or at least to indicate which of

---

43 See DTI Departmental Advisory Committee on Arbitration Law (report of Mustill Committee) 1989.

44 *Bank Mellat* v. *Heleniki* [1984] QB 291.

45 See Tupman ICLQ V. 38. p. 36.

two conflicting positions is correct[46]. But arbitration bodies generally do not assume such jurisdiction.

In addition to these particular problems, International Arbitration is known to be procedurally complex and generally slow and expensive even compared to litigation. This is on the basis that most International disputes are dealt with by a specially appointed Tribunal and generally receive much higher levels of administration than would be the case in comparable litigation. If, as a result of the common European construction market, the volume of these trans-national disputes increases materially (this being inevitable if the volume of work increases materially) there must be a serious risk that the present system will break down or will lead to a massive increase in delay and cost.

We suggest that a serious case exists for the European Commission to consider the creation of a European Court of Arbitration[47]. This would be modelled in the first instance on existing arbitration institutions, and would be specifically geared to the problems of the open market of the Community. Such a Court would need specific powers over problems and potential conflicts that exist in relation to national Courts. It may be that such a Court would initially limit its ambit to particular fields. In relation to construction disputes, the Court would need to embody the following features:

(i) Provision for the appointment of Tribunals and decisions as to which disputes should be within their jurisdiction.

(ii) Providing supervision of the Arbitration process.

(iii) Providing administration and interlocutory powers where these are not appropriate to be exercised by the Arbitral Tribunal.

(iv) Providing for the adoption of suitable rules of procedure, having regard to the parties and the particular disputes.

(v) Supervising questions of judicial review of the arbitration process including, where appropriate, reference to any national Court.

(vi) Supervising the enforcement of arbitral awards through national Courts.

(vii) Creating and publishing appropriate jurisprudence in commercial disputes and arbitration procedure.

Conclusions

The need for harmonisation within the European Community is clear. An open market cannot be achieved in the field of construction without

---

46 See I.N.D. Wallace ibid.
47 See also *Arbitration in a Single Unified Market:* A L. Marriott (1990) Arbitration V. 56. N. 2 p.88.

measures being taken to reduce or minimise disparity between different national systems. In principle, the problems faced by the European Community and its member states are no different from those which exist within the USA in regard to Federal and State Court jurisdiction and choice of applicable laws. Perhaps a closer study of the American solution would be warranted.

The question that exists in relation to the European Construction Market is what action should be taken by the European Commission to avoid a proliferation of trans-national disputes, perhaps of unprecedented complexity. It is evident that full harmonisation of commercial law is not an option, either generally or specifically in relation to construction. Nor is it practicable to think of achieving effective harmonisation solely through legislation. If the Product Liability Directive is taken as an example, the danger exists of creating one common level of liability throughout the community, accompanied by many different parallel forms of liability in every European State that may bear on the same transaction.

We suggest that, while some areas of construction law and practice are amenable to direct harmonisation, in other areas a more appropriate course would be to achieve commercial harmonisation through the vehicle of contracts. This approach has its own advantages in terms of flexibility and offering participation to the construction industry. We have sought to identify particular areas which might be approached on one or other basis.

An area which we identify as being of great importance is disputes and arbitration. The present international practice relating to construction disputes exists as a patchwork of measures, some reasonably satisfactory and others not, which presently work at a comparatively low volume of activity. We suggest that the problems generated by a common construction market will require a radically different approach, possibly involving the creation of a new Court structure.

This paper is necessarily written primarily from the point of view of English Law. The argument presented is derived principally from what are perceived to be the characteristics of the construction process, its organisation and management, and the types of dispute or issue which necessarily arise under any system. It is envisaged that the analysis could readily be extended and repeated in relation to other specific systems of law, but it is doubtful that any different conclusions would be reached.

Part VI

Dispute resolution

Developments in Arbitration 27

Sir Michael Kerr

Synopsis

This paper, which was delivered as the Keynote address at the Fourth Annual Conference, reviews the recent history of commercial arbitration, with particular reference to international developments and to the respective roles of the ICC and the LCIA of which the author is the current President.

Introduction

We live in an age in which the art or technique of commercial dispute resolution has become something of a learned topic and a business in its own right. The existence of the Centre of Construction Law, its syllabus, and indeed many of the topics covered in this volume, bear witness to this fact. The trend is apparent in all the main trading countries of the world, and it manifests itself in new legislation, reform of the courts and litigation procedures, competitive developments to attract and improve arbitrations, and in the search for new alternative methods of dispute resolution known compendiously as ADR.

Let us take a brief look at this scene. In the first 25 years after the war there was scarcely any change in the available dispute resolution procedures, either here or abroad, despite the compound proliferation of commercial contracts of every kind which inevitably gave rise to disputes. It was then the sheer pressure of numbers, and the inability to stem the tide with available resources and existing techniques, that led to all the changes which we have seen in the last 15 years. These remarks are mostly concerned with arbitration. But precisely the same trends towards change have been apparent in our courts in the last few years and are still being worked out. All this activity has one objective: to devise techniques of dispute resolution which are more effective from the point of view of the disputing parties, so that they may be attracted to national venues and processes which are effectively in silent competition with each other.

The 1979 Arbitration Act

The first great milestone in this development was the Arbitration Act

1979 in this country, which had a great direct and indirect impact in other parts of the world. It was a breathtaking piece of law reform, purely on the ground of expediency. The doctrine that only the courts could be the final arbiters on disputed issues of law, and the consequent technique of the "case stated" or "special case" procedure, had been enshrined for centuries as a rule of public policy in our law. Although our courts rarely characterise anything as a rule of public policy, this one was summarily swept aside for reasons of expediency, much resisted at the time, but with hindsight obviously right. The purpose, as declared by the Lord Chancellor when he introduced the Bill which led to the 1979 Act, "was to remove certain legal obstacles which at present stand in the way of London being used to its full potential as an international centre for arbitration."

The reason was that the existing law, enshrining our existing public policy, had become a deterrent to foreign lawyers and businessmen from arbitrating in this country. We had been the world centre for commerce and industry for centuries. And we had also enjoyed a predominance of the dispute resolution business, because this generally follows the trades in question, and the rules of our countless professional and trading organisations provided for arbitration here. But by the 1960's and 70's, in an expanding and increasingly complex commercial world, we were clearly losing out to other arbitral centres and institutions in which arbitration was perceived to be more effective. Why? Because it was there conducted in ways which were less complex, more direct, and quite unlike litigation.

The lead given by the 1979 Act was inevitably followed in other common law jurisdictions such as Hong Kong, Australia, Singapore and Canada. But this has so far been relatively unimportant, except domestically. Of far greater importance has been the independent development in the main civil law countries. The eighties have seen new legislation to deal with international arbitrations in France, Holland, Belgium, Switzerland and Spain. Italy has had a bill pending in Parliament for some 2 years, and of the important European trading countries only Germany is still hesitating. The objective of the new legislation in all these countries is to promote them as venues for international arbitrations by curbing the power of interference by the national courts under national laws, thus making the local process of international arbitration more autonomous, effective and attractive.

At the same time there have been constant changes within the established arbitral institutions. The 1985 Rules of the London Court of International Arbitration (LCIA), which combine the best of the civil procedures with the elimination of the worst in ours, are attracting a considerable volume of business. Perhaps in response to this trend, the ICC has done much to improve its own Rules and administrative processes. The American Arbitration Association (AAA) has recently sought to adopt a more international stance in order to play a role in this market. And against the background of the so-called USSR - USA Optional Clause Agreement, there is great competition for the coming proliferation of East-West arbitrations, although the Stockholm Chamber of Commerce is at present still the leading venue outside Moscow.

Meanwhile new would-be arbitration centres are springing up. They exist in Cairo, Kuala Lumpur, Singapore, Hong Kong, Sydney, Melbourne, Vancouver, Quebec, Bahrain, to mention but a few, and others exist under the auspices of Chambers of Commerce, such as the Euro-Arab Arbitration Congress. This seeks to offer a venue for the arbitration of disputes arising out of the Gulf war, although it is reliably reported that the major proportion of the contracts dealing with the reconstruction of Kuwait contain LCIA clauses.

UNCITRAL Model Law

Superimposed on all this is the United Nations initiative in the form of the UNCITRAL Arbitration Rules and, above all, the "Model Law". Its objective is simple and good: to provide a model which can be adopted or adapted in any country where the law and practice of arbitration is presently undeveloped or outdated. This of course applies to many of the "third world" customer countries to which "western" construction projects, goods and services are exported. The thought is that, with the adoption of the Model Law and an "open door" policy for international arbitrations conducted in their territory, they will be seen as acceptable new venues for international arbitrations. In the result, the adoption of the Model Law may have the effect that their suppliers may more readily accept arbitration clauses which specify the customer's country as the venue. With important potential new customer countries such as Russia, the independent USSR Republics, and the other Eastern states, there is clearly a long-term future for the Model Law.

In the interim, however, its main success has been in developed countries which are not traditional arbitration centres, but hope to attract arbitrations to them. Not content with the 1979 Act, the Model Law has been adopted in Hong Kong, Australia, Canada and now Scotland. Even in England we are already hopefully engaged on a further round of improvement by means of a new draft Arbitration Law.[1] Support for this initiative, including financial support, has had to come exclusively from the legal profession, because our government unfortunately lacks the vision of the responsible Ministries in other countries, and because our parliamentary procedures are

1 See paper 28

still far too cumbersome to permit the enactment of uncontroversial beneficial measures. Lack of money and parliamentary time is the constant excuse. And had it not been for a period of relative political truce during the last six months of the last Labour Government, we might by now not even have had the 1979 Act.

Construction Disputes

The effectiveness of all rules, institutional structures and procedures in the field of commercial dispute resolution is best measured, and indeed constantly measured in practice, by reference to what we compendiously call construction contracts. They provide an enormous source of disputes, and the greatest challenge to the problems of their effective resolution. With the potential for countless disputed issues of fact and law, and the consequential claims and counterclaims often involving vast sums of money, construction contracts, more than any other forms of agreement, call out for the best machinery to arrive at a fair decision with the minimum delay and cost to the parties. No other forms of contract provide a greater challenge. It is therefore one of the objectives of this Centre to study these problems and to seek to find the best solution for them.

What are the available solutions? The processes of international legislative reform and institutional improvement about which I have spoken cannot do more than to provide a better framework by way of background. The important question is how individual disputes are handled, and that depends mostly on the people involved. I have often thought, and sometimes half seriously advocated, that the art or technique of resolving complex commercial disputes has room for experienced lawyers or other professionals whom I call "disputologists", for want of a better way of describing what would be their function in individual disputes. This would be as follows. They would be appointed by the parties or by some agreed outside institution. They would then act as mediators, conciliators, amiable compositeurs, or in whatever other way which they might consider useful within the repertoire of ADR. Then, if and when these attempts at settlement fail, their function would change. They would then prescribe for the parties, who would be bound to accept their recommendations, the most effective adversarial procedure for the resolution of their particular dispute. Perhaps by litigation, such as by trial in the Commercial Court or by an Official Referee, possibly of preliminary or limited issues. Or, no doubt more usually, it would be by means of some form of arbitration, for which the disputologist would prescribe the composition and method of appointment of the tribunal and, if necessary, the choice of procedural rules.

One could then argue as to whether or not he or she would be disqualified from acting as arbitrator, but that is a detail. The important point is that the use of a "disputologist" in complex disputes would ensure two things. First, the full range of potentially useful ADR methods of settlement would be explored before resorting to any adversarial process. Secondly, and of the greatest importance in this context, the actual adversarial process used, if and when this becomes unavoidable, would be tailor-made for the fair resolution of the dispute in question, with the minimum delay and cost.

But at present, this is of course like Utopia. All these aspects are unfortunately nearly always pre-empted by the original arbitration clauses incorporated into contracts, often more or less automatically, as a matter of course, and with little thought. I will conclude by considering briefly how well or badly the common arbitration clauses appear to work at present, in particular in construction disputes.

I cannot speak for the domestic scene. When I was president of the Chartered Institute of Arbitrators, hardly any major construction disputes were referred to the Institute. And although I am sometimes asked to make appointments for some domestic disputes under the Rules of the LCIA, because they can be used for any purpose, in any venue and under any system of law, there have again been no domestic construction disputes in my experience. It would seem that the rules of the professional institutions, in particular of the ICE and the RIBA, meet the domestic demand, and that they are therefore presumably successful in achieving their objective.

ICC and LCIA Arbitration

But what of the international scene, of which I see a great deal? In practice the choice nowadays appears to lie mainly between the ICC[2] and the LCIA[3]. The ICC still has by far the largest share of current arbitrations. But if one could monitor the statistics of arbitration clauses which are currently incorporated into contracts, then there can be no doubt that the picture would be vastly different. And the LCIA is also constantly receiving inquiries from parties with ICC clauses in their contracts, asking if they can have their arbitration conducted under the auspices and Rules of the LCIA.

What then are the main differences between them? Not their Rules. Both give full flexibility and freedom to the tribunal, although the LCIA Rules are much more explicit in this regard. The main differences are in relation to cost, delay and (dare one say it) in some instances the suitability of the tribunal appointed in individual cases. Of these the difference in cost is incontestable, since the ICC charges "up front" deposits related to the

2 See generally *International and ICC Arbitration* ed Uff and Jones; Kings CCL
3 See op. cit paper 24 (B. Vigrass)

amounts at stake, of which a large proportion is retained for administration charges, and the surplus, plus the interest earned by the deposits, goes to the funds of the ICC. The LCIA charges only at cost, without reference to the amounts at stake, and the interest earned on deposits is credited to the parties. As regards delay, the requirement that the tribunal and the parties must draft and sign formal Terms of Reference for approval by the Court of the ICC, inevitably entails an initial delay which can easily take six months or more.

As regards the composition of tribunals, the ICC's choice tends towards professors rather than practitioners, and above all towards the choice of sole arbitrators or chairmen from countries which are not directly relevant to the parties or to the dispute or to the composition of the tribunal. In the result it is now a frequent and desirable practice for the parties or their nominated arbitrators to choose an ICC arbitrator or chairman, rather than to leave this choice to the ICC; and the ICC accepts this practice, subject to formal confirmation.

In all this the LCIA is fundamentally different. All appointments are made speedily and directly from the body of the most suitable available practitioners. Appointments are made within a matter of days from when the parties are ready, and the arbitrations can then get under way at once. Most would agree that in relation to its international contracts, the construction industry still has something to learn about suitable arbitration clauses. Perhaps resort to the ICC is too automatic in many cases. However, I entirely agree that what really matters is to get the right people to deal with individual arbitrations in the right way, and a mirror-image of litigation is fatal[4].

4 See paper 29

A New Arbitration Act 28

Arthur Marriott

Synopsis

This paper describes the evolution of a privately drafted Arbitration Bill which is designed both to fulfil the recommendations of the Mustill Report and to further the cause of Arbitration Law reform in this country.

Introduction

A private group has been established of which I am Chairman, to promote a new Arbitration Act in this country. The background to the venture which my colleagues and I have undertaken is now well known. Our initiative stems from the recommendation of the Mustill Report that we should have a new Arbitration Act. The Departmental Advisory Committee (DAC), which produced the Mustill Report, was appointed to consider whether we should enact the Model Law on International Commercial Arbitration. The Committee decided that it would not be in our interests for the Model Law to be enacted here for reasons which are elegantly and persuasively set out in the Report itself. However, a distinguished Swiss commentator[1], has described the Mustill Report as "timid", a view shared by many of our friends abroad, who also find it difficult to understand why the Model Law was rejected here, but accepted and enacted in Scotland. I should make clear that I am not a member of the DAC and do not speak for, or represent the views of that Committee in any way.

The UNCITRAL Model Law is part of a clear international movement, starting with the New York Convention of 1958, towards harmonization of the law and practice of international commercial arbitration. The trend internationally is to support the arbitral process by seeking to reinforce the autonomy and independence of the arbitration agreement and to promote flexibility and independence of arbitral procedure. There have been various recent statutes affecting international commercial arbitration in the developed and recognised arbitral jurisdictions, such as the 1979 Act in this country, the Act in France in 1981, designed expressly to enhance the

1 Professor Reymond

577

position of Paris as the headquarters of the ICC; in the Netherlands in 1986 and in Switzerland in 1987.

Both the 1979 Act and the Mustill Report were prompted by a desire, as paragraph 109 of the Mustill Report makes quite clear, to keep London in the van of the preferred venues for international commercial arbitration. While the Mustill Committee recommended against the enactment of the Model Law, it recognised that the very diffuse nature of English Arbitration Law led to confusion and uncertainty, which could militate increasingly against London as a preferred venue.

Proposals for Change.

To satisfy what were perceived as the needs of the international commercial community, Mustill summarized the recommendations for change in paragraph 108 of the Report, a paragraph which merits close study, as it expresses a clear and radical policy which the then Secretary of State accepted. Paragraph 108 provided as follows:

> "108 In these circumstances we recommend an intermediate solution, in the shape of a new Act with a subject-matter so selected as to make the essentials of at least the existing statutory arbitration law tolerably accessible, without calling for a lengthy period of planning and drafting, or prolonged parliamentary debate. It should in particular have the following features:
>
> (1) It should comprise a statement in statutory form of the more important principles of the English law of arbitration, statutory and (to the extent practicable) common law.
> (2) It should be limited to those principles whose existence and effect are uncontroversial.
> (3) It should be set out in logical order, and expressed in language which is sufficiently clear and free from technicalities to be readily comprehensible to the layman.
> (4) It should in general apply to domestic and international arbitrations alike, although there may have to be exceptions to take account of treaty obligations.
> (5) It should not be limited to the subject-matter of the Model Law.
> (6) It should embody such of our proposals for legislation as have by then been enacted: see paragraph 100.
> (7) Consideration should be given to ensuring that any such new statute should, so far as possible, have the same structure and

language as the Model law, so as to enhance its accessibility to those who are familiar with the Model Law."

In its Second Report of May 1990, and in correspondence with our group and in public statements, the DAC has explained and developed in greater detail the recommendations which have been made in paragraph 108. Thus, for example, in defining what is controversial, Mr. Justice Steyn[2] has made it clear that, despite his own views to the contrary (and, incidentally, the views of most practitioners) there will be no statutory immunity for arbitrators. It has also been made clear, that there will be no provision enabling arbitrators to act ex aequo et bono, and there will be no provision for consolidation. There will be no changes to the balance struck by the 1979 Act with respect to appeal on errors of law.

Fortunately, it has been made quite clear that the DAC is not interested in a mere consolidation of existing statute law, but wishes particularly to ensure that the recommendations of sub-paragraph 1 and sub-paragraph 7 of paragraph 108 are given full effect. The DAC attaches great importance, as does our private group, to the intention expressed in sub-paragraph 3, that the Act should be:

"set out in a logical order and expressed in language which is sufficiently clear and free from technicalities to be readily comprehensible to the layman";

and, to the recommendation in sub-paragraph 7 (the DAC having further considered the matter) that:

"any such new statute should, so far as possible, have the same structure and language as the Model Law, so as to enhance its accessibility to those who are familiar with the Model Law."

There would be little point in a private group spending much time and money in promoting a new Act independently of the DAC. It is the DAC's responsibility (and not that of our private group) to advise the Secretary of State on the implementation of the Mustill recommendations. In order to comply with the DTI's and DAC's requirements, our private group engaged what has come to be known as the "Bill Team", to be primarily responsible for the preparation of the draft. Originally, the Bill Team consisted of Mr. Basil Eckersley, a maritime arbitrator; Mr. Godfrey Carter, a retired Parliamentary Counsel who would prepare the draft itself; and Mr. John Evans, a retired solicitor from the DTI with great experience in instructing

2 now Steyn LJ

Parliamentary Counsel and in the legislative process. Mr. Eckersley was appointed on the initiative of my group; Mr. Carter and Mr. Evans were recommended to us by the responsible permanent official at the DTI.

It was clear from the outset, that we would need to have financial support from the arbitral community in order to fund the Bill Team. Accordingly, we approached a number of law firms and sets of Chambers. We had a mixed response. We received, for example, enthusiastic and prompt help from COMBAR and from certain firms of solicitors. But by no means all whom we thought would support the venture have done so. However, I am happy to say that eminent firms, many with strong construction industry connections, have been most generous with money and with time. Three of the large US law firms with offices in London and substantial international practices have supported the venture financially. I should have liked more support from the American legal community in London, but this has not been forthcoming so far.

We have had very considerable support and encouragement from a number of institutions with particular interest in arbitration. Thus, amongst others, the Chartered Institute of Arbitrators, The Law Society, the London Maritime Arbitrators Association, The Royal Institution of Chartered Surveyors and Lloyds of London have all helped us. But a surprising absentee from the ranks of those supporting this venture financially, is the Construction Industry. We have had no financial contribution from the Industry as such. I must, however, pay tribute to the initiative which led to the very successful CIC Conference on 1st February 1991[3] at which extensive comment was given from the Construction Industry's perspective on the principles and policy which should underlie a new statute.

First Draft Bill

At the beginning of this exercise, Lord Justice Mustill and I rather naively imagined that it would be relatively straightforward to prepare a sixty clause Bill which would follow the form and structure of the Model Law and satisfy the particular requirements of sub-paragraphs 3 and 7 of paragraph 108. In the Spring and Summer of 1990 the Bill Team worked to that end. Basil Eckersley who was convinced that the recommendations of Paragraph 108 could be given full effect, found that when advising it was simpler to draft what he had in mind by way of a statute and to explain his reasoning by way of commentary. He therefore did so and prepared a first draft in June 1990 which subsequently became the "26th November 1990 Draft" which many

---

3   The report and papers presented at the conference remain unpublished but accessible
    in the Library of the Kings Centre.

will have seen.

However, by the Summer of 1990, Godfrey Carter, had come to precisely the opposite view. He considered that paragraph 108 could not be put into effect if the conventional precepts of English legislation were to be followed. This placed my group in something of a dilemma which we sought to resolve (and did resolve) by asking the DAC to consider which route it wished to follow. At its meeting of November 1990 the DAC thus had a clear choice, namely, whether to follow the approach expressed by Basil Eckersley in his draft, or to adopt the recommendations of Mr. Carter. Godfrey Carter's recommendations were that there should be a conventional consolidation of existing legislation (which he had already prepared) and a Handbook of Practice published, as he put it, "by authority of the DAC" which would be a guide to the conduct of arbitration in this country with no statutory force, though perhaps persuasive authority.

The DAC rejected the Carter approach and endorsed the Eckersley approach of trying in simple and straightforward language to give effect to the provisions of paragraph 108. Accordingly, Godfrey Carter resigned from the Bill Team as, understandably, he felt he could not attempt what he regarded as the impossible. Mr. Justice Steyn and his colleagues continued to feel that only a draft prepared by former Parliamentary Counsel would be suitable to recommend to the Secretary of State. So my group was asked by the DAC to find another former Parliamentary Counsel. We have been fortunate in finding a replacement and the work of drafting has now begun again.

It is, I believe, clear from the experience we have had, that the major difficulty which confronts a private group in this country seeking to introduce new legislation, is to satisfy both the market place and those in Whitehall entrusted with the preparation of legislation. In our case, the task is, perhaps, easier given that the terms of paragraph 108 have been accepted by the Secretary of State and expressly envisage a statute in the form and structure of the Model Law and using language necessarily different from current English arbitration legislation. But, it is clear that without such a policy direction, it would be well-nigh impossible to produce a statute which involved a significant departure from the traditional approach to drafting.

By the end of November 1990 we had clear directions from the DAC as to how they wished us to proceed. I had indicated both publicly and privately several months before, that it was our intention, once we had a draft of some kind, to start an informal consultative process. We did so. This itself, represented something of a departure from the accepted approach. There were two reasons why an informal consultative process was both desirable and necessary. The first was that we needed to have the views of the domestic and international arbitral communities, given informally, as to what they thought of our attempt to give effect to the policy of paragraph 108 and, indeed, whether they thought that policy was worth giving effect to. Secondly, we needed to raise money, without which this exercise could not continue.

We were criticised in certain quarters for commencing an informal consultative process. The criticism has taken different forms, from those who believe that it is a mistake to consult at all, and particularly to ask foreigners, to those who consider that the process has aroused expectations which cannot be fulfilled. I confess I thought this latter opinion the most depressing criticism of all, but I was much encouraged by the radical and forthright terms of Professor Goode's Lecture on the Adaptation of English Law to International Commercial Arbitration[4]. Speaking in a personal capacity and not as a member of the DAC, Professor Goode urged the English arbitral community to be radical and far sighted in reform. He rightly emphasised the high regard in which English law and English Courts are held in other jurisdictions, but he stated that we must constantly guard against "arrogance or complacency". He reminded us that "we live in a highly competitive world" and that although

> "we may feel that our laws and procedures are superior to those of other states, if we cut ourselves off from outside influence we may discover sooner than we think that our ideas have become outmoded, and they are no longer seen to be responsive to the needs of the international business community".

He pointed out that, "we are all too often followers rather than leaders". The group found Professor Goode's speech a clear and welcome contrast to some of the criticisms made of us.

It was perhaps inevitable, given the large number of people to whom the 26th November 1990 draft was circulated, that confusion arose in some minds, as to whether our draft was a DAC draft or a private draft. That confusion was regrettable, but I think was quickly dispelled. Most people know that our draft, whilst representing the approach to 108 which the DAC wished to be followed, is not a DAC draft, but, rather, the basis of the Instructions to retired Parliamentary Counsel. But, much of the criticism of our efforts, has shown a fundamental misunderstanding of the nature of the enterprise which our private group has begun. The private group is not there merely to provide funds which would otherwise be provided by the taxpayer, so that the DAC and the DTI may implement the Mustill recommendations at the private group's expense. If the DAC had wanted

4   The Freshfields Lecture Arbitration vol 58 no.1 p21 Feb 1992

that, it would have organised its own funds.

Rather, this project is an attempt by the private sector, in close conjunction and collaboration with the DAC, to implement the policy of 108 taking full account of the views of the arbitral community in this country and abroad. It is of paramount importance that this distinction and our motives and objectives be clearly understood, for otherwise it will prove difficult to generate the financial and moral support from the arbitral community without which this exercise will fail. We recognise that the DAC has the ultimate power of decision as to what to recommend to the Secretary of State. It is to be hoped, that in exercising its power, the DAC will adopt the robust approach of Professor Goode. He has rightly expressed some of the concerns of practitioners about international commercial arbitration as practised in this country. But, the informal consultative process has, interestingly, revealed many more concerns which a proper implementation of paragraph 108 must address and allay.

Concern of arbitration users

Perhaps the most significant revelation of the informal consultative process, was that concern about arbitration in this country was more widespread in domestic than in international circles. Whether or not this country should enact the Model Law does not, frankly, concern the vast majority of those engaged in arbitration in this country. But they are wholehearted supporters, as the informal consultative process has revealed, of the policy of paragraph 108 of Mustill: particularly, that the language of the new statute should be sufficiently clear and free from technicalities to be readily comprehensible to the layman.

This should come as no surprise, when it is appreciated that the majority of arbitrations in this country are conducted by sole arbitrators who are not legally qualified. We see, for example, extensive conduct of arbitration in the construction industry by engineers, architects and surveyors. Arbitration in the construction industry, we believe, accounts for perhaps 30 to 35% of all domestic arbitrations. A highly important role is played by arbitrators and experts in the commercial property industry in this country. No less than 17,000 appointments of arbitrators and experts were made by the President of the RICS last year. Contrary, therefore, to the practice in many other developed jurisdictions, English arbitration is largely administered and practised by laymen. This is one of its great strengths and a tradition which paragraph 108 seeks to respect.

It also emerged that the Eckersley draft was widely welcomed. It is regarded as a first class attempt to express the policy of 108 and, in particular, to achieve the requirements of structure and language to which

I have made reference. Inevitably, and rightly, there was much detailed comment and criticism of certain provisions, but, broadly speaking, all those who studied the draft greatly admired it. Mr. Eckersley's draft has established the bench mark against which the users of arbitration in this country and abroad will judge any legislation which the DAC recommends. Whatever form the new legislation may ultimately take, it will fail to satisfy the requirements of the arbitral community if it does not address the concerns which the community has about the uncertainty of English arbitration law, language and procedure.

There is concern that arbitration here has become too protracted and expensive, particularly in resolving disputes in the construction industry. This is because procedure, at any rate hitherto, has tended to imitate High Court litigation with excessive emphasis on the discovery of documents and the orality of proceedings. Various attempts have, of course, been made to streamline procedures. Arbitrators have been resourceful and robust in seeking ways to shorten arbitrations and to render them less expensive. Mr. Justice Steyn has advocated procedural freedom to follow, for example, inquisitorial procedures and to disregard strict rules of evidence.

To an extent, the concern about arbitration in the construction industry goes wider than procedural difficulties, because it appears that there is a different attitude, and perhaps a different practice, in the exercise of the jurisdiction given to the Courts under the 1979 Act to review awards. Thus, it is felt that the NEMA[5] guidelines and the principles laid down by Sir Michael Kerr and Lord Justice Bingham in such landmark cases as *Universal*[6] and *Bulk Oil*[7] are not always fully followed in the Official Referee's Corridor. I do not intend in this talk to debate the pros and cons of the NEMA guidelines when applied to construction cases. There are clear doubts about the efficacy of the NEMA guidelines. The purist approach and language of Lord Diplock may not be suitable when applied to construction cases, as distinct from a charter party dispute. But, if a different practice has developed, then it is as well that be recognised and that the Court of Appeal and, if necessary, The House of Lords should have the opportunity to pronounce upon it.

The future course of arbitration in UK.

We have detected no great demand for fundamental change in the relationship between the arbitral process and the Courts. It is generally felt

5　*BTP Tioxide Ltd* v. *Pioneer Shipping Ltd. The Nema* [1982] A.C. 724.
6　*Universal Petroleum* v. *Handels* [1987] 1 WLR 1178
7　*Bulk Oil (Zug)* v. *Sun International (No 2)* [1984] 1 Lloyds Rep 531.

that the balance of policy struck by the 1979 Act is about right and that it is essential that the Courts continue to play both the supportive and supervisory roles in the arbitral process. The informal consultative process has also revealed a growing interest in Alternative Dispute Resolution. This reflects, to some extent, the concerns at the cost and delay of more conventional dispute resolution. I believe that arbitration is not part of ADR, because arbitration has as an essential characteristic, the principle of formal dispute resolution according to law. That is far from the underlying rationale of ADR. But, the informal consultative process has, I think, revealed that many engaged in arbitration in this country are very interested in seeing whether techniques developed in ADR can be applied to the arbitral process. I detect no great demand to go as far as in Hong Kong with provisions for conciliation built into the arbitral legislation. But, I think most practitioners in this country would welcome an enabling provision in the new Act which would permit arbitrators, with the consent of the parties, to decide ex aequo et bono. This would be in line with the practice of our continental colleagues and, I think, would also satisfy some of the residual concerns about London arbitration.

I also believe that the informal consultative process has revealed a measure of ignorance about the role of the DAC itself. There is general ignorance as to the method of appointment to the DAC and as to its precise function. Indeed, this has led to representatives of the Construction Industry saying that the Industry is insufficiently represented on the Committee. Some have said that the balance of the Committee, given the original terms of its appointment, is tilted too far in favour of the London international arbitral establishment. It is not for me to express an opinion as to whether these concerns are merited. I think it is sufficient to point out that they clearly exist and, that many believe that if the DAC, under its authoritative and experienced Chairman, is to realise the potential as an instrument for change and reform, which many feel that it has, it will have to broaden its composition and mandate.

This country has a long and distinguished tradition of arbitration, both domestic and international. We have been fortunate in having Judges and practitioners of the highest calibre with a profound knowledge of the arbitral process and of the needs of the commercial community. No matter what criticism we may make of the difficult language of the 1979 Act, it cannot be denied that the arbitral establishment responded remarkably quickly to what Lord Roskill rightly and trenchantly described as the notorious abuse of the case stated procedure. It is a considerable tribute to Lord Roskill, Lord Donaldson, Sir Michael Kerr, Mark Littman QC and others that the 1979 Act came so swiftly to correct an obvious and growing mischief.

We have, therefore, demonstrated in this country in recent years that we are able to change. But, with the admonition of Professor Goode well in front of us, we should ensure that the provisions of paragraph 108 of the Mustill Report are fully implemented. Thus, we can create the legislative framework within which arbitration law and practice in this country will develop in response to the needs of the commercial community in the next Century. For, as Lord Roskill also reminded us, the arbitral community exists to serve the needs of the commercial community. If we fail to do so, then we have no one to blame but ourselves, if the commercial community votes with its feet.

It is said that history has a habit of repeating itself and I am indebted to Johnny Veeder for drawing attention to the fate of the Arbitration Bill of 1885 presented by Lord Bramwell, assisted, amongst others, by Sir Montague Chalmers, Mr. Russell and Sir Courtney Sebert. This draft Bill of some 140 clauses set out, as Mustill & Boyd tell us, "to embody the whole of the law, as contained in reported cases as well as statute". It failed because it was considered too controversial and ambitious an exercise. A splendid opportunity was lost.

We are embarked on an ambitious and perhaps controversial exercise. We should not compromise on the provisions of paragraph 108 and allow our resolve to be weakened by the alleged difficulties of the legislative process. It would be a great set back if we were to fail. I do not believe that we will, for we know that we share with our friends on the DAC the common objective of implementing paragraph 108 of the Mustill Report and that we have the full support of the arbitral community in this country in trying to do so.

A pragmatic approach to arbitration 29
John Uff

Synopsis

The object of this paper is to examine the concept of cost-effective arbitration, and to discuss means of achieving it. It is suggested that the role of the arbitrator needs to be reconsidered. Proposals are made as to the approach likely to be conducive to efficiency in the arbitration process. Comparisons are made between arbitration, conciliation and litigation. The views put forward are based principally on the author's experience.

Introduction

Why bother with arbitration? The Courts offer greater certainty and their service is free; and if informal methods of dispute resolution are necessary, ADR is available. It offers a quick and cheap service with seemingly few disadvantages and much to commend it[1]. In contrast, arbitration can be slow, expensive, and uncertain both in terms of the result and the possibility of an appeal. If arbitration is to survive it must justify itself as a viable process.

What are the features of arbitration which justify maintaining it as a major means of commercial dispute resolution? They are twofold, it is suggested. First, arbitration ranks as legal proceedings, by which disputes are finally resolved, subject only to the possibility of subsequent judicial review. Whatever the merits of ADR in its various forms, its processes and its result are non-binding: it can resolve disputes only where the parties so agree. Secondly, as against the Courts, arbitration is bound by very few rules or conventions and is capable of offering limitless flexibility, including the choice of Tribunal, which may be selected for its expertise in the subject matter of the dispute. These two features are of cardinal significance and place arbitration in a special position in relation to trade and commercial disputes. A third major attribute, of a less positive kind, is the place which arbitration occupies internationally. In terms of trans-national disputes, arbitration offers possibilities for resolution of disputes not available in any individual state Court. The importance of arbitration internationally

1 See article by Frances Gibb The Times 2nd July 1991

dictates that the domestic process must also be fostered. No country can flourish internationally without the equivalent home-based institution.

It is evident that there is a substantial gap between the perceived qualities and opportunities of arbitration and its performance in practice. This point was expressed by a prominent construction lawyer in the following terms:

> "Although enormous progress has been made recently, UK arbitrations, particularly those in the construction field, still leave much to be desired. All too often they are allowed to assume a life of their own and what is already financially and emotionally taxing for a client, becomes a positive nightmare. Arbitration grew out of the need of persons of commerce to have a commercially viable dispute resolution procedure which could cope with disputes which the Courts were singularly unsuited for. Regrettably, over the years, the arbitration process has been highjacked by lawyers. Now all too often it has become a pale imitation of High Court procedure, to which it is supposed to offer an alternative. What is more, this pale imitation does not possess the sanction available to the High Court. As a consequence most lay persons with practical experience of an arbitration are usually badly affected by that experience and claimants and defendants alike who have embarked upon arbitration emerge sadder, wiser and poorer people."

The effect which the legal profession has had on the arbitration process is described in an article by a prominent engineer-arbitrator as follows:

> "Now the law has come to be recognised as a vehicle for winning cases. Lawyers use legal argument before an arbitrator to overcome the technical shortcomings of their client's case. Expert witnesses write long reports, frequently based on disputed facts. The full disclosure of documents, relevant and irrelevant, is commonplace. Lawyers indulge in protracted openings, and arbitration has become a mirror of court procedure, with the consequent increase in costs. It is not surprising that there is now an increasing advocacy for mediation and conciliation as means of settling disputes.[3]"

There is no shortage of opinions on what is wrong with arbitration. The

2 *Getting the best from ICC Arbitration*: Martin Harman. International & ICC Arbitration. CCLM King's Coll. 1989.
3 The Construction Disputes Resolution Group: Kenneth Severn. The Structural Engineer V.69 N.11. p.222.

problem which is addressed here is what can be done to bring the process back towards realising the true potential of arbitration. This involves two separate issues. First, the forms of procedure which should be adopted; and secondly, the means by which such procedures can be introduced. These issues are now addressed.

What procedures are appropriate?

It is easier to identify the shortcomings of arbitration procedure than to devise or specify more appropriate procedures. The traditional field of guidance for lawyers is to look to judgments of the court. Unfortunately, these are almost entirely restricted to cases where the procedure has been found wanting on the ground of some impropriety. The courts are not really concerned if the parties, aided or encouraged by the arbitrator, wish to throw their money away. It is therefore necessary to approach the issues as matters of principle.

As a broad goal, it is suggested that all procedures should satisfy a test of consumer acceptability. A useful, if modest application of this test would be to ask if the parties (especially the losing party) would, after undergoing the procedure, be prepared to use it again. Such is claimed for ADR, and it is difficult to see any reason why arbitration should not satisfy the same test. It is obvious, however, that arbitration will never achieve this objective unless the advantages which it possesses are to be optimised. How can this be achieved? In order to optimise the process, the particular objective to be achieved must be defined, and this may immediately give rise to conflicting views.

For example, a contractor who claims to have been under-paid may consider that the objective is to reach a decision as quickly and cheaply as possible. On the other hand, a major public authority which regularly faces claims by contractors, may see the objective as ensuring that any such claims are thoroughly and painstakingly investigated in order that the money is shown to be payable, as well as to deter others from speculative claims. Other apparently conflicting objectives could be listed. It may be that such conflicts come close to explaining the difficulty of devising acceptable procedures. What is clear is that an optimised procedure cannot fully reflect the aspirations of both parties: in this sense the procedure to be adopted can be regarded as part of the dispute itself.

It is therefore suggested that proper objectives can be formulated only from a neutral stand-point, not being that of either individual party. If concrete expression were required, the objectives should be those considered to be reasonably acceptable by an informed but neutral observer[4]. From

4 Perhaps corresponding to Sir Michael Kerr's "disputologist": see paper 27.

such a stand-point, it is suggested that the following general objectives can be identified as applicable to all or most commercial arbitrations:

(1) Cost: The procedure must have regard to cost and ensure that it is not disproportionate to the importance or monetary value of the case as a whole or of individual issues.

(2) Speed: The overall period from commencement to rendering an award, should be reasonable in relation to the issues to be investigated and the need to bring the dispute to a result.

(3) Hearing: The time to be allowed for any hearing, should be as short as is consistent with dealing properly with the issues. The rapidity which can be achieved in a hearing will be dependent on the degree of pre-preparation.

(4) Use of Expertise: It is of the essence of the arbitration process that the expertise of the arbitrator should be used to the maximum possible extent.

(5) Form and Formalities: No procedures ought to be adopted unless they are positively useful. Forms of procedure should not be adopted merely because they are familiar and/or available.

(6) Interruptions: These should be avoided wherever possible: it follows that the proceedings should be steered in a direction which minimises the possibility of un-programmed delays.

It is suggested that an appropriate or acceptable procedure is one in which the above objectives are optimised in relation to the particular dispute. To express this concept in a single expression, the procedure adopted will be "cost effective" in the sense of producing a procedure which is commensurate with the disputes in question.

The question of choosing an appropriate procedure will be discussed further below. It is appropriate at this stage, however, to consider whether there are examples of procedures which would satisfy these objectives. In commodity and trade arbitrations, particularly involving perishable goods or machinery in a transient condition, rapid procedures are available, colloquially referred to as "look-sniff" arbitrations. These involve one or more arbitrators being rapidly appointed and making an inspection of the subject matter of the dispute after consideration of the documentary evidence, often followed by the rapid issuing of an award on the quality of the goods or machinery in question. Such procedures appear to satisfy the criterion of customer acceptability. It is tempting to think that one reason for their success is that lawyers have little opportunity to become involved in the arbitration process. The problem that needs to be addressed, however, is how to foster and maintain the robust attitude represented by such procedures in more complex disputes involving heavy documentation, recollected evidence and technical issues.

Implementing cost-effective procedures

Having suggested that cost-effective procedures can be devised, the second question to be considered is by what means they can be implemented in an arbitration. It is necessary to stress that cost-effectiveness must necessarily involve the possibility of curtailment of the full English-style investigatory adversarial procedure as applied in litigation. In practice, parties will rarely object to this approach if it is put forward at the outset. Parties who have had to bear the financial consequences of a full investigation which in retrospect was not justified by the importance of the issues will rarely need persuasion. In the present context, the question is whether the parties' legal representatives be expected themselves to devise and adopt cost-effective procedures. Under present circumstances in the UK, it is suggested that the answer is no. If this is so, it follows that, if cost-effective procedures are to be implemented, it must be for the arbitrator to devise and apply them.

The reasons for this view are the following. First, lawyers representing parties in dispute have a primary duty to protect their clients' interests, and this means that they will seek to retain any procedure that might be used to the advantage of their particular client. This approach is facilitated if not encouraged by the fact that there is rarely any form of cost constraint on lawyers. Solicitors and Barristers have been known to criticise each other for their disregard of the clients' financial interests in terms of the cost of the proceedings. Neither is usually under any personal cost restraint, and it is uncommon for consideration to be given to how costs might be reduced (in stark contrast to most other fields of commerce). The lawyers' position is justifiable on the basis that, if the client has a good case, he will recover a substantial proportion of his costs. This position may be compared to that in the USA and in continental Europe, where an award of party-costs is the exception. Procedures commonly adopted by the parties and by their lawyers in these circumstances are markedly simpler and cheaper than those adopted in a similar dispute in the UK (see reference below to AAA Rules). Secondly, most lawyers are familiar with civil procedure as applied in the High Court and relatively unfamiliar with the possibilities of different procedures being applied in arbitration. Thus, neither solicitors nor counsel may have any useful experience of cost-saving procedures, and neither may have any incentive to pursue them. Perhaps the appropriate conclusion to draw is that costs rules applied both in litigation and in arbitration in the UK are an essential underpinning of the expensive legal procedures which tend to be adopted. For these reasons, under present circumstances, the parties and their lawyers will invariably tend to adopt conservative and expensive procedures, and it must therefore be the arbitrator who seeks to improve the position, if anybody is to do so.

If the parties' lawyers cannot be expected to adopt cost-effective procedures, the question arises what powers the arbitrator himself possesses to impose what he considers to be appropriate procedures, where this is against the apparent wishes of one or even both of the parties as expressed through their authorised representatives. If one of the parties is content to accept a truncated form of investigation, then the arbitrator has considerable powers "to determine how the arbitration is to be conducted from the time of his appointment to the time of his award, so long as the procedure he adopts does not offend the rules of natural justice"[5]. These rules require each party to be given a "reasonable opportunity" to present evidence and argument and to test the case against him[6]. But there is no right to conduct endless and exhaustive examination of witnesses, and there is considerable scope for an arbitrator to adopt a firm approach in determining how far the investigation of particular issues should be taken. In this regard, the arbitrator may need expressly to address the question of what is a "reasonable opportunity", and if necessary hear the parties on the question. It is thought most unlikely that the court would seek to impose any different view.

The power of an arbitrator to control proceedings has potentially been greatly enhanced by the abolition of the power of the court formerly contained in Section 12(6)(b) of the Arbitration Act 1950 to order discovery of documents[7]. The only relevant power is now that contained in Section 12(1) which provides that, in the absence of a contrary provision in the arbitration agreement, the parties:

> "shall ...... produce before the arbitrator ...... all documents
> within their possession or power respectively which may be
> required or called for, and do all other things which during the
> proceedings on the reference the arbitrator ...... may require".

The right to call for documents rests with the arbitrator, not the parties; the arbitrator has an undoubted discretion which must be properly exercised, but which may result in discovery being restricted or even refused[8]. The extent of discovery will usually be a material factor in the type of investigation which the parties can conduct and therefore the amount of their clients' money which will be spent, directly and indirectly.

What is the position if both parties or their representatives express a wish for full discovery and/or a full investigation of the issues, when the arbitrator

---

5   *Bremer Vulkan* v. *South India Shipping* [1981] AC 909, per Lord Diplock.
6   See Mustill and Boyd *Commercial Arbitration* 2nd ed. p.299-302, cited with approval
    by HH Sir William Stabb QC in *Town & City* v. *Wiltshier Southern* (1988) 44 BLR 114.
7   Courts & Legal Services Act 1990, s.103
8   See Mustill & Boyd p.324-326.

forms a different view? The convention is that the arbitrator should regard himself as the servant of the parties and do or order whatever the parties jointly wish. If the arbitrator considers that this course would impose a burden on him beyond that which he agreed to take on, for example, if the agreed procedure would require a much longer hearing than was contemplated at the time of his appointment, the arbitrator may resign, although he may, of course, decide to continue under the new conditions. What is the position if the arbitrator considers that the true interests of the parties require that he ought to maintain his view about the procedure? Can the arbitrator properly proceed on the basis that he knows better what are the parties' interests than the parties or their advisers? It is suggested that he can do so. The proposition amounts to no more than saying that it is the arbitrator who must determine the issues, and that process must encompass, to a degree, the way in which the issues are investigated. If the position is reached that the parties jointly express their disagreement and invite the arbitrator to resign, he will have no practical choice but to comply. However, before reaching this position, the arbitrator is under a continuing duty to "use all reasonable despatch in entering on and proceeding with the reference and making an award"[9]. This duty, it is suggested, requires the arbitrator to continue in accordance with his own views as to the proper conduct of the reference unless and until the parties agree upon inviting his resignation. The arbitrator will, in most circumstances, be justified in adhering to his position, provided that he considers the views and addresses of the parties as to the course he follows. For the parties to agree to invite the arbitrator's resignation is unlikely, the more so if any replacement is likely to take a similarly robust view of procedure.

In practice, where parties to commercial disputes appear before an arbitrator without legal representation, they are more likely to defer to the arbitrator's views about procedure. Indeed, their lack of experience may be such that they are content to leave the whole direction of the proceedings to the arbitrator. It is usually when lawyers are brought in that advice will be given about procedure. The arbitrator may find himself presented with an apparent agreement between legal representatives to adopt a form of procedure which is at variance with his own view. It is at this stage that the arbitrator must express his own views and, after considering the views of the parties' representatives, state his intentions as to the procedure to be followed. The arbitrator must rule on the procedure at an early stage and in a manner which is even-handed to the parties. For example, if the arbitrator intends to limit cross-examination in some manner, he must do so at the outset so that both parties are equally affected, and have the

9 Arbitration Act 1950 S.13(3).

opportunity to decide how best to advance their cases.

It is concluded that, if cost-effective procedures are to be achieved, the following propositions need to be accepted, both by the parties and by the arbitrator:

(1) The procedures adopted may fall short of a full and rigorous investigation;
(2) The parties may not by agreement restrict the power of the arbitrator to direct the procedure.

It is argued above that these principles are inherent in the appointment of an arbitrator. It is, of course, possible for the parties to include such principles within arbitration rules or within the arbitration agreement itself. Certainty as to these matters would facilitate further the process of achieving cost-effective solutions. It does, however, impose greater burdens on the parties and on the arbitrator, in that the parties place greater reliance on the arbitrator to conduct a fair hearing and to produce an acceptable award. It is important, therefore, that the parties should have confidence in the person appointed. From the arbitrator's viewpoint, these principles impose a positive duty to direct the arbitration in the right course, without the comfort of being able simply to leave the parties to "get on with the case". It will be suggested later that this is an important distinction between the arbitral process and the judicial process, and that the true nature of arbitration is in danger of being stifled through too close contacts with the courts.

Choosing appropriate procedure

It is suggested above that the arbitrator must himself be prepared to address the elements of cost-effectiveness in the likely absence of assistance from the parties. He must consider and if necessary devise procedures which are likely to meet the objectives suggested, in relation to the particular dispute with which he is engaged. The procedures to be adopted must be expressed in terms of orders and directions, and it is important that these are given at an appropriate time. This means that the arbitrator must take control of the proceedings at an early stage, before the legal representatives have decided for themselves (in the absence of any reference to the arbitrator) how they are going to proceed with the case. It is a frequent experience that the arbitrator hears little or nothing about the case for some months after being appointed, and is then informed at a procedural meeting that the parties have agreed the "usual" directions. They may even have gone through an exchange of pleadings without involving the arbitrator at all. Once the parties have embarked on such a course and have begun to expend the client's money, it becomes more difficult for the arbitrator to impose an effective influence. It follows that it will be in the interests of the parties for procedural meetings to be arranged at a very early date.

The particular procedure appropriate to achieving cost-effectiveness will depend on the details of the case, and will necessarily vary within wide limits. Some examples are suggested at the end of this paper to illustrate the types of procedure that might be adopted. It it proposed here to comment on a number of specific aspects of procedure where the arbitrator ought to be aware of the possibilities for achieving efficiency and expedition.

Duration of Hearing: It is usually a matter of surprise to parties unused to commercial arbitration that the proceedings are so slow and appear to have no time limit. Businessmen, and most professionals also, are well-used to working against commercially significant time limits. The idea that a building contract should permit the works to run for an indeterminate period would seem strange indeed. Why is it that parties so readily accept the idea of timeless arbitration? It is suggested that there is no need to do so and that it is up to the arbitrator to fix a "reasonable" time or at least to control the length of the hearing. In the event that one party or even both parties complain that they will not have enough time to present their cases, an acceptable solution may be based on the procedure often adopted in ICC arbitrations involving parties travelling from abroad, where a fixed length of hearing is of the essence. The solution usually adopted is the following:

(a)   evidence and submission are put into writing and served in advance;
(b)   written statements are taken as evidence in chief with no additional examination in chief normally being permitted;
(c)   the time available for the hearing is then divided equally between the parties to use for cross-examination, re-examination or making submissions, as they choose;
(d)   separate hearings may be arranged for evidence (cross-examination and re-examination) and for final submissions, which are initially delivered in writing;
(e)   at the close of such a "truncated" hearing, the parties may be given a further opportunity to make a written submission on any matters which they have not had an opportunity to deal with.

If such a procedure is to be adopted, proper directions must be given at a very early date and these must provide for the submission of bundles of documents for the arbitrators to read before the oral hearing.

Arbitrator using his own expertise: This has been seen as an emotive topic, as the issue comes before the courts only in circumstances where the arbitrator is alleged to have committed misconduct by so doing[10]. It is suggested that arbitrator must endeavour to use the expertise which he possesses, more especially if that is part of the reason for his selection as arbitrator. He must do so in a manner which complies with the requirements of natural justice, and this may involve informing the parties of the *prima facie* views which the arbitrator holds. However, for the arbitrator to retreat into the role of a passive judge involves a misconception of the role of an arbitrator which is bound to result in inefficiency and waste of opportunity. Where the arbitrator's expertise is legal, there will be little inhibition in using such expertise. The same ought to apply to technical expertise.

In practice, there is a considerable area of inhibition arising from use of party-appointed experts. This is frequently the case even where these experts cover the very field of the arbitrator's own expertise. It is possible that an arbitrator might be justified in refusing to receive evidence tendered by such experts.[11]. However, a much more convenient approach is to consider the matter at the outset when leave is sought to call experts[12]. As an alternative to refusing leave, it is submitted that the arbitrator may (and should) warn the parties that he may disallow the costs of any expert whom he finds to have been unnecessary, having regard to his own expertise. Provided the parties are sufficiently warned in advance, it is thought most unlikely that the court would be persuaded to interfere.

Interruptions: Applications for various forms of judicial review or intervention can have a most disruptive effect on the progress of an arbitration, which will in turn have serious cost consequences. The avoidance of delay in achieving finality at the conclusion of an arbitration has been addressed through the appeal procedure under the Arbitration Act 1979[13]. Applications during the course of the proceedings, particularly involving jurisdictional questions, can be pursued without any limitation. Jurisdictional questions frequently arise in construction disputes, where arbitration Clauses tend to be intentionally restrictive as to the issues which may eventually be brought within the arbitration process[14]. Under particular arbitration rules, such as those of the ICC, the arbitrators may be empowered to resolve finally such questions, which typically involve decisions of no greater complexity than whether notices have been given in time or whether particular claims are deemed to be included within notices given. Under

10 See *Fox* v. *Wellfair* (1981) 19 BLR 52, and 1989 Bernstein Lecture: Making effective use of the expertise of arbitrators. J.F. Uff.
11 See Bernstein Lecture op cit.
12 Civil Evidence Act 1972 S.2(4), 5(1)(2).
13 As interpreted in *BTP Tioxide* v. *Pioneer Shipping (The Nema)* [1982] AC 724.
14 See ICE Conditions, Clause 66 and FIDIC Conditions Clause 67. See particularly in regard to the latter Construction Contracts: I.N.D. Wallace (1986) Chapter 18.

English law, such decisions cannot be rendered finally by the arbitrator, in the absence of agreement, and recourse must be had to the court[15].

This question has been addressed in a submission on behalf of the Construction Industry Council to the DTI Advisory Committee on Arbitration Law[16]. A number of solutions are possible. The solution suggested in the CIC submission is for such jurisdictional questions to require leave so that the court would exercise a filtering role similar to that in relation to appeals. An alternative solution is for the parties to adopt rules which empower the arbitrators, finally to decide relatively "routine" jurisdictional questions .

Example of cost-effective procedure

To illustrate the proposals discussed above an example is given of a typical construction dispute which might ordinarily be dealt with in a conventional hearing lasting perhaps six to eight weeks involving oral speeches and evidence. The dispute is as follows:

"The contractor (Claimant) claims for disputed variations and for the balance of the final account which the engineer has been unable to finalise. The employer (Respondent) alleges defects in the contractor's work which gave rise to the need for additional or remedial work which the contractor claims should have been the subject of variation orders. The contractor says the defects arose from the design. The employer contends that the defects are of workmanship or alternatively that the contractor was responsible for the particular design element. The contractor says that the contract precludes such design liability. The repair/ additional work resulted in delay for which the employer has deducted liquidated damages."

This comparatively commonplace type of dispute gives rise to large numbers of issues and will typically generate voluminous pleadings, extensive discovery and a long and expensive oral hearing. It is suggested that an arbitrator taking control of such a dispute at the outset could resolve it in the following manner:

(1) The question of responsibility for the defects appears to be central to the issues and governs the question of additional payment and liability for

15 See *Christopher Brown* v. *Genossenschaft Osterreichischer* [1954] 1 QB 8.
16 See particularly paper by D.N. Keating: The need to avoid Delay (to be published).

delays. The arbitrator may know from his experience that if this issue is resolved, the remainder of the case could be settled.

(2) Particularly, the dispute over the final account, if wholly or mainly dependent on questions of valuation, can be economically argued by the respective quantity surveyors with the arbitrator resolving matters of principle.

(3) The arbitrator should consider whether the issue of defects should be dealt with by resolving issues of fact and then considering legal arguments on responsibility; or whether these matters should be dealt with together. Issues involving technical expertise (for example, why cracks occurred) could be the subject of a separate expert submission on behalf of each party.

(4) The arbitrator may therefore give procedural directions with the aim of bringing the defects issue to a resolution at the earliest stage, leaving the consequences (time and money) to be resolved later. The final account issue can be taken separately and should not be allowed to hold up progress on the central issue.

(5) In giving directions the arbitrator will have regard to the amounts at stake, and who is being kept out of money. Usually it will be the employer who is holding the disputed funds, and the directions should also have in mind the question of whether any further money can be paid to the contractor on an interim basis.

A comparison may be drawn between this suggested approach in the hypothetical case above and the "usual" directions likely to be agreed between the parties' lawyers which would be in the following form:

(1)   Points of claim 42 days;
(2)   Points of defence and counterclaim 42 days thereafter;
(3)   Points of reply and defence to counterclaim 28 days thereafter;
(4)   Discovery etc.

Such directions, which are closely modelled on the High Court procedure, are a convenient way of discovering the issues in a case. However, having discovered the issues in this way, it is then often too late to revert to a different approach, taking separate issues. Pleadings drawn in the above manner will be closely interlocked and the separation and subsequent definition of issues may leave difficult sub-issues to be resolved later. A material difference between commercial arbitration, particularly in the construction field, and general civil litigation, is that in the former case, the parties are usually well aware of not only the broad issues, but also of the many layers of argument and counter-argument, which may have been rehearsed in correspondence, meetings and pre-arbitration claims and submissions. It is often the case, at the outset of an arbitration, that the arbitrator knows practically nothing about the issues, the retained lawyers know a little, and the parties themselves know a great deal. In many cases, of which the above example is typical, the arbitrator and the parties' lawyers could contribute much more to the economic resolution of the case by discovering more about the issues before the procedure in the case is settled.

It is suggested, therefore, that a different approach to pleadings and procedural directions would be justified in many cases. Because they necessarily frame the issues in the case, pleadings should not be used as a means of finding out what the case is about. It may be preferable for the arbitrator to request a submission from each party, either written or oral, on what it sees as the issues in the case, and for the arbitrator to give further procedural directions after considering such submissions. If the legal representatives are not sufficiently instructed to deliver such submissions at an early date, experience indicates that the client can (and is often anxious to) inform the arbitrator what the case is really about. It is not suggested that legal representatives should be dispensed with, but that they should ensure that their presence does not prevent focusing on the real issues at an early stage.

There has been much discussion on the role and usefulness of advocates and legal representation in arbitration. Arbitrators must be cautious not to deny the right to proper representation[17]. However, there is no warrant or necessity for the arbitrator to draw a rigid distinction between submissions and evidence and to regard these as the exclusive function of advocates and witnesses. The breadth of the arbitrator's powers under Section 12(1) of the Arbitration Act 1950[18] is such that an arbitrator can invite assistance and information from any person prepared to speak on behalf of the parties, provided that he adheres to the basic requirements of fairness and equal treatment. To be in a position to direct the course of the arbitration purposively, the arbitrator must inform himself about the issues in the case. The traditional way in which counsel achieves this is to be "briefed", in writing or in conference. There is no reason why the arbitrator should not take a similar course with the aim of putting himself in a position where he is sufficiently informed to give directions. These steps, which will occur at the outset of the arbitration should not involve great expenditure in money or time, and their benefits may be considerable.

17 See *Town & City* v. *Wiltshier* op cit.
18 Compare also the express duty placed on the arbitrator under the ICC Rules, Article 14.1 to "proceed within as short a time as possible to establish the facts of the case by all appropriate means".

Resolution of issues

Few construction arbitrations ever reach a final award in the formal sense, i.e. the arbitrator resolving every outstanding issue. Most cases break down into a series of interim awards with the parties themselves resolving some of the issues. Frequently this takes the form of the arbitrator making findings or declarations relating to liability and the parties determining other matters such as quantum, interest and costs. More complex cases may be broken down into more detailed issues and sub-issues for separate resolution.

Where particular issues are to be determined, they are usually defined by the representatives of the parties. Their approach is often influenced by the attitude of the High Court towards such issues i.e. that they should be limited to "a point of law which, if decided in one way, is going to be decisive of litigation"[19]. No such limitations apply in arbitration. It is suggested that issues to be determined separately in arbitration should be approached on the basis of whether they are likely to result in a narrowing of the differences between the parties, particularly those which will involve considerable time and expense. The jurisdiction of an arbitrator to make interim awards[20] is in no sense limited to issues of law. An arbitrator may render interim awards on questions of fact or mixed fact and law as well as purely legal issues; and awards on fact may include or even be limited to questions of technical expertise. An arbitrator has a complete discretion as to the nature of preliminary or separate issues and it is suggested that such discretion ought to be used with a view to narrowing if not resolving what will otherwise be costly issues.

While existing arbitration legislation gives wide discretion as to the means of proceeding with an arbitration, it is undoubtedly true that the arbitrator's powers can be usefully enlarged by agreed procedural rules. The ICE Arbitration Procedure, introduced in 1983, contains many such additional powers, including rules for a procedure largely on documents[21] and a special procedure for issues dependent upon technical expertise[22]. A further matter which has been the subject of considerable debate is the power of arbitrators to order the payment of money on terms equivalent to Orders 14 and 29 in Part II of the Supreme Court Rules[23]. Experience indicates that

---

19 *Everett* v. *Ribbands* [1952] 2 QB 198, 206; and see also *Carl Zeiss Stiftung* v. *Herbert Smith & Co.* [1969] 1 Ch 93, *Waters* v. *Sunday Pictorial* [1961] 1 WLR 967, 974.
20 See Arbitration Act 1950 S.14
21 ICE Arbitration Procedure (1983) Part F: Short Procedure
22 ICE Procedure Part G: Special procedure for experts.
23 Refer to proceedings of a Conference on the new arbitration law organised by the Construction Industry Council (1st February 1991), particularly paper (unpublished) by D. Cornes: "*Powers and Interlocutory Measures*".

such a power can have a beneficial effect in allowing the ensuing arbitration proceedings to concentrate on the issues of principle dividing the parties rather than the immediate problem of cash-flow.

The procedures suggested in this paper, however, are not dependent on arbitration rules. They are suggested as part of the arbitrator's overriding power to control and direct the proceedings. The role of procedural rules is seen as a means of clarifying the arbitrator's powers and directing the attention of the parties to the possibilities for cost savings through the adoption of properly structured procedures.

Settlement and Conciliation

It has hitherto been the convention that settlement negotiations should be outside the arbitration arena, usually being expressly on a without prejudice basis. The convention is no doubt fostered by the belief that an arbitrator loses independence if he becomes aware of settlement negotiations. It is suggested that this approach is unwarranted and that arbitrators can properly become involved to a limited but significant extent.

The arbitrator should not participate in the settlement process by expressing views on the issues, but it is suggested that it is quite unnecessary to require him to remain aloof from or unaware of the process. For example, if the arbitrator forms the view that a particular issue is readily capable of settlement, (e.g. a simple difference of figures) there is no reason why he should not require the parties to attempt to resolve the matter by settlement before proceeding further with the arbitration. This approach is not unfamiliar in the High Court, but it is suggested that an arbitrator has the power to require the parties to take such steps as part of the means of defining the issues which he has to decide. The arbitrator may also, it is suggested, properly ask to be informed how far negotiations have proceeded on particular issues in order to decide how to proceed with the arbitration.

Arbitrators and Judges

It will be seen from the foregoing that there are significant differences and contrasts which should be recognised between arbitrators and judges. The obvious historical contrast is that most arbitrators have been and continue to be drawn from the relevant trade or profession, whereas judges are, by training, professional lawyers. In some countries, the arbitration system is seen as a means of escape from the burdens of the Court system. This is perhaps nowhere more obvious than in the USA, where oppressive Court procedures are notorious. The American Arbitration Association, in contrast, has evolved helpful and constructive arbitration rules which draw a stark contrast to Court procedures. For example, the AAA Construction Industry Arbitration rules[24] provide by Section 56 as follows:

> "The Hearing: Generally, the hearing shall be completed within one day, unless the dispute is resolved by submission of documents under Section 37. The arbitrator, for good cause shown, may schedule an additional hearing to be held within 7 days."

This quotation expresses the hope rather than the expectation in US construction arbitration. But the contrast to the UK experience is obvious. The distinction between arbitrators and judges can also be seen in the significantly different role of party-appointed arbitrators, whose function is usually taken to include safe-guarding the interests of the party who appointed them[25]. The English view that all arbitrators should be equally disinterested comes as a surprise to most foreign parties. A more pertinent comparison is the role of retired or former judges. In USA, such persons can find gainful employment advising on the likely outcome of trials, or even conducting mock trials. They appear, however, not to be in great demand as arbitrators, and do not play any prominent part in the development of arbitration. Similarly, on the continent of Europe, judges are only occasionally encountered as arbitrators[26]. In England, by contrast, there is an increasing trend in the appointment of former judges as arbitrators. It is relevant to ask whether this is a trend which should be supported[27].

While there are examples of former judges who have made successful careers as arbitrators, this may serve to foster the impression that arbitration is litigation in the private sphere: a view which would condemn arbitration to the role of an expensive second-class system. With respect to those former judges who work as arbitrators, it is suggested that the training and experience of English judges is inappropriate to the role of arbitrator in a number of significant respects. First, an English judge has little experience in initiating procedural steps. Their training is limited to the determination of issues raised by the parties themselves. Secondly, the deep seated tradition of litigation is to leave questions relating to efficiency or cost-effectiveness to the parties themselves. Thirdly, the role of the English judge is firmly rooted in the adversarial system, by addressing only the

---

24 As amended January 1 1991
25 *International Commercial Arbitration*, Redfern & Hunter, Ch.4, citing Simpson & Fox, *International Arbitration* (1959) p.88
26 There is a discernible preference for University Professors
27 The question is not new: see Keynote address of Lord Wilberforce in International and ICC Arbitration; CCLM King's Coll. 1990.

issues which the parties choose to raise. For these reasons it is suggested that the experience of judges does not best fit them for the wider roles suggested in this paper.

A further aspect of this question is the close relationship which has developed between arbitration institutions and the judiciary in England, particularly through the Chartered Institute of Arbitrators. In 1977, this Institute broke with sixty years of tradition in appointing distinguished lay arbitrators as President by appointing to the office Lord Diplock, who has been succeeded now by five other very senior members of the judiciary. In terms of the development of arbitration law and raising the public profile of arbitration, this policy can be seen as a success. However, attention ought to be drawn to the adverse consequences of encouraging lay arbitrators to look to judges as their role-model. It is to be doubted that liaison with the judiciary will result in arbitrators developing more efficient techniques. The converse is more likely to be true, namely that liaison with judges is more likely to persuade arbitrators to adopt a more passive and "judicial" approach to their work. It may be that the American approach of building barriers rather than bridges between the judges and arbitrators is the more appropriate.

Summary and conclusion

This paper addresses the questions of efficiency and cost-effectiveness in arbitration. There have been many calls for better procedures to be developed, but few constructive proposals. This paper suggests that arbitrators presently have wide powers to direct arbitrations in a manner more in keeping with the true interests of the parties and that if arbitration procedures are to be radically improved, the initiative must come from the arbitrators themselves.

In seeking to arrive at cost effective procedures, the following steps are suggested:

(1) The arbitrator should become sufficiently acquainted with the issues at an early stage so that procedural orders can be directed specifically towards economic management of the arbitration;

(2) The arbitrator should not regard himself as bound by any of the rules or procedures of the High Court. Specifically, an exchange of pleadings should not be ordered as a matter of course at the outset;

(3) The arbitrator should consider initially briefing himself by a written or oral presentation from each side aimed at defining the principal issues to be addressed in the arbitration. Thereafter, consideration should be given as to how these issues should be defined;

(4) The arbitrator should consider from the earliest possible date how the arbitration is to proceed, in relation to the identified issues;
(5) The arbitrator should consider whether and to what extent oral hearings are necessary or appropriate, and where this is so, who on behalf of the parties should present the cases;
(6) The arbitrator should have specific regard to the sums of money in issue, the complexity of particular issues and the cost of resolving them.

The question also needs to be addressed how arbitrators are to assume the role of achieving the efficient conduct of arbitrations. In the past the role of the lay arbitrator has been to use his expertise to resolve disputes as presented by the parties. The modern arbitrator, however, has to deal with skilled lawyers whose task is to preserve all the rights and interests of their clients, even though this may not be conducive to efficiency or cost effectiveness. Thus, whatever the position was in the past, arbitrators today require specific skills and techniques beyond those of a mere independent third party. The training of arbitrators is presently directed primarily towards obtaining a sufficient appreciation of the law of arbitration to avoid the pitfalls of misconduct. What is suggested is a new, more positive, role for arbitrators. This is likely to require the development of specialist arbitrators, whose main occupation is in conducting arbitrations[28]. What is needed from the Courts and judiciary is neither guidance nor leadership, but support for the development of arbitration as a process quite distinct from litigation, and for the evolution of efficient and, where necessary, radical procedures.

28 A situation which already exists in Maritime and Marine Arbitration, through the LMMA, and to a lesser extent in construction arbitration through the Society of Construction Arbitrators.

Mark McGaw

Synopsis

This paper reviews the history of the use of adjudication clauses in the construction industry; collects, summarises and contrasts the types of adjudication process which have been adopted; and discusses the relevant case law and considers the merits of the innovation.

Introduction

Adjudication is the procedure where, by Contract, a summary interim decision-making power in respect of disputes is vested in a third party individual (the Adjudicator)[1] who is usually not involved in the day-to-day performance or administration of the Contract, and is neither an Arbitrator or connected with the State.[2] Adjudication is an expert system forming part of the "contractual machinery".[3] It differs from mediation in that, to a greater or lesser extent, the outcome is binding on the parties and therefore its efficacy is not dependent upon the co-operation of both parties. It differs from arbitration in that the process is summary and may to some extent be inquisitorial, and the decision is ordinarily only an interim one. It is not subject to the Arbitration Acts 1950 - 79.

The use of adjudication in the UK construction industry standard forms is expanding. It has been said of adjudication that:

> "Its value is in making both sides think again before persisting with an arbitrary decision which can only generate a dispute. I have made recommendations for adjudicators when asked to do so, but afterwards the people appointed phone me and complain that they haven't had anything to do! My experience is that the mere knowledge of there being an adjudicator in the background

---

1   There is no reason why it could not be an organisation or panel of Adjudicators. Indeed there is one private form which uses a panel and such a system was advocated by R.B. Hellard in an article in May 1988 Arbitration.

2   Except in the GC/Works/1 model where the Adjudicator is an individual within the PSA organisation and therefore connected with the State.

3   See *Tubeworkers Ltd.* v. *Tilbury Construction Ltd.* (1985), 30 BLR 70 (C.A.).

to whom disputes can be referred makes the whole operation run
much more smoothly."[4]

It is being experimented with elsewhere. The recent Australian No
Disputes study carried out by representatives of the Australian construction
industry (other than the Architects), and generally accepted by that industry,
recommended that the initial determination of disputes should be performed
by an independent contract Adjudicator:-

"A person other than the person administering the contract
should be appointed in the contract as an adjudicator to ensure
that no conflicts of interest arise and that disputes are dealt with
on their merits, prior to the referral to arbitration or litigation....
Industry contracts of all types should provide for binding interim
decisions by an independent third party, with the potential for
this decision to be overturned after the stage of Practical Completion by an arbitral or court decision, if either party choose to
challenge it."[5]

At the moment adjudication is being judged on the basis of favourable
anecdotal evidence and limited case law. One of the reasons that I find the
concept of adjudication to be of interest is that it is being used in Contracts
between enterprises who bargain equally and at arms' length, as a mechanism to resolve primarily money disputes where there are no relevant non-
commercial considerations.[6] Hence there is a sort of pure "commercialness"

4   By Ron Denny, the former deputy director of the BPF, in an interview in Construction
     News, 13th June 1991. See also comments of Hugh Try in "A Builder's Conception",
     1988 Arbitration 11 at p 14 and a note in FASS Bulletin, Issue No. 13, August 1990,
     pp 12-13.
5   Reduction of Claims and Disputes in the Construction Industry - a Research Report
     (various authors) p.9.
6   ie moral, political, social, criminal law or consumer protection considerations.
     Therefore its performance would be judged solely on its efficiency, which can be
     judged on the basis of the sum of error costs (i.e. the consequences of incorrect
     decisions) and direct costs (fees and management time). See Richard Posner,
     Economic Analysis of Law, 3rd ed. (Boston, Little, Brown, 1986) pp 517-557, "*An
     Economic Approach to Legal Procedure and Judicial Administration*", (1973), 2 J.
     Leg. Studies 399. For a brief English introduction see C. Veljanovski, *The Economics
     of Law* (London, Institute of Economic Affairs, 1990). The writer considers that the
     vocabulary of economics promotes rational and functional legal policy if only
     because it challenges the unstated assumptions implicit in the normal vocabulary of
     legal reform. This paper is not a serious attempt to apply the economic method as
     practised by the Chicago School but the writer's perspective is influenced by it. There
     is an enormous body of writing particularly in the United States about judicial process
     and procedural law, and the comparison between inquisitorial and adversarial models.

to the situation which allows comparatively unfettered experimentation with mechanisms for efficient dispute resolution.

Adjudication is also interesting because it is being used in an industry which is cyclical, fragmented, highly competitive and labour-intensive. Performance of Contracts involves a great deal of communication, interaction and co-operation between numerous parties, creating the potential for a multiplicity of interconnected factual and legal issues.[7] In a difficult environment it is being used as a policing method. It is presumably as a result of the inherent commercial good sense of construction industry managers and Employers that this potential for difficult issues of fact and law has not led to even more litigation and arbitration than now exists. Perhaps the way forward, therefore, is to simulate by way of contractual procedures the kind of managerial approach which leads to most disputes being resolved before the lawyers hear of them. Managers do not act like Judges or Arbitrators even though each is a decision-maker. It is not obviously the case that all disputes must be dealt with judicially, rather than merely fairly or reasonably. An inquisitorial procedure operated by an expert over a short timescale may be better; this, it seems, is closer to how managers decide.

The construction industry operates on a rhythm of monthly interim payments intended to be about right, followed by a final and more precise adjustment after the projects are over. It is at least plausible that prompt adjudication, followed later by arbitration or litigation, stands a better chance of serving the dispute resolution needs of the industry, since it mirrors the Contract administration process itself.

History

It appears that use in the UK construction industry of an adjudication mechanism was introduced at the beginning of 1976 with amendments to the then widely used "Green Form" of nominated Sub-contract. Shortly thereafter the procedure was also added to the "Blue Form" of domestic Sub-contract. Both of these forms were used in conjunction with the JCT63 Standard Form of Building Contract.[8] In 1980 these amendments were

---

7   See a similar description in an article by J. J. Myers in [1991] Int. Bus. Lawyer 313.

8   Prior to the amendments which regulated set-off rights and introduced an adjudication mechanism the Green Form provided that "The Contractor shall...be entitled to deduct from or set off against any money due from him to the Sub-contractor (including any Retention Money) any sum or sums which the Sub-contractor is liable to pay to the Contractor under this Sub-contract." The Blue Form was the same except that it referred to "sums which the Sub-contractor is legally liable to pay". That wording had existed, it seems, at least as far back as 1950. The phrase "liable to pay" was

retained in the new forms of building Sub-contract, NSC/4, NSC/4a and DOM/1, issued by the JCT to replace the Green and Blue Forms, for use in conjunction with the JCT80 Standard Form of Building Contract which replaced JCT63. The 1976 amendments introduced elaborate provisions regulating Contractors' rights of set-off against Sub-contractors which necessitated the use of an Adjudicator to deal with disputes over set-off claims.

The introduction of these provisions regulating set-off was due to pressure brought to bear upon the NFBTE by representatives of the sub-contracting industry and especially, it seems, the now defunct Metal Windows Federation. The sub-contracting industry was concerned to minimise the ability of unscrupulous, financially pressed or simply heavy-handed Contractors to disrupt orderly cash flow under the Sub-contracts in view of the important House of Lords decision in *Gilbert Ash (Northern) Limited* v. *Modern Engineering (Bristol) Limited*[9] relating to rights of set-off against amounts due to nominated Sub-contractors under Architects' certificates.

Prior to 1971, it was generally accepted that the rights which a contracting party had at law to set-off or set up a claim as a defence in proceedings brought by the other contracting party applied as much to the construction industry as any other area of commerce.[10] As noted by Lord Diplock in *Gilbert Ash* at p.718:

"...it was the common practice in actions for sums due on interim certificates to set up breaches of warranty in diminution or extinction of that sum."

In that year, however, the Court of Appeal decided in *Dawnays* v. *Minter*[11] that monies certified under the Green Form represented a special type of debt to which the normal rules of set-off did not apply. This became known as "the rule in *Dawnays*' case" and was applied by the Court of Appeal in a further five decisions within the space of a couple of years[12]. The

interpreted to have the effect of restricting the right of deduction to "liquidated and ascertained sums established or admitted as due": Dawnays v. Minter [1971] 1 WLR 1205. This obviously suited the commercial interests of Sub-contractors.

9   [1974] AC 689
10   See eg *Hanak* v. *Green* (1958), 1 BLR 1 and the discussion in I.N. Duncan Wallace QC's *Construction Contracts: Principles and Policies in Tort and Contract* (London, Sweet & Maxwell, 1986) beginning at p.198.
11   [1971] 1 WLR 1205, 1 BLR 16
12   *Frederick Mark Ltd* v. *Schield* [1972] 1 Lloyd's Rep. 9, *GKN Foundations Ltd* v. *Wandsworth* [1972] 1 Lloyd's Rep. 528, *John Thompson Horseley Bridge Ltd.* v. *Wellingborough Steel and Construction Co. Ltd.* The Times, 23rd February 1972,

underlying principle for this so-called rule was stated by Lord Denning to be that cash was the lifeblood of the construction industry. The *Dawnays* case came to be regarded:

> "...not as a mere decision on the construction of a particular clause in a particular contract but as authority for a general principle of law applicable to all building contracts which contain provisions for payment of the price of the works by instalments."[13]

That trend was reversed by the House of Lords in *Gilbert Ash* which stated categorically that an Employer is entitled to exercise the normal rights of set-off which arise by operation of law against amounts due to a Contractor unless the Contract excluded those rights. As a result, if a plausible set-off claim was raised, a summary judgment or interim payment could not, to that extent, be obtained with the effect that the claimant would be faced with the unattractive prospect of having to proceed either to a hearing, if there was an arbitration clause, or trial if not. It will be remembered that the process whereby the procedures and *pace* arbitration were being made more complex and slow was picking up speed and the volume of litigation was starting to tax the resources of the judicial system.

The problem which was identified by the sub-contracting industry was that, unless a Main Contractor's rights of set-off were controlled by changes in the Sub-contract terms, there was much scope for abuse.[14] Unjustified or inflated claims to a right of set-off could be made for tactical or financial reasons with an eye to the tests applied on applications to the Courts for summary judgment or an interim payment.

The relevant provisions of the amended Blue and Green Forms, now found in substantially their original form[15] in DOM/1, NSC/4 and NSC/4a

---

Token Construction Co. Ltd v. *Naviewland Properties Ltd.* (11th May 1972, C.A., unreported) and *Carter Horseley (Engineers) Ltd* v. *Dawnays Ltd.* The Times, 5th July 1972.

13 Lord Diplock in *Gilbert Ash* at p.716.

14 See eg *"The Great Set To About Set-Off"*, John Parris, at 2 BLR (v) ("Egged on by modern accountants, whose philosophy is expressed in their slogan 'never pay anything until you have to' building owners as well as main contractors found it highly convenient to have a set-off claim to excuse delay in payment"). See also Chapters 14-16 of I.N. Duncan Wallace QC's *Construction Contracts: Principles and Policies in Tort and Contract.*

15 The Blue and Green Form provisions were clauses 15 and 16, and 13A and 13B, respectively. Taking the Blue Form and DOM/1, the main differences are: (a) under DOM/1 the Contractor's notice of set-off must be served 20 days, rather than 17 days before the money against which the Contractor proposes to exercise its right of set-off becomes due and payable. This is because the payments terms (clause 21) are now

at clauses 23 and 24 and NSC/C at Clauses 4.26 - 4.37, reflect this limited but worthy objective. All other areas of potential conflict were and are left to be resolved in the traditional way. This suggests that the adjudication mechanism was introduced not because of a fundamental re-thinking of the management of disputes but instead as a necessary part of the contractual machinery limiting rights of set-off. A blanket exclusion of set-off rights would have been quite rightly unacceptable. Someone was needed to administer the set-off provision and presumably it was thought that the most readily available person to do this, the Architect under the Main Contract, should not as a matter of principle become directly involved with the resolution of payment disputes at Sub-contract level.

Evidently it became JCT policy to incorporate a set-off adjudication mechanism into all Sub-contracts since all such forms introduced by it since 1980 have such a mechanism: DOM/2 (1981) (for use with the JCT81 Design and Build Contract), NAM/SC and IN/SC (1984) (the named and domestic Sub-contracts for use with the IFC84 Intermediate Form of Building Contract) and the JCT87 Works Contract (1987) (for use with the JCT87 Management Contract).

There are no statistics or studies which show how extensively the adjudication mechanism has been operated or how successfully. As discussed below, it appears that it was not necessary for the provision to be considered by the Courts until this decade[16] although the associated set-off provision has been before the Court on a number of occasions. The absence of judicial involvement over the previous 15 years indicates either that the mechanism was operating successfully or that the parties bypassed the provision in its entirety. There are some indications in the case law that, although the set-off notice procedure was indeed operated in these early years, dissatisfied Sub-contractors generally ignored the adjudication mecha-

17 days rather than 14 days as under the Blue Form; (b) under DOM/1 the Adjudicator is expressly empowered to direct some combination of the outcomes listed in clause 24.3.1.1 - .3. Under the Blue Form this power probably existed but it could have been argued to be ambiguous on that point; and (c) Clause 24.5.2 of DOM/1 (dealing with the situation where the Trustee-stakeholder is a deposit-taking bank) was new.

16   There are other cases where adjudication was commented on but they are all obiter dicta: *Finn Construction Ltd.* v. *Lakers Mechanical Services Ltd.* (C.A., unreported, 12th March 1981) ("It is a useful frill but above all a frill."), *Tubeworkers Ltd.* v. *Tilbury Construction Ltd.* [1984] QB 644 (C.A.), *Pillar PG Ltd.* v. *DG Higgins Construction Ltd.* (1986), 34 BLR 43 (C.A.), *Chatbrown Ltd.* v. *Alfred MacAlpine Construction Southern Ltd.* (1987), 7 Con. LR 131 (O.R.), aff'd (1986), 35 BLR 44 (C.A.), *ARC Concrete Ltd.* v. *Gee Walker & Slater Plc* (C.A., unreported, 25th July 1988), *Archital Luxfer Ltd.* v. *AJ Dunning & Sons (Weyhill) Ltd.* (1989), 47 BLR 1 (C.A.), *Hermcrest Plc* v. *G Percy Trentham Ltd.* (1991), 53 BLR 104 (C.A.).

nism and went straight to Court with a summary judgment application.[17] However these cases may be the exception and not the rule.

It is perhaps fair to say that to some extent the concept of adjudication has its origins in the ICE and FIDIC civil engineering forms which require a preliminary reference of disputes to the Engineer under the Contract, who is ostensibly independent of the parties. For instance, in the ICE form current at the time of the 1976 amendments to the Green and Blue Forms (the 5th), if a matter was not referred to arbitration within 3 months of notice of the Engineer's decision, it was final and binding. I doubt, however, that the proponents of the 1976 amendments had the ICE and FIDIC approach particularly in mind since the real innovations in the adjudication mechanism were (i) the use of someone who, like an Arbitrator, was not involved in the day-to-day administration of the Contract to make decisions and (ii) a detailed code of procedure. ICE and FIDIC had neither of those features.

Commercial men have never been enamoured of litigation or arbitration. However beginning in the early 1980's, and perhaps triggered by the explosion of construction litigation and arbitration and the accompanying growth of a claims industry, there was increasingly vocal dissatisfaction with traditional litigation and arbitration as mechanisms for the resolution of construction disputes.[18] This led to debate and awareness of ideas generated by a similar debate in the United States which had begun some years before. I will not describe that debate in detail but so-called "ADR" mediation techniques were one product of that debate.[19]

Contract policymakers started to re-examine the Contract administration process from the bottom up. They sought to identify the contractual and psychological factors which led to adversarial working relationships. Litigation and arbitration were both increasingly recognised as imposing

17 Eg. *Redpath Dorman Long* v. *Tarmac* (1981) Construction Law Digest Vol. 1-07-32 (Blue Form), *Tubeworkers Ltd* v. *Tilbury Construction* [1984] QB 644 (Green Form), *Chatbrown* v. *Alfred McAlpine* (1986), 35 BLR 44 (Blue Form), *Pillar* v. *D J Higgins Construction* (1986), 34 BLR 43 (NSC/4a), *Hermcrest Plc* v. *G Percy Trentham Ltd* (1991), 53 BLR 104 (DOM/1), *BWP (Architectural) Ltd* v. *Beaver Building Systems Ltd* (1988), 42 BLR 86 (NAM/SC), *Acsim (Southern) Ltd* v. *Danish Contracting and Development Co. Ltd.* (1989), 47 BLR 55 (Blue Form).

18 The objectives are similar to those which led, for instance, to the development of administrative tribunals - the pursuit of "cheapness, accessibility, freedom from technicality, expedition and expert knowledge": Report of the Committee on Administrative Tribunals and Enquiries (1957)(the "Franks Committee") Cmnd. 218, London: HMSO. See also the chapter by Karl Mackie, "Dispute Resolution: the New Wave" in *A Handbook of Dispute Resolution*, Karl Mackie (ed.), (London, Routledge and Sweet & Maxwell, 1991).

19 A survey of the history and developments in this field can be obtained from Karl Mackie (ed.), *A Handbook of Dispute Resolution*. See also J. Effron, "*Alternatives to Litigation: Factors in Choosing*", [1989] MLR 480.

significant direct costs, in the form of legal fees and wasted management time, and the less readily quantifiable (but equally real) indirect costs imposed by game-playing, instead of teamwork, during construction.[20] Adjudication, as a means of summary dispute resolution, was identified as one possible way to solve these problems.

Presumably for these reasons, during the 1980's adjudication clauses in a variety of forms were introduced into a number of Contracts to resolve a far wider range of disputes, in addition to the various JCT Sub-contract forms dealing with set-off claims: the ACA Form of Building Agreement (optionally, 1982), the Building Contract and Professional Engagements for use under the British Property Federation ("BPF") System (1983), the 1984 edition of the ACA Form (still optionally), JCT81 (optionally, 1988), GC/ Works/1 Edition 3 (1989), and the ICE's draft New Engineering Contract (1991).[21] Adjudication also spread to non-JCT Sub-contracts through the GW/S Sub-contract for use with GC/Works/1 Edition 2 (1985) and the New Engineering Sub-contract (1991). Apparently the experiment is viewed as a modest success. How successful is unclear because of the apparent lack of research and statistics. Successful dispute resolution does not naturally attract publicity. Perhaps in this instance no news is good news.[22]

As can be seen, adjudication has spread to many of the usual domestic building industry standard forms (other than the core Building Contract ie JCT80, and the JCT87 Management Contract) and was considered to represent best practice by Martin Barnes and therefore included in the New Engineering Contract. There are also adjudication clauses in increasingly frequent use in private forms of building or civil engineering Contract, particularly for infrastructure projects.[23] It should be added that Sub-

---

20 The CIRIA Draft Study of PSA Procurement Strategies (1988) stated that the BPF System is "...evidence of a profound dissatisfaction with the traditional building system, and [is] a determined attempt to put something better in its place".

21 The ICE Minor Works form (1988) introduced a form of non-binding conciliation. The ICE (6th) (1991) introduced both conciliation and a beefed-up interim decision-making role for the Engineer some of the language of which seems to have been influenced by forms using expert systems. The GC/Works/1 (3rd) has a rather uninspiring form of "adjudication" in respect of a restricted range of issues but the adjudicator is from within the Employer's camp and in any event no adjudication can proceed until the dispute is at least 3 months old.

22 An interview with Ron Denny, formerly deputy director of the BPF in Construction News, 13th June 1991, argues that in the case of the BPF adjudication clause the lack of litigation is an "outstanding record". See also Alan Shilston, "*Reconciliation in the Construction Industry*", August 1988 Arbitration 179, 187.

23 Five examples are cited here: Sainsbury plc (dubbed "JS89"), Channel Tunnel, Second Severn Crossing, Second Dartford Crossing, Birmingham Northern Relief Road. The Sainsbury's approach is appointment of an Adjudicator by the Chartered Institute of Arbitrators when the dispute arises, broad jurisdiction being conferred and

contractor representative organisations have been lobbying for the DOM/1 adjudication procedure to be extended to cover a range of other issues beyond set-off rights and there have been some suggestions by commentators that the procedure be adopted for JCT80 itself. Furthermore, in the literature and construction press there is increasing interest in the benefits of adjudication.[24]

There are similarities and dissimilarities between the variants. I attempt to summarise these in the following section and later in this paper comment, in the light of the limited case law, on the policy issue of whether expanded use of adjudication mechanisms should be encouraged. The case law dealing with adjudication clauses, all under the DOM/1 version, has not, it seems, been perceived to be encouraging, which must create the prospect that grassroots enthusiasm for adjudication will abate. This would be unfortunate because the bases for the decisions in those cases do not affect the underlying commercial logic of adjudication.

---

later litigation by any dissatisfied party (See article by Tony Bingham, Building, 15th March 1991, p.39). The Channel Tunnel contract provides for adjudication by a panel of three experts whose decisions are final and binding until revised by arbitration if the decisions are unanimous. The Second Severn Crossing Contract uses an Adjudication Panel. Unanimous decisions are final and binding for all purposes. Majority decisions of the panel bind until Award or settlement. If either party if dissatisfied there is concilation followed by arbitration. Arbitration cannot proceed before practical completion unless the panel fails to reach a decision or the Employer agrees. The Second Dartford Crossing approach, involves a single Adjudicator who has 35 days to make a decision. It has, by all accounts been quite successful. See, for instance Comment in New Civil Engineer, 1st November, 1990, p.21: "It [the adjudication panel] is a system which is proving highly satisfactory on Dartford Bridge, by all accounts, and is being pointed out by some industry commentators as the way forward in reducing the uncertainty which often bedevils major projects....A number of decisions have been called for and no-one seems to be contesting them. The contract has gone very quickly indeed with little apparent acrimony." Adjudication is favoured by the Department of Transport for BOT infrastructure contracts. Also possibly in use is a system of panel adjudicators described in an article by R. B. Hellard in May 1988 Arbitration p 108. The panel approach has become increasingly popular in Australia. Although in its infancy, adjudication is also in use in complex long-term construction contracts in the U.S.A., where it is recognised that the longer a dispute remains outstanding the more it takes on a life of its own. The Adjudicator is frequently given the title of "Referee": JJ Myers, *"Could Arbitration be Made a More Effective Method of Resolution of Construction Disputes"*, [1991] Int. Bus. Lawyer 313.

24 Eg Adjudication: Does it Offer an Alternative? (interview with Ron Denny, formerly deputy director of the BPF), Construction News, 13th June 1991 - "Many of the concepts in the BPF System have been gaining ground since the manual was first introduced.... Mr. Denny points in particular to its requirement for appointment of

The Adjudication Variants

A number of general comments applicable to all variants can be made. Every variant provides that when a dispute arises which falls within the scope of the adjudication provision either party may invoke a contractual procedure whereby an independent investigation, including receipt of submissions from the parties but no hearing, is carried out in respect of the dispute and a decision is issued. The process takes weeks rather than months or years. The decision is reviewable de novo,[25] usually in an arbitration, which proceeds in the normal way. Until that time, or sometimes only until practical completion, the parties are expected to comply with the decision. The Adjudicator is not otherwise involved in the day-to-day administration of the Contract. In most instances there is a single Adjudicator, identified in the Contract, but sometimes an Adjudicator is only appointed when the need arises. Adjudication panels are also in use, as is an alternative procedure whereby the Adjudicator can appoint Assessors in the appropriate discipline to assist him or her. Variables include the length of procedural time limits and the extent to which a detailed procedure and the intended effect of the decision is set out. The JCT form also creates a Trustee-Stakeholder role, enabling the Adjudicator to order one party to pay a sum to a Trustee-Stakeholder rather than the opposite party.

There are important differences in the approaches to jurisdiction. The JCT Sub-contract approach limits jurisdiction to the important question of set-off. Another approach, of which the BPF System Building Contract is typical, sets out a wide shopping list of issues to which the adjudication mechanism applies. In contrast, the BPF System professional appointments refer all disputes during performance to an Adjudicator who is only appointed once the need for an adjudication arises.

In each instance the Adjudication mechanism is a contractual system of third party intervention normally expected to be invoked by a party that would otherwise have either no remedy in the short term or face seeking relief from the Courts unassisted by the contractual machinery. Functionally, this process is to litigation and arbitration what the function of police powers, pre-trial detention and bail are to criminal proceeding, supplying interim solutions to questions which may take some time to resolve fully and finally. If and when invoked, the interim "final say" on disputes is taken away from either the Architect, Engineer or whichever party has the short-term tactical or financial advantage. It introduces a neutral third party to make such decisions in order to create a greater degree of actual or ostensible independence on the part of the interim decision-maker and presumably

---

25 Subject to the effect of *NRHA* v. *Derek Crouch Construction Co.Ltd.* [1984] QB 644 (C.A.).

therefore more objective administration of building or civil engineering Contracts. The reader is referred to the Appendix which contains a textual analysis of the variants referred to above.

Policy decisions to be made in designing adjudication provisions are the following:

(a) Whether the Adjudicator is named from the outset: The argument made in favour of naming the Adjudicator at the outset is that it is important for the parties to choose someone they know and respect. This is not completely convincing. The Adjudicator could simply become someone imposed by the Employer (or whoever has the greater bargaining power). Appointment by a third party ensures neutrality. Presumably the involvement of a body like the Chartered Institute of Arbitrators would guarantee a minimum standard of competence.

(b) Breadth of jurisdiction: A shopping-list approach to jurisdiction may create potential problems which would entitle one party or the other to derail the adjudication process or efforts to enforce any decision, by impugning the Adjudicator's jurisdiction The more complicated the contractual machinery the easier it is for one of the parties to put a spanner into it. If a triable issue can be raised as to whether an Adjudicator had jurisdiction then a Court is not going to give effect to it at the important interlocutory stage. That potential problem must be weighed against the perceived benefit of excluding certain disputes from adjudication. I am dubious of variants which effectively exclude valuation disputes. On a practical level, jurisdiction should extend to every dispute of the sort that can take on a life of its own or where it is considered that unacceptable unfairness arises from delays associated with traditional dispute resolution. For instance, all interim payment-related and extension of time issues should be covered. There may be practical disadvantages in giving jurisdiction to override decisions of the Engineer, Architect or Contract Administrator on matters such as the adequacy of the Contractor's temporary works or other design or specification issues, instead of just determining the rights and obligations arising from such decisions, including the financial consequences. Hence there may be merit in the New Engineering Contract's approach of awarding compensation or extensions of time for such decisions where wrongly taken instead of altering the decision. Obviously the process of settling on the best jurisdiction must involve examination of actual experience with existing forms.

(c) Procedure and time limits: Express provisions for submissions by the parties consistent with a summary inquisitorial process within short time limits, and strict time limits imposed on the Adjudicator are advisable. Procedure must be scrutinised to eliminate opportunities for one party to cloud the issues or a weak Adjudicator to avoid the proper discharge of his or her duties. The right form of procedure can reinforce the Adjudicator's authority. Appointment of a Trustee-Stakeholder is a good idea.

(d) Duration of binding force: The effect of the decision should never automatically lapse. It should remain in force until displaced by Award or Order. Whether it should become binding for all purposes unless some step is taken within a time limit following the adjudication is problematic. Known legal finality is desirable but the benefit may be a mirage since parties may simply as a matter of course take the necessary steps in order to reserve their position.

(e) Whether the decision should only be interim: It is best for the conclusiveness of the Adjudicator's decision to be interim only. This strikes the best possible balance between the desire of the honest party for a speedy result and a desire for the correct decision. I tend to agree with I. N. Duncan Wallace QC that the parties' "desire for a correct decision greatly outweighs any wish for speed and premature finality"[26] but adjudication with an interim binding decision shows that long term absolute correctness does not rule out speedy and practical short-term solutions. In any event, a right of recourse to an Arbitrator or to the Courts seems to be the trend. Absolute finality seems to be associated with variants where one party, the Employer, has greater influence than the other (GC/Works/1, the private forms). However, with some issues the interim status of a decision may create difficulties. Money can be repaid, but if the parties have acted on a decision in some other way (relying on an extension of time, carrying out the works in a particular way) a subsequent reversal may leave one party worse off than had an adjudication not taken place.

(f) Timing of Arbitration: If Arbitration is the forum for review de novo, to what extent is it to be available immediately, or deferred until after practical completion ? The arguments for and against are well known. To the extent that the solution adopted is a shopping-list approach, this creates potential jurisdictional problems.

(g) Extent to which the intended effect of the decision is stated: Clearly the more the better. Making the decision an "incorporated term of the contract" is prudent.[27] The wording must recognise the likelihood that one party or the other may try to argue that the decision is not fully effective in some way. Consideration should perhaps be given to replacing the usual complete re-hearing of the issues with limited reviewability, for instance by providing that the Adjudicator's decision is binding to the extent that and until it is held that no reasonable Adjudicator could have come to that decision. This

26 "*Control by the Courts: A Plea for More, Not Less*", (1990), 6 Arb. Intl. 253.
27 The optional Amendment 3 (1988) to JCT 81.

would be similar to the way that Courts of Appeal review the exercise of judicial discretion by lower Courts.

Other Developments in Contract Dispute Procedure

ICE Minor Works (1988)

Although it does not use an adjudication mechanism, the ICE Minor Works form contemplates "interim arbitration" pursuant to the ICE Arbitration Procedure 1983 which corresponds closely to adjudication. The Arbitrator is entitled to "rely upon his own knowledge and expertise to such extent as he thinks fit". There is also a "Conciliation Procedure" which, being a form of mediation, falls outside the scope of this paper.

The ICE Minor Works form allows arbitration to proceed during the course of the Works. Clause 11.7 provides that any reference to arbitration shall be conducted in accordance with the ICE Arbitration Procedure (1983) and unless otherwise agreed in writing shall follow the rules for the Short Procedure. Where the Arbitrator is appointed and the arbitration is to proceed before completion or alleged completion of the Works an interim arbitration is to be conducted (clause 24.1 of ICE Arbitration Procedure). The Arbitrator is to "apply the powers at his disposal with a view to making his Award...as quickly as possible and thereby allowing or facilitating the timely completion of the works (clause 24.2). In an interim arbitration the Arbitrator has the power to direct use of either the Short Procedure or the Special Procedure for Experts (Clause 24.7).

If the interim arbitration is completed before completion of the Works, or the relevant part thereof, the Arbitrator is to publish his or her decision within 14 days of completion of the interim arbitration (clause 24.3). The Arbitrator has a choice of issuing either:-

(a) a Final Award or an Interim Award;
(b) findings of fact;
(c) a Summary Award; or
(d) an Interim Decision.

Final or interim awards and findings of fact are stated to be final and binding in any subsequent proceedings. A summary award usually requires payment of an interim payment by one party to another or to a Trustee-stakeholder (Clause 14.1, cf Clause 6.1(c)). It is final and binding unless and until varied by any subsequent Award (clause 14.4). An interim decision is final and binding until such time as the Works have been completed or any further award or decision in the interim arbitration is given. Thereafter the interim decision can be re-opened in a subsequent arbitration.

Even an interim arbitration may not proceed especially quickly. The party seeking a speedy outcome must wait one month following service of a Notice to Concur before being in a position to apply to the President of the ICE for appointment of an Arbitrator. The aggrieved party will be lucky to have a first meeting with the Arbitrator within a further month. In proceeding with the interim arbitration the Arbitrator will proceed in accordance with the Short Procedure but this contemplates submissions and a hearing. Furthermore, it is arguable that a party intent upon delay may, at any time before the Award, require that the arbitration cease to be conducted in accordance with the Short Procedure. That depends upon whether the fact that clause 11.7 of the ICE Minor Works form says that the arbitration "unless otherwise agreed in writing shall follow the rules for the Short Procedure" means that either party, in accordance with those rules, is not in a position to require that they should not be followed. Accordingly, it seems clear that the ICE Minor Works form is not structured so as to be capable realistically of matching the speed of adjudication.

ICE (6th edition) (1991)

This adopts an approach in the disputes clause, Clause 66, similar to that adopted in ICE Minor Works except for the following:

(a) a first tier decision on a dispute is made by the Engineer, within one month of a Notice of Dispute being served. The Engineer's decision is "final and binding" until a conciliator's recommendation is accepted or the decision is revised by an Arbitrator, and the parties "shall both give effect forthwith" to the decision (clause 66(1)-(4)). There is no time limit for commencing either conciliation or arbitration that would have the effect of making the decision potentially binding and final for all purposes; and
(b) the eventual arbitration (which can also proceed before the works are complete) is also to be in accordance with the ICE Arbitration Procedure (1983) but clause 66 is silent as to which procedure is to be adopted.

This approach is essentially a development of the traditional approach under civil engineering Contracts of referring disputes to the Engineer before the parties proceed to arbitration. The availability of arbitration before completion is a significant change. Under ICE (5th), unless the parties otherwise agreed no steps were to be taken in the reference until completion or alleged completion of the Works except in relation to a clause 12 ground conditions claim or a financial claim. Under ICE (6th) clause 66(8)(d) there is a blanket entitlement to proceed notwithstanding that the works are not completed.

The Conciliator's recommendation is deemed accepted in settlement of the dispute unless either party proceeds to arbitration within one month of receipt of the recommendation. Since its effect is dependent upon the acquiescence of both parties, it is not an adjudication process. Clearly, the Engineer's decision is not adjudication, as I have defined it, since the Engineer is involved in the day-to-day administration of the Contract.[28] The arbitration procedure seems even more unlikely than under the ICE Minor Works form to be able to function as speedily.[29]

Bovis Trade Contract

Some mention must be made of the forms which were considered in the *Rosehaugh Stanhope* v. *Redpath Dorman Long*[30] and *Beaufort House Developments Limited* v. *Zimmcor*[31] cases. The contractual arrangement in both cases was that Bovis Construction Limited was appointed as Construction Manager and the Employer engaged various Trade Contractors. Clause 19(1) of the form of Trade Contract provided that if the Trade Contractor was in breach of its obligations to carry out the works diligently and in accordance with Bovis' directions and to complete the works by the agreed date or dates, then:-

"... without prejudice to and pending the final ascertainment or agreement between the parties as to the amount of the loss or damage suffered or which may be suffered..."

by the Employer, it must pay or allow to the Employer:

"...such sum as the Construction Manager shall bona fide estimate as the amount of such loss or damage, such estimate to be binding and conclusive upon the Trade Contractor until such final ascertainment or agreement...."

28 It remains to be seen whether, when consequential amendments to the FCEC Blue Form (the standard form of civil engineering Sub-contract) are made, some form of adjudication will be introduced. The FCEC appears (Comment, Construction News, 20th June 1991) to be under some pressure from FASS and the Conference of Construction Specialists to amend the payment clauses.
29 However, it seems to have been the starting point for the drafting of the disputes clause of one of the interesting private forms, used for the Second Severn Crossing, discussed above.
30 (1990), 50 BLR 69 (C.A.)
31 (1990), 50 BLR 91 (C.A.)

Clause 19(4) gave a similar right of payment or deduction of Bovis' estimate in respect of losses suffered by reason of the Trade Contractor's breaches, tortious acts or breaches of statutory duty. Clause 19(5) then required Bovis to ascertain the loss or damage suffered by the Employer, without prejudice to the Employer's rights under Clauses 19(3) and (4). It would appear that it was intended by Bovis that the Trade Contract should vest in Bovis a binding interim decision-making power in respect of, in effect, one category of dispute as one way of imposing its will on the Trade Contractors. It is not adjudication as I have defined it because Bovis was involved in the day-to-day administration of the Contract.

The broader policy question is whether such a role should be performed by a Construction Manager. Few Trade Contractors are apt to consider the Construction Manager to be independent of the Employer or likely to make a decision on a dispute without regard to its own best interests given its own potential exposure to claims by the Employer for mis-management leading to valid Trade Contractor claims. It is clear from the judgments that the Court of Appeal found repugnant this approach to interim dispute-resolution. The Court of Appeal accepted the Trade Contractor's argument that the Employer's rights under Clauses 19(3) and (4) were subject to the contingent condition that the Trade Contractor be in breach and that by its terms the contractual machinery did not empower the Construction Manager to make that determination, only to make an estimate of the consequent loss or damage. The Employers' claims for summary judgment were accordingly dismissed.

Presumably the apparent flaw in the Contract wording which led to the Construction Manager's estimate being of no effect could be remedied by providing that the Construction Manager was also entitled to decide whether the Trade Contractor was in breach, which decision would be binding and conclusive unless and until the issue was decided by the Court, assuming that the Contract's attempt to confer such a jurisdiction was effective.[32]

Case Law on adjudication

I have described the adjudication procedure of DOM/1 in particular detail in the Appendix because the two instances where the status of an Adjudicator's decision has had to be decided by the Courts both involved DOM/1. The first case dealing with the DOM/1 adjudication clause is *Archital Luxfer Ltd* v. *Horton Construction Limited*[33] from which some general policy

---

32   There was no arbitration clause and the parties sought to confer on the Courts the same power to open up and revise, so as to avoid the effect of *NRHA* v. *Derek Crouch Construction Co. Ltd.* [1984] QB 644 (C.A.).

33   (O.R., 24th January 1990, unreported)

conclusions can be drawn. His Honour Judge Fox-Andrews Q.C.'s reasons are brief.

Archital had been engaged by Horton in 1988 as glazing Sub-contractor on the DOM/1 conditions. By March 1989 there were claims and cross-claims between the parties. Archital was claiming an extension of time and Horton was claiming liquidated damages (ie indemnity in respect of exposure to the Employer for liquidated damages) and loss and expense. It appears that the Sub-contract works were not yet practically complete.[34] Archital applied for an interim payment under Clause 21 of the Sub-contract (and seemingly rendered their final account) which should have been paid within 17 days from when payment fell due. No payment was made nor was a notice of set-off under Clause 23 given by Horton.

After correspondence between the parties and at least one claims meeting, Archital purported to invoke the adjudication procedure, stating in its letter to the Adjudicator that "...no further payments are imminent. Therefore we must presume that they have decided on an informal invocation of Clause 23 of DOM/1". Archital's argument presumably was that Horton, by airing its position both in correspondence and at a meeting, must be taken to have considered it unnecessary to serve a formal notice of set-off. Horton's position on the summons was that its withholding of payment was pursuant to its rights under Clause 12, which relates to the parties' rights and obligations in the event of failure by the Sub-contractor to complete on time, and had nothing to do with Clauses 23 and 24.[35]

The reasons do not give any indication of whether Horton participated in the adjudication. Presumably it did not, given the position which it took on the summons. In any event, within 21 days, the Adjudicator decided that Horton should pay the full amount of the interim payment claimed by Archital. Horton failed to pay and Archital applied for summary judgment or alternatively an O.29 interim payment, on the basis that either the amount claimed was due as an interim payment under the Sub-contract or as an

---

34   The Official Referee granted judgment on the basis that Horton's defence was based upon a claim under Clause 12 for liquidated and ascertained damages which did not become due until failure to complete on time and "Thus the Plaintiffs...are entitled to immediate judgment" ie the time for completion had not yet passed. This is difficult to reconcile with submission of a final account.

35   This argument is no longer open to a contractor. See now *Hermcrest Plc* v. *G. Percy Trentham* (1991), 53 BLR 104 (C.A.) which held that Clause 12 only applied when the amount had been agreed between the parties and that compliance with Clause 23 was necessary. See however *Mellows PPG Ltd.* v. *Snelling Construction Ltd.* (1990), 49 BLR 109 (O.R.) (a right of deduction under Clause 21.3.1.2 of NSC/4 of damages for delay is separate from a right of set-off under Clause 23), *Acsim (Southern) Ltd.* v. *Danish Contracting and Development Limited* (1989), 47 BLR 55 (C.A.) (abatement claim not affected by Clause 23) and *Pillar PG Ltd.* v. *DJ Higgins Construction Ltd* (1986), 34 BLR 43 (C.A.) (Clause 23 applies to contractor's disruption claim).

amount due under an Adjudicator's decision.

The Court expressed surprise that Archital had not gone straight for summary judgment for the amount of the valuation rather than first relying upon the adjudication procedure.[36] The Court held, apparently on the basis that the Contractor was not relying on its rights of set-off under Clause 23, that the Adjudicator had no jurisdiction. There was no set-off claim to adjudicate upon. The Official Referee's reasons in this respect were as follows:

"It is the Defendants' contention that [the Adjudicator] had no jurisdiction.

I am in full agreement.

The Defendants' case however is put thus...:-

'If it be argued that the contract conditions by clause 23 thereof precludes such a defence as the strict provisions therein contained have not been complied with by the Defendants, the Defendants would submit that the Plaintiffs waived reliance on such strict conditions by themselves making application pursuant to clause 24 to the Adjudicator notwithstanding the lack of the appropriate conditions precedent as they well know....'

This might have relevance on an Order 14 or Order 29 application if the adjudicator adjudged that some lesser sum than the amount of the valuation was payable. But in fact on 5th June 1989 [the Adjudicator] adjudged that [the full amount of the valuation] was payable.

As [has] been noted the Plaintiffs claim for their monies was put alternatively on the 14th March valuation or on the adjudicator's judgment.

In these circumstances what occurred although irregular, has not in itself I find deprived the Plaintiffs of the right to the benefit of clause 23."

It appears that "these circumstances" were either the absence of jurisdiction for the Adjudicator, which therefore did not deprive Horton of its right to the benefit of Clause 23, or that the claim was alternatively based on the interim valuation. The Official Referee decided that since Horton only

36 It is likely that the reason was that in similar circumstances on another project Archital had tried an immediate summary judgment application, rather than using adjudication, and the claim had been rejected by both the Official Referee and the Court of Appeal on the basis that the contractor had raised an arguable set-off defence: *Archital Luxfer Ltd.* v. *AJ Dunning & Sons (Weyhill) Ltd.* (1989), 47 BLR 1 (C.A.). It was therefore not unreasonable for Archital to try adjudication the next time.

relied upon its claim under Clause 12, and Archital's obligation to pay under that clause only arose when it had failed to complete on time, Archital was entitled (presumably because the time for completion had not arrived) to immediate judgment for the amount of the interim payment application. Hence Archital succeeded notwithstanding that the Adjudicator's decision was a nullity.

Although not referred to, this decision on the Adjudicator's jurisdiction is in accordance with the Official Referee's own obiter dicta in *Chatbrown Ltd.* v. *Alfred MacAlpine Construction Southern Ltd.*, where it was said:[37]

> "The Sub-contract introduced a new concept, that of adjudication. In the event of a valid notice being given by the Contractor under Clause 15, a Sub-contractor who disputes the amounts specified by the Contractor in his notices may, if he fulfils such conditions, obtain a decision of an adjudicator as to the amount. I stress the word 'amount'. I find that when it is the notice that is being impugned and not the amount in the notice, the adjudicator would have no powers."[38]

This suggests that an interesting way in which to avoid adjudication is simply by not serving a notice of set-off. But of course that will expose the Contractor to a summary judgment claim, in which the Contractor will not be able to raise a set-off, but it would be open to it to resist the claim, for instance, upon the grounds described in *Acsim (Southern) Limited* v. *Danish Contracting and Development Ltd.* (1989), 47 BLR 55 (C.A.), that is, an abatement defence, as was noted by the Official Referee in *Archital*. The Official Referee was not asked to consider Acsim but made reference to it.

The general policy conclusion which can be drawn from *Archital* is that, if and to the extent that the jurisdiction of the Adjudicator is limited to specific issues (and even more so if the instigation of the procedure is dependent upon a formal step being taken by the respondent party), there is scope for parties to take opportunistic jurisdictional points with a view to resisting its enforceability. It is predictable that systems which depend on a formal procedural act by a party other than the one considering itself to be aggrieved will tend to be less robust.

---

37 (1986), 7 Con LR 131,134 (affirmed at (1986), 35 BLR 44)
38 See also comments to similar effect by Kerr LJ in *Tubeworkers Ltd.* v. *Tilbury Construction Ltd.* (1985), 30 BLR 70. Archital is also consistent with the general approach which the Court of Appeal used in the *Zimmcor* cases (see section on Bovis Trade Contract) where the ascertainment of the contractor's loss and expense was a nullity because jurisdiction had not been established since the fact of the underlying breach was a triable issue.

Clearly, when faced with an adverse decision of an Adjudicator, many parties will engage professionals to think up clever ways of making the decision unenforceable or at least not enforceable in the short term.[39] To the extent that the jurisdiction is more general, the risk of the benefit of a short, sharp procedure being lost will be minimised. The Adjudicator's jurisdiction derives from the terms of the Contract. When faced with an attempt to impugn that jurisdiction, the Court will apply normal rules of interpretation of Contract, which leave limited scope for purposive interpretation unless faced with the illogical consequence of a literal one.

The second case under the DOM/1 adjudication procedure is the Court of Appeal decision in *A. Cameron Limited* v. *John Mowlem & Co.*[40]. Cameron was Mowlem's roofing Sub-contractor for a development in Putney, West London. The company was engaged on the DOM/1 conditions of Sub-contract.[41] Mowlem served Cameron with a notice of set-off under Clause 23 for loss and expense totalling £52,800. The set-off claim arose out of a deduction of liquidated and ascertained damages by the Employer for which Mowlem blamed Cameron. At the time of service of the notice the amount next due as an interim payment was £1,462.50.

Cameron initiated the adjudication procedure a few days later (it was necessary for the parties to agree on an Adjudicator as one was not named in the Sub-contract). After reviewing the parties' submissions (which included a counterclaim by Cameron for £77,564.16) the Adjudicator decided that Mowlem should pay the full £52,800 to Cameron. The whole adjudication process took less than four weeks from service of notice of set-off. Mowlem refused to pay the £52,800. Mowlem did not, however, thereafter rely upon its claim to a set-off. The next interim payment due, £1,462.50, was paid in full as were all subsequent interim payments.

Having obtained a decision, apparently binding on the parties, which on its face meant that it was immediately to be paid £52,800, Cameron felt compelled to embark upon what must have proved to be costly Court proceedings culminating in a Court of Appeal decision 20 months after the Adjudicator's decision. The outcome was that the terms of the decision were not enforced. The Court of Appeal decision dealt with appeals from two Official Referee decisions[42]

(a) a decision of His Honour Judge Esyr Lewis QC refusing leave under s.27

---

39 In the same way that the deduction mechanism in the Bovis Trade Contract cases was demonstrated to be ineffective.
40 (1990), 52 BLR 42 (C.A.)
41 Not incorporating the 1987 amendments.
42 I wish to thank Simon Tolson of Fenwick Elliott & Burns for supplying copies of both Official Referees' decisions.

of the Arbitration Act 1950 to enforce the decision in the same manner as a judgment of the Court; and

(b) a decision of His Honour Judge Fox-Andrews QC granting Cameron summary judgment for £52,800 less the £1,462.50 paid by Mowlem rather than staying the proceedings and referring the claim to arbitration.

The Adjudicator's decision was described by the Court of Appeal as having:-

"an ephemeral and subordinate character which in our view makes it impossible for the decision to be described as an award on an arbitration agreement".

The Court accepted that certain of the usual factors indicating that the decision had an arbitral quality were present, but held that it was better to "focus upon the Sub-contract". The Adjudicator's decision had "an ephemeral and subordinate character" because disputes under the Contract (including those concerning set-off) were to be resolved ultimately by an Arbitrator since "an Adjudicator's decision is [only] 'binding ... until' determination by an Arbitrator."[43]

It should be noted that under DOM/1 at the same time that a Sub-contractor requests action by the Adjudicator, it must also give notice of arbitration to the Contractor. Article 3 of DOM/1 contains an arbitration agreement referring "any dispute or difference" to the arbitration and final decision of an Arbitrator. "Any dispute or difference" would include whether a Contractor was entitled to claim a set-off. In respect of such claims the Arbitrator is expressly entitled, under Article 3.3, to enter on the arbitration prior to practical completion and in doing so to exercise the powers given to the Arbitrator by Clause 24 to vary or cancel the Adjudicator's decision. It will be noted that the Arbitrator's jurisdiction is not simply to review the Adjudicator's decision - it is a complete hearing de novo but the Arbitrator can at an interlocutory stage take the step of varying or cancelling the interim decision of the Adjudicator. The fact that the two procedures start concurrently seems to have influenced the Court.[44]

The consequence of the decision not having an arbitral quality was that the registration and enforcement procedure under Section 26 of the Arbitration Act 1950 for arbitral Awards was not available. The Court of Appeal

---

43 Perhaps the Adjudicator's decision would have fared better if DOM/1 provided for it to be binding unless and until varied by agreement of the parties or Award of an Arbitrator since this would assist the argument that the decision was a final determination, but subject to a sort of condition subsequent.

44 This was described as a "powerful point" by the Official Referee.

therefore affirmed the decision of His Honour Judge Esyr Lewis QC refusing to grant leave to enforce the decision in the same manner as a judgment of the Court. This part of the decision is, in my view, correct. However administratively convenient it might be to the party which succeeded in the adjudication, the Contract taken as a whole indicated that it was not the parties' intention (or, rather, the intention of the drafters of the standard form) that the decision should have the status of an Arbitrator's Award. If they had so intended they could more easily have expanded the arbitration clause. It is questionable, however, to justify the Court's conclusion on the basis that the decision was only binding until a determination by the Arbitrator: see for instance comments by Lord Simon in *Arenson* v. *Casson Beckman* [1975] 3 All ER 901, 910 where he expressed the view that finality and conclusiveness are not necessary characteristics of arbitration.

In any event, it was presumably unnecessary to decide, for the purpose of disposing of that aspect of the appeal what the status of the decision was, if it was not an arbitral Award. An alternative tactic of Cameron, adopted after its initial application to the Official Referee for registration of the decision under s.26 of the Arbitration Act 1950 had failed, had been to rely upon the adjudication in support of an application for summary judgment.

This had been met with a cross-application by Mowlem to stay the action and refer the claim to arbitration since, as required by Clause 24 of DOM/ 1, Cameron had given notice of arbitration. This of course raised the issue of whether any sum was indisputably due to Cameron. His Honour Judge Fox-Andrews QC had given judgment "with some hesitation" for Cameron for the full amount claimed i.e. £52,800 less the £1,462.50 already paid by Mowlem. The Court of Appeal reversed that decision on the very simple and correct basis that by virtue of Clause 24.4.2 the maximum entitlement arising from the Adjudicator's decision was the amount due as an interim payment in respect of which the Contractor had notified an intention to exercise a right of set-off. That amount had been paid long before, so there was, in effect, nothing left for the Court to enforce.

It was quite clear from Clause 24.4.2 of the Sub-contract that the most the Contractor could be expected to pay was:-

> "the amount due from the Contractor under Clause 21.3 in respect of which the Contractor has exercised the right of set-off referred to in Clause 23.2",

that is, the gross valuation of the works (prepared by the Sub-contractor but subject to substantiation at the request of the Contractor) less retention, any cash discount and the amount previously paid. The Court correctly stated that:-

"we do not think that the claimed amount of a set-off premises that that amount is or will become due by way of an interim payment"

(and by the same reasoning that Mowlem was not estopped by its notice from denying that at least £52,800 was due) and that the Adjudicator's powers did not extend to determining the amount due as the next interim payment. The Adjudicator was only entitled to rule on the set-off claim itself.[45]

In *Cameron*, although the notice of set-off totalled £52,800, the amount due under Clause 21.3, i.e. the next interim payment, was only £1,462.50. Mowlem had paid that as well as subsequent interim payments. A set-off never occurred. It is submitted that *Cameron* v. *Mowlem* leaves completely open the question of the extent to which a decision by an Adjudicator under DOM/1 can be enforced by way of application for summary judgment.

The dismissal of the application for summary judgment and grant of the stay of the action is, therefore, of little general interest. The question is, what effect will Adjudicator's decisions be given by the Courts? As I have explained, there are no cases directly on point; *Cameron* v. *Mowlem* is not really of much assistance. Clearly this will to some extent vary from Contract to Contract but, where the Adjudicator has made a decision in the circumstances contemplated by the Contract, there is no logical reason why the Courts should not be expected to enforce or apply it to the extent that the Contract, on a proper construction, contemplates it. In a proper case, therefore, the Courts will rely upon an Adjudicator's decision as excluding any arguable defence to a claim and grant summary judgment.

It does not follow from the description of the decision as "ephemeral or subordinate" (and therefore not an Arbitrator's Award for the purposes of Section 26 of the Arbitration Act 1950) that the decision has no legal effect. Until the Arbitrator varies or cancels the decision, or determines the set-off issue in his or her final Award, the Sub-contract states that the decision "shall be binding" (Clause 24.2.1). This is "contractual machinery": Kerr LJ in *Tubeworkers Ltd.* v. *Tilbury Construction Ltd.*[46]; *NRHA* v. *Derek Crouch Construction Co. Ltd.*[47] If it had been necessary, I would have expected the Court to characterise it as an expert decision and/or the clause

---

45   As in *Archital* v. *Luxfer* where the absence of any attempt by the contractor to serve a notice of set-off under the set-off provision meant that the Adjudicator had no jurisdiction whatsoever.
46   (1985), 30 BLR 70
47   [1984] QB 644

as a "conclusive evidence" clause[48] but in any event produced by contractual machinery and to be given effect to accordingly, rather than by the Court substituting its own machinery for that provided by the Contract.

I would expect that if a Contractor disregarded the Adjudicator's decision, and proceeded to set-off its claim, a Court would grant summary judgment in a proper case[49] for the amount due as an interim payment. In doing so, the Court would be giving effect to the fact that the decision is stated to be binding to the extent provided by the Sub-contract until varied or superseded. The wording would enable the Court to hold that the Contractor is unable to raise any uncertainty as to whether the next interim payment is in fact indisputably due (to the extent that this issue has been dealt with by the Adjudicator) in order to defeat an application for summary judgment or an interim payment. The fact of service of notice of arbitration would not per se bar a proper claim for summary judgment for a sum indisputably due or an interim payment.

Clearly, there are perceived, rightly or wrongly, to be general problems with the utility of the summary judgment and interim payment remedies due to the availability of defences to such applications. However, that problem arises from the wording of the contractual interim payment and set-off machinery, and the relevant test on such applications (which is not part of the subject-matter of this paper), and has nothing to do with the adjudication mechanism itself[50]. There is no question of the Courts being hostile to adjudication mechanisms. See for instance the obiter dictum of May LJ in *Archital Luxfer Ltd.* v. *AJ Dunning & Sons (Weyhill) Ltd.*[51]:

> "In essence the latter [Clause 24 of NSC/4] were to enable him to give a swift but interim decision about the payment, repayment or securing of monies certified to be due to a Sub-contractor, but against which the main Contractor claimed a set-off, pending the final resolution of any dispute between the

---

48   See eg L. Collins and D. K. Livingstone, "Aspects of Conclusive Evidence Clauses" [1974] JBL 212 and pp 300-310 of D. Yates and A. J. Hawkins, Standard Business Contracts (London, Sweet and Maxwell, 1986). For the American experience of contracts expressing an Engineer's decision as final see J.J. Myers, "Finality of Decisions of Design Professionals Where the Contract Provides the Decision Will be Final", (1984-85), 2 ICLR 319.

49   ie subject to defences such as in *Acsim* v. *Dancon*

50   One commentator on the case proposed that DOM/1 should be amended either to permit immediate arbitration on all payment matters or to make failure to implement a decision a ground of determination: Guy Cottam, *Construction News*, 17th January 1991.

51   (1989), 47 BLR 1 (C.A.) at p.7

parties by agreement or after a reference to arbitration pursuant to the wide provisions of the arbitration clause...."

and the description of it by Donaldson LJ (as he then was) in *Finn Construction Ltd.* v. *Lakers Mechanical Services Ltd.*[52] as a "useful frill".

The Courts' likely attitude is, I suggest, reflected in the following passage in the judgment of Kerr LJ in *Tubeworkers*, supra, beginning at p.72 where, in the course of holding that where a nominated Sub-contractor had recovered summary judgment on an interim certificate because, at the time that payment became due, the Contractor had not yet fulfilled the requirements of a valid notice of set-off (it had not obtained an Architect's certificate of non-completion, but did shortly thereafter) it was inappropriate to grant a stay of execution of the judgment, he stated:-

"... the Adjudicator, in his absolute discretion and without giving reasons, may do a number of things to safeguard or deal with the position in the interim....

This is the background to the events in the present case....

[T]he Judge's order of a stay has ... put the plaintiffs in a worse position than they might possibly have been in if the defendants had been able to invoke, and had invoked, the machinery of Clause 13A. The reason is that, in that event, the immediate decision as to what was to happen pending arbitration would have gone to an adjudicator under Clause 13B, and he might possibly have ordered that all or part of the money certified as being payable to the plaintiffs was to be paid to them....

So what the learned Judge has done, in effect, is that he has replaced the contractual machinery agreed between the parties by the process of the courts in ordering a stay under Order 47. In my view, this is prima facie wrong. I say "prima facie" because, as already mentioned, there might be exceptional circumstances to justify it. But, generally speaking, I think that the relevant terms of the contract between the parties must be paramount and take precedence over the court's discretion under Order 47.

Of all the authorities to which we were referred, I found the most helpful one in this connection, in principle, to be the decision of this Court in *Northern Regional Health Authority* v. *Derek Crouch Construction Co. Ltd.* [1984] QB 644; 26 BLR 1. That was not concerned with the present form of Sub-contract, but it was, among other matters, concerned with the question whether

52 (C.A., unreported, 12th March 1981)

the Court could substitute its process by opening up an architect's certificate for the powers given by the contract to an arbitrator in that regard. It was held that there was no power to do so. For "arbitrator" in that context one can, I think, read "adjudicator" in the present context. The passages relied upon are to be found in the judgments of Dunn LJ and Browne-Wilkinson LJ in particular. At p.664[53] Dunn LJ said:

> 'The parties have agreed that disputes as to anything left to the discretion of the architect should be referred to arbitration, and Clause 35 gives wide powers to the arbitrator to review the exercise of the architect's discretion and to substitute his own views for those of the architect. Where parties have agreed on machinery of that kind for the resolution of disputes, it is not for the Court to intervene and replace its own process for the contractual machinery agreed by the parties.'

It is in particular that last section which I find of assistance in the present context."

Procedurally Efficient Contracts

It has been doubted whether there is a meaningful distinction to be drawn between conflicting interests and disputes: see comments by Lord Kilbrandon at p.918 and Lord Fraser at p.927 in *Arenson* v. *Casson Beckman*[54]. In any event, as a matter of contract policy, it would seem that conflicting interests and disputes should be treated as being part of the same continuum. Conflicting interests create the potential for a dispute in that, unless the parties agree on the proper method of reconciling those conflicting interests in specific instances, a dispute will gradually emerge. Viewed in this way, Architect's certificates, Adjudicator's decisions and Arbitrator's Awards all become simply component mechanisms, which may be incorporated into a contract design to channel the parties' rights and obligations in a more streamlined way. The alternative would be to leave the determination of all issues unregulated by contractual machinery, which means unrestricted factual disputes, unlimited collection and presentation of evidence, delay,

53 26 BLR 25,
54 But see comments by Lord Simon at p.912

adversarial procedure and full hearing rights.[55]

To a greater or lesser extent, the emergence of conflicting interests is inevitable under Contracts. Contracts are entered into because of perceived mutuality of interest; however there is never an identity of interest. The real question is the extent to which, and how, the design of a Contract should anticipate and accommodate conflicting interests. Some methods of procurement, for instance management contracting, were designed in an attempt structurally or substantively to reduce conflicting interests. The thrust of the relevant section of the recent Building Toward 2001 report is aimed at a substantive solution (eg identifying the need for "A new form of contract that arranges the resource groups of a construction project so that they all have identical goals of a timely, economical, profitable and high quality product"). That must involve a radical change to the parties' basic contractual rights and obligations. Although that may achieve the objective in some cases, it does not represent a complete solution. The increasingly vocal criticism of management contracting reflects the limitations of such solutions.

An alternative approach, which can be adopted either instead of or in conjunction with altering the basic structure of rights and obligations, is to try to accommodate conflicts of interest inherent in the system by designing , and contacting on the basis of, practical procedural solutions which strike the most effective balance between achieving the correct result and keeping the cost of the process to a minimum. If this is not done, conflicting interests

---

55 The conventional procedure of issuing certificates is an expert system. A certification mechanism is an evidentiary tool used primarily in contracts for the sale of goods, carriage of goods or for the supply of work and materials. The contract requires certain types of evidence, for instance a Q.S's valuation or a sample of material, to be processed by the certification mechanism, the end product being a formal statement of fact. It is used in order to preclude, or at least channel, evidentiary disputes by making conclusive, to the extent provided by the contract, whatever statements of fact or conclusions the contract machinery requires in order to operate effectively. The finality of the certificate in each case is to be derived from a construction of the contract as a whole, it being dependent upon the intention of the parties. However, in each instance, the certifier is acting in the capacity of an expert, vested with a decision-making power binding to a greater or lesser extent on the parties. Certification is an exercise in dispute prevention whereas adjudication is an exercise in dispute resolution. However, in my view there is no useful distinction between the two processes. Rather they represent two out of the full range of possible mechanisms that parties negotiating a contract can agree to regulate their respective rights and obligations during the performance of a contract. See the helpful discussion of certificates in K. Lewison, *The Interpretation of Contracts* (London, Sweet & Maxwell, 1989) at pp.283-295. The primary significance of certificates in construction contracts is that access to the contract enforcement procedures of the judicial system is greatly facilitated (although not ensured) by being able to rely upon a certificate to fulfil the applicable test on summary judgment and interim payment applications.

will be left to be resolved by supplementary agreement between the parties or, failing that, arbitration or litigation.

Use in leases of an expert decision to decide rent reviews amounts to treating the issue of the new rent as a conflicting interest issue rather than a dispute. It is obvious from the outset that arriving at a new rent is a process in which it would be unsafe to assume that the mutuality of interests which existed at the time of contracting will still exist at the relevant time and be sufficient in the natural course of events to lead to a supplementary agreement.

Other disputes, arising out of conflicting interests, arise from time to time out of leases and are dealt with by arbitration or litigation. It may be argued that types of disputes which arise occasionally can safely be left to be resolved following traditional patterns. However, where conflicting interests regularly and/or inevitably become acute, it is better for the contractual machinery to supply a tailored solution in the form of either certification or adjudication, depending upon the importance of complete independence and/or procedural rules.

The regularity of disputes during construction on a whole host of matters and the obvious inefficiency of the arbitral and judicial process in resolving those disputes within a sensible timeframe, points toward the need to adopt a policy dealing with them which in broad terms corresponds to the way in which rent reviews are dealt with, with suitable procedural changes.

Expert Decision-Making v. Arbitration

The most obvious alternative to contractual expert decision-making machinery is arbitration. Using an expert decision to resolve certain disputes under a Contract which already includes an arbitration clause seems to be a conscious policy decision. In order to judge that policy decision it is necessary to understand the respective legal ramifications of both methods of dispute resolution.

Arbitration is a procedure where, by Contract, either prior to or after disputes arise, the parties refer disputes for the decision of an independent person whose decision the parties agree to accept as binding. Arbitration has the following features:-

(a) The Arbitrator acts in a judicial or quasi-judicial capacity[56]. The

56 In *Arenson* v. *Casson Beckman* [1975] 3 All ER 901, 915, Lord Wheatley indicated the elements necessary for a judge or arbitrator to be acting in a judicial manner:-
(i) there is a dispute or difference between the parties which has been formulated in some way or another;
(ii) the dispute or difference has been remitted by the parties to a person to resolve in

Arbitrator must act on the evidence and arguments of the parties. Of course the Arbitrator can and indeed is normally expected to rely upon his or her own expertise but the Arbitrator does not conduct his or her own investigation. In other words, it is never an inquisitorial process: *Town & City Properties (Development) Limited* v. *Wiltshier Southern Limited*.[57] This probably means that the Arbitrator is immune from being successfully sued by either of the parties except in the case of fraud or collusion: *Sutcliffe* v. *Thackrah*[58], *Arenson* v. *Casson Beckman*[59]. The immunity is given on grounds of public policy.[60]

(b) There are statutory rights of appeal or to determination of a preliminary point of law:[61]

(c) The Court has a statutory jurisdiction to make certain interlocutory orders facilitating the arbitration process (eg appointment of an Arbitrator, discovery, subpoenas) and jurisdiction to remit the Award back to the Arbitrator and/or remove the Arbitrator on grounds of misconduct:[62]

(d) The Arbitrator's Award is registrable and thereafter enforceable as a judgment of the Court:[63]

(e) A provision obliging both parties to bear their own costs is unenforceable. The costs of the arbitration are in the Arbitrator's discretion unless the contrary intention is expressed. The Arbitrator's fee and the cost of the

---

such a manner that he is called on to exercise judicial functions;

(iii) where appropriate, the parties must have been provided with an opportunity to present evidence and/or submissions in support of their respect claims in the dispute; and

(iv) the parties have agreed to accept his decision.

It may be questioned whether this list really assists the inquiry of whether a judicial function is being exercised.

57   (1988), 44 BLR 109 (O.R.).

58   [1974] 1 All ER 859 (H.L.)

59   [1975] 3 All ER 901 (H.L.)

60   There is a possibility that the House of Lords may review this immunity at some stage, at least where the arbitrator is given a partial investigatory role by the parties, but it seems that, at least up to Court of Appeal level, an arbitrator will be safe: *Russell on Arbitration* 20th ed (London, Stevens & Sons 1982). Lords Fraser and Kilbrandon in Arenson were of the view that in principle there was no reason why a person appointed as arbitrator should be immune from an action for negligence in the exercise of that function. It has been argued that in view of the drastically reduced rights of appeal since 1979 public policy may require a cause of action against arbitrators: Mustill & Boyd, *Commercial Arbitration* at p 194. See also F.A. Mann, *"Private Arbitration and Public Policy"*, [1985] Civil Justice Q 257.

61   Arbitration Act 1979, SS.1, 2

62   Arbitration Act 1950, sS.10, 12, 22 - 25. ss.10 and 12 will be amended by Ss.101 and 103 of the Courts and Legal Services Act 1990 when these come into force.

63   Arbitration Act 1950, S.26

arbitration can be taxed:[64]

(f) There is a lot of case law and good texts on arbitration and therefore a fair degree of certainty as to the rights and obligations of the parties and the Arbitrator; and

(g) Arbitrators are in control of their own procedure subject to the terms, if any, regulating procedure set out in the arbitration agreement itself[65]. The only constraint imposed by the Courts is a duty of fairness and to give the parties an opportunity to be heard. The "legalism" of arbitration over the past decades is not inherent in the process. For instance there does not appear to be any reason why the same procedure as DOM/1 prescribes could not be used, with an Arbitrator substituted for the Adjudicator[66].

The basic features of contractual expert decision-making machinery are as follows:-

(a) The expert acts in a non-judicial capacity[67].

The expert carries out an independent investigation, is not necessarily required to receive submissions from the parties or, if received, to act on them and is not bound to disclose evidence from one party to another party: *Sutcliffe* v. *Thackrah* (Lord Salmon at p.882), RICS Guidance Note, *Top Shop Estates* v. *C. Danino*[68]. Fundamentally it is an inquisitorial procedure. It is, however, increasingly common for provision to be made for at least written representations to experts; see for instance *Palacath* v. *Flanagan*[69]. That, however, is up to the parties. This also means that the expert may be liable to the parties for negligence as well as fraud or collusion: *Sutcliffe* v. *Thackrah, Arenson* v. *Casson Beckman, Campbell* v. *Edwards*[70]. It is this

64   Arbitration Act 1950, ss.18, 19
65   See eg *Carlisle Place Investments Ltd.* v. *Wimpey Construction (UK) Ltd.* (1980), 15 BLR 108.
66   However, see *Town & Country Properties* v. *Wiltshier* where the Arbitrator went too far and was found to have adopted a valuation process rather than an arbitration.
67   There are a number of obscure references in the cases to the concept of a "quasi-arbitrator" (e.g. *Palacath* v. *Flanagan* (1985), 274 EG 143). This term has been used to refer to a person who, although he or she exercises a judicial function, has not been appointed as an Arbitrator under the Arbitration Acts: per Lord Morris in *Sutcliffe* v. *Thackrah* at p.689. See Lord Salmon in Sutcliffe at p. 882 where he refers to the concept of quasi-arbitrator as having been "invoked but never defined". There appears never to have been a case finding that a person acted as a quasi-arbitrator and probably no such separate classification has any legal significance: Hals. 4th ed Vol. 48, para 6.
68   [1985] 1 EGLR 9
69   (1985), 274 EG 143
70   [1976] 1 All ER 785 (C.A.) At one time it was thought that an expert was not liable in negligence: *Chambers* v. *Goldthorpe* (1901), 70 LJKB 482, the Court of Appeal decision in *Arenson* v. *Arenson* [1973] 2 All ER 235. This public policy immunity

exposure which explains the exclusion of such liability in the New Engineering Contract;

(b) There is no relevant legislation, and therefore no statutory right of appeal, statutory reviewing jurisdiction or specific statutory right of registration and enforcement of the expert decision. Enforceability or, conversely, reviewability, is a matter of contract[71]. Expert decisions are clearly reviewable on grounds of fraud or collusion but the extent of reviewability for error is somewhat unsettled. At one time it was thought[72] that an expert's decision could be set aside on the basis of mere mistake or miscarriage which could mean adding up figures wrongly, taking into account irrelevant facts or law or failing to take into account relevant facts or law, proceeding on the basis of an incorrect interpretation of the Contract or making errors of principle, or arriving at an extravagantly large or unreasonably small valuation. This gave the Courts a largely free hand to intervene, when they wished, and substitute its own judgment in most instances, particularly where the expert's decision was a "speaking" one. In consequence of *Sutcliffe* v. *Thackrah* and *Arenson* v. *Casson Beckman* holding that an expert was not immune from liability this was reviewed in *Campbell* v. *Edwards*[73] which considered the issue in a different way:

"It is simply the law of contract. If two persons agree that the price of property should be fixed by a valuer on whom they agree,

was held by the House of Lords in *Arenson* v. *Casson Beckman* to be contrary to "principle, sound authority, reason and justice". It may now be that where the expert is fulfilling a contractual function which an Arbitrator or Court would otherwise fulfil, the Court, given current trends in the law, may find some reason based upon a proper construction of the contract or the development of the vague concept of a quasi-arbitrator (see footnote 79) to create exceptions to this principle: *Arenson* v. *Casson Beckman* at p.947 and see also *Russell on Arbitration* at p.93. In practice, there may be difficulty in proving negligence or breach of implied term requiring the exercise of skill and care, and especially in the case of a non-speaking award. See for instance *Belvedere Motors Limited* v. *King* (1981), 260 EG 813. See also *Lubenham Fidelities* v. *South Pembrokeshire D.C.* (1986), 33 BLR 46 (C.A.) at p.55 where May LJ states that there is "no sufficient reason for differentiating ... between certificates which contained patent errors and those which contained latent errors" and p.54 where he refers to an architect as "the particular expert to whom the parties have chosen to entrust this function."

71 *Arenson* v. *Casson Beckman*, Campbell v. Edwards
72 *Dean* v. *Prince* [1953] 2 All ER 636
73 See also Lord Denning's views expressed in *Arenson* v. *Arenson* [1973] 2 All ER 235 where he stated that a certifier's and valuer's decision, at any rate where no reasons are given, was unimpeachable except in case of fraud or collusion: "[The parties] have made their bed and must lie on it, no matter how uncomfortable it may be - for one or other of them" (p.241) and *F. Baber* v. *Kenwood Manufacturing Co.* [1978] 1 Lloyd's Rep 175.

and he gives that valuation honestly and in good faith, they are bound by it. Even if he has made a mistake they are still bound by it. The reason is because they have agreed to be bound by it. If there were fraud or collusion, of course, it would be different. Fraud or collusion unravels everything. It may be that, if a valuer gives a speaking valuation - if he gives his reasons or his calculations - and you can show on the face of them that they are wrong, it might be upset."

The process of self-limiting the Court's jurisdiction continued in *Jones* v. *Sherwood Computer Services*[74], which developed a test based upon whether or not the expert departed from his or her instructions in a material respect. Whether or not the expert included reasons with the decision was irrelevant[75]. The Court in *Jones* v. *Sherwood* stated that the real question was whether it was possible to say from all of the evidence properly before the Court what the valuer or certifier had done and why he had done it. If the expert departed from the parties' instructions in a material respect either party could say that the decision was not binding because the expert had not done what he was appointed to do.[76] Enforceability is generally viewed as being facilitated by the Contract providing that the decision is incorporated into the Contract as a term. It is then used in support of an application for such relief by way of summary judgment, injunction etc as may be appropriate;[77]

(c) The quantification and recovery of the expert's fee depends on the terms of the engagement and the ordinary rules of civil procedure. Entitlement to award costs would require a contract term to that effect;

(d) There is relatively less case law, or at least it is spread over wider ground, and therefore, there is less certainty as to the enforceability of expert

---

74   [1992] 1 WLR 277
75   Followed in *Nikko Hotels* v. *MEPC* [1991] NPC 41.
76   See for instance *Jones* v. *Jones* [1971] 1 WLR 840 where the expert carried out his own valuation instead of employing someone else as required by the contract. See also *J T Sydenham* v. *Enichem* [1989] 1 EGLR 257 where the rent review valuation was set aside because the valuer had misinterpreted a user clause restrictively and *Apus Properties* v. *Douglas Henry Farrow Ltd.* [1989] 2 EGLR 265 where the valuer wrongly assumed a wider use as provided in the licence to assign than the more restrictive use in the head lease. It is difficult to reconcile these cases with the principle that the main mistake must be fundamental.
77   See eg JCT81 optional Amendment 3 and model clause in ICC Brochure No. 326 on Adaption of Contracts (October 1978) ("a final decision binding on the parties and ... deemed to be incorporated in the contract").

decisions and the duties of the expert to the parties;[78]
(e) The expert has, like an Arbitrator, a duty of fairness: *Sutcliffe* v. *Thackrah, Arenson* v. *Casson Beckman, Campbell* v. *Edwards*; and
(f) The expert is, like an Arbitrator, in control of how he or she performs their role subject to any terms of the Contract relating to procedure.

The common thread running through the use of expert decision-making is that the process is treated simply as part of the Contract machinery. Expert decision-making is used in a wide range of contexts involving either disputes or merely conflicting interests:

(a) accountants carrying out company valuations or valuers fixing the price of goods as envisaged by the Sale of Goods Act 1979, s.9;
(b) actuaries carrying out valuations for pension schemes;[79]
(c) chartered surveyors carrying out rent reviews;
(d) certifiers of quality under sale of goods Contracts;[80]
(e) certifiers of liability especially under on-demand performance bonds, which may even be one of the parties to the underlying Contract itself;[81]
(f) certifiers under building and civil engineering Contracts i.e. the Architect and the Engineer; and
(g) finally, of course, Adjudicators under building and civil engineering Contracts or professional engagements expressly or implicitly acting "as expert and not as arbitrator".

It is sometimes difficult to know whether a person is appointed as expert or Arbitrator. This is, strictly, a matter of construction and not one of description. So for instance in *Langham* v. *Brompton*[82] where a rent review clause made no reference to arbitration or to appointment of an expert. The clause provided for appointment of a "chartered surveyor" without specifying the capacity. The Court held that the person was required to act as an independent valuer i.e. an expert, and not as Arbitrator as the draftsman had used none of the language associated with arbitration which had been used in the clause immediately preceding the rent review clause.

---

78 Some guidance can be obtained from the following texts and in the cases cited: Bernstein and Reynolds, *Handbook of Rent Review*, (London, Sweet and Maxwell, 1990 revision), Clarke and Adams, *Rent Reviews and Variable Rents*, 3rd ed (London, Oyez, 1990), *Russell on Arbitration*, 20th ed, Mustill and Boyd, *Commercial Arbitration*, 2nd ed 1989, pp 300-310 of D. Yates and A. J. Hawkins, *Standard Business Contracts* (London, Sweet & Maxwell, 1986).
79 *Re Imperial Foods Limited's Pension Scheme* [1986] 1 WLR 717.
80 Eg *Lishman* v. *Christie & Co.* (1887) 19 QBD 333
81 Eg *Bache* v. *Banque Vernes* [1973] 2 Lloyd's Rep 437 (C.A.)
82 (1980), 256 EG 719

The practice of choosing an expert rather than an Arbitrator used to derive from the fact that use of an expert had the great advantage that it was not subject to the delays associated with the wide rights of appeal from arbitral Awards by way of stated case. Those rights are now greatly reduced. Use of experts to resolve disputes cannot really be justified on that ground. Further, the fact that an expert may be liable in negligence but not an Arbitrator is not necessarily a great advantage. This liability may be excluded by the terms of engagement and in any event review may be considered to be a preferable way of correcting any error rather than relegating correction to a negligence action.[83]

On the basis of the above, viewed legally and in the abstract, neither expert decision-making nor arbitration are obviously superior to the other. Most differences can be eliminated by Contract.[84] The central difference seems to be that the absence of statutory control (it being unlikely that the ruling in *Cameron* v. *Mowlem* will be reversed) gives a greater flexibility to expert decision-making machinery. Furthermore, expert decision-making is investigative rather than conforming to the common law judicial and quasi-judicial model.[85] For the purposes of a summary interim procedure, expert decision-making seems to have the edge.

Parallel Developments

The problem of increasing the efficiency of UK construction processes is primarily a managerial challenge. Spurred in part, perhaps, by the explosion of claims under construction Contracts, although also part of a wider trend over the last decade, there has been a real growth in awareness of the contribution of management to maximise the return on resources applied to the construction process.

Most disputes are founded in management shortcomings.[86] Adjudication can be viewed as a contractual procedure which simulates the methodology of managerial decision-making to resolve disputes. It is, therefore, in theory at least, a pragmatic solution to the problem of managing disputes arising out of the interaction of individuals from separate organisations tending to

---

83 See comments to that effect in Bernstein and Reynolds, *Handbook of Rent Review*, p.109
84 In particular, it is probably desirable that liability in negligence is excluded in the Expert's terms of engagement where resolving disputes.
85 If the use of adjudication spreads, conceivably its procedures might tend over time to take on the characteristics of arbitration with the possible consequence that the concept of quasi-arbitrator is developed and *Cameron* v. *Mowlem* is treated as a particular case on a particular contract.
86 Martin Barnes, *"Prevention is Better than Dispute"*, (1987) 4 ICLR 196.

have conflicting interests.[87] Adjudication is just one of a number of responses which have developed to meet the problem of disputes in the construction industry. It ought to be put into the context of other developments, some of which are complementary to it, others of which are competing as possible solutions to the problem. I identify below eight trends relevant to the construction industry which have developed over the same period in which adjudication has emerged as a mainstream method of dispute resolution:

(a) Attempts to renovate the arbitration process in response to the criticism that it had lost its time and cost advantage over litigation. I would point, for instance, to the ICE Arbitration Procedure (1983) and the JCT Arbitration Procedure (1988) in addition of course to the Arbitration Act 1979. A private bill to make further amendments is pending;

(b) A shift in some Contracts toward the availability of earlier arbitration (eg ICE (6th));[88]

(c) Discussion, awareness and some experimentation with ad hoc and contractual conciliation procedures (eg establishment of CEDR, ICE Minor Works, ICE (6th));

(d) The development of, or acknowledgement of, management as a distinct construction profession or role, and the associated tendency toward separation of design and administration (eg. the BPF System, the New Engineering Contract, the recommendations in the Australian No Disputes report), the growth of management-based contracts (eg JCT87, various construction management forms) and the more frequent appointment of second-tier advisers to second guess financial and managerial performance of the Employer's front line advisers;

(e) Attempts to introduce formula-based claims quantification (eg. "Brown" clauses, the withdrawn first version of GC/Works/1 Edition 3);

(f) The increased emphasis, in part insurance-driven, on quality and quality

---

87 See also, R. B. Hellard, "*ADR in Technical Contracts by Corporate Multi-Disciplinary Contract Adjudication*", 1988 Arbitration 108 ("It will be more sensible to make an overall analysis using the methodology and the thinking and practice of management to arrive at better procedures for resolving civil disputes increasingly the result of now even more highly developed and sophisticated industrial processes.")

88 See also the shift in the interpretation of phrases such as "whether a certificate is in accordance with the terms of this Sub-contract" (or similar) to include valuation disputes, thereby enabling arbitration prior to practical completion: *Farr* v. *Ministry of Transport* [1960] 1 WLR 956, *Dawnays* v. *Minter, Building and Engineering Standard Forms*, pp 184-5, 231, *Killby and Gayford Ltd.* v. *Selincourt Ltd.* (1973), 3 BLR 106, *Gilbert Ash, Costain International* v. *the A-G Hong Kong* (1983), 23 BLR 48, *C.M. Pillings* v. *Kent Investments* (1985), 30 BLR 84, *Lubenham Fidelities* v. *South Pembrokeshire D.C.* (1986), 33 BLR 39, 58, *Cameron* v. *Mowlem.*

assurance;

(g) Judicial "engineering" of the law through the retreat from *Anns* v. *Merton*[89] and self-limiting the exercise of its jurisdiction in *NRHA* v. *Derek Crouch*, in respect of certificates, and The *Nema*[90] in respect of appeals from arbitral Awards;[91] and

(h) Greatly increased pressure on the Courts for summary relief in the form of summary judgments and interim payments and the judicial response of self-limiting its jurisdiction to grant such relief.

It can be said that many of these reflect a general dissatisfaction with the status quo. In other words they represent a reforming urge which presumably can only increase as traditional insularity recedes with the development of the Single Market.

Conclusion

Surely it is the task of construction industry contract policymakers (be they representative industry bodies, leading executives, commentators and drafters) to make the essentially managerial decision as to the extent to which the risks associated with innovation are warranted by the anticipated benefits. Reform need not come from Parliament alone. That decision cannot be made without proper investigation and consultation with all relevant representative or academic bodies and the users themselves.

A Contract system (and associated methods of dispute resolution) which over-rewards games playing must penalise the fair Employer, the professional Consultant and the honest skilled Contractor, Sub-contractor or supplier alike. Debate in forums such as the Centre of Construction Law and Management or the Society of Construction Law in order to work toward the correct decisions, combined with broader awareness in the industry of alternatives to the status quo to increase the pressure for reform, may be the way forward. Strategies must be identified and adopted for orderly implementation, where necessary either by-passing or co-opting vested interests found to be satisfied with an inefficient status quo. The National Contractors Group's Building Towards 2001 report[92] asserts that:-

"A profitable secondary industry has evolved which has a vested

---

89   [1978] AC 728
90   [1981] 2 Lloyd's Rep 239
91   See I.N.Duncan Wallace QC's spirited criticism in "*Control by the Courts: A Plea for More, not Less*" (1990), 6 Arb.Intl.253. See also O.M. Fiss, "*Against Settlement*", (1984) 93 Yale L.J. 1073.
92   (1990) at p.13

interest in the games playing that takes place. It would doubtless be concerned that an increase in harmony will mean a reduction in the demand for its services."

The secondary industry referred to is, presumably, the legal and surveying professions, which provide no more or no less than the services which their clients request. Some clients may also be concerned about the consequences of an increase in harmony. Frequently claimsmanship is used as a crutch for the less competent Contractor or as a means of distorting the outcome of the competitive tendering process. Contracts are sometimes bought with the hope of making a profit on claims. Some Employers and their advisers can take advantage of their control over the purse strings to coerce Contractors unfairly.

Adjudication appears to be a promising solution, if only a partial one, to the problem of resolving conflicting interests on construction sites. I have attempted in this paper to pull together the relevant contractual and judicial developments in the area and to put adjudication into the context of a number of other developments in related areas of construction law and management. It would be helpful if further studies were carried out to establish the extent of use of adjudication in the industry and to replace anecdotal accounts of its success with reliable statistics, so that a true measure of its performance can be obtained.

If adjudication is as effective in practice as its proponents claim it to be then a measure of the industry's commitment to reforming itself may be the pace with which its use continues to expand. The following three developments are potentially the most important to the field of dispute resolution in the construction field in recent years:-

(a) *Cameron* v. *Mowlem's* finding that adjudication was not subject to the Arbitration Acts 1950-79;
(b) *Campbell* v. *Edwards* and *Jones* v. *Sherwood's* restrictive attitude to the reviewability of expert decision-making; and
(c) the deferential attitude to contractual machinery shown by *NRHA* v. *Crouch* and *Tubeworkers* v. *Tilbury Construction*.

Taken together, they create a legal environment for development of new and innovative private systems of dispute management[93] responsive directly to "the market". Those systems would look to the Courts primarily as a

---

93 There is already a movement toward a dissociation of the substantive issues in arbitration from the judicial system, leaving the judicial system's involvement largely procedural or concerning enforcement: see p.229 of Mustill & Boyd, *Commercial Arbitration*.

means of enforcing conclusive decisions arrived at by neutral third parties in the agreed manner. The systems would depend to a reduced extent on the Court's fact-finding and law-determining functions[94]. Most importantly, their arrival would mean that the hegemony of litigation and arbitration, which has arisen since the halcyon days[95] of the Victorian Engineer, would have been broken.

The net effect, if properly drafted,of adjudication mechanisms is that roughly the correct amount of money is likely to be in the correct pocket while one or the other party, if it sees fit to do so, pursues traditional remedies. By doing that, it addresses more effectively than any other dispute resolution procedure the reality that cashflow is the lifeblood of the industry. Enforced where necessary by the Courts, having the effect of lowering the threshold for (interim) recovery below the generally applicable (and therefore correctly high) standard under the Rules of the Supreme Court, adjudication becomes a privatised interim payment mechanism.

Appendix

Review of the Adjudication Variants

DOM/1 Standard Form of Domestic Sub-Contract (1980)

I start with DOM/1 since the limited case law is concerned with that set of conditions.

Subject Matter and Commencement

Due to the limited purpose for which the adjudication mechanism was introduced, the DOM/1 adjudication mechanism is limited in subject matter to disputes concerning set-off claims by the Contractor. There was no need to go any further to avoid the effect of Gilbert Ash. The adjudication mechanism is triggered by a dissatisfied Sub-contractor making a "request for action" by the Adjudicator[96]. The Adjudicator (and a Trustee-Stakeholder)

---

94   It is a fundamental principle of public policy that parties cannot by contract oust the jurisdiction of the Courts (*Lee* v. *Showman's Guild of Britain* [1952] 2 QB 329, *Re Davstone's Estates Ltd's Leases* [1969] 2 Ch. 378) but that does not prevent the parties from achieving this in large measure by selection of contractual machinery which, in the absence of fraud or collusion, will lead to the Courts not interfering.

95   See John Uff QC's interesting paper "*The Place of Law and the Role of Construction*" (Paper to Society of Construction Law).

96   The fee of the Adjudicator is paid by the Sub-contractor but the Arbitrator in the final Award will allocate responsibility for the fee between the contractor and Sub-contractor (Clause 24.8).

are named in the Contract documents (Clauses 24.1.1.2 and 24.1.2). At the same time as this request is made, the Sub-contractor must:-

(a) send a written statement setting out the reasons for disagreeing with the claim to a set-off, and particulars (quantified in detail and with reasonable accuracy) of any counterclaim arising out of the Sub-contract; and
(b) give notice of arbitration in respect of the same dispute (Clause 24.1.1.1 and .2).

There is a time limit for going to adjudication. The request must be sent within 14 days of receipt of a notice from the Contractor under Clause 23.2.2 of the Contractor's intention to set-off against any money otherwise due (ie against retention monies or a forthcoming interim payment), a claim for actual loss and/or expense incurred by the Contractor due to breach of or failure to observe the terms of the Sub-contract by the Sub-contractor. It appears that where the notified set-off claim exceeds the amount then due, a fresh notice is required every time a further set-off against a later interim payment is sought to be made (Clause 24.7).

Procedure

The adjudication procedure leading to a decision is quite summary:-

(a) Since the Adjudicator and Trustee-Stakeholder are named in the Contract documents there is no delay in obtaining the necessary appointments;
(b) The procedure contemplates submission of a statement by the Sub-contractor setting out the reasons why it disagrees with the amount of the set-off. If the Sub-contractor considers that it has a counterclaim it must also include details to the same standard as applied to the Contractor's notice of set-off, that is, quantified in detail and with reasonable accuracy;[97]
(c) It appears that only if there is a counterclaim by the Sub-contractor does the procedure contemplate submission of further material by the Contractor ("brief particulars of his defence to any counterclaim") beyond what is in the set-off notice unless the Adjudicator otherwise requires. In effect the Contract assumes that the Contractor has given in the original Clause 23 notice all details necessary adequately to justify its position on the set-off. Obviously, on a practical level, a Contractor will submit such further

---

97 Clause 23 requires that the amount of the claimed set-off be "quantified in detail and with reasonable accuracy" (clause 23.2.1) and that the notice supply the grounds on which the set-off is claimed (Clause 23.2.2).

material in the time available as it sees fit[98] and an Adjudicator will inevitably consider this, either in respect of whether the original notice of set-off was valid or whether the Sub-contractor's disagreement is justified; (d) The Adjudicator has a discretion to require "such further written statements ...necessary to clarify or explain any ambiguity in the written statements of either the Contractor or the Sub-contractor" (clause 24.3.1). That phrase does not appear to warrant the interpretation that only the author of a statement can "clarify or explain" that statement, but the "written statements" are those referred to in Clause 24, not the Contractor's notice of set-off. The Adjudicator, therefore, could request a statement from the Contractor to clarify something in the Sub-contractor's statement. A requirement for further statements does not extend the time limits;

(e) There is no hearing (clause 24.3.1);

(f) No reasons are given for the decision (Clause 24.3.1); and

(g) The whole procedure is quite quick. The most likely interpretation of the procedure is that it will take no more than 21 days[99].

98 See for instance *A. Cameron* v. *Mowlem* (1990) 52 BLR 42 (C.A.) where the contractor submitted both a defence to counterclaim and response to the Sub-contractor's statement of disagreement.

99 The Sub-contract is rather ambiguous as to the applicable time limit for reaching a decision. Clause 24.3.1 requires the Adjudicator to come to a decision:-
"Within 7 days of receipt of any written statement by the Contractor under clause 24.2 or on the expiry of [NB. not "or within 7 days of the expiry of" or "or the expiry of"] the time limit to the Contractor referred to in clause 24.2 whichever is the earlier".
Clause 24.2 provides that:-
"Upon receipt of the aforesaid statement the Contractor may within 14 days from the date of such receipt send to the Adjudicator...a written statement with a copy to the Sub-contractor setting out brief particulars of his defence to any counterclaim by the Sub-contractor."
As the expiry of the time limit under clause 24.2 approaches, strictly speaking the Adjudicator must start to do whatever work is necessary with a view to being in a position to issue a decision as soon as the deadline expires. By its terms, clause 24.3.1 does not allow the Adjudicator a further 7 days following the expiry of the time limit if no statement from the contractor is received. Effectively an Adjudicator must assume that the contractor will respond to the counterclaim, which will have the effect of allowing the Adjudicator a further 7 days to consider both sides.
A further problem of interpretation arises if the Sub-contractor does not advance a counterclaim. Even though clause 24.2 deals only with time for submission of material in respect of any counterclaim, is 14 days still to be counted when establishing when the Adjudicator is to come to a decision? Why wait 14 days for a statement that will never be submitted? The problem is that unless the 14 days is counted the Adjudicator would, apparently, be required to make an instant decision as soon as he receives the request for action, unless he asks the Sub-contractor for further information. It seems likely that the 14 days does apply and therefore the procedure will take 14 days where there is no counterclaim (clause 24.3.1 requiring a decision on the expiry of the 14 day time limit) or 21 days where there is and a statement by the contractor is submitted.

Decision and Enforcement

The decision to be made (in the Adjudicator's "absolute discretion" but also such as the Adjudicator considers to be "fair, reasonable and necessary") is as to whether the amount of the set-off claim may be retained, should be deposited with the named Trustee-Stakeholder, or should be paid to the Sub-contractor or some combination of these options[100]. By virtue of Clauses 24.4.1 and .2, the most that the Contractor is required to pay to a Trustee-Stakeholder or the Sub-contractor is the amount otherwise due from the Contractor as the interim payment in respect of which the Contractor sought to exercise the Clause 23 right of set-off[101].

Clauses 24.4.1 and .2 provide that where the decision requires the Contractor to pay a sum to either the Trustee-Stakeholder or the Sub-contractor, that payment is to be made immediately. The capacity in which the Adjudicator acts is not stated. However the Adjudicator's decision is stated to be "binding upon the Contractor and the Sub-contractor until the matters upon which he has given his decision have been settled by agreement or determined by an Arbitrator or the Court" (Clause 24.3.1).

The Arbitrator is free to vary or cancel the decision before issuing his final award (Clause 24.6). DOM/1 specifically contemplates arbitration commencing prior to practical completion in respect of set-off claims and Adjudicator's decisions[102]. If effective, the procedure enables a rough-and-ready distinction to be made between good and bad set-off claims at a relatively modest cost. The net effect of the time limits is that there is a reasonable prospect that a bad set-off claim can be disposed of quickly enough to prevent it from clouding the Sub-contractor's short-term entitlement to payment and in consequence delaying payment to any significant extent.

---

100 It is perhaps the case that Clause 24.3.1 could be clarified by inviting the Adjudicator not to order payment but rather to rule on whether and to what extent, taking into account any Sub-contractor counterclaim, the contractor may exercise set-off rights. The payment obligation arises, then, not from the decision but from the usual contract provision entitling a Sub-contractor to be paid interim payments.

101 The interaction of Clause 24.3.1 (decision by the Adjudicator in respect of the set-off claim) and Clause 24.4.1 (the contractor shall only be obliged to pay a sum no greater than the amount due as an interim payment or retention but for the set-off) is not completely unambiguous. See *Cameron* v. *Mowlem* (1990) 52 BLR 42 (C.A.).

102 Article 3.3 of the Articles of Agreement. The other issues listed at Article 3.3 are whether a payment has been improperly withheld or is not in accordance with the Sub-contract, the date of practical completion and entitlement to extensions of time, and the reasonableness of the Sub-contractor's objections to instructions. Article 3 was amended in 1987 and a new Clause 38 added but these changes did not alter the availability of immediate arbitration. Those amendments only apply if Amendment 4 applies to the JCT80 Main Contract. Clause 38 was further amended in 1989. Those amendments extended the availability of early arbitration somewhat further.

1987 Amendments

In 1987 amendments were introduced to DOM/1[103] for use only where the Main Contract was in a JCT80 form incorporating Amendment 4, issued in 1987[104].

The 1987 DOM/1 amendments made a number of adjustments to the regulated right of set-off in clause 23. For instance the amendment makes clear that the Contractor can set-off both loss and expense and damages and contemplates set-off of losses not yet actually suffered[105]. The way in which the timing of the deadline for the Contractor's notice of set-off is expressed is also altered but the net effect is the same[106].

The 1987 amendments also amend clause 24 itself:-

(a) brief particulars of the Sub-contract are also to be supplied to the Adjudicator by the Sub-contractor when requesting action;

(b) provision is made for appointment of an Adjudicator by the Sub-contractor from a list maintained by the BEC, in the event that the parties fail to name one in the Sub-contract, and the appointment by the Adjudicator of a deposit-taking bank as Trustee-Stakeholder if no Trustee-Stakeholder is named in the Sub-contract; and

(c) an attempt, probably only partially successful, has been made to clarify the wording dealing with the time limit for the Adjudicator to issue a decision[107].

---

103 Amendment 3
104 The relevant changes introduced by Amendment 4 to JCT80 are:-
  (a) simplifying the arbitration agreement in the Articles of Agreement (in accordance with general JCT policy) and transfer of the detailed provisions to a new clause 41;
  (b) giving the parties the option of selecting the RICS or the Chartered Institute of Arbitrators as the body appointing the arbitrator in the absence of agreement between the parties, reflecting, perhaps, the lessening influence of the RIBA and, unfortunately, the architecture profession;
  (c) incorporation of a change first introduced optionally in IFC84 whereby the parties agree that points of law arising during the reference and out of the award are to be determined by the Courts under the provisions of the Arbitration Act 1979, if the arbitration is held pursuant to the optional joinder of arbitration provisions.
105 The claimed loss and/or expense need not have "actually been incurred" at the time of service of notice, only "suffered or incurred". This is designed, it seems, to reverse the effect of *Chatbrown* v. *Alfred McAlpine* (1986) 35 BLR 44 (C.A.).
106 Rather than say "20 days before the money ... becomes due and payable" it now says "3 days before ... the payment from which the contractor intends to make a set-off becomes due". Because the payment terms are 17 days, the net effect is the same.
107 See footnote 73 for discussion of possible problems with the unamended wording. There seems to be a drafting or printing error in the amendment. Clause 24.3.1, where Amendment 3 applies, provides for the Adjudicator to issue a decision in accordance with the following timetable:-

Summary

In summary then the DOM/1 procedure creates a quick interim decision-making process for disputes. The decision-making power is vested by Contract in a third party, named at the outset by the parties, who is not otherwise involved in the day-to-day administration of the Sub-contract. The power is limited in subject-matter to claims to set-offs against interim payments due. It is intended to be binding, unless varied by the agreement of the parties or varied or cancelled by an Arbitrator, until superseded by an Arbitrator's Award. Arbitration on the set-off and decision is not deferred until after practical completion. In the main body of this paper I consider the limited case law under DOM/1.

NSC/4 and NSC/4a Standard Forms of Nominated Sub-Contract (1980)

An adjudication mechanism is included in clauses 23 and 24 of NSC/4 and NSC/4a, which replaced the Green Form, in substantially the same form[108] as under DOM/1 and hence the comments on DOM/1 apply equally here. Amendments to clauses 23 and 24 issued in 1987 substantially

"If ... no statement by the Contractor under clause 24.2 has been received by the Adjudicator within the time limit set out in clause 24.2, then within 7 days of expiry of that time limit, or
no statement by the Contractor under clause 24.2 has been received within that time limit then within 7 days of receipt by the Adjudicator of such statement...".
It seems that the second "no statement" should read "a statement". "That time limit" in the second Sub-clause must refer to the 7 day time limit for receiving a statement from the contractor. How can an Adjudicator receive a statement that has not been received? This would defer to infinity the expiry of the time limit under the second sub-clause for a decision. That would mean that there are two equally applicable limits - within 7 days of expiry of that time limit, under the first sub-clause, or infinity, under the second. Presumably the former will be applied. Furthermore no time limit is given for when a statement is given. If "a statement" is substituted for the second "no statement" the clause works naturally - the first alternative deals with the consequence of no statement having been received within 7 days (in which case the decision is due within a further 7 days) and the second alternative deals with the situation where a statement is received within 7 days (in which case the time limit will advance accordingly). I doubt that the error will prejudice the normal operation of the clause, through the application of common sense by the Court, but it appears that a correction is necessary to reflect clearly the JCT's intended meaning.
108 The only differences are in clause 23 dealing with the contractor's right of set-off:
(a) clauses 23.1 and 23.2 provide that the right of set-off against retention is "notwithstanding the fiduciary obligation of the Contractor under 23.9.1". Unlike NSC/4, DOM/1 is silent on the question of the capacity in which the contractor holds Sub-contractor retention; and
(b) no right of set-off "relating to any delay in completion" may be exercised unless

correspond to those issued in the same year for DOM/1 and are also intended to apply only where the Main Contract incorporates Amendment 4[109].

NSC/C was issued in 1991, to replace use of NSC/4 and 4a where Amendment 10 applies to the JCT80 Main Contract. The adjudication mechanism is in Clauses 4.26 - 4.37 and is virtually identical in terms to NSC/4 and 4a as amended in 1987[110].

BPF System for Designing and Constructing Building (1983)

Particularly interesting adjudication procedures are used in the modified ACE forms of Consultant's and Client's Representative's Engagements and the modified ACA Form of Building Agreement used in the BPF System for Designing and Constructing Buildings[111]. The contrast with the DOM/1 approach reflects the fact that the BPF adjudication provisions are the outcome of a process of attempting to re-think the management of the design and building process from the ground up whereas the DOM/1 approach is evolutionary, in the JCT fashion.

the architect's certificate of non-completion of the Sub-contract Works pursuant to clause 35.15 of the JCT80 Main Contract has been issued to the Contractor and Sub-contractor.

109 Amendment 4 to DOM/1. Under DOM/1 the time limit for the Contractor to notify the Sub-contractor of its intention to exercise a right of set-off was changed from "20 days before the money ...becomes due and payable" to "3 days before...the payment...becomes due". In NSC/4 the original wording was the same as that in DOM/1 but changed to "not less than 3 days before the date of issue of the Interim Certificate which includes...an amount in respect of the Sub-contract and for which...amount the Contractor intends to make the set-off". This change seems to be due to a decision to tie in more closely the timing of the deadline for notification with the approach to payment adopted in NSC/4 (clause 21) which differs from that in DOM/1.

110 The changes only eliminate certain possible ambiguities. The right of set-off is made expressly subject to the adjudication clause. The architect's certificate of non-completion is more correctly stated to be issued in accordance with the relevant provision of the main contract rather than Clause 12.2 of the Sub-contract. The word "latter" has been deleted from before "amount" in 4.27.2, presumably not making any change of substance. It now contemplates statements rather than only pleadings later being exchanged in the eventual arbitration. In Clause 4.32.2, the Adjudicator's decision is now to deal with the whole amount "notified" not the whole amount "set off", which must also not be a change of substance. In Clause 4.33.1, dealing with decisions requiring a deposit of an amount, it provides that the contractor shall not be obliged to deposit (rather than pay) a sum greater than the amount due as the next interim payment. Under Clause 24.5.1 funds on deposit have added to them "any interest thereon" rather than "the interest".

111 The ACA Form predated the BPF form but I have found it convenient to deal with the BPF version first.

Consultant's and Client's Representative's Engagement

I will first discuss the simpler adjudication provision under the Engagements.

Subject Matter and Commencement

The BPF Conditions of Engagement for Consultants Works and Conditions of Engagement for a Client's Representative, both at their respective Clauses 4, refer to an Adjudicator all disputes or differences arising out of the Engagement prior to the earliest of take-over or abandonment of the project, termination of the Engagement or completion of the services. Since the wording is the same in each Engagement, for convenience I will refer below only to the Consultant's Engagement.

The Adjudicator is not named at the outset. The Adjudicator is either agreed between the parties or, failing agreement within 10 days of a request to concur in the appointment of such a person, appointed by the Chartered Institute of Arbitrators. Although the BPF Manual uses that label "Adjudicator", in the Contract this individual is described simply as an "independent person".

The BPF System Manual recommends, at paragraph 3.8, that a single Adjudicator of disputes under the various Consultants' Engagements should be agreed at the beginning of Design Development (Stage 3) to enable disputes to be resolved quickly and simply. There is no obligation to that effect nor do the Conditions contemplate tripartite adjudication between the Employer, Consultants, the Client's Representative and/or the Contractor (or for that matter tripartite arbitration)[112].

The Manual also sensibly recommends that the Adjudicator "should be conversant with building development, design procedures, drawing office administration and fees" and that it be agreed that the cost of the Adjudicator's fee, calculated on a time basis per dispute, be shared equally. These points are not addressed in the Contracts themselves.

Procedure

There is no time limit for the Adjudicator to come to a decision nor is there any direction as to the extent of the due process rights of the parties which the Adjudicator must respect when coming to a decision.

112 In contrast, under the BPF Building Contract, tripartite arbitration is contemplated where there are related disputes between client and contractor, and between contractor and Sub-contractor.

Since it may be assumed that the Chartered Institute of Arbitrators will appoint one of its members, this together with the lack of time limits or other procedural guidelines, does appear to create the risk that, under pressure from one party or the other, the process could develop toward an arbitration-like procedure. This would, of course, introduce significant delay into the process, thereby frustrating to a great or lesser extent its objective. To this extent something closer to the DOM/1 model might have been preferred, perhaps with provision for the Adjudicator to grant extensions of time in appropriate cases. The Arbitrator-cum-Adjudicator is more apt to expedite matters if the Contract clearly indicates an expectation that he or she should do so.

If dissatisfied with the Adjudicator's decision, either party may refer the matter to arbitration. There is no time limit (other than the applicable statutory limitation period) within which this step must be taken unlike, as we shall see, under the BPF Standard Form of Building Contract. If notice of arbitration is given, the arbitration process cannot itself begin until after the period when disputes are to be dealt with by adjudication ends, that is, the earliest of the date of taking-over, termination of the Engagement or performance of the services. There is no scope for early arbitration and therefore no scope for early reversal of an Adjudicator's decision by an Arbitrator as is the case under DOM/1.

Decision and Enforcement

Given the referral of all disputes or differences to adjudication it was not appropriate, as it was under DOM/1, for the Consultant's Engagement to specify what decision is required. The nature of the decision would of course depend upon the nature of the dispute.

The Adjudicator acts "as expert and not as arbitrator"; DOM/1 is silent on this point. The Adjudicator's decision "shall forthwith be given effect" by the parties and is "final and binding" but only until the earliest of take-over, termination of the Engagement or performance of the services. Clause 4 provides, presumably for the avoidance of doubt, that the reference of a dispute to an Adjudicator "shall not relieve either party from any liability for the due and punctual performance of such party's obligations"[113].

By its terms, the Adjudicator's decision ceases automatically to be final and binding as soon as the earliest of the above events occur. This creates

---

113 Of course, until after the adjudication and arbitration neither party can be completely sure of what their respective obligations are, and so must make a judgment as to what is required of them, but that is no different from the situation whenever a contractual dispute arises during the performance of any contract.

a hiatus between the date of that event and any later arbitral Award, which might in some cases prove inconvenient[114]. It would, I think, have been better for the decision to be final and binding until varied or revised by the Arbitrator, as is the case with DOM/1.

Building Contract

There is also an adjudication provision in the BPF Building Contract which forms part of the contractual framework for the system. That Contract is an amended version of the ACA form of Building Contract originally issued in 1982.

The drafting follows a rather different approach from that used in the BPF Consultant's Engagement. There are considerable differences in complexity between the adjudication provisions of the Consultants' Engagement and the Building Contract. Whether this is due to subtly different policy considerations, or a different drafting team being involved, is not apparent. It does, however, follow the same general pattern of referring all disputes to an Adjudicator whose decision is final and binding until the right to open the reference to arbitration arises.

Subject Matter and Commencement

A quite different approach to defining the Adjudicator's jurisdiction is adopted. Clause 25.2 limits the subject matter of adjudications to:

(a) adjustment or alteration of the Contract Sum;
(b) extensions of time;
(c) whether the Works are being properly executed;
(d) availability of the contractual rights of termination;
(e) the Client's Representative's rights of access to the Works and workshops to test and inspect; and
(f) the reasonableness of any objection by the Contractor to a replacement Client's Representative and to execution of work or installation of

---

114 For instance an unsuccessful set-off claim could be resurrected after take-over and used to justify non-payment of the final instalment of fees. It also does not address the status of the parties' respective rights and obligations connected with the dispute once the decision no longer is binding. Presumably the question is academic unless an arbitration proceeds.

things by others[115].

Disputes relating to any proposed revised Schedule of Activities (upon which pricing of changes is based) are excluded. The Manual is silent on the rationale for this particular list of matters. What disadvantage there would have been in adopting the Consultant's Engagement's approach, referring all disputes and differences to the Adjudicator, is not clear. However, the list does include a large proportion, but not all, of the usual areas of dispute under the Contract. A notable exception, possibly, is disputes about the amount of interim certificates[116] other than as to the correctness of any adjustment of the Contract Sum to take into account, for instance, the effect of disruptive acts or omissions of the Employer or Client's Representative. There may be potential problems in the Adjudicator's jurisdiction which would entitle one party or the other to de-rail the adjudication process or efforts to enforce any decision, by impugning the Adjudicator's jurisdiction. If a triable issue can be raised as to whether an Adjudicator had jurisdiction then a Court is not going to give effect to it at the important interlocutory stage. That potential problem must be weighed against the perceived benefit of excluding certain disputes from adjudication.

Other differences from the Consultant's Engagement are that the dispute or difference must have arisen prior to Taking-over, so that adjudication continues to be the proper forum for dispute even after termination of the Contractor's employment. If the Building Contract had mirrored the approach taken in the Engagement this would not be the case. Further, the dispute or difference can be "arising out of or in connection with" the Contract whereas under the Consultant's Engagement the underlined words are omitted. The Manual does not explain the reason behind this difference for which there is no obvious rationale.

Unlike the position with the Engagement, the Adjudicator is to be named in the Building Contract (Clause 25.1). Why it was decided that the identity

---

115 It also refers to adjudication the reasonableness of any objection by the Contractor under Clause 4.1. Clause 4.1 gives the Client's Representative unqualified rights of access to works for the purpose of testing, inspection and examination. There is no right of reasonable objection. In the ACA Form of Building Agreement on which the BPF form was based there is such a right. Perhaps this is a drafting oversight. Having eliminated the right of reasonable objection the BPF did not delete the corresponding right to refer the matter to the Adjudicator.

116 See also the interesting history of the interpretation of the clauses governing the availability of adjudication prior to practical completion under ICE and JCT forms in respect of the amount of interim payments. It is now clear that it is available. This seems to be an issue on which employers and contract administrators want to have the short-term final word.

of the Adjudicator should be settled by negotiation at the outset, rather than, as under the Consultant's Engagement, left to subsequent agreement or failing agreement appointment by a third party institution, is not clear. In principle the same policy considerations seem to apply to both Contracts in this respect unless it was considered that disputes with the Contractor were more likely to arise than disputes with Consultants, warranting immediate appointment.[117]

Clause 25.1 allows the Adjudicator, on notice to the Employer, Client's Representative and the Contractor, to delegate his or her duties to another person. Clause 25.4 provides a mechanism for appointing a replacement if the named Adjudicator (or delegatee) fails, refuses or is unable to act[118]. Presumably this is justified on the basis that naming an Adjudicator from the outset creates the risk that that person will be temporarily unavailable when the dispute arises. Under the Consultant's Engagement this would be dealt with simply by selecting another candidate.

The Adjudication process is commenced by the dispute or difference being referred to the named Adjudicator (clause 25.2). There are no general time limits for commencement. The only time constraints are imposed in the limited circumstances described in clauses 7 and 17. Clause 7 sets out a procedure for attempting to agree the damage, loss and/or expense

117 There seems to be a discrepancy between the adjudication procedure outlined in the BPF Building Contract and Consultant's Engagement, and the System as described in the Manual. This may be due to the fact that the Manual was published some months before the contracts were finalised. At paragraph 5.1 the Manual states that "An Adjudicator is appointed for Stage 5 [ie Construction]. He may not be the same one appointed for Stages 3 and 4 because the skills required are different". In fact, the Adjudicator, if any, appointed in respect of disputes under the Consultants' Engagements (or Adjudicators, if the various parties have failed to agree to the appointment of an Adjudicator for disputes under all such appointments), ordinarily but not necessarily at the beginning of Stage 3, Design Development, will continue to act as Adjudicator of all disputes under those engagements, including those which may arise during and after Stage 5, unless some other arrangement is agreed. Arrival at stage 5 does not mean that the existing appointments lapse. The BPF Building Contract, signed at or about the commencement of Stage 5, requires that an Adjudicator be identified at the time of signature. That person will not necessarily be the same as the Adjudicator under the engagements and so two (or more) Adjudicators may become involved under different contracts where a problem gives rise to related disputes between the Client and the Contractor, and the Client and one or more of the Consultants and/or the Client's Representative. The Client, in particular, may be faced with conflicting binding decisions. Clearly, if common sense prevails that scenario can be avoided. The problem is that when disputes arise, common sense is not always perceived to be in all parties' interests.

118 In the event of failure or refusal to act, pursuant to Clause 25.4 and 25.5 the parties can obtain the appointment of a replacement Adjudicator and/or refer the matter to arbitration.

associated with disruptive or delaying events attributable to the Employer. Clause 17 sets out a procedure for attempting to agree the value of any instructions and the length of any associated extensions of time. Clause 7 provides that the right to refer a Contractor's estimate of its claim to the Adjudicator is deferred until 20 working days following notice from the Client's Representative either of acceptance of the estimate or of desire to negotiate, during which time the clause contemplates the parties attempting to agree the necessary adjustment of the Contract Sum. Clause 17 is similarly worded except that the negotiation period is 5 working days and for no apparent reason it only contemplates the Client's Representative referring the estimate to the Adjudicator.

Procedure

The Adjudicator is required to give written notice of decision within 5 working days of being requested by either party to do so. (clause 25.2) It will be recalled that under the Engagement there are no time limits for a decision. It is not completely clear whether this means within 5 working days of the request for adjudication or within 5 working days of a request for a decision. The Manual does not assist. The latter interpretation is more likely. The former interpretation would be convenient since if the nature of the dispute was such that it merited more than 5 days of deliberation the parties could delay their request for notice of decision. This would impose a tight timetable on the Adjudicator unless, in effect, the parties agreed otherwise.

The Adjudicator has power to request such oral or written statements, documents or information as the Adjudicator may determine (Clause 25.2). This does not defer the 5 working day time limit. Disputes concerning the existence of termination rights are given special treatment. If the dispute relates to an event upon which either the Contractor or Employer rely to justify commencement of the process of contractually terminating the Contract, and the dispute has been referred to the Adjudicator within 10 days of service of the associated Default Notice, the right in due course to serve a Termination Notice is suspended until the Adjudicator gives the decision. Furthermore, if no reference to the Adjudicator is made prior to service of a Termination Notice by either party, the entitlement to terminate is not subsequently open to challenge (Clauses 20.1 and 20.2). This is quite sensible.

Returning to the general provision, if either party is dissatisfied with the Adjudicator's decision, or if the Adjudicator has failed to give a decision, either party may within 20 working days of receipt of notice of the decision, or expiry of the time within which it should have been given, give notice of arbitration. Clause 25.6 contemplates tripartite arbitration between the Employer, Contractor and Sub-contractors or suppliers.

Decision and Enforcement

Clause 25.2 states that, without prejudice to the generality of his powers, the Adjudicator is entitled to adjust the dates for the Taking-Over of the Works or any section thereof and/or award damage loss and/or expense to either party. If the decision fixes a new date for Taking-Over the Contractor is to submit a revised time schedule within 10 working days of notice of the decision (clause 11.9) and if the new date is later than the date named in any certificate of non-completion issued by the Client's Representative the Client is to repay any liquidated and ascertained damages, plus interest, in respect of the period between the two dates (Clause 11.4).

The Adjudicator's decision is given substantially the same status as an Adjudicator's decision under the Consultant's Engagement. As with the Consultant's Engagement the Adjudicator's decision "shall forthwith be given effect to" by the parties and is "final and binding upon the parties" until the Taking-Over of the Works (NB not the earliest of Taking-Over and termination of the Contract). Also as with the Consultant's Engagement the Adjudicator is deemed to act "as expert and not as arbitrator" and a reference to adjudication "does not relieve either party from any liability for the due and punctual performance" of their obligations (clause 25.3). Clause 25.3 also provides, presumably for the avoidance of doubt, that the Contractor "shall proceed with the Works with all due diligence" even if the Adjudicator's decision is referred to arbitration by either party.

One important difference is that unless, as previously described, either party gives notice of arbitration within 20 working days of receiving notice of the Adjudicator's decision, the decision is final and binding (clause 25.5). Under the Consultant's Engagement there is no cut-off point for objecting to the decision.

There are aspects of the BPF System as a whole which are viewed, rightly or wrongly, as being contrary to the commercial and professional interests of certain sectors of the building industry and in consequence it is not used extensively[119]. I do not propose nor is it necessary here to comment on the merit of these objections. A review of the published comment on the System

---

119 Building Procurement Systems, issued by the Chartered Institute of Building indicates that the full BPF system is used for only 4 percent of developments. The extent to which parts of the system are in use is not known. The Australian study quoted at p.1 indicates that it is used for 8% of large scale projects in the private sector and that this percentage is expected to increase.

at the time of its launch indicates that commentators were generally complimentary about the adjudication provisions.

ACA Form of Building Agreement (1982)

The ACA Form of Building Agreement was issued in its original form in late 1982 and as noted above was the basis for the BPF Building Contract. A second edition was issued in 1984 and this was revised in 1990. In all versions there has been a choice of three alternative dispute clauses (clause 25). In its current version the first choice follows the BPF model, adjudication by a named third party followed by arbitration. The second provides only for an expert decision by the Architect followed by arbitration. The third is litigation of all disputes. It is, of course, important that the parties decide on one of these options at the outset. Too often, that does not happen, with the inevitable confusion about how disputes are to be resolved.

In the first alternative, a necessary minor adjustment is made to reflect the increased role of the Architect in place of the BPF Client's Representative. However, there are no significant differences from the BPF Building Contract adjudication provision. The comments above in the section on the BPF Building Contract are equally applicable.

The second alternative is interesting. The Architect takes the place of the Adjudicator. It is in certain respects conceptually similar to the role of the Engineer in respect of disputes under ICE and FIDIC. It contemplates the Architect making an expert decision in respect of a list of disputes prior to Taking-Over of the Works slightly different to that under the first alternative. The Architect is not entitled to rule concerning the entitlement of either party to terminate the agreement but otherwise can adjudicate on all of the BPF issues. Additionally the Architect can resolve disputes as to:

"... the construction of this Agreement, or... any other matter or thing of whatsoever nature (including any matter or thing left by this Agreement to the discretion of the Architect the withholding by the Architect of any certificate to which the Contractor may claim to be entitled or any issue as to whether or not any certificate is in accordance with the provisions of this Agreement)".

The rationale behind the differences in the lists is unclear. Under the second alternative the Architect is to decide on all disputes. The provision gives the Architect's decision the same status and finality as an Adjudicator's Award under the BPF option. The parties have 20 working days to give notice of arbitration failing which the decision is final and binding. The arbitration agreement, Clause 25.4, appears to contemplate arbitration only of those disputes or differences in respect of which any decision of the Architect has not become final and binding. The clause lacks the additional wording found in the BPF option which also refers to arbitration "all disputes or differences arising out of or in connection with the Agreement or the carrying out of the Works". Clause 25.4 provides that " all disputes or differences in respect of which a decision (if any) of the Architect has not become final and binding under clause 27.3" shall be referred to arbitration. Presumably this will be interpreted so as not to limit the scope of the Arbitrator's jurisdiction to the list of issues previously referred to the Architect for adjudication. Any other interpretation would create the possibility that some disputes would slip through to the Courts. Although the option is headed "Alternative 2 - Arbitration", Clause 23.2 provides that headings shall not affect the construction of the Agreement so the heading cannot be used to justify that conclusion.

Perhaps the most significant difference between the 1984 and 1982 versions[120] is that in the 1982 version the Adjudicator and Arbitrator were to be one and the same person unless the parties agreed to the contrary[121]. The ultimate arbiter of the parties' rights would be settled from the outset and therefore the identity would be influenced by the parties' respective

---

120 The 1984 edition substantially adopted the changes to adjudication made in the BPF form. The differences between the 1982 and 1984 versions are as follows:- (a) implementing a BPF change, in the 1984 version the Adjudicator is given the power to delegate his or her duties; (b) in the 1982 version the Adjudicator had the power to determine which party was to bear the costs of the reference. The 1984 version is silent on this point; (c) the 1984 version added to the Adjudicator's jurisdiction the reasonableness of any objection by the Contractor to a replacement architect/ Supervising Officer (as in BPF), to an instruction to permit the execution of work or installation of things by others (as in BPF) and to instructions to sublet work to a person named in the instruction (under the BPF there is no right of objection); (d) implementing a BPF change in the 1984 version the time periods are expressed as working days; (e) The architect is also to be notified of the Adjudicator's decision in the 1984 version; (f) The 1982 version lacked the express power to adjust taking-over dates and award damages, loss and/or expense; (g) implementing a BPF change, in the 1984 version Clause 25.3 requires both the Contractor and the Employer, not just the Contractor, to give effect to the decision; (h) implementing a BPF change, clause 25.3 provides, for the avoidance of doubt, that reference to an Adjudicator does not relieve either party from liability for their performance obligations; (i) implementing a BPF change, in the 1984 version the Chartered Institute of Arbitrators, not the ACA, are to appoint a replacement Adjudicator failing agreement between the parties; and (j) implementing a BPF change, in Clause 25.5 the time limit for reference to arbitration following a refusal or neglect to adjudicate is clarified.
121 Presumably the party which succeeded at the adjudication stage will be unlikely to agree to a different person as Arbitrator.

bargaining power. The arbitration would in effect become a review by the Adjudicator of his or her own decision. In subsequent editions the Adjudicator and Arbitrator are different persons[122]. It is clear from published comment that the lack of popularity of this form is not due to the incorporation of an adjudication mechanism, although there was criticism of the fact that in the first edition the Adjudicator and Arbitrator would be the same person.

It is of interest to note that the ACA Form of Sub-contract (1982 and all subsequent revisions) does not contain an adjudication mechanism. Clause 10.4 provides that the Contractor's right to set-off is not in any way limited or excluded. The disputes clause, Clause 15, presents only the two alternatives of arbitration or litigation.

Clause 15.4 provides, however, that:

"Where an Adjudicator has been appointed pursuant to the provisions of the Agreement [the Main Contract], and any decision of the Adjudicator is final and binding on the Contractor under the Agreement, such decision shall also be final and binding on the Sub-contractor and the Contractor under this Sub-contract until after Taking-Over or alleged Taking-Over of the Works or termination or alleged termination of the Sub-contractor's employment under the Sub-contract."

This applies only if the arbitration option is selected. Where arbitration is selected, the reference shall not be opened until after Taking-Over, alleged Taking-Over or termination or alleged termination of the Sub-contractor's employment unless the parties otherwise agree (Clause 15.1).

DOM/2 Standard Form of Domestic Sub-Contract for Use in Conjunction With JCT81 (1981)

The DOM/2 conditions incorporate, with amendments, the DOM/1 conditions by reference. The set-off and adjudication provisions, clauses 23 and 24, are virtually identical[123], as is the arbitration clause. The 1987 amendments to DOM/1 amended DOM/2 pursuant to Amendment 2 to DOM/2.

Optional amendments to JCT81 itself which incorporate an adjudication

---

122 Except in the unlikely event that the parties agree that they will be.
123 The one change is the deletion of "DOM/1" in Clause 23.4 in the phrase "The rights of the parties to the Sub-contract in respect of set-off are fully set out in Sub-contract DOM/1...".

mechanism are discussed below.

IN/SC Standard Form of Sub-Contract for Use in Conjunction with IFC84 (1985)

IN/SC adopted at Clauses 21 and 22 a regulated set-off and adjudication provision substantially corresponding to those contained in the unamended DOM/1[124].

Amendments corresponding to those issued in 1987 to DOM/1 were issued in 1989[125]. Arbitration can proceed immediately. The Clause regulating arbitration, Clause 35, does not defer the arbitration of any disputes. Clause 35 was amended in 1989 by Amendment 3 (which also amended the set-off and adjudication provisions) but did not effect any change to the availability of early arbitration.

NAM/SC Sub-Contract for Sub-Contractors Named Under IFC84 (1985)

The identical NAM/SC set-off and adjudication provisions are also found at Clauses 21 and 22. The clauses were amended in the way that DOM/1 was, in 1989 when the conditions were reprinted, rather than by a separate amendment. Availability of arbitration is the same as under IN/SC[126].

GW/S Standard Form of Sub-Contract for Use in Conjunction with GC/Works/1 Edition 2 Where Building Works are Being Carried Out (1985)

The terms of GW/S derive from a combination of the provisions of DOM/1 and NSC/4 and the need to pass down the obligations owed by the Contractor to the Authority under the provisions of GC/Works/1 Edition 2. The relevant clauses are Clauses 68 to 70. Clause 69 of GW/S is essentially identical to Clause 23 of DOM/1 (before it was amended in 1987) and hence adjudication is restricted to issues relating to set-off claims.

The DOM/1 set-off and adjudication procedure contained in Clauses 69 and 70 of GW/S is supplemented by Clause 68 where the Sub-contractor is

---

124 Clause 21.1 does not expressly contemplate deduction from retention unlike Clause 23.1 of DOM/1.
125 Amendment 3 for use where Amendments 1-3 apply to the IFC84 Main Contract.
126 The arbitration clause amendments were issued in 1988, a year earlier than those to IN/SC.

nominated. If the Contractor has incurred an "authorised set-off"[127] it gives notice to that effect to the Sub-contractor if it considers that all or part of this is attributable to the Sub-contractor (the "Sub-contractor's share"). The adjudication mechanism applies only to the question of the Sub-contractor's share not to the validity or amount of the authorised set-off itself. How that distinction is to be maintained in practice is difficult to see. No new form of Sub-contract or amendments to GW/S have been issued for use in conjunction with GC/Works/1 Edition 3.

JCT 87 Works Contract (1987)

The Works Contract set-off and adjudication provisions, Clauses 4.33 to 4.44, most closely correspond to those in NSC/4 and 4a, as amended in 1987. The material differences are as follows:

(a) Clause 4.34.1 (corresponding to the amended Clause 23.2.1 of NSC/4 and 4a) refers to a "claim for loss and/or expense and/or damage". It includes neither the pre-1987 wording "which has actually been incurred" nor the 1987 wording "which he has suffered or incurred". This is due, it seems, to the peculiar position of a Management Contractor in that the real claim is ultimately that of the Employer, which the Management Contractor does not itself incur; and

(b) NSC/4 and 4a, as amended, require issue of an Architect's certificate of non-completion before a delay-based claim can be deducted. Clause 4.34.1 of the Works Contract version requires the Management Contractor to have responded in writing to each notice of delay from the Works Contractor and to have notified the Works Contractor of its failure to complete under Clause 2.11.

The extent of availability of early arbitration is the same as under NSC/ 4 and 4a.

JCT81 (1988)

Following representations from the BPF, in 1988 the JCT issued Amendment 3 which contained optional supplemental provisions to JCT 81. These

---

127 A deduction by the Authority under GC/Works/1 Edition 2. The "Allocation of Provisions-Sources" in the GW/S Conditions states that Clause 68 is derived from Clause 43 of GC/Works/1 Edition 2, which by its terms simply reserves the Authority's right to deduct or set-off from any payment any amount due to the Authority.

represent the JCT's first venture, albeit through an optional provision, into adjudication of disputes in the context of a Main Contract. Presumably, it was prepared to concede this, if only optionally, because there is no Architect under JCT81. Through lack of statistics I am unable to state the extent to which this optional provision has been used. There are a number of similarities and dissimilarities with the BPF adjudication provision:-

(a) The issues referred to the Adjudicator differ. Most significantly neither extension of time issues nor rights of termination are to be adjudicated upon. However, all issues relating to whether instructions are empowered or any consent, statement or agreement has been withheld which is not to be unreasonably withheld or delayed are subject to adjudication (S1.2);

(b) The procedure commences with a notice from one party to the other. By 14 days later both parties are to submit statements. Within a further 14 days the Adjudicator may require any further information or documents from the parties and must indicate when he or she expects to give a decision. There is no overall time limit for that decision (clause S1.3.1 - .2). As with the BPF Building Contract, specific treatment is given to valuation of change instructions and direct loss and/or expense claims by deferring for a period of time the commencement of adjudication;

(c) As with the BPF System the Adjudicator acts as expert and not as arbitrator but, so that "its legally binding nature is secured" (Guidance Note), the decision is "deemed to be a provision of this Contract (an Adjudicated Provision) and such Adjudicated Provision shall be final and binding on the parties unless referred to arbitration" within 14 days of receipt of the decision (clause S1.3.3 - .4);

(d) Each party bears the Adjudicator's fee in equal proportions (clause S1.7). Clause S1.6 provides that each party bears its own costs; and

(e) Under Article 5 arbitration can proceed prior to practical completion in respect of the usual wide range of issues.

The innovation of deeming the decision to be a Contract term, thereby governing the rights of the parties from then on, is one which warrants consideration for incorporation in other variants.

GC/Works/1 Edition 3 (1989)

An unconvincing adjudication provision, Clause 59, was introduced in the 3rd Edition of GC/Works/1. Its principal features are that:-

(a) adjudication is unavailable in respect of any dispute, difference or question other than a matter as to which a decision is expressed to be final and conclusive. That effectively excludes, for example, interim payment issues;

(b) the dispute must have been outstanding for at least 3 months. It contemplates only the Contractor proceeding to adjudication;

(c) the Adjudicator is selected by a person named in the Contract and in practice connected with the Employer, from within the Authority. The "independent adjudicator" is not to have been associated with the letting or management of the Contract;

(d) a decision is made within 28 days of the Contractor's notice of adjudication;

(e) clause 59(6) attempts to permit the Adjudicator to have regard to the extent to which the parties have "acted promptly, reasonably and in good faith"; and

(f) the decision is binding until completion or abandonment of the works or determination of the Contract.

Arbitration cannot proceed until after completion or abandonment of the works or determination of the Contract and is unavailable in respect of any final and conclusive decision. Presumably this approach to disputes can be rationalised on the basis of the special position of the State and its agencies[128]. I doubt that there is anything of potentially wider application here. In drafting Edition 3 the PSA was influenced by the BPF System but the overriding effect of the system of "final and conclusive" decisions under GC/Works/1, the questionable deferral of adjudication for 3 months and the internal appointment of the Adjudicator makes this a less attractive model.

ICE New Engineering Contract and Sub-Contract (1991)

One of the features of the New Engineering Contract is the division of the role of the Engineer into its constituent elements of project manager, designer, supervisor of construction and Adjudicator. In particular the introductory booklet at page 5-6 states that:

"...the dual role of the Engineer as manager of the project on

128 The general view of GC/Works/1 is that all of its editions, and its predecessor CCC/ Works/1, were slanted in favour of the State. For instance it is said that these forms "have reflected the best interests of the agency [the PSA], with little regard to the views of contractors required to use it": Derek Simmonds, *Construction News*, 16th November 1989. On the other hand I.N. Duncan Wallace QC (eg in Chapter 1 of *Further Building and Engineering Contracts* (London, Sweet & Maxwell, 1973) and *"Contract Policy for Money"* in Construction Contract Policy (London, C.C.L.M., 1989)) and V. Powell-Smith (in GC/Works/1 Edition 3 (London, BSP Professional Books, 1990)) are generally favourably disposed toward it.

behalf of the Employer and adjudicator of disputes which he himself has caused (if only in the sense of not having given in to the wishes of the Contractor) appears to be becoming less tolerable as the incidence and severity of disputes rise....[U]sing a separate Adjudicator can be a significant contribution to reducing the incidence and severity of disputes. There are many situations outside the United King⌐¬m where this detachment is regarded as an advantage by the Employer....The Adjudicator is named in the Contract, and uses no more complicated or quasi-legal procedures in carrying out his work than the Engineer would have done in carrying out the procedures formerly required of him by the 'Engineer's decision' clause in the traditional ICE Conditions of Contract."

The adjudication clause, Clause 90, is one of the "core" provisions of both the Contract and Sub-contract. Its principal features are:-

(a) the Adjudicator is named from the outset;
(b) the right to proceed to adjudication arises on either party disagreeing with an action of the Project Manager or Supervisor or considering it to be outside their authority. This right must be exercised within 4 weeks of the action (Clause 90.1). If there is a related dispute under a Sub-contract the Contractor can also refer that dispute to the Adjudicator and the two disputes are treated as one (Clause 90.4);
(c) the Adjudicator makes a decision as to the correctness of the action and if it was not correct, decides what action should be taken and the time and cost consequences (Clause 90.2). The only submissions to the Adjudicator which the Contract contemplates is submission by the Project Manager of "the information upon which the disputed action was based" (Clause 90.2). Presumably the dissatisfied party will also include some information in making the reference, but submission of material by the Supervisor, where the dispute relates to an action by him or her, is not contemplated;
(d) even though disputed, the disputed action is to be implemented; the Adjudication process deals with the rights arising from the action and its implementation rather than whether the action should be implemented. As stated in the Guidance Notes, "The Adjudicator does not alter decisions made by the Project Manager. If he disagrees with a decision made by the Project Manager, he will say so and award the Contractor compensation for the fact that the decision was wrongly taken. He will not, however, overturn the Project Manager's decision. Exceptions to this are in respect of amounts certified for payment, other financial decisions and in certain circumstances, extensions of time." The decision is due within 4 weeks of the matter being

referred to adjudication (Clause 90.3);
(e) a party dissatisfied with the decision has 8 weeks in which to refer the
matter to arbitration (Clause 91.1). There are no terms deferring the right
to proceed to arbitration in respect of certain disputes. The Clause does not
otherwise address the status or binding effect of the decision;
(f) formal terms of appointment for the Adjudicator are contemplated. It is
important to note that Clause 90.5 contemplates that the Adjudicator will be
immune from liability in respect of the discharge of his or her responsibilities;
and
(g) the fees of the Adjudicator are shared equally.

The Sub-contract's adjudication provision, also Clause 90, takes a
similar approach. There are potential problems with the approach of
focusing the right to adjudication, and therefore to arbitration, on disputes
regarding actions of the Project Manager or Supervisor[129]. It would seem
that the jurisdiction of either the Adjudicator or the Arbitrator should be
expanded, since otherwise some disputes seem likely to require litigation,
which from a review of the Guidance Notes does not seem to have been an
intended result.

These sorts of points can be dealt with in the future. As part of the process
of consultation the form was issued as a draft, albeit a very glossy draft.
However, their existence reflects the risks associated with starting with a
clean sheet of paper. The policy decision to be made is whether the likely
litigation and arbitration costs arising from problems of detailed interpretation which, however good the drafting effort, realistically are likely to result,
are more than balanced by the perceived overall efficiency gains from restructuring the contractual aspects of civil engineering.

---

129 The approach taken may be influenced by European contracting practices as they
relate to the position of the Engineer.

Developments in procedure 31
of the Official Referees

Judge Peter Bowsher

Synopsis

"It was the Official Referees that were the trail blazers in the abandonment of trial by ambush": so stated Lord Griffiths[1]. In this paper a practising Official Referee reviews the history of reform and the current procedures in use in Official Referees business. The Official Referees welcome suggestions for further improvement.

Introduction

An early scene in the film "Brothers in Law", based on a book by the late Judge Harry Leon Q.C., shows Ian Carmichael playing the stammering tyro barrister in a minute court with Victorian furniture and architecture, presided over by an Official Referee, Sir Hugo Cramp, perched on a low dais hardly wide or deep enough to support his small desk. After a short dialogue moving quickly from exaggerated patience to testiness, the mythical Sir Hugo exclaimed that it was intolerable that there should be no Scott Schedule when there were 50 items in dispute and added, "You had better put your heads together. I shall rise for 10 minutes after which I shall expect to hear that you have reached a compromise." Those who practised before the Official Referees in the 1960s will have recognised that scene as a perfect depiction of many an incident in their own experience. Sadly, many think that it is still accurate today.

The appointment of the last of the Official Referee knights, Sir William Stabb Q.C. in 1969, soon joined by HH. Judge Edgar Fay Q.C. in 1971, began a new era when the Official Referees turned from discouraging litigants to devising new procedures to encourage the efficient and just despatch of business[2]. The popularity of the court has grown ever since. Since the time of William Stabb and Edgar Fay, we have also moved away from the depressing Victorian architecture and furniture of "the Corridor"

---

1 Journal of the Chartered Institute of Arbitrators (1991) August, page 168, "*Civil litigation in the Nineties*".

2 Some of those procedures have been adapted and recommended for use in Group Actions, - "Guide for use in Group Actions", Supreme Court Procedure Committee, May, 1991, Lord Chancellor's Department, 26, Old Queen's Street, London SW1

to our new quarters at St. Dunstan's House.

The Interventionist Court

Some still hold the old fashioned image of the judge as one with little experience of initiating procedural steps, who leaves all questions relating to efficiency or cost effectiveness to the parties themselves. There may still be some few English judges moulded in that image, but the Official Referees are not included among them. The Official Referees are deeply concerned about efficiency and cost-effectiveness in litigation, and by their involvement in preparation of litigation for trial they seek to translate their concern into action.

One advantage to which the Official Referees have clung (against substantial opposition) is their personal supervision of preparations for trial of the cases in their lists. An interventionist attitude to the conduct of interlocutory hearings has given rise to developments in procedure which have now permeated out through the whole of the civil justice system in England and Wales.

Extension of work undertaken

The techniques adopted by the Official Referees have attracted new areas of work. The Official Referees are specialist judges. Their speciality is complex litigation. As a result they try most of the construction cases in the High Court. Those construction cases include claims by and against architects, engineers and surveyors. But the Official Referees' work is not confined to construction cases. At Appendix A[3] there is a list of categories of work typically heard by Official Referees. We hear an increasing number of claims regarding computer hardware and software.

Official Referees exercise both first instance and appellate jurisdiction:

(i) Official Referees have "the same jurisdiction, powers and duties as a High Court judge (including the power of committal and discretion as to costs)": in addition, they can and do hear cases wherever they wish[4]. It is not sufficiently widely appreciated that Official Referees can and do hear cases in part or in whole outside London, and also travel for views of the subject-matter of litigation.

(ii) Unlike High Court judges (other than judges of the Commercial Court)

---

3 Reproduced from the note in the Supreme Court Practice, 1991, 36/1-9/13.
4 R.S.C. O.36 R. 4.

the Official Referees also have for many years exercised jurisdiction to sit as arbitrators under section 11 of the Arbitration Act, 1950, as now amended by the Courts and Legal Services Act, 1990, section 99.
(iii) Applications for leave to appeal from arbitrators and appeals from arbitrators are required by R.S.C. O. 73 to be referred to the Commercial Court. Such appeals are referred to Official Referees by the Commercial Court when the appeal concerns subject matter normally dealt with by Official Referees. That practice became routine in 1984 without being questioned, and when it was questioned it was approved by the Court of Appeal: *Tate & Lyle Industries* v. *Davy McKee* [1990] 1 QB 1068. We have a procedure for dealing with those appeals very speedily once they are referred to us.
(iv) All Official Referees have been appointed to sit as High Court judges and in that capacity as well as in their capacity as Official Referees may hear any first instance case in the Queens Bench Division (apart from cases in the Crown Office list which are heard only by judges specially nominated for that work) as well as appeals from Masters and District Judges.

The Official Referee has jurisdiction over cases within the jurisdiction of the High Court throughout England and Wales, and indeed the jurisdiction may extend to deal with property and incidents around the world. Although the Official Referees' Courts are in effect the courts for the construction industry, our work embraces subjects far beyond construction including (to take just some examples from recent cases), computers (hardware and software), the testing of welds for gas rigs in the North Sea, boat building, deck machinery on Royal Navy destroyers sailing throughout the world, pipeline construction, erection of navigation beacons in the Clyde for nuclear submarines, an irrigation system in Nigeria, dealings in put and call options, a wide variety of sale of goods cases, problems in the construction of an art gallery in Glasgow, a gas rig in the North Sea, a tower block in Hong Kong, Liverpool Cathedral, Great Ormonde Street Hospital, other hospitals, the Emerald Oil Field, environmental pollution, misrepresentation on sales of shares, and partnership actions. The sums of money involved in Official Referees' cases are usually larger than the amounts in issue in many cases in other parts of the High Court.
In some respects the jurisdiction of an Official Referee is wider than that of a High Court Judge. An official Referee may hear both Chancery and Queen's Bench cases. A High Court judge does not have jurisdiction to hear Official Referees' cases. Moreover, order 36 rule 4(4) provides that an Official Referee may hold a trial "at any place which appears to him to be convenient". An ordinary judge can only sit in approved court buildings or in other places specially approved by the Lord Chancellor.

Original Jurisdiction replaces Derivative Jurisdiction

The manner in which cases come before Official Referees has changed markedly. The jurisdiction was once wholly derivative, but is now in practice almost wholly original.

In the nineteenth century, when most civil trials were tried by judge and jury, issues of fact unsuitable for jury trial were referred to an Official Referee for inquiry and report. The referring court would usually, but not invariably, adopt the report and incorporate it into its judgment. That procedure is completely dead, but it is still authorised by R.S.C. O. 36 rr. 8 and 9. Those rules should be revoked.

As long ago as 1884, the Queens Bench Division and the Chancery Division were authorised to transfer whole actions to the Official Referees for decision and final judgment. That procedure is still to be found in R.S.C. O. 36 r. 3. This is still a live procedure and is indeed the jurisdiction used by the Commercial Court to transfer applications for leave to appeal and appeals from arbitrators. But the procedure is otherwise used much less frequently than in the past, mainly because the majority of litigants who wish to come before the Official Referees use the direct procedure now available[5]. Litigants who start their action in the Chancery Division or the Queen's Bench Division are less welcome to the Official Referees because the Official Referees prefer to control the litigation before them from the very outset.

In 1982, litigants were given the power to bring an action before the Official Referees not in any derivative way but directly to an Official Referee by issuing a writ out of the Chancery or Queen's Bench Division and marking it in the top left hand corner, "Official Referees' Business"[6]. Actions so begun might be transferred by the Official Referee to the Chancery or Queen's Bench Division or to the County Court: transfer from the Official Referees under the new distribution of business rules following the coming into force of the Courts and Legal Services Act, 1990 will continue to be decided on all the relevant criteria, including complication of fact or law, and not just on a financial basis[7]. Marking the writ "Official

---

5 Lord Mustill and Mr. Stewart Boyd QC still say, wrongly, in the second edition of their book on Commercial Arbitration (1989) (at page 271) that,".. from 1889 until 1925, inquiries and trials by referees were governed by sections 13 to 17 of the Arbitration Act 1889, under the general rubric 'References under order of the Court'. This derivative jurisdiction of the Official Referees nowadays constitutes almost the whole of their business, although their proceedings no longer bear any resemblance to the process of arbitration." In fact, very little of the jurisdiction of the Official Referees is derivative. The overwhelming bulk is from direct issue of process by the litigant.

6 Order 36 rule 2(1).

7 High Court and County Courts Jurisdiction order 1991 (5.1. 1991 No. 724 L.5) articles 2 and 5; practice Direction [1991] 1 WLR 643.

Referees' Business" has become the most popular way of starting actions before the Official Referees, and has become even more popular since the opening of the Official Referees' Registry on the third floor of St. Dunstan's House upon our move to that building in October, 1988.

The Scott Schedule

If the 1960s were a brief low period in our history, it would not be right to regard everything that went before as lacking in innovation. There was after all the remarkable invention of the Scott Schedule by Mr. George Scott (1920 -1933). The success of that invention has sadly been the source of many of our troubles. So great is the fame of the Scott Schedule that many otherwise well informed lawyers think that we spend our time poring over Scott Schedules, counting bent nails and cracked bricks. After nearly four years as an Official Referee, I am beginning to lack the energy to explain that the Scott Schedule is a valuable tool for bringing the parties to define the issues and to reach sensible agreements and that I have only once come close to working through a Scott schedule filling in the right hand column headed "Official Referee's Comments". Even in that case, the issues went far beyond the Scott Schedule. The Scott schedule is now widely used in all divisions of the court and throughout the world in complex litigation of all types.

It is usually possible, by trying representative items, or by encouraging agreement on all points apart from a few points of principle, to avoid point by point consideration of the Scott Schedule.

Experts' Reports

Even in the 1960s there was a great leap forward in the practice of the Official Referees. An enormous change was made regarding expert evidence. That change was enshrined in the Practice Direction of the Senior Official Referee, Sir Walker Kelly Carter Q.C., published in 1968, and still printed in the White Book as the last Practice Direction given by a Senior Official Referee,[8] though obsolete in many respects. The process of its obsolescence is typical of many procedural changes initiated by the Official Referees. The Official Referees, often prompted by court users, have from time to time initiated important procedural changes relying on the inherent jurisdiction of the court and without any change in the rules. After the

---

8 [1968] 1 WLR 1425;[1968] 2 All E.R. 1213: Supreme Court Practice, 1991,36/1 - 9/ 12

success of those procedures has been demonstrated in practice, other judges
of the High Court have wished to adopt them and rules of procedure have
applied those procedures to the whole court. At that stage, someone else
usually claims the credit for inventing the procedure in the first place. Sir
Walker Kelly Carter's Practice Direction requiring the disclosure of expert
evidence was considered at the time by practitioners outside the Official
Referees' Corridor to be revolutionary and seriously subversive of the right
of the parties to prepare their case under the cloak of privilege and then at
the trial to ambush the other side who were unprepared to answer the case
mounted against them. The direction was in the following terms:

> "Where a party intends to adduce expert evidence, he should
> produce to the other party his expert's statement of proposed
> evidence, together with any reports, plans, models, calculations,
> etc., relevant to it, for agreement if possible. Failing such
> agreement, the other party should deliver to the first party a
> written statement setting out particulars of the matters not
> agreed. Where both parties intend to adduce expert evidence,
> each should follow this procedure. Failure by any party to follow
> this procedure may result in a special order as to costs".

The Official Referees' practice has become the foundation for much of
what is to be found in R.S.C. order 38 rules 35 to 44. We see in Sir Walker
Kelly Carter's direction the beginnings of the disclosure of experts' reports,
the urgings that the experts should try to reach agreement, and the requirement that if agreement is not reached a statement should be prepared stating
what is not agreed. There we have the genesis of the three elements which
are now required universally of experts in our courts, disclosure, attempts
to reach agreement, and formulation of the degree to which there is
disagreement. In the threat of a special order as to costs, Kelly Carter
revealed that there was no authority for the Practice Direction beyond the
inherent jurisdiction of the court and the general ability to penalise in costs
anyone behaving unreasonably.

We still have the common law rule that reports of experts prepared for the
purpose of pending or contemplated litigation or in connection with the
obtaining or giving of legal advice are privileged from disclosure[9]. But
following Sir Walker Kelly Carter's Practice Direction, we were given the
Report of the Committee on Personal Injuries Litigation[10] and the Seven-
teenth Report of the Law Reform Committee on Evidence of Opinion and

9 *Worral* v. *Reich* [1955] 1 QB 296
10 Cmnd. 3691 (1969) paras 277 - 283.

Expert Evidence[11], which resulted in the Civil Evidence Act, 1972 and the new rules of court drafted pursuant to that Act by the late Master Elton. Those rules restrict the right of parties to call expert evidence in much the same way as was enforced first by the Official Referees.

Without Prejudice Meetings of Experts

It is now common form in every case in which there are expert witnesses (that is, in almost every Official Referee case) to order that the experts should meet without prejudice for the purpose of trying to agree facts and narrow issues. That form of order was initiated by His Honour Judge Newey Q.C. in 1981 building on experience of an order which he invented in 1980 as Inspector at an inquiry to decide whether there should be a second terminal at Gatwick Airport[12]. Conscious that he had no express power under the Rules of Court to make such an order, he persuaded parties to consent to his making such orders. The other two Official Referees of the day, Judges Stabb and Hawser, began to make such orders but on an increasing number of occasions neglected to ask for the parties' consent, and no one objected, no doubt on the basis that such orders could be made under the inherent jurisdiction of the court. In 1982, the Official Referees asked for express authorization for this practice but were refused. The practice was continued. The success of the continued practice persuaded the Chancery Division and the Commercial Courts by 1986 that they would like to imitate it but they were reluctant to do so without express authority. As a result, in 1986, the Lord Chancellor agreed that express power should be granted to the Official Referees, and to the Chancery Division and to the Commercial Court. That power was granted in R.S.C. O. 38 r.38(3) and was later extended to the whole of the High Court[13].

On some very few occasions there has been dispute as to the legal status of what was agreed at an experts' meeting[14]. The problem usually arises out of lack of clarity in the definition of the authority given by the parties to the experts to negotiate on their behalf.

Statements of Witnesses of Fact

A similar story emerged with the exchange of statements of witnesses of

---

11 Cmnd.4489 (1970).
12 British Academy of Experts Newsletter, June,1991, page 60.
13 R.S.C. (Amendment No. 2) 1986 (SI 1986 No. 1187).
14 *Carnell Computer Technology* v. *Unipart* (1988) 16 Con LR 19; *Richard Roberts Holdings* v. *Douglas Smith Stimson* (1989) 22 Con LR 94.

fact. Also in 1981, the Official Referees began, with the consent of the parties, to order that Statements of Witnesses of Fact be exchanged before trial, and usually before the Experts' Meeting. This had been the practice in some international arbitrations, but it was the first use of the practice in the courts. Once again, it was done without express authority, and as time went by, the parties tended not to be asked for their consent. In 1986[15], the practice was authorised by R.S.C. O. 38 r. 2A for the Official Referees, the Chancery Division, the Admiralty Court, and the Commercial Court. In 1988, R.S.C. O. 38 r. 2A was extended to the whole of the High Court[16], including the Queen's Bench Division. As with experts' reports, questions were raised about privilege[17]. As with experts' reports, the position is very simple. The original statement taken from a witness is privileged, the later statement offered for exchange is not privileged, but it remains confidential to the parties until put in evidence[18].

An order that a witness statement should stand as evidence in chief should not be made as a matter of course[19], but will be appropriate very commonly in cases coming before the Official Referees, so that oral examination in chief is either eliminated or at least very substantially reduced in length.

Interlocutory Summonses

Like the judges of the Commercial Court, the Official Referees hear all interlocutory summonses relating to their cases. The shorter summonses are heard before 10.30 am., starting between 9.30 and 10.00 a.m. The longer summonses are heard on Fridays, also starting between 9.30 and 10.00 am.

Judges who have the privilege of conducting the interlocutory proceedings in actions assigned to them can and do undertake an interventionist role, not always popular with lawyers. A summons for directions is rarely limited to the decision of applications made on behalf of the parties. For example, the Official Referee may, and frequently does, suggest that there should be an early trial of a preliminary issue, such as an issue to determine whether the claim should properly be brought in contract or on a quantum meruit: such an issue is not capable of deciding the whole action, but it will enable the parties to limit discovery and the preparation of evidence to one of the two alternative claims.

15 S.I. 1986/1187.
16 S.I. 1988/1340.
17 *Comfort Hotels Limited* v. *Wembley Stadiums Limited* [1988] 1 WLR 872.
18 *Fairfield Mabey* v. *Shell U.K. Limited and another* [1989] 1 All ER 576; *Black and Decker* v. *Flymo* [1991] 1 WLR 753; *Prudential Assurance* v. *Fountain Page* [1991] 1 WLR 756
19 *Mercer* v. *Chief Constable of Lancashire,* [1991] 1 WLR 367 and see RSC O38r2A

There is no doubt, however, that there is room for more interventionism by the Official Referees. It will be necessary for the court to instil in litigants and their representatives some questioning of the cost effectiveness of the procedures adopted by the lawyers. Lawyers assume that they must examine and challenge every minute detail of the opposing case without ascertaining whether that is what the client wants and what he is willing to pay for. As a result, discovery of documents, for example, as presently conducted in litigation is far too wide in its range and far too deep in its examination of detail. In many cases limits could properly be imposed by the judge on discovery.

I have developed a form of Summons for Directions which is set out at Appendix B. There are two orders in particular to which I would draw attention because they deal with situations where the Rules of the Supreme Court have failed to take account of the special position of the Official Referees' jurisdiction. Both the time for service of a Civil Evidence Act Notice and the time for service of a Notice to Admit Facts are linked in the Rules of Court to the date for setting down of an action[20]. The time for setting down an action in the Official Referees' court is within 14 days after the notice of intention to defend or the order for transfer. Either date is likely to be too early from a practical point of view for notices concerning the evidence, and for that reason, the Official Referees will readily grant extensions of time under their powers granted by R.S.C. O. 3 r.5. To encourage use of these helpful procedures, I make such orders as a matter of form. So far as the Notice to Admit Facts is concerned, I acknowledge some useful prodding from Davies, Arnold and Cooper[21].

Written note of Counsel's opening and closing speeches

Since 1981, the Official Referees have asked for written notes of counsel's opening submissions. It has also often been found useful to have a short adjournment at the end of an unusually complex trial to enable counsel to prepare written notes of their closing submissions, summarising the submissions on complex fact and law. It is a hallmark of the Official Referees' work that it is complex[22]. That complexity extends both to law and fact and the complexity of the law in recent years has dictated greater dependence on the excellent counsel practising before the Official Referees.

The roller-coaster of the law of tort travelled by the Court of Appeal and the House of Lords, from *Dutton* v. *Bognor Regis Urban District Council*[23]

20 R.S.C. O. 38 r. 21 and R.S.C.·O. 26 r 2.
21 Construction Industry Law Letter, May, 1991
22 R.S.C.O 36 r. 1.
23 [1972] 1 QB 373

via *Sparham Souter* v. *Town and Country Developments (Essex) Limited*[24] and *Anns* v. *Merton London Borough Council*[25], *Pirelli* v. *Oscar Faber*[26] and many other cases of the Court of Appeal and the House of Lords through to *D & F Estates Limited* v. *Church Commissioners for England*[27], *Department of the Environment* v. *Bates*[28], *Murphy* v. *Brentwood District Council*[29] and still continuing, has been concerned overwhelmingly with Official Referees' cases. As a result, in very many cases coming before the Official Referees, the judge has been shooting at a moving target so far as the law is concerned, and written submissions by counsel have been invaluable as regards clarity, saving of time at the trial, and provision of opportunities for thought before trial.

The law of tort is not the only area of developments in the law with which the Official Referees are concerned. For an example of a contract case of general importance on the nature of set-offs starting before an Official Referee see *Modern Engineering* v. *Gilbert Ash*[30]. In *Rush & Tomkins Ltd.* v. *G.L.C.*[31], a decision of an Official Referee was overturned by the Court of Appeal and restored by the House of Lords. That decision is of general importance on the topic of privilege in relation to discovery of documents.

An appeal to the Court of Appeal relating solely to the practice of Official Referees is of interest: *Northern Regional Health Authority* v. *Crouch*[32]. The Court of Appeal held that the Official Referees were wrong in law to assume jurisdiction to open up and review architects' certificates. Some of the statements in the Court of Appeal suggest that there was a degree of pragmatism in the judgments, in that there was a desire to reduce the amount of work before the Official Referees so as to reduce the length of their lists. Having made such a statement, Lord Donaldson M.R. said[33]:

> "If this reduction in the length of the lists does not occur or seems unlikely to occur, urgent consideration should be given to conferring on the Official Referees a power ... to enable the Official Referees, whether sitting as such or as arbitrators, to refer or sub-refer, the 'nuts and bolts' of the suit to a suitably qualified arbitrator for enquiry and report. This would result in

24 [1976] QB 858
25 [1978] AC 728
26 [1983] AC 1
27 [1989] AC 177
28 [1991] 1 WLR 73
29 [1990] 3 WLR 413
30 [1974] AC 689
31 [1989] AC 1280
32 [1984] QB 644
33 at pages 674,675

the Official Referees becoming, in effect, the construction industry court, having the same relationship to the construction industry as the Commercial Court has to the financial and commercial activities of the City of London. It could decide questions of principle of general interest, leaving it to the individual arbitrators to apply those principles to the details of individual disputes".

The power to make references for enquiry and report to a suitably qualified arbitrator or on specific topics has not yet been granted. It would be most valuable in dilapidations claims and in a number of other cases. The practice adopted by the Official Referees of opening up architects certificates which was disapproved by the decision of the Court of Appeal in Crouch has now in effect been given qualified statutory approval by the legislature by the Courts and Legal Services Act, 1990, section 100, provided all the parties to the arbitration agreement consent[34].

As a further example of the great reliance by the Official Referees on the submissions of the very skilled counsel appearing before them, I do point out that there is now a large number of specialist and valuable reports in addition to the Law Reports and the All England Reports which do give us guidance. It is pertinent to cite from the first volume of the Construction Law Reports, in which the editors wrote:

"We have been concerned that much more attention should be paid to the judgments of the Official Referees. The Official Referees' court has now become in effect a specialist construction industry court, one of the few in the world .... Most of the cases which come before the Official Referees involve complex and technical issues of fact but may also involve difficult and important questions of law. It is important that the guidance which emerges from the court should be generally available .... We plan to report all Official Referees' decisions containing points of construction law".

---

34 Section 100 provides for a new section 43A to the Supreme Court Act, 1981 in the following terms:
"In any cause of matter proceeding in the High Court in connection with any contract incorporating an arbitration agreement which confers specific powers upon the arbitrator, the High Court may, if all parties to the agreement agree, exercise any such powers".

Typed judgments handed down

The Official Referees' reserved judgments do of necessity tend to be rather long. Most of us hand down our typed judgments without reading them out. In that way we save many hours of court time. The interests of justice are preserved by providing copies of the judgments to the parties beforehand and offering copies free of charge to any spectators or court reporters in court when the judgment is delivered. The Supreme Court library now keeps a copy of each reserved judgment of the Official Referees. Every typed judgment of an Official Referee is produced on a word-processor (IBM Compatible/Wordperfect 5.1) either by the Official Referee himself or by our shared secretary. I have made an offer to the Court of Appeal that if ever they should find it helpful to be provided with a computer disk of any of our judgments, I would endeavour to see that they are provided with such a disk. I have not yet been asked for such a disk.

Documents accepted by Fax

Since our move to St. Dunstan's House, the Official Referees have been able to receive documents by fax. The fax number is: 071 936 7428. As a matter of common form, for over three years, we have been receiving by fax agreed orders, affidavits, lists of authorities, notes of openings, and other messages. I am not aware of any other part of the High Court where fax is used in this way. The Lord Chancellor's Department has agreed to set up an experiment in the use of Lix, a system of computer to computer communication, in the Official Referees' courts early in 1992.

Submissions and documents on computer disk

Some counsel hand in a computer disk containing their opening submissions and chronology. That is an immense help both in keeping control of the case as it progresses and in writing the judgment. There could be a considerable saving of costs to the parties, and probably also a substantial increase in profit margins for the professionals involved in litigation, if all the documents created especially for the litigation were exchanged both in hard copy form and on computer disk. That class of documents would include pleadings, Scott Schedules, statements of witnesses of fact, and experts' reports. Official Referees have no power to make any order to that end, but they do have powers of persuasion. There are technical problems of compatibility between systems used by those who are equipped with the necessary technology. There is also a fundamental constitutional principle to be observed, that access to the courts by litigants in person should not be limited to litigants in person who own computers. That principle should not prevent the court from requiring those who put themselves forward as qualified to represent litigants before the court to equip themselves with up to date professional tools.

Litigation Support

There is a strong movement to persuade solicitors to bring the bulk of their documents into court on some form of computer disk rather than in the bulky files which now encumber our Courts.[35] Many solicitors, experts, and lay clients are anxious for a change of practice. This is a complex subject. A revolution will soon occur and the Official Referees will again be in the lead. A sub-committee of the Official Referees Solicitors Association has been formed to try to reach agreements which will overcome the difficulties in the way of using existing technology to the full.

Computerised Case Management

The Official Referees would benefit from adopting a system of case management. The Court of Appeal has just moved onto its second system, RECAP. If the Official Referees' system were computerised, they would be able (by requiring the lodging with the court of certain documents such as lists of documents, experts' reports and witness statements) to identify those cases which were lagging behind on the deadlines for preparation for trial and at the same time identify the likely peaks and troughs in effective cases coming up for trial. A recommendation that there should be a feasibility study of such a computerized system for the Official Referees was made in 1988 by a working party of the Society for Computers and Law led by Mr. Sean Overend (now His Honour Judge Overend). There are marked differences in procedure between the conduct of a case before an Official Referee and the conduct of other civil litigation. Many of those differences spring from the requirement of RSC Order 36 rule 6 that the summons for directions be issued and a date for trial be applied for at a very early stage, whereas in the Queen's Bench and Chancery Divisions the summons for directions comes at quite a late stage in the action. As a result, the Official Referees do eliminate many, though by no means all, of the delays arising elsewhere from the lack of court control over the timetable for the litigation. If, like the Court of Appeal, the Official Referees had a suitable computer and programme and trained staff to operate it, they could eliminate even

---

35 For a recent account of some systems, see "Technology in the Courtroom", Clive Davidson, New Law Journal, 19, July 1991, vol. 141 No. 6513, page 1011.

more delays because they could more easily review the whole case load and detect backsliders. The thinking of the Official Referees is in line with the views expressed by Lord Griffiths in *Department of Transport* v. *Chris Smaller* [1989] 2 WLR 585H:

"I, for my part, recommend a radical overhaul of the whole civil procedural process and the introduction of court controlled case management techniques designed to ensure that once a litigant has entered the litigation process, his case proceeds in accordance with a timetable as prescribed by rules of court or as modified by a judge"[36]

Lord Griffiths has made it plain at a recent seminar that the court controlled case management techniques should be organised by computer.

In advance of computerization, a small administrative change might with advantage be made without a computer. R.S.C. O. 36 r. 6 requires that in proceedings before the Official Referees the Summons for Directions shall be issued within 14 days of the Defendant giving notice of intention to defend or of the order for transfer. Sometimes, that order is disobeyed, either through ignorance or deliberate disobedience, with the result that the trial date is deferred unnecessarily for many months and as a result lawyers and the courts are brought into disrepute. To avoid this delay, when the Official Referees' Registry receives either a notice of intention to defend or an order transferring proceedings, the Registry should of its own motion issue a date for the hearing for directions without waiting for the issue of a Summons for Directions. This proposal is unpopular with many solicitors who feel that they know best when to press a case forward, but experience of complaints from litigants of delay and lame excuses from solicitors for those delays suggests that if parties wish to litigate before the Official Referees they should submit to the discipline of the Official Referees in the preparation of the case from the earliest stage.

Conduct of Trials

As a result of changes pioneered by the Official Referees and now accepted throughout the High Court, trials are conducted with the maximum amount of openness. The exchange of Statements of Witnesses of Fact and of Experts' Reports has led to less technicality in pleadings. Ever since the

36 See also the Report of the Review Body on Civil Justice, 1988, Cm 394 paras 223 to 228.

Scott Schedule was invented in the 1920s the Official Referees have paid little regard to the technical rule of pleading that you do not plead to particulars. Parties are regularly required to plead to almost all particulars, though the pleading to details may be timed for a late stage in the preparations for trial. Now that all the evidence is disclosed, there seems to be little point in listening to tedious arguments that a request for further and better particulars of a pleading would offend the rule that a party should not be required to disclose evidence in his pleadings, or that a request for particulars should be framed as an interrogatory rather than as a request for particulars.

On the Thursday before a trial is due to start, the court usually expects to receive documents which reveal the whole of the case which the parties intend to produce at the trial. Those documents would include:

1. Note of the opening by counsel for the Plaintiffs;
2. Chronology;
3. Pleadings;
4. Statements of witnesses of fact;
5. Experts' reports;
6. Bundles of relevant documents;
7. If the bundles are voluminous (and they usually are), core bundles.

Counsel's opening and chronology are also frequently lodged on disk. The practice of lodging documents of this sort is yet another practice which has now, since 1 July, 1991, been adopted for use throughout the High Court[37].

I have to confess that I find it difficult to derive any benefit from documents being read out to me. Happily the number of counsel appearing in the Official Referees' Courts who think that there is some ritual benefit in reading out documents is decreasing, and in any event, I decline to take part in the ritual.

Suggestions how statements of witnesses of fact can best be dealt with at the trial have been reported in *Fairfield Mabey* v. *Shell U.K. Limited* and another[38]. In the same report are some observations on how counsel may be able to reduce the length of trials by giving notice to witnesses on the other side of questions which may be asked in cross-examination which would require some research before they could be answered. This device can save much time at the trial, and it also reduces the heavy burden which can be imposed on a witness by a casual request, "Can you give me an answer to that question by tomorrow morning?" The witness usually agrees to such requests, even if his agreement will keep him out of his bed until the early

37 RSC Order 34 rule 9
38 [1989] 1 All ER 576

hours of the morning.

Closed Circuit Television Camera

In Court 8 in St. Dunstan's House we have a television camera with a zoom lens pointing down at the desk beside the witness box. That camera can show to everyone in court by means of high definition monitors both large plans and small details on those plans or photographs. It is no use putting a poor photocopy of a photograph under that camera, but amazing detail can be revealed from good quality prints. The same equipment can be used to show video-tapes. These may be recordings of evidence, such as the opening up of a roof or an inspection of a drain, or alternatively they may be a demonstration by graphics which form part of counsel's opening. We hope that more equipment will be provided.

Computer assisted transcripts

All trials are recorded mechanically by tape-recording, and interlocutory proceedings can also be recorded on request. In longer cases, it would be a great saving of money to the parties if a daily transcript were provided at the expense of the parties so that the speed of the proceedings is not limited by the ability of the judge to write down the evidence in his notebook. Even better than an ordinary daily transcript would be Computer Assisted Transcription (CAT). There are shorthandwriting companies using this system already. The system provides not only a daily typed transcript but also daily the provision of computerised information which enables computerized searches to be made through the evidence. It is difficult to persuade parties that it would be a saving of money to use this system in the Official Referees Courts. I am sure that in appropriate cases savings would result, and if the parties decide to use the system it can and will be put into operation. The Society for Computers and Law hopes to sponsor a monitored trial of such a system, in an Official Referee's Court in 1992.

Appendix A:

Classes of actions commonly heard by Official Referees
(Supreme Court Practice, Note: 36/1 - 9/13)
- (a)　civil or mechanical engineering;
- (b)　building and other construction work generally;
- (c)　claims by and against engineers, architects, surveyors, accountants and other such specialised professional persons or

bodies;
(d)   claims by and against local authorities relating to their statutory duties concerning the development of land or the construction of buildings;
(e)   claims between neighbouring owners and occupiers of land in trespass, nuisance and liability under *Rylands v. Fletcher*[39];
(f)   claims between landlord and tenant for breach of repairing covenants;
(g)   claims relating to the quality of goods sold or hired;
(h)   claims relating to work done and materials supplied or services rendered;
(i)   claims involving the taking of accounts especially where these are complicated;
(j)   claims relating to the supply and use of computers;
(k)   claims arising out of fires.
(l)   environmental claims.

Appendix B: Order For Directions

1.   Trial: the Fixture   Estimated Length
2.   Defence and Counterclaim to be served by
3.   Reply and Defence to Counterclaim if so advised to be served by
4.   Discovery by lists to be exchanged by
5.   Inspection on 3 days notice.
6.   Plaintiff to serve a Scott Schedule of defects and damages by
7.   Defendant to serve a Scott Schedule of defects and damages by
8.   Plaintiff and Defendant to respond respectively to the other party's Scott Schedule by
9.   Statements of witnesses of fact to be filed with the Court and offered for exchange by
10.   Experts of like disciplines to meet without prejudice to try to narrow issues and agree facts by
11.   Experts to seek to agree a joint statement indicating those parts of their evidence on which they are, and those on which they are not, in agreement.
12.   Leave to the parties to call expert witnesses limited to [per party on condition that their reports shall have been filed with the Court and exchanged by
13.   The time for service of any Civil Evidence Act Notice pursuant

to RSC O.38 r. 21(1) shall the same as the time for filing and exchange of statements of witnesses of fact.

14.   The time for service of any Notice to Admit Facts pursuant to RSC O.27 r.2 is extended to 21 days after the time for filing and exchange of statements of witnesses of fact.

15.   Agreed bundles and written note of Plaintiffs' counsel's opening to be lodged with the Court by 4p.m. on the Thursday before the date for trial stated in this order.

16.   Pre - Trial Review

17.   Liberty to Restore. Cost in Cause

Index

Index